ART
CONTEXT AND CRITICISM

SECOND EDITION

ART
CONTEXT AND CRITICISM

SECOND EDITION

JOHN KISSICK
Penn State University

Brown & Benchmark
PUBLISHERS

Madison Dubuque, IA Guilford, CT Chicago Toronto London
Caracas Mexico City Buenos Aires Madrid Bogota Sydney

Book Team

Publisher *Rosemary Bradley*
Senior Developmental Editor *Deborah Daniel*
Associate Marketing Manager *Kirk Moen*

Brown & Benchmark
PUBLISHERS

Brown and Benchmark Publishers, A Times Mirror Higher Education Group, Inc. Company
President and Chief Executive Officer *Thomas E. Doran*
Vice President of Business Development *Russ Domeyer*
Vice President of Production *Vickie Putman*
Vice President of Sales and Marketing *Bob McLaughlin*
Director of Marketing *John Finn*

Times Mirror
Higher Education Group

Chairman and Chief Executive Officer *G. Franklin Lewis*
Executive Vice President and Chief Operating Officer *James H. Higby*
President of Manufacturing and Senior Vice President *Roger Meyer*
Senior Vice President and Chief Financial Officer *Robert Chesterman*

Library of Congress Catalog Card Number: 95–76184

ISBN 0–697–26613–3

This book was designed and produced by
CALMANN & KING LTD.
71 Great Russell Street, London, WC1B 3BN

Editor Melanie White
Designer Karen Osborne
Picture Researcher Carrie Haines
Maps by Eugene Fleury

Typeset by Bookworm Typesetting, Manchester, UK
Printed in Singapore

10 9 8 7 6 5 4 3 2 1

Front cover: Georgia O'Keeffe
Black Hollyhock, Blue Larkspur 1929
Oil on canvas, 36 x 30 in (91.4 x 76.2 cm)
The Metropolitan Museum of Art, New York
George A. Hearn Fund, 1934 (34.51)

Back cover: Detail from a Jain manuscript
of the Uttaradhyayana Sutra, Western India c. 1460
Opaque watercolor on paper
© Victoria & Albert Museum, London

Frontispiece: (detail) Angelica Kauffmann
Self-Portrait Hesitating between the Arts of Music and Painting 1794
Oil on canvas, 4 ft 10 in x 7 ft 2 in (1.47 x 2.18 m)
Nostell Priory, Yorkshire

CONTENTS

1

INTRODUCTION
Page 15

THE BEGINNINGS OF ART
Page 37

5

ARTS, ISSUES, AND INNOVATIONS IN THE BAROQUE ERA

Page 225

6

REASON AND REVOLUTION

Eighteenth- and Early Nineteenth-Century Art in Europe

Page 281

7

THE MODERN WORLD AND ITS ART

Page 319

8

ART IN THE AMERICAS

Page 371

9

ART IN THE TWENTIETH CENTURY

Page 401

10

CONTEMPORARY ART, ISSUES, AND IDEAS

Page 451

MAPS

TIMELINES

FOCUS ON
MEDIA AND TECHNIQUES

ACKNOWLEDGMENTS

An art text of this breadth requires the support and insights of many individuals. It has been my good fortune over the past two years to work with the editors Deborah Reinbold and Rosemary Bradley at Brown & Benchmark, whose kindness, sincerity of vision, and inexhaustible patience often strengthened my resolve and provided the support necessary for such a project to come to fruition. As research assistant and capable author of the accompanying teachers' guide, Kathleen Dlugos has given to this book her keen sense of intelligence, purpose, and critical clarity. My thanks also go out to Melanie White, who anchored the production of this book with enthusiasm and thoughtfulness, and to the various reviewers who have helped shape its contents.

If learning is indeed a product of social interactions, I have been particularly blessed with good friends and insightful colleagues. There are many individuals who participated, either directly or through inspiration, in the development of this text and to acknowledge everyone is perhaps impractical. However, I would be remiss if I did not thank a few special people who have been beacons of sanity, intelligence, and support throughout this ordeal. Penn State colleagues Micaela Amato, David Brown, Charles Cave, Charles Garoian, James Hopfensperger, Thomas McGovern, Sallie McCorkle, Brent Oglesbee, Chris Staley and Director Jim Stephenson continue to be an inspiration to me in both their lives and their art. I have also had the good fortune to be able to rely on a supporting cast of caring and understanding friends and family: Joseph Ansell, Chris and Madonna Buffett, Steve Holysh, John Jansen, Leo Kamen, Jamie, Cathie, Emily, and Matthew Kissick, Peter Kissick and Pauline Ryan, and the Geohabs have all had a special role in the writing of this book, and to them I am particularly grateful. Finally, my heartfelt thanks to Nicole Alper for her patience and support during the revision.

If a text is the product of its author, this author is likewise a product of his influences — none more so than my parents. They have instilled in me a respect for the educational process, and given me the strength to challenge it when necessary. If human culture is a searching for human dignity and integrity, it is through the thoughts and loving deeds of my parents that I have come to understand such terms. This book is dedicated to them.

Thanks to the following professors who read the manuscript and shared valuable insights: Donald J. Alexander of Louisiana State University, Dr. George Anderson of Miami-Dade Community College — North Campus, Richard H. Axsom of University of Michigan — Dearborn, Vince J. Bodily of Ricks College, James L. Burgess of Salisbury State University, Ronald V. Clayton of Southeast Missouri State University, Jerry Coulter of James Madison University, Brad Cushman of Southeastern Oklahoma State University, Susan R. Dixon of Ithaca College, Douglas R. George of University of New Mexico, Gary Goldberg of Midwestern State University, Nancy S. Hemmingson of Central Michigan University, Eugene M. Hood, Jr. of University of Wisconsin — Eau Claire, Carol Janson of Western Washington University, Sandra L. Johnson of Citrus College, Klaus H. Kallenberger of Middle Tennessee State University, Patricia N. Kieft of Salem State College, Joni Kinsey of Washington University, Marybeth Koos of Northern Illinois University, Kathryn Kramer of Purdue University, John W. Linn of Henderson State University, Anne H. Lisca of Santa Fe Community College, Caroline S. Loeb of Central Michigan University, Jan Maher of Guildford Technical Community College, Robert Adams Mansfield of San Diego State University, Marc Moulton of University of Northern Iowa, Helen Phillips of University of Central Arkansas, Mary Ann Popovich of Lorain County Community College, Carl Purcell of Snow College, Ronald D. Rarick of University of Indianapolis, Ron R. Reynolds of Arkansas Tech University, James T. Rocha of University of San Diego, Debra Shingledecker of Butler County Community College, Peter J. Smith of Purdue University, H. J. Wassell of Colorado State University, Nancy L. Wicker of Mankato State University, Bille Wickre of Albion College, Ardelia Williams of Indiana Wesleyan University, Sallie Zimmerman of Nassau Community College.

PREFACE

In considering the proposition to write *Art: Context and Criticism* I was inevitably forced to confront a number of questions of content and direction at the outset. Perhaps no single issue so completely preoccupied me as that most fundamental question of all: Why thrust upon the world yet another "introduction to art" text when a veritable glut of such books already exists? The answer I developed, on both a professional and a personal level, is, I believe, the foundation of this book, and this is the time and place to give a brief outline of its *raison d'être*.

Most activities grow out of a need, and the execution of this book is no exception. To put it bluntly, I decided to write *Art: Context and Criticism* because I was extremely frustrated by the quality of the basic art and art appreciation offerings that exist for today's demanding university environment. For the most part, I have found that these works fall into two rather specific camps: the dogmatic connoisseurship of the traditional introduction to Western art books, and the supposed "new age" texts, which embrace the issue of plurality at face level and so supply the student with virtually no notion of how art functions in a social and historical context. Each of these book styles has its own particular strengths, but each also posits a world view sometimes at odds with the principles of art as an integral part of our consciousness.

Take, for instance, the traditional art history introductory text. Since the development of art history as a scholarly pursuit, there has been an implicit notion that the canon of great works was founded in and upon the Western tradition. As a result, the cult of masterpieces we were all weaned on reflects a general cult myopia, placing the idea of art next to supposedly compatible terms such as form, aesthetics, and beauty, and excluding those that do not fit neatly into such a framework (women, peoples of color, etc.). The result has been a decidedly narrow view of the power and dignity of art as predominantly a Western rather than simply a human need. However, what this system did grant was an effective picture of continuity and evolution through history — ideas that are particularly enticing from the point of view of an educational system structured in the same way.

Recently, there has been an attempt to correct the errors and omissions of the past with texts that espouse a plurality of views, with an emphasis on inclusivity. The idea is to allow objects and images from various cultures to share the stage of cultural significance with the "old standards" without the sometimes troubling deliberations of quality and value. Though this promotes a greater degree of visual awareness of the contributions of traditionally disenfranchised groups, it does little to suggest how they have been historically understood or oppressed by other ideas, and where their own particular biases originate. The result is a relentless bombardment of images without any underlying structure, and one that relegates the social significance of art as an idea to the very corners of the discussion.

Art: Context and Criticism is an attempt to walk that precarious line between continuity and inclusivity. Of course, these notions are often seen as diametrically opposed in spirit, and thus it is in the dialogue between these critical positions that I see the text functioning. At the outset, it will become clear that my method of handling this treacherous path is to place considerable weight on the idea of art as a socially generated idea, carrying with it the values of its historical situation and telling us, as a modern audience, about our own values and biases. To do this effectively, I have made the conscious decision to pare down (though not eliminate) many of the discussions of formal techniques in favor of what those techniques and formal biases actually mean. This way, many of the students' original predispositions toward art can be viewed and indeed dissected as documents of their historical situation.

The general structure of this book follows a roughly chronological path, exploring the development of ideas about art and attempting to expose their social, political, and theological underpinnings. There are, however, times when a chronological approach is technically impossible, and in these instances I have attempted to develop more sweeping themes in the hope that drawing parallels to other periods will be of some assistance to the reader. To facilitate such discussions, I have attempted to bring in the thoughts and words of art critics, philosophers, and historians as well as of the artists themselves. I believe that the result is a broader, more diverse offering, introducing the art student to other authoritative voices.

One particularly difficult area in writing any "introduction to art" book is how to present new trends and insights effectively. I am thinking in particular here of women's art and the art of African-Americans — two groups who have suffered in older books. Simply (or better, simplistically) to place the work of artists from these groups beside old favorites from the Western canon is not always appropriate or even beneficial to the just causes of inclusivity and cultural fairness (a practice very popular among the "new" style of texts). Take, for instance, the problem of women's art: many, indeed most, of the artists in question were either forbidden entry to the various art academies or censored from fundamental classes such as figure drawing. To compare an intimate painting by Rosalba Carriera with a Rubens (after all, they were roughly contemporary) not only is unfair but implicitly suggests and reinforces a hierarchy of quality based on standards of chauvinism. The same is true with the presentation of other disenfranchised groups, and obviously there are no easy answers. To include is thus to misrepresent; to treat separately is to ghettoize. With this in mind, I have tried conceptually to have my cake and eat it too, showing images of women artists alongside their male counterparts in the book proper, while devoting part of Chapter Ten to the problems and interests of feminist criticism. Likewise, Chapter Ten considers African-American art and art criticism, which I hope will contribute to greater class discussions. I am sure there will be those who find fault with this layout, but I can think of no other way in which to present the information fairly and with dignity, considering the inevitable length restrictions of the book.

I believe that this is a workable format for the introductory teaching of art and one that reinforces today's most accepted critical and theoretical positions. However, I am not so naïve as to think that the book does not also reflect its social and historical position. I make no apologies for this, for one can write only from the stance of one's own age and values, and I am certainly no exception to this rule.

I do hope that the information presented will move students to reconsider how art can be a vital component of their lives, and how inanimate objects and images can make a fundamental difference to the way we view ourselves and our world.

John D. Kissick
University Park, April 1991

Preface to Second Edition

The second edition of *Art: Context and Criticism* presents the reader with an expanded overview of the social and contextual issues that have shaped and continue to shape modern culture. The inclusion of many pages of new material, along with dozens of new images, has lent considerable breadth and clarity to the content of the text. Headings and paragraph structure have likewise been redesigned and reworked with the student reader in mind, all of which makes for a more complete, diverse, and readable account of the visual arts.

In revising and expanding the first edition, I have paid considerable attention to the helpful comments of several insightful reviewers and have attempted when possible to include their suggestions. The most significant change comes in the guise of the new Chapter Ten on *Contemporary Art*, which has been dramatically expanded from the previous Epilogue and includes discussions of modern performance, installation, and video art, postmodern architecture, political art, and issues of revisionism and censorship. Other additions include: new technical discussions on items as diverse as *art elements* (found in the expanded introduction), *drawing* (in Chapter Six), and *photography* and *lithography* (in Chapter Seven). Diversity issues have likewise been addressed and expanded throughout the text, including the addition of Ancient Chinese and Indian cultures in Chapter One, expanded coverage of Hindu and Buddhist art in Chapter Three, women artists such as Frida Kahlo, Emily Carr, and Georgia O'Keeffe in Chapter Eight, and new sections on modern African-American artists such as Renée Stout and Betye Saar. Finally, discussions on philosophers and art writers, popular among the reviewers, have been increased to cover a broader range of topics.

John D. Kissick
University Park, January 1995

SUPPLEMENTS FOR THE INSTRUCTOR

The integrated teaching package of ancillary materials is available to instructors using *Art: Context and Criticism*. Please contact your Brown & Benchmark sales representative or call 800–338–5371 to obtain these supplements, or to ask for further details.

Instructor's Resource Manual and Test Item File

The Instructor's Resource Manual is designed to assist instructors as they plan and prepare for classes. Included are chapter summaries, learning goals, lists of key terms, discussion topics, essay questions, and ideas for optional activities. The revised Test Item File appears at the end of the Instructor's Manual and contains chapter specific objective-type test questions that may be photocopied and used for quizzes or tests. Also included is a list of videotapes, recordings, videodiscs, and their suppliers.

MicroTest III

The questions in the Test Item File are available on MicroTest III, a powerful yet easy-to-use test generating software available for DOS, Windows, and Macintosh. MicroTest III allows instructors to generate tests and quizzes, and customize questions, headings, and instructions.

Call-In/Mail-In/Fax Service

Instructors may use Brown & Benchmark's convenient call-in/mail-in/fax service to generate tests. Select questions from the Test Item File at the end of the Instructor's Manual. Then call 800–338–5371, or mail your selections to Educational Resources at Brown & Benchmark Publishers, 25 Kessel Ct., Madison, WI 53711, or fax your request to Educational Resources at 608–277–7351. Within two working days of receiving your order, Brown & Benchmark will send by first-class mail (or Fax) a test master, a student answer sheet, and an answer key for fast and easy grading.

Slides

A set of 50 high-quality color slides correlated to the text or a museum-specific videodisc, available free to qualifying adopters.

Videos

Qualifying adopters may select video(s) from the Brown & Benchmark video catalog.

Brown & Benchmark Art Transparencies Set

A set of acetate transparencies is available with *Art: Context and Criticism*. The set includes illustrations of art elements and principles; architectural styles; media; and maps.

TECHNOLOGY PRODUCTS

Culture 2.0

Developed by Cultural Resources, Inc., Culture 2.0 © takes interdisciplinary humanities students on a fascinating journey into humanity's cultural achievements via Hypercard © software. Available for purchase in either IBM PC or MAC formats, this seven-disk program gives students access to essays, almanacs, visual, and musical examples. For each time period, categories include history, politics, religion, philosophy, art, and music, which provides an interactive Socratic method of learning for students. Culture 2.0 also features note-taking capabilities, report capabilities, and a student workbook for more guided learning. Contact your Brown & Benchmark sales representative or call Educational Resources at 800–338–5371 for ordering and purchase information.

Explore the Humanities

Currently under development by Brown & Benchmark, this CD-ROM series will soon be available for purchase. **Explore the Humanities!** provides you and your students with a fully interactive exploration of many of the arts, ideas, and societies discussed in *The Humanities in Western Culture*. For further details, call your local Brown & Benchmark sales representative.

KEY TO SYMBOLS AND EXPLANATION OF PRONUNCIATION GUIDE

Many of the more in-depth discussions of materials and techniques are now boxed to ensure their easy location and are signposted in the main text with the symbol □. Other discussions of materials and techniques are marked by the symbol ● at the start of the relevant paragraph.

A Pronunciation Guide has been added at the end of each chapter and is intended to provide the reader with an acceptable pronunciation for difficult and unfamiliar names and terms. It uses a simple phonetic system, which includes the following symbols:

oh = long o, as in obey
ah = a, as in father
th = th as in them
eye = long i as in nice
eye (n) = consonants after eye appear in parentheses for clarity
n in lowercase at the end of stressed syllables = nasal n as in gahr-SOHn.

INTRODUCTION

■ I.1 Pietro Perugino
The Delivery of the Keys (detail) 1482
Fresco
Sistine Chapel, The Vatican, Rome

We know that the tail must wag the dog,
for the horse is drawn by the cart;
But the Devil whoops, as he whooped of old:
"It's clever, but is it art?"
RUDYARD KIPLING, *The Conundrum of the Workshops*

This is a book about art. Now, given the plethora of introductory art texts that fill the shelves of book stores, and further taking into consideration the health of forests, you might rightly ask, "Why another introduction to art book?" My justification for writing this text is straightforward: to facilitate a more modern, multi-faceted, and diverse approach to the understanding of art. Granted, looking at art is a difficult business these days. Once time-honored methods and supposed truths are falling by the wayside in the wake of recent debates. To replace them, we are now constructing a more tolerant, inclusive view of the role and importance of art in culture, a view that takes into consideration differences as well as similarities and sees art not as a series of masterpieces whose value is etched in stone but as a collection of visual documents that enables us to grasp the fundamental notion of humanity. To do this, it is essential to reconsider how and why we have come to perceive art — and indeed culture in general — the way we do, and further, what implicit value judgments we embrace when we accept such standards. This is no easy task, and to be effective in pursuing it, we shall have to reconsider the nature of certain "truths" in the light of their original historical context. In this light, I hope that the ideas presented here will contribute to your greater understanding of the complexities of culture.

THE POWER OF IMAGES

A story is often told of a man who allowed his perception of people to be openly swayed by outward appearances. Like many of his friends, he equated an individual's physical appearance with certain character attributes: external features were thus considered an excellent indication of one's merits. For example, he readily accepted such arbitrary traits as a projecting voice, stiff formal posture, and cold, penetrating eyes as admirable qualities for a leader, and time after time he would search out political candidates who corresponded most closely to this ideal. As a result, he supported a leader of considerable formal stature, believing him to be uniquely qualified, and naïvely relegated the politician's actual ideas to the furthest corner of his mind. The outcome was, of course, disastrous, and as a story this is meant to teach us just how deceptive prejudicial determinations can be. The story often ends with the leader becoming a tyrant who then goes on to banish the poor old man from the kingdom for his naïve views.

Twentieth-century history has sadly proven that we have yet to learn the lesson of this simple story, and the study of human affairs provides one glaring example after another of how the images one sees, the sounds one hears, and the interchanges one engages in are rarely as simple as they at first appear. (Need one look any further than the horrid dichotomy between Nazi politics and pageantry [Fig. **I.2**] in pre-Second World War Germany?)

Though most individuals will acknowledge that external appearance can give an indication of the character of an object, an image, or even a person, few would consider it the most reliable or accurate way of gauging meaning. On a more personal level, human beings desperately desire to be understood as more than a facade — our ideas, feelings, and aspirations are at least equally representative of our sense of "self." It has often been said that an individual's thoughts and social activities very much determine their outward appearance. If you need proof of this, consider something as simple as one's choice of clothing — a decision that is taken daily. Human beings are social animals, and as such we are self-conscious about how we appear to others. A considered choice of clothing is one of the many ways in which people attempt to project a specific kind of character to the world at large; it is a choice that is both conscious and manipulative.

(such as Ralph Lauren and Calvin Klein [Fig. **I.3**]) successfully promote clothing intended to reveal the wearer's self-image, his or her deliberately chosen persona — hence the term fashion "statement." Yet even this desire to project a certain image to the public is not as straightforward as it may first appear, for often other, less obvious circumstances influence decision making. Consider again the example of fashion: certain kinds of clothing and certain makers' products are inevitably more expensive than others, which makes these items more accessible to those with greater disposable income. In this scenario, the chosen fashion can become a projection not only of character traits but also of economic status. Sometimes the dictates of fashion are more insidious: they establish models of attractiveness that bear little realistic resemblance to the average person. Such dichotomies may be at the heart of a fantasy world

■ **I.2 Drummers of the Hitler Youth Movement at Nuremberg, September 1933**

Fashion and the fashion industry are illuminating examples of how complex social pressures can become intertwined with an activity as simple and seemingly innocuous as getting dressed. A brief look through fashion magazines such as *Vogue* or *Gentleman's Quarterly* provides the reader with a potpourri of clothing advertisements that sell not only sophisticated apparel but a lifestyle, even a body, to match. If the clothes one wears are an extension of one's personality, the choices themselves become a projection of those characteristics the individual finds *attractive*. Many of the most popular fashion houses

■ **I.3 Calvin Klein advertisement, 1993**

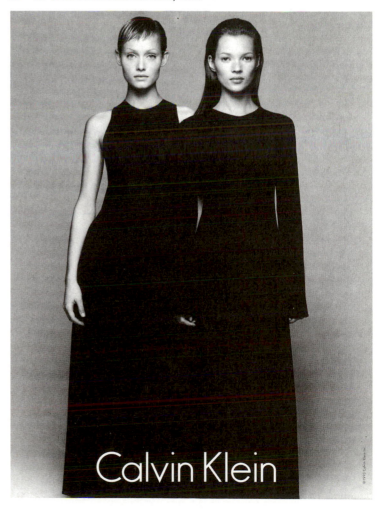

effective for the selling of merchandise, yet they also suggest a level of expectation and conformity that is clearly disconcerting.

In these examples it is possible to observe some intrinsic links between the idea of appearance and the sometimes complex and often unnoticed foundations on which it rests. To recognize these relationships is to understand better the workings of the world, and to do so effectively requires critical inquiry.

Although the history of fashion apparel is in itself a fascinating story of visual ideas, the purpose of this text is to introduce the subtleties of thinking that surround the "fine arts" — a term that will be discussed at length throughout the book. However, the analogy to fashion is a useful one, for if one agrees that "what one sees is not always what one gets," the same underlying issues surface once again in any discussion of art — namely, the problem of determining what it means for something to be attractive or popular, and how that in turn is based on other issues of historical and social interest. What exactly does it mean for something to be attractive? What makes something appear beautiful or important over several generations? And further, where do the traditional standards of excellence in art originate? These are difficult ques-tions, not easily answered by a trip to the neighbor-hood museum, but since they reflect the very essence of art in culture, it is imperative that a critically aware viewer consider them fully.

From where do we get our notions of art? As read-ers of an art appreciation text, it is quite possible that many of you may hold very specific ideas on the nature of art — perhaps embodying those ideas in a specific example — a well crafted landscape painting or figure sculpture against which other works of art are measured. The assumption is that art is something that takes *talent*, patience and hard work and thus should be appreciated for the considerable skills of its maker. Another assumption held dear by many a viewer is that art is supposed to look "like some-thing." Since abstract art appears to have little or no reference to everyday life, it is often either dismissed as incomprehensible or lauded as otherworldly. Even the very teaching of art is grounded in exercises from observation, under the assumption that technical skills will make the student a "better" artist. (Take, for example, Fig. **I.4**, a leaf from a "learn to draw" book, which typifies such an approach.) Who is to say that rendering objects from observation has anything to do with art? An even better question might be to ask

■ **I.4** *"Portrait drawing with ease"* reproduced from *Drawing on the Right Side of the Brain* by Betty Edwards

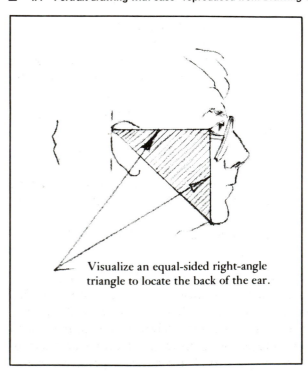

Visualize an equal-sided right-angle triangle to locate the back of the ear.

Back of eye

Back of ear

Eye-level to chin equals back of eye to back of ear.

why it is that creating an illusion of three dimensions on a flat surface has been so intriguing to so many people for so many years. Obviously, such ideas had to come from somewhere, and they must have been based on a commonly held belief as to the nature of art — what it was, and how it was useful to a society. Once again the analogy to fashion resonates, for if art is produced, taught, and even sold under particular assumptions about quality and attractiveness, it follows that art must be at least as susceptible to external pressures as any other expression or "statement." A study of art thus provides a looking-glass into the history of what it meant, and indeed means, to be human.

VIEWING ART AS LANGUAGE

Visual images are one of the most basic forms of communication available to the human community. It is through the eyes that the world is known in its most immediate and accessible state, and it is from this firsthand experience of nature that ideas were originally formed. Yet communication is a surprisingly complex, multi-faceted event; the successful transmission of even the simplest of ideas from one person to another requires that the exchange pass through a series of subtle operations.

The noted linguist Roman Jakobson was one of the first theorists to provide a comprehensive analysis of the structure of the communicative act. This study of sign systems, generally referred to as *semiotics*, takes into consideration six components specific to human interaction. Take, for instance, a friendly conversation with an acquaintance. To begin the process of communication one participant addresses the other: the *addressor* (1) says hello to the *addressee* (2). Between these two participants a *message* passes, "hello" (3); a shared *code* that makes the message intelligible (4) — let us assume both participants understand English; the *medium* of communication (5) means the actual spoken words; and finally there is the *context* of the conversation (6) — perhaps an introductory greeting. If any one of these six distinct aspects of communication breaks down, the interchange of ideas will in all likelihood cease. For instance, if one of the two participants does not understand English (the code), communication will be difficult. Likewise, if one of the

participants enters into the conversation at mid-point and is not privy to the context of the ideas, they will "misunderstand" the message, and again communication is thwarted. The exchange of ideas is thus never as simple and complete an experience as one might at first assume.

Since visual images are created by individuals, exist in the world, and are viewed by others, they inevitably become the focus of possible communication, and as such enter into a series of operations identical to that of oral or written traditions. Traffic lights are but one of literally thousands of examples of visual communication the average person confronts on a daily basis. If all members of society did not possess the same shared code (the code being red equals stop, yellow warning, green go), chaos would ensue. It is not that red "is" stop, since red is a color, but rather that members of that society have been brought up to identify such a color, when situated in that given medium (a traffic light) and in such a context (an intersection), as "meaning" stop. If one of those variables is taken away, red no longer means stop; indeed, depending on the culture and context, it might well be comprehended as "go." This same set of operations goes on every time an individual looks at a piece of art. For example, in schematic form, an examination of Mary Cassatt's *The Bath* (Fig. **I.5**) of 1891 would be constructed in the following way:

Addressor: the artist (Mary Cassatt)
Addressee: the viewer (person X)
Message: the tenderness of the relationship between mother and daughter, the innocence of the child, the nurturing character of woman, etc.
Code: traditional Western pictorial devices such as shallow illusionistic space, modeling to produce volume, the influence of Japanese prints introduced in the late nineteenth century
Context: 1891 painting produced by a woman artist, now situated in a late twentieth-century museum environment
Medium of communication: a 39½ x 26 in (100.2 x 66 cm) oil painting

Note how many possible variables there are within the context of communication: the message is dependent on characteristics of both the addressor's and the addressee's own histories, and even the context spans two very different eras. In fact, the only stable aspect of this whole operation is the physical painting itself.

■ I.5 Mary Cassatt, *The Bath* 1891
Oil on canvas, 39½ x 26 in (100.2 x 66 cm)
The Art Institute of Chicago, Robert A. Waller Fund

England) are removed from twentieth-century experience. To understand the code and context is to avail oneself of one of the true treasures of literature; to plunge freely into the writing without an "appreciation" of how communication works is to lose a considerable amount of what the author has to offer. The same is certainly true of the visual arts, in which code and context also combine to promote clearer communication and meaning. After all, isn't that why one takes the time and invests the energy to look at art?

One might think from this discussion that "pure" communication can exist once all the various operations are working in sync. Unfortunately, this is never completely possible, since each of the variables has a frustrating propensity to change or shift. The most obvious example of this occurs in the lives and experiences of the participants. Since no two individuals possess identical experiences, educational backgrounds, social surroundings, family structures, etc., their view of the world is never exactly the same. If you need proof of this, consider how often supposedly "eyewitness" accounts of crimes differ from one another, even though the witnesses are absolutely sure of what they saw. Another famous example is the co-called Grecian Urn (Fig. **I.6**), on which two faces converge to create a vessel shape in the space between them. Depending on the viewer or the context, this image has chameleon-like characteristics, changing its identity from vessel to faces. In this way, the viewer becomes an integral part of the overall creative process, since it

Consider this schema within the context of another art form: literature. Anyone who has struggled through Chaucer's *Canterbury Tales* will tell you that written English has changed a great deal over the past 600 years. Take, for instance, the opening lines from the "Prolog:"

Whan that Aprille with his shoures soot
The droghte of Marche hath perced to the roote,
And bathed every veyne in swich licour,
Of which vertu engendred is the flour;...

Some parts of the manuscript are virtually impenetrable to today's casual reader, since both the code (late Middle English) and the context (fifteenth-century

■ I.6 Grecian Urn

is the viewer's set of assumptions that ultimately gives meaning to any object or image. In other words, the viewer is a vital player in the process of constructing meaning, and thus in the making of art.

The previous semiotic breakdown of *The Bath* can likewise provide some insights into the methods and strategies of the art critic. As was noted, each variable in the construction plays a fundamental role in understanding the whole. Said another way, each communicative component can provide the impetus for a series of investigations, which in turn may influence the interpretation and evaluation of the work of art.

Consider the six components once again in light of the previous discussion. For instance, perhaps the viewer has a specific interest in the life of Mary Cassatt and chooses to investigate how the painting of *The Bath* coincides with issues prominent in the artist's life. Understanding the work within this cloak of autobiography will have significant ramifications for its interpretation. Likewise, viewing the painting as a manifestation of gender relations during the later half of the nineteenth century will offer very different opportunities for interpretation. Each communicative act thus inevitably opens up to a variety of interpretative strategies and positions. These structural components inherent in communication are generally coupled with the following critical methods:

Addressor: a consideration of the artist; biographical criticism, psychoanalytic criticism based on the artist's life, writings etc.
Addressee: criticism based on how audiences perceive works of art; viewer-response criticism, audience evaluation
Message: the study of symbols, subjects, iconography, or cultural variances
Code: formal criticism, the study of conventions
Context: social/political criticism, the historical interpretations of the work of art
Medium: the study of materials, conservation

Note that many of the components are open to any number of methods of evaluation. For instance, a study of the subject matter (message) may involve the interpretation of a storyline or a symbol. Yet once initiated, this process may itself be open to a series of critiques, as symbols do not exist outside specific contexts and codes. In short, the interpretation of a work is, like the making of art, a complex and highly creative activity.

ART AND ITS CODES

It is the availability of a shared code that allows images, words, and other forms of expression to become intelligible. A significant amount of one's early life is spent learning codes, be it the English language or street signs. A child learns to express itself through these codes; without them, it is nearly impossible to function in society. Like other forms of communication, art has a series of codes that makes its images, objects, and buildings intelligible to others.

Consider Jan Vermeer's *Woman Holding a Balance* (Fig. **I.7**) of c. 1664, which utilizes several established pictorial devices (which are called *conventions*). Is it possible to identify any aspects of the coding in this work? Today, we are so accustomed to looking at the world through the mediating eyes of history that it is often difficult to ascertain the nature of reality from the series of codes developed to describe it. *Woman Holding a Balance* is a good example. The considerable charm and convincing design of the painting leave the viewer vulnerable to one obvious manipulation — the viewer perceives, even if only for a fleeting moment, that there is depth "in" that flat surface. If asked to examine this item as a physical object, you would be likely to respond that it is a series of colored oil-paint marks on a flat surface of stretched canvas. Yet asked what you "see," your response would probably be very different: a woman standing at a table in an interior space with daylight flooding in from the side. The transition from paint on canvas to woman in room requires a set of presumed notions about what certain combinations of paint and color "mean." It requires, in short, a code.

In this particular case, the code seems easy to access, since we have been brought up to "see" such images as visual equivalents of our own experience of the world. But is this really the case? Eizan's *Courtesan Misado of the Tama-ya (House of the Jewels)* of c. 1810 (Fig. **I.8**) also describes a female figure in an interior scene, yet the deep space and natural light of the Vermeer are nowhere to be found. Both images convey much the same information, yet each operates within very different assumptions about how a flat surface can best describe a scene. In Vermeer's Netherlands of the seventeenth century, it would be difficult to convince an audience that there was much merit in the Eizan print, since it did not attempt to

■ I.7 Jan Vermeer
Woman Holding a Balance
c. 1664
Oil on canvas
16¾ x 15 in (42.5 x 38 cm)
National Gallery of Art,
Washington, D.C.
Widener Collection

▶ I.8 Eizan
*Courtesan Misado of the
Tama-ya (House of the Jewels)*
c. 1810
Oban color print
Private collection

model the figure in the round and possessed no perspectival space — both of which are essential to producing a convincing illusion of space. In Eizan's Japan of the eighteenth and early nineteenth century, Vermeer's painting would have been viewed as an insensitive dismissal of the characteristics of flat design, which emphasizes line, color, and pattern. Though space is certainly implied in the print (through devices such as overlapping), it is always within overall design considerations. Who was/is right? The answer is both, but to understand how and why, it is necessary to expand the earlier definition of a code to accommodate these wide variations.

A VOCABULARY LESSON

One reasonably certain aspect of communication is that its codes both embody and are susceptible to the pressures of change. This should make sense: a language incapable of adapting to new situations would simply become irrelevant. This seemingly obvious detail has in fact considerable ramifications for the understanding of art, for if codes are by nature dynamic and changing, understanding the fundamental components of a pictorial code can provide a variety of insights into the art in question. In other words, deciphering a work's code and further recognizing how various codes are employed for specific kinds of communication are at the very heart of understanding art. It is necessary here to digress briefly into a discussion of some of the fundamental components (sometimes called *elements*) employed by artists.

Line

There is perhaps no simpler or more rudimentary method for expressing oneself in visual form than through the use of line. By definition, a line is the path made by a moving point. Perhaps a more instructive definition could be that a line is a purposeful mark, which implies a meaning beyond its own physical presence. Consider handwriting — what is it but a series of marks connected as lines, which when

organized in certain collectively understood configurations suggest a message? Since lines in the visual arts perform essentially the same function, it is right to expect from such marks the same communicative potential and nuance.

Lines can possess a variety of characteristics, depending on their shape, density, rhythm, and angularity, and the materials that have produced them. Further, the context in which they appear and the message they are attempting to transmit can influence their perceived character. Consequently, the method one uses to describe a subject or emotion is hugely important to an idea's reception. Line, being a building block for the expression of a visual idea, thus provides an opportunity to consider the artist's possible intent and the potential meanings implicit in his/her method of execution.

Consider the following three examples in which line plays a fundamental role in how one interprets meaning: Vincent van Gogh's *Grove of Cypresses* (Fig. **I.9**), Henri Matisse's portrait of *Charles Baudelaire* (Fig. **I.10**), and Mel Bochner's *Vertigo* (Fig. **I.11**). Each of these works uses line in a distinct and suggestive manner, and they inform one's viewing experience in very specific ways.

In Van Gogh's drawing, the cypress trees were produced through groupings of parallel, undulating, and curvilinear lines. Here line is used to approximate, or give voice to, the artist's subjective impressions of the landscape, and in particular to the distinctive shape and *texture* of the southern French cypress. The *proximity* of these lines to one another determines the *density of value*, the *relative darkness* or lightness of the area (see Fig. I.13). Through this simple device van Gogh created an illusion of light and shade playing off the surface of the cypress, which in turn animates the space and makes the viewer aware of an illusion of depth into the picture plane. The artist also varied the *relative thickness* of his line, which again creates variations in value that suggest movement and rhythm. Finally, the absence of straight lines or hard angles gives the drawing a vine-like, organic quality that speaks metaphorically of a wild and untamed kind of growth. In short, the methods employed by van Gogh in producing this drawing have had an enormous effect on how the viewer perceives its meaning.

Henri Matisse's portrait of *Charles Baudelaire* also used line for very specific means, but his method of execution differed greatly from the textural mark making of van Gogh. Matisse, who once said that art should be like a comfortable chair to a tired business-man, produced a pared down and yet extraordinarily refined portrait of the great French writer. Unlike van Gogh, who varied line thickness and shifts in value, Matisse chose to use a single character or *measure* of line, which remains uniform throughout the drawing. This relative sameness of line places greater visual emphasis on the quality or *direction* of the marks. Some of the lines make long, sweeping curves, such as the diagonal of the collar and the jaw; others are more abrupt in their change of direction as in the upper lip. This expressive device is called *line speed*, and it is used to move the eye across the surface of the drawing to create a very tangible visual rhythm — something that is often pleasing to the eye.

Matisse also managed to provide the viewer with a strong suggestion of depth through the simple move-ment of *exterior lines* into *interior spaces*. A good exam-ple of this device can be seen on the left side of the

■ I.9 Vincent van Gogh
Grove of Cypresses 1889
Reed pen and ink over pencil on paper
24¼ x 18¼ in (62.4 x 46.4 cm)
Art Institute of Chicago
Gift of Robert Allerton, 1927.543

■ I.10 Henri Matisse
Portrait of Baudelaire (plate, page 136) from
Poésies de Stéphane Mallarmé, published
Lausanne, Albert Skira & Cie, October 1932
Etching, printed in black, composition 12 x 9 in
(20.5 x 22.9 cm) (irreg.)
Collection, The Museum of Modern Art, New York
The Louis E. Stern Collection
Photograph © 1996 The Museum of Modern Art,
New York
© Succession H. Matisse/DACS 1996

■ I.11 Mel Bochner
Vertigo 1982
Charcoal, conté, crayon, and pastel on sized
canvas, fixed with magna varnish
9 ft x 6 ft 2 in (2.74 x 1.88 m)
Albright-Knox Art Gallery, Buffalo, New York
Charles Clifton Fund, 1982

drawing, by following the path of the vertical defining the side of the poet's head down to its finish at the upper jaw. At the top, the mark is used as *outline*, which is roughly defined as the enclosing of a two-dimensional space by following the external border of an object — it provides the general shape of an object but tells nothing of its spatial character. Recall the exercise you might have done in primary school, where you traced around your hand: the resultant image gave a decent enough approximation but had frustratingly little descriptive potential as it told nothing about the quality, thickness, or personality of the hand. Matisse circumvented this problem, often associated with such distilled methods of drawing, by

allowing some of his external (*out-*) lines to follow their natural course into the interior, suggesting form and thereby producing a more engaging description of Baudelaire. With the simple turn of a line, the artist constructed a convincing suggestion of space, turning *shape* (a two-dimensional closed description) into *form* (a three-dimensional or illusion of three-dimensional description) without sacrificing any of the restrained elegance of his drawing.

Mel Bochner's use of line has many of the same visual characteristics as the previous two examples, but in this case the lines are no longer subservient to some recognizable content — they *are* the content. The artist used a variety of marks, differing in texture, density, and measure. In *Vertigo*, dramatic changes in line direction create very abrupt shifts across the picture plane. Into this high-strung configuration, he added something generally referred to as *visual history*, a process of *overlaying lines* in which initial marks are diminished by either erasing or being covered. The result is a visual record of the drawing process, including all the decisions made by the artist in the production of the work. The consequences are significant: instead of simply concentrating the viewer's attention on an illusion of space, it confronts the viewer with something more physically tangible — a record of the very activity of producing a composition. Taken a step further into the realm of speculation, one could rightly claim that in Bochner's work the illusion of space is supplanted by an actual material- or time-oriented space (since it is a record of an activity and its thought processes).

Value

In the previous discussion of van Gogh's *Grove of Cypresses*, passing mention was made of the artist's use of line proximity as a means to create a variety of values between black and white. By definition, value is *the contrast in light and dark that a line suggests against its ground*. In the value scale (Fig. **I.12**), the viewer may experience such a contrast as a series of grays between black and white. Black, white, and the grays between them are referred to as *neutrals*, in that they are said to possess *no color quality*, differing from each other only in the quantity of light they reflect. Such changes in value can be produced in a number of ways: by pressure exerted on the drawing tool, the closeness of one line to another, the relative thickness of a line, overlapping of marks, etc. Jacques Villon's *Portrait of a Young Woman* (Fig. **I.13**) done in drypoint, is a good example of the variety of means available to an artist for achieving gradations in value. In this work, the interaction of thick versus thinner, more delicate lines, varying line pressures, and the

■ I.13 Jacques Villon
Portrait of a Young Woman (*Portrait de Jeune Femme*) 1913
Drypoint, printed in black, pick: 21⁹/₁₆ x 16¼ in (54.8 x 41.3 cm)
Collection, The Museum of Modern Art, New York
Gift in Memory of Peter H. Deitsch
Photograph © 1996 The Museum of Modern Art, New York

overlapping of lines (called *cross-hatching*) all contribute to the production of a variety of values that enables the subject to be defined in illusionistic space.

Value is an important component in any description of illusionistic space, as it provides the artist with an opportunity to create *edges* (the point at which one value meets another), a device that mimics the way one perceives the world. In communities in which representing the world in a naturalistic manner is highly valued, the production of images with value gradations is fundamental. As this text demonstrates, cultures have either accepted or rejected this technical convention according to whether it suits their collective needs.

■ I.12 Value scale in gray

white   high light   light   low light   medium   high dark   dark   low dark   black

Color

Though the consideration of value is of primary significance for any artist interested in producing a "life-likeness," the fact remains that we perceive the world not in black and white but in a multitude of variations of color. Further, the materials with which the artist works are produced and exist in the real world and thus possess color. Throughout this book, there are discussions of theories of color as they have evolved within specific historical circumstances, but perhaps here a brief overview of color terminology may be of some benefit. Keep in mind that these terms are for the most part nineteenth- and twentieth-century inventions and consequently had little to no influence on artists before this period. (For a lengthy discussion of this issue, see Chapter Seven's section on color theory.)

Here, the discussion of color is limited to the realities reflected in the impure, everyday material properties of paint, pigment, ink etc., since the theoretical physics of color has little bearing on how color is used in the visual arts. In mixing pigments, a vast number of color variations can occur, and in order to facilitate some understanding and appreciation of their specific character, it is essential to identify *color property*. A look at a simple *color wheel* (Fig. **I.14**) may help here.

The color wheel presents a ring, constructed from three anchoring or *primary colors*: red, yellow, and blue (Fig. **I.15**). Theoretically, all other color is produced from the mixing of these primaries with the exclusion or inclusion of light. Consider the color orange. It appears on the wheel half way between the primaries red and yellow, from which can be inferred that its constituent makeup is 50 percent red and 50 percent yellow. Likewise, the colors green and purple exist in similar positions between the primaries yellow-and-blue and blue-and-red (Fig. **I.16**). These colors are identified as *secondary* and are surrounded by *intermediate colors*, which are produced by mixing the

■ **I.14 Color wheel**

■ **I.15 Primary triad**

■ **I.16 Secondary triad**

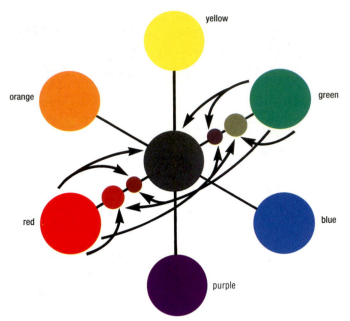

■ **I.17 Complementary wheel with lines leading to deep gray**

50 percent primary and 50 percent secondary colors that stand next to each other on the wheel.

In the center of the wheel stands deep gray (since black is defined as the complete absence of light and thus theoretically cannot be produced through mixing actual color), which is known as *neutralized color*. To produce a true neutral, artists often mix together equal parts of two colors that are positioned directly across from each other on the wheel, called *complementary colors* (Fig. **I.17**). Red and green are thus considered complementaries, as are blue and orange, purple and yellow, etc. Anyone who has tried mixing blue and orange will probably debate the ability to get a dark gray from such a blend. This is primarily because paints, pigments etc. are not pure color but are materials that exist, even in their purest states, with impurities. It is here that theory gives way to practical

experience, as artists must learn many of their mixing skills through trial and error. As a consequence, color mixing is often one of the most fundamental and yet most challenging skills a painter may have to develop.

Given the vocabulary, one may begin to describe color properties in more meaningful ways. All color has three defining properties: *hue*, *value*, and *intensity*. Hue is simply the name of color wheel colors — no sandstone or maize here. The practical reason for this is standardization. Value, as was previously discussed, is a means of discussing a color's relative lightness or darkness. Consider the hue blue, which can exist in a variety of different conditions ranging from a very light "powder" blue through a deep "midnight" blue. The blue referred to when discussing its condition on the color wheel is called its *normative value*, with "powder" blue existing at a lighter value, and "midnight" below normative. A color whose situation can be described as lighter than normative is called a *tint*, and that which falls below is referred to as a *shade*. To make matters even more confusing, each normative color also possesses a value that differentiates it from other colors. For instance, the value of the hue yellow is much lighter in value than blue. The schematic (Fig. **I.18**) illustrates this premise, in which a variety of hues is lined up across the top of the previous value scale in order of relative value.

The final property of color is its intensity, sometimes called its *saturation* or *chroma*. This generally describes a color's *purity*, with a hue being at its most intense at normative on the color wheel. As a color loses its intensity, it moves towards neutral. A color theorist might describe the mixing of two colors that are located directly across from each other as the simultaneous diminishing of intensity (neutralizing). The following schematic provides a clear example of what all this means in visual terms (Fig. **I.19**).

■ **I.18 Hues on the right side of the color wheel arranged according to gradations on the gray value scale**

| white | high light | light | low light | medium | high dark | dark | low dark | black |

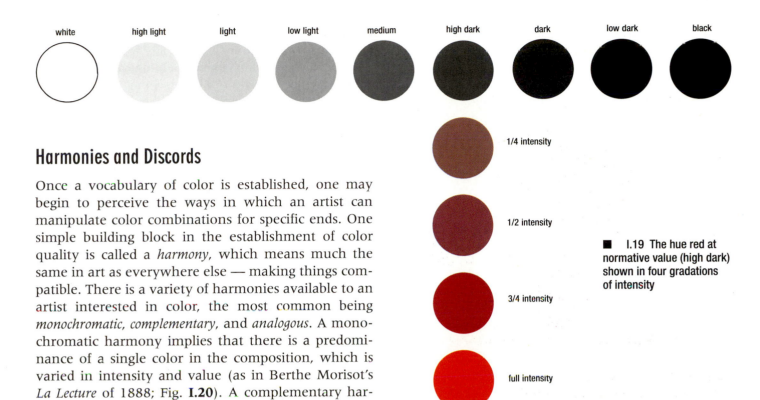

white high light light low light medium high dark dark low dark black

Harmonies and Discords

Once a vocabulary of color is established, one may begin to perceive the ways in which an artist can manipulate color combinations for specific ends. One simple building block in the establishment of color quality is called a *harmony*, which means much the same in art as everywhere else — making things compatible. There is a variety of harmonies available to an artist interested in color, the most common being *monochromatic*, *complementary*, and *analogous*. A monochromatic harmony implies that there is a predominance of a single color in the composition, which is varied in intensity and value (as in Berthe Morisot's *La Lecture* of 1888; Fig. **I.20**). A complementary harmony is one in which complementary colors and

1/4 intensity

1/2 intensity

3/4 intensity

full intensity

■ I.19 The hue red at normative value (high dark) shown in four gradations of intensity

■ I.20 Berthe Morisot
La Lecture (*Reading*) 1888
Oil on canvas
29¼ x 36½ in (74 x 93 cm)
Museum of Fine Arts,
St. Petersburg, Florida
Museum purchase in memory of
Margaret Acheson Stuart

their contingent values are used to counterbalance and sometimes neutralize the visual weight of each other. A typical complementary harmony is red-green, used by Vincent van Gogh in his *Night Café* (Fig. **I.21**). Finally, an analogous harmony is a composition in which a section of the color wheel is emphasized, such as a yellow-orange-red or a red-violet-blue. In these harmonies, the secondary colors often play a crucial visual role in connecting discordant primaries.

In the above examples, color is chosen to create a unified and harmonious whole. The result is often an impression of stasis, balance or equilibrium — at least in terms of color. In other cases, an artist might consciously attempt to disturb such a visual equilibrium by using color combinations that do not connect in a harmonious fashion, choosing instead to allow these disharmonies or discords to create a sense of tension or vibration (as in Matisse's *Study for the Joy of Life*; Fig. **I.22**). Yet what is most clear from the previous

■ **I.21** Vincent van Gogh
Night Café 1888
Oil on canvas
28½ x 36¼ in (72.4 x 92.1 cm)
Yale University Art Gallery, New Haven
Bequest of Stephen Carlton Clark, B.A. 1903

■ I.22 Henri Matisse
Study for the Joy of Life 1905
Oil on canvas
18 x 22 in (45.7 x 55.9 cm)
Statens Museum für Kunst,
Copenhagen
© Succession H. Matisse/DACS
1996

examples is that this basic vocabulary of color, line, value, and their combination is highly susceptible to interpretation and thus is primary to any discussion of art. But one must be equally careful not to let such considerations obscure an even more fundamental observation: that since such techniques exist in the world and are used by artists and challenged from time to time, they are also inherently social. As a result, even a discussion of a subject as seemingly innocuous as line or color must be understood contextually: the elements mean something different to each age.

THE CHANGING FACE OF QUALITY

Let us now reconsider a question posed earlier in the introduction: what makes something valuable or attractive to a society, or even generations of people? Is it possible for certain items to possess an intrinsic beauty or merit that can traverse cultural differences and the boundaries of time?

The Vermeer-Eizan comparison is a useful starting-point, for it is clear that, during the time of their making, neither culture would have assigned much merit to each other's art — the code from which visual communication begins and value is assigned simply was not accessible. From this example, it is apparent that even the most basic standards for assessing quality in art are very much dependent on time and place. In other words, what is art today was not necessarily art yesterday, and may not be art tomorrow, since the notion of art is always contingent upon a series of culturally derived ideas — ideas that present themselves not only in the subject matter or even materials of art but in the very visual code itself. Where do these codes originate? Quite simply, they develop and evolve from within the culture.

The term *manifestation* is often used to describe the important relationship between the way in which one visually describes the world and the greater discourse of ideas and social influences that makes this description possible. These visual strategies, which help produce an accessible visual code, are called *conventions*.

Conventions are the specific tools used to form a visual or other cultural code. Conventions are also

■ **I.23 Masaccio**
Virgin and Child 1426
Wood, 53¼ x 28¾ in (135.3 x 73 cm)
National Gallery, London

inherently social in nature; they come into existence through common agreement and are maintained through custom. What do conventions look like? Sometimes they appear as technical considerations, such as those of line and color; often, conventions have symbolic significance. A familiar example might be the gold halo (Fig. **I.23**), which was an accepted feature of Christian art for many centuries. The halo *motif* (motif meaning a recurring image or theme) was used as a visual equivalent for the aura (inner glow) holy personages were supposed to possess. Viewers are accustomed to "seeing" these gold discs as halos and as a result are cued in to the painting's possible subject matter. The blue dress of the Virgin is used in a similar manner: the color blue was symbolic of heaven, and its use throughout much of Christian art was a reminder of Mary's nature. Both these visual considerations are conventions — visual manifestations of then contemporary notions about the nature of God and the Christian religion. It is irrelevant whether or not Christ and the saints actually walked this earth with gold-leaf plates attached to their heads, or that Mary's wardrobe included only variations of blue — these are conventions that are to be understood as part of a larger visual code, which, when accessible to the viewer, makes the process of communication more complete or enriched.

Sometimes conventions are more subtle and complex than relating an idea to a color. Throughout history, there have been conventions so persuasive and pervasive that it has been difficult to view the world through art without them. This is true of an idea called *linear perspective*. First perfected by the Romans and then rediscovered in the Renaissance, linear perspective is a geometric system for representing depth on a two-dimensional plane. One-point perspective, in which all receding lines converge upon a single "vanishing point," was by far the most popular method of describing space in the early Renaissance. Note how in Perugino's painting of the *Delivery of the Keys* (Fig. **I.24**) the scene unfolds in a very predictable, through perceptually impossible, manner from the central door, positioned above Christ as he gives the keys of Rome to the first pope, St. Peter. The balance and predictability of this design are due in part to the artist's strict adherence to the "rules" of perspective, which, when applied in such a manner, help suggest deep space. However, this device does much more than simply create the illusion of space: it

■ I.24 Pietro Perugino
Delivery of the Keys 1482
Fresco
Sistine Chapel, The Vatican, Rome

further implies the unfolding of the entire world around the all-knowing view of the spectator. This is certainly not the world as we know it, but rather a carefully contrived, artificial, and rationally ordered world, in which all things are granted a specific place in the larger design of nature and in which the entire universe seems little more than an extension of the viewer's gaze. That this notion parallels the Renaissance view of man as the center of all things and the world as an unfolding of human consciousness should come as little surprise, since all conventions, in art or other subjects, are attempts to embody a community's world view in concrete form. (A discussion of linear perspective will take place in greater detail in Chapter Four.)

In the twentieth century, the idea of a world conforming to a logical pattern has taken a severe beating, and one-point perspective now seems more interesting as cultural history than a fruitful way of looking at the world — it has been replaced by conventions more appropriate for the current outlook. Nevertheless, during its time, perspective was an important feature of a much larger visual code, and by studying its relationship to other ideas, it is possible to understand how issues of quality in art have evolved, and further, what they meant during various historical periods and across disparate cultures. It is for this very reason that this book devotes a considerable amount of time to discussing the nature of conventions in various societies.

THE GOOD, THE BAD, AND THE UGLY

If quality is contingent upon a series of socially generated assumptions about the nature of good and bad or better and worse, any discussion of quality as it pertains to art is always fixed to a given age and cultural context. Since quality is first and foremost an idea, its criteria are susceptible to influences from within a given society; everything from politics to the weather can have an effect on what is perceived as good and

what as bad in a work of art, and throughout history this has proven to be the case.

Take, for instance, the example of the French Academy in the seventeenth century, when the ruling king, Louis XIV, and his minister Colbert designed a whole national art program to parallel the aspirations of the aristocracy. By carefully controlling all commissions and denying work to artists who operated outside the established code, they successfully determined the course of quality in French art for many years. What were those attributes of quality? A strong emphasis on drawing, solid forms, restrained color, balance of parts, clear design, and elevated subjects — which deliberately corresponded to the political notions of order, rationality, resolve, and firm structural management (see Fig. 5.28). Since these were seen as fitting attributes for the nation, their manifestation in art soon became equated with ideas of quality. The French Academy did not like work that elevated the status of the average citizen, notably the essentially middle-class representations of contemporary Dutch painting (such as Vermeer's *Woman Holding a Balance* [see Fig. I.7]); the democratic nature of such art seemed an affront to the God-given authority of the Crown. Eventually, this attitude

toward good art was replaced by a different conception of quality, based on an alternative set of values generated by changing social, political, and intellectual conditions.

Such apparent fickleness is inherent in virtually every collective human activity. Even such supposedly eternal codes as Christianity have changed enormously over the past centuries, due exclusively to social pressures (even the Bible itself is the result of debate and compromise). In fact, the very nature of art is dynamic, in flux, and never fixed, and that is why it has survived as an idea, indeed an essential part of the human community, since the dawn of consciousness. In other words, though art may indeed encompass an abundance of subjects, it is fundamentally about being human, and "being" has meant something different in every community.

■ I.25 Pierre Andre Brouilet
A Clinical Lesson at La Sâlpetrière 1887
Oil on canvas
Faculté de Médecine, Lyon

MAKING AMENDS

Despite the occasional setback, it appears that civilization is beginning to embrace a more inclusive, rather than exclusive, view of the world. Individuals once pushed to the periphery of cultural significance because of their gender, race, religious affiliation, or sexual preference are now actively participating in mainstream cultural debates, and the results have been both inspiring and important. Yet the road to change is arduous and difficult, particularly when there is an "accepted" view of history to compete against — a history of achievement and ideas based on white, male, European standards of truth, excellence, and quality.

Since art embodies such notions, it too has undergone a dramatic re-evaluation since c. 1975, as critics and historians alike try to uncover less savory aspects of Western civilization implicit within its visual culture. For instance, where are all the women artists throughout history? Why does the history of Western art seem to exclude the work of visible minorities? And why are women so often portrayed in the history of art as helpless objects of desire, rather than as active, capable participants (Fig. **I.25**)? These are not simple questions, yet they strike at the center of art making and its role in society. This book attempts to address such concerns within the context of a traditional view of art history — and this apparent contradiction requires further explanation.

PLOTTING THE COURSE

The organization of a text will often expose the particular biases of the person who writes it, and at least to this extent, this book is no different from any other. The decision to write the text in a chronological format (beginning with prehistoric society and moving toward the current age) reflects the nature of art and art making as a dynamic endeavor, influenced by the ideas in which it circulates. Without a basic understanding of the relationship between art making, art thinking, thinking, and finally being, it is virtually impossible to appreciate how art functions as an expression of a culture. Though it is certainly interesting to know how artists carved stone or how brush marks can be made to look like clouds, to study art simply as a series of techniques is to miss the point; those techniques are relevant only *because* they are grounded in culture and its ideas. In this way, a study of conventions as diverse as color theory and perspective may afford some insights into why certain ideas and groups have been excluded from the story.

This text is written as a general overview of the history of art making as a collection of ideas, concentrating on the relationship between art and society. To this end, the final chapter addresses several significant issues now dominating the cultural arena. The substance of Chapter Ten includes discussion of women's art, Post-modernism, revising art history, and other pertinent concerns, and it is meant as a critical revision to the text proper. This format is not without its flaws, yet it has been my conscious decision to err on the side of ideas, rather than give the impression that art appreciation is simply a matter of recognizing technical prowess.

Like a work of art or any other aspect of culture, this text reflects the pressures and influences of its age. I make no apologies for this. It is, however, my hope that this short journey through the history of art and ideas will make you a more critically aware viewer — with regard not only to art but also to the world in general. If art is to have any significance in this day and age, it must be made applicable to our lives; otherwise it becomes little more than a useless relic. By seeing art as an extension of ourselves and our society, rather than as something apart and superfluous, we become active participants in culture — and it is through our cultural expressions that we collectively define what it means to be alive. There are few occupations as precious as this.

Pronunciation Guide

Mel Bochner   mel **BAHK**-nur
Pierre André Brouilet   pyer **AHN**-dray broo-**LAY**
Charles Le Brun   sharl luh-**BROON**
Mary Cassatt   kuh-**sat**
Eizan   ay-**ZAHN**
Vincent van Gogh   van-**GOH**
Masaccio   muh-**SAH**-chee-oh
Henri Matisse   ahn-**REE** mah-**TEES**
Pietro Perugino   **PYE**-troh per-oo-**JEE**-noh
Jan Vermeer   yahn vur-**MAIR**

1

THE BEGINNINGS OF ART

1.1 The Great Pyramids at Giza, Egypt, c. 2650–2575 BC

"Where shall I begin, please your majesty?" he asked.
"Begin at the beginning," the King said, gravely,
"and go on till you come to the end: then stop."
LEWIS CARROLL, *Alice's Adventures in Wonderland*

The human species is notorious for viewing the world as an extension of itself. Thus history and art take on a certain organic unity: they are born, they live, and, with the species, they will someday die. For an introductory book on art as a collection of ideas, it is necessary to designate a *beginning*, but the questions of exactly where and when are not easily answered. In fact any concept of a beginning in art is laden with assumptions about the production of art itself, which changes with each generation. Keeping this in mind, this first chapter will attempt to examine some fundamental relationships necessary for image and object making and to begin what will be a text-long discussion on the nature of art.

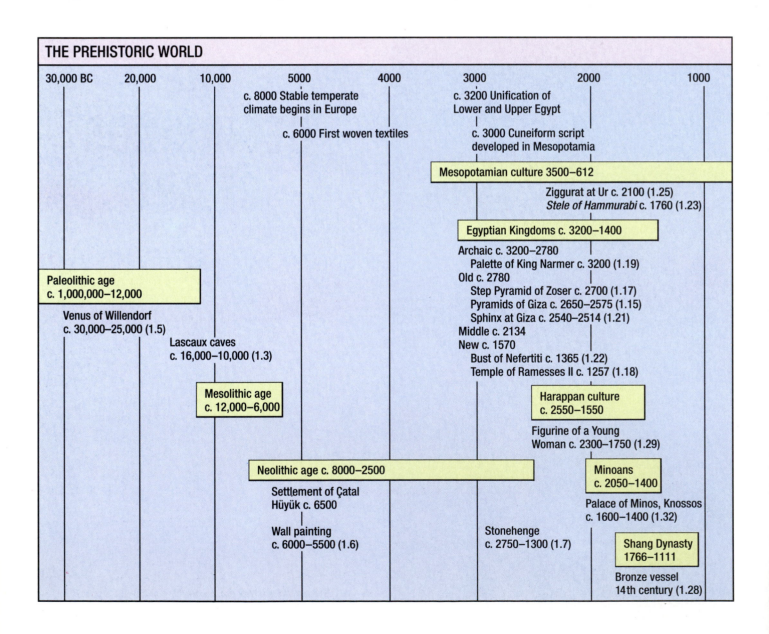

THE PREHISTORIC WORLD

30,000 BC	20,000	10,000	5000	4000	3000	2000	1000

c. 8000 Stable temperate climate begins in Europe

c. 6000 First woven textiles

c. 3200 Unification of Lower and Upper Egypt

c. 3000 Cuneiform script developed in Mesopotamia

Mesopotamian culture 3500–612

Ziggurat at Ur c. 2100 (1.25)
Stele of Hammurabi c. 1760 (1.23)

Egyptian Kingdoms c. 3200–1400

Archaic c. 3200–2780
Palette of King Narmer c. 3200 (1.19)
Old c. 2780
Step Pyramid of Zoser c. 2700 (1.17)
Pyramids of Giza c. 2650–2575 (1.15)
Sphinx at Giza c. 2540–2514 (1.21)
Middle c. 2134
New c. 1570
Bust of Nefertiti c. 1365 (1.22)
Temple of Ramesses II c. 1257 (1.18)

Paleolithic age c. 1,000,000–12,000

Venus of Willendorf c. 30,000–25,000 (1.5)

Lascaux caves c. 16,000–10,000 (1.3)

Mesolithic age c. 12,000–6,000

Harappan culture c. 2550–1550

Figurine of a Young Woman c. 2300–1750 (1.29)

Neolithic age c. 8000–2500

Settlement of Çatal Hüyük c. 6500

Wall painting c. 6000–5500 (1.6)

Minoans c. 2050–1400

Palace of Minos, Knossos c. 1600–1400 (1.32)

Stonehenge c. 2750–1300 (1.7)

Shang Dynasty 1766–1111

Bronze vessel 14th century (1.28)

■ 1.2 Prehistoric Europe

THE NATURE OF ART

On the surface, there might appear few obstacles to finding the beginning of art. Surely one simply starts with the cavemen and moves forward? This seems fair enough — that is, of course, until one is asked to determine which objects and artifacts constitute art and which do not. Consider this problem in terms of an example. Suppose one generally assumes that art is any handmade artifact. Using this rather simple definition, it would not be incongruous to consider an arrow head or an ax as a strong candidate for the label *art*. Indeed, since such items are often on display at prestigious museums, they must hold some value. Yet if this is the case, why are these ancient items considered more *art-like* than an ax in a local hardware store? Few, if any, would consider a power drill as worthy of art status. Almost immediately, one is forced to concede that art must be more specific than a handmade object. But what, then, are its parameters? It is within this context that the history of ideas becomes essential to any fruitful discussion of art.

Contrary to conventional wisdom, which presumes that there are eternal, fixed standards for virtually all human endeavors, art has always existed in a state of flux. Since art is first and foremost based on ideas, its very survival is contingent upon its ability to change with the times: art today was not necessarily art yesterday and might never be art again.

This contemporary mindset has certain repercussions for any discussion of history. If, for instance, a culture considers art as decoration, it is only logical that it should search through history for examples to reinforce such claims. One need look only as far as fourteenth-century Florence (see pages 179–182) to see how popular ideas tend to distort history to support one's own needs. Sometimes the art of a previous age can be used to manipulate an audience, as when, in the 1930s, the Italian dictator Benito Mussolini cited Roman culture as a precedent for his authoritarian regime and attempted to construct virtual facsimiles of antique art and architecture for a modern audience. To Mussolini, as well as less despotic types such as Thomas Jefferson, the ideals of Classical civilization were reincarnated for deliberate political ends that would effectively evoke concepts such as pride, power, stability, and destiny. Here the pedestrian notion of a fixed and static history shows itself in practice to be as malleable as clay, shaped by each generation to suit its own needs. History, and thus art history, is as much a projection of the present as it is authentic documentation of the past.

MAKING IMAGES IN THE PALEOLITHIC AGE

If art history is a dynamic concept shaped by present views, it is fair to assume that any designated starting point for the origins of art will embody certain aspects of the way in which today's culture has come to understand the nature of art and art making. Like most other surveys, this text will begin with two fairly popular examples of early visual culture, the Lascaux caves (Fig. **1.3**) and the so-called *Venus of Willendorf* (see Fig. 1.5), but in doing so it will further consider what such choices say about the current situation.

Consider the issue of human survival. It is a commonly held assertion that the most elementary activities necessary for the continuation of life are those of sustenance and procreation. Without one, it is impossible to conceive of the other, and without both, extinction is inevitable. Even the idea of consciousness

■ **1.3 Main hall, or "Hall of Bulls"** c. 16,000–14,000 BC, Lascaux caves, France has had to evolve from the overriding necessities of finding food and continuing the species. Art, on the other hand, is an act of consciousness. Even in work that claims inspiration from a spiritual or inner experience, the processes of selecting and editing imply at least a basic consciousness of the meaning of the activity and its context. Simple as it may seem, within this rather crude set of circumstances one can speculate about the possible origins of art. If eating and reproducing are essential characteristics of the human species (and every other organism for that matter), and art is an act of consciousness that arises out of the fulfillment of these necessities, it would be reasonable that the first visual expressions of consciousness should come through images or objects associated with sexuality or the hunt. In locating examples of such a correlation between basic survival and the expression of it, perhaps one may legitimately claim an appropriate starting point for the discussion of art.

The Lascaux Caves

In 1879, a series of Paleolithic-era cave drawings were accidently discovered by a Spanish archaeologist near Altamira, Spain. Though not authenticated until 1902, the Altamira find paved the way for a series of impressive discoveries, culminating in the 1940 discovery at Lascaux. The Lascaux Caves in the south of France are considered among the most exquisite and well-preserved examples of **prehistoric** culture. Inside the impressive tunnel complex there remains a vast array of *drawings* that date back 15,000 to 20,000 years. Anthropologists are still debating the meaning of these images, but it appears that they served some function relating to the hunt. The Paleolithic peoples were essentially migratory, since the stabilizing influence of agriculture was not yet a feasible alternative; their very existence relied on the success of the hunt. Two consequences follow on from such a basic level of survival: the first is a reverence for the food supply (together with a respect for the natural order of things and a giving of thanks for the coming of the herds) and the second is the necessity of moving to find food. It is within this context that Paleolithic communities first produced visual expressions.

The hunt was most likely a central focus in these early communities, and beasts of prey became the focus of enormous attention and admiration, particu-

larly since human lives depended on them. It is from these conditions that their religion and art evolved. Religion explains and orders the universe around a set of collectively assumed principles of reality, so if the reality of 15,000 BC was survival through the hunting of wild animals it was only natural that the hunt would be preceded by a ritual contemplation and appeasement of the animal's spirit. Such rituals were of considerable significance for these early communities; they provided an important arena for transmitting knowledge and history between generations. Visual expressions of the hunt were produced to serve as surrogates and objects of contemplation for the most basic experiences of life. The *Black bull* (Fig. **1.4**, on page 42) visually exemplifies this early organic relationship between the human community and its prey.

The series of caves that make up the Lascaux complex are remarkably well preserved. Their images utilized two primary *methods* of drawing: **solid shape** and **contour**. Due in part to the consistent pattern of contour drawing overlapping solid shape (note how in Fig. 1.3 one bull is superimposed over the other), historians now speculate that the solid images were the first to be produced, with the contour drawings appearing perhaps even centuries later. Although everything from the animal's anatomy to its coloring and scale was sensitively considered in terms of the natural world, these early image makers were apparently also aware of the suggestive qualities of the cave surface itself; many a bulge or crevice on the stone surface was used to imply a part of the subject's anatomy.

The consistent use of this pictorial device throughout Lascaux and other Paleolithic cave complexes has given some credence to the *image by accident* hypothesis, popular since the Renaissance as a possible explanation for the original impulse of art. The argument, first suggested by the Renaissance scholar Leon Battista Alberti (c. 1404–72), takes as its premise the notion that art began with the recognition of striking resemblances between objects (say a tree trunk or boulder and a face or animal); when someone added another element (perhaps a stick to suggest horns, or a pebble to suggest a head) to the natural occurrence in order to complete the likeness, art was born. This argument helps explain the vivid relationship between the cave wall surfaces and the subsequent placement of images in Paleolithic art.

The contour-drawing elements in the Lascaux caves exhibit a further development of the early visual language of image making. The desire to reuse wall space already decorated with solid-shape designs may have caused a later painter to delineate only the exterior edge of a bull or some other subject on top of the earlier images so as not to destroy their visual identity. As a result, line was added to the visual repertoire. Even in such early examples, it is possible to see the expressive possibilities afforded by line: the meeting of slow curves (such as the inverted *C* shape of the neck of the bull) with more angular joints (such as the front legs) gives the image an appealing rhythmic flow, which further entices the viewer to follow the path of the line around the animal. This visual quality (**line speed**) though still in its infancy at Lascaux was an important preface to later drawing conventions.

The Venus of Willendorf

The so-called *Venus of Willendorf* (c. 25,000 BC; Fig. **1.5**), perhaps the oldest surviving three-dimensional depiction of a human body, is approximately 8,000 to 10,000 years older than the images at Lascaux and exhibits notably different characteristics. (Venus was once a catch-all label for virtually any unidentifiable female nude in earlier European scholarship.) The figure is portrayed in the round, possessing volume and interacting with real space — the features that are now recognized as essential characteristics of the art of **sculpture**. Like all three-dimensional forms, the *Venus of Willendorf* may be viewed from any angle, a process that mimics the viewer's experience of the world.

Since, among over 200 surviving Paleolithic figurines, there is not a single male statuette, such statuettes as the *Venus of Willendorf* were probably fertility symbols. The expressive description of the body brings the symbolic intentions of the carving into sharp focus. The massive breasts and bulbous stomach suggest the life-giving qualities of the woman as childbearer. The faceless, downward-turning head of the figurine, which denies personality or

■ 1.5 *Venus of Willendorf* c. 30,000–25,000 BC
Lower Austria
Limestone, height 4½ in (11.5 cm)
Naturhistoriches Museum, Vienna

individuality establishes the image as a more general expression of sexual power.

Note that this fertility statuette is based less on the natural observation embodied in the bulls at Lascaux than on some more generalized, perhaps abstract consideration. It appears that, with god forms, the image maker was under less pressure (or had less interest) in producing an image that corresponded to something in nature; instead, emphasis was probably placed on creating images that appeared as embodiments of power and mystery, manipulating forms to accentuate their other-worldliness. As a result even at this early date there was apparently a process of conceptualization with regard to image making. The scale seems to appear as such: as the depicted forms move from animal life, through humans, to cult figures and godheads, their visual identities become increasingly abstract, with certain features accentuated and others diminished.

■ 1.4 Black bull c. 16,000–14,000 BC
Lascaux caves, France
Paint on limestone
Total length of bull 13 ft (3.96 m)

From such examples as the cave paintings and venus figures, it is clear that visual images were deliberately used as sources of order and understanding in the world. The visual description of figures and animals seems to have paralleled the development of religion as a means of appeasing an often hostile environment, and though it is unclear whether the initial representation of images inspired a devotion to their subject matter or whether speculation about the nature of the world precipitated the production of images (more likely), the result was significant.

The question as to why certain subjects were portrayed in two dimensions and others in three is equally challenging. Small stone carvings may certainly be tucked away in times of travel, and considering the migratory nature of these early communities, the choice of materials and scale might simply have been practical considerations. There is also the possibility that three-dimensional work was thought to mimic more effectively the physical reality of the human body (though this does not explain the two-dimensional character of the human and animal forms at Lascaux). The cave drawings are more likely to have been a transitory form of image making — perhaps even a ritual of mock creation intended to insure a successful hunt.

If the argument that the drawings were to make sure a hunt was successful is valid, it supports the current notion that image makers had special status in the tribe, since they were responsible for initiating such rites. This position has important ramifications for the way in which Western culture has come to view the role of the artist in early societies. It insists that artists are supremely *gifted*, their talents having been *given* to them by some higher order, and that they perform a function vital to the community. However, implicit in such a view is the contrary ancient notion that artists are up to no good, competing with the gods for creative supremacy. It is quite common in the history of culture to hear tales of magnificent technicians conspiring with the devil to enhance their power (the violin virtuoso Paganini is said to have sold his soul to the devil in exchange for greatness). A less elevated position views the artist as little more than a trained craftsperson, whose abilities are fostered through simple trial and error. Most likely, the true nature of creative activity lies somewhere between the two extremes.

It appears that, in earliest times, technical skills (how to produce a bull that appears to be running, how to carve a certain type of stone efficiently, etc.) were passed down from one generation to the next, allowing for the continuation of certain motifs and most likely securing a privileged position for the image maker in the community. In a sense, this dynamic of image making is a perfect analogy of life itself; the uneasy, sometimes volatile relationship between ideas, tradition, and individuality has unmistakable parallels to the trials and tribulations inherent in all social beings.

SECURING THE HOMEFRONT: THE NEOLITHIC AGE

The survival of the Paleolithic peoples depended primarily upon the hunt, and since the animals in question were usually migratory, so too were the hunters. For any dramatic shift in civilization to occur, it was necessary for at least a few communities to call one location home long enough to develop structures, decoration, and the all-important time to contemplate their place in the world. The breakthrough came in around 8000 BC, during the Mesolithic (Middle Stone) Age, when a number of disparate communities developed the notion (perhaps accidentally) that chasing dinner was far less appealing than cultivating it. There is some anthropological evidence to support the claim that changing climatic conditions around the Mediterranean basin had a profound effect on social developments at the time. The argument posits that a warming trend led to a more abundant food source, which in turn provided incentives to stay in one place long enough to settle. The discovery of agriculture — the precept that nature can effectively be controlled and manipulated — was to have important effects on the way in which the human community viewed itself and its art.

In the absence of the development of agriculture and the domestication of animals, the world would most certainly have been a very different place. With the advent of agriculture came the necessity for permanent dwellings, which, without the constraints of

■ 1.6 *Image of a Hunter* c. 6000–5500 BC
Detail of wall painting in the main room of Shrine A.III.1
Çatal Hüyük, Turkey

portability and scale, led to the development of more elaborate crafts. Perhaps the greatest impact of agriculture on society was the formation of communities that led to the organization of what is called civilized society. The word *civilization* comes from the Latin root citizen, which means town dweller. It is, therefore, not surprising that the human community has come to understand civilization based on the interrelations between people and ideas, rather than through concrete events and objects.

While communities were gaining increased confidence in their ability to manipulate their immediate environment during the early Neolithic period, their visual expressions were gaining a degree of consideration and complexity. This telling shift in sensibility (or the way one views the world) is most apparent in the obvious re-evaluation of the human versus animal configuration in early Neolithic wall painting. The *Image of a Hunter* (Fig. **1.6**) found in a recently excavated shrine at Çatal Hüyük, Anatolia, presents a visual response to the role of the human in the world dramatically different from the Lascaux imagery.

At Lascaux, emphasis was placed on the vitality of the animal figures — the few humans described in these early drawings played subordinate roles in the overall world picture. The mysterious comings and goings of the herds must have been a source of wonder for these early people, and it is understandable that these animals (on whose lives the survival of the community rested) would be expressed in the dominant position. Yet as the community's relationship to the world slowly changed from subordinate to master, so too did the representation of that relationship. In the drawing from Çatal Hüyük, a new type of figure emerges, full of a vibrance reminiscent of the Paleolithic animal renderings. Even the very abundance of human figures in these works signals a departure from the earlier isolation of the past, and it gives an indication of the growing importance of community and social organization during the period. The natural hierarchy of power was changing in the Neolithic world, and one may cautiously speculate that the drawings reflect such a confidence, not found in earlier representations.

Two-dimensional representation was not the only visual revolution to take place during the era. The cultivation of the land brought about an increased sense of place, since one could survive in the same location for many years if conditions remained adequate. The cycle of birth, death, and renewal held particular importance to these early farming communities, as survival shifted from the luck of the hunt to the mysterious workings of the seasons. One result of this need to appease the natural world (which could bring famine or flood to the fragile community) was the construction of belief systems based on the workings of natural phenomena. The importance of worship and ritual to the health and welfare of the community seems to have made monuments an essential part of each town.

The term **architecture**, like its companion *art*, is difficult to define. It is common to define architecture as the art of designing space — an activity that includes everything from interior design and garden construction to skyscrapers and stadiums. Its linguistic sources are in the ancient Greek roots of *archi* meaning rule and *tecture* meaning construction or building, and it was used during that period to define structures of decidedly more purpose and influence than basic housing. By design, it was often larger in scale, more central in its role in the community, and usually more permanent than its domestic counterpart. In other words, there was the implicit assertion that architecture embodied certain specific features of the community in which it was built. Today the term architecture is used to define virtually all building

■ **1.7** (above) Stonehenge c. 2750–1300 BC
Salisbury Plain, England
Diameter of circle 97 ft (29.6 m)
Height 13 ft 6 in (4.1 m)
(below) Plan of Stonehenge

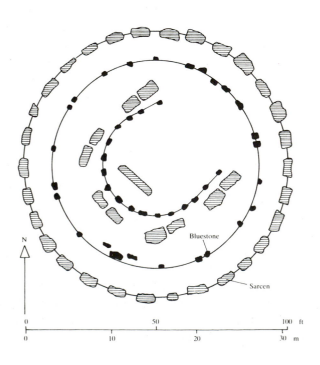

construction, including basic housing, which suggests a conscious re-evaluation of the domestic environment — an extension of the concepts of both individuality and private property. In this way, architecture exposes itself as no less susceptible to social pressures than any other culturally significant term.

Stonehenge

One of the most famous surviving Neolithic-style building structures is Stonehenge in southern England (Fig. **1.7**). The site actually supported a number of different structures over its 1,400-plus years of intermittent construction, and today it stands in approximately the same configuration as it did around 1300 BC. Most likely constructed as a shrine, the outer of its two concentric rings has the distinction of being laid out in exact accordance with the directional path of the sun at the summer solstice. This celestial consideration is indicative of the Neolithic community's growing awareness of natural phenomena and the cycle of the seasons. Perhaps,

FOCUS ON

Post and Lintel Construction

One of the earliest and most rudimentary of architectural devices, post and lintel construction (Fig. **1.8**) is defined as any vertical form (called a post) that is arranged in such a manner as to support a horizontal form (lintel) on its crown. It is from this simple building motif that the convention of the supported ceiling emerges.

■ 1.8 Post and lintel construction

however, its most important attribute is its very survival: Stonehenge remains one of the earliest surviving examples of public architecture in Northern Europe.

Stonehenge was a vital part of the local inhabitants' world, which was, no doubt, why it has proved more permanent than virtually any other item produced by the culture. It is also an excellent example of **post and lintel construction** □ a technical cornerstone of much of subsequent Western architecture. At Stonehenge, massive stones (called megaliths, meaning big stones) were propped upright to create a circular order of posts, on which a series of lintel stones once sat, enclosing the ring. The ingenuity and sheer will necessary to execute such an enormous and cumbersome building project have made Stonehenge the subject of legend; today it is still a matter of speculation how the community actually found, transported, and erected the massive stones, but the very fact that the complex was built at all is striking evidence of the community's need visually to express the binding relationship between themselves and their immediate, sometimes hostile environment.

PREHISTORIC AND PRIMITIVE CULTURES

Before continuing any further in this discussion, it is necessary to clarify the important distinctions that exist between the terms **primitive** (popularly used to identify and label the visual artifacts produced by certain cultures in recent times) and **prehistoric**. While the term *prehistoric* means *before historical documentation* and implies no value judgment on the work itself, the same cannot be said of the term *primitive*. Taken at face value, *primitive* implies that something is in an early stage of development, from which more complex associations may evolve. Yet in recent times the word has come to embrace a significant amount of visual material that possesses both considerable development and great insight — its primitiveness being little more than its obvious difference from mainstream Western culture. By the late nineteenth century, the term *primitive* had taken on a decidedly *social Darwinist* connotation (social Darwinism being an attempt to apply evolutionary theory to social organization) and it supported the notion that human communities developed in sophistication for biological as well as social reasons. To be labeled primitive was to be considered of less value and less significance or to be romanticized as pure and untainted by socializing influences. The use of the term *primitive* as a descriptive tool came to imply assumptions about both quality and importance.

Today, there remain small pockets of communities that continue with the same sort of social organization as Neolithic peoples. Why these communities survived intact for so long is open to speculation; their steady extinction during the years of Western colonialism may suggest that it was their isolation from larger population centers (and their influences) that very much determined their unchanged nature over centuries, even millennia. For this reason, such communities provide vital insights into the relationship between early social organization and the production of visual culture, which in turn provide clues about the nature of art and art making.

The opening up of Africa and the South Pacific during the nineteenth century signaled the beginning of the end for the few remaining Neolithic-like communities in the world. Until they came into contact with Europeans, many of the indigenous peoples of central Africa, Australia, and earlier the Americas had capably survived without need of dramatic change in their social organization. The Australian Aborigines are one such example. Destined to live as scavengers and hunters by the extreme conditions of the Australian outback, for them the issue of change meant one of constant adaptability rather than dramatic shifts of organization (under such extreme conditions, change was a very real gamble, since failure could result in death). Here, conditions similar to those confronted by the earliest human communities existed well into the twentieth century.

Despite some very real differences in social structure, there are striking similarities between the ancient Lascaux Caves images and the more recent visual culture of the Australian outback. In Fig. **1.9**, which shows an Aboriginal rock painting, the subject matter once again shows clear indications that human experience is understood within the larger context of the natural world to which the community is inextricably bound. In Aboriginal art it is common to see animals described in what might be called *X-ray* images; the subject is viewed with its internal organs clearly visible — a conceptual shift that has little to do with what the animal looks like, and everything to do with what the animal is understood to mean. The kangaroo is depicted as a symbol of life, whose complex system of organs supports both the miracle of life within its own body and, by providing food for the community, insures the continuity of life.

The hunting motif is not the only recurring image that connects the ancient communities of the prehistoric era to the traditional communities of the current age. The concept of fertility has always been closely associated with survival, and thus it is not surprising that there is an abundance of images of the mother and child throughout these close-knit societies. The *Woman and Child* (Fig. **1.10**) produced in Cameroon c. 1912 is a good example. Here the female figure suggests the continuity of life, embodying the child-bearing qualities of woman as essential to the community's survival. The relationship between suckling child, bound to the nourishing breast of its mother,

■ **1.9 Aborigine rock painting, Australia**

■ 1.10 Kwayep of Bamana Village
Woman and Child c. 1912
Bamileke Kingdom, Cameroon
Wood, pigment
Height 25¾ in (65.4 cm)
Musée de l'Homme, Paris

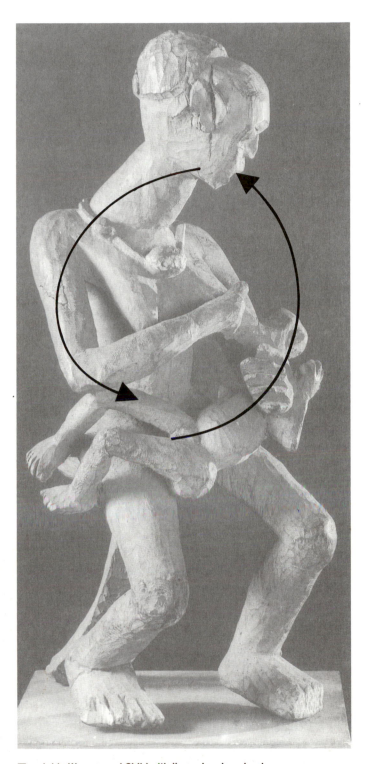

■ 1.11 *Woman and Child* with lines showing circular motion of the composition and woman, whose crouched body and extended neck visually enwrap and protect the infant, suggests a most basic bonding — on both a bodily and a psychological level. Note how the eyes of the mother and the pointing of the left breast fix attention on the head of the child, whose cradled body creates a *V* form. This line or visual rhythm is then met at the child's knees by the mother's right arm, which moves the viewer's eye up through the neck and back to the head. The resultant visual motion is that of a unified circle, interlocking parts in a satisfying and obvious manner (Fig. **1.11**). Like its companion fertility imagery, the mother and child motif continued to occupy a central and prominent position in the community's visual expressions.

Ancestor worship is yet another manifestation of a community's desire for continuity from one generation to the next. This belief often takes on characteristics peculiar to a community, but there are general

■ **1.13 Plastered skull c. 19th century** AD
Sepik River, New Guinea
Lifesize
British Museum, London

■ **1.12 Neolithic plastered skull c. 7000** BC
Jericho, Jordan
Lifesize
Archaeological Museum, Amman, Jordan

similarities from which one can draw certain conclusions for visual expression. One is the method of expressing reverence in visual form through the manipulation of the corpse of the deceased. Like the modern ritual of *making up* a corpse before a funeral the ancient rite was an excellent example of the breadth of visual needs in a culture and shows how issues such as mortality can become manifest in a body.

Another notable interest in such forms of ancestor worship is the desire to *trap* or keep the spirit of the dead within the shell of their previous body. A fascinating example of this approach, consistent over thousands of miles and thousands of years, can be seen by comparing two skulls, one found at Jericho (Fig. **1.12**) dating to 7000 BC and the other from nineteenth-century New Guinea (Fig. **1.13**). On the surface, both appear to allude to the same concern with the sanctity of, and the need for protection from, the spirit of the dead (in such societies, spirit is found in all things).

In the case of the New Guinea example, it appears that the plastering of skulls is used to keep the internal spirit of the dead confined within. This also had the added benefit of gaining a sense of control over the living spirit inside the dead corpse — much like holding someone captive inside a prison. In each case, a reconstruction of the facial features of the deceased is modeled in plaster over the bone, with various embellishments (sea-shell eyes, graphic facial markings, etc.) added to give the image greater impact. In this type of visual expression, one can speculate how later artists and their societies came to view objects as embodiments of personalities and then finally ideas. At the simplest level, the makers of these images have attempted to enclose, or more specifically embody, the spirit of the dead within an inanimate object. This simple form of what might be called a visual strategy (since this was obviously considered a method of dealing with the problem of quieting the dead) became a chief preoccupation with later image making, and it set an important precedent for the way in which societies have come generally to define art.

These examples show that the social and environmental conditions in which human beings live impact how they produce and conceptualize their creative expressions. If we do not accept that objects are created by individuals who are influenced by the specific concerns and beliefs of their cultures, we might ask the question, why is it important to study art in the first place? If we do accept this, however, then it is clear that a fundamental link exists throughout the world and throughout different ages between the visual arts and the historical contexts in which their creators lived.

ART AND THE DEVELOPMENT OF MORE COMPLEX SOCIETIES

It was stated earlier that visual expressions are always produced within the confines of time and place. Since human beings exist at a certain point in time, are schooled within the context of a current range of ideas, and participate and socialize within set boundaries, it is inevitable that their activities reflect that age.

If this is the case with individuals, it seems only logical that the objects they manufacture also reflect such conditions. This is certainly the case with basic items such as pots and utensils, which reflect a community's most basic functional requirements for living. Such objects of *material culture* are often excellent indicators of a society's requisite daily rituals, and as a consequence they become objects of immense interest to anthropologists. Yet objects of utility are often poorer conductors of historical issues than their non-functional counterparts, since their physical requirements make them so form-specific. There are, however, items that seem to change with time, evolving and dissolving as periods change. It is to these items that meaning is commonly assigned, since they reflect their creators (who in turn reflect their times), and thus the quality of human existence during their creation.

Meaning and Utility in Monuments

There are two important issues to consider when attempting to address such visual forms: the ideas of **self-referentiality** and of **audience**.

The Great Pyramids at Giza (Figs. 1.1 and **1.15**), built between 2650 and 2575 BC, were erected as burial monuments at the height of Egyptian civilization. In examining the three structures, one is immediately struck by their overwhelming presence, for they visually emanate a certain intelligible difference from their surroundings. On the surface, they appear to have no obvious function, and as a result the viewer is forced to consider them in terms of their own intrinsic characteristics. An object is self-referential when its form is derived primarily from considerations outside function. Consider this in the light of a simple tool such as a corkscrew. The spiral form of a corkscrew, which is derived from a very specific requirement — to pull a cork out of a bottle — refers first to its function. This is not to say that such an item cannot be appreciated for its formal characteristics but simply that the form evolves first out of a functional need, and its formal character is a necessary result of such considerations.

It has been rightly said that no item is without reference to the outer world; it is simply a matter of identifying the range and effect such references have on the formal character of the object. Consider this example: placing the Great Pyranids at Giza side by side with an equally colossal structure such as the Glen Canyon Dam, Arizona (Fig. **1.16**) may initially force one to apply very different standards in addressing the work. The Glen Canyon Dam is understood and appreciated for its function as a huge water obstruction, developed to hold back vast quantities of water. Thus its form is derived almost exclusively from its function. Its long sloping wall, massive vertical thrust, and awesome sense of mass are all tied directly to the need to hold back water. Though it is certainly true that such structures (indeed all material culture) can grant an observant viewer vast amounts of other information (such as construction practices, the environmental effects of increased energy demands on the environment, etc.), its form remains tied to its utility.

The Great Pyramids present a different scenario for the viewer. Since on the surface such structures appear to have little grounding in obvious utility, they are often considered in terms of formal principles, and the **intent** of their construction. When objects are divorced from obvious function, they begin to embody the circumstances from which they are created and thus open themselves up to a dialogue with the viewer on a more pronounced psychological, intellectual, and instinctive level.

There are, of course, problems with such generalizations when discussing art. The most obvious flaw in the self-referentiality argument is that in reality no item functions in a state of complete self-enclosure; even the most seemingly neutral and contentless creations are necessarily situated within an elaborate context of other issues. Look once again at the Great Pyramids. It is true that there appears little functional need for these monuments, but it is absolutely incorrect to claim that they exist without reference to then popular ideas and issues, or that they evolved in a vacuum. It is known, for instance, that the form of the pyramids is derived from an older form of burial chamber, called a *mastaba*, which was a four-sided sloped construction with a flat top and an access hole

■ **1.14 Ancient Egypt, Middle East, and Mesopotamia**

■ 1.15 The Great Pyramids at Giza (right) Cheops c. 2650 BC, (center) Chefren c. 2600 BC, (left) Mycerinus c. 2575 BC

■ 1.16 Glen Canyon Dam, Arizona. Height 710 ft (216 m), Length 1,560 ft (475 m)

■ 1.17 Step Pyramid and Palace (restored) of King Zoser c. 2700 BC. Saqqara, Egypt

that led on a vertical axis into the ground. These chambers were originally adapted from early domestic architecture and are in keeping with the Egyptian notion of the sanctity of the dead in the afterlife. Slowly, with the rise of the pharaohs, the *mastaba* form developed a stepped or piggyback appearance (Fig. **1.17**), adding height and visual force and suggesting the presence of authority granted to the deceased ruler in the afterlife. From this design, it was simply a matter of making the slopes of the stepped walls even to achieve the traditional pyramid form. So in this regard the form does make obvious reference to the prevalent ideas of its age; even if it does not display a primary functional use, it did not simply emerge in a social and intellectual vacuum. At this point one may begin to comprehend an important characteristic of art and art making: an object created outside the realm of functional considerations becomes a powerful agent for the expression of issues in which it, its creator, and its audience are immersed.

The notion of audience is an intrinsic part of the art process. Whenever individuals approach a work of art (or any situation for that matter), they bring a multitude of experiences and learning to bear upon the work in question. As was discussed in the Introduction, the dynamic is akin to a conversation, the work of art performing a communicative link between artist and viewer. In this sense the work of art is a point of arbitration, and as such it has aspects of both artist and viewer within its realm of meaning.

Of course, no two people have identical histories or experiences, and thus the communication is never complete. It is in essence a constant process of re-creation every time an individual enters into a dialogue with the piece. Further, artists are never in complete control of their part of the conversation either, since they too are required to enter into some form of a relationship with their materials. In other words, attaching specific meaning to a piece is always a tricky business; that fact has significant ramifications for later art.

As Neolithic communities grew, there came a need for more complex systems of social organization. It is difficult to pinpoint how leadership was originally determined in those days — perhaps by brute strength, or even the luck of the draw, one can't be sure. Subsequently, political systems evolved, with a hierarchy of individuals guiding the fate of the community. Although positions of power were often sanctioned through the various godheads and religious organizations, the stability of the regime always rested upon the assumption that the leaders had special rights to their offices. One of the ways to enforce such beliefs was to initiate a series of highly visible reminders through the use of buildings and images. Public monuments are a testimony to society's need to communicate with itself, and in more complex societies, the monument became a reminder of the role and fate of the individual in the world — a world all too often controled by relationships of power.

The Rise of Egyptian Civilization

Egypt was one of the first locations to show signs of more complex forms of Neolithic social organization. Along the banks of the River Nile, there was enough fertile soil in an otherwise arid environment to allow the development of highly specialized communities. Though there is evidence of a Neolithic culture in the Nile basin from 7000 BC, historians date the beginnings of an organized Egyptian kingdom to around 3000 BC, initiating a 2,500-year reign until its collapse under Persian rule in 500 BC.

Historians typically separate the Egyptian civilization into three distinct eras: the Old, Middle, and New Kingdoms. To this might be added an important consolidation period, which predates the Old Kingdom and at which time (roughly 3170–2685 BC) the two distinct communities of the Upper and Lower Nile were forcibly assimilated into a unified kingdom under the legendary King Narmer. The Old Kingdom (c. 2686–2182 BC) is noted for the rise of a centralized authoritarian government centered around a pharaoh, who in the relative order of things was situated somewhere between a god and a mortal (an idea consistent with Neolithic cultures). The *Giza pyramid complex* (see Fig. 1.15) is an excellent example of the ambitious building program emerging from the economic prosperity of the post-unification period. Further, the very immensity of such structures is indicative of the forceful cult of authority perpetuated around the pharaoh.

However, this prosperity did not last. By c. 2180 BC economic decline (some suggest brought about by the very same building programs) and regional divisiveness apparently led to the collapse of central authority in the area. The Middle Period (c. 2050–1786 BC) marked the reconsolidation of the Egyptian Kingdom and with it the development of important trade routes that helped economically augment a sometimes precarious reliance on agriculture from the flooding Nile. This in turn provided the resources for the spectacular building projects of the New Kingdom (c. 1575–1085 BC), such as the Temple of Ramesses II (Fig. **1.18**). The reign of Ramesses dynasty marked the pinnacle of the New Kingdom; subsequent dynasties were increasingly diminished in influence. By 500 BC, the Egyptian kingdom was in Persian hands, and in 332 BC Alexander the Great completed its collapse.

■ 1.18 Abu Simbel
Temple of Ramesses II c. 1257 BC
Sculptures height approx. 67 ft
(20.4 m)

Though these historical periods differ greatly in a number of respects, they remain strikingly consistent in at least one aspect: their approach to representing the world and their unique place in it. This consistency of vision is fundamental to any understanding of Egyptian art and architecture, and it provides unique insights into the relationship between art and culture in more advanced societies.

Egyptian Art and the Idea of Permanence

As the previous overview suggests, Egyptian civilization was not a static entity but one that endured the same fluctuations in political, economic, and social climates as any other society. Thus, given the hypoth-

esis that art both comments on and reflects its particular historical situation, it would seem presumptuous to expect similar fluctuations in its visual culture. Yet the truth of the matter is that, throughout 2500 years of Egyptian civilization, there remained a rather static or fixed manner in which the Egyptians envisioned their world.

Consider two tablets, produced almost two thousand years apart: the *Palette of King Narmer* (Fig. **1.19**) of c. 3200 BC and a wall **relief** from the Temple of Sethos I (Fig. **1.20**) of c. 1300 BC. The former is arguably the oldest *historical* work of art known today — since specific historical events can be linked with the storyline, and individuals can be identified, it is considered an historical document. Commemorating

■ 1.19 *Palette of King Narmer* c. 3200 BC
Hierakonpolis, Egypt. Slate, height 25 in (63.5 cm). Egyptian Museum, Cairo

■ 1.20 Wall relief from the Temple of Sethos I
Abydos, Egypt, c. 1300 BC
Sandstone

the unification of Upper and Lower Egypt, it depicts in various sequences King Narmer's triumphant control over the will of his enemies and his subsequent establishment of the Egyptian kingdom.

The palette is carved in a relief manner on both sides of the slate slab, with the visual information laid out in such a manner that a viewer is invited to consider the images as a somewhat symbolic account of the events proper. This use of specific images to suggest more complex ideas is fundamental to the later notion of written language, and its early connection to pictorial symbols can clearly be witnessed in this work. Take, for instance, the image of King Narmer, ominously standing over a kneeling, subservient figure on the obverse side of the palette. The obvious distortion of scale between ruler and defeated suggests power and control, while the generalized features of the victim further imply not a specific character but perhaps the personification of Lower Egypt itself. Thus these images act not just as simple representations of events but also as embodiments in pictorial form of more involved ideas.

It is from these conventions that Egyptian hieroglyphs emerged, with certain images denoting various noises or words that connect in various manners to suggest particular ideas. What is perhaps most remarkable about the palette is its clarity of design or lack of superfluous decoration, affording the viewer access to an abundance of information. The exaggerated appearance of the figures and the use of a differentiated scale combine in an abstract manner to create an image that is strikingly clear, inventive, and suggestive — the very dynamic of communication.

Unlike the previously discussed Neolithic objects, there is in the palette design a set of *conventions* or an understood visual *language* which emerges out of a communally assumed set of symbols. Until this point, art performed an essentially ritualistic function, making tangible the workings of an otherwise hostile world. Yet in this very early example of Egyptian art, a move toward a more didactic or instructional character in the visual imagery is clear — something generally referred to as **narrative**.

Narrative involves the progression of one idea to another, often encompassing time and thus a series of events. To arrange images in narrative, it is necessary to identify clearly a direction of movement, suggesting a possible entrance into the plot, as well as an exit. Because a full understanding of an object depends on its being observed from various angles, the ancient Egyptians probably decided that three-dimensional images were poor conductors of a progressive storyline. As a result, it seems that emphasis shifted toward flat design, in which one image could be effectively placed next to another and understood with the brief scan of the eye.

Today's common Western-script is derived from this simple format, and it is through the progressive scanning of simple illustrations that written language has emerged. Language is, in fact, nothing more than a commonly accepted set of conventions from which ideas are transferred from one individual to another. This simple notion has had a profound effect on the way in which one views two-dimensional art, and it helps form the basis of an understanding of the different qualities and possibilities afforded by two- and three-dimensional work. The result certainly caught the attention of ancient Egyptians, who were so taken by this method that their hieroglyphs changed remarkably little during their civilization.

Monuments to Power

One inevitable repercussion of the rise of politics in complex social organizations is the sometimes subtle, but more often obvious, development of authority. Today, the public generally relies on the media for information about political leaders and their agendas, considering them in most cases a relatively accurate source. Yet it is also clear that government agencies spend millions of dollars each year bolstering their media image and learning to use it to their advantage, and thus the media are also seen as a valuable tool in the dissemination of government policy. In other words, since the media (like art, and every other human endeavor for that matter) are a product of their environment and time, they will inevitably find themselves bound to that system. In 3000 BC there were no television sets or newspapers to extoll the virtues and aspirations of those in authority, so instead energies were poured into mammoth and highly visible work projects. The result was a series of some of the most impressive monuments the world has ever known.

Next to the Great Pyramids at Giza stands one of the most famous of Egyptian monuments, the Great Sphinx (Fig. **1.21**). Historians have speculated that the head of the Sphinx was modeled on the head of

■ 1.21 Great Sphinx at Giza, Egypt, c. 2540–2514 BC
Limestone, height 65 ft (19.8 m), length 240 ft (73.2 m)

■ **1.22** Bust of Queen Nefertiti c. 1365 BC
Painted limestone
Height 19 in (48 cm)
Egyptian Museum, Berlin

the pharaoh Chefren, with a lion's body — a common signifier of immortality — attached to it. The lion was then, a **symbol** (a communally accepted set of meanings associated with a form), and when specifically attached to a personality it became part of the character's **iconography** (the history of meanings associated with a figure). Such imposing sights did much to enhance the public reverence paid to leaders, and give a good indication of how monuments functioned; it is, indeed, hard not to feel moved and dwarfed beside such displays. The success of this form

of communication may give some indication of why there was so little change in Egyptian culture during its 2,500-year span. The belief in a divine right of kings probably enforced such forms of *language* as ordained from above and subsequently caused a degree of stasis in the art community. When this kind of display was coupled with the ever-present Egyptian preoccupation with death and the afterlife, it is no wonder that little innovation took place.

There was, however, one period in Egyptian history that proved an exception to this rule: the reign of Akhenaten, who came to power in 1372 BC. In instituting such reforms as monotheism (the belief in one god rather than many) and establishing an air of relative freedom and prosperity within the community, he transformed the complexion of Egyptian art. The result was a striking manifestation of this new tolerance: the rise of naturalism, an art based on observation. The most famous example of naturalistic art from this period is the portrait bust of Akhenaten's wife, Queen Nefertiti (Fig. **1.22**). Here conventions developed over the preceding two millennia gave way to an art based on individuality rather than uniformity, paralleling the social and political ethos of the age.

This move to naturalism was short-lived. Within two generations of Akhenaten's rule, traditional Egyptian conventions were once again being employed by artisans, suggesting a return to more authoritarian kinds of governance, which was to be the norm until the fall of Egypt to the Persians around 500 BC.

The development of representation may be dated to the period following the completion of the Sphinx, the head of which was fashioned after one of the important leaders of the age, Chefren. This is the first time that a specific name (and thus a personality) may be attached to an image. Unlike Neolithic figurines, which remained generic and thus somewhat universal in identity, the emphasis on producing a likeness meant that objects could now be charged with more specific meaning and often evoke very particular responses. As the Sphinx shows, the subtle streamlining of the viewer's response is an excellent way of bringing other issues into play when responding to a piece — a consideration that will be more fully explored in the next chapter.

Mesopotamian Cultures

Egypt was not the only location in which more complex social arrangements took place. The area between the Tigris and Euphrates rivers (historically referred to as Mesopotamia) provided enough fertile soil to support another series of developing cultures between the years 3500 and 612 BC. The first people to settle the area were the Sumerians, who appear to have been quite technologically and socially developed. Archaeologists credit them with inventing the wheel, constructing the first school and library, and employing the first historian. Like the Egyptians, the Sumerians recognized that water (and its availability) was essential to such arid environments, and as a consequence initiated a series of remarkable irrigation routes to ensure the health and development of herds and crops. But perhaps the greatest lasting achievement of the Sumerians in terms of visual culture was the development of writing.

The *Stele of Hammurabi* (Fig. **1.23**), with its elaborate series of marks carefully carved into soft basalt, is the logical extension of earlier pictures in series, in which a narrative progression of recognizable images provided the framework for a coherent thought (Fig. **1.24**). This more simplified script (called **cuneiform** after the wedge-shaped characters made by the writing tool) enabled the Mesopotamians to engage in and transmit more complex thoughts than ever before, since the abstract configurations gave scope for a wider degree of variation in expression and an economy of space.

Sumerian architectural projects were equally impressive. Most Sumerian architectural effort (like that of the neighboring Egyptians), was focused on impressive temples and monuments celebrating the gods and supporting the established power structure. Perhaps the best known of Mesopotamian architectural forms is the *ziggurat* (Fig. **1.25**), a massive fabricated mountain-temple built of brick. It is an excellent example of how the Sumerians, and later the Assyrians, were able to combine existing ideas in architecture with town design to create an overall urban environment imbued with religious significance.

■ **1.23** *Stele of Hammurabi*, 1760 BC
Basalt, height 7 ft 4 in (2.23 m)
Louvre, Paris

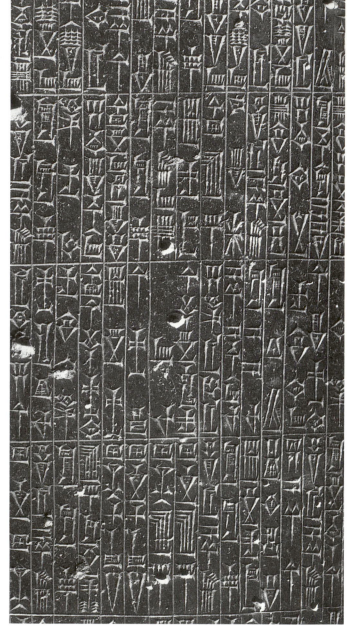

■ 1.24 Detail of the *Stele of Hammurabi* c. 1760 BC
showing (left) upper part of Stele and (right) the Inscription of the Law Code

The ziggurat was usually located at the center of the fortified Sumerian town, and rose high above the plain, suggesting both monumentality and authority. A richly decorated temple sat atop this mass of bricks and was connected to the town by way of long processional staircases, all of which surely gave the impression of ascension, as if the structure were an intermediary between heaven and earth. As the focal point of the community and a striking and forceful addition to the landscape, the ziggurat must have provoked wonder in contemporary travellers. Historians consider the Sumerian ziggurat as the probable visual impetus behind the biblical story of the *Tower of Babel*.

Sumerian rule in Mesopotamia began to decline by 2000 BC, replaced by the Babylonian and then the

■ **1.25** Ziggurat, Ur, c. 2100 BC
Fire brick over mud bricks
210 x 150 ft (64 x 45.7 m)
Original height at base 70 ft (21.3 m)

■ **1.26** *Dying Lioness*
Assyrian, from the North Palace of Ashurbanipal, Nineveh, 645–635 BC
Limestone, height 14 in (35.6 cm)
British Museum, London

Assyrian peoples. The Assyrians were noted as both highly disciplined and vicious when it came to waging war. Predictably then, there is a noticeable emphasis in the surviving artifacts on the harsh realities of death, sacrifice, and power. A very well known and often cited example of this rather stark characteristic of Assyrian art is the *Dying Lioness* (Fig. **1.26**). The potency of this image clearly lies in its unabashed nat-

uralism, as the arrow-pierced lioness is forced to drag her limp body across the picture plane in a condition that can only be described as that of agony. How different is this from the Egyptian depictions of death and dying! Here the move from received conventions (such as the schematicizing of the figure in Egyptian art) and towards naturalism (images based on observed reality) seems both right and poignant in addressing the heroic and the defiant in death — attributes highly desirable in a warrior culture.

Ancient China

According to recent archaeological data, there is clear evidence to support the claim of *simultaneous social development* in diverse locales across the globe between 3000 and 1000 BC. During that period of unprecedented cultural development in Egypt and Mesopotamia, there were other cultures beginning to organize in similar social configurations to the east. In particular, the *Shang Dynasty* in China (1766–1111 BC) and the *Harappan* culture in India (2300–1750 BC) marked decisive breaks from the Neolithic cultures that had preceded them.

The Shang Dynasty was the first recorded historical period in Chinese history. Evidence suggests that the first Shang settlements were probably located along the fertile Yellow River, later branching out to encompass a vast expanse of land to the south-west, covering most of presentday China. The Shang leader, like that of the Egyptians, had the designation of a god-king, who exerted influence over all matters in the community. At the heart of such theocratic rule lay ritual, and where there is ritual, there is art. Despite years of advanced archaeological research, scientists have yet to find a single Shang-era artifact to suggest any kind of artistic enterprise (even folk pottery) outside that of the ruling class. It appears that in that period artisans were concerned primarily with producing ritual objects to be buried with the ruling class for the afterlife, and as a result the surviving Shang Dynasty artifacts come predominantly in the form of decorated vessels and other utilitarian objects presumed useful to the dead in their next life.

A look at an early period Shang Dynasty artifact demonstrates the influence lost-wax casting had on vessel production and decoration at the time. The three-legged vessel cast in bronze from the fourteenth century BC (Fig. **1.28**) is indicative of early attempts at

■ **1.28** Bronze vessel, *li-ting*, 14th century BC
Height 8 in (20.3 cm)
Ashmolean Museum, Oxford

■ **1.27** China c. 1100 BC

FOCUS ON

Bronze Casting

One of the most significant technical developments to occur during the Shang Dynasty was *bronze casting*. Though by no means the first community to use the alloy in the production of objects (finds suggest bronze had been used in the vicinity of Lake Baikal centuries earlier), Shang artisans were the first to explore the expressive possibilities afforded by the material. Bronze is produced through the smelting of copper with small amounts of tin or antimony, which help harden the metal. Most likely, the recipe was found by accident and then perfected through trial and error. The Chinese added lead (an agent that has a lower melting temperature than copper and thus helped in the pouring of the bronze), which in turn enabled workers to design and execute more elaborate items. The results were the famous gray-brown color of Chinese bronzes of the period and the remarkably intricate detailing on their surfaces.

Casting in bronze during the Shang Dynasty required the pouring of molten copper (mixed with tin and lead) into an enclosed cavity. There were two processes typically employed in the construction of a bronze cast object, either *piece mold* or *lost wax*. In the piece-mold technique, a model is constructed in clay and hardened, then clay molds are taken from the original in sections and keyed together to make a completed mold. The bronze is then poured into the mold, filling the cavity and solidifying to take on the shape and character of the model. Lost-wax casting involves the production of the model in soft wax, which allows for very subtle carving and detail work. The wax is then covered in layers of a liquid-like clay slip, which falls into every undulation on the surface of the original. When the wax is burned out of the slip cast, it leaves a cavity into which the bronze is poured. Because of the character of slip and its ability to grant very fine detailing in the cast, the lost-wax process became increasingly popular during the middle and late periods of the Shang Dynasty, and it was the primary technical motivation behind much of the late-style vessel work.

The Culture of the Indus Valley

As with the Shang Dynasty, little remains of the ancient Harappan culture that once flourished in the Indus Valley, now in India and Pakistan. The culture was all but obliterated during the Aryan invasions of 1500 BC, so much is left to speculation. The Harappan community apparently developed along predictable lines: settlements along a fertile plain with access to a river, expansion into and conquest of neighboring areas, an entrenched polytheism and a central ruler with massive power. It is also clear that the production of artifacts was much in keeping with what is known of such early cultures: a reliance on utilitarian goods and ritual items such as figurines that could be used in worship. A remarkably well preserved sculpture from the period is the *Figurine of a Young Woman* (Fig. **1.29**) which dates to between 2300 and 1750 BC and has the singular reputation of being the

■ **1.29 Figurine of a Young Woman**
From Mahenjo-daro,
Harappan culture,
c. 2300–1750 BC
Copper
Height 5½ in (14 cm)
National Museum, New Delhi

casting through piece molds. The linear elements have a wonderfully controlled, organic quality somewhat suggestive of a mask. In this example, the reciprocal relationship between technical innovation and artistic production is clear. It also has important ramifications for understanding art as a deeply social activity, for if artistic expression is fundamentally tied to materials and thus technique, it is likewise possible to claim that *how* one makes a work of art is potentially indicative of the given social dynamics. In the production of a work of art, the materials used and the techniques embraced reveal a considerable amount about that period. Thus these bronze vessels are fascinating conduits for understanding Shang Dynasty culture.

■ 1.30 India c. 1100 BC showing sites of Harappan civilization

only metal figure yet discovered at Harappan sites. Made of soft copper and standing a mere 5¹/₂ inches (approx. 13.5 cm) high it was most likely used in ritual. Yet in its vivid description of a young woman it also suggests a lively interest in observation among artists of the period — something very different in character from the Shang Dynasty Chinese to the north-east.

Today, very little is known of these people, their origins and their customs. By 1500 BC Aryan invasions had destroyed the Indus Valley community, replacing it with what appears to have been a vacuum of visual culture and a ruling class with little interest in the production of artifacts. It was not until the conquests of Alexander the Great in the late third century BC that there was any sort of cultural reinvestment in the visual arts in India, and with it the development of Hinduism, Buddhism, and Jainism (see pages 149–164).

The Minoans and the Mycenaeans

Until the late nineteenth century, little was known of the communities to the west of Egypt and Mesopotamia other than through legend. The discoveries of Mycenae (by Heinrich Schliemann in 1876) and Minoan culture (by Arthur Evans in 1900) forced historians to reconsider the influences of these communities on the development of later Greek culture. Despite tireless research by archaeologists, there is still

■ 1.31 Wasp pendant from Mallia c. 1700 BC
Gold, width 1⅞ in (4.5 cm)
Archaeological Museum, Heraklion, Crete

very little known about the two powers. Arthur Evans's discovery of the Palace of Minos (which was apparently so complex a configuration of rooms that it survives in later Greek legend as the site of the labyrinth of the Minotaur) seems to date the culture from around 2000 to 1400 BC, when the community fell under the political control of the Mycenaeans and diminished as an important trading center. It appears that, unlike their Egyptian counterparts, the Minoans showed little interest in large-scale monuments. Instead, an abundance of smaller and more precious objects was produced, probably to ornament the body (Fig. **1.31**). The same interest in decorative design can be found in contemporary wall painting, which shows an enthusiastic embracing of the forms of nature, and a vivid interest in color (Fig. **1.32**). In the decorative beauty and celebratory character of this work, it is clear that the traditional struggle between self and world had, by 1500 BC, become increasingly harmonious and controlable.

■ 1.32 Throne Room in the Palace of Minos, at Knossos, Crete, c. 1450 BC

SUMMARY

Evidence from some 15,000 years of early civilization points to the fact that the desire to create images with reference to experience was a major preoccupation with early artists. The examples here give a good indication of the perceived power of visual images to enhance the various communities' understanding of their place in the world — an anchor that would help them fix their identity. With each breakthrough there came a greater degree of sophistication, and with each increased degree of sophistication there came the inevitable change in the status of human beings in their world. Greater consciousness necessarily leads to introspection, and as a result the natural world is slowly subsumed into a world of human thought. This development, now called humanism, is the stuff of the next chapter.

The origins of art are situated deep within the mysterious recesses of the early human community and in people's desire to express consciousness of their environment, their lives, their very humanness. Though today it is possible only to posit reasonable hypotheses for the earliest construction of images and objects, it is apparent that such activities were central to the formation of early societies and their sense of self. With the shift from Paleolithic to Neolithic social organization, and its emphasis on more stable agricultural conditions, the scale and magnitude of art and art making increased dramatically. The result was the beginning of a binding relationship between artistic practice and the greater society's fluctuating social and political pressures. Thus art became both a fundamental expression and a vivid document of the history of human culture.

Suggested Reading

Over the past two or three decades, there has been a dramatic re-evaluation of prehistoric and prehistoric-like cultures in both history books and anthropological surveys. Much of this is an attempt to rid older reference aids of their implicit cultural biases (as was discussed with regard to the term *primitive*) and provide a fairer appraisal of the communities and their visual culture. The secret, then, is to utilize texts that are more up to date, since they are more likely to give a balanced view (a good hint for all texts).

Amiet, Pierre: *The Ancient Art of the Near East* (New York: Abrams, 1980).

Groenewegen-Frankfort, H. A. and Ashmole, Bernard: *Art of the Ancient World* (Englewood Cliffs, NJ: Prentice-Hall, 1972).

Pronunciation Guide

Akhenaten ah-kuh-**NAHT**-uhn
Çatal Hüyük **CHAH**-tuhl hoo-**YOOK**
cuneiform kyoo-**NEE**-ih-form
Harappan huh-**RAP**-uhn
Lascaux la-**SKOH**
mastaba **MAS**-tuh-buh
Mycenae my-**SEE**-nee
Paleolithic **pay**-lee-oh-**LITH**-ik
Stele of Hammurabi **STEE**-lee uhv ham-uh-**RAH**-bee
Willendorf **VIL**-en-dorf

Glossary

architecture (*page 45*) Commonly defined as the art of designing space. Its roots are in the Greek *arch* (meaning higher or better) and *tecture* (meaning construction or building), but the term is popularly used to address virtually all facets of the organization of spaces (landscapes and interiors, for example, as well as buildings).

audience (*page 51*) The viewer of an object who completes the process of communication between themselves, the artist, and the art, thus playing an intrinsic part of the art-making process.

bronze casting (*page 65*) A method of replicating a form through the production of a shell, usually of clay, into which a molten copper-tin alloy is poured. The most popular method for bronze casting is the lost wax technique, in which an object is formed in wax and covered in clay, and then the wax model is melted away, leaving a perfect impression.

contour drawing (*page 41*) Delineation of only the edge of the subject to prevent destruction of an image below.

cuneiform (*page 61*) A Mesopotamian script derived from pictures arranged in a narrative order named after the wedge-shaped marks created by the writing styles. The ancestor of the modern Western script, it is the logical extension of earlier two-dimensional designs.

iconography (*page 60*) The meanings and symbolic associations attributed to a figure or idea.

intent (*page 51*) The interests of the artist as perceived by the audience, or why an artwork was made.

line speed (*page 43*) The ability of line (depending on its characteristic thickness or relative angularity) to suggest motion in a drawing or painting.

narrative (*page 58*) The progression of an idea from one image to another, often implying a passage of time.

post and lintel construction (*page 47*) Any vertical form (post) that supports the horizontal (lintel) on its crown, from which the later convention of the supported ceiling was derived.

prehistoric (*page 41*) Meaning before historical documentation.

primitive (*page 47*) A value judgment used to identify and label the visual artifacts produced by certain cultures in recent times as less sophisticated, and thus of poorer quality.

relief (*page 56*) Often acheived through carving or casting, it is the rise of material above a two-dimensional plane, or the cavity created below the plane, which enables forms to be articulated through light and shadow.

sculpture (*page 43*) Objects produced in the round, possessing volume and interacting with real space.

self-referentiality (*page 51*) An object or image that appears to serve no practical or obvious function, and as a result the viewer is forced to consider it in terms of its own intrinsic characteristics.

solid shape drawing (*page 41*) Color applied uniformly across a plane, making the image appear solid and separate from its surroundings.

symbol (*page 60*) A set of communally accepted meanings associated with a form.

2

THE ART
OF THE
CLASSICAL
WORLD

■　2.1　Ritual passagae into a mystery religion
Wall painting from the Villa of the Mysteries
Pompeii, mid-1st century BC

Fair Greece! Sad relic of departed worth!
Immortal, though no more; though fallen, great!
LORD BYRON, *Childe Harold's Pilgrimage*

The word *classical* is often used to convey "authentic," "a standard of excellence," or "a work of enduring importance." Given these parameters, one might consider it suitable for a specific work of art, such as Shakespeare's *Hamlet* or Handel's *Messiah* — two pieces that have continued to inspire audiences for centuries. But if an entire era is to be described as classical, it is necessary that a series of truly extraordinary events take place within the context of an historical period, and further that later cultures accept such ideas and documents as a standard against which others are tested. It is in this context that the Western world has come to understand the societies of ancient Greece and Rome, and it is as a result of such admiration that today they are embraced as Classical.

It is virtually impossible to contemplate the fate of Western art without the influence of ancient Greek and Roman culture. *Classicism* is a popular and recurring term throughout art history; in many ways it is used to describe work that attempts to evoke or resur-

THE CLASSICAL WORLD

1000 BC	500	0	AD 300

494–480 Persian invasions of Greece

431–404 Peloponnesian War

44 BC Julius Ceasar assassinated

31 BC Battle of Actium

AD 79 Mount Vesuvius erupts

Protogeometric period c. 1000–800

Amphora c. 950 (2.8)

Etruscan civilization 700–500

Apollo of Veii c. 520–500 (2.33)
Sarcophagus from Cerveteri c. 520 (2.34)

Republican Rome c. 500–27

Porta Augusta c. 2nd cent. (2.36)

Temple of Portunus late 2nd cent. (2.38)

Geometric period c. 900–600

Dipylon vase c. 750 (2.10)

Archaic period c. 600–480

Basilica at Paestum c. 550 (2.18)
Peplos Koré c. 530 (2.13)
Anavysos Kouros c. 530 (2.14)

Villa of Mysteries murals c. 60 BC (2.46)

Classical period c.479–323

Kritios Boy c. 480 (2.25)
Parthenon c. 447–438 (2.19)
Doryphorus 440 (2.27)
Apoxyomenos c. 330 (2.2)

Roman Empire 27 BC–AD 330

Ara Pacis 13–9 BC (2.39)
Colosseum AD 72–80 (2.43)
Arch of Titus AD 81 (2.41)
Pantheon AD 118–128 (2.44)
Constantinople becomes capital of Empire AD 330

Hellenistic period c. 323–31

Dying Gaul c. 230–220 (2.31)
Barberini Faun c. 220 (2.32)
Winged Victory of Samothrace c. 180–160 (2.28)

■ 2.2 *Apoxyomenos* (the *Scraper*)
Roman copy of original Greek bronze c. 330 BC by Lysippus
Marble
Height 6 ft 9 in (2.05 m)
Vatican Museums, Rome

■ 2.3 Michelangelo Buonarroti
David 1501–4
Marble
Height 14 ft 3 in (4.34 m)
Galleria dell'Accademia, Florence

rect standards favored in the heyday of Greek and Roman culture. Consider this example. The term *Renaissance* (which literally means "rebirth") is commonly used to identify a cultural situation in Europe centuries removed from the Classical era, when the ideas and art forms of ancient Greece and Rome were emulated, and discussions of quality were inevitably based on those standards. Compare Lysippus' *Apoxyomenos* (the *Scraper*) of c. 330 BC (Fig. **2.2**) with Michelangelo's *David* (Fig. **2.3**) of 1501–4. This may give some indication of the breadth of influence

Classical culture had on Renaissance thought. Yet it also accentuates this book's working premise that all art embodies ideas — and in this way quality can be seen not as some static code but as the relevance of a particular idea to a given situation. If this is indeed the case, what is there inherent in Classical culture that has continued to inspire artists for centuries? What does this obsession tell us about any absolute notion of quality in art? In attempting to address these issues, this chapter will, in the process, develop some basic foundations for later discussions on Western art.

THE ART AND IDEAS OF ANCIENT GREECE

The history of ancient Greece spans a considerable period of human history, from its beginnings in the Iron Age culture of Athens around 1000 BC to its demise in 146 BC with the sack of Corinth, which marked complete Roman control of the area (Fig. **2.4**). Between these two dates there rose a civilization of considerable energy and sophistication, the likes of which, it has often been argued, have never been seen again. Yet why is it that Western society has historically embraced the art of Greece as a standard of quality, and is a society's political and intellectual sophistication necessarily any indication of the relative merits of its art? These are questions worth considering, for if art has no specific relationship to other issues, it is irrelevant. It is incumbent upon any student of Western civilization to consider fully the weight Classical concepts such as freedom and humanism have exerted throughout history — ideas embodied in its art and culture. As this chapter will point out, Greek art is about the human condition and its social organization, and in this way it differs distinctly from civilizations in which art was confined to religious ceremony, ritual objects, and the burial chamber.

There are three basic concepts that form the foundations of an understanding of Greek art: movement away from **idealism** toward greater **naturalism**, a preoccupation with form and **perfect proportion**, especially in depicting the human figure, and representation of people and objects aiming at **realism**.

■ **2.4 The Classical World showing sites and cities**

Naturalism

In Greek art, human actions were carried out by gods and heroes who, for the most parts, looked and behaved like human beings — compare Praxiteles' *Aphrodite of Cyrene* (Fig. **2.5**) with the *Shiva Nataraja, Lord of the Dance* (Fig. **2.6**) of the Hindu tradition. Unlike their contemporaries in other cultures, Greek gods were almost always depicted in human form — though notably idealized. In other words, one immediately recognizes these images as derived from the human figure, but it is safe to assume that the average citizen of ancient Athens or Cornith possessed far less inspired features. Like the super-heroes of today's comic books, these figures were *idealized* to imbue them with a greater degree of stature and significance. In this way, the imagery addressed not so much the specific attributes of an individual as the more universal characteristics of the human form as accepted by the culture of the day.

■ 2.6 *Shiva Nataraja, Lord of the Dance* c. 1000 AD
Early Chola Dynasty
Bronze
The Metropolitan Museum of Art
Harris Brisbane Dick Fund, 1964

■ 2.5 Praxiteles
Aphrodite of Cyrene
Roman copy of 4th century AD original
Height 5 ft (1.52 m)
Museo Nazionale Romano, Rome

There are virtually no supernatural features (such as fire-breathing or multiple limbs) used in depictions of the deities in Greek art. This clearly separates them from the work of Egypt and the Near East, where attention was usually focused on death and the supernatural experience.

The Human Form

Greek artists often depicted their figures as nudes, calling attention to the humanness of their subjects. This consciousness of the body helps accentuate the Greek culture's decisive break from contemporary societies, in which the nude was utilized primarily for erotic or ritualistic impact.

In Greek society, athletes and warriors trained naked, and the body was generally admired and appreciated without any moralizing censorship. This is not to say that later viewers (for example, the early Christians, as will be fully explored in Chapter Three) did not come to look at the work with some suspicion; rather it suggests that discussions of morality are often more indicative of the values of later historical periods than they are of general perversion within Greek culture.

The human body has long been used as a gauge of self in relation to the world. One interacts with the world through a variety of bodily experiences: sight, smell, hearing, taste, and touch. Perhaps one of the least acknowledged but most fundamental manners in which individuals interact with their world is through measurement and scale. In societies before the Greeks, the comparison of the figure to external stimuli such as trees or sacred objects provided the basis for idealized measurements in art. The Greeks established an important precedent in shifting interest away from "ideal measurement" to that of perfect proportion.

How are these different? It is true that both provide the artist with a set of assumed notions about the figure — pictorial standards formed outside the experience of the individual in question. What is different about the two concepts is the degree to which they are based on a desire for internal harmony. Ideal

■ **2.7 Polyclitus's Ideal Proportions**

measurements can come from whatever set of natural or supernatural sources is deemed important to that community.

Consider the Bible story of Noah's Ark, in which God dictated that the vessel should be 300 cubits long, 50 wide and 30 high — a cubit corresponding to the length of the human forearm from elbow to the tip of the middle finger. These standards provide vital information on the relative dimensions of the piece with regard to the human body, yet say little about how such measurements corresponded to any greater principle of harmony. In Greece, emphasis was placed less on standards than on the interrelationships within human experience. Proportion supports the idea of an internal harmony, rather than imposing sets of standards or restrictions that are gathered from external or arbitrary considerations (Fig. **2.7**). In short, the movement toward perfect proportion in Greek art coincided with the community's increasing self-consciousness — a disposition evident in almost every aspect of Greek cultural life.

Realism

The problem of representation is perhaps the most crucial feature in the understanding of Greek art and ideas. As the discussion of the Classical age continues, it will become increasingly apparent that its art shows a distinct and undeniable move toward greater naturalism, or what is sometimes inappropriately described as realism.

What exactly is realism in art? On the surface, the description appears simple enough, but implicit in such a term is the idea that the human community understands the nature of reality, and that art is about representing this truth. Is that what Greek artists were attempting to do when they produced images such as the *Scraper* (see Fig. 2.2)? The question of representation is a tricky one, yet it has had a profound influence on the way in which one views art. A short digression into the nature of realism and naturalism is perhaps in order.

If one accepts the premise that realism is an attempt to imitate experience or "reality," one thing that is certain is that cold marble is nothing like warm flesh. So in this respect the Classical sculptor was a poor conductor of reality. If the sculptor fails to achieve reality, the painter is even less successful,

since his/her world of three dimensions is a complete illusion. Given this, it is highly doubtful that Classical artists actually saw themselves creating reality. But if this was the case, why did so many attempt to represent the world in such an exact manner? Obviously, there was at least some intent on the part of Classical artists to sculpt, paint, and create architecture with overt references to the world of everyday experience.

If one concedes that this consistency was not the result of a series of random acts, it is difficult not to conclude that the subjects in question must have related to a variety of ideas about life in general. Reality may be defined as a commonly held understanding about one's position in the world, and the art of reality as an expression of those concepts — and not a static truth. In this sense, most visual artifacts address the nature of reality as seen through the eyes of an historical period. So, in further discussions of images and objects that correspond to the world of everyday perception, this text will use the term naturalism.

The movement toward greater representational accuracy is certainly one of the most interesting and important developments in Greek art. Today, the very act of "looking" at an object before drawing, sculpting, or painting its image may seem so ridiculously simple that one takes for granted the important shift of consciousness that must necessarily have taken place on the part of the artist.

Why did this notion of deliberate representation seldom occur in art until the era of Classical Greece? One feasible answer to this historical riddle can be found in the changing relationship between gods and humans in Greek communities during the period. In Greek society, the movement toward greater representation implies less reliance on the role and interference of deities in everyday events. In other words, as Greek society began to take greater responsibility for its affairs, it left the gods to represent the community's history and ideals, so that they figured less in everyday events. Predictably, then, the monster-like images of the pre-Greek age gave way to greater glorification of the human condition, reaching its height in depiction of the human form. It is within this context that the shift toward representation becomes clear, reflecting the society's greater degree of independence from the awesome and inexplicable powers that generated earlier art.

THE ORIGINS OF GREEK ART: 1000–600 BC

The Greeks were by no means a unified community. The geography of Greece is severe, and its mountainous terrain made the transport of peoples and ideas initially difficult. By 1000 BC, the powerful Mycenaean empire had collapsed, leaving these Greek communities to fend for themselves. Each area, isolated from its neighbors by physical obstacles, slowly developed its own centralized governing structure. As peace continued, so did these "city-states" flourish, creating an unprecedented degree of wealth and autonomy in the area.

Pottery

To put it mildly, the beginnings of Greek art were neither particularly auspicious nor inspiring. The best surviving examples of early Greek art come in the form of pottery, which served the practical function of holding items or liquids. Though the construction of these vessels is in itself fascinating and worthy of attention, it is the decoration on their surface that holds significance for the history of representational art.

One of the earliest surviving vessels from the beginnings of Greek culture is an amphora (a storage jar with two handles protruding from either side of the neck) dating from c. 950 BC (Fig. **2.8**). Pottery from this initial era in Greek art is termed "protogeometric" in that its decoration signals the rise of the more obsessive geometric stylings that soon followed. By 800 BC, the simple designs of the earlier age had given way to more complex configurations.

■ 2.8 Protogeometric amphora c. 950 BC
Clay, height 21¾ in (56 cm)
Keramelkos Museum, Athens

■ 2.9 Geometric pitcher c. 800 BC
Clay, height 31¼ in (80 cm)
National Archaeological Museum, Athens

Semi-circles and circles blossomed into zigzags, checkerboards, and a variety of maze-like meanders. The obsessive quality of this work (Fig. **2.9**) suggests that the early artists were searching for a way to bring some form of subject matter into the monotony of earlier surfaces.

An important development in Greek pottery came in the eighth century BC, when human figures began to appear within these dense geometric patterns. This development signaled the rise of human content in Greek art — a subject that has preoccupied Western art ever since. The famed Dipylon vase (Fig. **2.10**) of c. 750 BC is one of the earlier surviving examples of the figurative motif in Greek art. The stylized silhouettes (Fig. **2.11**) mark a subtle but decisive break from the earlier geometric decorations, affording artists the opportunity to use the pottery surfaces to indulge in storytelling. Like present-day stick figures, these early attempts are more a shorthand suggestion of the body than a definitive representation, but they nonetheless serve the important function of describing an event in time and space — the beginnings of recognizable subject matter in Greek art.

Sculpture

Sculpture has long been considered one of the most significant achievements in Classical Greek culture. It was produced in either bronze or stone, both of which are capable of surviving years, even centuries, in harsh environmental conditions. The very survival of these sculptures inevitably leads to their acceptance as a representation of the age, and thus their images have become part of the collective cultural vocabulary. Current knowledge of Greek art comes from the

◄ 2.10 Dipylon vase (Attic geometric amphora) c. 750 BC
Clay, height 50 in (150 cm)
National Archaeological Museum, Athens

■ 2.11 Detail of Dipylon vase c. 750 BC showing stylized silhouettes study of these surviving artifacts and supporting documentation, so it is not unreasonable to speculate that the present consensus on the aims and ideas of Greek art is only partially accurate. For instance, it is certain that painting (independent, non-decorative painting) played a significant role in Greek culture (texts of that era warmly praise certain paintings), but the lack of surviving examples makes it difficult to speculate on the intent of the artists.

Figurative art emerged in Greece around the eighth century BC as a logical extension of the earlier decorative motifs. During the eighth and seventh centuries, the Greek city-states began to establish important trade links throughout the Mediterranean region, which in turn stabilized the economies of the area. One such influential trading partner was Egypt — a kingdom with a significant legacy of outstanding visual monuments and images. The migration of

■ 2.12 *Kouros* c. 600 BC
Island marble
Height 6 ft 1½ in (1.87 m)
The Metropolitan Museum of Art
Fletcher Fund, 1932 (32.11.1)

■ 2.13 *Peplos Koré* c. 530 BC
Parian marble
Height 3 ft 11⅔ in (1.2 m)
Acropolis Museum, Athens

Greek settlers to the region allowed for a certain degree of cross-fertilization between cultures. It is in this source that one may see the origins of Greek sculpture.

The earliest surviving Greek statuary pays direct homage to contemporary Egyptian cult figures, though with some notable exceptions, such as the *Kouros* (Fig. **2.12**) of c. 600 BC. Such stone figures as these — most likely used as funerary monuments for cemeteries; the female types called **Koré** (Fig. **2.13**), the male **Kouros** — exhibit many of the same generic features as the earlier Egyptian models, including a stiff frontal posture and relatively little articulation of joints. The figures do possess a degree of suggested motion in their clenched fists and advanced legs. These forms, which keep a certain visual connection to their original block shape, are generally identified as **closed-form** sculpture; **open-form** work engages its surrounding space as an extension of the sculpture — an issue in later Greek art. Yet, even in its infancy, Greek sculpture exerts a certain degree of body awareness; the description of the musculature and the nudity of these figures mark a dramatic departure from their Egyptian ancestry. This shift of consciousness on the part of Greek artists paved the way for a series of remarkable investigations in the following two centuries. It was here that the significant development of representational art occurred.

ARCHAIC ART: 600–480 BC

The period between 600 and 480 BC saw unprecedented movement in Greek culture, including its visual artifacts. The so-called *Archaic era* (archaic meaning belonging to an earlier or outdated period) has unfortunate connotations of inferior quality, yet it remains crucial to the formation of Greek art. As is almost always the case, the revolution in art coincided with equally important social changes that took place in the various Greek communities. The successes of trade and commerce within the area brought into existence a whole new merchant class, which in turn took power away from the earlier hereditary rulers. With such political change came an increased emphasis on the economy, a concern for personal prosperity, and the development of a certain intellectual freedom, giving individuals a sense of control over their destiny. This concept of "freedom" corresponds nicely with the changes that were taking place in Greek art, in which depictions of humans were characterized by a similar loosening of restrictions — one of those frequent cases in which it is possible to ask whether art mimics life or life art. Perhaps it will suffice to say that something was in the air, and both culture and politics were inevitable expressions of this changing climate.

Sculpture

The Anavysos Kouros (Fig. **2.14**) of c. 530 BC embodies the new sense of artistic individuality that permeated sixth-century Greek culture. The pose is certainly reminiscent of the earlier kouros statues; the Archaic convention of engaging the viewer's space by projecting the figure's leg forward (implying movement toward the viewer, as if walking) is still present as a way of diminishing the closed-form nature of earlier stone figures, and the face remains stylized and impenetrable. There is, nevertheless, a noteworthy difference in the handling of the body. Here the anatomy is conceived with a degree of accuracy impossible without keen observation — a significant conceptual shift on behalf of the artist, who must have moved from a reliance on traditional formulas or conventions for the description of the body to observation from life. A good example of this reconsidering of previous conventional codes toward a more naturalistic image can easily be seen in the comparison of "head to total height" ratios between the "New York" Kouros (see Fig. 2.12) and Anavysos Kouros: the earlier presents a somewhat stunted and overexaggerated presence of the head in its 1:6 ratio, while the latter's 1:7 is much more in keeping with actual human proportions.

■ **2.14 Anavysos Kouros**
c. 530 BC
Marble
Height 6 ft 4 in (1.93 m)
National Archaeological
Museum, Athens

Vase Painting

A similar move toward greater representational accuracy occurred in vase painting during the period, and it supports the claim that any idea as important as freedom will find its expression in a variety of materials and techniques.

By the middle of the sixth century BC, rigid geometric designs had slowly given way to more suggestive descriptions of the human form. However, it was not until the end of the century that artists were finally able to free their figures from the flatness of the pottery surfaces. The turning point came with the introduction of the **red-figure style**, a simple inversion of the previous **black-figure style**. As the first examples of Greek vase painting which date back as far as c. 600 BC attest, figure forms were painted in black slip on the terracotta surface. The result was a series of silhouette figures situated on a clay background (which was often red or orange after firing). This technique found its most profound expression in the hands of artists such as Exekias, whose figures show a remarkable degree of subtlety — particularly considering the restrictions of the technique (Fig. **2.15**).

For forward-looking artists, the problem of such a style lay in the solid silhouettes' inability to suggest much illusion of volume or detail, so consequently they looked rather flat. Earlier artists had attempted to scrape back into the figures with a sharp stylus to

■ 2.15 Exekias
The Suicide of Ajax c. 525 BC
Black figure vase
Height 21 in (54 cm)
Musée des Beaux Arts, Boulogne

■ 2.16 *Skyphos by Hieron*, painted by Makron showing Paris abducting Helen, c. 500–480 BC
Height 8½ in (21.5 cm)
Museum of Fine Arts, Boston
Francis Bartlett Donation

create linear effects, but the technique was awkward and often resulted in stiff and unconvincing images. The answer came in the simple reversal of "figure" and "ground" colors: the background terracotta was now painted black, leaving the figures open. (Today, the terms *figure* and *ground* are often used to describe the relationship that necessarily exists between an object [figure] and its environment [ground], or the interaction of objects and space on a flat plane.) This advance enabled artists to use a brush to describe the interior features of the form, instead of the previous reliance on an awkward scraping tool.

A good example of the obvious advantages afforded by such an inversion can be seen on an Athenian cup, *Skyphos by Hieron* (Fig. **2.16**), painted by the artist Makron in c. 500–480 BC. Here the artist capably depicted a rather complex arrangement of parts by utilizing a range of descriptive devices available through the new freedom of open red figures. Much like the strides being made in sculpture during the period, the red figure innovation in vase painting can be seen as yet another expression of an increasing self-confidence on the part of early Greek society.

Architecture

Sculpture and vase painting were not the only visual arts to exhibit dramatic movement during the Archaic era. The increased prosperity and expansion of the Greek states brought about a vast array of impressive building projects. Peering through the looking-glass of history, there is certainly no shortage of examples of societies in which economic stability has expressed itself in the desire to build monuments. Human beings instinctively seek out the secure and the stable, looking for anchors in a crisis-ridden world. Stability in turn grants the individual a sense of place and contact with the immediate community, and it is in such a situation that individuals function most productively. Given this natural inclination, architecture becomes much more than simply a way of designing a building. As a stable structure and a focus for the community, it inevitably expresses certain truths about that community.

Until the seventh century BC, the little architecture produced in Greece was apparently constructed from crude and impermanent building materials such as mud, grass thatching, and undressed stone. This is of course speculation, since none of it remains today, but

had more sophisticated constructions and techniques developed, buildings from that era would in all probability have survived. With increased trade and commerce from abroad, the Greek people were brought into direct contact with the impressive civilizations of Egypt and Mesopotamia — both of which had long-established building programs. Soon, economic prosperity gave the Greek cities the resources to compete on a similar level, leading to the development of a monumental building style.

The first specifically Greek style of architecture to emerge during the later part of the Archaic era was the austere **Doric order**, □ which had its roots in an

---

FOCUS ON

The Doric Order

In the Doric order (Fig. **2.17**) columns rest directly on the floor or *stylobate* and taper upwards like tree trunks. At the top of the *shaft* is the *capital* which forms both the head of the column and the transition to the horizontal lintel. On top of this is the *entablature* which comprises three distinct parts. The first is the *architrave*, a band of rectangular blocks immediately supported by the columns, and above this stands the *frieze* which consists of alternating blocks of relief sculpture or painting (the *metope*) and vertical bands (the *triglyph*). Above this is the *cornice*, on which sits the crowning *pediment*, a triangular-shaped construction that forms the roof.

A Entablature
B Column
C Cornice
D Frieze
E Architrave
F Capital
G Shaft

1 Metope
2 Triglyph
3 Guttae
4 Abacus
5 Echinus

stylobate
stereobate

■ **2.17 Components of the Doric order**

■ 2.18 Basilica at Paestum, Italy, c. 550 BC

earlier timber post and lintel design. This was the standard from which all variations of Classical building design emerged.

What kind of an effect does such a design have on a building? The Basilica at Paestum (Fig. **2.18**), which dates from c. 550 BC, is one of the oldest surviving examples of the Doric order, and it grants some basic insights into the fundamental visual characteristics of that style. Almost immediately one senses a burden of weightiness, emphasized by the relationship between the columns and entablature. Although the shape of the Doric column probably derived from the natural upward tapering of timber, this example demonstrates how early attempts at mimicking the lightness of organic forms often had the opposite effect. Here, the columns appear visually compressed by the burden they support. However, this squat quality seems to have been curtailed somewhat as the Doric order became a more frequent choice of architectural

arrangement and as builders became more aware of the strength and structural possibilities afforded by the design. Thus such initial visual problems can probably be attributed to structural overcompensation; the architects simply did not trust thin columns to hold up the heavy entablature. As the Greeks became more familiar with the properties of stone, they were better able to judge the distribution of mass over an area, giving designers more confidence in leaner column construction. The end result was a taller, more effective, and more dignified structure, which was to embody the new Classical era (see Figs. 2.19 and 2.20).

Even 2,500 years after its inception as an architectural motif, the Doric order still inspires thoughts of integrity and austere authority — it evokes "power." And for these very reasons it has remained the preferred style for modern government buildings and banks.

CLASSICAL ARCHITECTURE AND THE ACROPOLIS COMPLEX

The Parthenon of Athens (Figs. **2.19** and **2.20**) was constructed as a temple to Athena, the goddess of wisdom, and as such it set out consciously to embody the intellectual pursuits of mathematical harmony and precision implicit in the Greek world view. Though today only a shadow of its former glory, it nonetheless exhibits symmetry, balance, and a sense of system — attributes that had evolved with the greater self-confidence of Greek community. It is in the subtleties of this design that the efforts of its creators, Ictinus and Callicrates, are most clearly illustrated. Take, for instance, the swelling curvature of the Doric columns, called the *entasis*, which bulges to its thickest girth approximately one-third of the way up the cylinder form, rather than tapering predictably from the bottom of the column, as was the case with the timber-style Doric-construction columns at Paestum. This design was meant to suggest connec-

tions to the human form, evoking parallels to the human hip in a standing figure. The result was a series of columns that can best be described as muscular, organic, stoic, and most certainly body-like — an extension of the very centrality of the human position in Greek thought.

■ 2.20 Plan of the Parthenon

columns of peristyle

■ **2.19 Ictinus and Callicrates**
Parthenon 447–438 BC
Acropolis, Athens

■ **2.21 The Erechtheum 421–405** BC
Acropolis, Athens

■ **2.22 The Porch of the Maidens
from the Erechtheum 421–405** BC

The Ionic Order

The second of the Greek orders to emerge, the Ionic order (Fig. **2.23**) is a hybrid design combining the earlier Doric style with Persian and Egyptian sources. The double-scroll motif (called the *volute*) at its crown disperses the vertical thrust of the tall and slender column and, together with the simple base between column and floor, gives it a lighter and more elegant appearance than the Doric style. It is quite probable that the volute design was derived from the palm or another organic element, since the Persians and Egyptians often used floral and vegetal designs in their architecture.

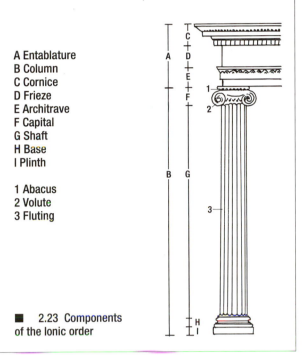

A Entablature
B Column
C Cornice
D Frieze
E Architrave
F Capital
G Shaft
H Base
I Plinth

1 Abacus
2 Volute
3 Fluting

■ **2.23 Components of the Ionic order**

The Corinthian Order

The third of the Greek architectural orders to emerge, the Corinthian order (Fig. **2.24**) was developed as an effective visual solution to the problem of corner columns, which can be viewed both from the front and the side. The Corinthian column presents the capital in the round, following the shape of the column shaft and making the transition from front to side consistent and flowing. The rising layers of acanthus leaves likewise provide a gentle, subtle transition from the visual weight of the architrave to the precariously thin shaft of the Corinthian column. A later Roman variation, called the *Composite order* reinserted the Ionic volute within the round acanthus flourish, providing a dynamic, if perhaps congested, hybrid of the previous orders.

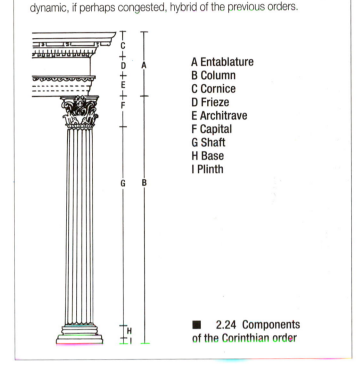

A Entablature
B Column
C Cornice
D Frieze
E Architrave
F Capital
G Shaft
H Base
I Plinth

■ **2.24 Components of the Corinthian order**

While the Doric order followed predictable lines from earlier architectural traditions around the Mediterranean its graceful counterpart, the **Ionic order** □ was firmly rooted in the East. Again, one may attribute such stylistic similarities between cultures to the increased importance of trade beyond the Mediterranean, which had initiated contacts in Persia (today Iran and Afganistan) by 500 BC.

The Ionic order shares many structural challenges with the older Doric style but differs dramatically in its visual presentation. For comparison's sake, consider the visual differences between the Ionic Erechtheum (Fig. **2.21**), built between 421 and 405 BC, and its neighbor the Doric Parthenon (see Fig. 2.19), which reside together on the Acropolis in Athens. How very different is the impression one receives from the Erechtheum. Instead of impressing the viewer by the sense of a heavy load bearing down on the muscular Doric design, the columns in this structure appear both light and elegant. The columns give the impression less of weight than of burdenless ease, and the relaxed intersection between column and entablature almost defies the mass it must obviously endure.

When Ionic work is compared with examples of the Doric order, human associations are once again obvious, but the suggestion appears more stereotypically feminine, with its softer curves and gentle transitions — a point not lost on the Greeks. One of the most fascinating designs to emerge with regard to this bodily association is the Porch of the Maidens (Fig. **2.22**), which stands attached to the Erechtheum. Here the implicit reference to the human body becomes explicit in the carved human supports, echoing humanity's own basic and intrinsic relationship to the world.

CLASSICAL SCULPTURE: 479–323 BC

Nowhere is the Greek notion of freedom and self-confidence better illustrated than in the remarkable achievements of sculpture between 479 and 323 BC, the period commonly referred to as the Classical age. From 494 to 480 BC, the Greek states suffered two attacks at the hands of Persian forces — first under Darius (whose armies were defeated by the Athenians at the famous Battle of Marathon) and then by his son Xerxes. Before falling in defeat, the Persians successfully captured and sacked Athens, and in the process destroyed most of the previous era's monuments. With little left standing, the Athenians initiated an enormous rebuilding program, culminating in vast enterprises such as the new Acropolis complex. However, sculpture affords a clearer sense of the vitality that captivated post-war Greece (and in particular Athens).

In the sixth century, artists had contrived to instill "life" into the traditional koré and kouros figures, which probably originated in Egypt. One of the breakthrough achievements of the early fifth century BC was a marble figure popularly known as the *Kritios Boy* (Fig. **2.25**). It was partially destroyed during the Persian assault on Athens and later rather clumsily restored. Very recent conservation work has now stripped away the later accretions to reveal the work of the Classical sculptor unadorned. Very few individual artifacts so clearly embody the shifting consciousness of an age — a fact that reiterates the working premise of this book that art is an idea best understood within its historical context.

Comparison between the Anavysos Kouros (see Fig. 2.14), of 530 BC and the *Kritios Boy* demonstrates the changes that took place over a fifty-year time span. The *Kritios Boy's* more naturalistic representation of the human form in space can be attributed partly to the relaxation of the stiff frontal pose of the earlier kouros pieces, and is a conscious attempt to activate the figure in its surrounding space. The head and body twist slightly, and the weight of the body shifts onto the back leg, allowing the front leg to rest free. This combination of free and engaged leg later came to be known as the *contrapposto* pose in Renaissance art and has subsequently been endowed with great significance as an embodiment of Western

values in visual culture. Within its original context of Greek art, the subtle twisting and shifting of weight was apparently merely a comfortable and natural posture for a human, and thus one tends to attribute specifically human characteristics to the work.

Another difference worthy of mention is the pensive expression of the *Kritios Boy*. Gone is the broad smile that typifies so much of the earlier work, and in its place there is a discernible meditative quality. To some degree, this shift of sensibility can be attributed to a keener observation of the human face, as artists began to rely more on the study of specific nuances and less on stereotypes. For example, in earlier Archaic sculpture, the human lips were represented as two symmetrically arranged parts, the top lip mirroring the bottom. This balanced design is what causes the so-called "Archaic smile" evident in much of the period's sculpture — a convention based on earlier abstractions of the human form rather than on observation (since the upper and lower lips are not identical in humans).

In general, the *Kritios Boy* exhibits a degree of anatomical inspection noticeably absent in previous figurative sculpture. This is particularly evident in areas such as the joints. No longer is the human form rendered as a stiff, inflexible corpse; instead the intersection of parts in the human body (joints such as the knees, hips, and shoulders) suggests elasticity and dynamism, as well as introspection and concentration on the part of the artist. Some scholars point to this change as an indication of a greater degree of introspection on the part of all Greek citizens with regard to their position in the world, as they entered a period of war (the Persian Wars were probably in progress when the *Kritios Boy* was produced), while others see such observation as a natural result of increasing Greek interest in the science of the human form. In any event, there emerged with the *Kritios Boy* a new manner of perceiving the body in three dimensions.

One of the most famous representations of athletic pursuit is the *Discobolos* — the *Discus Thrower* (Fig. **2.26**), which was produced, probably around 450 BC, by the Athenian sculptor Myron. Today the work is known only from a Roman copy, and it seems that the original was in fact a bronze not a marble. Even

■   **2.25** *Kritios Boy* c. 480 BC
Marble
Height 2 ft 9 in (0.85 m)
Acropolis Museum, Athens

■ 2.26 Myron, *Discobolos* (the *Discus Thrower*) c. 450 BC
Roman copy of bronze original. Marble, height 5 ft (1.52 m)
Museo Nazionale Romano, Rome

so, the intent of the artist seems clear. The work shows the unmistakable release of the figure from its previous closed-form confines, the result of which is the further dismantling of the stiff, frontal Archaic pose in favor of a more imposing gesture. Also, the modest interest in anatomical accuracy noted in the *Kritios Boy* achieves a degree of subtlety and rigor in the *Discobolos*, as the twisting of muscles and tendons accentuates the stresses imposed upon the figure.

The choice of a powerful, limber athlete as subject matter may originally have had something to do with an actual commission (perhaps it was to be placed outside a sporting hall), but it also enabled the artist to indulge in a series of observations and speculations on the human body's structure as it moves through

■ 2.27 Polyclitus
Doryphorus (the *Spear Bearer*)
Roman copy after Greek original of 440 BC
Marble
Height 6 ft 6 in (1.98 m)
Museo Archeologico Nazionale, Naples

space. Given Myron's obvious interest in musculature and the skeletal structure, one might assume that the *Discobolos* is a highly naturalistic representation of the human form; in reality, nothing could be further from the truth. Studies by Classical scholars on the viability of the pose have found that a human could not hold such a position without painful dislocation. In addition, a decidedly impersonal approach to the character indicates an interest not in the idiosyncrasies of a given model but more in the generalization of humanness based upon the observation of a number of individuals — in other words, idealization. The comparison to a present-day store mannequin is valid here, for there is much in common between the two types of figure. Like the mannequin, whose proportions are based more on accepted ideals of the perfect figure than on the average body, these powerful Greek physiques conformed to the contemporary standards of perfection and idealism. For both figures, form is determined by very social and intellectual considerations.

The idealization of the human form was brought to new heights in the work of the sculptor/theoretician Polyclitus, whose *Doryphorus* — the *Spear Bearer* (Fig. **2.27**) was allegedly executed as a model to illustrate his theory of internal proportion in the human figure. To Polyclitus, ideal beauty was achieved through a correct understanding of internal harmony, symmetry, and balance, and around 450 BC he set out to produce a formula for the depiction of the perfect figure (see Fig. 2.7), an experiment that had implications far exceeding the human form. For artists such as Polyclitus, beauty was not to be found in the everyday but in the abstract idea of perfection to which one aspired. Thus these sensual, powerful bodies can be understood as artistic manifestations of a pervasive Greek interest in defining their position in the world.

However, ideals such as harmony and balance become increasingly difficult to manage when a society's external affairs are in chaos. At the very heights of artistic activity, there were already indications of the culture's imminent demise.

PLATO AND ARISTOTLE LOOK AT ART

There is always some difficulty in describing the ascension of Greek art as a move toward greater naturalism. Even during the fifth and fourth centuries BC, great minds contemplated the very validity of representational art. The Greek move toward representation was much more complex than a simple reproducing of visual experiences: it involved a degree of selection and discrimination definable as idealism. Yet the question remains: to what extent were the Greek artists consciously attempting to reproduce their tangible, visible world, and further, to what end? This issue interested the Greek philosopher Plato (427–347 BC), whose Tenth Book of The Republic wrestled with the legitimacy of artistic practice.

Plato described artistic practice as an attempt to imitate the world of "sense-experience" (what one experiences through sight, smell, etc.). In Plato's world view, nature is organized in tiers, with ideal forms existing beyond the reach of limited human comprehension. Below these absolutes there stand poor imitations. Unfortunately, this is the world in which mortals live and function — the world of sense-experience.

Given Plato's premise that visual artists do little more than copy whatever is in front of them, they are in essence producing reproductions of reproductions. Thus the artist is responsible for creating an even less truthful description of reality, since its source is already an imitation. Plato exemplified this idea by describing the reality of the bed in a descending order of truthfulness. First, there exists the "ideal" bed, which is inaccessible to humans. Next, there is the carpenter's bed — a copy of the idea of bed but of poorer quality, since it is an imitation produced by an imperfect craftsperson. Lastly, there is the artist's representation of the bed, which is based on the carpenter's bed in the world of sense-experience. It is further removed from the "real" bed and is consequently of the poorest quality. Thus, Plato concluded, artistic activity is a vain and lowly ambition, since it only furthers an inferior experience.

Plato was obviously suspicious of the role of the artist, and he saw his contemporaries as little more than imitators of sense-experience. But was that actually the case? In considering the sculptural examples already described, it is hard to believe that artists were simply and arbitrarily copying from sense-experience. Concepts such as balance, harmony, and proportion often contributed to the production of art, and it seems safe to say that the artists believed themselves to be engaged in something more considered than simple reproduction

A good example is the *Doryphorus* (see Fig. 2.27). Since it was executed to illustrate a theory of proportion, it might be better to equate it with the work of the carpenter who makes the bed, as the *Doryphorus* did not derive exclusively from sense-experience but also from the world of ideas. In taking the best aspects of a number of sources and redistributing their content, the artist created an object that aspired to true

"form" rather than an imitation of an imitation. Plato simply believed that not enough art aspired to such heights and that too much was derived from inferior sources.

Later Greek philosophers, such as Aristotle (384–322 BC), reworked the severe Platonic critique of visual art by attempting to reconcile representation with the contemplation of the art object. Aristotle was somewhat suspicious of Plato's metaphysical leanings and attempted to ground art within sense-experience as a prerequisite to higher knowledge. Here art is still seen as derivative, but of the human soul rather than simply of brute experience. One might call this a watered-down metaphysics, but it is valuable because it explains humanity's inclination to "read into" Greek art a degree of human insight that has little to do with imitation.

LATE CLASSICAL AND HELLENISTIC ART

In 431 BC, the Peloponnesian War brought about an extended period of turmoil and chaos in Greece. When the dust settled in 404 BC, Athens had been displaced as a political, economic, and military center, though it still retained cultural significance. It was not until 338 BC that order was restored to the mainland, when the Macedonians, under Philip of Macedon, successfully unified most of the Greek cities. With his subsequent assassination in 336 BC, power was transferred to his energetic son Alexander (born 356/5 BC) — soon to be called "the Great." Though he survived only another thirteen years, Alexander spread Classical civilization to the far corners of Greek territory. From this "Hellenization" (dissemination of Greek culture) under Alexander derives the name of the era. It was to be the last gasp of energy for Greek culture, and it provided an important impetus for later developments in Roman art.

The Hellenistic age lasted less than 200 years, from the death of Alexander the Great in 323 BC to the rise of the Roman Empire with the Battle of Actium in 31 BC. Between these two dates there emerged an identifiably different sensibility in Greek art, one that emphasized emotion over restraint, individuality over idealism, and personal patronage over the needs of the state. Changing economic and social conditions

set important precedents for Hellenistic art, many of them attributable to a shifting awareness of the artists' position in their community and the greater world of ideas.

If one were generally to attach the concepts of harmony and order to the Classical age, the terms emotional turmoil and technical exuberance typically describe the Hellenistic period. In terms of technical prowess, there can be little doubt that Hellenistic sculptors understood the craft of stone carving better, and even took it further, than earlier artists, as the dramatic *Nike*, the *Winged Victory of Samothrace* (Fig. **2.28**), so visibly attests. These sculptors displayed considerable skill in their sensual depiction of clinging drapery; the expressive implication of wind raking across the body of the *Nike* only heightens one's appreciation of its vitality and movement.

Though the earlier advances in proportion and balance were not lost with these artists, they were certainly offset by an equally strong interest in expressive character. Harmony, once of primary concern to Classical designers, now retreated in favor of overt dynamism, grounded more in the tangible aspects of the everyday than in the lofty concerns of Plato and Polyclitus. The delightfully unpretentious statue of a *Child Playing with a Goose* (Fig. **2.29**) of the

■ **2.28** *Nike — Winged Victory of Samothrace* c. 180–160 BC
Marble, height 8 ft (2.45 m). Louvre, Paris

third century BC is one such example of the culture's increased grounding in the here and now and in those aspects of humanness more directly in touch with the senses. At the same time, the plight and fancy of the individual took on heightened significance in the subject matter of these last centuries, which may have had something to do with the new market for portraiture.

In the Classical era of Greek art, most if not all important monuments and works of art were produced for public buildings and thus public consumption. The artist's patronage came directly from the oligarchy of leaders (the powerful élite), so there developed a necessary correlation between art and the collective interests of the demos (free Greek people). In fact, public patronage was the major factor behind the lofty choice of subject matter. After the death of Alexander, his empire was quickly divided into a group of rich kingdoms, and with this came the establishment of a new ruling class and wealthy business community. It appears that few considered the Athenian attempts at democracy worthy of salvage, and patronage quickly fell into the hands of those who could afford the luxury of images and monuments. One significant result of this shift in patronage was the increased demand for portraiture, which paid reverence to the patron rather than necessarily to an idea (Fig. **2.30**).

■ 2.30 Roman portrait head of Alexander the Great
1st half of 2nd century BC
Marble
Height 16 in (40.6 cm)
Archaeological Museum, Istanbul

■ 2.29 *Child Playing with a Goose*
Roman copy of a 3rd century BC composition
Marble
Height 2 ft 9 in (0.85 m)
Capitoline Museum, Rome

■ 2.31 *Dying Gaul*
Roman copy after an original bronze c. 230–220 BC
Pergamum, Turkey
Marble, lifesize
Museo Capitoline, Rome

One of the more interesting repercussions of this new "individualization" was the range of emotions now considered worthy of depiction in art. Examples ranged from the heroic *Dying Gaul* (Fig. **2.31**) to the unencumbered sensuality of the *Barberini Faun* (Fig. **2.32**) which capture the complex nature of human experience in a much more definitive manner than the more Classical embodiments of, say, Polyclitus. Here the figure is presented not as an abstract ideal but as an embodiment of humanity's most fragile, sensuous, and sometimes tragic experiences. This is as close as Greek culture would come to true naturalism, and it effectively characterizes the increasingly introspective and uncertain nature of the once indomitable Greek spirit.

The Hellenistic period has sometimes been defined as one of moral and artistic decay, in which order and discipline gave way to embellishment and excess. In some ways, the period has suffered (as has the Baroque era, which will be discussed at length in Chapter Five, pages 225–279) from the general consensus that order and harmony are necessary for the production of art, rather than disquiet and emotion. It is certainly true that Hellenistic artists were adept at playing on emotions, and often this lack of subtlety leaves the modern viewer with little more to admire than the sculptor's technical ability in handling marble. But this was a culture and a people in transition: in a world in which order and idealism appeared increasingly suspect and peace was at the best of times precarious, it is certainly understandable that visual culture should exhibit a similar convulsion of ecstatic highs and introspective lows. Unable to reconcile the previous idealism with their contemporary world, artists resorted to elaborate technical formulas rather than the search for expressive new modes. Hellenistic art lacked the optimism and conviction of its predecessors, which was the belief that thought and action could result in universal harmony. In that regard, its outlook seems sadly familiar.

■ **2.32** *Barberini Faun*, Roman copy of a Greek original of c. 220 BC
Marble, over lifesize. Staatliche Antikensammlungen, Munich

THE TRANSITION TO ROME

One of the most frequent criticisms of Greek culture is that it was unable to reconcile intellectual ideals with practical considerations. Even Athens, supposedly the pinnacle of Greek sophistication and democracy, was always just a stone's throw away from chaos and war. No doubt, the contributions of the Greeks to civilization were enormous, but it was the Roman Empire that insured the primary position of Classical culture in the Western tradition.

Etruscan Art

There were two primary sources for Roman culture: the Etruscan civilization and Hellenism. The Etruscans remain one of the most mysterious and least understood societies in history. It is known that by 700 BC they had established themselves in northern Italy and that through trade and agriculture they soon prospered. It appears that early Etruscan art possessed a tremendous degree of skill and craftsmanship, and as commercial links grew, so too did the foreign influences on its art. Before long, aspects of contemporary Greek art began to have an impact on Etruscan design. The *Apollo*, from the Portonaccio Temple in Veii, c. 520–500 BC (Fig. **2.33**) is an excellent example of the combined sensibilities. It most likely derived from the kouros figures of Greece, but unlike its predecessors, this Apollo exhibits a degree of psychological power missing in the early Greek models.

The finding of large Etruscan burial complexes (referred to as necropolises, meaning Cities of the Dead) just north of Rome at Tarquinia and Cerveteri supports claims that the civilization had an elaborate burial cult. Yet archaeologists speculate that the Etruscans unlike their contemporaries, understood death as yet another transition in the soul's restless journey. This might explain the rather orderly "urban" design that characterizes the necropolis, as well as the rather contented expressions on the figures which often recline upon Etruscan sarcophagi (Fig. **2.34**).

The indebtedness of the Etruscans to Greek culture did not, however, end with sculpture; architectural conventions also provided the impetus for many a

■ **2.33** *Apollo* from the Portonaccio Temple in Veii c. 520–500 BC
Terracotta
Height 5 ft 9 in (1.75 m)
Museo Nazionale di Villa Giulia, Rome

■ **2.34** Sarcophagus from Cerveteri, c. 520 BC
Terracotta
Length 6 ft 7 in (2 m)
Museo Nazionale di Villa Giulia, Rome

building program. Such was the case with the arch □. Though the arch form had certainly been known to architects and builders for centuries (2,500 years earlier the Egyptians were already using it for burial chambers), the Etruscans followed the lead of the fourth-century Greek models and are credited with having been the first to feel comfortable combining it in monumental architecture. The early second-century BC Porta Augusta in Perugia (Fig. **2.36**) is an excellent example of the integration of the arch form into the environment of traditional Greek architectural orders.

The Rise of Rome: Art of the Republican Era

In 616 BC, Rome was little more than a rural outpost of Italic peoples, with little to suggest such an auspicious future. It was in that year that the Etruscans began a century-long "occupation" of the city, one that would forever change the fortunes of the Western world. According to Roman tradition, the Etruscans never occupied the city but simply played a significant part in its cultural order. Others disagree, citing this view of history as little more than a form of Roman revisionism bent on preserving ethnic superiority. Whatever the case, it is clear that Etruscan involvement in the daily affairs of the city brought about unprecedented prosperity and diversity, and with it the kind of development befitting a commercial center. New trade routes were soon established, and for the first time Italic Romans were brought into contact with the outside world. Within 100 years, the Romans had successfully learned all the lessons of trade and organization from their captors, and by 510 BC they had rid themselves of Etruscan influence. This was to mark the beginning of the end for the Etruscan civilization, as it slowly gave way before the aggressive Roman machine. Nevertheless, emotional introspection and love of the natural world remained an identifiable feature of Roman culture long after the demise of the Etruscans, and it is to them that Roman art owed some of its most captivating characteristics.

FOCUS ON

Arch Construction

The arch (as well as the vault and dome, which were derived from it) is a structural device that allows an opening in a wall, roof, etc. to exist without supports (Fig. **2.35**). The arch consists of a series of carefully cut stones, called *voussoirs*, which butt one against another to create a semicircle. The central voussoir, called the *keystone*, exerts pressure down through the arch, holding the form in place. Builders constructed such arches by way of a wooden support called *centering*, a semicircular device pushed up into the interior of the arch that kept the stones from collapsing inwards until the keystone was put in place.

Despite its fragile appearance, the arch form is structurally very secure once in place, and it gave architects the ability to cover great expanses of space. Combined with the transplanted Greek discovery of what came to be called *opus caementicium* (concrete) — a cheap and readily available compound of materials such as sand, clay, and stone that was easy to produce and could be formed into a variety of solid forms — the arch was the technical impetus behind the later great Roman building projects.

■ **2.35 Arch construction**

■ **2.36 The Porta Augusta, Perugia, 2nd century** BC

The period between 510 and 44 BC saw tremendous change in Italy and the surrounding territories. Rome, becoming increasingly powerful and self-confident with each military campaign, began to occupy enormous areas of land; by the first century BC, the entire Hellenistic world had fallen under its control. Local crafts remained intact, and often the very best craftspeople were sent to Rome or other important centers to engage in a vast array of building and decorative projects. This gave the general impression of a cultural continuum from Hellenistic to Roman rule, which proved itself to be a shrewd political as well as artistic maneuver.

One of the most interesting aspects of this inherited Roman art to emerge from the "Republican" (from *res publica*, commonwealth) period, 500–27 BC, was the accepted use of art as propaganda. As in the Greek and Egyptian civilizations, art and power were inextricably linked, since expensive art and architectural projects required tremendous financing and a large workforce, items often available only to the powerful. As the large-scale political regimes gave way to smaller and often less ambitious kingdoms, so too did the scale and use of the art. With the emergence of the Roman Republic, an interest in the grand project was rekindled. Art and architecture spoke of the

■ **2.37** *A Patrician Holding Portrait Heads of his Ancestors* c. 15 BC
Marble, lifesize
Museo Capitoline, Rome

power, majesty, and infallibility of the Republic — ideas the Romans saw embodied in the great Hellenistic capitals of Antioch and Alexandria.

During this early period, portraits were particularly popular with the patrician (ruling) class as an extension of the Roman ideal of individual veneration and responsibility. *A Patrician Holding Portrait Heads of his Ancestors* (Fig. **2.37**) exhibits the peculiarities of such design; the patrician's figure is most likely a copy from Hellenistic sources, on top of which is positioned a highly naturalistic representation of the individual. Unlike the previous Greek examples of figurative sculpture, this high-ranking civic official is not at all idealized; his wrinkles and warts are very much in evidence — an obvious extension of the Roman virtue of individuality. Once again, the notion of naturalism and its representation is always a matter of contingency, never a fixed and static thing. This disposition toward the specific over the ideal or general on the part of the Romans may be indicative of their aspirations as a people.

Republican architecture possesses a similar assortment of influences and innovations. One of the oldest surviving buildings from this era is the Temple of Portunus (Fig. **2.38**) in Rome, which was constructed in the late second century BC. At first glance, the structure appears to possess many of the attributes of earlier Greek buildings, including Ionic columns, a traditional pediment and frieze, and a design based on a sweeping 360-degree view of columns, sometimes referred to as peripteral. There is, however, one marked deviation from the original Greek design, and that is the use of **engaged columns**, which are actually non-structural decorations on the exterior wall. It appears that the Romans inherited from their Etrusco-Italic ancestors a temple design history derived not from peripteral but from frontal considerations, with conventions such as a high podium, steps located only at the front of the building, and an evident back wall — a design that gives a very specific directional character to one's interaction with the structure. The engaged column is thus a fascinating example of visual cross-fertilization and an important transitional motif between the Etrusco-Italic and Greek influences (hence the term "pseudo-peripteral" used to describe many of these structures). It effectively completes the exterior rhythm of vertical forms supporting the entablature, while keeping the wall intact — a practical solution for a practical people.

■ 2.38 Temple of Portunus, Rome, late 2nd century BC (Formerly called the Temple of Fortuna Virilis)

AUGUSTUS AND THE EMPIRE

In 44 BC, the assassination of Julius Caesar began a period of conflict and disorder in the Republic. Power was finally consolidated in 27 BC, when Octavian became emperor and initiated a new era in the Roman world — now called the "Empire." Octavian took the name Augustus, and it was under his astute leadership that Rome reorganized, beginning what would prove to be the period of greatest prosperity in Roman history.

Architecture

Peace and relative calm allowed Rome to concentrate on restoring pride and prestige to the regime. Soon massive building projects were begun with the aim of visually and psychologically reinforcing Roman authority. The artistic embodiment of this new regime was the *Ara Pacis* (Fig. **2.39**), the Altar of Peace. Here the delicate relief sculptures promote an image of the Empire and its leader as both pious and peace-loving (Fig. **2.40**). Perhaps the most interesting aspect of this altar is its obvious borrowings from earlier Classical Greek sculpture. As early as 9 BC, artists already recog-

nized the implications of using or evoking styles of previous ages and could successfully use them to political as well as artistic ends. The deliberate stylistic use of Classical relief sculpture gave artists (and thus Augustus himself) the opportunity to draw parallels between the lofty ideals of Athens and the aspirations of the new Empire. Yet despite the decidedly Greek overtones, the *Ara Pacis* remains essentially Roman in character.

■ 2.39 Ara Pacis Augustae, Rome, 13–9 BC
Marble. Outer wall approx. 34 ft 5 in x 38 ft x 23 ft (10.5 x 11.6 x 7 m)

■ **2.40** Detail of the Ara Pacis Augustae 13–9 BC, showing the procession of the Imperial Family

■ **2.41** Arch of Titus, Rome, AD 81. Marble, height 47 ft 4 in (14.43 m)

The Arch of Titus (Fig. **2.41**) is characteristic of Rome's popular form of monument. It took as its source the long tradition of arch and vault construction handed down from the Etruscans, and it possesses a rather monolithic authority when set in the middle of a road. Apparently the tradition of constructing wooden and floral arches for victory parades originated much earlier, but as with much that the Romans touched, it became grander and much more permanent — echoing the qualities of authority and longevity that symbolized the Empire. Like today's war memorials, these triumphal arches were erected to commemorate an event; at the height of the Empire, it is said there existed over fifty within Rome's city limits. The Arch of Titus commemorates that Emperor's successful recapture of Jerusalem after the Jewish revolt in AD 66–71. The surfaces are decorated with narrative relief carvings describing the triumphal procession (Fig. **2.42**), the presentation of the spoils, and an image of Titus riding in his chariot.

Perhaps the most famous architectural project initiated during the reign of Vespasian (AD 69–79) was the monumental *Flavian Amphitheater* (Fig. **2.43**), better

■ **2.42** Detail from the Arch of Titus, AD 81, showing the Menorah procession

■ **2.43** Flavian Amphitheater, also known as the Colosseum, Rome, AD 72–80
Concrete (originally faced with marble)
Height 160 ft (48.8 m). Diameters 620 ft (189 m) and 513 ft (156.4 m)

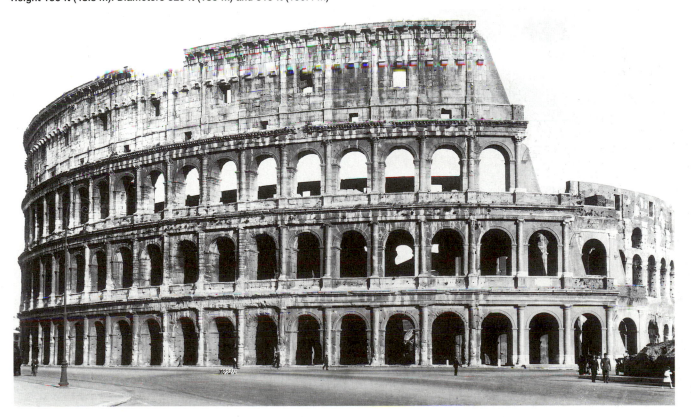

known today as the *Colosseum*. The choice of location for the amphitheater was symbolic: it was constructed directly on top of Emperor Nero's infamous gardens, which were to most of Rome's citizens a painful reminder of the previous administration's flagrant corruption and general malaise. Thus Vespasian's "arena of courage" was a direct challenge to the perceived decline of the Empire. It was dedicated by Vespasian's son, the Emperor Titus, a year after his father's death in AD 80.

The Amphitheatre is a massive structure. The problem architects faced in confronting such an imposing construction was how to provide a convincing sense of rhythm and rise in a building that expanded horizontally in such a cumbersome way. The solution lay in an inventive stacking of the traditional architectural orders, which in ascending order rise from the muscular, burden-bearing Doric, through the graceful and fluid Ionic, to the refined and delicate Corinthian and then finally the structurally superfluous, highly decorative Corinthian pillasters. The result is a sense of acsending lightness to the facade, which effectively circumvents the overpowering horizontal and ground-hugging nature of the structure.

The interior engineering of the amphitheater is nothing short of remarkable and is a vivid illustration of a Roman disposition towards the development of sophisticated technical solutions for building problems. Side by side, tunnel vaults led from the eighty entrance arches on the ground floor into interior staircases, which in turn led to the upper observation decks. Seating capacity was approximately fifty-thousand spectators, with no obstructed views! The arena floor lay on top of a series of tunnels, from which gladiators and/or animals could enter the ring of combat. Further, the infield could be flooded by way of an elaborate plumbing system, enabling mock naval battles to be waged in the center of Rome.

■ **2.44** Pantheon, Rome c. AD 118–28, height of Portico 59 ft (17.98 m)

oculus

Plan and section
of the Pantheon

■ **2.45** Interior view of
the Pantheon c. AD 118–28
showing the dome

Until the time of Constantine (AD 285–337), at least one part of Nero's gardens survived intact — a massive sculpture or *colossus*, which stood next to the amphitheater. As a consequence, the term was predictably applied to the structure as well. As with most of Rome's great monuments, centuries of pillaging building materials and just plain wholesale destruction (one of the Renaissance's most dubious distinctions) have left the Colosseum little more than a skeleton of its former self. Today it exhibits little of its original glory, though it remains a popular attraction with visitors and pilgrims and a poignant reminder not only of the immense skill of Roman engineering but also of the Romans' insatiable need of spectacle.

The Pantheon (Figs. **2.44** and **2.45**), built at the order of the Emperor Hadrian, is one of the greatest surviving examples of Roman engineering and architecture. It is also one of only a very few examples of dome construction that remain intact from the days of the Empire, and it gives an indication of the immense power of architecture. The structure was built as a temple to all the Roman gods (pantheon means "every god") and thus possesses several significant attributes considered fundamental to the Roman world view. The *oculus* (a small circular opening at the very center of the dome) is one such example of the happy marriage of structural interests and the need to embody ideas; it is suggestive of the eye of Jupiter, who orders the world, while having the practical function of illuminating the interior space.

In terms of technical innovation, a dome is simply the intersection of several arches arranged around a central axis (an arch rotated 180 degrees), and thus it was a logical extension of earlier activity. However, the centering skeleton necessary for the pouring of such a vast amount of concrete is still admirable to this day, making the structure a singular example of Roman ingenuity and perseverance. The result is breathtaking. Unlike monumental Greek entablatures, which rested flat on supporting columns, the dome allowed for a much grander and more expansive interior. The dimensions speak for themselves. Compare the Parthenon in Athens (see Fig. 2.19) with the Pantheon: the Parthenon rises 34 feet (10.3 m) from floor to entablature over a vast amount of floor area, whereas the Pantheon rises 142 feet (43 m) and is exactly the same distance in width, owing to the spherical form from which it is derived. This exact correlation between height and width gives the structure a unique symmetry and balance, and it remains one of the crowning achievements of Roman architectural engineering.

■ **2.46 Ritual passage into a mystery religion**
Wall painting from the Villa of the Mysteries, Pompeii, mid-1st century BC

■ 2.47 The Room of the Masks
Wall painting from the House of Augustus on the Palatine Hill,
Rome, c. 1st century BC

ROMAN WALL PAINTING

It is a standard opinion that Roman painters were more successful at adopting earlier innovations than at providing new styles and solutions in themselves. However, the discovery over the past few centuries of Roman wall paintings may give one reason to reconsider the traditional position. These murals are virtually the only evidence of the state of painting in Classical society.

The best examples of Roman painting come from the ancient city of Pompeii, which was covered and preserved virtually intact by the volcanic ash and debris from Mount Vesuvius when it erupted in AD 79. Although this event was a huge catastrophe, it has proven to be of great value for art historians, who now have exquisite examples of remarkably well-preserved painting from the preceding period. The wall paintings from the Villa of the Mysteries (Fig. **2.46**) give a good indication of the quality and technical abilities of painters during the Roman Empire. It appears that ideas such as depth and the description of forms in illusionistic space were well entrenched in Roman painting. Also, painters seem to have understood the capabilities of painting to describe a narrative progression, and hence there is no shortage of storytelling.

A more telling example of the expertise and technical prowess of the Roman painter can be seen in the recently discovered Room of the Masks (Fig. **2.47**) in Rome. In this wonderful series of **murals**, there exist the first surviving examples of perfect one-point perspective — a mathematically derived technique for describing space, and one that did not surface in Western painting again for another millennium (see the discussion of perspective on pages 184–191). It is impossible to say whether the Romans developed such sophisticated techniques on their own or derived them from earlier, perhaps Greek, sources; whichever is the case, these paintings remain essential to the story of Roman art.

The decline of the Roman Empire has been the subject of great debate, and it is difficult to pin its demise down to one cause. Some blame the huge bureaucratic machine (still a popular excuse) for the atrophy that plagued late Rome. Others have made mention of the huge percentage of non-Roman troops needed to police the Empire — most of whom had little interest in or loyalty to Rome and did little to stop its decay. There are those who see the shifting of power from Rome to Constantinople in AD 330 as the decisive blow; others argue that this move secured the continued health of Roman civilization until the Renaissance. Whatever caused the decline, the Romans left a legacy of building and art that has survived to this day and has provided generation after generation with inspired notions. In short, it has played an essential role in the construction of Western culture. Few have influenced the course of history as dramatically as have the Greeks and Romans, and it took an even greater authority to dismantle their legacy. That authority, claimed by the successor to the Romans, was the perceived will of God — the substance of the next chapter.

SUMMARY

The ideas first exhibited in Greek and then Roman culture have become essential components of Western art and culture. Within the difficult notions of freedom, responsibility, and political organization there lie the cornerstones of later Western thought, its particular value system, and its notion of art. In Greek art, the development of complex forms of social organization found its voice in the culture's representations. Such manifestations as a new attitude toward the value of observing from nature, the philosophical belief in the existence of ideal forms, the visual conventions of proportion and internal harmony, all contributed to a world view centered by the gaze of the human community. Roman art appropriated Greek culture into more pragmatic arenas, such as political monuments, portraits, and complex engineering projects, all of which admirably reflect the enormous potential for images and objects to engage the community on both a social and a private level. Classical conventions have continued to affect and direct aspects of civilization to the present day: the Classical age indeed provided the foundations on which all subsequent Western culture was built. Yet a closer study of the Classical era also makes clear that relationships between art and society are often those of power; the values generated by a community are thus also a reflection of the greater interests of those who control its policies.

Suggested Reading

The Classical world has been the subject of more writing and speculation than perhaps any era in the history of the Western world, so there is no shortage of suitable texts available.

Boardman, J., Griffin, J., and Murray, O.: *The Oxford History of the Classical World. Volume one: Greece and the Hellenistic World* and *Volume Two: The Roman World* (Oxford and New York: Oxford University Press, 1988). Gives a good overview of the arts as part of Classical thinking.

Haynes, Denys: *Greek Art and the Idea of Freedom* (London and New York: Thames & Hudson, 1981).

Robertson, Martin: *History of Greek Art* (Cambridge: Cambridge University Press, 1975).

Sheppard, Anne: *Aesthetics* (Oxford and New York: Oxford University Press, 1988). A clear and lucid introduction to early and Classical aesthetics.

Pronunciation Guide

Anavysos Kouros **ahn**-uh-**VEE**-saws **KOO**-raws
Aphrodite **af**-ruh-**DY**-tee
Apoxyomenos uh-**pahk**-see-oh-**MEE**-nuhs
Callicrates kuh-**LIK**-ruh-teez
Dipylon dy-**PY**-lahn
Doryphorus **dor**-uh-**FOR**-uhs
Erechtheum **air**-ek-**THEE**-uhm
Exekias ek-**SEK**-yuhs
Hieron **HY**-uh-**rahn**
Ictinus ik-**TY**-nuhs
Koré **KAW**-ray
Kouros **KOO**-raws
Kritios **KRIT**-ee-aws
Paestum **PES**-tuhm
Polyclitus **pahl**-in-**KLY**-tuhs
Pompeii pahm-**PAY**
Praxiteles prak-**SIT**-uh-leez
Shiva Nataraja **SHEE**-vuh nah-tuh-**RAH**-juh
Skyphos **SY**-fuhs

Glossary

black-figure style (*page 82*) In early Greek pottery, the painting of figures in black slip on terracotta surfaces, which were then scratched into with styluses to articulate forms. This style was followed in the middle of the sixth century BC by the subtler **"red-figure style."**

closed-form (*page 80*) Sculptural forms that keep a certain visual connection to their original block shape; generally sculptures that have little articulation and do not visually activate the surrounding space, giving the appearance of being self-enclosed.

Corinthian order (*page 87*) A Greek architectural order notable for its modelled acanthus leaf motif and rounded capital.

Doric order (*page 83*) The first architectural system developed by the Greeks, and also the sturdiest and plainest looking. This was the standard from which all variations of Classical building design emerged.

engaged columns (*page 100*) Non-structural decorations used on exterior walls in Roman temples, thus imitating Greek temple design while preserving an enclosed interior space.

idealism (*page 74*) A tendency in art in which representational images, often the human form, conform to an ideal aesthetic standard rather than to a naturalistic or individualistic one.

Ionic order (*page 87*) A more refined and slender version of the earlier Doric design, its most noteworthy feature is the double-scroll "volute", which acts as a mediation point between the entablature and the column.

koré/kouros (*page 80*) A generic term for Archaic Greek figurative sculpture (the female types called "koré," the male "kouros"), much of which exhibits features evident in earlier Egyptian models, including a stiff frontal posture and relatively little articulation of joints.

mural (*page 107*) A large scale painting often applied to a wall or other architectural surface.

naturalism (*page 74*) An attempt to imitate the world of everyday perception, or as things exist naturally.

open-form (*page 80*) Sculptural work that projects into and engages with its surrounding space. Many such pieces show little suggestion of their original source shape (see closed-form, Chapter 1).

perfect proportion (*page 74*) A system of determining the scale of a figure based on an interrelationship of parts within the body. Proportion supports the idea of an internal harmony, rather than imposing a set of standards or restrictions on the body, gathered from external considerations.

realism (*page 74*) A commonly accepted understanding of one's world. The art of reality is an expression of how one understands the world, not necessarily contingent upon what one sees (*see* **naturalism**). In this sense, most visual artifacts address the nature of reality as seen through the eyes of an historical period.

red-figure style (*page 82*) The opposite procedure of the **black-figure style** evolving in the mid-sixth century BC. In this style the artist paints the background areas in black slip, leaving figures in terracotta, which are then articulated through painted lines, giving the figures a greater sense of form and detail.

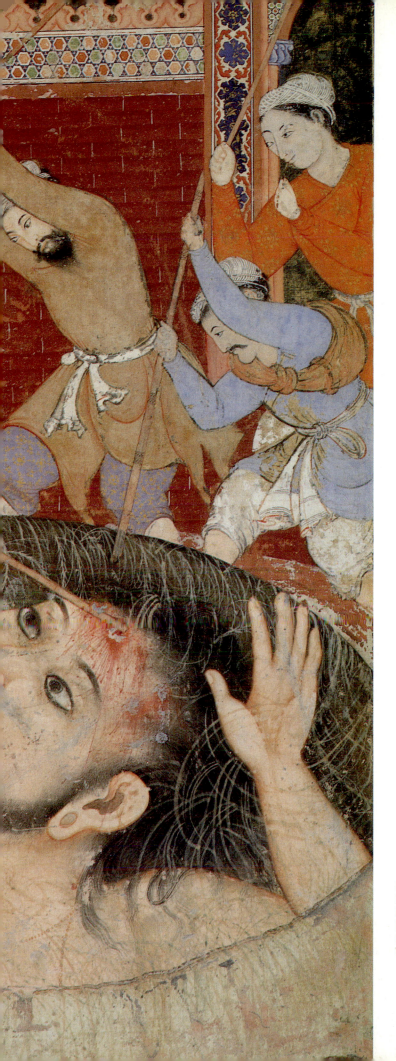

3

ART AND RELIGION

The visual worlds of Judaism, Christianity, Islam, Hinduism, and Buddhism

■ 3.1 Detail from *Gardeners Beating the Giant Zamurrad*
From the *Romance of Amir Hamza*
Mihal Period, 1555–79
Paint on cloth
26 3/8 x 19 5/8 in (67 x 50 cm)
Victoria & Albert Museum, London

All things are artificial,
for nature is the art of God.
SIR THOMAS BROWNE

Previous chapters have demonstrated how the visual arts operate within an historical context. Since a community is the sum of its goals, beliefs, and aspirations, any ideology that attempts to explain the fundamental meaning of life has an important and dramatic relationship with art and art making. Such is the case with art and religion. Every faith has had to establish some form of a dialogue (whether it be tolerant or intolerant) with the visual arts, and through often lively deliberations each has contributed to the present understanding of art.

The primary focus of this chapter will be on the five major faiths of the modern world: Buddhism, Christianity, Hinduism, Islam, and Judaism (Fig. **3.2**). Each faith is here considered as a "theory" of existence and reality, rather than as fact set in stone, and as both a foundation and an extension of the civiliza-

tion from which it once emerged, granting the greater human community insights into the mysterious workings of the world. Like art, religion both shapes and expresses those desires and needs that make meaningful each person's short time on earth. A typical understanding of art changes dramatically from one religion to another, and challenges some well-entrenched ideas and stereotypes.

THE JEWISH TRADITION

Since the Classical traditions coincided with an outpouring of culture around the Mediterranean basin between 700 BC and AD 330, it is perhaps appropriate to begin this discussion of religious art in roughly the

■ **3.2 Distribution of the major religions in the world today**

RELIGIONS OF THE WORLD

2000 BC	1500	1000	500	0	500	AD 1000
HINDUISM c. 2500 BC Origins in Indus Valley				2nd cent. BC Bhagavadgita	Shri Ranganatha Temple 5th cent. (3.49) Goddess Ganga c. 500 (3.45)	711 Muslim invasions begin	Kandariya Mahadeva Temple c. 1000 (3.47) *Shiva Nataraja* 11th cent. (3.46)

| **JUDAISM**

1900–1700 BC?
Abraham | 1300 BC
Moses

1010–970 BC
David, King of
Judah and Israel | Ivory lions of Samaria
c. 722 BC (3.4)

37 BC Roman
occupation of Holy Land | AD 70 Jerusalem falls to Rome
The Diaspora

Dura Europas AD 245 (3.5) |

CONFUCIANISM

551–479 BC Confucius

c. 500–600 Japan
imports Confucianism

BUDDHISM

c. 563–483 BC
Gautama Buddha

Great Stupa at
Sanchi 3rd cent. (3.53)

AD 160 Buddhism
reaches China

Seated Buddha
c. 2nd–3rd cent (3.55)

520 Start of
Ch'an Buddhism

c. 6th cent. Buddhism
enters Japan

c. 1140 Introduction
of Zen Buddhism

Jun Dish
c. 12th cent.
(3.58)

CHRISTIANITY

AD 0–33 Jesus

AD 51 First church

325 Council of Nicaea

Hagia Sophia,
Constantinople 532–37 (3.14)

c. 675–749 John
of Damascus

c. 1000 Development
of cathedrals
St. Sernin (3.23)
St. Denis (3.27)
Chartres (3.31)
Notre Dame (3.30)

ISLAM
570–632 Muhammad
Mosque of Damascus c. 715 (3.40)
Mosque of Cordoba 786 (3.44)
750–1258 Cultural peak

same geographic vicinity and at approximately the same time. While the Ancient Greeks were contemplating laws, democracy, and other such matters, another people, located in what is today the state of Israel, left an equally indelible mark on human civilization. They were the Jews, and it was from their rich religious tradition that the faiths of both Christianity and Islam eventually sprang. To understand fully the complex nature of Western art, it is necessary to discuss the Jewish interpretation of images and their use, for the Jewish philosophy of art created a strong precedent for the younger faiths that followed.

It is popular to describe traditional Jewish art theory as essentially anti-art. Though this label is not altogether correct, there are specific reasons why the religion distrusted visual images. Judaism is a religion of **iconoclasm**, which simply means that it considers the creation or veneration of representational images an illegitimate activity — against the will of God. (In a more strict sense, iconoclasm may also mean the destruction of images.)

The Old Testament tells how Moses received the Ten Commandments on Mount Sinai but later, in a fit of rage, crushed the precious stone tablets on which they were incised after witnessing his people worshipping a golden idol depicting the god Baal. Thus an important precedent for the Jewish suspicion of images was established. The second of the ten laws warns against the construction of "graven images." In art terminology, this translates as a denial of representational imagery on the grounds of blasphemy.

Why were the Jews so restrictive in their tolerance of the visual arts? One reason was probably their need to develop a culture distinct from their polytheistic neighbors. A polytheistic faith is one in which a number of deities are granted special privilege in the worship of a people. Many religions develop as polytheisms, worshiping various items such as the sun, moon, water, fire, etc. Judaism was perhaps the first religion to develop as an absolute monotheism — meaning a belief in one God. This distinguished Jews from other cultural groups and provided the impetus for a distinctive society.

The God of the Old Testament was transcendent, invisible, and apart from the world. His power lay in the ability to create and destroy — activities also associated with art making. Most polytheistic faiths were centered around physical manifestations of gods that survived in literal and figurative form. The god Baal from the Exodus story is a good example. These deities were worshiped by way of physical images, and thus the objects and representations became an essential part of worship. Given this, it is hardly surprising that many of the world's more developed polytheisms (such as Hinduism) have a rather distinct legacy in the field of the visual arts. Yet in Judaism, the transcendent nature of God (invisible, omni-present) denies the very possibility of describing him (*and in Judaism it is clearly a him*) in physical form. Further, the Jewish community's outright dismissal of polytheism made them suspicious of the use of visual images in worship — something central to their polytheistic neighbors. One may cautiously speculate that the early Jewish distrust of images had a lot to do with this historical connection between the visual arts and the religious polytheism rampant in most of the cultures of the Mediterranean basin.

The explanation in the preceding paragraph is what might be called the "traditional" justification for iconoclasm or the denial of representation in Judaism. Yet there are other, perhaps less obvious reasons for the establishment of such strict laws. One is the nomadic lifestyle of the early Jews. For a wandering people sustained by an unforgiving environment, art projects were obviously impractical and consequently meaningless. It seems that nomadic societies tend to develop rich oral and musical traditions, while the lack of secure grazing lands makes permanent architecture and art work difficult if not impossible undertakings. The Jewish culture is a good example of a society that flourished along very predictable artistic

■ 3.3 Model of Jerusalem in the Second (Herod's) Temple period showing the Second (Herod's) Temple with surrounding courtyards

■ 3.4 Ivory Lions of Samaria c. 722 BC. Collection of Israel Antiquities Authority

lines; the creative magic of poetry and music was firmly implanted in the faith at an early stage and was recorded in such works as the Psalms. There was, however, a brief period in Jewish history in which its people enjoyed a degree of stability and economic prosperity, and the results in the field of art making were significant.

Though often soaked in blood, the reign of King David made possible a consolidation of disparate tribes and a brief (very brief) disappearance of war from the area. This meant that the subsequent rule of King Solomon was one of marked prosperity and growth. This in turn led to the development of communities that grew along more stable lines than those of the nomadic shepherd. As the city of Jerusalem began to flourish, with it came the need for a more permanent architecture. The opportunity was indeed unique for a group that had survived as nomads for centuries, and they aspired to create monuments fitting to their culture and their God. The result was the building of the first Temple by King Solomon c. 950 BC. This was destroyed in 586 BC, and a second Temple (Fig. **3.3**) was built in the later sixth century BC, which was restored by Herod the Great and destroyed by the Romans in AD 70.

The Temple was the central focus of the faith, housing the Ark of the Covenant — God's contract with the Children of Israel. Contemporary descriptions of the project show that it included items such as golden cherubim, which were placed at the entrance to the structure. This means that the steadfast ban on image making of the Ten Commandments

(reiterated in Deuteronomy: IV, 17–18) was obviously not strictly observed by them. Archaeological evidence supports such claims, as witnessed in a pair of ivory lions (Fig. **3.4**) from Samaria that were probably fashioned by the Jewish people.

What does this apparent contradiction say about art making in the development of the Jewish faith? One obvious conclusion is that iconoclasm was never completely adhered to as a tenet of the faith. This partially explains the occasional lapse into representation that occured from time to time in Judaism. With specific regard to the Temple, perhaps permanent settlement, social stability, and material prosperity had an important effect on the production of art in the community. When the culture flourished with the establishment of peace and prosperity in the region, images seem to have emerged, and along with them a limited tolerance of representation.

Whatever the reasons may have been for such a deviation, it was certainly short-lived. In 586 BC the Babylonians sacked Jerusalem, destroyed the Temple, and led the Children of Israel into yet another extended period of captivity. The result was a virtual vacuum of artistic activity for the next few hundred years.

During the first century AD, the Hebrew theologian Philo of Alexandria (c. 30 BC–AD 45?), a thinker profoundly influenced by the philosophy of Plato, deliberated on the nature of the Jewish God. In his writings the idea of a transcendent, invisible God — with significant ramifications for Jewish art found perhaps its greatest apologist. Like Plato, Philo saw

God as a universal perfection, unencumbered by material and thus impossible to represent. This contrasts with earlier, more anthropomorphic notions of God (who, according to the Genesis story, supposedly made man in his own image), yet historical circumstances within the Jewish community at the time made such theological pronouncements at the very least a comfortable fit. Albeit commenting only on the nature of God and not on the more general issue of representation, the result of this marriage of Jewish and Classical traditions (generally referred to as the Masoretic tradition) was a more orthodox interpretation of the role of imagery in the synagogue.

Jewish Art

What is one to make of the Jewish contribution to art in the light of the previous discussion of iconoclasm? When considering such issues, it is helpful to consider a couple of factors that may have contributed to such a discrepancy between religious law and later artistic practice. One is separation. As history so cruelly

points out, the Jewish people had little opportunity to develop as a distinct nation. The Babylonian Captivity was only one in a number of setbacks. It was followed by the invasion of Alexander the Great and then the Romans, which led to an angry uprising and the eventual Diaspora (meaning dispersal) in AD 70, to all intents and purposes ending Jewish occupation of Israel. The forced migration of Jews to all areas of the Roman Empire and beyond led to the fossilization of religious law as a common thread between peoples growing further and further apart geographically. Following on from this, there was both a more rigorous application of iconoclasm in the synagogue and also the establishment of more relaxed art in the secular world.

There were, however, notable exceptions to this rule, and they underscore the tenuous and often shifting relationship between theory and practice with regards to representation within the Jewish community. The discovery in 1932 of the town of Dura Europos (Fig. 3.5) in Mesopotamia forced archaeologists and religious historians alike to reconsider

■ **3.5 West wall with the Torah niche, Dura Europos, AD 245**
Tempera on plaster, approx. 40 ft (12.2 m). Reconstruction from the National Museum, Damascus

■ 3.6 Curtain for the Ark of the Torah, Mannheim, Germany, 1728
Velvet, silver thread embroidery
Collection Israel Museum, Jerusalem

assumptions about Jewish art. The synogogue, constructed around AD 245, was decorated with scenes from the Old Testament presented in a manner reminiscent of both Roman and early Christian sources. Art historians speculate that the compositions, which possess a likeness to contemporary murals, were probably taken from a pattern book or series of conventional drawings that were then circulating within the Jewish community. This suggests that there was a greater interest in representational imagery than contemporary writings allow.

In the case of Dura Europas, it is possible to hypothesize why such a deviation from orthodoxy took place. Located in the hinterlands of the Roman Empire, in Mesopotamia (modern day Iraq), the small frontier town was a minor trading center and as such became a melting pot for several religious ideologies. Further, the isolated character of Dura Europas' geographic situation meant that an adherence to orthodoxy was constantly tested by the town's own inner dynamics. One such pressure and influence was most certainly the Christian and Classical cults, with their reliance on representational imagery as an integral part of ritual. In both format and stylization, the synogogue murals are clearly derived from period sources, and thus it seems probable that the murals were as much a positive response to the art the Jewish community saw around it as they were any outright or calculated rejection of dogma.

From the sixth century onwards there were synagogues that embraced representational aspects as part of the interior decoration. For the most part, however, art for religious ceremony was essentially reduced to calligraphy and ornamentation of the Torah (Fig. **3.6** on page 117). As in Protestant Christian iconoclasm (which will be more fully discussed in Chapter Five, see pages 226–233), the Judaic prohibition of representational images in worship did not prevent artists from creating work for everyday enjoyment. The result was a marriage of practical considerations and religious law that neither denied the authority of the faith nor prevented those who felt inclined to produce images for other functions from doing so. Thus the history of Jewish art is the result of practical compromise rather than religous sanction. In this way, the Jewish community was able to embrace art making as a fundamental part of life, while retaining a strong degree of suspicion about its aims.

THE CHRISTIAN TRADITION

It is perhaps appropriate to begin this discussion of Christian art by remembering that Christ was a Jew. To Christians, however, he was the fulfilment of Jewish prophecy, and also the Son of God. This belief had enormous repercussions for both the formation of the religion and its art. Although the God of the Children of Israel was invisible and transcendent, in Christianity the "word" (*logos* in Greek) had become flesh: through Christ, God was made visible and lived among his people. This meant that God possessed an image — an identifiable whole that could be reproduced through representational imagery. This was to be the basis of a distinctly Christian philosophy of art.

Jewish interest in forming a distinct culture and Jewish iconoclasm, an extension of the need for religious identity, were also features of the first Christians, who were themselves Jews, having either followed Jesus as disciples or had contact with some of the earliest missionaries. The displacement of Jewish Christians in the Diaspora of AD 70 meant that the subsequent history of the Christian faith was that of the "Gentiles" — those from cultures not directly descended from Christ's own Jewish heritage. This ended the strict iconoclasm of the very beginnings of the Christian Church and moved the faith into communities in which visual images were both sophisticated and historically accepted, such as Corinth and Rome. Soon, early missionaries began to adopt regional styles of expression (such as the making of visual images) to help converts better understand the significance of Christ's resurrection. From within this sometimes difficult and often controversial meeting of Christianity and native culture (in particular Classical society), Western art began to blossom.

Images and Imagery

One of the first debates to ensue in the new Christian Church was the consideration of art forms. The discussion, highlighted by the debates of Origen and Clement of Alexandria in the third century, centered around the relative merits of both two- and three-dimensional art work within the context of the Scriptures. This debate quickly established important precedents in Christian art, and it provides an interesting starting point from which to discuss the various

■ 3.7 *Good Shepherd* late 3rd century AD
Marble (restored)
Height 39 in (99 cm)
Vatican Museums, Rome

ways in which one may experience art. The issue was whether or not art in general, and sculpture in particular, was a legitimate form of expression for the pious Christian, and the outcome of the deliberations initiated a shift away from three-dimensional art toward painting for the best part of a millennium.

One of the more conclusive resolutions to come out of this debate was the opinion that painting was the most appropriate medium for representing the Christian faith. The logic went as follows: painting was essentially an illusion, and understood by all as simply a design born of experience but incapable of duplicating experience. In other words, its flatness was so obvious that theoretically it could not deceive the viewer as three-dimensional reality. Now, anyone who has felt the eyes of a portrait watch them as they move around a room, may have something to say about the ability of flat planes to give the viewer a believable representation of reality. However, what is essential here is the notion that painting and representation are justified on the grounds that they do not attempt to duplicate reality — they have no volume and thus do not exist in a real space.

Sculpture, with its emphasis on forms existing in real space and having discernible volume, did not fare quite so well under the critical eye of the early Church. It appears that sculpture came too close to pagan idolatry for many of the early Christians, who wanted to assert a very specific identity within the Gentile communities. Some of the first Christian excursions into sculptural forms, such as the *Good Shepherd* marble of the third century (Fig **3.7**), exhibit this tenuous relationship with their Classical sources — a resemblance that no doubt made the pious uneasy. Between the third and sixth centuries, most Christian sculptural projects took the form of relief work, decorating sarcophagi and other essentially flat surfaces with shallow, narrative-like representations that were in sympathy with the tenets of two- rather than three-dimensional ideas. During the first years of the Christian faith, the existing sculptural traditions of Gentile communities, such as that in Rome, were arguably so refined and convincing that they provided many iconoclasts with visible proof of the power of sculpture to compete with the handiwork of God. Later, even painting and two-dimensional art were not excluded from attacks by those who saw all representational art as a direct challenge to the creative authority of God.

Being a Christian in the early years of the faith was not easy; indeed, it was a capital offense in Rome. One of the results of the relentless persecution was the need for secrecy with regard to rites and practices, and this led to a very interesting development: "camouflaged symbolism," which could be read and understood on a number of levels without revealing its true intentions to the wrong people. A good example of such symbolism is *Christ as the Good Shepherd* (Fig. **3.8**). Though the story of the Good Shepherd is firmly entrenched in Christian lore, the subject was also a popular one in pagan mythology (such as the Greek story of Hermes Criophorus — the ram carrier). By a careful choosing of subject matter with a variety of possible meanings, Christian sites of worship innocently appeared as rooms decorated with scenes from popular myths; the images were ambiguous enough to hide their real intent.

Many of the most popular Christian symbols have their origins in pagan imagery: items as diverse as the dove (the Holy Spirit), the fish (baptism, Christ), the sun (truth), the feast (the Eucharist), and the shepherd (Christ) can all be traced back to earlier cultures

■ 3.8 *Christ as the Good Shepherd* mid-4th century AD
Wall painting from the Catacombs
of SS Pietro and Marcellino, Rome

■ 3.9 *Tombstone with Fishes* 3rd century AD
Stone fragment from Catacomb of St. Domitilla, Rome

(Fig. **3.9**). The end result of this intermingling of pagan iconography with early Christianity was the development of a hybrid system of symbolic language and imagery from which later artists drew inspiration.

Early Christian Architecture

In 313, with the Edict of Milan, the Emperor Constantine successfully introduced Christianity as the official religion of the Roman Empire, and for the first time the young faith was able to exist without the threat of persecution. Almost immediately, Christianity became a public institution, and with its new status came a degree of authority and stability. The first major development to evolve from this recognition was a drastic re-evaluation of the scale and impact of religious art. Within a few years of Constantine's rise to power, officially sanctioned churches were being built on the sacred sites of Christendom. The church — "Christ's house" — quickly became the sustained focal point for Christian art interests, and thus surviving architecture affords special access to some of the most important qualities of the faith.

Old St. Peter's Basilica (Fig. **3.10**) was one of the first architectural expressions of the new faith. Built in Rome from about AD 333, it was designed to house various relics from the Apostle Peter's martyrdom and was held in particularly high regard by the faithful as a place of contemplation and pilgrimage. The design was simple and austere, and it laid the foundations for Church architecture for many centuries. It appears

■ 3.10 Cross section showing the nave of Old St. Peter's Basilica, Rome (reconstructed) c. AD 333–90

■ 3.11 Floor plan of Old St. Peter's Basilica c. AD 333–90

from archaeological evidence (the actual structure was destroyed in the Renaissance to make way for the current St. Peter's Basilica) that the faithful entered the shrine through an enclosed courtyard (*atrium*), which was attached to the **basilica** proper. The interior plan was evidently modeled after the secular architecture then popular in Rome (the so-called "basilica design") and is likely to have been a reflection of the earlier Christian sites of worship, which were generally the homes of the faithful. As a result, the "house of the faithful," or "God's house," tended to follow a very particular Roman legacy, mirroring not so much temple architecture as the intimacy of the domestic housing that had been the meeting place of the early Christian community.

To understand the fundamental structure of the basilica plan, it is necessary to consider further the union of form and function as each pertains to the complex proper (Fig. **3.11**). The basilica was constructed with a long central *nave* that helped focus attention on the services conducted at the far end of the church. The nave was intersected by the *transept*, originally designed as a means of creating space around the altar so that the congregation could be

more centralized. It also had the added benefit of visually isolating the tomb of a saint (in this case Peter) from those lesser figures buried in the nave, as well as serving the practical function of allowing pilgrims access to the shrine without interrupting normal services. Later the transept was introduced further down the nave to make a cross form (symbol of the crucifixion) rather than its original *T* shape.

To light the building, windows were placed on a second level, which rose above the central portion of the nave (called the *clerestory*). This ingenious device gave worshipers the impression that natural illumination (whether it implied Plato's notion of light as the symbol of wisdom or the divine light of the New Testament) was a sign of God's grace. The design enabled natural light to fall from above rather than raking on the diagonal or horizontal, which inevitably cast strong directional shadows — a problem sidestepped by placing relatively few windows on the first level. The result of such experimentation between sacred and secular architecture set an interesting precedent for later Christian building projects; its symbolic language continues to inspire architects to this day.

The ability of basic elements such as directed light and a cruciform ground plan to evoke an emotional (some would say spiritual) response in a viewer may give an indication of the psychological power of architecture. It also points to the uneasy realization that, if art can enlighten and transform for the good the viewer's world, it can also influence for less worthy ends. There is little doubt that good religious architecture effectively manipulates the faithful, and Christianity quickly learned the all-important lessons that had inspired the architects of the Great Pyramids at Giza and the Acropolis in Athens — that spaces and images (architecture and art) not only inspire the masses but often control them. It is in these terms that one comes to understand the grandeur of perhaps the greatest visual expression of the Christian faith: the cathedral.

The development of the cathedral in Christian art is a slow and arduous one, but its beginnings can be traced back to building programs such as Old St. Peter's Basilica in Rome and contemporary churches. In 326 Helena, mother of Constantine, made a pilgrimage to the Holy Land in search of the locations of Christ's birth and Passion. The result was the consecration of specific sites: the Church of the Nativity in Bethlehem and the Church of the Holy Sepulchre in Jerusalem. The Church of the Holy Sepulchre (Fig. **3.12**), which was built c. 345, has much in common with the design of the Old St. Peter's Basilica in Rome, including the long nave with a transept placed at one end, and the clerestory that housed the ever-important windows. But the significance of this building project lies in its combination of the basilica plan (derived from Roman secular architecture) with a domed expanse — a structure used in major Roman monuments and civil buildings such as the Pantheon (see Fig. 2.44) and thus commonly associated with

■ **3.12 Church of the Holy Sepulchre, Jerusalem (reconstructed)** AD **345**

FOCUS ON

Dome Construction

In structural terms, a dome (Fig. **3.13**) is simply the intersection of several arches around a central axis. In its earliest use, the dome rested directly on a cylindrical wall called a *drum*, which transferred the massive weight directly on to the floor. As building projects increased in size, the drum was replaced by the *pendentive* — a triangular shaped segment of vaulting that effectively transfers the stress away from under the dome, and disperses it over a greater expanse of sturdy columns. The result is a stronger foundation, capable of supporting the vast weight of a monumental dome.

■ **3.13 Dome construction**

power □. This dome, which covered the supposed site of Christ's entombment, gave the church a degree of visual stature and prominence not easily discernible in the original Basilica of St Peter.

The dome motif had been the preferred structure for the burial chambers (mausoleums) of the great Roman emperors, and the use of such a device suggests that early Christian architects were attempting to evoke the same form of reverence for Christ's life. Even the Roman triumphal arch eventually found its way into church architecture, forming both a visual and a structural transition between the nave and *apse* (the front section of the church, usually separated by the transept in basilica-style buildings). Architecture, which is often considered a relatively neutral and practical art, is thus far more value-laden than one might suppose.

Hagia Sophia

On 11 May 330, Constantine made the ancient eastern city of Byzantium (today Istanbul, Turkey) his new capital, renaming it Constantinople. This fresh start enabled the weak Roman Empire to purge itself of its immediate history of conflict and instability, and it helped establish a new image of the state and its religion. The shift of capital marked the beginning of both the Byzantine era (named after the old city) and an uneasy relationship between Church and state that has continued to the present day.

The crowning architectural achievement of the Byzantine age is undoubtedly Hagia Sophia (Figs. **3.14** and **3.15**) and though today it appears significantly altered (its conversion to a mosque precipitated the addition of four large minarets on the exterior and the dismantling of the mosaic works on the interior walls), it remains one of the truly magnificent visions of the young faith. Construction of "the Church of Holy Wisdom" began in 532, and it was to be the glory of the Christian world. It was conceived in accordance with the principle of light as a metaphor for wisdom.

The structure was almost 41 feet (12.5 m) higher than the Pantheon in Rome, which then had the largest dome of its kind in the world (Fig. **3.16**). The most impressive feature of the work is the immense expanse the dome covers. Until this point, domes had

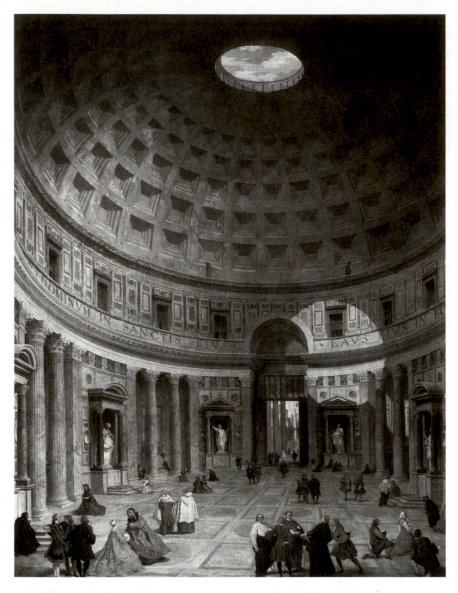

■ 3.16 Giovanni Paolo Pannini
Interior of the Pantheon c. 1740
Oil on canvas
4 ft 2½ in x 3 ft 3 in (1.28 x 0.9 m)
National Gallery of Art, Washington, D.C.
Samuel H. Kress Collection

▶ 3.17 Interior view of Hagia Sophia AD 532–37

often rested directly on a cylindrical *drum*, which extended the vertical field of the dome directly into the floor. This was suitable for less ambitious projects, but a larger dome meant increased strain on the drum, which had to support great weight on a relatively small base. Hagia Sophia circumvented this structural deficiency by placing the drum on another support, called the *pendentive*.

Once the architects had successfully grounded the weight of the dome, light (the symbol of wisdom) was used to accentuate the interior volume of the structure. To do this, forty windows were situated between the dome and the drum, giving the impression that the dome floats above its support. The impact is breathtaking, as light appears to support the expan-

sive ceiling and contradict the massive weight of the roof. At this point, it is hard not to experience awe at the consummate poetry of space. Here Christ visually supports Heaven (which in this case is the dome interior), and the structure becomes its own living metaphor of the majesty of the faith (Fig. **3.17**).

The symbol of light had a continued effect on art making throughout the early years of the faith. Christianity also relied heavily on previous artistic and architectural traditions in its search for a grand visual expression. Early Christian architecture is a good example of such a dynamic. Architects consciously invested their buildings with a variety of deliberate quotations from assimilated cultures (the basilica format from Roman secular architecture and

the dome, which was associated with imperial monuments), while developing more specifically Christian concepts, such as the divine quality of light. Since light had the ability visually to lift ceilings and speak of the mercy and wisdom of God, it became imperative that these two-dimensional arts should disseminate a similar kind of religious association. It was at this point that the age-old technique of mosaic established itself as the favored medium among early Christian artists.

Mosaic and Cloisonné

● **Mosaic** is a very practical form of art making. Colored stone, glass, or ceramic *tesserae* are adhered to surfaces such as floors, walls, and ceilings, becoming more or less permanent fixtures. The first documented mosaic works were floor designs, executed somewhere around the eighth century BC in simple black and white pebble designs. Soon, accessibility to rarer colored marbles allowed for a remarkably subtle range of tone and coloration. Like a rug, a mosaic floor gave the interior space of a building a more decorative appearance than bare plaster or mud, and it had the added incentive of needing almost no upkeep. Early Christian mosaics obviously derived much of their technical prowess from Roman precedents (for example, the *Head of Autumn*, Fig. **3.18**, from the late second century AD, which bears a resemblance to early Christian designs), yet the art form quickly took on other, more "theologically sound," associations. Take, for instance, the decree of the Emperor Theodosius II in 427, which forbade the exhibition of images of Christ on the floor. The idea of

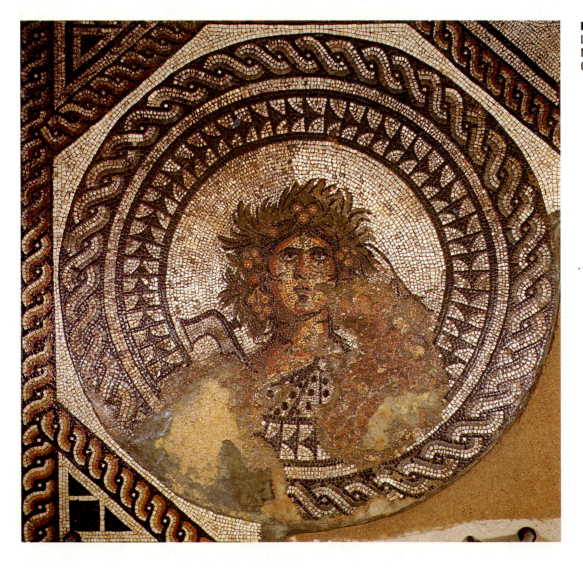

■ 3.18 *Head of Autumn*
Late 2nd century AD
Mosaic from Cirencester,
Gloucestershire

■ 3.19 *Cross, Stars and Evangelists Symbols* Vault of the Galla Placidia, Ravenna, 5th century AD

positioning a sacred figure such as Christ below that of the sinning human (and in the case of floor mosaics, this was exaggerated even further by stepping on that image) became blasphemy, and it opened the way for regulations governing the appropriateness of certain forms of composition — ideas commonly called decorum.

Unlike wall painting, in which surfaces remain somewhat flat and static, the rough textures of glass and stone make mosaic surfaces undulate in an uneven manner. In more complex and sophisticated mosaic programs, care was taken to place tesserae at subtly different angles. The development of glass tesserae gave artists even greater freedom with regard to color and glass had the further advantage of reflecting light. The combination of the uneven surfaces and

the reflective qualitites of glass and stone made the material ideally suited to lighting effects. In the Mausoleum of Galla Placidia and the Baptistery in the Italian coastal town of Ravenna, such illumination came primarily in the form of candles, with their warm, golden glow. As a result of the necessary relationship between light and the mosaic medium, the interior spaces of these buildings possess many of the same dynamic qualities as the candle — something of profound interest to both artists and church officials attempting to evoke the presence of God in these spaces. The beautiful interior vault in the Mausoleum of Galla Placidia (Fig. **3.19**) is a particularly fine example. The gold tesserae dance in candlelight, and the vivid blue surroundings provide a dynamic counterpoint to the rich symbolic imagery.

■ 3.20 Cover of a Reliquary for the Preservation of the True Cross
Cloisonné enamel. Limburg an der Lahn, Germany

● Another popular medium for the Christian artist was cloisonné enamel work (Fig. **3.20**). It had very specific technical complexities that did not easily translate into subtle modulations of tone and color, and like mosaic, it had important repercussions on how Christians continued to render figures.

Cloisonné enamel is produced by firing enamels into pockets formed on the surface of the metal. The result is a relatively flat form, in which the noticeable outline surrounding the color tends to discourage the viewer from reading these figures as representations of three-dimensional objects. The clarity of design and strength of vision make these items at once striking, and like mosaic, they helped set in motion a standard of design that lasted well into the next millennium.

The Icon

The most significant two-dimensional art form produced by early Christians is arguably the **icon**. As visual representations, most icons possess the same pictorial qualities as both mosaic and cloisonné enamel: flatness of design, strong transitions of color, and abstracted figures, all of which enable the image to function on a number of levels simultaneously. For instance, an image can be rendered in a manner that enables a viewer to learn from it (it has a didactic function), while concurrently evoking emotional responses very different from the probable effect on original audiences.

Icons grow out of such a situation. Early Christian art was primarily concerned with converting the masses, and used visual images to help tell stories about the life and deeds of Jesus Christ. Since clarity was of utmost importance for such missionary work, the best images became extremely illustrative. Further, since these images came out of a narration (the Bible), the subjects were always grounded in history (or "historical circumstance") and were thus removed from the viewer by time. As group worship became more important in Christianity, there was a greater need for images and objects that not only reinforced aspects of Christian teaching but also provided a more introspective and contemplative focus. The meditative function of art was achieved by simply reorienting some of the features of the previous didactic format. Artists first removed the figures from the narrative, allowing the subject to exist in what is referred to as "non-historical time." In other words,

when a background scene is removed from a figure, the subject is portrayed without a sense of placc and is thus capable of entering into personal communion in the present tense (Fig. **3.21**). The early Church scholars agreed: since Christ had died and risen, he could be portrayed in the present, emphasizing both the resurrection and the omnipresence of God. This eventually led to the portrayal of the Virgin, the saints, and the apostles in non-historical time, allowing them also to remain fixed in the present. Inevitably, this whole movement toward a more personal and meditative art led to the exaltation of the image *as* the essence of God; in other words, the pictures quickly took on the role as intermediaries to the Divinity and became an important part of the process of worship.

Stylistically, the icon developed with many of the same qualities as other early Christian art. Icons were produced in a variety of materials, ranging from mosaic and enamel to carved ivory reliefs and tempera paintings on wood panels (Fig. **3.22**). The design was, and remains, most often flat, with highly abstracted features that are both a predictable extension of the strong graphic tendencies of the earlier act, such as enamel work, and a necessary severing of the relationship with simple representation (which is based exclusively in the world of everyday perception and thus of little meditative value). The most recognizable features of these images (such as the penetrating, almond-shaped eyes and the gaunt, descriptive faces) are attempts to find a visual vocabulary capable of evoking the spiritual in the everyday. If 1,500 years of a still vital and uninterrupted tradition are any indication of the power and authority these images possess for Orthodox Christian communities (icon makers still hold to these precepts), one may conclude that this format of picture making has succeeded in evoking the universal in the specific.

An Apology for Images

As the history of icons illustrates, it does not take long for images and picture making to become a complex business, entangling within one image a host of other, seemingly unrelated, issues. The question then becomes one of differentiating between worshiping what the image is supposed to evoke, and simply worshiping the image as a manifestation of God (which Christians claim is idolatry). This issue came

■ 3.21 One of several icons of *Our Lady of Vladimir*
Icon, early 15th century
Attributed to Andrei Rubiev
Vladimir Museum of Art, Russia

to a head in 726, when Emperor Leo III ordered the destruction of a mosaic figure of Christ over the palace gate in Constantinople, and replaced it with a simple cross. This was followed four years later with an official decree forbidding the use of icons of Christ or the saints in worship. Leo III based his argument on the Second Commandment, and in so doing quickly lit a fire of controversy within the religious community — many members of which saw his action as a blasphemous denial of Christ's fulfilment of prophecy and the termination of the old law. Regardless, iconoclasm soon became a general preoccupation.

One eloquent individual formulated the basis of an argument to counter the claims of the iconoclastic authorities. His name was John of Damascus (c. 675–

■ 3.22 Icon of the Mother of God
16th-century copy of the 13th-century original
Detail from central panel

749) and his passionate apology for imagery is an excellent example of the sometimes antagonistic but often crucial relationship that exists between art and theory.

John of Damascus based his argument on Classical Greek thought, applying Platonic idealism to Christian principles. He started with the premise that appreciating visible beauty is a necessary step in the appreciation of the absolute (which in this argument was equated with God). Since the absolute is apprehended only by the soul, the visual form is perhaps one of the few references to God comprehensible to the human. Thus, John argued, a good picture could rightly guide the worshiper toward the absolute — but as a path, not as an end in itself. He asserted that the image was only a poor prototype, and simply a trigger for greater and more beautiful thoughts.

This theory may help clarify the role of icons in church services, and it is an argument that remains popular to this day. Thanks in part to John's defence of figurative art through the employment of Platonic arguments, the development of a lively Christian art had a firm theoretical underpinning.

Christian Art of the Romanesque Period

As Europe converted to Christianity, the expressions of faith became decidedly more diverse. Two major art forms in particular stand out as significant achievements within the context of Christian religious art: the medieval cathedral and the illuminated manuscript.

For all their great size and complexity as constructions, underlying the medieval cathedrals was a unified vision, deriving from many of the notions previously discussed in connection with Christian architecture: the symbolic nature of the design, the importance of light, and the intimate relationship between art and worship. The medieval cathedral is a striking testimony to the rising grandeur of Christianity after the passing of the millennium, and its ability to negotiate between the often mutually exclusive interests of aesthetics and brute mechanics makes it one of the crowning achievements of the age.

It is not difficult to equate height with a quest for the heavens and with society's search for the absolute. The skyscraper has often been called the modern cathedral because of the way it reaches up to

■ 3.23 Exterior of St. Sernin, Toulouse, France, c. AD 1080–1120

■ 3.24 Interior of St. Sernin, Toulouse, France

■ 3.25 Pentecost scene, tympanum, Abbey Church of La Madeleine, Vezelay, France, c. 1120–1132 the sky, and the same premise was very much in the minds of medieval architects after the passing of the millennium. After years of warring, the Church and its secular benefactors began rebuilding with a vigor and enthusiasm unparalleled since Roman times. This era has been known since the nineteenth century as the *Romanesque* period (meaning Roman-like) after the renewed interest in monumental architecture reminiscent of the glory of the old Roman Empire that occurred between the tenth and twelfth centuries.

The architecture combined Roman stone arches with exterior sculptural decoration, and provided the impetus for revitalizing a form of Church architecture that had changed relatively little since the building of Hagia Sophia (see Fig. 3.14). The massive stone arches and masonry walls were able to support more weight than previous projects, and this resulted in even larger interior spaces (Fig. **3.23**). However, higher structures meant more mass exerted on the walls (which had to support those weighty stone arches) and necessitated thick and awkward piers. As the image of the interior of St. Sernin (Fig. **3.24**) suggests, a necessary result of such practical building considerations was the relative lack of windows, since such gaps made the walls less structurally sound. In the quest for a majestic interior space, architects were forced to sacrifice light, which had been such an important aspect in earlier architecture.

One interesting result of this lack of adequate interior illumination was the transferring of images to the exterior surfaces of the building (Fig. **3.25**). The delicate nature of the painting medium made it impractical for most exterior settings, but stone relief sculpture was both resilient to climatic conditions and easily integrated into the various surfaces of the facade. There was, in fact, very little interest in interior decoration for churches in northern Europe; in other words, relief sculpture was a way of keeping images alive during a period in which church interiors appeared inhospitable to art. This development initiated a dramatic shift in Christian policy toward three-dimensional art forms, and it marked the resurrection of sculpture as a major force in Western art. The stone figures share many abstract traits with mosaics and icons, but they also serve as reminders of the human body's association with architecture.

A good example of this is the figure of the prophet Jeremiah (Fig. **3.26**) that stands at the entrance to the

■ 3.26 *Jeremiah*, from St. Pierre, Moissac, France, early 12th century

Church of St. Pierre, Moissac, France. Carved around a functional support, the figure bends and undulates in such a manner that one immediately concentrates on the burden of weight on its shoulders. Thus, by manipulating a figure and successfully integrating it into the thrusts of the architectural structure, the anonymous sculptor created a visual reminder of Jeremiah's prophecies as the foundations of Christ's coming, and the support for his home.

Abbot Suger and the Gothic Cathedral

By the twelfth century, the concept of light had become an integral component of the symbolic program of the Church. However, as Romanesque cathedrals such as St. Sernin suggest, technical skills often trailed well behind the aesthetic and theological aspirations of the time. This was particularly the case in northern Europe, where limited sunlight accentuated the cavern-like atmosphere of Romanesque struc-

■ 3.27 Abbot Suger
Facade of the Church of St. Denis, France, begun 1134, consecrated 1140

tures. The problem lay in introducing light into the buildings. The obvious answer lay in the construction of more and larger windows, yet this in turn meant having to reconsider the height of cathedrals, as their massive vaulted ceilings required walls of great strength to support their weight and windows only lessened that structural integrity. In short, the metaphors of light and height required a new architectural language. The answer was supplied in the work and writings of one Abbot Suger, who in redesigning the Cathedral of St. Denis near Paris (Fig. **3.27**) set in motion an architectual vocabulary now defined as Gothic.

The term *Gothic*, like many of the titles given to historical periods, is more a relic of a later era than it is descriptive of the late-medieval culture of northern Europe. In fact, the term originated during the Renaissance as a pejorative to describe work that appeared crude and irrational to contemporary eyes. The term obviously referred to the infamous Goths who sacked Rome in AD 410 and in the process were seen, at least in Renaissance eyes, to have destroyed Classical culture. Yet, in reality, Gothic art was nothing of the sort. Indeed, in examining the work of the period's greatest theorist-architect, it will become clear that the Gothic cathedral was the culmination of earlier attempts to reconcile architecture and religion, and remains perhaps its greatest expression.

The beginnings of the Gothic style date to 1134, the year in which Abbot Suger, an advisor and close confidant of Kings Louis VI and VII of France, was given the task of redesigning the Abbey of St. Denis, a church that held special significance for court and country as the burial place of French kings. It appears that Suger was acutely aware of the need to produce credible solutions to earlier architectural problems. He began by adding a massive front entrance hall (*narthex*), only a bay and a half deep, in front of the nave. It rose, in the words of the eminent architectural historian Vincent Scully, "...like a great banner, an enormous signboard hung in front of the old church...". The new facade was crowned by two towers and anchored in the middle by a large rose window, the first of its kind in Christendom.

The rose window is uniquely medieval in sensibility, combining the "perfect shapes" of the Christian world — the circle and the square, in setting the rose within its frame. The circle and the square had, since the first-century BC Roman architectural theorist

Vitruvius, been considered fundamental, even archetypal shapes, since by design they mimicked the parameter of the outstretched human body. To the medieval mind, the circle held awesome symbolic potential: the miraculous proportioning of the human body implied not only the centrality of man in God's world but also the human as central to all other principles of order and beauty. Though it is popular to credit the later Renaissance era with such metaphysical formulations, it is clear that Suger was acutely aware of Platonist writings on the subject. There can be little doubt that such contemporary musings found their way into the narthex design.

From the interior, the light of the rose window shone directly upon the king's chapel — a tiny space in which the king could stand, a striking silhouette, in the center of the brilliant circular wall of light. Positioned thus, the implication was that the king could be envisioned as the man of perfect proportion and consequently in touch with the order of the universe. Here Suger capably combined heavenly and earthly authority in one symbolic gesture, anchored in a large circular passage of light.

Suger also turned his attention to the entrance arches or portals (now called *royal portals*) of the facade, enlarging their size to spread out between the front piers and in the process suggest the triumphal arches of Ancient Rome. The twin towers were probably derived from the church architecture of the Rhineland, which had, since the ninth century, often included a castle attached to the apse. Their inclusion in the St. Denis facade had the dual effect of implying an historical lineage from the Emperor Charlemagne to the French kings and providing a balanced frame for the central rose window. Together, these three elements — the twin towers, the royal portals, and the rose window — became signature components of the French Gothic facade throughout the twelfth and thirteenth centuries.

To Abbot Suger's mind, the ideal cathedral was one that illuminated its interior with heavenly light; in other words, a cathedral with vast sections of wall filled with glass. Yet to do this required a series of architectural innovations, capable of increasing the height of the building while decreasing the load on the walls. Thus, in redesigning his church's *ambulatory* (situated behind the altar), he added a new technical convention to the architectural vocabulary: the **ribbed vault** ☐.

FOCUS ON

The Ribbed Vault

A ribbed vault is constructed by way of a series of intersecting pointed arches that, when assembled, provide a structural skeleton (*ribs*) of a vaulted ceiling (Fig. **3.28**). The pointed arch differs from more traditional rounded arches (such as those pictured in the interior of St. Sernin) in that it can rise to any height without requiring an equal width span. This meant that Suger's builders were afforded the opportunity of exploring spectacularly high interior spaces. Further, since the ribs also possess great weight-bearing potential, the surfaces of the vault (sometimes called the *webbing*) could be made of relatively light materials, decreasing the weight of the ceiling and thus the load on the walls. The pointed arch also possesses less of an outward thrust than its rounded counterpart, which means that, once again, less of the span's weight is loaded on the walls. This in turn enables more wall space to be devoted to glass. The physical result was higher buildings, lighter ceilings, and more glass. Perhaps more importantly in Abbot Suger's era of symbolism, the transcendent quality of light now flooded the cathedral.

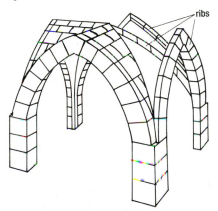

■ **3.28 Illustration of a Gothic ribbed vault**

The effect of such an innovation on interior spaces is readily discernible by contrasting the Romanesque St. Sernin and the interior of a Gothic structure such as Chartres Cathedral (Fig. **3.31**), begun fifty years after the redesign of St. Denis. The initial impression is that of an architectural forest: the movement from the heavy column-like piers, to the colonnettes that rise from their capitals, to the ribs that carry this linear progression up to the top of the ceiling, speaks of trunks and branches, nature and growth. Indeed, during the Romantic era of the nineteenth century it was popular to suggest that the forest-like quality of these interiors was in fact the last spiritual vestige of northern pre-Christian nature cults. Though this is clearly incorrect in terms of development, the uncanny

The Flying Buttress

The flying buttress (Figs. **3.29** and **3.30**) is an external armature that helps deflect much of the structural strain caused by rib vaults away from the primary walls of the building. This buttress technique allows for a greater distribution of weight, which in turn enables architects to reconsider the thick walls that had been such an integral feature of earlier Romanesque building. This in turn enabled a more skeletal wall structure, and with it the introduction of stained glass.

■ **3.29 Cross section of a flying buttress**

■ **3.30 Exterior side view of Notre Dame, Paris, 1163–1250 showing flying buttresses**

■ **3.31 View of the nave from the interior of Chartres Cathedral, France, 1194–1220**

▶ **3.32 Interior view of the Upper Chapel of La Sainte-Chapelle, Paris, 1243–48**

upward momentum of interiors such as that at Chartres is certainly reminiscent of a canopy of trees.

Once the ribbed vault was in place, all that remained to make Abbot Suger's dream of a cathedral of light a reality was further to divert the ceiling weight away from the walls. If this still considerable load could be significantly lessened, more glass could be utilized in the construction of the walls without sacrificing structural integrity. The answer was to come by way of a supporting armature called the **flying buttress** □. The result was, and indeed still is, pure and heavenly light — the light of wisdom, familiar from Hagia Sophia — finding its greatest Christian expression in the Gothic cathedral.

Glass and Books

One of the most opulent and exquisite examples of Gothic architecture is the Sainte-Chapelle (Fig. **3.32**) in Paris, built between 1243 and 1248. Though considerably smaller than many of the cathedrals of the

■ 3.33 Notre Dame de Belle Verriére
Interior detail from Chartres Cathedral, France, early 13th century

▶ 3.34 The Initial "B" from Psalm I of the *Munich Psalter* c. 1200
10⅞ x 7⅞ in (27.4 x 18.8 cm)
Bayerische Staatsbiliothek, Munich

time, this chapel stands out as arguably the best example of the concepts of medieval luminosity and majestic height left intact today. Colored (*stained*) glass replaced the cement and stone of the early constructions; the once solid, if perhaps somber, cathedral interior was transformed into a lively and delicate skeleton enveloped by light. Here technical innovations and aesthetic considerations united in one of the truly great expressions of faith and humanity. The cathedral, reaching skywards toward God and illuminated by God's holy light, effectively transcends simple building construction and becomes a living example of Christian art in physical, concrete form.

Once windows were in place, artists began to turn their attention to the possibilities of colored glass. Through relatively simple means, glass could be cut into various designs and attached to lead borders, producing images that glow when pierced by the sun's rays. This enabled coloristic effects impossible with

mosaic and wall painting, and allowed artists to introduce two-dimensional art into the church interior (Fig. **3.33**).

Stained-glass images are characteristically more abstract than icon images, with strong color contrasts. This is a common occurrence in early Christian art, due in part to the technical demands of the materials and the importance of making the images legible to the average worshiper. Pictures were a means of communicating ideas to an often illiterate public, and it is not surprising that artists found themselves more concerned with clarity of intent than with subtly rendered figures. A good analogy here is to the relationship between handwriting and printed type. People often enjoy producing very personal forms of script, and sometimes go so far as to "read into" these marks all sorts of autobiographical information, but when it is necessary to communicate a message or thought to another person, a more generic and predictable form of script is most appropriate, with as little deviation from the norm as possible; hence the popularity of type. This is the point behind much of the simple, straightforward design of the early Church and the seemingly strict adherence to very limited motifs. The beauty of this work lies in how individual artists worked within the confines of these practical considerations.

In Europe the book was one of Western civilization's few links with the thoughts and deeds of the past (the Moors and Islamic scholars likewise kept libraries, but these were inaccessible to most Western eyes). The luxury of the printing press was not available to the Europe of the Middle Ages (movable type was not invented until 1447), so each text had to be patiently recopied by hand. The process could, and often did, take years, and thus books became an extremely valuable item, housed in the security of monasteries and the dwellings of a few cultured rulers, and accessible to very few. The importance of these texts (often works of philosophy and religious commentary) made them understandably precious, and thus they became predictable repositories for decoration and embellishment. The *illuminated manuscript* provided artists with the opportunity to work in a labor-intensive and intimate manner — in a medium very different from the awkward materials of glass and stone. The result was work (Fig. **3.34**) that illustrates the intricate patterning and painstaking detail that typify this form of art making.

The history of Christian art after the Middle Ages is one of developing representation, as the faithful began to investigate the relationship between humans and their physical world. Developments such as perspective and illusionistic rendering began to obsess Christian artists by 1400 (see pages 184–191), ushering in a new age in Western art referred to as the Renaissance. This meant that pattern — a form of art and a way of looking at the world that was very different from the aspirations of the Renaissance — was to find its greatest religious expression not in Christianity but in Islam.

ISLAMIC ART

In 622 an Arab prophet named Muhammad fled from his native Mecca to the northern city of Medina. In doing so, he ushered in a new age and a new religion — Islam.

Islam belongs to the tradition of monotheism initiated in the Mediterranean basin by Judaism and then Christianity, and it shares some of the same history. Unlike the Judeo-Christian heritage, it relies exclusively on a book, the Koran, as the undisputed word of God, given to the world through the prophet Muhammad. This has certain repercussions for Islamic art, including the basic concept of the artist or creator, which one often takes for granted. As a religious community evolving out of a virtual vacuum of visual art activity, Islam provides a fascinating case study of how art develops around, and then reacts to, existing notions of beauty and decorum.

Like the ethnic Jews before them, the Bedouin (the native peoples of the Arab peninsula) were a nomadic society, with little practical interest in architecture or the cumbersome visual arts. What little they had was decorated simply, and for the most part the culture survived through oral means and music. A good example of this lack of interest in visual arts in Bedouin society is the absence of actual words to define art forms. Since there was little practical use for such expressions, no linguistic equivalents for concepts such as painting or sculpture developed. Instead, the word *musawwir*, meaning fashioner, was used as a catchall term for any visual expression.

Islamic history begins with Muhammad's exile in Medina — in fact, year one in the Islamic calendar coincides with 622 in the West, pointing to an outright dismissal of the earlier era. (Muslims call this time the *jahiliyyah*, meaning the time of ignorance.) So central is the Koran to the faith that it quickly became both the source for later art and the law for its execution. Early Islamic scholars looked to the holy book for guidance with regard to the visual arts, but it is difficult to find any overt support or denial for the creation of images in the text. One story is the Koran's reference to Jesus fashioning a bird out of clay, and then breathing life into it and letting it free. This passage may suggest the awesome power of images and the creative act, but perhaps it also warns against such activities unless sanctioned by God.

The ambivalence of such passages gave early scholars little to go on, but certain pragmatic considerations helped clarify the status of art in Islam. One such reality was the fact that the Koran simply did not lend itself well to narrative illustration. It reads much more like the Psalms, the Proverbs, the laws of Leviticus, and the Epistles of the Bible, which by their very format are difficult to translate visually. Thus the idea of representational art as a vehicle for narrative held little interest or practical merit for the faith.

The Hadith (traditions about the Prophet) was compiled some years after the death of Muhammad, and as a document it probably reflects the interests of another time and even other cultures. Unlike the Koran, it is explicit about the repercussions for the pious of indulging in representational art. One dramatic example from the text will suffice to illustrate this point: "Those who will be most severely punished on judgment day are the murderers of a prophet, one who leads men astray without knowledge, and the maker of pictures." This placing of blame on the artist as a blasphemous competitor with the creative powers of God is probably an early attempt at justifying iconoclasm. Logically, if God is the sole source of inspiration behind any creative act, it follows that the artist's creation is simply an extension of God's will and thus his or her art a glowing example of God's magnificence. Recent scholarship on this important text suggests that it was compiled for the most part outside Arabia, in areas such as Persia and India (which had become part of the Islamic empire), where representational imagery was already present. Such new adherents to the Koran may have desired an identifiable separation between their polytheistic pasts (and the images that surrounded such worship)

■ **3.35 The rise of Islam**

and their new faith, much as the Jews had, before them.

Christian Byzantine culture was flourishing around the Mediterranean basin during the rise of Islamic culture, and as the Muslim community aggressively flexed its military and political muscle, it quickly assimilated many of the Christian towns and subsequently their Byzantine heritage. Though by most accounts it appears that Muslims began by appreciating, and in some cases even emulating, Byzantine art, as the fighting continued, admiration was quickly consumed by hatred and suspicion, and Christian art forms fell out of favor. The Islamic community saw Byzantine icons and mosaic works as idolatrous, and in retrospect this is certainly understandable, considering the Christian community's own inability to come to a consensus on their value and legitimacy. This had a recognizable effect on the developing art of Islam, as its adherents consciously avoided the blasphemies of their enemies.

Calligraphy and Arabesque Design

Shortly after the initial conquests of Christian territory, Islamic culture began to develop an art program based almost exclusively on decoration, as artists desired a symbolic language different from that of other cultures, and a unique expression of the faith.

An interesting way to study this development is by examining early coinage from the period. Once Islam occupied the so-called "fertile crescent" and began expanding to cover most of the territory between eastern Europe and the Sinai peninsula, there came the need for an all-inclusive monetary system. The conquerors began by removing Christian symbols from the existing coinage, which was then followed by the removal of typical Greek-style portrait busts (similar in design to modern coins). In 699 a decree insisted on Islamic coinage with no links to other cultures. This was obviously not an easy undertaking.

The unique aspect of Islam is, of course, the centrality of the Koran as the undisputed word of God in written form. This meant that the script of the Koran

■ 3.36 (above) Dirham or drahm minted in Basra AD 694–95 (below) Dirham minted in Abarqubedh, Iraq, AD 702–03 The American Numismatic Society, New York (1975, 270.1) (1949, 163.946)

► 3.37 Glass Mosque Lamp Inscribed with quotes from the Koran Syrian, 14th century Early glass painted in enamel colors Height 11³/₈ in (28.5 cm) Diameter 10 in (25.5 cm) © Victoria & Albert Museum, London

(written in "the miraculous gift of Arabic") was in some way a visual artifact of God's communiqué to the world. The miracle of script in a community that relied exclusively on oral traditions made Arabic at once a central and important part of the Islamic culture. When the written language of the Koran was accepted as a legitimate symbol of the faith, **calligraphy**, the art of drawing language, quickly became the most important visual document of the culture. By 750 the motif had found its way onto coinage (Fig. **3.36**).

Calligraphy is arguably Islam's greatest visual expression. To the faithful, Arabic was a language designed and instituted by God himself through his mouthpiece Muhammad, and calligraphy its human expression. Scholars note that, before the birth of Islam, there was no accepted written script among the nomadic Bedouin community, most likely because of

the long tradition of oral histories and the practical consideration of traveling light. With the arrival of God's word in its final form, there came a need for more permanent documentation, since the proliferation of such truth relied on a fixed and unchanging source. As a consequence, the vitality of God's transmission through Muhammad quickly became inextricably linked with the development of script, to the point of becoming a logical extension of God's gift to the world — hence the popular phrase "the miraculous gift of Arabic." Though it started out with only the most utilitarian of motives, script soon took on important ramifications for art. Kufic script (the earliest and most common manifestation of Arabic) has many of the same qualities as vegetal patterning, yet the unpredictability of the lines separates it from more all-over and static patterns with which it is often associated (Fig. **3.37**).

By the eighth century, Arab Islam was for the most part free of representational imagery (many of the conquered areas, such as Persia and India, still embraced figurative images, most likely because of their strong pictorial traditions). Abstract patterning, then, was one of the few available outlets for visual explorations. The term **arabesque** is often used to describe the great abstract designs initiated by these Islamic artists, and it refers specifically to the combination of calligraphy and intricate, mathematically precise compositions. This art form breaks down into two basic areas of design: vegetal and geometric.

Vegetal design was considered an appropriate symbol of growth, change, and movement — the basic vocabulary of life. The ivy plant and the grape vine are typical of these organic motifs, their wandering, cursive branches good examples of abstract design in nature. These patterns probably originated in Persia, and with the conquests they quickly became popular throughout the Islamic world as eloquent reminders of life's flow and unpredictability (Fig. **3.38**).

Geometric design has its origins in Arabia and the great developments in the field of mathematics that surfaced during the eighth century. Appearing visually predictable, angular and hard-edged, it came to represent the static, fixed, and stable ideas of the faith. It also had the added bonus of providing clarity and balance to any visual composition (Fig. **3.39**). When combined, the vegetal and the geometric motifs were understood to represent life and growth within the framework of order — the sensitive pictorial equivalent of the Islamic faith (Fig. **3.40**).

■ **3.38** Details of the tile work from the Lotfollah Mosque, Isfahan

■ **3.39** Geometric designs from the Dome of the Rock, Jerusalem, late 7th century AD

One of the most striking examples of design on a flat plane is the combination of arabesque elements infused with script (Fig. **3.41**). In these compositions, one may appreciate the considerable visual force of some of the most simple principles of design — principles that continue to inspire designers to this day. For

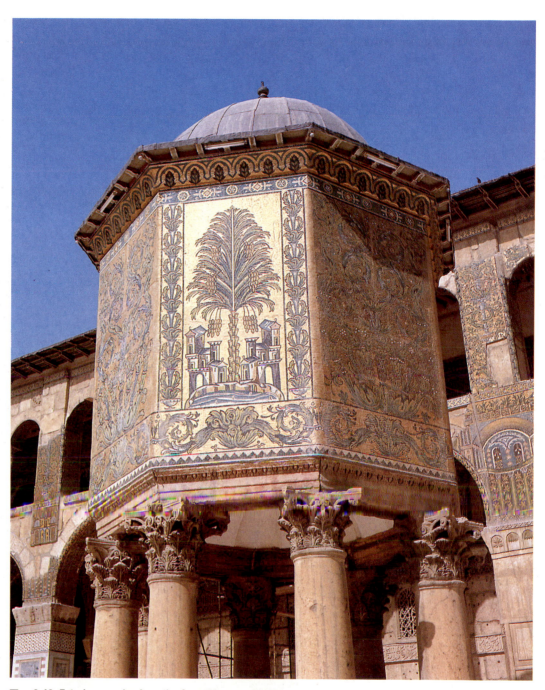

■ 3.40 Exterior mosaics from the Great Mosque of Damascus c. AD 715

instance, straight lines of predictable and consistent thickness and tone immediately evoke static and rational qualities on the picture plane. This visual framework provides a field on which other activities (scribbles, forms, etc.) can be measured and stabilized. A good example of this type of design is the grid, which breaks down the plane into smaller, often identical, compartments. Once the grid is in place, any mark or scribble placed on top of it will set up an interesting discord, and the structure of the grid attempts to stabilize the activity of the gesture. The Islamic vegetal design undulates in and out of the predictable geometric framework much as lives pass through time, and in this way the overall design is a reminder of humanity's own relationship to the static realities of life, death, and the need for faith.

The most dynamic gesture to grace these intricate designs is that of calligraphy, the word of God made visible through script. These sporadic, sensual lines dance through the field of vegetal and geometric pat-

terns, providing the viewer with an obvious counterpoint. On the most basic visual level, the marks demand attention because they are different from the pattern on which they exist; they are a form of "language" different from the arabesque design. In the case of Islam, it is a profound difference because it refers directly to the Koran, which in turn refers directly back to God. If arabesque design is a visual

■ 3.41 Leaf from a manuscript of the Koran c. AD 1000
Probably by Ali-ibn-Hilal, Baghdad
7 x 5¼ in (17.7 x 13.5 cm)
Reproduced by courtesy of the Trustees of the Chester Beatty Library, Dublin

■ 3.42 The Great Mosque and Minaret of al-Mutawakkil, Samarra, Iraq, AD 847–48

■ 3.43 Floor plan of the Great Mosque and Minaret of al-Mutawakkil, Samarra, Iraq

equivalent of life's harmonious balance, the dynamic visual quality of script connotes humanity's own persistent need for faith. In any event, arabesque design and calligraphy remain Islam's most profound visual expressions, and they remain virtually unchanged to this day. If great religious art can be said to perform as a contemplative act and an expression of one's relationship to the unknown, in Islam abstract design has consistently satisfied artists and viewers on both levels.

Architecture

Traditional Islamic architecture presents the viewer with similar visual suggestions. The format of most mosques (from *masgid* or *masjid*, meaning roughly worship or place of worship) is based on a relatively simple rectangle, oriented in such a manner as to lie directionally in line with the holy city of Mecca. Mosques usually consist of three sections: a courtyard (*atrium*), a covered sanctuary, and a tower (*minaret*), from which the *muezzin* (crier) calls the community to worship. In order to facilitate the Islamic worshiper's ritual prayers, which are to be performed while facing Mecca, the *qibla* (the direction faced by the faithful) wall at the end of the sanctuary always faces east. In the center of the *qibla* the *mihrab* (sacred niche) is located.

One of the earliest examples of this simple, though by no means simplistic, architecture is the Great Mosque and Minaret of Samarra (Fig. **3.42**), which was constructed between 847 and 848. Though now

only a shadow of its former glory (excavations suggest that the inner walls were once covered with golden mosaics), the structure is a clear example of the period's architectural philosophy, and it remains the largest of its kind in the Islamic world. The floor plan (Fig. **3.43**) demonstrates the predictable, symmetrical character, suggesting such psychological equivalents as stability, clarity, anchoring, and perhaps the eternal character of God's law.

Encompassed within this complex lie row upon row of columns, dispersed throughout the sancturay in seemingly endless succession. Like most architectural developments, these posts were first and foremost the products of functional need — they held a roof over the sanctuary to protect the worshipers from the intense sun. But their striking visual character was not overlooked by either architect or theolo-

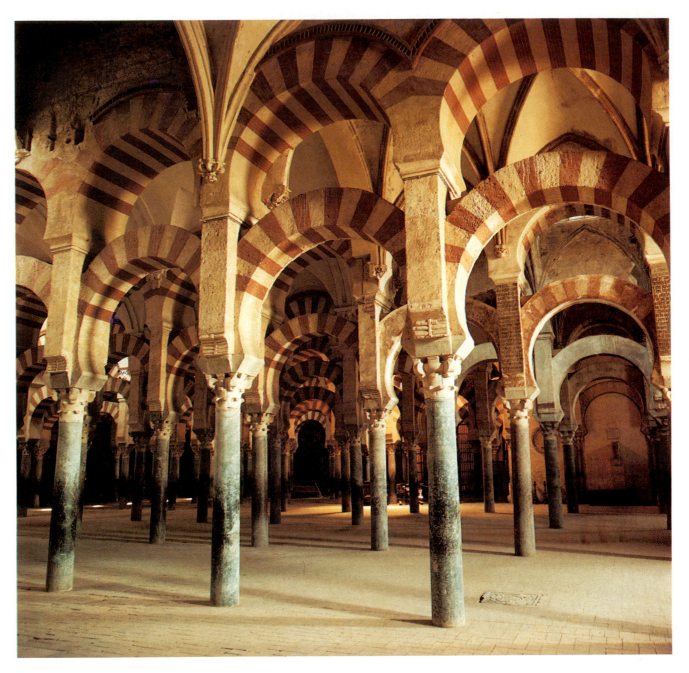

■ 3.44 Interior of the Mosque at Cordoba, Spain, begun AD 786

gian; the array of columns, with their curved vaulting, provided a fitting counterpoint to the rigid format of the predictable rectangular skeleton. An interior scene from the Mosque at Cordoba (Fig. **3.44**) illustrates the visual impact such a repeated motif has on one's perception of space within the confines of the rectangle. Like arabesque patterning and Kufic script, the interest in repeated gestures or pattern within the defining boundaries of a strict, easily understood geometric form such as a rectangle, makes these excursions into architecture visually satisfying while remaining meaningful as a vivid reminder of God's eternal order in a world of seemingly endless possibilities.

HINDUISM AND THE CULT OF IMAGES

It has been said that nearly all Indian art can be considered religious in one way or another, and the practice of art making a spiritual endeavor. Thus it is understandable that historians have until very recently found it difficult to distinguish between art and religion in traditional Indian culture. As the principal religion of India, Hinduism stands out as both the oldest continuous religious tradition in the modern world (dating as far back as 2500 BC) and the most devoted to visual forms.

As a faith, Hinduism emphasizes the centrality of a single god who, unlike the God of Israel, exposes itself through myriad manifestations, including male, female, and animal forms. The primary focus of Hinduism is on the cycle of reincarnation, in which right conduct may lead to a better situation in the next life. This emphasis on birth, death, and rebirth is both the crux of Hindu social and moral codes and a viable explanation for the abundance of fertility images in its visual culture, and it points to a faith obsessed with notions of transience and transition — important features in its art.

The polytheistic nature of the faith has made representational imagery a necessary and rich part of ceremonies and rituals. Many gods means many identities, all of which are differentiated in worship by an image. Unlike the traditions of Judaism and Islam, which place emphasis on the transcendent nature of the deity and thus its incompatibility with pictorial representation, Hinduism's emphasis on the multiple manifestations of the "Supreme Being" allow for a great many representations.

The history of Hindusim is, then, the history of image making in Indian culture, and in this way it provides some interesting parallels to Christian art.

In general, Hindu art theory emphasizes the role of art as embellishment or idealization. There are texts that outline proper procedures for the rendering of forms; these coincide with the ideal nature of the deities in question. In this context, poor art is that which deviates from the prescribed forms, or art that emphasizes the particular over the universal. This is reminiscent of two traditions already discussed: the idealism of Classical Greece and the rigid pictorial structure of Christian icon painting. The relationship between Hindu and Greek culture is not an incidental one, for conquests by Alexander the Great brought the Indus valley into direct contact with Classical models as early as 327 BC. The idealized form recurs with regularity throughout the history of art, and its cross-cultural significance should give some indication of the ability of art to tackle such abstract concepts. The relationship between Hindu art theory and early Christian thought is perhaps less obvious but still intelligible. The sanctioning of specific forms of representation by the Christian Church gave Western artists little room for expression. In these restrictive confines, the test of great art is its ability to transcend the dictates of decorum. In this way, Hindu and early Christian artists engaged in a similar type of artistic activity, in which meaning is found in the meditation on established codes rather than in innovation.

An Historical Context for Hindu Art

The history of Hindu art is inseparable from the history of India, yet Indian art is by no means solely Hindu. This fact has provided more than its fair share of troubles for researchers seeking clearly delineated relationships between religion and art, for India is not only the center of Hinduism but also the original homeland of both Buddhism and Jainism, and in many examples of art the distinctions are blurred. This being said, the relationsip between historical events, religious orthodoxy, and the production of art in the Indian sub-continent is vital to an understanding of Hindu art and requires further examination.

Unlike Christianity and Islam, it is impossible to pinpoint the exact beginnings of the Hindu faith, as it grew somewhat organically from sources, which date to around 1500 BC in the culture of the Aryans who displaced the earlier Harappan culture. The Aryans brought with them an established religious tradition centered upon ritual sacrifices, meant to appease the deities who were considered the personification of the forces of nature. The *Rigveda*, the oldest surviving religious text in the world, dates to the period between 1500 and 1000 BC and in its 1028 hymns describes in lively detail the traditions surrounding the pantheon of gods.

■ **3.45 The river goddess Ganga, from the lintel of a temple at Beshnagar, India**
Gupta, c. 500
Buff sandstone
29 x 15½ x 6 in (73.5 x 39.3 x 15.4 cm)
Museum of Fine Arts, Boston
Charles Amos Cummings Bequest Fund

By the eighth century BC, Aryan culture had undergone a significant transformation in its religious character. The process of acculturation and assimilation had a profound effect; ritual sacrifice in worship was slowly replaced by concepts of penance and self-denial, an understanding of sacred texts and the concept of devotion (*bhakti*). These concepts, today readily identifiable with Hinduism (or, as it is sometimes referred to, Brahmanism) and Jainism (a religion that places paramount importance on a life of non-violence) were in place by the beginnings of the Christian era. However, it was not until the decline of Buddhism in northern India during the Gupta period (AD 320–415) that Hindu art finally came to prominence.

Sculpture

One of the most evocative features of Hindu art from the Gupta and post-Gupta periods is the overt sensuality of the god and goddess figures. This convention dates back as far as 200 BC to the *yakshi* (f) and *yaksha* (m) sculptural figures of northern India themselves probably descendants of the fertility gods and goddesses of the Indian Neolithic period. Such *yakshe* sculptures, said to be tree spirits, are often distinguished by their voluptuous, rounded surfaces and unabashed sexual character, and they are said to display the "quality of inner breath" (*prana*), which grants them harmony with the fertility of the earth. They were also understood as conduits between humans and their world, the personifications of the laws of nature.

Through the following millennium, these fertility figures underwent a series of mutations at the hands of both Hindu and Buddhist artists. One such example is a relief sculpture of the river goddess Ganga from around AD 500 (Fig. **3.45**), in which the previous tree spirit has been transformed into a symbol of water. This is done by combining the established *yakshi* figure convention with an animal symbol — in this case a beast that is part elephant, part crocodile, called the *makara*. Together, woman and *makara* represent the sacred River Ganges, the sculpture paying symbolic reference to the river as both a life-giving and life-sustaining entity.

Perhaps the most famous of Hindu sculptural conventions is that of *Shiva Nataraja* (Fig. **3.46**), which began in south India in the twelfth century and is still

■ **3.46** *Shiva Nataraja*
11th or 12th century bronze
Height 32¼ in (82 cm)
Museum Rietberg, Zurich
Von der Heydt Collection

Sitting on the top of Shiva's tongue-like protrusion of hair is a small mermaid creature. This is Ganga, now fully integrated into the once separate *makara* form. Here the metamorophosis is complete, and it gives some indication of the natural, organic manner in which the iconography of Hinduism was visually constructed. The development of the Shiva image, with its multiple hands and various accoutrements, probably followed a similar path.

Architecture

A tremendous amount of Hindu iconography centers around three manifestations of the central power: Shiva, Vishnu, and Vishnu's subsequent manifestation in the form of Krishna. Since each god is present in both the heavenly and material (earthly) realm, places such as temples hold special significance for Hindus as dwellings of the deities. From temple architecture one can learn much about how Hindu artists have viewed the relationship between art and religion. Typical examples are the Kandariya Temple (Figs. **3.47** and **3.48**) at Khajuraho in northern India, and the Shri Ranganatha Temple (Fig. **3.49**), near Madras, which is a typical southern building.

■ **3.47** Kandariya Mahadeva temple
Khajuraho, North India, c. AD 1000

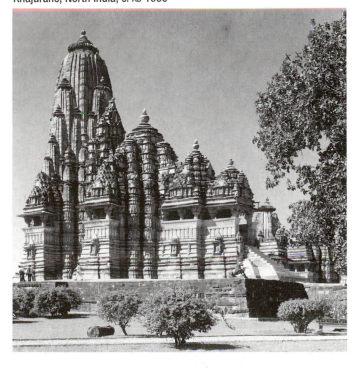

manufactured today. Here Shiva, the great creative and destructive force in the universe, is portrayed as Lord of the Dance. As the abundance of detail might suggest, this exquisite bronze sculpture is a veritable catalog of Hindu symbols. Shiva dances wildly on a ring symbolic of the cosmos, which shoots forth from the mouths of *makaras* at the base. The creative force of the cosmos is complemented by flames of destruction, which edge the circle and which Shiva holds in one of his four hands. This hand-held fire in turn complements the drum in his right hand, a symbol of the creative force of the dance. Beneath the god's right foot lies a dwarf of ignorance holding a poisonous serpent, in the process of being crushed by the illuminating power of the dance. The dwarf looks up, his eyes fixed in the direction of Shiva's extended left hand, which grants a blessing. Together, these examples (and many more) suggest a cyclical, complementary, and balanced view of the world, as Shiva's creative and destructive natures are kept in a perpetual state of equilibrium.

■ 3.48 Cross-section of the Kandariya Mahadeva temple c. AD 1000

The Kandariya Temple was built around 1000 as a shrine to Shiva, here symbolized in the form of a lingam, or stylized phallus, and the great stone image of primal force is the central focus of the temple construction. The temple complex was built to emphasize the vertical thrust of the lingam, and the participant's journey through the temple interior is a psychological ascent to the embodiment of Shiva.

Viewed from the exterior, the roofs of the three inner halls rise in ascending order towards the inner chamber (*shikhara*), in which the phallus is kept. The immediate impression is one of verticality, and the diagonal movement of the roofs helps focus attention on the primacy of the *shikhara* (see Fig. 3.48). This is reiterated by the height of the platform on which the temple is constructed, reinforcing the already obvious heavenward thrust of the complex. There is also the impression that one is viewing some form of ideal or heavenly mountain, devoid of the imperfections of nature.

One enters the mountain by way of the cave, finding the center of the lingam deep within the "womb" of the earth (the actual room that houses the lingam is called the *garbha-griha*, the womb room). The allusions to both moutain and sexual union are appropriate in this case and are accentuated by over 850 individual sculptures, many of which are in erotic poses. The Kandariya Temple is a wonderful example of how intelligent design can evoke very convincing bodily associations in the minds·of the faithful. Here the primal creative power of Shiva is successfully

integrated into the structure of the temple design, and the result is a very pleasing union of religion and art.

The Shri Ranganatha Temple is devoted to the ancient god Vishnu (the great heavenly king who descends to earth periodically in a number of guises to maintain cosmic stability). Today it stands as the practical result of centuries of change and rebuilding, though the original design is said to date back to the fifth century. The temple covers an immense 156 acres (385 ha) and includes seven rectangular walls arranged concentrically around the *garbha-griha*, which houses the image of Vishnu. It holds approximately 42,000 permanent residents, most of whom live inside the first wall.

As one continues toward the center, the hustle and bustle of daily life give way to fewer and fewer distractions. The overall design is reminiscent of a maze, with its center hidden from view. The worshiper is required to follow a series of alleyways to reach the inner sanctum, supporting the impression that Vishnu appears only to those who specifically seek him out. Here the experience is one of descent rather than ascent (as was the case in the Kandariya Temple), as the worshiper peels off layers of the outer world to find the sanctum and union with the god. Again, the obvious analogy to the body and the revealing of self through a carefully orchestrated journey is evident, and it further reiterates the rather impressive abilities of architecture to embellish a religious experience.

■ 3.49 Plan of the Shri Ranganatha temple, South India 5th century AD

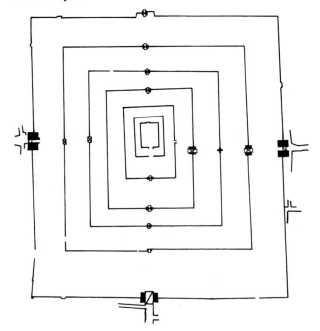

Indian Painting

Though there is no archaeological evidence to support the claim, contemporary writings suggest that painting was an important component in the illumination of sacred texts as far back as the writing of the *Rigveda*. There are, of course, practical reasons for this absence: since paper was not used in India until late in the fourteenth century, artists used palm leaves, which deteriorate with age and humidity, as surfaces for painting. Another consideration is the advent of Islam in northern India, carried by way of invading Turks, Afgans, and Persians from the tenth century onwards. During this period of conquest, much Hindu, Buddhist, and Jain work was apparently destroyed. The oldest surviving manuscripts date from the late eleventh century.

A Jain manuscript (Fig. **3.50**) from c. 1460 gives some indication of the prevailing conventions. Flat and decorative, with only a limited palette of color, it appears that the artists followed formal guidelines in the making of their paintings. An interesting development is the depiction of the head in profile, with both eyes shown; it predates the experiments in simultaneous viewing by the Cubists Pablo Picasso and Georges Braque by about seven hundred years (though, as Chaper Nine shows, their intentions were somewhat different).

The development of trade routes between India and the Arab peninsula had a profound effect on Indian painting. First, the use of paper rather than palm leaf (which was rough and unpredictable as a surface) facilitated a more detailed and ornate composition. Trade also brought into India color pigments

■ 3.50 Detail from a Jain manuscript of the Uttaradhyayana Sutra, Western India c. 1460
Opaque watercolor on paper
© Victoria & Albert Museum, London

that were not indigenous to the area, such as blue, which was to become the most popular ground for later painting. Finally, trade and conquest brought with them the images and techniques of other lands. In the case of Indian painting, it was Persian manuscripts, with their high degree of precision, crisp linear elements, and remarkable, sometimes microscopic detail, that became the standard from which to develop. Indeed by the sixteenth century, the Mughal ruler Akbar had initiated a state school of art, in which Hindu artists could work side by side with Persian masters. Several breath-taking paintings survive from this period, such as *Gardeners Beating the Giant Zamurrad* (Fig. **3.51**), many of which indicate an

interest in both detail work and portraiture. Inevitably, these conventions found their way into the fabric of Hindu art, most notably in celebration of the cult of the god Krishna.

An incarnation of Vishnu, Krishna is one of the most popular deities in the Hindu pantheon. His playful character has made him a favorite subject of Hindu artists, and the great narratives from which they draw inspiration are ideally suited to the demands of painting. Some of the most beautiful of these Krishna narratives were produced by an eighteenth-century artist named Manaku, whose illustrations for the *Gita Govinda* formed the basis for later Indian painting.

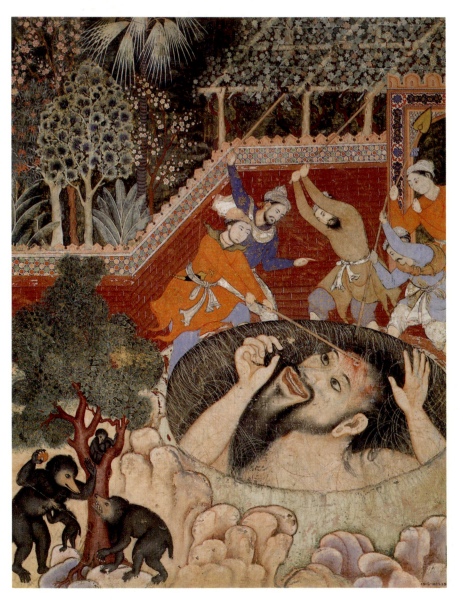

■ 3.51 *Gardeners Beating the Giant Zamurrad*
From the *Romance of Amir Hamza*
Mihal period, 1555–79
Paint on cloth
26⅜ x 19⅝ in (67 x 50 cm)
© Victoria & Albert Museum, London

▶ 3.52 *Krishna and Radha in a Grove* c. 1780
from the *Gita Govinda*
Gouache on paper
4¾ x 6¾ in (12 x 17 cm)
© Victoria & Albert Museum, London

A good example of Manaku's virtuosity is the image of Krishna and Radha from the *Gita Govinda* (Fig. **3.52**). Consistent with Hindu art theory, the figures and the environment are idealized, and the graceful handling of the forms is indicative of the lushness and sensuality often associated with Indian manuscript painting. In the ideal world, it is always spring, and thus the paintings typically exude the brilliant colors of the most perfect of seasons, including the symbolic blue of Krishna himself. This is paradise, a place in which gods and humans live in intimacy, and here art can provide a vehicle for flights of religious fancy. This is not representation but a highly developed tradition of abstraction, in which art can become the springboard for meditation and rapture. In Hindu art, this is the very essence of quality.

ASPECTS OF THE BUDDHIST ART TRADITION

One of the most fascinating and dynamic religious art traditions is that of Buddhism. It encapsulates such a wide range of stylistic inventions and philosophical viewpoints that this survey will unfortunately have to concentrate on only a few fundamentals.

Buddhism derives from the teachings of Gautama, a fifth-century BC Indian prince and sage who achieved profound wisdom and complete enlightenment by finding the "middle path" between excess and denial. Traditional Buddhism teaches of a world in flux, in which truth is achieved through a process of extinguishing one's ego or soul, which is the root of all suffering. When Buddhists speak of enlightenment, they are describing a dismissal of self. This traditional form of Buddhism is described as extrabodily, in that it attempts to move beyond the everyday. This is, of course, very different from most Western religions, in which the shocking reality of daily existence and its manifestation in guilt and faith sustain the sinner. In Buddhism, this endless cycle of birth, death, and rebirth is ended only through the realization of *nirvana* and a letting-go of the world.

Early Buddhist Art and Architecture

Buddhist figurative art did not surface until after the first century AD, and its rise coincided with the beginnings of the veneration of Gautama as a deity. Early on, orthodox Buddhism saw the Buddha as embodied in his message — to understand him was to see him. Another problem for early Buddhist art was the admission that, when the Buddha died, he achieved complete extinction in *nirvana* and thus could not be legitimately endowed by art with any likeness of a body. This accepted truth denied figurative representation, but it did allow for the establishment of a system of symbols that claimed no likeness but simply evoked an idea.

Historians speculate that the first monuments erected after the death of the Buddha were large mounds called *stupas*, probably derived from earlier, perhaps Harappan burial mounds. They appeared for the first time during the rule of King Ashoka (273–232 BC), who after converting to Buddhism erected 84,000 such *stupas* to mark the sacred sites

■ **3.53 Great Stupa at Sanchi, India, 3rd century BC– 1st century AD**

and secure the holy relics of the faith. Sometimes these monuments existed as little more than crude piles of rock, but often they were auspicious. A good example of *stupa* construction from the period of Ashoka is the *Great Stupa at Sanchi* (Fig. **3.53**), considered by many to be the greatest Buddhist monument in India. The mound measures 60 feet (approx. 20 m) in diameter and is over 25 feet (approx. 8.5 m) high. Later additions included an ambulatory perched on the side of the mound and a large set of stone railings. As a visual reminder of the Buddha, the *stupa* form obviously traveled well: architectural historians suggest that it was the basis of the later pointed pagodas of Burma and tiered pagodas of China.

As early as 450 BC, symbols such as the wheel (the *dharma chakra*) became an established part of Buddhist meditation, conjuring ideas of both the cyclical nature of existence and the veneration of the Buddha through his teaching. Another famous symbol is that of the footprint, which is associated with the Buddha's missionary journeying and his presence in nature. The lotus is the most complex and prevalent of the major symbolic representations of Gautama's teaching, and depending on one's orientation to the object or image, its meaning alters. Viewed from above, its rounded shape and circular heart represent the "essence of all," and when seen from the side above the water line, it is a vivid reminder of spiritual rebirth.

By about 100 BC, artists had begun combining such symbols to imply the presence of the Buddha (Fig. **3.54**). Thus from the footprint, lotus form, and wheel the viewer inferred the presence of the Buddha, rather than simply seeing separate symbols. Slowly, artists had found a way of describing the body of the Buddha through symbolism, signaling a shift toward a more sophisticated description of his bodily form.

Buddhist Figurative Art

The emergence of figurative art in Buddhism coincided with the beginning of the veneration and worship of the Buddha as an object of devotion. Early Buddhism stressed austerity and discipline, and its inflexibility to everyday demands gave little incentive to the average person to follow its noble path. The teaching of the law (*dharma*) slowly gave way to devotion (*bhakti*), and with it came the emergence of Mahayana Buddhism between the years 100 BC and AD 100. With a new emphasis on love and adoration not found in earlier orthodox Buddhism, objects of veneration quickly became an important part of worship. Here, Buddhist art made a conceptual move back into the context of the older Hindu tradition from which it had emerged — a process of conventionalizing the teachings into a complex iconography.

The development of figurative art in Buddhism coincided with two other historical events of some note. One was the development of the cult of Krishna in Indian Hinduism, with its emphasis on love and devotion and its popular use of imagery. The other was the effect of Alexander the Great and Greek culture on India and central Asia. The Greeks brought with them a figurative tradition already well

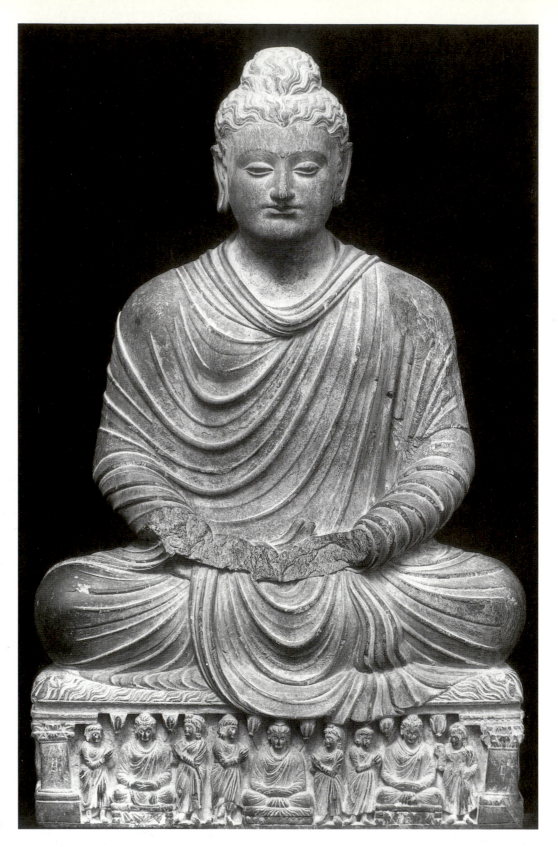

■ 3.55 *Seated Buddha* from
Gandhara, Pakistan,
2nd–3rd century AD
Dark grey schist
36 x 22½ in (91.4 x 57.1 cm)
Seattle Art Museum
Eugene Fuller Memorial Collection

entrenched in religious ceremony, and the influence of Western sources is very evident in the development of Buddhist statuary (Fig. **3.55**). The combination of these influences and events, along with an increased desire to make the teachings of the Buddha more accessible and meaningful to the populace, led to the emergence of visual images of the Buddha by about AD 100.

The seated Buddha image remained virtually intact as an image format for the next two millennia. Upon first observation, one is immediately struck by the symmetrical posture of the figure. Its stability and balance are attributes of the Buddha's harmony, perfection, and ideal character at enlightenment. Its posture, the ancient Indian yogic "lotus position," suggests discipline and strength. Such figures also retained much of the earlier Buddhist interest in symbolism, using such devices as hand gestures and special decorative marks to evoke specific ideas. One such gesture (*mudras*) is the commonly depicted outstretched right hand with the palm up, which symbolizes blessing and reassurance. In the case of the Gandhara *Seated Buddha* it is the *dhyana-mudra* with upturned hands held in the lap, designating meditation and serenity, that is depicted. An even more striking example of symbolic suggestion is the *ushnisha*, the extra lump on the Buddha's cranium, referring to an auxiliary brain that accommodates his supreme wisdom. In much of later Buddhist statuary, the evolution of this symbolic gesture results in the head's becoming highly abstracted, and it gives a good indication of how representation is itself nothing more than a set of conventions agreed upon by a community (Fig. **3.56**).

As Buddhist figurative art became more popular and widespread, the image of the Buddha changed from a lifelike Greek-style statue, to a more abstract, frontal, and schematic form. This development paralleled a similar process of abstraction in Christian art during the Byzantine era, as artists attempted to discover a clear and transcendent language for the description of forms. As in Orthodox Christianity, Buddhists soon developed a canon (fixed standards) for the production of religious imagery. The *Kama Sutra* was one such text, outlining such important considerations as proportion, which would allow art work to transcend the imperfections of this world. These proportions have little to do with naturalistic human anatomy, so in this respect the figures do not aspire to represent the physical Buddha but stand as representations of ideas.

Buddhist art is not, however, restricted to simple three-dimensional concerns. In areas such as Nepal and Tibet, banner illustration became a popular format for figurative motifs. Since monastic orders often migrated on a seasonal basis to avoid the biting cold, the cumbersome nature of three-dimensional work made it impractical. The banner, on the other hand, was both convenient and portable, and it quickly took on the form of a visual record of the order. Though

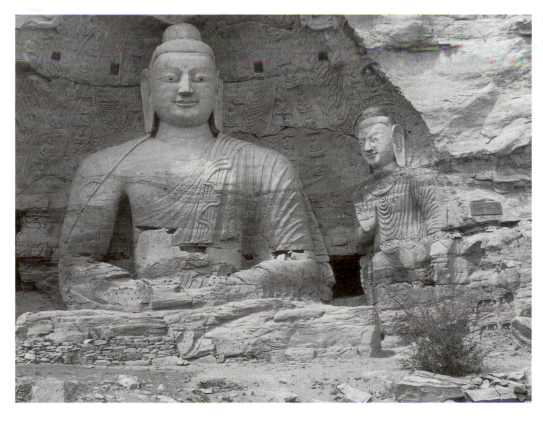

■ **3.56** *Colossal Buddha with Attendant Buddha*
Yung Kan, China c. AD 460–70

■ 3.57 *Tathagata Buddha*
Tibet, 13th–14th century
Opaque watercolors on cloth
36¼ x 26⅞ in (92 x 68 cm)
Los Angeles County Museum of Art
Nasil and Alice Heeramaneck Collection
Museum Associates Purchase

banners (*thangkas*) have religous significance, they were for the most part painted by lay people, many of whom spent years working on single pieces. As the banners became increasingly complex, they took on greater meditative value to the monks, who often used the illustrations as part of the process of refining their spiritual vision, and became permanent parts of the monastery (Fig. **3.57**).

Buddhist Painting in China

By AD 100 Buddhism had reached China, coming into contact with other sophisticated religious traditions, the most prominet being Taoism and Confucianism.

The Tao (Way) placed primary importance on the naturalness of action (*wu wei*) and the harmonious relationship between humanity and the universe. Therefore, the virtues of intuition and spontaneity anchor Taoist philosophy. Ch'an Buddhism (the most popular form of Buddhism in China) was deeply influenced by this concept, and it changed the way in which artists viewed both traditional techniques and the tools for making religious art.

Confucianism had less direct influence with regard to Buddhist art than its Taoist counterpart, but it did provide artists with an important convention that was essential to later Buddhist art: poetry. As a socially constructed religious philosophy, Confucianism supported the idea of filial piety and loyalty through the writing and exchanging of verse, sometimes on a daily basis. As the custom developed, this essentially social activity soon took on deeper significance, prompting many observers to believe that poetry was an intuitive and natural outpouring, capable of leading to enlightenment. Such greetings were often combined with small drawings or a simple painting, and as the reputation of poetry grew, so too did that of

■ **3.58 Jun Dish**
China, 12th century
Ceramic
Diameter 6¾ in (17.1 cm)
Ashmolean Museum, Oxford

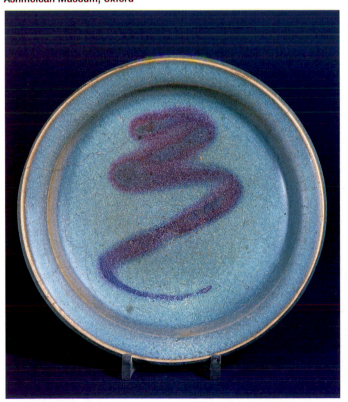

illustration. Art, like poetry, was granted special status as a form of revelation about human nature. Here, the secular arts of calligraphy and drawing took on religious significance and placed increased emphasis on the meditative value of the actual activity of painting (Fig. **3.58**).

Early Chinese Art Theory: The Idea of Spirit

One of the earliest Chinese treatises to consider this symbiotic relationship between calligraphy and painting was the sixth-century commentary of Hseih Ho, whose *Ku Hua P'in Lu* (Old Record of the Classifications of Painters) poses six considerations when judging the merit of a painting. They are:

1 *Spirit resonance* or vitality, meaning the transmission of life-affirming energy from the artist to the subject through the brush.

2 *Bone method*, the quality of the marks made by the artist when executing the work of art. A consequence of effective spirit resonance, the term probably refers to the ancient Chinese method of "reading" the character of an individual through an evaluation of their bone structure. The term is poetically applied here to the structural foundations of the painting, namely the drawing elements.

3 *Correspondence to the object*: the manner in which the artist depicts his forms, and their ability to suggest the natural world.

4 *Suitability to type*, which has to do with the proper application of color.

5 *Division and planning*: the compositional organization of a painting.

6 *Transmission by copying.*

Hseih Ho's *Ku Hua P'in Lu* makes plain the interests and aspirations of artists during the rise of Buddhism and reveals art's assimilation into the secular structure of Chinese life. Though these critical judgments were clearly to be applied to all aspects of Chinese painting, it is interesting to note the high regard *spirit* is given in the deliberations. Indeed, according to the author, if spiritual resonance is missing from the work, the other five considerations are a moot point. This gives some indication of how deeply imbedded the "Middle Paths" of Buddhism and Taoism were in the fabric of Chinese secular life. It also suggests that the superior artist would possess an implicit, spiritual understanding of nature. An outstanding example of this sensibility in visual form can be seen in

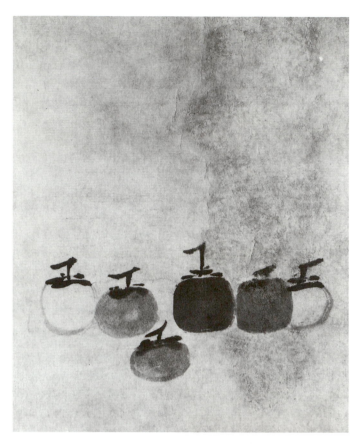

▲ 3.59 Mu Ch'i's
Persimmons
Late 13th century
Ink on paper
15 x 14¼ in (38.1 x 36 cm)
Daitokuji, Kyoto

Persimmons (Fig. **3.59**) of Mu Ch'i (active 1269), in which description and expression are held in perfect equilibrium. Here the act of painting — sensitive painting, that is — takes on a highly meditational and devotional quality that was to have implications for artists well into the twentieth century.

As the foregoing discussion suggests, the Eastern view of nature differed considerably from Western interpretations. In Western society, it is popular to see nature as something to shape, fashion, or beat down if need be. In this view, the world is the supreme embodiment of intellect (i.e. God) and thus can be ordered and manipulated according to certain rules. In traditional Eastern thought, nature is cruel, dispassionate, and unconquerable. Unlike their Western counterparts, Eastern artists felt a certain degree of religious awe toward their environment — devoid of intellect. Thus, in the Eastern view, the very best and most truthful art is that which attempts to assimilate itself into the workings of nature rather than be its opposition. In Chinese Ch'an Buddhism, a landscape painting is an embodiment of Gautama's teaching, and the artwork, like nature itself, is a manifestation of the eternal truths (Fig. **3.60**).

■ 3.60 Emperor Hui Tsung
The Five-Colored Parakeet
Handscroll, ink and
colors on silk
21 x 49½ in (53.3 x 125.1 cm)
The Museum of Fine Arts,
Boston
Maria Antionette Evans Fund

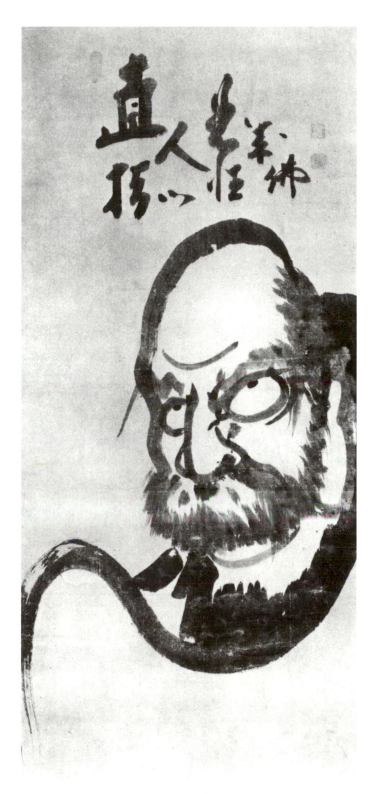

■ 3.61 Hakuin Zenji
Bodhidharma
Ink on paper
Private Collection

Japanese Zen Painting

When Buddhism arrived in Japan around the sixth century, the Ch'an view of nature became established in the Japanese monasteries. Zen Buddhism (the Japanese equivalent of Ch'an) is the most intuitive of all forms of Buddhist art, placing the naturalness of the act above all else. In an enlightened state, a Zen practitioner successfully unifies subject, content, and form into one absolute harmony — all of which is brought about by an intuitive response to environment. Alan Watts, one of the first Westerners to explore Zen Buddhism, summed up Zen painting when he stated: "The painting itself is a work of nature...using controlled accidents, paintings are formed as naturally as the rocks they depict" (A. Watts, *The Way of Zen*, Vintage Press, 1957, p. 174). Here art is as much a work of nature as it is a representation of it (Fig. **3.61**).

To understand this important concept (which will recur in Chapter Nine's discussion of modern art) it is necessary to understand what is commonly called a "non-dual" experience. The age-old Chinese symbol of **yin and yang** (Fig. **3.62**) is perhaps the best way to describe the idea. Shown as opposites, these shapes nevertheless combine to create a perfect harmonious whole — the decline of one is supported by the rise of the other. This image can be applied to a variety of situations, but the most common is that of intuition versus rationality. According to the symbol, humanity attains harmony by finding the perfect equilibrium between these two extremes. The artistic ideal, then, would be the combination of naturalness and human thought, and in Zen painting that quality is achieved through the relationship between artist, materials, rational conception, and the accidents of nature.

What exactly did the Zen artists mean by the idea of harmony? First, consider the rational processes inherent in the making of art: one sits down, determines what one wants to paint, and then attempts to execute this design with the available materials. The

■ 3.62 *Yin* and *Yang*

■ **3.63 Calligraphic ox hair brush and Western bristle brush**

tools will determine to what extent the artist can control the marks on the paper, and it is in these materials that the essence of Zen harmony is achieved. Take, for instance, a typical tapered bristle brush used in ink painting. Unlike a Western brush, which is often shaped to provide its user with the maximum degree of precision and predictability, the brush of the Zen artist is shaped to hold ink, as well as being extremely sensitive to pressure — which gives the line an unpredictable quality (Fig. **3.63**). If it is worked in a hesitant or unsure manner, such a brush blots or empties its ink; hence it is a tool shaped specifically for spontaneity and confidence. Even the handmade paper on which such marks are made is an extension of the natural world, since it reacts differently with each

■ **3.64 Gyokusel Jikhara, *Circle* (Void)**
Brush and ink on paper

application. Together, these simple materials become the messengers or embodiments of the intuitive truth that the Zen artist hopes to capture. When these features are combined with the polarity of black marks on white paper, the stage is set for the profound gesture. Briefly, then, in Zen painting the non-duality of existence is realized through a very sophisticated relationship between chance (the materials) and choice (the hand).

The most deliberate and perhaps quintessential symbol of Zen Buddhist art is the circle or "marvelous void" (Fig. **3.64**). Here the image of wholeness and connectedness is painted with great authority, only to find its path mediated by the "happy accidents" of the tools. Rationality and intuition, nature, and nurture, universe and self, or whatever else one may choose to call this harmony, this is one of the great expressions of balance and humanness in the history of civilization. Though many have attempted such an integration between their lives and the mysterious world around them, few have been able to achieve anything quite so profound and so sparse as the Zen circle.

SUMMARY

It is fitting that this short discussion of religious art should end with the circle painting, for embodied in its simple gesture is the wrestling between the known and unknown that forms religous art. Though the diversity of approaches and theories has changed dramatically from religion to religion, there remains a constant: the desire for an art that can eloquently speak the truth while simultaneously manufacturing it. Perhaps that is the real motivation behind iconoclasm, but it is also what has historically given art its authority. If harmony can be achieved through spirit and mind, the next chapter, on the Renaissance, will show how Western society created its own equivalent to the Zen circle — Michelangelo's *David* (see Fig. 4.37).

Religion is generally understood as the human community's attempt at constructing some greater truth or rationale for existence in an often dispassionate and cruel world. Thus art as a vivid expression of humanity's cultural needs and thoughts, perhaps more clearly illustrates this important relationship.

Through the examination of five of the world's

most important religions, it has become apparent that each community fashions its images around certain basic assumptions with regard to its personal and communal relationship with God. In some cases, such as Islam and Judaism, the very act of producing likenesses was/is seen as a blasphemous attempt at competing with God's power to create and destroy; in others, images appear as a fundamental component of the faith and the process of worship. It appears that the suspicion of images is determined very much by the nature of the faith, particularly its monotheistic or polytheistic character. Yet in all faiths there is an undeniable attempt to make an art that acts as both an inducement to worship and meditation and an accurate suggestion of God's will and order in the world. In this way, the religious arts remain perhaps the clearest indications of how humanity has historically contemplated the mind of God.

Glossary

arabesque   (*page 143*) Meaning "Arab-like," it is commonly used to describe Islamic ornamental work, which combines vegetal and geometric configurations into a unifed composition.

basilica   (*page 121*) An early form of Christian church architecture based on Roman secular designs, which set precedents for later Christian building projects. It typically consisted of an outer courtyard (*atrium*) and a closed colonnaded hall.

calligraphy   (*page 142*) Literally the art of writing, it is the written word or words as a visual document.

flying buttress   (*page 136*) A supporting armature used on Gothic cathedrals to take the strain of the vast vaulted ceilings. The buttress distributed the mass of the building away from the walls to the area around the foundation, allowing architects to build higher and more structurally sound churches, with more window space and thus greater light in the interior.

icon   (*page 129*) Literally meaning image, the term is generally used to describe representations of the Christian pantheon, particularly those with metaphysical connotations produced under Orthodox Christianity.

iconoclasm   (*page 113*) The practice of denying representational imagery, often on moral or religious grounds. However, the term literally means image-breaking, the destruction of an already produced image.

mosaic   (*page 126*) The art of creating images using colored pieces of stone, terracotta, and glass "tesserae." This art form was originally used to decorate the floors and walls of buildings.

yin and yang   (*page 163*) Described as the unity of opposites and popular in Taoism and Buddhism, this circle symbol combines its halves to create a perfect harmonious whole — the decline of one is supported by the rise of the other.

Suggested Reading

Some of the best texts on religious art are books on the history of religion, since they place artists and their visual expressions within the context of faith. However, there are also some excellent surveys that specialize on religous art.

Gough, Michael: *The Origins of Christian Art* (London: Thames & Hudson, 1973).

Graber, O.: *The Formation of Islamic Art* (New Haven: Yale University Press, 1973).

Moore, A.C.: *Iconography of Religions* (London: SCM Press, 1977).

Rowland, B.: *The Evolution of the Buddha Image* (New York: Abrams, 1963).

Scully, Vincent: *Architecture: The Natural and the Manmade* (London and New York: St. Martin's Press, 1991). An excellent examination of Christian architectural innovations.

Pronunciation Guide

cloisonné   **kloy**-zuh-**NAY**
Cycladic   suh-**KLAD**-ik
dharma chakra   **DAR**-muh **CHAHK**-ruh
Dura Europas   **DUR**-uh yoo-**ROH**-puhs
Gautama   **GOW**-tuh-muh
Hagia Sophia   hah-**GEE**-uh soh-**FEE**-uh
jahiliyyah   **jah**-hee-**LEE**-uh
Kandariya Mahadeva   **kahn**-duh-**REE**-yuh **mah**-huh-**DAY**-vuh
Mahayana   mah-huh-**YAH**-nuh
La Sainte-Chapelle   lah **sant**-sha-**PEL**
shikhara   shee-**KAR**-uh
Shri Ranganatha   shree **rahn**-guh-**NATH**-uh
Tao   dow
Tathagata   **tah**-thuh-**GAH**-tuh
Vézelay   **vay**-zuh-**LAY**

4

ISSUES AND IDEAS IN RENAISSANCE ART

■ 4.1 Paolo Uccello
Rout of San Romano c. 1450 (detail)
Tempera on wood
6 ft x 10 ft 5¼ in (1.8 x 3.2 m)
National Gallery, London

> *Painting is not only a science, it is even a divinity,*
> *because it transforms the painter's mind into something*
> *similar to the mind of God.*
>
> LEONARDO DA VINCI

In 1860 the Swiss historian Jakob Burkhardt wrote his influential text *The Civilization of the Renaissance in Italy*. He argued that European culture was "reborn" in the late fourteenth century after having lain dormant for almost 1,000 years (since the fall of the Roman Empire). Such a rebirth, or *renaissance*, signaled a new emphasis on individuality and a recentering of culture around humanistic interests rather than devotion to God. This marked a dramatic shift in European civilization after the medieval dominance of religious ideals of self-denial and left a legacy of learning and humanism, of which the visual arts are perhaps its greatest manifestation. Although the term **renaissance** has been violently debated since its origin in Burkhardt's text, it is now commonly associated with European culture from c. 1400 to 1600.

If it is at all possible to localize the aspirations of an entire era in one specific locale, in the early Renaissance that locale was Florence. The city was something of an anomaly during the late fourteenth century, for it had a strong economy and one of the most progressive political systems of its age, moving

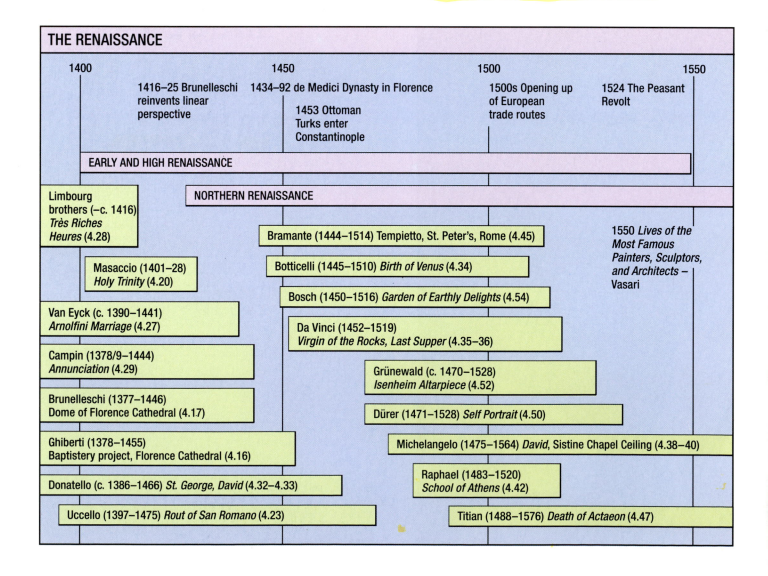

THE RENAISSANCE

1400	1450	1500	1550
	1416–25 Brunelleschi reinvents linear perspective	1434–92 de Medici Dynasty in Florence	1500s Opening up of European trade routes	1524 The Peasant Revolt
		1453 Ottoman Turks enter Constantinople		

EARLY AND HIGH RENAISSANCE

NORTHERN RENAISSANCE

Limbourg brothers (–c. 1416) *Très Riches Heures* (4.28)

Bramante (1444–1514) Tempietto, St. Peter's, Rome (4.45)

Masaccio (1401–28) *Holy Trinity* (4.20)

Botticelli (1445–1510) *Birth of Venus* (4.34)

Bosch (1450–1516) *Garden of Earthly Delights* (4.54)

Van Eyck (c. 1390–1441) *Arnolfini Marriage* (4.27)

Da Vinci (1452–1519) *Virgin of the Rocks, Last Supper* (4.35–36)

Campin (1378/9–1444) *Annunciation* (4.29)

Grünewald (c. 1470–1528) *Isenheim Altarpiece* (4.52)

Brunelleschi (1377–1446) Dome of Florence Cathedral (4.17)

Dürer (1471–1528) *Self Portrait* (4.50)

Ghiberti (1378–1455) Baptistery project, Florence Cathedral (4.16)

Michelangelo (1475–1564) *David*, Sistine Chapel Ceiling (4.38–40)

Donatello (c. 1386–1466) *St. George, David* (4.32–4.33)

Raphael (1483–1520) *School of Athens* (4.42)

Uccello (1397–1475) *Rout of San Romano* (4.23)

Titian (1488–1576) *Death of Actaeon* (4.47)

1550 *Lives of the Most Famous Painters, Sculptors, and Architects* – Vasari

■ 4.2 Renaissance Italy

from its previous medieval feudal system to a burgher oligarchy (*Signoria*). Located on the road between Rome and the northern centers of commerce, Florence was ideally situated for the development of trade, and it soon became an enticing center for many of the Western world's most powerful financial institutions. Recognizing the importance of the city's trade guilds to the well-being of all its citizens, elected officials from each of the seven most economically influential guilds formed a "representative" government for the whole of Florence. This insured the continued prosperity of the city-state and kept the affairs of government directly related to economic policy. The result was an efficient and energetic community that had both the resources and the intellectual aspirations to become the new center of Western culture.

Florence's prosperity coincided with a significant shift in attitude toward education and intellectual curiosity. One notable result was the re-emergence of philosophy and the Classical languages of Greek and Latin in daily study after centuries of neglect. Influential Florentines were exposed to many of the great Classical thinkers, whose works were not readily available in the Middle Ages. This in turn created a new generation of enlightened citizens.

THE RISE OF LEARNING

There is no shortage of frustration for a historian studying the origins of the Renaissance. It is, obviously, impossible to pinpoint any one specific social or technical condition as the impetus for the Renaissance. Rather, it is sensible to see the rise of Renaissance culture as an outgrowth of an assortment of disparate events and ideas surfacing during the end of the fourteenth and beginning of the fifteenth century. To understand clearly the singular dynamic that permeated Florentine culture around 1400, it is necessary to look into some of the contemporary historical issues and consider some precedents that anchored such activity.

On 29 May 1453, the Ottoman Turks entered the golden city of Constantinople, signaling the end of the Christian Byzantine culture. Like most collapses, the process of moral and intellectual decay within the walls of the city had been slow but steady in the years leading up to the fall, and by the beginning of the fifteenth century, the scholarly community had begun a steady migration toward the West, finding sanctuary in the numerous universities that had sprung up in Europe over the previous two centuries. One such center was Florence, which hosted the latter half of the ecumenical council of 1438–9 that attempted a reconciliation between Eastern Orthodoxy (centered in Constantinople) and Western Catholicism (centered in Rome). Many of the Eastern dignitaries and intellectuals remained in the city after the meetings,

including the celebrated Genisthos Plethon (c. 1389 –1464), sometimes called Gemistos, who tutored the Florentine leader and patron Cosimo de' Medici.

This migration of scholars was indeed significant, for it reintroduced certain Classical thinkers into Western culture. In particular, the rekindling of interest in Plato made popular once again the notion of ideals and *idealism*, as opposed to an earlier medieval interest in **empiricism** (which emphasized observation of natural phenomena over abstract speculation and devotional mysticism). One consequence of this shift was a dramatic reconsideration of the structures of society and culture — subjects that would form the foundation of Renaissance art.

It is one thing to be able to lecture to a small, interested, and typically affluent audience on a topic such as Plato; it is an entirely different story making such information available and digestible to the greater populace. Throughout the Middle Ages, the written tradition (including such works as the Bible, a few commentaries, and some authorized works of philosophy) had been kept alive by scribes and calligraphers who patiently recopied by hand the texts in various monastery libraries. In that sense, the monks were perhaps the only continuous link between that era and the great thoughts of the past. However, such projects were extremely labor-intensive, making these documents highly prized and rarely available for study.

In 1457 the German Johann Fust printed the first surviving dated book, a Latin edition of the Psalms. Using the then new movable-type process invented by his father-in-law, Johann Gutenberg, he successfully distributed and popularized a text that had until then been in the hands of only a very few. By 1500 over half a million printed books were available across Europe, and they helped spread new intellectual ideas throughout the continent (Fig. **4.3**).

By the fifteenth century the world was also becoming a considerably smaller place. The invention of navigational tools such as the stern rudder and the astrolabe made travel easier and more reliable. For example, the North Atlantic was now opened as a trade route, linking the British Isles and Scandinavia to the large commercial centers in the south. As with the introduction of printed text, this dramatic increase in communications between nations enabled the quick proliferation of ideas and works of art across Europe — and subsequently into the New World.

Jonas missus est in mare·z zeglutit a pisce·Jone
primo ca.   Jonas zer zphet ward geworffen in das
mozr vnd von zem walfisch verschlicket.

Scöa figura·

¶Sepulturam xpi etiam filij Jacob pfigurauerüt.
Qui fratrem suum Joseph in cysternam miserunt·
Filij iacob fratrem suum sine causa vsqz ad mortem
ozerunt· Ita iuzei fratrem suum xpm gratis odio ba
babuerunt· Filij iacob fratrem suum p triginta zenarijs venzebant· Juzei xpum pro triginta zenarijs
iuda emebant· Filij iacob tunicam fratris sui dilace
muerüt· Juzei carnem xpi virgis flagellis spinis cla
uis verberauerunt· Tunica ioseph nõ sensit aliquam
penam vel zolorem· Sed caro xpi in omnibz mebris
sustinuit passionem· Tunica ioseph vsqz ad talos ze-
scenzebat· Et in xpo a vertice vsqz ad talos nulla sa/
nitas erat·Filij iacob tunicã ioseph sanguie ezi asp-
gebant·Sed iuzei tunicam Cristi pzopzio sanguine
pfunzebant· Filij Jacob patrem suum nimis turba
uerunt·Sic iuzei marie tristiciam maximũ intulert
Joseph fratribus suis qz in eo zeliquerant zelaxauit·

■ 4.3 *Jonah and the Whale*
Illustration from "Speculum humanea
salvationis"
German, 15th century
Woodcut
The Metropolitan Museum of Art,
Harris Brisbane Dick Fund, 1923 (23.26.2)

INDIVIDUALITY AND HUMANISM

Perhaps the most important concept to come out of all the innovative developments and economic factors of the late fourteenth century was a renewed belief in the power and the majesty of the human being. The nineteenth-century historian Burkhardt claimed that it was an interest in individuality that separated the Renaissance from the Middle Ages in which God had been the center and the axis of all power and dignity. The human, created in perfection but fatally flawed by desire (as evidenced in the story of Adam and Eve; Figs. **4.4** and **4.5**), lived in the shadow of God through the sacrifice of his son Jesus Christ. The result was a world view deeply entrenched in guilt and obedience, and one in which individuality was seen as a gross indulgence of vanity for all except kings and princes, who remained to all intents and purposes above the strict precepts of the Church.

The Renaissance seems to have liberated many of the pious from much of the restrictive dogma of the Middle Ages, thanks in part to economic considerations. With the various technical innovations in place, trade and commerce throughout the continent increased significantly, which in turn brought about the slow development of the competitive marketplace. Earlier teachings had made the acquisition of wealth appear a hindrance to salvation, and in its place put poverty and humility as attainable goals. Yet the success of commerce and the trade guilds in many

■ 4.4 *Adam and Eve Reproached by the Lord*
Relief from the bronze doors of Hildelsheim Cathedral c. AD 1015
Approx. 23 x 43 in (58.4 x 109.2 cm)

■ 4.5 Bronze doors with scenes from the Old and New Testaments,
c. AD 1015
Hildesheim Cathedral, Germany
Bronze
16 ft 6 in (5.03 m)

■ 4.6 *The Bank's Counting House*
Manuscript illustration
Courtesy of the Trustees of the British Library, London

of the more developed communities afforded a better
standard of living for some and a more humane organization of society, all of which in turn helped justify
such a system on solid moral grounds (Fig. **4.6**). Also,
the rich could afford to engage in a variety of guilt-
assuaging charities and cultural activities. The art
patron is an excellent example of such supposedly
philanthropic activity; it was through the donations of
the rich that many a cathedral obtained its art.

The Body

The human figure embodied many of the traits implicit within this new social order. For instance, depiction of the human nude made an undeniable resurgence in the fifteenth and sixteenth centuries, after being absent from Western art since antiquity. The reasons for this seem clear: the human body was intrinsically connected with pleasure during the Middle Ages. According to dominant religious doctrines of the period, bodily pleasures were to be avoided as a way of atoning for the guilt of the original sin of Adam and Eve. By the middle of the fifteenth century, this chaste outlook began to give way to a more natural and perhaps more realistic point of view, in keeping with the freedom being exercised in the areas of economics and social matters. Subsequently, the issue of the body as a symbol of sexuality became equated not so much with sin as with nature, and it assumed the visual role as a reminder of the majesty and centrality of human form as God's creation (Fig. **4.7**).

■ **4.7** Antonio del Pollaiuolo
Battle of Naked Men c. 1465–70
Engraving, 15½ x 23½ in (38.4 x 59 cm)
The Metropolitan Museum of Art
Joseph Pulitzer Bequest, Purchase 1917 (17.50.99)

Giotto and the Liberation of the Figure

Giotto di Bondone (c. 1266–1337) is always cited as the artist who initiated the decisive pictorial break that culminated in the so-called "rebirth" in the visual arts. He is best known for his monumental frescoes in the Arena Chapel, Padua, which illustrate the lives of Christ and the Virgin. Perhaps the most memorable of the various scenes is the *Lamentation* (Figs. **4.8** and **4.9**) of c. 1305, in which the dead Christ is presented to the faithful. Viewed alone and out of its historical context, it is difficult to see why this work was so radical, yet at the time it marked a significant shift in the way in which art was produced.

To appreciate Giotto's achievement and its repercussions on later art, it is useful to compare his work with contemporary representations of the same theme. First consider the *Madonna Enthroned* (Fig. **4.10**) by Cimabue (c. 1240–1302?), painted between 1280 and 1290. In this painting, there is an obvious adherence to the Byzantine tradition of figurative abstraction and the flattening out of space (which allows for a clearer reading of the image). However, in this work, unlike that of Cimabue's predecessors, there are some marked departures. Though the space is shallow and not particularly convincing, the painting nonetheless attempts to situate its figures within a

■ 4.9 The Arena Chapel, Padua, showing frescoes in situ

constructed depth of field. This illusion of three-dimensional space is further accentuated in the drapery that wraps the body of the Virgin; unlike in previous images, it corresponds to the implied roundness and volume of the figure. Also, the scale of the piece is an unprecedented 12 ft 7 in by 7 ft 4 in (3.84 x 2.24 m) — much larger than most Byzantine images. As a result, the painting functions on a very different level with its audience: it reflects an heroic affirmation of faith and the power of the Church, rather than an intimate personal correspondence

■ **4.10 Cimabue**
Madonna Enthroned c. 1280–90
Tempera on panel
Approx. 12 ft 7 in x 7 ft 4 in (3.84 x 2.24 m)
Uffizi Gallery, Florence

FOCUS ON

Tempera

Tempera is among the oldest of artistic media, with examples dating back thousands of years. As a material, tempera is little more than pigment combined with a water soluble "binder," which allows for a fluid application, and enables the pigment to adhere to the painting surface. The traditional binder for tempera is egg yolk, which when mixed with pigment and water produces a paint which dries very quickly and doesn't crack. The advantage of such a material was that it enabled the artist to have a remarkable degree of control, as layers of color are built up slowly through repeated applications of brushstrokes. The disadvantage (and it would prove difficult to overcome after the development of oil paint) was that tempera's quick drying time made blending and subtle transitions nearly impossible, and as a result artists "en masse" turned to the easier and arguably more suitable oil medium.

The typical method of an artist working in tempera is as follows:

1 *Priming* This initial stage involved preparing the painting surface (wood, board, canvas) with *gesso*. Traditionally made with marble dust (though today most commercial preparations are latex based) gesso is a white paint that gives the surface a uniformity, smoothness, and just enough "tooth" to accept tempera.

2 *Underdrawing* The design is then transferred to the prepared surface by scratching through a preliminary cartoon, or light drawing.

3 *Underpainting* General areas of color are then applied to the surfaces, in some cases time-tested "recipes" are used to enhance the final painting. A good example of this was the use of *terre verte* (green earth) as underpainting for flesh in the Middle Ages. The belief was that a green undertone helped make the flesh appear more vibrant and lifelike (a good example of intuiting complementary colors long before scientific color theory). This helps explain the rather sea-sick look of many of the period's madonnas and saints, where underpainting has been exposed.

4 *Final layers* It is at this point that the intricate color schemes and layers of paint are employed, often with small brushes. The surface dries to a matte finish.

---

between the viewers and their faith. The result is noteworthy, and it leads to the work of Cimabue's younger contemporary, the Sienese artist Duccio di Buoninsegna (c. 1255–c. 1318), who between 1308 and 1311 painted his own version of the *Madonna Enthroned* (Fig. **4.11**) for the altar of Siena Cathedral.

Duccio's painting shows many of the Byzantine mannerisms evident in the work of Cimabue. There is still little variation in scale between figures (which implies that all the figures exist on the same plane, which in turn flattens out the painting), and there remains a certain degree of abstraction and schematic design in the scene. There is, however, a notable departure in the rendering of volume in the work, and further, a concentration on facial expressions that produces an engaging sense of emotion and tenderness. The soft folds of the drapery and the contemplative expression of the Virgin reveal the emergence of a new type of figure — the emotional counterpart to the compositional innovations of Giotto. In other words, with the Duccio painting one senses not only the liberation of the figure from the flatness of the panel but also an increased awareness of the personality of the subject — both of which seem to imply a more general acceptance of the idea of individuality.

■ 4.11 Duccio
Madonna Enthroned c. 1308–11
Tempera on panel
Height 6 ft 10 in (2 m)
Cathedral Museum, Siena

It is not unusual for texts on the history of art to take the work of Giotto as a turning point in Western art. Indeed, many of the most important attributes of Renaissance culture are inextricably linked to the artist's attempts at constructing a more convincing sense of space on a painted surface. But why was it so important and revolutionary for an artist to create a convincing illusion of depth in painting? And further, what does this development reveal about Giotto's historical circumstances? Consider his version of the *Madonna Enthroned* (Fig. **4.12**), which is contemporary to Duccio's version. Giotto placed much greater emphasis on the description of mass and volume in the work — illusionistic elements only mildly suggested in the previous examples. The most common way to produce an illusion of volume is to convince the viewer that elements within the scene exist in light and shadow. Giotto's successful use of light as a tool in the modeling of items enabled the inner space of the painting effectively to recede, liberating the figures from the surface.

The term "liberation" is indeed appropriate here, for it asserts the freedom of the figure from the Byzantine insistence on flat, embedded design — a pictorial concept with parallels to the increasing sense of individuality in fourteenth-century Italy. For the first time in almost 1,000 years, both artists and their painted figures became individuals in the most basic sense of the term, liberated from the flattening dictates of previous "good taste." An example of this is the issue of authorship or *attribution* that suddenly surfaced for the first time in Western art since the Classical age. Today we know the names of these important figures; Cimabue, Duccio, and Giotto are recognized as "individuals" of achievement rather than anonymous contributors to the greater glory of the Church (which was previously the fashion in a world centered around concepts of piety and humility).

As the work of Giotto demonstrates, new ideas were developing which, by the fourteenth century were making their way into the cultural arena. Yet the decades after the death of the artist provided little conclusive evidence that a rebirth had indeed taken place. The century had seen its share of misery, with war and religious intolerance, but perhaps the most devastating event to darken the period was the terrible Black Death, which made its way across Europe from Sicily in 1348, ending in Scandinavia in 1350. In

■ 4.12 Giotto di Bondone, *Madonna Enthroned* c. 1310
Tempera on panel, 10 ft 8 in x 6 ft 8 in (3.25 x 2 m)
Uffizi Gallery, Florence

that period, it is estimated that Europe lost 40 percent of its population. One Sienese writer summed up the agony and destruction of the day when he stated, "No one wept for the dead, because everyone expected death himself."

If it is possible to set aside the huge cost of human suffering brought about by the plague, there is evidence to suggest that the drastic decline in population had some beneficial effects on the economy and the standards of living in the late fourteenth and early fifteenth centuries. Fewer people meant more jobs, more food, and better wages for the workforce, and a greater share of what the land produced was now going back into the pockets of the survivors. Although records do not indicate any significant resurgence in gross economic product, the alteration in per capita affluence shows that the plague indeed contributed in an odd way to the success of the Renaissance.

The Florence Cathedral Complex and the Aims of Art in 1400

It was not until 1400 that Church authorities in Florence decided to continue work on their beloved cathedral. The first of many projects to be initiated was a competition for a pair of bronze doors for the Baptistery, started in 1401. This was one of the great competitions of the age, and it pitted two of Florence's most talented young artists against each other: Filippo Brunelleschi (1377–1446) and Lorenzo Ghiberti (1378–1455). The competition asked several artists to submit a design of cast bronze on the biblical subject of the sacrifice of Isaac. The decision of the jury reveals much about the new "look" that was capturing the imagination of the era.

Brunelleschi's *Sacrifice of Isaac* (1401; Fig. **4.13**) was a dynamic and busy composition. Though the artist made some attempt to produce an illusion of depth in

■ 4.13 Filippo Brunelleschi
Sacrifice of Isaac 1401
Gilt bronze
21 x 17¹⁄₂ in (53.3 x 44.4 cm)
Museo Nazionale del Bargello, Florence

■ 4.14 Lorenzo Ghiberti
Sacrifice of Isaac 1401
Gilt bronze
21 x 17¹⁄₂ in (53.3 x 44.4 cm)
Museo Nazionale del Bargello, Florence

the relief, there is a notable insistence on the foreground plane, which gives the impression of a simple relief rather than a convincing spatial arrangement. If one compares this with Ghiberti's winning entry, it is possible to speculate on the criteria the jury deemed important and on what they aspired towards.

Though Ghiberti's *Sacrifice of Isaac* (Fig. **4.14**) conformed to the same design requirements as Brunelleschi's entry (stipulated in the competition guidelines), the results were somewhat different. Instead of the tight grid format utilized by his most formidable competitor, Ghiberti implemented a dramatic diagonal thrust across the middle section of the relief, resulting in a more startling depiction of space and depth within the work. Such a recession of space also gave him the opportunity to manipulate sharply the various sizes of his figures with regard to their relative positions in relation to the viewer. Such "foreshortening" is best seen in Ghiberti's handling of the figure of the Angel, which pierces the foreground plane from its origin in the background. This more natural approach ·to the positioning of figures must have found greater favor with the jury than Brunelleschi's more stable composition.

It took Ghiberti almost twenty-five years to complete the first commission for the north doors of the Baptistery; then he was offered the job of creating another set of bronze panels to adorn the east doors. The two works cover some forty years of cultural flux, and the change of attitude on the part of the community (and subsequently the artist as a member of that community) can be witnessed by comparing the two projects. First, the east doors are much more regular in styling and lack the medieval quatrefoil frames that graced the surface of the north doors — which results in a more refined and somewhat restrained series of works. The recent rediscovery of **linear perspective** also found its way into Ghiberti's late work — a technical innovation for the systematic design of illusionistic space that was ironically initiated by his one-time competitor Brunelleschi. The result is a series of works that exhibits a much more airy and expansive inner space than the earlier panels from the north doors.

A good example of this increased sense of depth can be seen in the *Story of Jacob and Esau* (c. 1435; Fig. **4.15**) from the east doors (Fig. **4.16**) — which the young Michelangelo once aptly called "the Gates of

■ **4.15 Lorenzo Ghiberti**
Story of Jacob and Esau c. 1435
from the "Gates of Paradise,"
Baptistery of Florence Cathedral

4.16 Lorenzo Ghiberti
"Gates of Paradise" c. 1425-52, Baptistery of Florence Cathedral

Paradise." In the new work, Ghiberti allowed for the figures to integrate into the deep illusionistic space of the relief, creating a much more relaxed and naturalistic portrayal of the subject. The attempts at rendering architectural motifs in space further refined the illusionistic quality of the piece. What is more, the earlier compositional exuberance of the sweeping diagonal (witnessed in the *Sacrifice of Isaac*) gives way to a more harmonious and subtle design. This marriage of architectural motifs and closely observed figure modeling became an increasing preoccupation with many of the artists following in Ghiberti's footsteps, and it set the stage for some of the most prominent innovations of the latter part of the fifteenth century.

The unsuccessful bid for the Baptistery doors commission was not the end of Brunelleschi's relationship with Florence, and perhaps his initial loss was the Renaissance's gain, in that his later discoveries in architecture were to prove exceptionally valuable.

At the time of the competition of 1401, the cathedral proper was still unfinished. The problem was how to bridge the enormous area of the central tower of the original design by Arnolfo di Cambio (c. 1245–1302), without the use of flying buttresses, which were out of the question because of their obvious incompatibility with the beautiful Romanesque marble exterior. Between the years 1417 and 1420 Brunelleschi studied many of the ancient building projects in Rome (such as the Pantheon [see Fig. 2.44]), and suggested that a dome could in fact be built without the visual distraction created by buttressing. His answer was the implementation of classical vaulting techniques and a project that would take another sixteen years to complete (Fig. **4.17**).

Brunelleschi's innovative design provides further evidence of the new sensibility in Florence around 1420. It succeeded in addressing the needs of both art and technical interests through a clear understanding of not only Classical but also medieval building techniques, creating a sense of harmony rather than the typical discord that often follows such mergers. Brunelleschi understood that the principles of buttressing were useful in spreading the enormous weight of a dome over a greater expanse — thereby alleviating much of the stress on the walls and foundations of the structure. He thus concluded that the tall supporting walls of the dome had to be constructed with *tribunes* (small offshooting extensions from the original walls), which, like the buttress, would act to disperse weight over a wider area. In this way, Brunelleschi manipulated the basic tenets of medieval cathedral construction to serve the interests of the new church.

Clearly, however, it was the dome itself that created most awe in the community. No such structure had been attempted in Europe since antiquity, and never before on such an immense scale. Brunelleschi's solution was to create a dome within a dome, which would support the exterior weight effectively while removing the need for interior armatures or any other superfluous accessories that would distract from the simplicity of the construction. The outer dome was thus constructed as a light skin or cover, exhibiting great visual authority over the Florence skyline while resting almost exclusively on the smaller interior skeleton. The result was a resurgence in dome architecture, since now architects possessed both the skill and technical expertise to attempt structures that only years before had been thought impossible.

What may one conclude from Brunelleschi's technical breakthrough in the light of the previous discussion of the Renaissance? First, it must be remembered that, had it not been for a renewed interest in Classical thought and culture, it is doubtful that artists such as Brunelleschi would have sought inspiration from Roman architecture such as the Pantheon. It was not that artists and architects had not been interested in such building solutions before this period, but simply that most looked toward a more "spiritually sound" influence. The dome is by design a stable and symmetrical structure — attributes that visually mimic the emerging Renaissance ideals of harmony and equilibrium over the obedience and superstition that had marked the previous age. In this way, the innovative dome construction constitutes a vivid reminder of the greater influences and aspirations of the day.

■ **4.17 Filippo Brunelleschi**
Dome of Florence Cathedral 1420-36
Height of dome 367 ft (111.86 m)

Linear Perspective and other Renaissance Conventions

The word perspective comes from the Latin verb *perspicio*, meaning to see clearly or look through. Today the term is commonly used to describe a geometric system for depicting depth on a two-dimensional plane (called linear perspective), but its original meaning put a more general emphasis on the "life-likeness" of a given representation. In aspiring to life-likeness, there is an underlying assumption of a certain truthfulness implicit to this system — an idea that should be put in context at the very outset of this discussion. The depiction of space on a two-dimensional plane is not truth but convention; its validity as a method of interpreting visual experience is not absolute. However, the notable popularity of the system from the Renaissance through the nineteenth century makes it an interesting example of the inter-relationship between art and convention.

According to the Renaissance writer and critic Giorgio Vasari (1511–74), pictorial space re-emerged in Europe around the end of the thirteenth century in the work of Giotto. It was he who first attempted the

■ 4.18 Giotto di Bondone
St. Francis Drives Away the Demons from Arezzo
Instituto Italiano d'Arti Grafiche, Bergamo

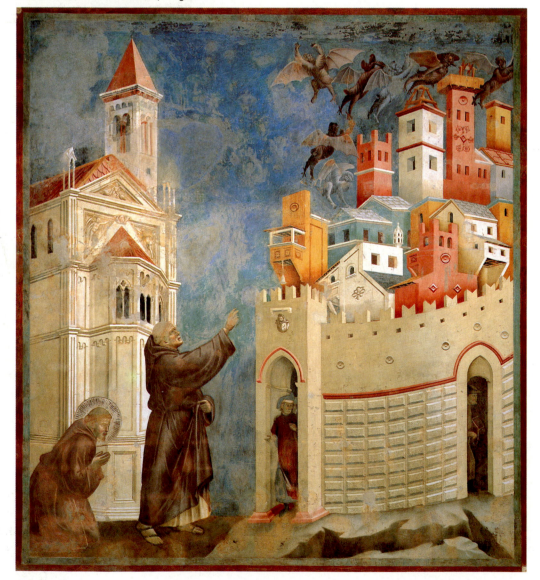

devices of **foreshortening** (the visual contraction of an object that extends back in space) and **scale diminution** (the reduction in scale of objects as they move away from the picture plane) to produce an illusionistic space within his painting.

These concepts are clarified by Giotto's *St. Francis Drives Away the Demons from Arezzo* (Fig. **4.18**), in which he positioned two figures in the immediate foreground of the scene and other characters in the middle or background. Note that the distribution of figures in space appears convincing due to Giotto's willingness to "shrink" elements as they recede in depth. This technique mimics everyday perception, as things closest to us appear larger than those in the distance.

The reception such revolutionary depictions received during their day is an interesting example of how the seemingly natural act of perception is tied to certain preconceptions about reality, which are themselves based in convention. The early Renaissance writer Giovanni Boccaccio (1313–75), in discussing the merits of Giotto's painting in his famous literary work *The Decameron*, stated: "…many times the visual sense of men was misled by the things he made, believing to be true what was only painted." Perhaps the idea of being misled by the rather shallow and often illogical space of a work such as *St. Francis* seems an absurdity in an age of such illusionism as 3-D movies and compact discs, but at the time such images were apparently quite deceptive.

Ideas about why this phenomenon occurred vary, but one of the soundest is a theory developed by the twentieth-century psychologist Rudolf Arnheim, whose intense studies of composition have led to a new understanding of the relationship between art and the science of perception. Arnheim claims that any progress in pictorial lifelikeness creates an illusion of life itself. He takes the example of how the public first reacted to the technique of moving pictures in the 1890s, when it was quite common for viewers to scream at a moving image of a locomotive coming toward the foreground of the screen. Since the resultant image from this new medium appeared as a revolutionary departure from earlier images of its kind, the initial response of the public was to perceive it as "more real" and act accordingly. If a moving picture had such a reception, Giotto's simple foreshortening might well have given his audience a similar visual thrill.

■ 4.19 Ambrogio Lorenzetti
Scenes from the Legend of St. Nicholas
Panel. Uffizi Gallery, Florence

After Giotto's preliminary excursions into the field of illusionistic space, many competent artists began to utilize the techniques with greater freedom and skill. Within a few years of Giotto, Ambrogio Lorenzetti (1280–1348) had already far advanced the basic skills of his predecessor (such as in his *Scenes from the Legend of St. Nicholas*; Fig. **4.19**). His complex renderings of

...hn 1428

n)

■ **4.21** *Holy Trinity with the Virgin and St. John* 1428 showing perspective lines

cityscapes and intricate building items such as staircases allowed for a much more convincing (if somewhat inconsistent) space within the confines of the painting.

Vasari claimed that the system of linear perspective was reinvented by the painter-sculptor-architect Brunelleschi. His discoveries placed an increased emphasis on the viewer's gaze and set in motion a codified system by which to render space. Between 1416 and 1425 the artist produced two perfect examples of his discovery, which operated much like public peep-shows. In these demonstration pieces, he painted an accurate depiction of the church of San Giovanni in Florence, which was separated from the viewer by a partition with a small peep-hole cut out in the middle. Directly opposite this hole was a mirror, in which was reflected the painted scene, which rested on the back of the partition. The result was an image that seemed to recede into space. By aligning the viewer's vision with his own centralized convergence of lines (thanks to the small peep-hole), it is said that the artist found the all-important "vanishing point" (the point at which lines receding back into space converge) that had been lost for over 1,000 years. Though neither of the two showpieces survives to this day, their reputation was well known to many of the leading artists in Florence at the time. Painters such as Masaccio (1401–28), Piero della Francesca (1416–92), Giovanni Bellini (c. 1431–1516) and Andrea Mantegna (1431–1506) claimed to have followed the discoveries of Brunelleschi during the period, and many went on to produce even more spectacular results including the further development of volume in painting.

Among the early masters who capably assimilated the complementary notions of volume and perspective was Tommaso di Giovanni di Simone Guidi, better known as Masaccio. In his short life he produced some of the most important paintings of the early Renaissance. He is perhaps best known for his fresco of the *Holy Trinity* (Fig. **4.20**) of 1428, the year of his death. In this work the important innovations of Giotto were assimilated into a more rigorous and rational depiction of space, clarified through a steadfast insistence on symmetrical composition (Fig. **4.21**). Here symmetry and balance become the visual equivalents of the principles of harmony and moderation — precepts very much in keeping with an era and a people bent on reconciling body and soul after the piety of the Middle Ages.

The merging of volume and perspective was of course inevitable, particularly since each technique often had to rely on the other to produce a convincing representation of space. Masaccio was one of the first to understand this relationship, and his painting of Christ in the *Holy Trinity* is one notable result. The artist's use of linear perspective in rendering the surrounding architectural framework effectively created a deep central space, suggesting area both in front of and behind the Christ figure. Masaccio then reasserted this space by modeling his figure in light and shadow, which reaffirms the viewer's anticipation of space in the work. This is a reciprocal relationship, since each device relies on the other to produce a convincing illusion; in other words, flat figures in a perspectival scene, or figures with volume on a flat background, will not succeed in convincing the viewer.

The compositional rigor of Masaccio was not the only significant characteristic of his painting. He had likewise learned from the earlier Duccio and successfully integrated emotional content into the sometimes too predictable demands of balance and symmetry. The results are paintings such as the *Expulsion from Eden* (Fig. **4.22**) of 1427. The sense of deep shame is present in these nudes, and they suggest a naturalism unparalleled at the time. Together, these two attributes, idealism (embodied in mathematical constructs such as perspective) and naturalism (the artist's eye for detail and expression), were to form the basis of much of later Renaissance art theory, in which quality distinguished itself through a harmonious interchange between observation from nature and contemplation of perfection and beauty.

Masaccio was a student of nature, and his works exhibit a much closer observation of shadows, anatomy, and emotional gestures than any of those of his Italian predecessors. Once observed, these figures

E
F
B   orence

■ 4.23 Paolo Uccello
Rout of San Romano c. 1450
Tempera on wood
6 ft x 10 ft 5¼ in (1.8 x 3.2 m)
National Gallery, London

were nonetheless assimilated into "higher" or loftier considerations. The dominating concern of pictorial balance is but one of the many reliances on idealism over naturalism. In harmony, a great painting could glorify both God and the cultural aspirations of the day; in discord, it became either a static academic exercise or an unintelligent arrangement of imperfect objects. In Masaccio there is at least the attempt to integrate one aspect into the other, and the result eventually led to the theories and works of Leonardo da Vinci and Michelangelo.

Another contemporary of Brunelleschi was the artist Paolo Uccello (1397–1475). He too was obsessed by the possibilities of linear perspective. In his *Rout of San Romano* (Fig. **4.23**) of c. 1450, the results of his investigations seem completely absorbed, though perhaps overly contrived. Note how the broken shafts of the various lances and other weapons that litter the foreground fall neatly to the vanishing point of the painting, and how the tidy positioning of the fallen soldier again draws the viewer's eye back to a predictable central focus. The result is a clear depiction of space receding from the immediate foreground, but its less than subtle manipulation of the viewpoint makes it a somewhat obvious solution to the problem of "lifelikeness," and thus in the end less satisfying.

In the year 1500 another great craftsman of the Renaissance, Leonardo da Vinci (1452–1519), began a treatise on art that remained unfinished at his death and was not circulated until 1542. In it the artist-scientist attempted to define and discuss many facets of the art-making process, of which perspective was given special consideration. One of the famous discussions of perspective centered around what became

■ **4.24 Albrecht Dürer**
Alberti's Veil 1525
Woodcut from Dürer's *Perspective and Proportion* 1525

■ **4.25 Albrecht Dürer**
A Variation on Alberti's Veil 1525
Woodcut from Dürer's *Perspective and Proportion* 1525

■ **4.26 Brook Taylor**
Leonardo's Window
From *New Principles of Linear Perspective*, published 1811
British Library, London

known as "Leonardo's window," a device that enabled the painter to see and then translate elements from life onto a flat surface. The idea itself was not really new: the art theorist Leon Battista Alberti (c. 1404–72) had used a similar device called a veil, whose transparent grid of string bound on a frame enabled him to transcribe a given scene, as Figs. **4.24** and **4.25**, contemporary woodcuts, illustrate. However, it was Leonardo who first attempted a codified statement on the subject. He wrote: "Perspective is nothing else than seeing a place or objects behind a pane of glass, quite transparent, on the surface of which the objects that lie behind the glass can be drawn. These can be traced in pyramids to the point in the eye, and these pyramids are intersected by the glass pane." Fig. **4.26**, from a nineteenth-century text on perspective, shows how this might have looked to Leonardo.

Through the research initiated by artists of the early Renaissance era, there continued to be dramatic advances in the rendering of illusionistic space on the two-dimensional plane. By far the most significant result of the years of patient research was the general implementation of both one- and multiple-point perspectives as convenient "rules" from which to develop depth. So convinced were artists that linear perspective was the correct and accurate method for depicting nature that it was not until the late nineteenth century that the idea was really challenged.

However, by the early sixteenth century the ingenious Leonardo had already noticed faults in the system and mathematical paradoxes implicit within its method. The results of his complex investigations need not concern us here; suffice it to say that even its supposed infallibility was an illusion. Nevertheless, the feat of creating a logical space on a two-dimensional plane remains a remarkable achievement, particularly when one takes into account the amazingly short period of time it took Renaissance artists to rediscover what had been lost for over a millennium in Europe.

Naturalism in Northern European Art

If the paintings of Masaccio and the architecture of Brunelleschi can be said to have epitomized the goals and aspirations of early fifteenth-century Florentine society, it can be claimed that the painter Jan van Eyck (c. 1390–1441) likewise captured the spirit of northern Europe during the period — with very different results. Consider one such image, his famous *Arnolfini Marriage* (Fig. **4.27**) painted in 1434, roughly contemporary with Masaccio's paintings. (Arnolfini was an Italian merchant attached to the Medici bank in the Netherlands which gives an idea of the prominence of Florentine banks throughout the continent.) From this example, it is obvious that very different artistic conditions prevailed in the northern centers that had little obvious reference to the aspirations of the south.

Unlike Masaccio's idealization of form and composition, evident in his *Holy Trinity*, (see Fig. 4.20), van Eyck's painting gives paramount emphasis to minute observation. Van Eyck studiously described the natural world with a precision unparalleled during the age. Art historians such as E. H. Gombrich have claimed that van Eyck saw art as a mirror of nature, in which faithful reproduction of all its intricacies was necessary to capture the wonder of creation. In the painting of the wedding portrait of the Arnolfini, van Eyck reflected this interpretation of northern art as a mimic of the natural world. Everything from the fur trim of the cloaks to the wood paneling speaks of close observation. Though different in approach from the rigid compositional harmonies of Masaccio's *Holy Trinity*, it nonetheless marks a departure from the earlier Gothic styles at that time still prevalent in the North. Van Eyck's delicate manner of observing and then transcribing the most seemingly insignificant features of clothing and ornament should lead one to believe that there were specific reasons why he and other northern European artists adopted such a manner of painting, and this was the case.

In the thirteenth century, the establishment of universities meant that texts once hidden away in monasteries were circulating to a wider public. This led to an increased interest not only in ancient scientists and philosophers but also in the form of illustration that ornamented these texts. The result was the emergence of a pictorial style very similar to the aims of the monastic artists of the past: intricate, complex arrangements with an eye for detail and a delightful vibrancy of color — all of which had a tremendous effect on the artists of the day. Unlike their contemporaries in the south, in cities such as Florence, ideal forms (based on Platonic scholarship) were less important than considerations such as ornamentation and empiricism.

◄ **4.27 Jan Van Eyck**
Arnolfini Marriage (Giovanni Arnolfini and His Bride) 1434
Oil on panel
32¼ x 23½ in (81.9 x 59.7 cm)
National Gallery, London

■ **4.28 Limbourg Brothers**
Crucifixion in the Darkness of an Eclipse
From the *Très Riches Heures du Duc de Berry* c. 1416
Tempera on vellum
11⅜ x 8¼ in (29 x 21 cm)
Musée Condé, Chantilly, France

There are, of course, reasons for this difference in sensibility between northern and southern centers. One issue was the popularity of Classical Antiquity within the communities; though it was embraced in Italy, northern intellectuals and artists appear to have been less convinced of its merits. This in turn probably reflected centuries of monastic learning, based on the study of logic, mathematics, and rhetoric that propelled northern Europe towards a more grounded metaphysics — traits that found their visual equivalent in the highly observed, naturalistic paintings of the period. Further, unlike Italy, in the north there was no tradition of large-scale **fresco** work (due to the practical considerations of moisture, light, and climate). This relative absence of painting, other than in manuscript illustration, meant that northerners preferred the more precise manuscript techniques.

An outstanding example of this identifiably northern preoccupation with ornamentation and keen observation is the *Très Riches Heures du Duc de Berry* (Fig. **4.28**), a manuscript of 130 images painted by the Limbourg brothers sometime before 1416. In the remarkable *Crucifixion in the Darkness of an Eclipse*, an image that measures little more than this page, the artists rendered the subtle personal interactions and extreme pathos of the Crucifixion in a manner that is both natural and jewel-like. The result is a world in microcosm.

The high degree of naturalism in northern painting had other, perhaps less obvious, associations, the most important of which was rise of *symbolic content*. By placing a profound faith in the observable world, northern artists and intellectuals alike implied that God was manifest not only in biblical narratives but in the very nature he created. Thus items as diverse as flowers, food, even insects were worthy of consideration, since, at least by implication, they suggested God's design. Inevitably, this process led to the development of a complex array of symbolism, in which elements from the natural world came to replace traditional narrative sequences in the telling of stories. In this way, a picture of a landscape could be read both for its apparent lifelikeness and its symbolic content. This process of replacement or "standing in for" is called *metaphor*, and it once again suggests that pictorial developments are part of a larger set of issues that surround the art making process.

■ 4.29 Robert Campin, Triptych of the *Annunciation* c. 1425–30 center panel, The Annunciation; left wing, Kneeling Donors; right wing, Joseph in His Workshop. Oil on wood, center panel 25¼ x 24⅞ in (64.1 x 63.2 cm). Each wing 25⅜ x 10¾ in (64.5 x 27.3 cm) The Metropolitan Museum of Art, New York. The Cloisters Collection, 1956 (56.70)

It is possible to recognize this development of complex, symbolism in the *Annunciation* (Fig. **4.29**) by Robert Campin (1378/9–1444), which dates to 1425–30. The most striking factor in this image is its vivid clarity, as if every element were the subject of careful meditation. In particular, the careful description of light and shade, and the weightiness of even the shadows, suggests that the act of looking took precedence over all other pictorial concerns. This is a sensibility different from that of, say, Masaccio (roughly a contemporary), who constructed pictorial space in his work to conform to a geometrically derived system — namely linear perspective. The result is a sometimes truncated, unpredictable space in Campin's *Annunciation*, yet one in which every component is given equal visual weight.

One result of this certain clarity of description is that the eye races across the surface of the painting in search of meanings, moving from item to item as if each were an important component of the story — as it is. Take for instance the lily on the table: it has three flowers, two open, one about to bloom, suggesting the Trinity (Father, Son, and Holy Spirit), with Jesus (Son), whose birth is the subject of this sacred "announcement," yet to flower. The plume of smoke that rises from the extinguished candle likewise tells a story: it suggests both a specific moment in time and also a holy presence. Light is a symbol of God, and in this sense the announcement of Christ's coming into the world provides the possibility of divine illumination (witnessed by the small Christ form that enters the room from the top left as a ray of light). There is also the possibility of the candle's being a wedding candle, in which case its extinguishing suggests that the marriage (of Mary and the Holy Spirit) has been consummated.

Such multiple interpretations of objects exponentially enrich these paintings, yet their effectiveness as symbols lies very much in the way in which viewers experience these highly naturalistic scenes. The degree of detail provided in objects brings an inevitable degree of focus or attention to them; they become players in a story rather than props in a scene. In other words, the quality of the painting plays an integral part in how one sees, and consequently understands, the picture's meanings.

Oil Painting

Though the invention of oil paint is still hotly debated, many scholars credit van Eyck with being the first documented painter to use oil as a binder for his pigments. Before this time, artists typically ground their colors (usually derived from various minerals or vegetal roots) and then added a liquid substance to bind the mess together and create a fluid material. The choice binder of the time was egg yolk, the viscosity of which made the paint opaque; it was also quick drying. This meant that subtle blendings and glazes of color were for all intents and purposes impossible. Instead, tempera was usually applied in a series of linear cross-hatchings, one color on top of another (Fig. **4.30**). The resulting paint, while brilliant in color, often lacked subtlety.

Van Eyck must have been dissatisfied by the speed of the drying process — perhaps because it did not allow an artist the time to blend colors successfully or create luminous effects. The solution was not particularly earthshattering: he simply replaced the egg yolk with a binder that had a slower drying time, which enabled the artist to work over an area for days instead of minutes. The suspension of the ground pigment in the translucent oil medium further increased the intensity of the colors, in that it allowed light to penetrate the surface and reflect the various underlayers of paint. The result was work that possessed a closer perceptual intensity to one's experience of nature, and painting that could now embrace a very wide array of subtle differences and fluctuations (Fig. **4.31**).

■ **4.30 Detail of Cimabue's** *Madonna Enthroned* 1280–90 showing handling of tempera paint

■ **4.31 Detail of Van Eyck's** *Arnolfini Marriage* 1434 showing oil paint technique

ART PATRONAGE AND THE HIGH RENAISSANCE

The rise of individual wealth throughout Europe during the fifteen century had an important influence on the course of art making in the Renaissance. After centuries of artists' working directly with the Church or state, now private citizens began to commission art projects as a way of solidifying their social, and sometimes even moral, position in the community. Often such families also possessed enormous political influence, and as a result much of the patronage granted to many of the Renaissance's most influential artists was tied in some way to the success of such figures in the marketplace and in government. One such family was the Medici, who between the years 1434 and 1492 controlled the city-state of Florence through a combination of political expertise and financial prowess, thanks to their highly profitable banking company.

The first member of the family to rise to prominence was Cosimo de' Medici (1389–1464), who held power from 1434 to 1464. Cosimo reaped the significant benefits of a prosperous banking enterprise and was able to secure for himself the very best scholars and teachers to cultivate his interests in the humanities. Of the many studies pursued during the period, Classical philosophy played a decisive role in later events — and in particular the neglected works of Plato. Finding Platonic scholarship almost non-existent in the city at the time, Cosimo enticed some of Constantinople's most brilliant scholars to Florence with offers of good pay, decent lodgings, and a safe haven from the dangers of the East. He funded a new Chair in Greek at Florence's "Stadium" (university). Thanks to this all-important economic boost, Platonism became a dominant artistic and philosophical force amongst the city's élite — an influence that would determine the path of much of future art theory.

The Medici are perhaps best known for their patronage of the arts. Cosimo was the first of the Medici rulers to fund elaborate commissions, the results of which both beautified the city and possibly assuaged some of the guilt that Christians associated with usury. Cosimo had a particular fondness for sculptural projects and the result was a long and profitable relationship with one of the great sculptors of the age, Donato di Niccolo Betto Bardi, better known as Donatello.

Donatello

Donatello (c. 1386–1466) was a prolific sculptor, and his work offers an insight into the state of sculpture in the middle of the fifteenth century. Though art in the round posed problems very different from those of two-dimensional images, there were certain unmistakable parallels in sensibility beginning to emerge between the two forms. During the Middle Ages, sculptural projects were often seen as simple extensions of architecture, and as in much of the painting at the time, emphasis was placed on legibility and decoration over naturalism — which was seen as a vain attempt to duplicate the perfections of God. With the rekindled interest in the idea of universal laws that govern the natural world (a popular preoccupation with many in the increasingly Platonic Florentine intelligentsia), sculpture began to move back toward a more naturalistic three-dimensional format.

One of Donatello's earliest attempts to integrate such ideas into carved stone was his *St. George* (Fig. **4.32**) of 1415–17. Conceived as a niche sculpture, it was probably never intended to be viewed from all sides, thus the frontal nature of the work can be attributed more to the specifics of the commission than to any omission on the artist's part. Yet note the monumental sense of volume and mass the figure possesses. Further, the proportions of the figure suggest a keen observation of nature and anatomy rather than a reliance on traditional graphic equivalents, which tended to schematize the figure for the demands of legibility. In essence, Donatello effectively produced a work that unified Christian subject matter with the sculptural traditions of antiquity — a reasonable aspiration for such an avid participant in the weekly discussions on Classical thought initiated by his patron, Cosimo de' Medici, during the early years of his rule.

Many historians consider the bronze sculpture of *David* (Fig. **4.33**) of c. 1432 to be Donatello's most important work. Created with the intention of being seen from all sides, this figure, like Giotto's painted equivalents, was liberated from the confines of past decorum. In this work, the gesture itself was a dramatic departure of some historical note. The swinging of the hip — the so-called **contrapposto** pose already encountered in the *Doryphorus* (see Fig. 2.27) — engages one leg while resting the other, and it gives the impression of deliberate confidence and

■ 4.33 Donatello
David c. 1432
Bronze
Height 5 ft 2½ in (1.58 m)
Museo Nazionale del Bargello, Florence

■ 4.34 Sandro Botticelli
Birth of Venus c. 1482
Tempera on canvas
5 ft 7⁄8 in x 9 ft 1½ in (1.75 x 2.78 m)
Uffizi Gallery, Florence

grace. There is an undeniable celebration of the human figure implicit within this work; its convincing gesture and sensuous modeling produce a dynamic image of young virility and heroic defiance. It is also difficult to miss the rather provocative sexuality in this piece; it neatly parallels the steady decline of medieval prudery in favor of the body as the center of consciousness — and the attainment of pleasure as a worthwhile pursuit. There is little in the history of Christian art before this period to compare with the ease and sensuousness of Donatello's *David*, and it points to a crossroads in a religion that by the end of the Renaissance found itself severely compromised by its importation of other popular views.

Botticelli

Cosimo de' Medici died in August 1464, leaving the leadership of the city in the hands of his son Piero, who himself lived only another five years. The short period of Piero's rule was beset by political tensions, and thus emphasis was placed more on the Medici family's survival than on celebrating a city and a culture through its often generous art patronage. There was, however, one artist of some considerable note who came to prominence during Piero's term in office — the painter Sandro Botticelli (1445–1510).

Botticelli's reputation flourished under the patronage of Piero's successor, Lorenzo the Magnificent (1449–92), after the former's early death in 1469. The reign of Lorenzo has come to be known as the golden age of Florentine culture, and his death signaled the decline of Florence as the center of the Renaissance. A pragmatic politician and a cultivated patron of the arts, Lorenzo initiated some of the most impressive commissions of any age. This period of intelligent and sympathetic patronage also corresponded with a tremendous amount of artistic activity within the city walls. The result was spectacular.

One of the important works to come out of this invigorating environment was Botticelli's *Birth of Venus* (Fig. **4.34**) of c. 1482. The choice of subject matter was unprecedented in its embrace of Classicism. Although artists of the period were interested in Classical thought, their subject matter remained in the domain of traditional Christianity. However, regardless of the less than religious implications such a painting might have, Botticelli's Venus possesses many of the same pictorial qualities as contemporary religious works. The reason for this is straightforward: by the late fifteenth century, the interest in nature had led many to believe that the Classical myths possessed the same extraordinary wisdom as their great philosophies. Venus, traditionally the bearer of divine beauty to an imperfect world, took on obvious symbolic associations with the Virgin.

Though Church decorum could not accept the portrayal of the Virgin as a nude, the use of Classical myths provided a convenient opportunity to further the growing relationship between Classical idealism and Christian morality. The result was a work that has come to embody the harmonious marriage of Christianity and Classicism, mystery and reason, the sacred and the profane, in the graceful emergence of Venus from the ocean. Botticelli continued to produce these allegories throughout his career, but none equaled the Venus in its embodiment of the dynamic of the age.

Botticelli was but one of many artists of note to benefit from Lorenzo de' Medici's patronage during the late fifteenth century. Two others who enjoyed similar support were Leonardo da Vinci (1452–1519) and Michelangelo Buonarroti (1475–1564), both of whom lived in Florence during the rule of Lorenzo. Together, their works have come to epitomize the Renaissance sensibility in its grandest and most inspired form, and it was in their creations that the era found its greatest expression.

Leonardo da Vinci

Leonardo moved to Florence as a young man and stayed there until 1483, when he was appointed to the court of Milan. Leaving Florence as he did at only thirty years of age, little of his great work had yet been executed, but it remains significant that he passed through the city of Florence when he did, and his work retains many of the interests and pictorial devices then popular in the city. Perhaps the most noteworthy development to come out of Leonardo's early stay in Florence was an interest in linear perspective, which had, by the late fifteenth century, become a predominant concern with many painters. Another important influence in the early development of Leonardo was the centrality of Platonic scholarship, which appears to have deeply affected the subsequent course of the artist's thinking. Together these factors provided the necessary impetus for many of the later discoveries and theories that were to secure his reputation forever as one of the most truly remarkable people of any age.

One of the most striking of all Leonardo's paintings is the *Virgin of the Rocks* (Fig. **4.35**) of c. 1484. Almost immediately, one is struck by the developed sense of illusionism within the confines of the picture plane. The organic landscape and naturalistic interior combine to give the piece a deep, mysterious space without the static and often awkward reliance on perspective lines (as noted in Uccello's *Rout of San Romano* [see Fig. 4.23]). Through keen observation, Leonardo was able to note such perceptual subtleties as how objects move toward a more neutral blue-gray as they recede in space, and how images become less clear in the distance. This portrayal of space with regard to these rather elementary observations is called **atmospheric perspective**, and though now commonplace, only a few artists had yet broken away from the mannerisms of earlier traditions and attempted to harness such findings to their own paintings.

Leonardo da Vinci considered these observations from nature as fundamental to knowledge, and their implementation into art a decisive move toward a more ideal vision. For many, observation provided little of interest outside the most fundamental necessities such as proportion, but for Leonardo the natural world provided the underlying blueprint for the workings of the universe. Since painting had the ability to transform a viewer's experience of the world, the artist was afforded the possibility of contemplating ideals. In other words, since artists did not have to rely exclusively on the visual experience of nature to produce their images, their choice of subject and its presentation granted the viewer special access to a world perhaps closer to a universal truth than that in which they ordinarily existed.

For Leonardo, the power of art lay very much in the basic premise that the artist possessed a privileged and necessary position in the community. This did not

■　4.35　Leonardo da Vinci
Virgin of the Rocks c. 1484
Panel
6 ft 6½ in x 4 ft (1.99 x 1.22 m)
National Gallery, London

■ **4.36 Leonardo da Vinci**
Last Supper c. 1495–8
Mural painting
14 ft x 28 ft 10½ in (4.26 x 8.8 m)
Refectory, S Maria delle Grazie, Milan

necessarily mean that the artist's imagination was in itself authoritative: Leonardo, like many of his contemporaries, abhorred such indulgences as gross vanity. Instead, he placed importance on a correct experiencing of phenomena, from which the viewer could then access the implicit connections and workings of the natural world. The balance between natural observation and artistic license was thus paramount, and in Leonardo's work it finds some of its greatest expressions.

This all-important construction of a painting is perhaps best envisioned in Leonardo's famous *Last Supper* (Fig. **4.36**) of 1495–8. Though the painting stands in a horrid state of disrepair due to dampness and Leonardo's own disposition for experimenting with painting media, the composition remains clear. The scene portrays Christ's presentation of the sacraments and the acknowledgment of his later betrayal at the hands of Judas. The group that congregates around the back of the table part from the central figure at the news, creating a heightened focus on Christ. The various figures are richly modeled and show a keen observation of facial expressions and bodily gestures. However, ultimately this painting's success rests on the pivotal figure of Christ — a compositional arrangement that embodies Leonardo's theoretical standards.

Leonardo positioned Christ as the central figure in this work, in keeping with his divine status and importance to the subject matter. His presentation in the center of the table also corresponds with the central vanishing point for the receding perspective lines that enclose him. A simple experiment will perhaps clarify this concept. Take a straight edge and place it on either of the diagonal lines that are created by the meeting of the side walls with the ceiling. Now draw a line across the image, and then do likewise with the other side, forming an *X* on the painting. You may also do likewise by connecting the lines formed by following the receding diagonals of the top of the various doorways on either side of the table. The axis perspective lines meet at the head of Christ, the vanishing point, the personification of God, the implied universal truth; Jesus thus becomes the origin and center of the world. By utilizing such a mathematical system with consummate skill, Leonardo successfully painted an image of harmony and idealism within Christian dogma.

Michelangelo's Figurative Ideal

Michelangelo Buonarroti was an artist of remarkable versatility, and his accomplishments spanned the disciplines of painting, sculpture, architecture, and poetry. Though most of his important work was executed in Rome after 1505, he produced works of considerable note while he was still in Florence. By far the most influential of all his early work is his heroic depiction of the Old Testament figure *David* (Fig. **4.37**), created between the years 1501 and 1504.

Michelangelo's *David* has long been considered one of the great depictions of ideal beauty. It stands at over three times life size and was carved from a single piece of Carrara marble that had lain unused behind Florence Cathedral for over a century. The clarity of anatomical observation and the grandeur of the pose make clear that Michelangelo was no simple imitator of the earlier Donatello but possessed tremendous skills and sensitive insights into both sculpture and the human condition — issues embodied in the massive stone figure.

The polarities or "dialectic" of existence were a constant point of interest for Renaissance artists and scholars, who attempted to find a single, unified vision that could engage both the Classical and Christian traditions. In the works of Leonardo, this uneasy balance found its parallels in the delicate harmony between naturalism and systems of reason, in keeping with the struggle between experience and faith. The unification of apparent opposites has of course been a part of almost every cultural tradition in the world, witnessed in societies as diverse as those of Taoist Asia (with the symbol of yin and yang) and the Western tradition of the unity of body and soul. Michelangelo's *David* is one such work of art that attempts, within the confines of a single body, to find perfect harmony and equilibrium.

Scholars often talk of the split nature of *David* — his body consciously separated into the *vita activa* and the *vita contemplativa*, the active and the contemplative life. This can be seen by running a vertical line up the middle of the figure, which splits the sculpture into two seemingly separate personas. The right half of the body is the side of action. His strong, outstretched right arm cradles the rock that will kill his enemy, Goliath and make the young warrior king of Israel. His right leg, engaged and holding the considerable physical and psychological weight of his entire

■ **4.37** Michelangelo Buonarroti
David 1501–4
Marble
14 ft 3 in (4.34 m)
Galleria dell'Accademia, Florence

body, again echoes the necessity of brute action. The right side is the foundation of David's existence, as it visually supports his upright, living posture. The left side does much the opposite. The left arm gently holds the sling over his shoulder, relaxing the very instrument of action (and in this case of death) in that eternal moment of thought. The left leg, free of the weight of activity that bears down so heavily upon the *vita activa*, is left forever weightless. The result is a vivid personification of an era, and its contrapposto gesture subsequently came to symbolize the body in perfect harmony.

THE "HIGH" RENAISSANCE IN ROME

During the fifteenth century, the papacy consolidated its religious authority after surviving nearly two centuries of rather shaky existence, and by the turn of the century, it again possessed the resources to commission large, expensive art projects. These works were seen as glorious reassertions of the Church's dignity and authority over its people, and its importance demanded the attention of only the best artists. With his reputation already established, the young Michelangelo was summoned to Rome from his Florentine home in 1505 for the greater glory of the Church.

Pope Julius II, concerned with his rapidly declining health and convinced that he deserved a magnificent tomb, commissioned Michelangelo to produce a lavish future resting place for his bones. The project was never completed, but the offer of working on such an elaborate sculptural commission was enough to entice the artist to the Holy City. Little did he know at the time that most of his days were to be spent on major painting projects that he neither liked nor wanted. It was with this disposition that the sculptor was virtually commanded to begin his most famous work — the ceiling of the Sistine Chapel in the Vatican (Fig. **4.38**). It is claimed that when Michelangelo caught word that he was being ordered to spend the next four years of his life painting a ceiling, he immediately fled Rome, only to be brought back by a papal edict. He miraculously finished the entire 131 x 41 ft (39.9 x 12.5 m) ceiling in less than four years — with virtually no assistance.

In general, social, economic, and political circumstances play an important role in shaping, and even determining, the standards of quality on which a particular work is judged, but in approaching the work of the Sistine Chapel ceiling, even the most skeptical of social historians cannot help but be reminded of the will and determination of the human spirit that seems to stand apart from the most considered of theories and explanations. The Sistine ceiling is a monument to Michelangelo's tenacity and perseverance, and it is a reminder of the intangibles that so modestly inspire important and influential works.

The art historical problems surrounding the Sistine ceiling are perhaps too numerous to be of much use in such a brief discussion, but its iconography does help to illuminate the artist's disposition toward his subject matter. Though extremely difficult to describe, the basis of the iconography of the work is threefold: the ancestry of Christ, Old Testament and pagan prophecies of Christ's coming, and scenes from the creation of Man and other stories from Genesis. The figures are the rough two-dimensional equivalents of Michelangelo's earlier *David*, but his obvious exaggeration of much of the anatomy is not altogether incompatible with his sculptural work (Fig. **4.39**). Such abstractions were probably Michelangelo's way of compensating for the height and awkward character of the ceiling surface, which called for more dramatic and legible figure-types. In any case, the overall effect is one of heroic grandeur and herculean will. The most famous of these images is the *Creation of Adam* (Fig. **4.40**), which occupies the central position in the intricate composition. The concentration of the entire composition upon a single, energized space that weaves between the outstretched fingers of God and Adam is without doubt one of the most poignant and dramatic "pauses" in all art.

■ 4.38 Michelangelo Buonarroti
Sistine Chapel ceiling (after cleaning), the Vatican, Rome, 1508–12
Fresco, total 131 ft x 41 ft (39.9 x 12.5 m)
© Nippon Television Network Corporation, Tokyo, 1995

1 Ezekiel
2 Creation of Eve
3 Cumaean Sibyl
4 Creation of Adam
5 Persian Sibyl
6 God Separates the Water and Earth and Blesses his Work
7 Daniel
8 God Creates the Sun and the Moon and Plants on Earth
9 Jeremiah
10 God Separates Light and Darkness
11 Libyan Sibyl
a Lunettes above the windows with portraits of the ancestors of Christ and scenes from the Old Testament

▼ 4.40 Michelangelo Buonarroti *Creation of Adam*
Detail from the Sistine Chapel ceiling (after cleaning), the Vatican, Rome, 1508–12
© Nippon Television Network Corporation, Tokyo, 1995

▲ 4.39 Michelangelo Buonarroti
Detail of lunette after restoration
Sistine Chapel ceiling 1508–12
The Vatican, Rome

Raphael

While the melancholic genius of Michelangelo wrestled away the years between 1508 and 1512 suspended many feet above the Sistine Chapel, there was another artist in the same Vatican complex whose name was to become synonymous with great painting. Raffaello Sanzio, called Raphael (1483–1520), was born in Urbino and trained at the court of the Duke of Urbino before moving on to Florence in 1505. There he produced several accomplished pictures of the Madonna and other saints, such as his early *St. Catherine of Alexandria* (Fig. **4.41**) of 1507. Though there is an indebtedness to Leonardo in Raphael's description of the landscape background, the work displays an emotional sensitivity and quiet

■ 4.41 Raphael
St. Catherine of Alexandria
c. 1507
Oil on panel
National Gallery, London

■ 4.42 Raphael
School of Athens 1508
Fresco
26 ft x 18 ft (7.92 x 5.49 m)
Stanza della Segnatura, Rome

tenderness all his own. In Raphael's work, even at this early point, the ideal had become a psychological embodiment, in which subjects possess not only the physical attributes of beauty but also the emotional characteristics of inner harmony. It is this remarkable depiction of solemnity and dignity that has endeared Raphael to so many viewers for nearly five centuries.

In 1508, Raphael moved to Rome where he soon found favor at the court of Julius II. Among the works he was commissioned to produce for various rooms in the Vatican, the best known were executed for the library. The *School of Athens* (Fig. **4.42**) of 1508 is one

of four frescoes that decorate the walls of the Stanza della Segnatura (where important documents were signed), and it stands alongside other depictions of the great passions of the age: law, poetry, and theology. It is a homage to the Classical philosophical tradition, anchored by the towering figures of Plato and Aristotle, who stand together in the center of the composition. Plato (on the left) strides forward while pointing to the heavens — a reference to his belief in ideal forms. He is flanked by Aristotle, whose downward-pointing hand is a visual reminder of his steadfast belief that all knowledge is based in observation

Fresco

The term *fresco* has been used throughout much of this chapter in reference to painting — a material process by which the likes of Giotto, Michelangelo, and Raphael produced their most important work. But what exactly is fresco? And how does it differ from other forms of painting? It is the process of painting water-immersed pigments onto wet, freshly prepared lime plaster. Though it is common to think specifically of the Renaissance when discussing this practice, the technique had been known to artists of different cultures for many years and is thought to have evolved from processes used in Byzantine mosaic work. Recent archaeological evidence from India now verifies that the painting of pigments onto wet plaster is well over 3,000 years old.

Fresco painting has long been favored as a technique by painters. First, the drying of the colored pigments into the plaster makes for an extremely solid bond, literally embedding color into the ceiling or wall and drying rockhard. A second practical consideration is the matt finish of the dry colored plaster, which allows for a surface free of the glare and reflection commonly associated with oil painting. This is particularly handy when producing an image on a wall or a ceiling that will be viewed from a number of angles, where different light sources often pose reflection problems. Another handy feature of the technique is that, once dry, the image is part of the wall rather than a painting on its surface and can be washed without losing much of its initial impact. There is, however, a downside to this attribute: such large painting surfaces usually come into contact with all sorts of atmospheric pollutants from candlesmoke to car exhaust, all of which significantly damage the fresco surface.

Both Raphael and Michelangelo used fresco in a manner typical of most artists. The seams of each day's plaster application are still visible in these works, and they give interesting insights into the remarkable proficiency of these artists in producing such stunning details and luminous color effects over a very short period of time. Unlike a painter in oils, who has the leisure to reconsider and rework ideas over a period of days or even months, the true fresco painter has only a few hours. Once the color is in the plaster, it is there for good (short of chiseling the initial painting off the ceiling or wall).

There were, however, in use two adaptations of the traditional practice of fresco painting that became increasingly popular during the period: *lime water* and *secco*. Lime water is a clear water mixed with a very small amount of plaster. This solution is then mixed with the pigment to produce a more chalky or pastel-like color. By varying the palette between lime-water and clear water, the artist is able to achieve a greater degree of subtlety than in traditional fresco. The other technique, secco, refers to the application of color on dry plaster. Though Michelangelo used this additional aid sparingly, it allowed for the intensification of a color area after the initial plaster had taken hold. It takes a confident painter to execute imaginative and inventive work in fresco, and these artists' skill in producing such lively work under such decidedly harsh conditions only reiterates the notion of a sizable talent.

(empiricism). Both the environment and its figures are heroic, and the work demonstrates the breadth of Raphael's skill as both a draftsperson and an imaginative thinker. It is also one of the most convincing and seemingly natural depictions of space using one-point perspective to emerge during the period, a feat of technical brilliance that further concentrates the viewer's attention on the deep space in which these figures interact.

Architecture

There was a spirit of expansion and grandeur in the Rome of the early sixteenth century that did not end in painting. Several commissions attracted considerable interest, but perhaps, none more so than the scheduled rebuilding of St. Peter's. The Old St. Peter's Basilica, originally built during Constantine's rule, had, by the late fifteenth century, fallen into poor repair. Centuries of neglect had diminished the beauty of the structure, and it became apparent that a new basilica was desperately needed to restore the image of the Church. In 1506 the architect Donato Bramante (1444–1514) was awarded the prestigious commission, but he died many years before the final, compromised completion of the project.

Bramante envisioned the focal church of Christendom as having a domed central plan (Fig. **4.43**). Such a form paid visual homage to the great building projects of antiquity, and Bramante was particularly inspired by the famous Pantheon (see Fig. 2.44); its proximity to the Vatican allowed for vivid comparisons. The architect also had the good fortune to learn from Brunelleschi's important engineering advances in dome construction that had enabled the earlier completion of Florence Cathedral. The overall impression was one of a deliberate evocation of the antique within the context of the new humanistic Church. In fact, the only "leftover" from earlier Romanesque and medieval structural plans was the stabilizing Greek cross floor plan — a form that suggests that the institution of the Church (the building proper) rests squarely on the foundations of faith (the cruciform foundation).

Bramante's intentions are now known only through drawings, since the actual building was never completed as designed. However, his vision of a harmonious and fully integrated architecture does live down to this day in his engaging Tempietto

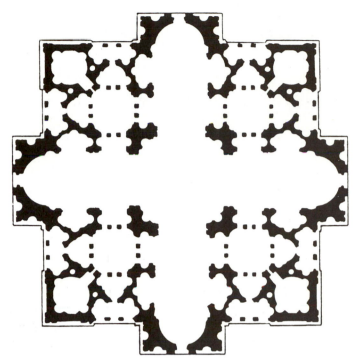

■ 4.43 Donato Bramante
Floor plan for the new St. Peter's
Basilica, Rome 1506

returned to Bramante's centralized basilica design, which indicates that even late in his life Michelangelo still had a strong affection for the virtues of **symmetry** and balance. His greatest contribution to the project was the dome (Fig. **4.45** on page 210) — an immense structure he lived to see completed (something unknown in previous centuries, when a lack of engineering techniques made such projects span many lifetimes). St. Peter's was to undergo a series of other design alterations, including the construction by Carlo Maderna (1556–1629) of a long nave and elaborate entrance in 1606, and finally the execution of the piazza by Gianlorenzo Bernini (1598–1680) in 1663 (see Fig. 5.21). The result is a structure that embodies not one but several sensibilities and interests. Though the simple design first initiated by Bramante became all but lost in the trappings of other ages, the basilica proper remains a monument to the marriage of humanism and Christianity, and to an era's quest for harmony and equilibrium.

■ 4.44 Donato Bramante
Tempietto completed after 1511
San Pietro in Montorio, Rome

(Fig. **4.44**), the "Little Temple" authorized in 1502 and completed after 1511. Here, many of the same issues are reiterated in the Classically derived, domed structure. The building is of some art historical significance in that it was one of the first such structures to be designed and carried out with strict regard to Classical building principles. It likewise exhibits the characteristic Renaissance qualities of symmetry, balance, simple design, and a harmonious interplay between parts. If Michelangelo and Raphael can be said to have embodied the Renaissance spirit in painting and sculpture, it is to Bramante that one must turn when considering architecture.

Almost as soon as Bramante was dead, his basic central design for St. Peter's was altered. Several important artists were assigned to the project over the next years, including Raphael and a talented designer named Giuliano da Sangallo (1443–1516), who added a long nave and some side aisles to Bramante's plan. The result was a break with his centralized Greek cross foundation, relying on a more traditional Latin cross design.

In 1546 Michelangelo assumed control of the project. He found Sangallo's additions intolerable and was given permission to rework the plans. He

■ **4.45** View of St. Peter's, Rome, begun 1546

ART CRITICISM IN THE RENAISSANCE: VASARI

One of the most important literary documents of the Renaissance period and its art is a text called *Lives of the Most Eminent Painters, Sculptors and Architects* (first edition 1550, second edition 1568), written by the painter and architect Giorgio Vasari (1511–74). In this classic text, Vasari discussed the rise of Antique Classicism in Renaissance Italy and provided some interesting insights into the lives of many of the most important artists of the day. As a document of its time, it is unique.

Vasari saw his era (sixteenth-century Italy) as the artistic culmination of experiments that had been taking place since Giotto and his first attempts to construct space on a two-dimensional plane. According

to Vasari, before Giotto there was only the black hole of the Middle Ages, a period of cultural decline from the "Golden Age" of Antiquity. It is clear that Vasari, like most of his contemporaries, embraced Classicism and its humanistic values as necessary points of departure for great art. It also provides a clear indication of the period's bias against the artistic goals and aspirations of the Middle Ages (and, in Vasari's words, "its indifference to fame"), despite the era's significant achievements. Vasari described the development of Renaissance art as a series of technical and intellectual achievements leading up to Leonardo da Vinci, whose pivotal innovations signaled the end of experimentation and the beginning of what Vasari described as "perfection in our own times" — a perfection manifest in the work of Michelangelo.

Like many of his contemporaries, Vasari embraced an art that placed the humanistic values of individualism, idealism, and synthesis above all else. Predictably, this premise had ramifications for the artistic persona. As translator of these established "truths" in visual form, the Renaissance artist was not merely a craftsperson involved exclusively with technique but a thinker of the highest caliber. Vasari clearly supported this notion and took great pains to describe the significant artists of the period as within the realm of genius, rather than simply illustrators or carvers.

The most significant institutional manifestation of this trend towards the intellectualization of artistic practice came in the establishment of the Florence Academy of Design in 1563. Vasari was instrumental in promoting the idea of a school for artists and is known to have been supportive of the Academy. Here, in what amounted to a liberal arts environment, artists were encouraged to study Classical texts and ideas as well as their technical exercises. This institution, together with Vasari's insightful, sometimes dubious and always enchanting writing, suggests a cultural climate very much in flux during the sixteenth century, and one with huge significance for later art.

PAINTING IN VENICE IN THE SIXTEENTH CENTURY

Rome was not the only Italian city to enjoy prosperity during the sixteenth century; the port republic of Venice also flourished as a result of recent advances in shipping and trade. Venice was the gateway to the East, and it supplied much of inland Europe with an assortment of items from abroad. Also, improvements in rudder-steering techniques and navigational aids had enabled the Venetian merchant marine to travel to what were once thought impossible destinations such as America and the Orient. The result was tremendous economic and political growth, which in turn attracted many artists to Venice in search of patronage.

During the early sixteenth century, Venice was the richest, most productive, and most heavily populated city in Italy. There appears to have been an abundance of commissions available to artists during this period, and art became highly influenced by the diverse historical background of the city. Venice had perhaps the closest relationship to the northern centers of commerce of any of the Italian cities, thanks predominantly to its trade connections. The city also received an influx of Eastern artistic styles, including icon painting from Constantinople. The result of such diverse influences was a keen interest in color — an element in painting that was secondary to the principles of linear perspective and compositional clarity in the courts of Florence and Rome. Both the medieval North and the Byzantine East had a legacy of rich coloration in their art, and Venice's proximity to such

images had a significant influence on tastes in painting. This issue was pushed even further by the overwhelming use of the new medium of oil by prominent Venetian painters.

Oil paint, a technical development out of early fifteenth-century Flanders, had made its way via the trade routes to Venice by the middle of the century. This new material was ideally suited to the needs of the Venetians, who had great difficulty in maintaining fresco paintings because of the damp conditions that prevailed in their "floating city." The plaster content in fresco did not dry effectively in such conditions, and the results were paintings of little quality and almost no longevity. Oil paint, on the other hand, could withstand damp conditions without much damage. When this practical consideration was combined with a historical disposition toward highly saturated color, the result was the emergence of a particular brand of painting quite unlike that of either Florence or Rome.

The term "sensuous" has often been used to describe Venetian artists' painting, and it refers to the dynamic play of light and color on the surfaces of observed objects. Many have speculated that this textural interest in light derived from Venice's proximity to the sea and the unpredictable effects of reflections on colored surfaces that often illuminate the city. This may indeed have had an unconscious effect on Venetian painting.

Though light had played a part in the modeling of

■ **4.46** Titian, *Le Concert Champêtre* c. 1505
Oil on canvas, approx. 3 ft 7¼ in x 4 ft 6¼ in (1.09 x 1.37 m)
Louvre, Paris

forms in both Roman and Florentine painting, it was held to be of less significance than clear linear design and ideal proportion. The evolution of the liberated figure from its flat surface has interesting parallels with the elevation of individuality during the rise of the Renaissance — ideas that germinated alongside the idealist philosophy. Venice's interest in such matters was always tempered by a more northern preoccupation with the minute observation of nature derived initially from a medieval fascination with the empiricism of Aristotle. This led to an interest in details such as texture and bold color that were perhaps too harsh or discordant for those not used to such a Venetian sensibility. It is within this context that the painter Titian made his break with past interests, using light to interject a degree of subjectivity in the observable world.

Titian

Tiziano Vecellio (c. 1488–1576), known as Titian, was by far the most prolific and traveled of the port city's painters, and his work capably embodies the Venetian style. He is best known for his sparkling use of light and color, attributes very much in evidence in his *Concert Champêtre* (c. 1505; Fig. **4.46**). There is an undeniable subjectivity in this work that is very different from the paintings of, say, Raphael, and it speaks of a view of individuality rooted in the North.

The Venetian style appears plainly in Titian's *Death of Actaeon* (Fig. **4.47**), painted late in his career. Initially, it appears quite unlike other paintings of the age. The coloration is subtle yet saturated, and the figures are rendered with more consideration of their immediate environment than of any specific convention such as proportion. Perhaps most importantly, there is a tangible playfulness and lyricism to the work; the painting is firmly committed to the interrelationships between paint handling, color, and the dramatic effects of light upon objects. Few painters during the era handled paint with the freedom and spontaneity exhibited by Titian, and the result was a degree of unity between the medium (oil paint) and the personality of natural daylight — both could caress surfaces while breaking down the materiality of other objects by their sheer intensity. (If you need proof of this, place an item in front of the sun and attempt to study its outline. You will quickly note how the rays of the sun affect your ability to perceive the object — a phenomenon commonly referred to as *halation*.) The *Death of Actaeon* is a good example of this warm bathing light, a light that is transformed into an almost physical entity by Titian's paint.

■ 4.47 Titian, *Death of Actaeon* c. 1560
Oil on canvas, 5 ft 10¼ in x 6 ft 6 in (1.78 x 1.98 m)
National Gallery, London

NORTHERN EUROPEAN PAINTING IN THE HIGH RENAISSANCE

Though the Renaissance ideals of harmony, individuality, and humanism may seem to have melded perfectly with the aspirations and interests of the Italian states of the fifteenth and sixteenth centuries, sometimes dramatic cultural differences prevented the northern European centers from embracing such issues wholesale. Instead, the so-called Renaissance "ideals" were tempered by a long northern tradition of piety, restraint, and suspicion — developed through the severity of the Middle Ages. By the end of the fifteenth century, political and religious dissent were already beginning to make possible a very different artistic path for the North.

Throughout the Renaissance, the northern centers (those to the north of the Alps) provided a sympathetic intellectual climate for some of the more important scientific studies of the age — a climate that also embodied such attitudes in its art. Like the Venetian character of Titian's art, the North's passionate interest in the sciences can be traced back to a general respect for Aristotle's empirical methods, popular in the monasteries and universities of the Middle Ages. Fundamental to such a doctrine was the belief that all inquiry and learning should be based on valid observations of nature, and on the practical application and testing of hypotheses through experiments. Thus throughout the Middle Ages, many artists and scientists were drawn to observed experience, and such fundamental attitudes were inevitably reflected in their activities.

Dürer

Any survey of Renaissance art would be incomplete without a discussion of the accomplishments of the German artist Albrecht Dürer (1471–1528). An artist of tremendous range and technical skill, Dürer executed a body of work that reflects a competence in both painting and printmaking.

Trained as a wood engraver, Dürer found himself very much at ease with the often limiting constraints of that form of printmaking □. Considering the tedious labor and obvious limits imposed by such a primitive process, Dürer's *Christ Bearing the Cross* (Fig. **4.49**) is a remarkable feat. With works such as this, Dürer revolutionized printmaking to the point at which it possessed a strength of vision usually confined to painting. Further, his use of a reproducible process for the generation of images (in effect making multiples of what was once a unique image) enabled his works to travel freely throughout Europe, quickly establishing his reputation as a master draftsperson.

The rise of printing processes in the fifteenth century also coincided with the growing religious and social unrest in the North that culminated in the Reformation. Dürer's prints were popular among many of the same northern clergy who within a few decades found themselves forever severed from the Catholic Church. The print had a wonderfully democratic side, as images could be easily read, interpreted, and even discussed by groups with little or no access to great art. In this regard, the reformer Martin Luther's written texts and Dürer's prints can be seen as parallel visions in bringing doctrine to the masses.

Dürer's paintings from around the turn of the century share many of the painstaking qualities of his printed works, but the greater subtleties and color afforded by oil paint allowed for depictions of even greater psychological depth. There resulted works such as the provocative *Self Portrait* (Fig. **4.50**) of 1500, which immediately resonates as a rather striking resemblance to the stereotyped medieval image of Christ. This parallel was obviously intentional, for Dürer went to great lengths to depict himself in a typically Christ-like frontal pose with solemn gaze — features usually associated with the mystery of Jesus's sacrifice. This may give some indication of Dürer's faith in the sacredness of the art activity; like many in the Renaissance, he believed in the power of images as a source of contemplation and greater truth, and as a result, he too celebrated the special character of the artist. However, the German artist also grew up in a cultural environment that envisioned artists as faithful and humble reproducers of God's world and his abundant creations. The merging of these contradictory positions explains the strange transformation of personality that takes place in the portrait — the genius of artistic creation tempered by a will to servility. Given this dynamic, Dürer's art may be viewed as exuberance tempered by a lonely relationship to faith; a character-type that found many a kindred spirit in the Renaissance in the North.

Dürer was one of several northern artists who took an interest in the artistic developments in Italy. Between 1505 and 1507, he traveled to Venice, where it appears he was involved in many a lively debate on aspects of contemporary art theory and the technical subtleties of perspective. Though Dürer was understandably impressed by Venetian painting, he later returned home to concentrate more fully on his printed works.

FOCUS ON

Woodcut, Wood and Metal Engraving

Woodcut is a relief printing process in which a print is made by carving away the areas of a wood block which are not to be printed and inking the remaining relief surfaces. Next a piece of paper is placed on top and when pressure is applied across its surface the image is transferred. When the endgrain rather than a lengthwise slab of wood is cut, the process is called wood engraving.

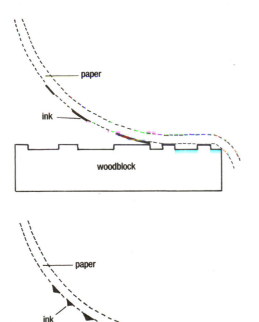

■ **4.48 Diagrams of woodcut (*above*) and metal engraving (*below*) techniques**

In metal engraving a multiple of an image is produced by scoring a metal plate with a burin to create lines. Ink is rubbed into the scored surface and dampened paper is then pressed against the surface, pushing the paper into the ink filled troughs which creates the print.

■ **4.49 Albrecht Dürer, *Christ Bearing the Cross* 1498–9
Woodcut
British Museum, London**

Perhaps the greatest of Dürer's late works is the engraving depicting a *Knight, Death, and the Devil* (Fig. **4.51**) of 1513. Here the considerable technical prowess of the artist reached full maturity in the subtle transitions of tone from deep black through the lightest grays, giving the print a sense of depth and volume usually associated with painting. In **metal engraving**, Dürer did not have the benefit of drawing directly on the surface of the plate and then carving away the waste (as in woodcut or wood engraving). Instead, he relied solely on his vision, creating the composition in reverse (so that it would print the right way round), using nothing but an awkward engraver's tool called a burin to carve into the surface. Despite the rather formidable odds against achieving such subtleties, Dürer arrived at one of the great depictions of the triumph of will over temptation, typifying a new age and a new attitude.

■   4.50 Albrecht Dürer
Self Portrait 1500
Oil on panel
25 7/8 x 18 7/8 in (65.5 x 47.8 cm)
Alte Pinakothek, Munich

■ 4.51 Albrecht Dürer
Knight, Death, and the Devil 1513
Engraving
9⅝ x 7½ in (24.4 x 19 cm)
The Metropolitan Museum of Art, Harris Brisbane Dick Fund, 1943

■ 4.52 Matthias Grünewald, *Isenheim Altarpiece*, center panel with Crucifixion c. 1510–15
Oil on panel, center panel 8 ft x 10 ft (2.4 x 3 m)
Musée Unterlinden, Colmar

Grünewald

If Dürer can be said to have personified the uneasy balance of sensibilities between northern self-consciousness and Italian humanism, the paintings of the artist known as Grünewald (c. 1470/80–1528) were firmly entrenched in the traditions of the North. Little is known about him — his name is thought to have been Mathis Neithardt-Gothardt, and few of his works survive, but his masterpiece, the *Isenheim Altarpiece* (Fig. **4.52**) of c. 1510–15, remains one of the most captivating and emotional portrayals of the Crucifixion in Western art.

The lack of historical documentation on the artist says much about Grünewald's character. Unlike Dürer, whose whole life is known through his various writings, diaries, and numerous works, Grünewald wrote little, perhaps nothing, and produced only a few works before abandoning painting to fight in the 1525 Peasants' War in Germany. (It is even possible that he stopped producing religious art altogether in his later years, since he sided with a fanatical Protestant sect in the war against Catholicism.) Grünewald's work shows little desire to revolutionize art. In the *Isenheim Altarpiece*, the haunting disposition of an earlier Europe is rediscovered in an only

■ 4.53 Detail from the *Isenheim Altarpiece* c. 1510–15 showing the body and wounds of Christ

vaguely familiar Renaissance guise — its voice punctuated by thoughts of death and forgiveness rather than by the perfections of beauty and harmony. It is the work of an artist who chose freely from current technical innovations but whose intent lay squarely on the shoulders of medieval piety.

A detail from this work (Fig. **4.53**) gives even greater insight into Grünewald's punctuated vision. Here the naturalism of the North is pushed to its logical limits; the green body and the festering wounds speak of death as both awesome and awful. This is certainly not the Renaissance ideal of Michelangelo or Raphael; instead, the body's disintegration provides an interesting counterpoint. From his figures, it is apparent that Grünewald was familiar with both linear perspective and the rendering of volume, but he used them only in so much as they granted him greater emotional clarity. The result is a degree of representation very different from the idealism of Florence and Rome. The centralized Christ is almost twice the scale of the other figures in the scene, and the emphasis on particular body parts as flashpoints of agony is apparent when one compares the hands and feet of Christ with those of Mary. This abstraction of features for expressive ends, like the reworking of the body to fit the interests of art, was of course no less arbitrary or natural than the idealizations of Michelangelo — the cultural mindset was simply different. This form of abstraction drew much of its psychological power from the conventions of earlier medieval art, but the adept modeling and manipulation of light (Renaissance conventions anchored in the liberation of the figure) enabled a far more convincing depiction of suffering and resurrection to be produced.

Bosch

Another artist of considerable imagination and insight during the first years of the sixteenth century was the enigmatic Dutch painter Hieronymus Bosch (c. 1450–1516), whose outlandish depictions of sin and the afterlife remain some of the oddest and most private visions ever produced. His *Garden of Earthly Delights* (Fig. **4.54**) of between 1505 and 1510 is a highly intricate and compulsive description of the sins of the flesh. Like Grünewald, Bosch used naturalism as a base from which to embark on visions both bizarre and moralizing. The distortions of the figure types and

■ 4.54 Hieronymus Bosch
Garden of Earthly Delights triptych 1505–10
Prado, Madrid
Left panel: *Garden of Eden,* 7 ft 2 in x 3 ft (2.18 x 0.92 m)

Center panel: *The World before the Flood*
7 ft 2 in x 6 ft 4 in (2.18 x 1.95 m)

Right panel: *Hell*
7 ft 2 in x 3 ft (2.18 x 0.92 m)

the various metamorphoses of human to animal to inanimate object are both celebrations of observation and imaginative departures from tradition.

Little was written about Bosch's work during the period, and one can only speculate as to the intention of his complex symbolism. However, as with the works of Grünewald, his contemporary, the strong moralizing character of Bosch's paintings plants them firmly in a Europe far removed from the idealist visions of the South. The degree of religious fervor embodied in the works of Grünewald and Bosch anticipated the religious turmoil and conservatism that later found their voice in the Reformation. In this light the *Garden of Earthly Delights* may be read as an appropriate northern response to what was seen as the excesses of the Italian Renaissance.

It is perhaps fitting that this discussion of Renaissance art should end with the northern artists, for their work reveals the emergence of a very different sensibility arising by the middle of the sixteenth century. Their reservations about Italian art and its reliance on Antiquity rather than on the Scriptures paralleled a growing distrust of papal authority and a growing sense of nationalism in the North. The result was a revolution that laid the foundations of modern Europe — creating a decidedly different role for the artist in society. In its wake, the period called the Renaissance, with all its lofty hopes and aspirations, came to appear awkwardly impractical. By 1630, the Renaissance style had to all intents and purposes lost its initial edge and rigor, settling on mannerisms more predictable than invigorating. The seventeenth century's religious, political, and economic turmoil marked a new Western order, characterized by the rise of nation states and the slow decline of the authority of the Church — an era called the Baroque.

SUMMARY

The Renaissance has historically held a prominent position in texts on Western art. The period between the mid-fourteenth and mid-sixteenth centuries is generally viewed as the culmination of a "rebirth" of humanistic pursuits and a freeing of the artist from the restrictive dogma of the medieval Church. The status of art, and indeed the artist, shifted significantly, and today's views on both are based very much on certain assumptions about the role and rationale of art in culture that were first developed during the Renaissance. It was in the Renaissance that the role of the artist went from simple maker (suggesting an anonymous craftsperson) to that of creator (suggesting individual genius) — an appellation once reserved only for God. As a consequence, art took on greater significance, becoming not only an expression of its age and its means of production but also the very embodiment of genius. In this way, the Renaissance played a fundamental role in shaping the way we think about art.

Suggested Reading

The Renaissance has long been a favorite subject with art scholars, and so there is no shortage of texts on it.

Baxandall, M.: *Painting and Experience in Fifteenth Century Italy* (London/New York: Oxford University Press, 2nd edn, 1988).

Chastel, A.: *A Chronicle of Italian Renaissance Painting* (Ithaca: Cornell University Press, 1983).

Freedberg, S.J.: *Painting in Italy 1500–1600* (Harmondsworth/New York: Penguin Books, 1971; revisions 1979).

Snyder, J.: *Northern Renaissance Art* (New York: Abrams, 1985).

Wright, Lawrence: *Perspective in Perspective* (London: Routledge & Kegan Paul, 1983). An informative look at the history of perspective.

Glossary

atmospheric perspective (*page 199*) A convention for developing depth within a painting by making objects appear less defined as they recede in space.

contrapposto (*page 197*) A figure pose first developed by Polyclitus with his *Doryphorus* model in Classical Greece, it combines a "fixed" or "engaged" leg with a "free" leg — a motion that creates a sway in the hips and is subsequently counterbalanced by the upper torso.

empiricism (*page 170*) A philosophical position holding that one can gain knowledge and insights into existence through the close observation of nature. Originating in the writings of Aristotle, it had sweeping implications for the study of science in the Middle Ages.

foreshortening (*page 185*) A convention for depicting illusionistic space in painting. The technique involves the visual contraction of an object as it moves back in space.

fresco (*page 193*) A painting method by which colored pigments immersed in water are applied to fresh plaster, which absorbs the paint and dries rockhard. The method was particularly popular for decorating interior spaces during the Renaissance.

linear perspective (*page 180*) A geometric system for defining items in space. It implies that all lines receding back into space have their point of origin at a central vanishing point or points, depending on the circumstances.

metal engraving (*page 215*) The process by which a multiple of an image is produced by scoring a metal plate with a burin to create lines. Ink is rubbed into the scored surface and dampened paper is then pressed against the surface, pushing the paper into the ink filled troughs, which creates the print.

Renaissance (*page 168*) Meaning "rebirth," it is generally used to define the period in European culture between 1400 and 1600, when there was a renewed interest in Classical scholarship and art.

scale diminution (*page 185*) Used in painting, it is the reduction in scale of an object as its position from the picture plane changes. Together with *foreshortening*, it is used to suggest space.

symmetry (*page 209*) A compositional device to produce balance between parts through offsetting items on either side of the center.

tempera (*page 176*) The mixing of pigment with a binder (historically egg yolk) creates tempera paint. During the Renaissance, the use of oil instead of egg yolk resulted in the development of oil paint.

wood engraving (*page 215*) A relief printmaking method whereby areas not to be printed are carved out of a flat wood surface, leaving the intended image raised to take ink.

Pronunciation Guide

Gianlorenzo Bernini **jahn**-lor-**EN**-zoh ber-**NEE**-nee
Giotto di Bondone **JAW**-toh dee bohn-**DOH**-nay
Sandro Botticelli **SAN**-droh baht-uh-**CHEL**-lee
Donato Bramante doh-**NAH**-toh brah-**MAHN**-tay
Filippo Brunelleschi fee-**LEE**-poh broo-nuh-**LES**-kee
Michelangelo Buonarotti **my**-kel-**AN**-juh-loh **bwon**-uh-**RAW**-tee
Cimabue chee-**MAHB**-way
Duccio **DOO**-chee-oh
Albrecht Dürer **AL**-brekt **DUR**-ur
Jan van Eyck yahn van **EYE(K)**
Lorenzo Ghiberti lor-**EN**-zoh gee-**BAIR**-tee
Isenheim **IZ**-uhn-**heye(m)**

Ambrogio Lorenzetti am-**BROH**-joh lor-uhn-**ZET**-ee
Masaccio muh-**SAH**-chee-oh
Cosimo de' Medici **KAW**-zee moh day **MED**-uh-**chee**
Antonio de Pollaiuolo an-**TOH**-nyoh day **pohl**-ly-**WAW**-loh
Raphael **RAF**-ee-uhl
Renaissance **REN**-uh-**sahns**
Giuliano da Sangallo jool-**YAHN**-oh dah sahn-**GAH**-loh
Titian **TISH**-uhn
triptych **TRIP**-tik
Paolo Uccello pah-**OH**-loh oo-**CHEL**-oh
Georgio Vasari **JYOR**-joh vah-**SAHR**-ee
Leonardo da Vinci lee-uh-**NAHR**-doh duh **VIN**-chee

5

ART, ISSUES, AND INNOVATIONS IN THE BAROQUE ERA

■ 5.1 Nicolas Poussin
Arcadian Shepherds (detail) c. 1660
Oil on canvas
34¼ x 47¼ in (87 x 120 cm)
Louvre, Paris

Beginning reform is beginning revolution.
THE DUKE OF WELLINGTON

The origins of the word **Baroque**, as the era of European art after the Renaissance is known, are not clear, and today one can only speculate as to the original intention of the title. It may have come from the Italian *barocco*, meaning a complex problem, or even the Portuguese *barroco*, meaning an irregularly shaped pearl, but what both roots imply is an interest in decoration or complex configurations — something very different from the harmonious mindset commonly associated with the art of the Renaissance. It is, however, clear that the title was given to the period later, probably as a dubious descriptive term.

The seventeenth and early eighteenth centuries saw an unprecedented degree of nationalism and commercial venture develop in the major centers of Europe. In this relatively short period, the ideals and religious preoccupations of the West expanded past the boundaries of Europe and began to envelop the Americas and the Far East. It was the period of merchant forces and diplomacy, and in its subsequent flourish it planted the seeds of revolt that would forever change the face of politics as it was then known. In such a climate, art became perhaps the ultimate expression of individuality — this was the era of Rembrandt and Rubens, of Velázquez, Poussin, and Bernini, and with them came some of the most admired masterpieces the Western world has ever known.

Like the enraptured Renaissance, the Baroque was a period of tremendous artistic activity, though with decidedly different aspirations. The reasons for this are complex, and in approaching the art of the age within the context of the massive social, political, and philosophical upheavals of the time, the subtle pressures that influenced the nature of art and art making will become clear. To gain an idea of the historical background, one must start by examining a discussion that preoccupied much of Rome in the year 1541 — the year in which Michelangelo finished his fresco of the *Last Judgment* (Fig. **5.2**).

THE "LAST JUDGMENT" AND ROME IN 1541

On 31 October 1541, Pope Paul III unveiled Michelangelo's recently completed *Last Judgment* in the Sistine Chapel — twenty-nine years after the completion of his masterly ceiling (see Fig. 4.38). The new work had taken seven years to complete and, once viewed by the public, it initiated a furious debate that was to last another twenty. At the center of the debate was the question of "decorum" — in other words, the appropriateness of Michelangelo's choice of figures for the needs of the chapel. The significance of the argument was that it saw a questioning of the validity of figuration and the role of images in the Church for the first time since the Middle Ages. This sudden readdressing of decorum, in an age that had witnessed unprecedented freedoms for intellectual and artistic curiosity, signaled the emergence of a very different attitude in Europe. In a letter dated November 1541 (shortly after the unveiling of the aforementioned fresco), Nicolo Sernini wrote to Cardinal Gonzaga with regard to the reception afforded the *Last Judgment*: "The Theatine fathers are the first to say that it is not good to have nudes displaying themselves in such a place...others say that he has made Christ beardless and too young, and that He does not have the majesty which is suitable for Him, and so there is no lack of talk."

A cool breeze of restraint and suspicion had swept over a once exuberant Church, its Renaissance values, and its art, and behind it was a man named Martin Luther.

The Reformation

On 3 January 1521, the German Augustinian canon Martin Luther was officially excommunicated from the Church for heretical teachings (Fig. **5.3**). The severe condemnation of Luther's activities was the result of a series of highly critical observations launched against the Church in 1517 in the form of ninety-five propositions, now known as the *95 Theses*. Tacked to the door of Wittenberg Cathedral, these complaints called for an end to the corruption that

■ 5.2 Michelangelo Buonarroti, *Last Judgment* 1534–41
Fresco, altar wall of the Sistine Chapel, Rome. 48 ft x 44 ft (14.6 x 13.4 m)
The Vatican, Rome. © Nippon Television Network Corporation, Tokyo, 1995

was by this time increasingly common in the Church. The protest was a culmination of many years of frustration for northern European Christians, who saw the Church enjoying increased revenues while remaining unmoved by the plight of its "flock;" the situation was further complicated by an administration riddled with corruption and hypocrisy. The religious revolt led by Luther came to be known as *Protestantism* (as its followers were protesting), and the subsequent Reformation dramatically altered the face of European culture, including its art.

Luther's teachings had enormous cultural repercussions, ranging from public education to music and art. Perhaps his greatest achievement, apart from his religious reforms, was his work for greater literacy among all classes. The Lutheran emphasis on the "word" of God as translated through the Bible made it imperative for all Christians to have access to the written text. Luther's translation of the Bible into his native German was thus of significance in that it was an attempt to give back the responsibility of faith to the individual, rather than see it arbitrated through an elaborate construction of ceremonies conducted by the Church. This democratization of faith led to other reforms, such as access to education — an idea with huge moral implications. In a similar vein, many Protestant congregations found it appropriate to use music to instruct the common people. Luther's emphasis on music as a vehicle for both celebration and teaching led to his writing of hymns — a genre

■ **5.3 Hans Holbein the Younger**
Hercules Germanicus 1520
Colored woodcut
Zentralbibliothek, Zürich

■ **5.4 Simon Guillain (after Annibale Carracci)**
Paintings for Sale 1646
Etching

■ 5.5 Religious affiliations in Europe c. 1600

that found its greatest expression in the works of the German Lutheran Johann Sebastian Bach (1685–1750).

One area in which the doctrines of Protestantism allowed for little tolerance was in the field of visual arts. The militant iconoclasm of Protestantism was a reaction to what it perceived as the Catholic (i.e. unreformed) Church's reliance on mystery and symbolism that were often unintelligible to the general public. However, this denial of imagery within the sanctuary of the Church had other, more positive, side effects for the development of art. The slow but steady drying up of commissions from the once reliable patronage of the Catholic Church in the Protestant North contributed to the emergence of art in the commercial marketplace, where it could be sold, as a commodity, to a rising middle class (Fig. 5.4).

Between the years 1517 and 1520, Luther's published writings sold an amazing 300,000 copies — and this in a Europe in which very few could read. The recent invention of movable typeface and printing

techniques enabled the dissemination of information over large areas in a relatively short period of time, and by the middle of the sixteenth century, a considerable area of Europe had come under the influence of the Reformation spirit. Since that time, the religious boundaries that divided Europe's various Protestant denominations from their Catholic heritage have remained relatively unchanged. Britain, much of Germany, the northern Netherlands, most of Switzerland, and all of Scandinavia became Protestant states, while France, Spain, Portugal, Italy, southern Germany and Austria maintained their allegiance to the Pope (Fig. 5.5) for both religious and decidedly political reasons. These geographic divisions also contributed to the pictorial and cultural variety that marked Baroque art, making it one of the richest periods in the history of the visual arts.

This diversity of styles and concepts between the years 1600 and 1750 was the result not so much of the Reformation as of the defensive posture of the Catholic Church after suffering this onslaught of harsh and militant criticism. It was through the

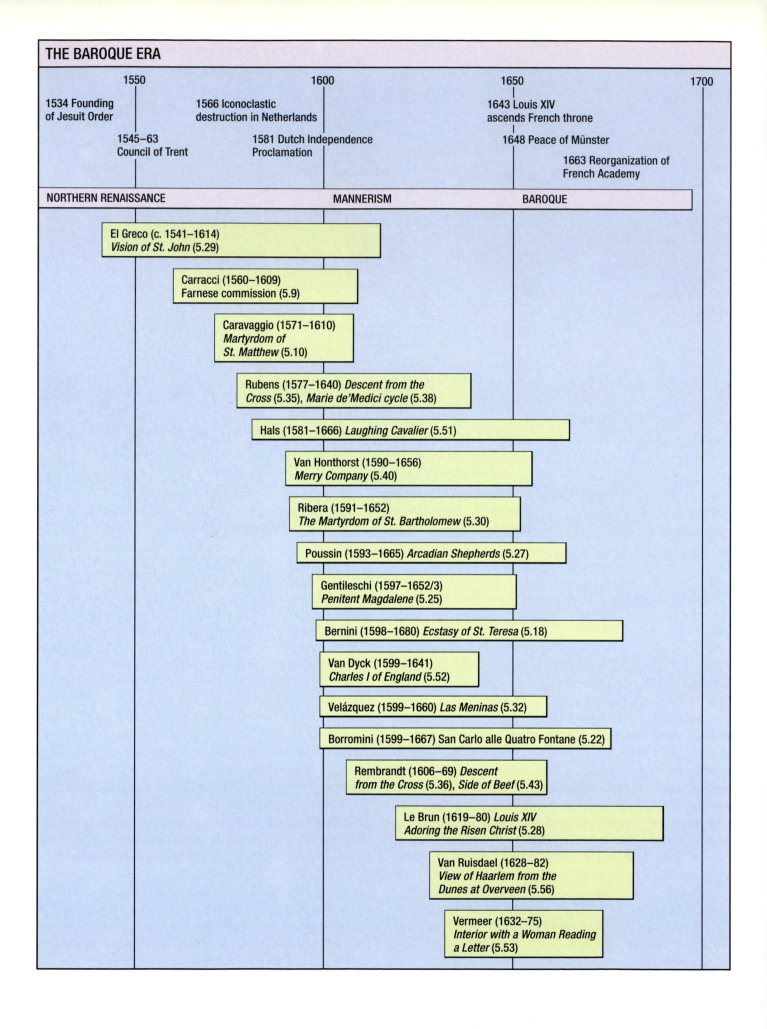

THE BAROQUE ERA

| 1550 | 1600 | 1650 | 1700 |

1534 Founding of Jesuit Order

1566 Iconoclastic destruction in Netherlands

1643 Louis XIV ascends French throne

1545–63 Council of Trent

1581 Dutch Independence Proclamation

1648 Peace of Münster

1663 Reorganization of French Academy

NORTHERN RENAISSANCE　　　　**MANNERISM**　　　　**BAROQUE**

El Greco (c. 1541–1614) *Vision of St. John* (5.29)

Carracci (1560–1609) Farnese commission (5.9)

Caravaggio (1571–1610) *Martyrdom of St. Matthew* (5.10)

Rubens (1577–1640) *Descent from the Cross* (5.35), *Marie de'Medici cycle* (5.38)

Hals (1581–1666) *Laughing Cavalier* (5.51)

Van Honthorst (1590–1656) *Merry Company* (5.40)

Ribera (1591–1652) *The Martyrdom of St. Bartholomew* (5.30)

Poussin (1593–1665) *Arcadian Shepherds* (5.27)

Gentileschi (1597–1652/3) *Penitent Magdalene* (5.25)

Bernini (1598–1680) *Ecstasy of St. Teresa* (5.18)

Van Dyck (1599–1641) *Charles I of England* (5.52)

Velázquez (1599–1660) *Las Meninas* (5.32)

Borromini (1599–1667) San Carlo alle Quatro Fontane (5.22)

Rembrandt (1606–69) *Descent from the Cross* (5.36), *Side of Beef* (5.43)

Le Brun (1619–80) *Louis XIV Adoring the Risen Christ* (5.28)

Van Ruisdael (1628–82) *View of Haarlem from the Dunes at Overveen* (5.56)

Vermeer (1632–75) *Interior with a Woman Reading a Letter* (5.53)

Council of Trent, which met intermittently between 1545 and 1563, that Catholicism began its purge of internal corruption, and in its wake there emerged a revitalized Church. The most obvious result of this new celebration of papal authority was the launching of large and elaborate commissions — items that were to set the standards for Baroque art.

The Counter-Reformation

The brief sack of Rome in 1527 and the rising tide of Protestant insurrection is an appropriate place to begin a discussion of the Catholic resurgence. The Counter-Reformation was, as the name implies, an attempt to fight back against the militancy of the Protestant North (Fig. **5.6**). The Church began to rely heavily on missionary service to expand both its pocket and its authority, and the founding of the Jesuit Order in 1534 was the first of a number of decisive steps taken to counter the recent inroads of the radicals. Emphasis was placed not on esoteric symbolism and unintelligible ceremony but on a directness and clarity of teaching, so that even the humblest could come to understand the chief tenets of the faith.

For the Church of the Counter-Reformation, art worked on two levels: it was didactic and it served as propaganda. One of Luther's complaints was that Christian worship had become inaccessible and mysterious to the common people. Ceremonies had become nothing more than a grand theatrical production with little substance and even less relation to the Scriptures. The Council of Trent attempted to rectify this obvious inconsistency between the commissioned art of the time and its public, by placing greater emphasis on more direct and intelligible works — governed first by moral standards and then by aesthetic interest. The result was a series of debates that ended with a specific decree issued at the last meeting of the Council in December 1563. It explicitly stated: "By means of the stories of the mysteries of our Redemption portrayed by paintings or other representations, the people [should] be instructed and confirmed in the habit of remembering, and continually resolving in mind the articles of faith." By viewing art that surrounded them in worship, the pious could gain greater insight into the articles of faith, and in this way art functioned as a teaching device — very much in keeping with Luther's objective in writing hymns.

■ 5.6 Anon. *Luther as the Wolf in the Fold* c. 1525 Woodcut. Print Collection; Miriam and Ira O. Wallach Division of Art, Prints and Photographs The New York Public Library; Astor, Lennox and Tildes Foundations

Artists working under the patronage of the Catholic Church during the early sixteenth century were heirs to an abundance of visual conventions developed over the previous century. As a result, technical formulas such as perspective and ideal proportion soon became the focus of further manipulation at the hands of artists who desired a more personal, if somewhat idiosyncratic, form of representation. The label **Mannerism**, often applied to the art of this transitional period, refers to an emphasis on stylistic virtuosity and complex design over the principles of restraint, idealism, and equilibrium — the catchwords of the previous generation.

■ 5.7 Parmigianino, *Madonna with the Long Neck* c. 1534
Oil on panel, 7 ft 1 in x 4 ft 4 in (2.15 x 1.32 m), Uffizi Gallery, Florence

A clear example of this exaggeration comes in the work of Parmigianino (1503–40), whose so-called *Madonna with the Long Neck* (Fig. **5.7**) shows the elongation of both body parts and perspective characteristic of the changing spirit of the era. The impossible proportions and exaggerated perspective (note the tiny figure in the bottom right corner, which is supposed to imply background) posit theatricality over naturalism, and the result is an oddly lyrical, even erotic, rendering of the Virgin and Child.

Another aspect of painting to come under consideration was color. One of the most striking departures from the early Renaissance norm of color harmony is a work by Jacopo da Pontormo (1494–1556), the *Deposition* (Fig. **5.8**) of c. 1528, in which exaggerated figure types and highly active color (consisting of

■ 5.8 Jacopo Carucci da Pontormo, *Deposition* c. 1528
Oil on panel, 11 ft x 6 ft 6 in (3.35 x 1.98 m)
Capponi chapel, Santa Felicita, Florence

bright pinks, light blues and acid yellow-greens) resonate with a blatant, and often disquieting, contrast.

It was within this artistic climate that critics placed
Michelangelo's *Last Judgment* (see Fig. 5.2), with its
almost supernatural rendering of space and its
demanding, disjointed, and psychologically challenging composition. Moreover, the unabashed nudity of
the figures spoke as much of eroticism as it did of

idealism. These were works ripe with the stylistic
ingredients considered so insidious to Luther and his
followers, and their exotic character and obscure subject matter only further corroborated the Protestant
insistence that art served its own god, rather than
Christ. Soon the Catholic Church too felt the pressure, and between 1559 and 1565 drapery was added
to many of the figures in the *Last Judgment*.

■ 5.9 Annibale Carracci, Ceiling, Farnese Gallery 1597–1604
Fresco, 67 ft x 20 ft (20.42 x 6.09 m). Farnese Palace, Rome

CLASSICISM VERSUS NATURALISM

Two distinct currents that emerged in the late sixteenth century determined the direction for much of the Baroque era: a Classicism derived from the antique, and an invigorated **naturalism** that found at least its inspiration in the edicts of the Council of Trent. Both began in the Rome of the Counter-Reformation, and though each was in keeping with the spirit of the reformed Catholic Church, their sensibilities were very much in conflict. That these two contradictory attitudes arose simultaneously is not surprising, particularly in the light of the continued interest in the antique throughout the 1500s, and the developments in the description of space and volume in both painting and sculpture. What is interesting is how each of the early practitioners attempted to reconcile these inclinations with the "new spirit" of the Church.

Carracci and Caravaggio

Much of the impetus for developments in the Baroque can be traced back to two contemporaries whose contrasting works set precedents that were still followed well into the nineteenth century. Thus in comparing the work of the Classicist Annibale Carracci (1560–1609) and the "naturalist" Michelangelo Merisi da Caravaggio (1571–1610), the various mutations of the Baroque aesthetic begin to emerge.

In 1597 Annibale Carracci was awarded the commission for decorating the reception hall of the Farnese Palace (Fig. **5.9**). The work took almost seven years to complete — the same length of time it took Caravaggio to complete a series of paintings for the Contarelli Chapel (Fig. **5.10**). The results could not have been more different. The strong contrasts of light and shade and the violent directness of the composition made Caravaggio's paintings at once controversial; in contrast, Carracci's steadfast reliance on Antique sources and Classical modeling appears a direct recapitulation of High Renaissance ideals. However, what the artists had in common was a desire to push their art to a higher level of emotional content; their images possess an unprecedented directness and clarity, signaling the rise of a new sensibility in Counter-Reformation art.

The personalities of the two artists were diametrically opposed: Carracci was withdrawn and brooding, his younger competitor dramatic and violent. The story of Caravaggio's life is almost as exciting and theatrical as his paintings, and his violent existence no doubt had some effect on his work.

Shortly after the Contarelli Chapel commission was finished, Caravaggio murdered a fellow citizen, having argued with him over a game of racquets. He fled to Malta, where he enjoyed prestige as a court painter until a fight with a police officer landed him in jail. He subsequently escaped, only to run into more trouble in Naples, where yet another quarrel left him seriously wounded. He died of fever on his way back to Rome in 1610. This story has all the intrigue of an adventure novel, but it also points to an artist of violent emotions with little interest in the accepted etiquette of his day — personality traits that found their resolution in the striking innovations of his work.

Through the Council of Trent, it was made clear that Church art was to follow the path of clarity and directness, making intelligible the various biblical stories and parables that were so often the subjects of great commissions. Caravaggio's answer to this demand was a critical reworking of the traditional techniques of rendering volume through the deliberate manipulation of light and shade, known as **chiaroscuro**.

Chiaroscuro (Italian for "light and shade") is a term used in painting and drawing to describe the convention of using light to enhance the volume of objects. As a picture-making device, chiaroscuro mimics the visual world; light and shade are, of course, fundamental to a perception of space, and shadows and highlights help the viewer determine surfaces and indicate volume.

Consider this example. Place an item on the desk next to your reading light; note how the beam of light falls on the nearest surface of the object facing the light (creating a highlight), and shadows on the planes that face away. By manipulating the lamp head, it becomes apparent that the contrasts between highlights and shadows are particularly acute when the light source is both strong and directed, making such a situation ideal for dramatic effects. If it is possible to appreciate the visual theatricality of such a light source from this example, consider the ramifications for painting.

Caravaggio's *Conversion of St. Paul* (Fig. **5.11**) of 1600–1602 is one such breathtaking study in the dynamic character of light and the artist's theatrical use of high contrast chiaroscuro, called **tenebroso**. The once implicit heavenly light that softly shone in Leonardo da Vinci's painting has become in Caravaggio's work an explicit reminder of God's presence. Like a flash of lightning, the artist has suggested the very moment of St. Paul's conversion, focusing physical and psychological attention on the central figure by the erratic nature of the gesture and enveloping him in a shroud of darkness like an actor

◄ 5.10 Caravaggio
Martyrdom of St. Matthew
c. 1602
Oil on canvas
10 ft 9 in x 11 ft 6 in
(3.23 x 3.5 m)
Contarelli Chapel,
San Luigi del Francesi, Rome

► 5.11 Caravaggio
Conversion of St. Paul
1600–02
Oil on canvas
7 ft 6½ in x 5 ft 9 in
(1.2 x 1.4 m)
Cerasi Chapel,
S Maria del Popolo, Rome

on stage. The result is a work that appears unapologetically dramatic, high keyed, and penetrating — attributes in keeping with the new spirit of renewal and accessibility sweeping over the Catholic Church.

Although the chiaroscuro modeling could claim some implicit sympathy with the "new" Church, Caravaggio's unorthodox use of models and interest in minute details often brought him into conflict with the tightening noose of decorum. In attempting to produce authentic representations of biblical figures (who were themselves often peasants and laborers), he went to painstaking lengths to describe every aspect of their physiognomy. The results were representations of martyrs and disciples with dirt on their

■   5.12 Caravaggio, *Death of the Virgin* 1605–6
Oil on canvas, 12 ft 1 in x 8 ft ½ in (3.68 x 2.45 m), Louvre, Paris

■ 5.13 Annibale Carracci, *The Triumph of Bacchus and Ariadne* 1597–1600
Detail from the Farnese Gallery ceiling, Rome

feet, and Virgin Marys who resembled not the idealized figures of Raphael but those of simple, poor Roman mothers. One particularly enlightening altercation of this sort surrounded Caravaggio's painting of the *Death of the Virgin* (Fig. **5.12**), in which the figure of the Virgin was derived from the body of a drowned prostitute (apparently to get the authentic look of a dead body). Predictably, this offended the sensibilities of many Church officials, who considered such depictions blasphemous and lacking in true devotion.

Comparisons between the life and work of Caravaggio and his rival Carracci could not be more extreme. Carracci, thirteen years older than Caravaggio, lived a relatively secure life and enjoyed a considerable reputation as a painter. Historians typically point to him as a major, and perhaps even the primary, figure in the re-establishment of Classical virtues in painting. Until the nineteenth century, his famous Farnese Gallery fresco cycle (see Fig. 5.9) was considered, along with Michelangelo's Sistine Chapel (see Fig. 4.38) and Raphael's Stanza della Segnatura (see Fig. 4.42), as one of the truly great works in the whole history of art.

Carracci had formidable talents as a technician, and his thorough knowledge of the principles of drawing, combined with an observant eye for Classical proportions, gave him the singular advantage of recognizing the subtleties of the Antique often overlooked by his contemporaries. The result was a body of work that injected a strong dose of Classical refinement and a lively, celebratory character to what had only decades before been a monotony of lofty and uninviting compositions. His unique ability to combine Classical picture-making devices and motifs with a clarity and exuberance befitting the new spirit of the Counter-Reformation makes Carracci's achievement as dramatic in stature as Caravaggio's chiaroscuro. He became the other half of the era's equation — a second possibility afforded to the artist in the age of reform.

Since Caravaggio's naturalism faced a major obstacle in the doctrine of decorum, it may appear odd that the Farnese Gallery (Fig. **5.13**) did not suffer the same criticisms for its less than subtle joviality. In pondering the overwhelming acceptance of this work during an era of reform, it may be helpful to consider two other points: the difference between public and private commissions, and the difference between the grand tradition of fresco and the emergence of oil painting.

The Farnese Gallery, part of a magnificent mansion built by Cardinal Odoardo Farnese, was of course a private building and not necessarily bound by the decrees of decorum issued by the Church. The subject matter, full of popular myths then familiar to most guests, could be justified as serving a double purpose — celebrating the wonder of life and love and at the same time allowing for a degree of moralizing through symbolic associations with the Bible (circumstances reminiscent of the early Church during its years of persecution). Though such subject matter exhibits at least a mild affinity to the elaborate narratives so harshly criticized in the Mannerist era, its uncompromising use of Classical sources (many of

■ 5.14 Annibale Carracci
Assumption of the Virgin
1601
Cerasi Chapel,
S Maria del Popolo, Rome

these poses are direct copies of Classical sculpture) made it appear ultimately controled and thus acceptable.

Another recognizable difference between the Contarelli Chapel and the Farnese Gallery is the consideration of materials. Both artists had a working knowledge of the materials and techniques of the age, but Caravaggio worked almost exclusively in oil on canvas, while Carracci is perhaps best known for his fresco painting. The issue of materials may on the surface appear relatively inconsequential when compared with many of the other variations that separate the artists' images, but it is nevertheless illuminating in any consideration of the reception their work received.

Since the early Italian Renaissance, fresco had enjoyed a reputation as the medium of the grand commission, since it was most flexible to the decorative demands of interior church architecture. The most noted artists — those capable of winning prestigious competitions — were thus forced to use the rather awkward medium. The ability to produce quality results under often extreme conditions (such as lying on one's back or straining the neck for ceiling work) was considered the mark of a true master, and subsequently fresco developed a strong mystique as the medium of the great artists.

In contrast, the relatively new medium of oil painting, capable of far more dramatic shifts in color and texture and able to sustain repeated workings, was considered inferior to fresco. The canvas stretcher frame, which was transportable and thus could be bought and sold like any other object, tended to be looked upon as technically less demanding — though few would quarrel with the view that it gave the painter greater freedom. It would be difficult to visualize Caravaggio's theatrical lighting and deep chiaroscuro in terms of fresco; his *form* (oil on canvas) and *content* (the dramatic spaces and violent gestures) are inextricably linked. However, this did not stop many critics of the day from ranking him behind Carracci, who produced admirably in the difficult medium of fresco. When Carracci did paint in oil, his work shows an awareness of the dramatic effects produced by an extended tonal range missing in his fresco work, and the result is a deeper, more volumetric series of forms (Fig. **5.14**).

THE ART CRITICISM OF BELLORI

Giovanni Pietro Bellori, born in Rome in 1613, wrote many years after the death of both Carracci and Caravaggio, yet his critical work reflects an enthusiasm for idealism rather than the naturalism so popular in the Italian Baroque. Bellori was one of the leading scholars of the time, holding the position of Commissioner of Antiquities in Rome from 1670 to 1695, and this no doubt influenced his opinions. He is perhaps best known for his *Lives of the Modern Artists*, published in 1672. Here he not only described some of the leading figures of the day but also recorded a series of critical observations on the then current state of art.

In his preface to *Lives of the Modern Artists* Bellori presented a brief but influential treatise on the nature of art. Though not particularly original, the short text quickly became a model for art criticism during the Baroque period, and it is enlightening as a justification of Classicism in art. Bellori's concept of art shows a clear sympathy for ideal forms, and in the works of Carracci as well as the earlier Raphael he found perfection.

Bellori began his treatise by describing a world in which the Earth is still positioned at the center of all things. Writing almost fifty years after Galileo's revolutionary observations had displaced the Ptolemaic conception of the universe, Bellori implicitly adhered to the earlier astronomer's views. This apparently reactionary stance had important ramifications for Bellori's theory. Regarding the universe beyond the atmosphere as a place untainted by decay or time, he believed that certain "ideals" (prototypes for each thing in the universe, created by God) found their true reflection only in the realm of the heavens. The opposite of this abstract world of perfection is life on Earth, where time and decay corrupt such true reflections, leaving only vulgar facsimiles (a view derived from Plato). Enter the artist. It is the artist's role to form an example of superior beauty and then use that prototype to beautify his/her depictions of earthly objects. By effectively implementing such a concept of divine or heavenly beauty, the artist had the ability to improve on the corrupt images of nature and provide a window to heaven.

Bellori used a then popular story from Pliny to illustrate his point. He told how the ancient Greek painter Zeuxis, hoping to depict the legendary beauty of Helen of Troy, sought out the five most beautiful maidens in the city of Croton and then copied the best parts of each model. In this way he was able to assemble a human form more beautiful than any that existed in nature (remember that, in Bellori's theory, the natural world is plagued by imperfection and decay). As a rather outrageous addition to the myth, Bellori further claimed that the famous Trojan War was fought not over the real Helen but over the sculpture depicting the idea of her beauty. Seeing the idealized art of the Greeks as an expression of acute selection and synthesis, Bellori believed it was a treasure chest of valuable lessons for the artists of his era. For this reason, he is categorized as a devout Classicist.

Given Bellori's blatant sympathy for Classical design, it should come as little surprise to find him an avid supporter of artists such as Carracci, whose idealization of form and heavy reliance on Classical imagery pleased him. In Carracci, Bellori saw an artist who exemplified the Classical tradition of synthesizing disparate parts of imperfect ideals (namely the human body) to produce a more profound and eternal beauty. The emphasis was to be placed not on direct observation of an imperfect world and its corrupt reflections but on assimilating parts of this imperfection into a higher conception of the idea. As a result, although Bellori was moved by the work of Caravaggio, he saw such painting as having less sophistication and merit. Bellori believed that Caravaggio had erred by taking the natural world as a true reflection of the idea rather than something that was aspiring to real beauty. Caravaggio saw true spirituality (perhaps, he would even claim, the idea) in the images of daily life, and he took great pains to depict these events in even the most religious of pictures. Bellori saw only imperfection and corruption in the dirty feet and tattered clothing of the naturalist painting of the Italian Baroque. To him, it was the artist's duty to reach toward ideals that spoke of God and the eternal, rather than depicting the common and the defective.

Bernini and the Baroque Sensibility in Sculpture

If Caravaggio and Carracci can be said to have contributed to the arguments between naturalism and classicism that preoccupied much of the Baroque age, perhaps the most successful integration of these ideas came in the work of the sculptor-architect Gianlorenzo Bernini (1598–1680). No other artist during the Baroque era so completely dominated his or her discipline as did this virtuoso, whose sculpted figures, came to personify the very spirit of the Counter-Reformation.

Born in Naples, from an early age Bernini possessed tremendous technical skill in modeling. His *David* (Fig. **5.15**), of 1623–4, sculpted between the ages of twenty-five and twenty-six, evokes comparisons with the *Davids* of Donatello and Michelangelo. Each work encapsulates the ideals and aspirations of its day. The sinuous body and graceful gesture of Donatello's bronze (Fig. **5.16**) speak of the break with the stiffness and grim determination of the Middle Ages. Michelangelo's *David* (Fig. **5.17**) is quintessentially heroic, his gigantic body and sensuous musculature the very idiom of human self-confidence in the High Renaissance. By comparison, Bernini's sculpture, neither complacent nor particularly grand, takes on a combativeness and an offensive posture; here the body appears poised to attack and defeat. This suggested dynamism points directly to the confident social and political climate in Counter-Reformation Rome. The clarity of vision and directness of the figure in its engagement of surrounding space are reminiscent of the naturalist Caravaggio. One could easily imagine confronting this *David* and feeling the need to duck out of the way of the stones about to come from his sling. This agitation of the area around the figure was in fact very new to sculpture, and its provocative engagement of the space amplified the viewer's relationship to the art. This was the very essence of the Baroque.

Bernini's technical skill is also worthy of consideration, for it reveals the influence of Caravaggio. His captivating use of light and shade through the technique of "undercutting" gave his cold marble figures an emotional vitality on a par with the very best chiaroscuro in painting. To appreciate fully such an advance in sculpture, it is necessary to consider in greater depth stone carving as it was practiced in the seventeenth century.

■ 5.15 Gianlorenzo Bernini
David 1623–4
Marble, height 5 ft 6¼ in (1.7 m)
Borghese Gallery, Rome

■ 5.16 Donatello
David c. 1430–2
Bronze, height 5 ft 2½ in (1.58 m)
Museo Nazionale del Bargello, Florence

■ 5.17 Michelangelo Buonarroti
David 1501–4
Marble, height 14 ft 3 in (4.34 m)
Galleria dell'Accademia, Florence

Baroque Stone Carving

Stone carvers use relatively simple tools to execute their art. The process is a *subtractive* one, which means that pieces of material are removed from the original form to produce an end result (clay or wax modeling is thus usually considered an *additive* process, since one builds up a form). By hammering stone chisels of various shapes and sizes into the quarried stone, the artist can often produce quite astounding representations of other materials. For many centuries and in many cultures, the stone of choice for delicate carving has often been marble, since its cleavage and molecular structure allow for a relatively soft yet stable material capable of withstanding heavy blows. It can also be highly polished,

which made marble particularly good for interior work, where there was often a demand for greater finish.

Marble sculpture made a marked resurgence in European art during the Italian Renaissance, having been absent for several centuries. Medieval artists had worked predominantly gray limestones, granites, shales, and cement to complement the materials chosen for cathedrals and other buildings. Also, the stone's exposure to severe environmental conditions did not facilitate the use of an expensive material most noted for its polish. This set of circumstances changed dramatically in the Renaissance with the opening up of large interior commissions, which in turn precipitated the reintroduction of fine marble (quarried in great abundance in Italy) on a much

■ 5.18 Gianlorenzo Bernini, *Ecstasy of St. Teresa* 1645–52. Marble, height approx. 11 ft 6 in (3.5 m)
Cornaro Chapel, S Maria della Vittoria, Rome

FOCUS ON

Undercutting

Michelangelo likened carving to liberating a figure from its stone captivity. If this was a feeling shared by sculptors of the day, prehaps it could be said that Bernini's figures leapt from their prisons. The emotional gestures and agitated surfaces give the impression that the figures are indeed flesh and blood. The drama of the scene is caught entirely by the convincing portrayal of movement, produced by a series of deep cuts into the marble surface that catch and reflect light. These deep spaces of shadow are produced by a technique called "undercutting" — a method of manipulating the descriptive character of light on stone.

Undercutting is a technique of creating deep cuts in stone to produce shadow; the result suggests movement and dynamism, as the surface is transformed by light and shade capable of expressing the most dramatic of gestures (Fig. 5.19).

■ 5.19 Diagram of undercutting

A cross-section of a typical sculptural surface which shows undercuts at different places.

A cross-section of a typical sculptured surface shows how the sculptor avoids creating unwanted shadows by carving surfaces at nearly right angles to allow light to strike both sides of the form.

Bernini's remarkable *Ecstasy of St. Teresa* (Fig. **5.18**) is a witness to the dramatic potential of such a development. Note how the draperies of the enraptured saint take on the lightness of cloth, and how the scene itself is wrapped within a turmoil of lines created through the inventive use of shadow. Bernini was also aware of the coloristic possibilities afforded by marble, and he used striking variations of the pink, white, green, and black varieties to produce spectacular results. One such example is his execution of the tomb of Pope Alexander VII (Fig. **5.20**) of 1671–8, in which traditional white marble figures are juxtaposed against colored marble drapery, striking black pedestals, and the ever-present symbol of Death — the skeleton. This is the Baroque sensibility in all its glory: the newly rediscovered confidence of the reformed Church finding its visual manifestation in what was once a crude block of quarried stone.

■   5.20 Gianlorenzo Bernini
Tomb of Pope Alexander VII 1671–8
Marble and cast bronze
The Vatican, Rome

greater scale. However, there was also a decidedly conceptual side to this argument; the historical connotations of marble were very much in keeping with the popular aspirations of the day. Observing marble as the stone preferred by ancient Greek and Roman stone carvers (the ruins of their work littered the Roman landscape), many sculptors began not only to emulate the images but also to use the materials of the past, in the hope of evoking a similar sensibility □.

BAROQUE ARCHITECTURE

Considering Bernini's rather formidable skill in engaging space and working materials, it was perhaps inevitable that he would from time to time embrace architecture as well. The most notable of these excursions was his design for the piazza of St. Peter's in Rome (Fig. **5.21**). The monumental project saw the passing of three popes before its final completion, by which time there had been a total reworking of the ceremonial entrance. Relying on many of the techniques and innovations of Renaissance architects, Bernini nevertheless allowed his engaging sense of novelty to guide him. As a result, the unorthodox combination of Doric and Ionic orders and the dramatic sweep of the colonnade (which psychologically heightens the pilgrim's anticipation of the church) appear very much in keeping with his quintessentially Baroque sensibility.

Bernini's decidedly different response to the problem of activating space was a departure from previous Renaissance norms. Here, space is arranged for what can be described only as kinesthetic (sensation on a nervous or muscular level) ends; Bernini's deliberate manipulation of the viewers' sense of rhythm and motion as they progress toward the steps of St. Peter's is thus a logical extension of his sculptural strategy — space as a psychological tool. This notable departure in the construction of space from the relative stasis of Renaissance models perhaps epitomizes the rise of a specifically Baroque architecture.

■ 5.21 Gianlorenzo Bernini, Piazza of St. Peter's begun 1663 Height of facade 147 ft (44.81 m), width 374 ft (114 m)

Borromini's San Carlo alle Quattro Fontane

Though Bernini had virtually no contemporaries to rival his work in sculpture, there were architects who matched his abilities in designing buildings. The most famous of these was Francesco Borromini (1599–1667), whose work may rightly be described as "Baroque." The excessive detailing and intricate patterning of his facade designs show yet another vein of Baroque decoration, one whose popularity increased during the next two centuries. A fine example of this incessant desire for greater complexity is Borromini's facade of San Carlo alle Quattro Fontane (Figs. **5.22** and **5.23**), finished in 1667. This structure marks a notable departure from the building conventions that had preoccupied the Renaissance imagination (symmetrical composition, balance, clear quotation from Classical sources). The undulating surfaces and

■ **5.22 Francesco Borromini**
San Carlo alle Quattro Fontane, Rome
Begun 1638, facade finished 1667
Width of facade 38 ft (11.58 m)

■ **5.23 Plan of San Carlo alle Quattro Fontane begun 1638**

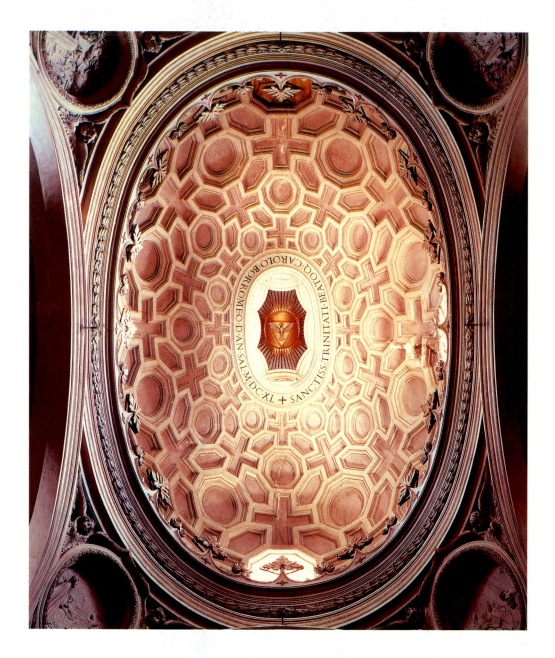

■ 5.24 Francesco Borromini Detail of Dome from interior of San Carlo alle Quattro Fontane

dramatic play of light and shade within the facade of San Carlo point to an architect with sympathies for the issues that appear to have preoccupied Bernini in his sculptural work. In fact, one may even go so far as to claim that Borromini's architectural work has more in common with Bernini's sculptural interests than do Bernini's own architectural designs.

The interior dome of San Carlo (Fig. **5.24**) further confirms Borromini's singular abilities in the designing of dynamic space. The oval form of the dome is a dramatic departure from the typical circular motif; its suggestive compression and the speed of its end curves create an almost uncanny pulsing sensation. Yet, despite the compression, the dome remains light — almost floating — due to the architect's inclusion of a row of hidden windows at the base. The interlocking of cross and circle forms, which illusionistically decrease in scale as they rise up from the base, accentuates the otherworldly quality of the design. Though later architects extended the emotional possibilities afforded by such conventions in a variety of interesting ways, few achieved the convincing coupling of energy and harmony that is displayed in San Carlo.

THE INFLUENCE OF ROME

Throughout history, certain cities have fallen in and out of favor as meeting places for artists and artistic ideas; at different points in the history of Western art, Athens, Constantinople, Florence, Paris, and New York have all taken on this role. In the early 1600s, Rome was the cultural focus. The great demand for artists to work on the numerous major commissions centered around the regenerated Church led to many an artist's pilgrimage to Rome. With the possible exception of artists from the Protestant North, most artists spent a part of their formal training in the ancient city. Here, many of them were brought into contact with the works and ideas of both Caravaggio and Carracci, as well as other distinguished artists from outside Italy, and these encounters inevitably led to artistic debates that continued outside the city — particularly in Spain and France — until the mid-eighteenth century.

Caravaggio's rigorous naturalism did not always

■ 5.25 Artemesia Gentileschi
Penitent Magdalene 1619–20
Oil on canvas
Pitti Palace, Florence

serve him well with his patrons, but it did leave an indelible mark on many of the artists of the age. A group of artists, sometimes referred to as the Caravaggisti after their reliance on the pictorial devices of the master, used the technique of strong contrast chiaroscuro with varying degrees of skill and innovation. One such artist was Artemisia Gentileschi (1597–1652/3), whose *Penitent Magdalene* (Fig. **5.25**) of c. 1620 embraces the dramatic potential of deep chiaroscuro with somewhat more reserve.

Perhaps the most noted practitioner of dramatic light and shade was the French artist Georges de la Tour (1593–1652). The calm that permeates his paintings is an emotional departure from the sometimes violent gestures of Caravaggio, but his use of candlelight is an innovative progression from the raking light evident in his predecessor's work. The results are often breathtaking, as his *Joseph the Carpenter* (Fig. **5.26**) of c. 1645 attests.

Another French artist greatly influenced by the art of Rome was Nicolas Poussin (1593–1665), who chose a path very different from that of de la Tour.

■ **5.26** Georges de la Tour
Joseph the Carpenter c. 1645
Oil on canvas
4 ft 10⅛ in x 3 ft 3¼ in (1.3 x 1 m)
Louvre, Paris

■ 5.27 Nicolas Poussin, *Arcadian Shepherds* c. 1660
Oil on canvas, 34¼ x 47¼ in (87 x 120 cm). Louvre, Paris

While de la Tour was a Caravaggist, Poussin's sympathies lay with Carracci and his Classicism. To Poussin, much of Baroque art was decadent and excessive, and throughout his life he aspired to a harmony and Classicism even more stringent than Carracci's.

The results are illuminating. In his *Arcadian Shepherds* (Fig. **5.27**) of around 1660, Poussin used mythic Arcadia, the Greek golden land of peace and contentment, as the setting for a painting about death and Classical notions of mortality, depicting a group of humble Arcadian shepherds as they stumble upon a tomb. Inscribed on the tomb's face are the prophetic words *Et in Arcadia Ego* — "Even in Arcadia, I [meaning Death] am to be found." Clearly Poussin was interested in the philosophical confrontation between the life of the ego and the brutal reality of death, which, though dramatic in its implications, is painted with a restraint and timeless contemplation.

The demands for absolute control and clarity may indeed give the painting an air of contrivance, and it is known that the artist went to almost absurd lengths to plan every aspect of his pictures (including the modeling of detailed wax figures and the construction of intricate miniature stage sets to plan his compositions), yet this is also what makes the work appear so timeless and satisfying to the eye. The painting makes few pretensions toward naturalism; instead it aspires to an image of perfect solidity, control, and restraint — ideas anchored in the belief that art is about timeless ideals. Further, this work acted as a strong critique of the emotionalism of Poussin's contemporaries, such as Artemisia Gentileschi and other Caravaggisti, making clear his sympathy for the cool detachment he saw epitomized in the Antique.

Art Theory and the Reorganization of the French Academy

Poussin's steadfast order and clarity were not only characteristics of Baroque Classicism; they also came to embody a nation's entire art program. The story of the development of the French Academy and its relationship to the reign of Louis XIV is perhaps one of the clearest examples of the manipulation of artistic enterprise in the name of political expedience. The implicit control of artists and their work by the state calls into question the role of patronage as it pertains to art making, and is thus worthy of some consideration here. At the height of its influence the French Academy had the ability not only to dictate commissions and schooling but also to determine the very concept of art through its teaching of theory. In exposing the reality that even art theory is not immune to the overriding concerns of power and political convenience, the French Academy is an illuminating microcosm of the subtle relationship between art and society.

The death of Cardinal Mazarin, first minister to the young Louis XIV, in 1661 ushered in a dramatic new era in the history of France. By declining to replace Mazarin with another first minister, the King took complete control over the governing of the nation. Astute enough to recognize the limits of his own capabilities, he then appointed Mazarin's assistant, Jean Baptiste Colbert (1619–83), as chief adviser — a post he would hold for some twenty years. Though most noted for his economic reforms and Machiavellian politics, Colbert also managed to change the course of the visual arts in his country for the next half-century. Under his critical eye, the artist in France became yet another cog in the large propaganda machine that helped establish and glorify the rule of the so-called "Sun King."

Colbert fully believed that the arts should follow the goals of national unity and power, serving to propagate these ideas as a state cultural industry. To carry out this program, in 1663 he appointed the French artist Charles Le Brun (1619–90) to oversee the Academy during its reorganization. Together they dictated the interests of French art and by way of their distinguished positions were able to direct virtually every important commission. In a country that was centrally governed, all money for art programs affiliated with building projects or important portraiture could be given to artists and works in sympathy with the political aims of the King. The result was an era of homogeneity in the field of virtually all French arts (except literature) — and perhaps nowhere so obviously as in the visual arts, where patronage was a necessity for survival.

To establish such steadfast rules for artists, both Le Brun and Colbert recognized the importance of providing training for those who aspired to paint or sculpt or be architects. The Academy filled this essential role as "bearer of truths," espousing the virtues of correct craft and correct intent. One of the major influences on this theoretical stance was rationalism, perhaps best known today through the work of the great French thinker René Descartes. Art, according to the Academy, could be learned through the application of certain rational principles, which could be expressed in words and would thus be intelligible to anyone. These new principles can be summarized as an adherence to certain characteristics of Classical art, such as the reliance on rational processes and systems such as ideal proportion, linear perspective, and deliberate execution. What the Academy rejected was the emotional inclinations and the dramatic postures of the Italian Baroque, and in particular that of Caravaggio and his followers.

There are many ways in which to justify the emergence of such sympathies on behalf of the Academy. Some historians point to the French disposition for the principles of rationalism, and the then current interest in the relationship between art and science. A more telling reason may be Louis XIV's own feeling that such art had an intrinsic relationship with the religious aims of the Counter-Reformation, and thus was not suitable for secular projects such as his palace of Versailles. By the time of Le Brun's appointment to the Academy of St. Luke in Rome in 1675 (pointing to the increasing influence of French art throughout Europe), this agenda had become the accepted orthodoxy of French art.

With respect to some of the finer features of the theory of art taught within the French Academy, many of the ideas were not new. The Academy generated a view of art that was primarily for the mind and not for the eye. Art was to be considered an intellectual pursuit, to be followed and understood by educated people. This position was in keeping with many earlier claims that painting is essentially imitation but is different in that, through intelligently choosing

■ 5.28 Charles Le Brun, *Louis XIV Adoring the Risen Christ* 1674
Oil on canvas
Musée des Beaux-Arts de Lyon

subjects from the disorder of nature and reorganizing its most beautiful parts (*à la* Bellori), the artist could establish new images of greater understanding and perfection. The Academy warned against an overzealous regard for color, which was of interest to the eye and not the mind. The artist should keep instead to issues such as form and outline, which were constants and could be rationally analyzed.

The order of merit within this system is telling. The noted twentieth-century expert on French Baroque Anthony Blunt described the hierarchy as follows:

first, the artists of Classical Greece and Rome; second, Raphael and his followers; third, Poussin; then, at the other end of the scale, Titian and the Venetian painters (whose interest in color apparently led them to frivolous painting without substance); and finally the Dutch, whom the Academy considered little more than direct imitators of an unordered and chaotic world — their indiscriminate portrayal of the irrational and the unbeautiful, like that of the Venetians, showed a lack of understanding of the rational principles evident to those of sound intelligence.

What can one learn about art from such an historical situation? Certainly this development illustrates the relationship that necessarily exists between a patron and an artist. In a period such as the seventeenth century in France, the granting of lucrative commissions became an expedient way of developing a virtual dictatorship of taste. Art, sustained and somewhat dependent on large commissions, faced compliance with the interests of the Academy or risked falling into disrepute. In this manner, art quickly became assimilated into the power structure of its patron; both its technical aims (form) and its subject matter (content) rightfully became the psychological property of the state. The Classical sensibility so firmly adhered to by the Academy was thus as much a political device as it was an aesthetic concern, in that it theoretically proposed a form of stability, rationality, and heroic proportion in keeping with the aspirations of those in power. Here, then, the supposedly neutral theories of an art academy took a decidedly political twist, and the work became yet another form of cleverly disguised propaganda.

A representative example of the Academy in action is Le Brun's painting of *Louis XIV Adoring the Risen Christ* (Fig. **5.28**) of 1674. Here the lofty standards of the Academy came to fruition in a technically superb and politically correct rendering of the artist's three masters: Christ, the Sun King, and Colbert (lower right).

Spanish Painting

Another country deeply influenced by the art of Rome was Spain, which is noted for its Baroque painting. One of the more interesting artists of the period (particularly to modern eyes) was a Greek immigrant named Domenicos Theotocopoulos, called El Greco (c. 1541–1614). Little is known of his life, save from a few documents and a couple of outrageous comments. (He is attributed with having offered to paint over Michelangelo's *Last Judgment* when he was in Rome, claiming that Michelangelo was "a good man, but he could not paint.") He appeared in Toledo, home of the Spanish Inquisition, early in 1577, after studying with Titian in Venice, and remained in the city for the rest of his life.

El Greco is often said to have embodied the Counter-Reformation spirit, and his spiritual zeal and ecstatic vision found their visual equivalent in elongated, flamelike figures, flickering color, and tumultuous environments. His *Vision of St. John* (Fig. **5.29**) of around 1610 is a good example of his singular ability to suggest visionary rapture. Here, Heaven and Earth convulse at the moment of Revelation, and El

■ 5.29 El Greco, *Vision of St. John* c. 1610
Oil on canvas, 7 ft 3 in x 6 ft 4 in (2.2 x 1.9 m)
The Metropolitan Museum of Art, New York. Rogers Fund, 1956

■ 5.30 José de Ribera, *The Martyrdom of St. Bartholomew* c. 1639
Oil on canvas, 6 ft x 6 ft 6 in (1.83 x 1.98 m). Prado, Madrid

Greco's eccentric, Mannerist figure types quiver and twist at their awaiting judgment. The result is painting that expresses rapture, rather than illustrating it.

José de Ribera (1591–1652) was another artist interested in the dramatic intensity of Caravaggio's painting, and like Caravaggio he painted religious figures in sometimes startling detail (Fig. **5.30**). To this brew of contrasting light and shade, Ribera added his own characteristically Spanish disposition for strong emotion, a combination that produced a body of work that parallels the psychological intentions of Caravaggio as closely as that of anyone during the age.

However, the most dominant figure in Spanish art during the height of the Baroque was the more subtle Diego Velázquez (1599–1660), whose scenes of court life provide a strong counter to the brutal naturalism of Ribera. No doubt Velázquez' eye for detail and his incessant observation of character evolved from Caravaggio, but here the results are very different.

One reason for this divergence was Velázquez' singular use of color, a sensitivity derived more from Titian than from any of the popular naturalist painters (who continued to shroud their paintings in dark shadow). His portrait of *Pope Innocent X* (Fig. **5.31**) of 1650 demonstrates the results of this happy marriage in the shimmering satin garment and striking color combinations that fill the picture plane. In Velázquez' portraits, Venetian color found its rightful place alongside the steady observation of a Caravaggio, producing work uncompromising in its naturalism and subtle in its palette.

■ **5.31** Diego Velázquez
Pope Innocent X 1650
Oil on canvas
4 ft 7 in x 3 ft 9¼ in (1.4 x 1.15 m)
Galleria Doria Pamphilli, Rome

■ 5.32 Diego Velázquez
Las Meninas (*The Maids of Honor*) 1656
Oil on canvas
10 ft 5 in x 9 ft (3.2 x 2.7 m)
Prado, Madrid

Perhaps Velázquez' most famous court portrait is *Las Meninas* (Fig. **5.32**), the *Maids of Honor*, painted in 1656. The relaxed pose of the five-year-old Princess Margarita and her maids makes for court portraiture very different from the norm. It is as if the viewer has stumbled, almost accidently, upon an intimate moment in the life of the Spanish court. It is also a complex composition, which includes the artist, peering from behind his canvas on the left, and the patron King and Queen reflected in the central background mirror. The eccentricity of the scene leads one to sev-eral hypotheses as to the artist's intentions: was he actually in the act of painting the King and Queen, as suggested by the mirror that would place them in front of the Princess? Is it a novel way of producing a family portrait by inserting the royal couple in the reflection rather than situating them with their child? In any event, *Las Meninas* is a brilliant exercise in por-traiture, an original compositional arrangement and an example of an exquisite sense of color and nuance, making it one of the true masterpieces of the Baroque period.

DUTCH AND FLEMISH ART

While the Counter-Reformation can be said to have provided the impetus for the dynamism of the Italian Baroque, the Reformation was equally influential, changing forever the way in which people thought about art. The breaking away of the Low Countries (today Belgium and the Netherlands) from Spanish control between 1573 and the Peace of Münster in 1648 provided the necessary context for a drastic reorientation of art and patronage, and it created in its wake the foundations of today's art market.

In the sixteenth century, the Low Countries were ruled by Spain, which felt justified in taxing its subjects to help finance overseas conquests. By the end of the sixteenth century the Spanish government's excessive taxation of the Netherlands had inevitably led to increased tensions. The small lowland country was the site of many industrious ports and was blessed with a practical geographic position, close to Britain, France, Scandinavia, and the Atlantic Ocean. Though relatively few in population, the Dutch had shown themselves extremely capable in commerce and seamanship, occupations that afforded them the opportunity to develop an affluent middle class without the bloodshed that is so often a part of economic self-determination.

Another economic factor that contributed to Dutch prosperity was the influence of the marketplace — an idea based upon the free exchange of goods produced by individuals or groups and bartered in a forum. Yet economics was not the only bone of contention between the Dutch and Spanish: another was religion.

By the late sixteenth century, the Protestant Reformation had reached the northern provinces of the Netherlands in the form of Calvinism, a denomination in which artistic iconoclasm was a major characteristic. Known for their severity and dogmatism, Calvinists forbade the use of imagery in places of worship, considering it idolatrous and further evidence of the corruption of the Catholic Church. A popular preoccupation of Calvinists during the militant sixteenth century was to tear down and burn church art, leaving once magnificent interiors whitewashed and spartan. The most famous of these purges was the iconoclastic destruction of 1566, which destroyed a considerable amount of liturgical art in the major Dutch centers. (The result can be witnessed in a work by Pieter Saenredam [1597–1665], depicting the *Interior of St. Bavo, Haarlem* [1637; Fig. **5.33**].) Soon thereafter, the Dutch Church collapsed as a reliable source of patronage for the arts, and artists were forced to turn elsewhere to make a living.

The answer lay in the hands of the affluent middle class, who desired small paintings to hang in their homes. Soon artists found themselves developing pictorial strategies in keeping with the demands of their customers, and concentrated on depicting scenes of domestic life rather than the immense heroic subjects familiarly associated with southern Baroque painters. This contrast may be appreciated by a comparison between a work by Gerard Terborch (1617–81), *Boy Removing Fleas from His Dog* (Fig. **5.34**) of c. 1658 and Annibale Carracci's work from the Farnese Gallery (see Fig. 5.9).

■ 5.33 Pieter Saenredam,
Interior of the Choir of St. Bavo's, Haarlem 1637
Oil on oak panel
27³/₅ x 21½ in (70.4 x 54.8 cm)
Copyright Worcester Art Museum, Massachusetts
Charlotte E. W. Buffington Fund

■ 5.34 Gerard Terborch
Boy Removing Fleas from His Dog c. 1658
Oil on canvas
13½ x 10⅝ in (34.4 x 27.1 cm)
Alte Pinakothek, Munich

Such circumstances also had a notable effect on subject matter, as grand religious works slowly gave way to more modest still-life, landscape, group portrait, and everyday life (*genre*) paintings, in keeping with the interests of the clientele. Artists were now content to find art and spirituality in the everyday, rather than relying exclusively on grand mythological themes and biblical stories.

The marketplace provided the perfect setting for the selling of art — painting in particular. In entering the marketplace, art took on a number of practical features that changed both the criteria and the context of the work. It was a move away from the large-scale commissions of Caravaggio and Carracci toward a more intimate and practical art in keeping with the modest quarters of the purchasers. However, while the marketplace was influential in bringing about such dramatic changes, it required the added vehemence of early Calvinism to grant it moral justification.

The political upheaval created by the excessive taxing of the Netherlands, and the Spanish government's strong links with the Catholic Church, provided a suitable setting for a revolt by the North, with its dominant middle class and Calvinist religious sympathies, against its faraway landlords. The northern provinces' quest for self-determination led to their secession in 1609 after a truce with Spain. The subsequent collapsing of excise tax in the six northern provinces (Holland being the most prosperous) allowed for a tremendous period of growth in the area, and it is to this period of Dutch art that historians assign the title "Golden Age." After 1609, many Catholics, fearing religious persecution in the North, migrated south into the Flemish provinces still held by Spain and were consequently able to practice Catholicism without interference. The subsequent split in the Spanish Netherlands thus fell almost directly along religious and economic lines, and it provides an ideal context from which to study the relationship between art and ideology.

Rubens and Rembrandt Paint the "Descent from the Cross"

The Flemish artist Peter Paul Rubens (1577–1640) and the Dutch artist Rembrandt van Rijn (1606–69) have come to personify the legacy of Baroque art, and in many respects each embodied the particular sensibilities of the fractured Spanish Netherlands. Rubens,

■ 5.36 Rembrandt van Rijn, *Descent from the Cross* c. 1633
Oil on canvas, 36¼ x 27½ in (92 x 69.2 cm). Alte Pinakothek, Munich

who distinguished himself not only as an artist but also as a diplomat and scholar, is best known for his grand commissions, such as the altarpieces for Antwerp Cathedral and the massive Marie de' Medici cycle (see Fig. 5.38) of 1622–5. Rembrandt, who also enjoyed considerable praise and attention from contemporaries, never traveled and had few close associates. Even their manner of work and choice of subject offer striking comparisons. Only once did the two artists attempt a similar composition, and in their contrast these paintings have come to embody the artistic ideas generated by and through each artist's complex historical situation (Figs. **5.35** and **5.36**).

Rubens painted his *Descent from the Cross* (see Fig. 5.35) between the years 1611 and 1614, shortly after completing a massive and complex commission for another altarpiece, called the *Raising of the Cross*. The thirty-one-year-old artist was called back to his native Antwerp to execute the commission, which forced him to abandon his studies in Rome, where he had already developed a considerable reputation for his capable modeling of forms. Once in Antwerp, he, like most artists engaged on large-scale commissions, set up an *atelier* (studio with assistants) — an enterprise that soon shipped its products to clients across the continent as Rubens' reputation flourished.

Rubens' *Descent from the Cross* is a vast painting, and its sheer scale and massive figure types give the work a dramatic sense of presence and strength. In this work Rubens openly acknowledged his debts to other artists with whom he most certainly came in contact during his time in Italy. The massive figures call to mind the Classical borrowings of Carracci, the sensuous paint handling pays direct reference to Venetian art, and the theatrical light source shows a thorough understanding of chiaroscuro. Yet the allusions go further than simple stylistic conventions. The main figure of Christ — gestural and outstretched — is derived from the central figure of the famous *Laocoön* (Fig. **5.37**), only in reverse.

Discovered in 1506, and an exquisitely preserved example of Antique sculpture, the *Laocoön* was admired by early seventeenth-century viewers as a supreme representation of suffering and pathos in a visual form. Rubens, by directly alluding to famous Greek sculpture, was thus able to further the tragic and heroic nature of the Crucifixion — a point that would not be lost on most of his patrons, who had come to know the Classical sculpture through circulated engravings popular during the period. The frieze-like placement of figures on the immediate foreground only served to reiterate this Classical orientation, and when combined with the striking prototype for his dead Christ, the altarpiece became a champion of Counter-Reformation dogma. This mixture of Christian and Classical iconography (complementing contemporary Neo-Platonism) situates Rubens's choice of subject firmly within the new spirit of the Church. Further, when one considers the great role of the Catholic Church in Flanders as a focus of nationality (the northern provinces being, of course, predominantly Protestant), it is understandable that such activity would become invested with a degree of social and cultural relevance beyond its subject matter.

■ 5.37 Hagesandros, Athenodoros, and Polydorus
Laocoön and His Two Sons 1st century AD
Marble
Height 8 ft (2.44 m)
Vatican Museums, Rome

Like most artists of his era, Rubens did his share of private portraits and smaller commissions, but his most noteworthy achievements remain in the form of large-scale commissions. One of the most famous of these is the Marie de' Medici cycle (Fig. **5.38**), which contained twenty-one paintings once completed. Painted between the years 1622 and 1625, there is a notable departure from Rubens' previous work into a more graceful, sensuous, and painterly manner. Gone are most of the Classical allusions, and the figure types now resemble the living nude rather than age-old marble. These are not portraits in a conventional sense but represent their subject as dominating a mythological world of gods, nymphs and obedient peasants. The world of the painting with its complex allegory is arranged according to principles of power and privilege and is thus intensely political, setting out an ideal to which the original owner of the painting wished the real world to aspire. These expansive commissions — difficult to paint and labor-intensive

■ 5.38 Peter Paul Rubens, *Triumph of Juliers* from the *Marie de' Medici* cycle c. 1622–25
Oil on canvas, 14 ft 11 in x 9 ft 6 in (3.94 x 2.95 m)
Louvre, Paris

— were within the grasp of only the very rich, who used such images to establish and secure an aura of privilege.

Since his death, Rubens' reputation in art circles has enjoyed the highest of acclaim, as well as meriting the most deliberate of criticism. Today his prestige as the quintessential Baroque painter appears to be in decline. Some speculate that this may have much to

do with more middle-class modern tastes, which typically embrace art produced within similar circumstances (such as the Dutch Baroque, see pages 258–260). Perhaps Rubens' work embraces a lifestyle and an aura of privilege no longer fashionable, and as a result his work is viewed as decadent. (Note once again that it is one's own set of socially defined values that determines the worth of a work of art.)

The most common complaint about Rubens' work is also one of its most illuminating features. The figures, which play an increasing role in Rubens' paintings, are often considered unsightly as body types. Today the term "Rubenesque" refers more to a plump and fleshy figure than it does to any other stylistic convention. In one respect, Rubens' refusal to conform to Classical female prototypes can be taken as a reassertion of a northern inclination toward naturalism. On the other hand, portraiture of this period clearly indicates that the majority of women did not possess the figurative attributes of Rubens' nudes. Was Rubens, then, viewing his female figure-types as embodiments of sensuality and nature or did they indeed derive from another source? These are provocative questions, not easily answered, yet they amply reflect the modern appreciation of these figures. At least one thing is clear, and that is the simple truth that Rubens was unparalleled in his free and unencumbered use of the oil-paint medium. No artist had ever given flesh such an organic reality and handled complex compositional problems with such apparent ease.

Rembrandt knew of Rubens' *Descent from the Cross* by way of the engraving by Lucas Vorsterman, whose faithful reproduction was widely known throughout Europe. By 1630 the Flemish master had not only established a considerable reputation in his own country but was also revered in the Dutch provinces to the north. The Dutch writer and critic Constanin Huygens considered Rubens "the greatest painter in all the Netherlands" and claimed that his influence was recognizable in the works of many of the artists of the North. Rembrandt was one such artist. Thirty years younger than Rubens, he entered into an art world in which the achievements of the Italian Baroque were fully understood; its conventions were commonplace in most of the European art centers. The tradition of chiaroscuro, carried on by the followers of Caravaggio, was particularly popular in the northern Netherlands at the time of Rembrandt's emergence as an artist.

By the 1630s, the city of Utrecht had become known for its community of Caravaggisti — the most prominent artists being Gerrit van Honthorst (1590–1656), Dirck van Baburen (c. 1595–1624), and Hendrick Terbrugghen (1588–1629; Fig. **5.39**). In particular, the Utrecht Caravaggisti contributed a specific convention to Dutch painting that was to become essential to the young Rembrandt: the use of the **repoussoir** figure — one or more silhouetted figures situated in the immediate foreground facing away from the viewer and thereby creating a more convincing sense of space in the middleground area. This convention also gave the work an increased sense of intimacy; the viewer was now an implied bystander to the activities within the painting, behind other deliberately positioned spectators.

A good example of this convention can be seen in Honthorst's *Merry Company* (Fig. **5.40**) of 1620, in which the dark figure on the left side acts as a gauge of space on the foreground plane, projecting an impression that the light source and the other players rest in the middleground. This dramatic device found its maturity in the work of Rembrandt, who by 1633 had started to work on a series of Passion pictures for the Prince of Orange.

■ **5.39** Hendrick Terbrugghen
St. Sebastian attended by St. Irene 1625
Oil on canvas
4 ft 11 in x 3 ft 10½ in (1.49 x 1.19 m)
Allen Art Museum, Ohio; R. T. Miller, Jr. Fund, 1953 (53.256)

■ 5.40 Gerrit van Honthorst, *Merry Company* (*The Prodigal Son in the Brothel*) 1620
Oil on canvas, 4 ft 6 in x 7 ft (1.37 x 2.13 m)
Uffizi Gallery, Florence

Viewing the paintings of Rubens and Rembrandt side by side, there appear marked differences between the artists in both stylistic approach and emotional sensibility. Though Rembrandt paid explicit homage to the work of the Flemish painter through his allusion to the Christ gesture, his painting was not only a reworking of the Rubens altarpiece but also a complete transformation of the subject matter. Gone are the Classical heroics of the Rubens works, and in its place is a quiet, solemn, and intimate portrayal of the descent of the dead Christ. The extreme musculature of the Jesus on the Rubens altarpiece — so much in keeping with the revival of the Church — finds its opposite in the pitiful figure in Rembrandt's *Descent from the Cross* (see Fig. 5.36). This, like the Christs of Grünewald, is a portrayal of a limp and lifeless corpse, a figure of sacrifice rather than of Classical heroics.

The extreme pathos is further intensified by the illumination of the middleground; it situates the scene not in the immediate and confrontational foreground (as in Rubens' painting) but to the back, not immediately accessible to the viewer. This scene does not celebrate or confront with large figures and explosive gestures; instead it patiently embraces the spectator. Even the color is subdued, leaving the scene to quiet contemplation rather than imposing itself on the public. This is Rembrandt's private searching made public, and in both its quiet resignation and its haunting mood, it anticipates many of his later great paintings.

Rembrandt's level of inquiry is perhaps best felt in his engaging series of self-portraits, executed from the 1620s through to his death in 1669. They are fascinating documents of an artist as both subject and object

■ 5.41 Rembrandt van Rijn
Self Portrait with Saskia on His Lap c. 1635
Oil on canvas, 5 ft 8⅜ in x 4 ft 3½ in (1.01 x 1.31 m)
Gemäldegalerie, Dresden

Portrait (Fig. **5.42**) of the late 1650s exhibits a very different sensibility; charm has given way to a more complete and penetrating portrayal of endurance and perseverance in the face of time.

Popular mythology has embraced Rembrandt as a brooding, intense individual — the perfect stereotype of the romantic artist. Little of this has any basis in fact, but his paintings, and indeed paint handling, have often been used to support these claims. Paint handling (the application of paint onto the canvas or panel) was often ignored by Baroque artists, who saw any reliance on materials as a distraction from the so-called "higher principles" of composition and rendering. In Rembrandt's work, the method of applying material is inseparable from the subject matter — and thus the meaning of the painting.

The famous *Side of Beef* (Fig. **5.43**) of 1655 is an excellent example of Rembrandt's skill in integrating the paint into the very subject of the work; the often

■ 5.42 Rembrandt van Rijn
Self Portrait c. 1659
Oil on canvas, 33¼ x 26 in (84.4 x 66 cm)
National Gallery of Art, Washington, D.C.

of contemplation, and in their extreme intimacy, they provide the viewer with singular insights into the dynamic psychological potential of painting. Rembrandt's close and unrelenting observation of the ageing process — in both physical and emotional terms — is comparable in its riveting honesty only with the self-portraiture of his fellow-countryman Vincent van Gogh over two centuries later.

Two examples, taken from very different periods in Rembrandt's life, exhibit this move toward greater introspection. The *Self Portrait with Saskia on his Lap* (Fig. **5.41**) of c. 1635 is one of the truly engaging portraits of the young artist during his early successes, as Rembrandt poses with his bride Saskia in an uncharacteristic scene of celebration and joviality. Though the smile on the artist's face seems slightly awkward, the scene is one of the all too few examples of Rembrandt's charm as a genre painter (a painter of scenes of everyday life). In comparison, the *Self*

■ 5.43 Rembrandt van Rijn
Side of Beef 1655
Oil on canvas
37 x 27⅛ in (94 x 69 cm)
Louvre, Paris

■ 5.44 Detail of *Side of Beef* showing the build up of paint

thick and textured paint makes demands on the viewer's attention. One possible explanation for Rembrandt's desire to put such large amounts of paint on his canvas is perhaps the way in which it molds and models the carcass; the paint then becomes a metaphor for meat, and its sinewy application reaffirms the texture and structure of the animal. Whatever the initial reasons may have been for constructing this painting in such a manner, the use of the paint nevertheless gives the viewer an intimate chance to retrace the work process of the artist. When paint is applied in such a way, the gestures of the brush or knife are often very visible. By examining such traces, one is then equally conscious of both the work process and its eventual result (Fig. **5.44**). In many areas of the painting, the viewer is privy to

Rembrandt's gestures with the brush, and through them comes to a further appreciation of the artist's relationship to the work.

Rembrandt and the Art of Etching

Though Rembrandt is best known as a painter, he was also an extremely accomplished etcher, with a lively and lucid line quality that culminated in a series of moving and intimate prints. His etchings are perhaps unparalleled in their marriage of technical skill and emotional insight, and are interesting for both their inventiveness and their sheer visual energy. It is true that the use of **etching** ☐ as a technical process did not begin with Rembrandt, but in his adept hands it arguably found its greatest expression.

FOCUS ON

Etching

The process initially began by covering an iron plate with a thin layer of melted wax, which served as a resist, keeping the plate surface protected from its later immersion in an acid bath. Having prepared the plate, the artist would lightly scratch into the soft wax surface, removing its thin skin and exposing the metal base. The plate was then soaked in a bath of diluted acid, which reacted to the exposed iron and created a trough — the longer the plate's exposure to the acid, the deeper the "bite." The final step in this process was the removal of the resist (the wax skin), leaving behind an "etched" design on the metal surface. At this point, the plate would be inked and fed into the press like an engraving (Fig. **5.45**).

■ **5.45** Diagram of etching plate process

A cross-section of a plate which shows all surfaces coated with an acid-resistant resin.

The coating is then scratched with a steel burin to form the lines of the design.

The plate is then immersed in acid and the scratched lines (unprotected by the resin) become etched into the metal surface.

The resin coating is then removed and the plate is wiped with ink. This ink fills the lines of the design and these lines are forced from the plate onto paper under pressure in a printing press.

Etching (which comes from either the old High German word *azzen* or the Dutch word *etsen*, both meaning to bite, hence to eat) was first practically applied to printmaking in the early sixteenth century, when techniques borrowed from armor decorators enabled artists such as Dürer to begin producing a new type of printed image. As a technique, etching involves many of the same principles as metal engraving, such as the wiping of the plate, the embedding of ink below the surface of the metal, and the printing of the image in a press. However, with etching the artist engages in a further chemical process that alleviates many of the frustrating difficulties inherent in engraving.

A key player in the development of etching was the French artist Jacques Callot (1592/3–1635). Most noted for his strikingly impartial depictions of the atrocities of war, he was also a master craftsperson who extended the then restrictive boundaries of etching through the use of some inventive new techniques. In one of his first important works, the *Great Fair at Imprunita* (Fig. **5.46**), he carefully depicted over 1,100 figures in a neatly constructed composition. In developing such a scene, Callot introduced two innovative technical devices to the etching process: a change of ground to resist the acid and a new scratching tool. Frustrated, like his predecessors, by the traditional wax ground that gave an uneven bite and was too soft to allow for detailed work, he substituted a harder varnish (then used in the making of musical instruments). This change of material allowed artists to generate a more subtle line quality and an easier reproduction of the intended image. When this innovation was combined with the introduction of the *echoppe* (a cylindrical drawing tool with one end cut to produce a rounded point like an engraving tool), the result was a freer and more workable medium, capable of both tremendous accuracy and spontaneity.

With these technical innovations already in place by the time of Rembrandt's birth, the Dutch artist was able to manipulate and develop further the young medium — in his hands, etching was more than a technique for reproducing images: it was a valid basis and starting point for the making of art. The result is nothing short of breathtaking. Introduced to the various printmaking processes while still in his twenties, Rembrandt took to etching immediately. The quality of line afforded by the acid-biting technique enabled him to produce a wide assortment of expressive marks, using such varied instruments as nails and spikes to make drawings in the resist. His earliest attempts, such as his *Self Portrait by Candlelight* (Fig. **5.47**), already exhibit the strength and emotional vibrance of an artist set on expanding the boundaries of etching.

▲ 5.46 Jacques Callot, *Great Fair at Imprunita* 1620
Intaglio, 16 ¹⁵/₁₆ x 26¹/₄ in (43 x 66.7 cm)
The Metropolitan Museum of Art
Harris Brisbane Dick Fund, 1917 (17.3.2645)

◄ 5.47 Rembrandt van Rijn, *Self Portrait by Candlelight* 1630
Etching
Staatliches Museum, Berlin

By the time Rembrandt reached Amsterdam in 1631, he had begun experimenting with "state prints" and "selective wiping," both of which grant the viewer privileged access to the artist's work process. The term *state print* refers to the initial printing and subsequent changing of an etched plate — a process that demonstrates the movement of an artist's idea over a period of time. By printing the plate at different times in the working out of a pictorial problem, the artist has the opportunity better to consider a decision without the inevitable loss of the original image.

A clear example of Rembrandt's use of the state print can be seen in his *Christ Presented to the People* of 1655. The first state of this print (Fig. **5.48**) depicts the silent Christ as he is brought before the people of

■ **5.48** Rembrandt van Rijn, *Christ Presented to the People* 1655, Etching (first state)
The Metropolitan Museum of Art, Gift of Felix M. Warburg and His Family, 1941 (41.1.34)

Jerusalem. Below him are gathered the vengeful crowds, who stand to judge him. Though one may appreciate the skill of the drawing and the lightness of touch present in the artist's portrayal of these figures, Rembrandt obviously felt them a distraction to the viewer. In attempting to clarify the composition and complement the subject matter, he removed the centralized crowd, opting instead for the deep, cavernous hollow that better focuses attention on the Christ fig-

ure. By scraping back into the copper plate (which had by this time replaced iron) and slowly burnishing down the etched lines, Rembrandt was able to remove almost all trace of those original figures — leaving only "ghosts" as a reminder of their presence (Fig. **5.49**). By executing the print in this manner, the viewer is granted intimate access to the private world of a great artist at work.

When the final state was ready to print, Rembrandt

■ 5.49 Rembrandt van Rijn, *Christ Presented to the People* 1655, Etching (last state)
Reproduced by Courtesy of the Trustees of the British Museum, London

would then manipulate the ink spread on the plate, allowing for an uneven wiping of the surface to give each printed image a particular character of its own. The result was a sometimes hazy clouding of the image, in keeping with the artist's use of chiaroscuro.

Rembrandt's prints are among the great treasures of the period, and today they still attract attention as works of consummate skill and feeling. In assimilating the technical innovations of his time and combining them with the insights and vision of a great artist, Rembrandt produced printed works for which there is little comparison. Though he is generally regarded as a great painter, his skills as a printmaker were equally revolutionary and are equally admirable.

Portraiture and other Genres: Hals, Van Dyck, Vermeer

Though Rubens and Rembrandt were by far the most prolific and esteemed of the artists of the divided Netherlands, there were others of note who also contributed to this so-called "Golden Age" of painting. One of the most famous was Frans Hals (c. 1581–1666), whose vibrant brushwork was particularly revered by nineteenth-century artists.

Hals was a portrait artist, and his work runs the social gamut, from images of the unusual and the downcast, to vast group portraits of the well-to-do. One such portrait is the *Banquet of the Officers of the St.*

■ 5.50 Frans Hals, *Banquet of the Officers of the St. George Militia Company of Haarlem* 1616
Oil on canvas, 5 ft 8⅞ in x 11 ft 5½ in (1.75 x 3.5 m),
Frans HalsMuseum, Haarlem

George Militia Company of Haarlem (Fig. **5.50**) of 1616, depicting a men's social club cleverly disguised as a militia brigade. Hals' talents in organizing space and creating ambience and sparkling color are very much in evidence in this work; they were qualities in considerable demand during the period. Perhaps a more dramatic example of his enormous skill as a painter can be seen in his so-called *Laughing Cavalier* (Fig. **5.51**) of 1624. His slashing strokes, which seem to suggest rather than model, complement the dramatic contrasts of color and tone in his painting. The result is a body of works that embrace the act of painting as much as they do the descriptive function of the portrait. With Hals one may rightly use the term "impression-like," because his work glorifies the beauty of the passing moment and the charm of the little event — the very pictorial qualities the nineteenth-century Impressionists embraced.

On the other side of the Flemish-Dutch border emerged an artist of very different sensibilities, the portrait painter Anthony van Dyck (1599–1641), who worked with a clientele slightly more inclined to the grand commissioned portraiture of old than the seem-

ingly spontaneous outpourings of Hals. Implicit within this assumption (that a particular style or manifestation of painting can correspond with the needs or aspirations of a given class or clientele) is the idea that art carries a series of subtle value considerations often left unacknowledged. At least in this respect, Hals and van Dyck provide a fascinating looking-glass into the explicitly social nature of portraiture.

One of van Dyck's most interesting works is the 1635 portrait of *Charles I, King of England* (Fig. **5.52**). Van Dyck's ability to imbue grace and esteem in the personality of his sitter is truly remarkable. Unlike his master Rubens (in whose studio he had briefly worked during the years 1618–20), van Dyck situated his figure not in some grand allegorical composition but in a moment of quiet pleasure, as befitting his stature as ruler over the landscape he surveys. Whereas Hals' excited brushwork created a slightly shifting and dynamic image, van Dyck's refined and delicate manner only heightened the already present aura of dignity and authority. Here, the relationships between material handling, composition, and subject

■ 5.51 Frans Hals
Laughing Cavalier 1624
Oil on canvas
33¾ x 27 in (86 x 69 cm)
Reproduced by permission of the Trustees, The Wallace Collection, London

matter combine to produce a package suitable for the social and political needs of the sitter. Thus van Dyck's paintings, like those of his contemporaries Rubens, Rembrandt, and Hals, entered into the larger context of issues and class distinctions that were already beginning to surface — finding their culmination in the bloodbaths of the eighteenth century's revolutions. Van Dyck's creation of an imagery of royalty and dignity operated as effective propaganda.

However, such dignity, maintained by the portrait, was insufficient to prevent Charles' execution in 1649 during the English Civil War. So in the end, van Dyck perhaps did more for his sitters than the history books could, presenting them as civil and dignified human beings at a moment in time.

Today, one of the most popular of the Dutch Baroque painters is Johannes (Jan) Vermeer (1632–75), whose reputation was saved from obscurity in

◄ 5.52 Anthony van Dyck
Charles I, King of England 1635
Oil on canvas
8 ft 8¾ in x 6 ft 9½ in (2.66 x 2.07 m)
Louvre, Paris

► 5.53 Jan Vermeer
Interior with a Woman Reading a Letter c. 1662–4
Oil on canvas
18⅓ x 15⅓ in (46.5 x 39 cm)
Rijksmuseum, Amsterdam

the nineteenth century after almost 200 years of neglect. Few artists have captured the quiet moments of domestic tranquility better than he, and his meticulous rendering of the effects of the cold northern light of morning is utterly convincing. Vermeer turned his attention predominantly to genre scenes — concentrating on everyday activities rather than formal portraiture. Since these scenes were not person specific, they appealed to a number of prospective buyers — in keeping with the strictures of the market, in which the Dutch artist had to compete. His *Interior with a Woman Reading a Letter* (Fig. **5.53**) of c. 1662–4 is one such intimate portrayal. The cool colors of the scene — a variety of muted blues and yellows — are somewhat typical in Vermeer's work. Behind the woman there hangs a large map — a reminder of the

■ 5.54 Camera Obscura in cutaway view 1646, engraving
Museum of Photography at George Eastman House
Rochester, New York

might and prestige of the Dutch merchant fleet — which acts both as a development of subject matter (perhaps she is reading a letter from a loved one far away) and as a deliberate use of geometric form to strengthen the composition. Some 250 years later, another Dutch artist, Piet Mondrian (1872–1944), was to cite Vermeer as an influence in his development of geometric abstraction.

Little is known about Vermeer's life, and from the very small body of work that survives it appears that he was not particularly prolific. It is probable that he employed a technical device called a *camera obscura* (Fig. **5.54**) in the production of his highly illusionistic pictures. This rather rudimentary device is little more than an enclosed box form illuminated by a small hole in one of its walls. As a result of the physical properties of light, the beam that passes through this hole projects onto the opposite interior wall all the elements of the exterior environment, only upside-down — an almost exact duplicate that can then be traced by the artist. This helps explain the breathless representational clarity of Vermeer's work, while also accounting for the peculiar, almost abstract quality of light that filters through many of his paintings.

It is clear from the multitude of calendars, posters, and picture books on Vermeer currently available that these scenes of quiet, domestic, middle-class virtue continue to strike a modern (or perhaps a nostalgic) chord; perhaps his work reflects a kind of solitude and tranquility, a pictorial release from current anxieties. Vermeer's paintings have been successfully assimilated into the tastes of the late twentieth century, and in that way they too document some of the thoughts

and aspirations of the present age. In the mid-twentieth century, Rubens was the most prized and respected of the Baroque artists; today many find him excessive. Though it is probable that Vermeer's reputation will decline over the next decades, the necessary re-evaluation of his work in the late nineteenth century has left the world a little more at peace with itself.

The Dutch art community distinguished itself in a vast array of subjects. There were flower painters such as Willeboirts Bosschaert (1573–1621), Jan de Heem (1606–83/4), and Rachel Ruysch (1664–1750; Fig. **5.55**), still-life artists such as Willem Heda (1594–1860) and Pieter Claesz (1597/8–1661), landscape painters such as Aelbert Cuyp (1620–91) and Jacob van Ruisdael (c. 1628–82; Fig. **5.56**), and even those who specialized in farm animal paintings, such as Paulus Potter (1625–54). This subject specialization became very popular with artists over the next generations, as developing a sound reputation in one area of

■ 5.55 Rachel Ruysch, *Flowers in a Vase* 1698
Canvas, 23 x 17½ in (58.5 x 44.5 cm)
Städelsches Institut, Frankfurt

■ 5.56 Jacob van Ruisdael, *View of Haarlem from the Dunes at Overveen* c. 1670
Oil on canvas, 22 x 25 in (55.8 x 63.5 cm)
Mauritshuis, The Hague

expertise was essential to their survival in a competitive marketplace (mimicking the specialization of labor going on in all sectors of society). Few ventured into such dramatically different avenues as Rembrandt, but then again, few had his great skills. Yet this short era in the history of Western art (approximately 1600–1680) produced some of its greatest paintings, cultivated in an economic and political climate very different from that of the previous era. The Dutch "experiment" is one of the great examples of the interplay between social and economic realities, and the culture that derives from its body. In its breadth and foresight, the Dutch Baroque set the stage for the modern idea of art.

THE DECLINE OF THE BAROQUE

In 1689 the Dutch Stadholder William III, Prince of Orange, and his wife, Mary Stuart, became the monarchs of England and Scotland. This political shift came at the end of the so-called Golden Age of the Dutch. The exhaustion of the Dutch economy caused by years of warfare against Louis XIV's French armies coincided with a more general retreat from the aggressive expansion of trade and commerce that had marked the Golden Age. Competition from England, France, and the Baltic states challenged Dutch supremacy on the seas, and more conservative schemes came to replace the lively speculative invest-ment that had been a feature of the Amsterdam financial markets. Stylistic innovation in the arts also slowed with the stagnation of the economy, signaling the end of the Golden Age of Dutch painting.

The decline of energy that marked the end of the Baroque era affected the arts as well as the political aspirations of the dominant groups in each European nation. The period was characterized by contradiction rather than unity; Reformation verses Counter-Reformation, aristocratic patronage versus the bour-geois marketplace, and the grand-style decorative program versus the bawdy genre scene (Fig. **5.57**). Yet the sheer output and energy of this period were among the most decisive and unifying characteristics of the seventeenth century.

Louis XIV, the Sun King began building his great palace at Versailles in 1661. It was to be the clearest expression of the Baroque age in its scale, grandeur, and excess. It was also to be the ultimate symbol of power befitting the stature of its owner. On his deathbed, he left his great-grandson, Louis XV, with a prophetic indictment of both the excesses of his

patronage and the art it produced. It is perhaps fitting that this chapter should end with his chilling words: "My child, do not imitate me in my taste for building; it spells the ruin of the people."

SUMMARY

There are few periods in the history of Western art to compare with the Baroque for vitality and sheer output. A century and a half of political and religious turmoil had a profound effect on Europe's view of the role of art in society, and helped set the stage for modern conceptions of the art market and the autonomous creator. With the significant shift in patronage that began to occur during the period, art, which had formerly reflected almost exclusively the desires of the Church, now began to cater for a more broadly based market. In this way, the art of the Baroque period set an early but important precedent for the slow release of culture into the growing middle class.

Suggested Reading

Blunt, Anthony: *Art and Architecture in France 1500–1700* (Harmondsworth and New York: Penguin Books). Useful survey of the period.

Enggass, R. and Brown, J.: *Italy and Spain 1600–1750: Sources and Documents* (Englewood Cliffs, NJ: Prentice-Hall, 1970). For those interested in original documents from the era, including artists' statements and critical writings.

Hyatt Major, A.: *Prints and People* (Princeton, NJ: Princeton University Press, 1971). Informative and well written text on etching and engraving.

Rich, J. C.: *The Materials and Methods of Sculpture* (New York and Oxford: Oxford University Press, 1947; reprinted New York: Dover Books, 1975). Contains useful information on technical aspects of the Baroque such as stone carving.

Rosenberg, J., Slive, S., and ter Kuile, E. H.: *Dutch Art and Architecture 1600–1800* (Harmondsworth and New York: Penguin Books).

Saff, D. and Sacilotto, D.: *Printmaking: History and Process* (New York: Holt, Rinehart, & Winston, 1978). Informative text on etching and engraving in the Baroque period.

Wittkower: *Art and Architecture in Italy 1600–1750* (Harmondsworth and New York: Penguin Books).

Pronunciation Guide

Baroque   buh-**ROHK**
Jacques Callot   zhahk ka-**LOH**
Caravaggio   **kar**-uh-**VAH**-joh
Caravaggisti   **kar**-uh-vah-**JEES**-tee
Annibale Carracci   ahn-**NEE**-bah-lay kuh-**RAH**-chee
chiaroscuro   kee-**ahr**-uh-**SKOOR**-oh
Jean-Baptiste Colbert   zhan ba-**TEEST** kawl-**BAIR**
Artemisia Gentileschi   **ahrt**-uh-**MIZ**-ee-uh **jen**-tuh-**LES**-kee
Simon Guillain   see-**MOHN** gee-**YAYN**
Gerrit van Honthorst   **GER**-uht vahn **HAWNT**-hawrst
Parmigianino   **pahr**-mih-jah-**NEE**-noh
Jacopo da Pontormo   **YAHK**-oh-poh dah pohn-**TOR**-moh
Nicolas Poussin   **NEE**-koh-lah poo-**SAN**
repoussoir   **ray**-poo-**SWAHR**
Rembrandt van Rijn   **REM**-brant vahn-**REYE(N)**
Jacob van Ruisdael   **YA**-kop vahn **ROYS**-dahl
Rachel Ruysch   **RA**-kel roys
Pieter Saenredam   **PEE**-tur **SAN**-re-dahm
Gerard Terborch   **GAY**-rahrt ter-**BORK**
Hendrick Terbrugghen   **HEN**-drik tur-**BRUHG**-uhn
Diego Velázquez   dee-**AY**-goh vuh-**LAHS**-kays

Glossary

Baroque (*page 226*) A term used to identify the period in Western art from c. 1600 to c. 1750. Its linguistic origins indicate something complex, intricate, or irregular, and it most likely refers to the increase in emotional content and exuberant composition after the restraint of the Renaissance.

chiaroscuro (*page 235*) From the Italian "light and shade," it is a technique for suggesting three dimensions by modeling figures in highlight and shadow.

etching (*page 267*) Derived from the old High German word *azzen* or the Dutch *etsen* to eat, it is a printmaking process that involves the drawing of lines into a resist already painted on a metal plate. Drawing removes the resist, exposing the metal, which is then submerged in acid (called "biting"). The exposed metal is then eaten into, leaving a series of lines "etched" in the metal. When the plate is inked, printing will faithfully reproduce the original lines.

Mannerism (*page 231*) A transitional period between the High Renaissance and the advent of the Baroque (c. 1600) characterized by stylistic virtuosity and compositional complexity over conventions of restraint and idealism.

naturalism (*page 235*) Art that draws from the world as it exists in perception, without idealization (often opposed to the precepts of Classicism, which forms ideals from natural phenomena).

repoussoir figure (*page 264*) An object or figure placed in the immediate foreground of a composition whose purpose is to direct the viewer's eye into the picture.

tenebroso (*page 236*) The theatrical application of light and shade in painting to provide strong contrasts and emotional effects.

6

REASON AND REVOLUTION

Eighteenth- and Early

Nineteenth-Century

Art in Europe

■ 6.1 Jacques-Louis David
The Oath of the Tennis Court (June 20, 1789)
Musée Carnavalet, Paris

With terrors round, can reason hold her throne,
Despise the known, nor tremble at the unknown?
Survey both worlds, intrepid and desire,
In spite of witches, devils, dreams and fire.

ALEXANDER POPE

"My child, do not imitate me in my taste for building; it spells the ruin of the people." With those prophetic words, the dying King Louis XIV of France ushered in an age of doubt and conflict that would signal the slow but steady demise of the Baroque era. He was talking, of course, about the Palace of Versailles (Fig. **6.2**), that example of aristocratic indulgence and deified power that was to preoccupy the French imagination during its sixteen years of construction (1669–85) and subsequent decades of debt. At its height, Versailles housed almost 4,000 servants and encompassed thousands of acres of carefully groomed "nature." Today it stands as one of the most exquisite examples of Baroque sensibility in architectural form, and in retrospect perhaps the most inane. Although the bloodbath which has come to be known as the French Revolution was still a century away from the completion of Versailles, the palace's image and aura planted a symbolic seed in the hearts of the masses — revolution.

■ **6.2 Louis Le Vau and Jules Hardouin-Mansart**
Palace of Versailles 1669–85
Garden Facade

VERSAILLES AND THE DECLINE OF BAROQUE

As a building, Versailles is quintessentially Baroque, with a fittingly French accent. As exteriors go, the palace stands as a monument to the lasting virtues of symmetry, order, and restraint — the very principles Louis XIV admired in artists such as Poussin, on whom he modeled the ethos of his French Academy. The facade extends for almost half a mile (about 800 m) and the dominant horizontality of the design is interrupted only by the inclusion of several small pavilions articulated with standing columns that jut out slightly from the face of the structure. It is in essence a monument to Classical design. However, on the inside, opulence reigned (Fig. **6.3**). The analogy

to a body is both fitting and appropriate here, and it says much about the subsequent decline of the Baroque era in Europe.

By the middle of the seventeenth century, the initial inroads of the Counter-Reformation spirit (in which art was certainly an influential player) had begun to level out, and as a result art production turned increasingly away from the patronage of the Church. The demise of the Church's moral authority in an increasingly rational world coincided with the rise, and subsequent wealth and autonomy, of the European nation states and their colonies. By the end of the seventeenth century, authority rested not in

■ 6.3 Jules Hardouin-Mansart and Charles Le Brun
The Hall of Mirrors
Interior of the Palace of Versailles, begun 1678

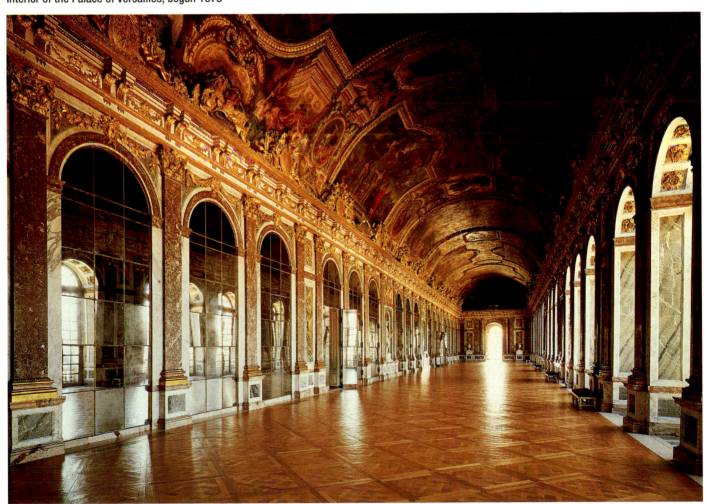

the will of God but with the might of armies and the whims of royalty. Although the world might not have looked different, power now rested in more pragmatic hands.

The earlier discussion of ancient Egyptian art argued that monuments existed as visual demonstrations of the status quo. In order to produce a monument, one needs funding, land, and laborers. So the people in a position to acquire all these can, and often do, produce visual objects and images that reflect their interests. The absence of monuments to people of color and to women throughout the history of American art bears out this contention. The larger the project, the greater the funding, and thus many of the most elaborate structures in history are reflections of the interests and ideas of those in positions of power. Cathedrals were erected in a similar way and with similar psychological intent. However, religious buildings have had the added benefit of a supposedly moral underpinning, that effectively diverts criticism away from the less savory issues of excess and onto the questionable moral character of the critic. In nation states, such forms of criticism were often considered treasonous — affronts to the authority of those in power.

Within this context one man began to examine the tricky relationship between art and power — a course that set important precedents for later art criticism. His name was Jean-Jacques Rousseau, and his target was Versailles.

■ 6.4 Europe c. 1730

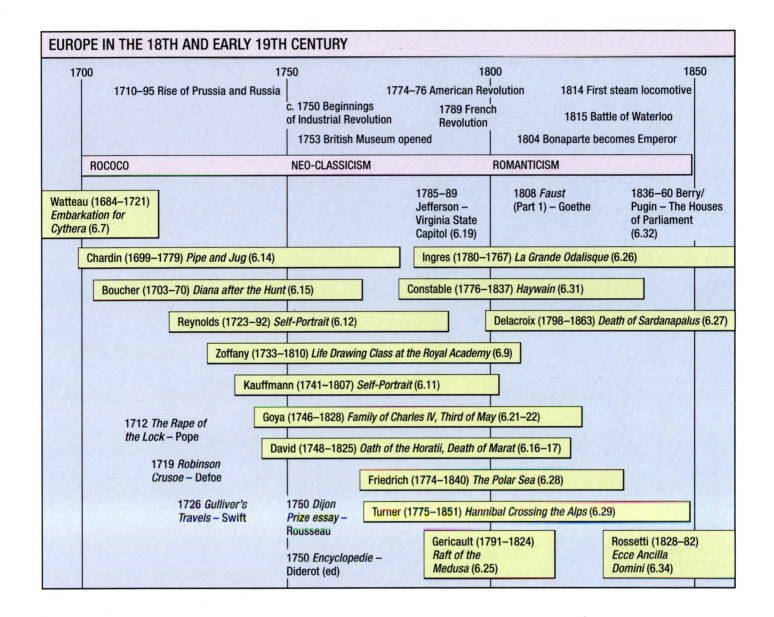

EUROPE IN THE 18TH AND EARLY 19TH CENTURY

1700	1750	1800	1850
1710–95 Rise of Prussia and Russia		1774–76 American Revolution	1814 First steam locomotive
	c. 1750 Beginnings of Industrial Revolution	1789 French Revolution	1815 Battle of Waterloo
	1753 British Museum opened		1804 Bonaparte becomes Emperor

ROCOCO	NEO-CLASSICISM	ROMANTICISM

Watteau (1684–1721) *Embarkation for Cythera* (6.7)

1785–89 Jefferson – Virginia State Capitol (6.19)

1808 *Faust* (Part 1) – Goethe

1836–60 Berry/ Pugin – The Houses of Parliament (6.32)

Chardin (1699–1779) *Pipe and Jug* (6.14)

Ingres (1780–1767) *La Grande Odalisque* (6.26)

Boucher (1703–70) *Diana after the Hunt* (6.15)

Constable (1776–1837) *Haywain* (6.31)

Reynolds (1723–92) *Self-Portrait* (6.12)

Delacroix (1798–1863) *Death of Sardanapalus* (6.27)

Zoffany (1733–1810) *Life Drawing Class at the Royal Academy* (6.9)

Kauffmann (1741–1807) *Self-Portrait* (6.11)

1712 *The Rape of the Lock* – Pope

Goya (1746–1828) *Family of Charles IV, Third of May* (6.21–22)

David (1748–1825) *Oath of the Horatii, Death of Marat* (6.16–17)

1719 *Robinson Crusoe* – Defoe

Friedrich (1774–1840) *The Polar Sea* (6.28)

1726 *Gulliver's Travels* – Swift

1750 *Dijon Prize essay* – Rousseau

Turner (1775–1851) *Hannibal Crossing the Alps* (6.29)

1750 *Encyclopedie* – Diderot (ed)

Gericault (1791–1824) *Raft of the Medusa* (6.25)

Rossetti (1828–82) *Ecce Ancilla Domini* (6.34)

Rousseau's Critique of Versailles

Rousseau (1712–78) is best known for his idea of the "noble savage" — a person living free of the corrupting influences of society and education. This ideal followed the premise that individuals are by nature good and it is social constructs that inevitably corrupt. Living as he did in a country in which virtually every aspect of "high" culture was overseen by the Crown, Rousseau understood implicitly the need of the aristocracy to maintain a cultural status quo. (Consider the discussion in the previous chapter of the intentions of the French court in the reorganization of the French Academy in 1663.) Rousseau saw this arrangement as a microcosm of the world's problems; the dominating influence of sanctioned culture further alienated the people, replacing "natural" feelings with "correct" feelings, given to the people by those in power. In 1750 Rousseau gave substance to these thoughts in an essay on Versailles that remains one of the most penetrating readings of the structure ever written.

Rousseau's use of the "forbidden" topic of Versailles (the government censors were understandably uneasy with any critical discussion of the subject), and in particular the gardens (Fig. **6.5**), is an indictment not only of aristocratic power but also of the human desire to control the world. Rousseau under-

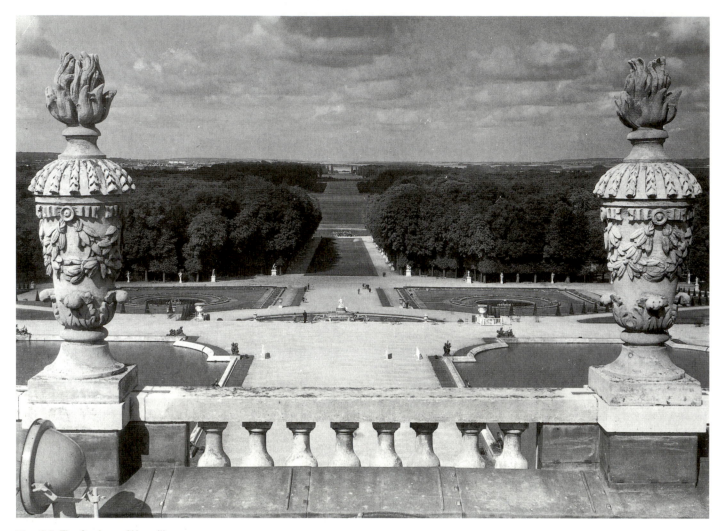

■ **6.5 The Gardens of Versailles**
planned 1661–8, executed 1662–90

stood the connection between the control of nature and the control of people, and set about, within the context of the Versailles gardens, to draw on such parallels (Fig. **6.6**). In his Dijon Prize essay of 1750, he wrote:

A stroll through the gardens of Versailles represents a direct challenge to man's impulse toward virtue and an invitation to join in collective corruption...A society which can ordain such a travesty of nature must by definition be corrupt. Our gardens are adorned by statues and our galleries by paintings. What would you expect to be shown from these masterpieces of art, exposed to the admiration of the masses? Great men who have defended their country or those still greater who have enriched it with virtue? No, these are all images of the aberrations of the heart and mind, carefully selected from mythology in order to have models of misconduct...this is the work of the arts that secretly exert their influence in the governmental chambers.

Apparently, Rousseau understood art as both a tool of corruption and an unconscious representation of the larger corruptions of the age. This is indeed a balanced interpretation, as art is viewed in this critical model as both manipulating and manipulated. Yet consider a more positive extension of such a theory. If, as Rousseau claimed, art has the capacity to corrupt, it must by extension have the ability to inspire, and it was this very dynamic that was to perplex and captivate both artists and critics for the next 200 years.

■ 6.6 André Le Nôtre
Plan of the Gardens and Park of Versailles
17th-century engraving

THE ROCOCO

Few periods in art history continue to bring out such violent reactions from modern viewers as that which spanned most of the eighteenth century up to the French Revolution — a period commonly referred to as the **Rococo**. The term, once again dating from a later period, derived from a negative value judgment, the word *rocaille* — a delicate and ornate form of shell and rock work used to decorate walls and floors, thus denying anything more profound than a trivial and decorative character to the art of the period. In today's vocabulary, Rococo has come to mean tasteless, gaudy, and contentless decoration, and subsequently few are willing to admit to a liking for such fancies. As with Versailles, Rococo art embodies an age and a sensibility far removed from our own, but it nonetheless set in motion a precedent for the explicit and the pleasurable that has survived in some facets of art to this day.

Watteau

One of the great masters of this period was Jean-Antoine Watteau (1684–1721), whose *Embarkation from Cythera* (Fig. **6.7**) of 1717 embodies some of the complex concerns of the late Baroque age. The painting is loosely about a pilgrimage to the shrine of Venus on the island of Cythera, where the reward is love without any restraints. The subject might be considered too trite and gratuitous in the present cynical age, but for Watteau the concept of profane love was inextricably intertwined with other issues of the period — the ideas of freedom and human nature.

■ 6.7 Antoine Watteau, *Embarkation from Cythera* 1717
Oil on canvas, 4 ft 2¾ in x 6 ft 2¾ in (1.28 x 1.89 m). Louvre, Paris

Until that time, the conventions of Western art had strictly excluded the explicit presentation of passion and eroticism. The declining influence of the Church and the creation by Louis XIV and his successors of a large court with dwindling political and executive roles led to an increasingly elaborate and luxurious court culture. While philosophers examined the possibilities of rational argument, artists, like their courtly patrons, concentrated on exploring the possibilities of human relationships and feelings, especially courtship and love.

One of the most popular complaints about a painting such as *Embarkation from Cythera* is its apparent delicacy — a technical exuberance considered by some as inherently "feminine" in sensibility (or so said the eighteenth-century critic Diderot). As early as 1713, the British critic the third Earl of Shaftesbury claimed that looking at a Rococo painting was much like looking at a woman's dress, which, he said, would "make effeminate our Tastes, and utterly set wrong as to all Judgment and Knowledge in the kind." One can surmise from this claim that high or good art is supposedly about rational, sturdy, moral (read masculine) virtues — the virtues of the academies and of the governments that supported them — and not about profane love. This implicit male/female polemic continued to taint art language for the next 200 years, and today it is still disturbingly common to understand ideas of delicacy and momentary rapture as inherently feminine insights in art.

Watteau wanted to create an image of love embodied in a relationship between a couple, a bond that the world could not disturb. His paintings are about freedom and insight, the psychological moment and the electricity that is desire. It is in essence about being human, and in creating such paintings he wrested art from the constraints of decorum to produce an effective image of the age. It is ironic that Watteau of all people let loose some of Rousseau's noble savage in his intimate portrayals of love, particularly since Rousseau had little faith in the powers of art to act as an instrument for truth. However, in another respect, it placed both characters within the context of an age increasingly enchanted by issues of freedom and nature, and their works were necessarily extensions of those issues.

Watteau's intimate portrayals of frail and sometimes buffoon-like harlequins suggest the characteristic atmosphere of the Rococo period. The idea of the masquerade and the individual as an actor playing a role is never far from the heart of Watteau's paintings. His choice of the actor as subject had a long and established literary tradition by the eighteenth century. The actor existed in two realms, had two lives, had two distinct natures — one free of set conventions (life on stage, life in masquerade), the other within society's codes. In Watteau's paintings, such a masquerade becomes an analogy to duality — the relationship between self and world, discipline and desire, and all the other opposites. Watteau's embodiment of this predicament is the Harlequin — the comedian lover. His painting *Gilles* (Fig. **6.8**) demonstrates the melancholy that is conventionally supposed to afflict the lover, and it gives some indication that these supposedly frivolous works are perhaps more penetrating than one might originally have assumed. In any case, with Watteau the psychology of profane love — of what it means to be and feel human — enters into the realm of appropriate art.

■ **6.8 Antoine Watteau, *Gilles* (undated)**
Oil on canvas
6ft ⅝ in x 4 ft 10¾ in (1.84 x 1.49 m)
Louvre, Paris

MORALIZING TONES: DISCOURSES ON ART

Rousseau was not the only scholar to have problems with the cultural status quo during the late eighteenth century. Throughout Europe there began a dramatic re-evaluation of artistic practice, which provided the community with a much needed dialogue on artistic responsibility. Two of the most outspoken critics of the age were the British artist Sir Joshua Reynolds (1723–92) and the French writer Denis Diderot (1713–84), whose discourses on art provided an important context for the development of nineteenth- and twentieth-century critical thinking.

Reynolds and the Royal Academy

It is difficult to separate Joshua Reynolds from the institution of the Royal Academy, of which he was president from its inception in 1768 until his retirement in 1790. Unlike the French Academy, set up and operated within an arm's length of the court, the Royal Academy was somewhat more autonomous, if less influential (Fig. **6.10**). As in virtually all academies then, the Royal Academy's membership and attitudes reflected the values of the time. A fascinating

■ 6.9 Johann Zoffany
Life Drawing Class at the Royal Academy 1772
Oil on canvas
3 ft 4 in x 4 ft 10 in (1.02 x 1.47 m)
Copyright Her Majesty the Queen,
Windsor Castle

■ 6.10 *George III and his Family Viewing*
the Royal Academy Exhibition at Somerset Place 1788
Engraving, Guildhall Library, London

group portrait of the members (Fig. **6.9**) by one of their number, Johann Zoffany (1733–1810), shows them during a discussion of the nude. Noticeably absent from the proceedings, since women were not then allowed to draw from the nude, are the two women members of the Academy, Angelica Kauffmann (1714–1807) and Mary Moser, whose portraits hang above on the right. (This point will be taken up in greater length in Chapter Ten.) As president, Reynolds initiated the tradition of delivering an annual address to the students and members of the Royal Academy — a tradition that resulted in a series of fifteen discourses, which survive as one of the most significant statements on art in the late eighteenth century.

Two parallel issues preoccupied Reynolds throughout his discourses, and they show clearly how the Academy mirrored the concerns of the period. The first was art education — the idea that art could be effectively taught. (If this appears a rather moot point, consider that even today the liberal education of the artist is not without its critics.) Reynolds steadfastly believed that art was a matter of applying certain principles (rules) to the observation of nature, and that these principles were acquired through a disciplined study of the great masters. The discourses on art became the first authoritative system in the English language for the academic training of the artist, and even today the concept and structure of the art school are in many ways a reflection of these influential lectures.

The belief that art is a problem-solving, intellectual exercise is very much an eighteenth-century idea, and it derives from a popular love affair with the

■ **6.11 Angelica Kauffmann**
Self-Portrait Hesitating between the Arts of Music and
Painting 1794
Oil on canvas
4 ft 10 in x 7 ft 2 in (1.47 x 2.18 m)
Nostell Priory, Yorkshire

scientific method that appeared to make the whole world knowable. To be of sound merit, art had to be guided by the same principles as all other disciplines — the pursuit of truth through reason, hence an investigation of nature through study. Royal Academy training thus involved more than basic studio exercises: it encompassed a variety of literary and philosophical considerations. If the early results of this kind of training were sometimes dubious, it was perhaps because officials of the Academy were unable to understand artistic practice as a sensitive barometer of cultural pressures, and not simply its secretary.

Reynolds also believed that it was the artist's role to capture nature's "timeless forms" from the everyday and then, through exposing truth, to educate and enlighten the viewer. This is, of course, Classicism at its height and shows how little opinions had changed since the time of Bellori. Reynolds warned against the evils of simple imitation (needless to say, the Dutch masters of the early Baroque were reviled in his writings) and instead called on artists to delve deeper into the true "nature" of things. How does one do this? Simply by learning how to decipher nature's code, which comes through patient deliberation and study. Here the discussion has come full circle: nature's essential characteristics are available only to those who have studied its principles, and thus education becomes an essential part of being an artist.

One artist trained under the Academy was Angelica Kauffmann, one of only two women originally allowed membership. Her work openly embraced many of Reynolds' and the Academy's theories, such as a timeless (though some would claim overly artificial) quality, being enhanced by such devices as symmetry, a correct understanding of the human form, and the elevation of both subject and concept (Fig. **6.11**).

Reynolds' discourses were intended as a manifesto for his new Academy, claiming for British painting and artistic theory equal status with the French and Italian Classical schools. The ultimate inappropriateness and perhaps even unattractiveness of Reynolds' theories to British artists are evidenced by the very small number of classically conceived history paintings at the Academy's own exhibitions. Sir Joshua's own painting was far less portentous than his discourses, and the results, especially in portraiture, if less dramatic, were far livelier and more captivating in the long run (Fig. **6.12**).

■ 6.12 Sir Joshua Reynolds
Portrait of the Artist 1773
Oil on canvas
4 ft 2 in x 3 ft 4 in (1.27 x 1.01 m)
Royal Academy of Arts, London

Diderot

Denis Diderot has long been considered the father of **journalistic art criticism**, and his brisk essays on the artists of his age point to a critic with a shrewd eye and a moralizing point of view. Diderot's writing is full of what might be called "secular morality," which placed high value on art that was instructive, socially useful, and elevating. Given these parameters, it seems only right that Diderot should have moved to a more popular and accessible form of criticism (a journalistic style) later in his life, producing, among other pieces, nine outstanding reviews of the Paris Biennial Salons between 1759 and 1781.

Diderot's criticism seems to blur distinctions between ethics and aesthetics, and in this respect he was very much a man of his time. Diderot understood truth in art as not merely the resemblance of nature but a position of moral rightness. Consequently, he spent most of his time developing critiques of story-lines and arrangements, paralleling in sensitivity the Rousseau-inspired paintings of his contemporary, Greuze (1726–1806), whose moralizing narratives were an affront to the Rococo *joie de vivre* (Fig. **6.13**).

What did such criticism sound like? Consider these extracts from Diderot's *Pensées détachées* (meditations), which illuminate his bias: "Every work of sculpture or painting must be the expression of a great principle, a

■ 6.13 Jean Baptiste Greuze, *The Village Bride* 1761
Oil on canvas, 3 ft x 3 ft 10½ in (0.91 x 1.18 m). Louvre, Paris

■ 6.14 Jean-Baptiste-Siméon Chardin
Pipe and Jug (undated)
Oil on canvas
12½ x 16½ in (31.7 x 41.9 cm)
Louvre, Paris

lesson for the spectator — otherwise it remains mute;" and, "A question which is not as ridiculous as it may seem: is it possible to have pure taste, when one's heart is corrupt?" Today, it is hard to find a critic overly concerned with an artist's purity of heart; indeed, most would agree that moral intention does not always lead to great art. However, in the period directly preceding the French Revolution, the question of intention on the behalf of artists was tied into the greater question of the morality of the cultural machine itself. Needless to say, Diderot saw little good coming out of the playful Rococo stylings so popular at the French court.

Who, then, did Diderot champion? For him, the French painter Jean-Baptiste-Siméon Chardin (1699–1779), whose scenes of the pious middle class and their various accoutrements (notably his still lifes) exuded virtue and vitality (Fig. **6.14**). Diderot wrote, "Here is the man who truly understands the harmony of color and reflections. Oh, Chardin! What you mix on your palette is not white, red or black pigment, but the very substance of things." Here truth to experience is seen as truth to oneself and thus truth to the viewer; in one sweeping gesture, the critic has

given moral authority to a painting of inanimate objects! Diderot's use of the word "understand" with regard to Chardin's vision is yet another indication that the artist's vision is part of a deeper and more truthful view of the world. Given this point of view, it is understandable that a moralist such as Diderot would find Watteau's contemplations on the nature of love trivial, if not immoral. What he failed to realize is that morality often confuses impressions of true "nature" and that ethics are a social construct. In other words, truth to nature is not always morally uplifting, and sincerity to truth is often a difficult thing to swallow.

Both Reynolds and Diderot point to a sensibility far removed from the present age, and if both seem a little too optimistic and moralizing in their appraisals of art, perhaps it is because they (like most of their contemporaries) believed that the adherence of all to rational principles was an attainable ideal, which would result in the development of a code of ethical conduct. The tranquil certainties of Diderot, Reynolds, and their contemporaries were to be dramatically displaced by a series of violent and uncontainable revolutions.

THE BIRTH OF THE PUBLIC MUSEUM

One of the most significant, yet often neglected, developments in eighteenth-century culture was the conscious exhibiting of fine art and artifacts for the appreciation of the general public. The idea of a *museum* (its roots in the word mausoleum, implying the housing of dead or no longer produced items), intended solely for the exhibition of objects, was based on the private galleries and sculpture gardens of the Renaissance, in which wealthy collectors of antiquities displayed their treasures. Through the seventeenth and early eighteenth centuries, collections of paintings and sculpture flourished throughout Europe, and it became common to open these private galleries to scholars as a way of promoting public erudition (and, of course, showing off the collections, which, then as today, were considered an indication of taste and status). Nevertheless, despite general good will on the part of many of the collectors, the collections were still essentially private.

The first truly public or national museum came into existence in 1753, when an Act of Parliament authorized the purchase of Sir Hans Sloane's collection of natural objects. With it, the British Museum was born. According to a declaration presented at its inaugural reception of 1759, the collection was to be a truly public institution, freely accessible to "all studious and curious persons." Although the museum had no permanent home for another sixty years, it set an important precedent for the democratization of works of art — one that was followed in other European cities.

The first work of public museum architecture to be constructed in the wake of the British Museum was the Museum Fredericanum in Kassel, Germany, named after its patron, Frederick II, Landgrave of Hesse, in 1769. The museum combined the traditional notion of the picture gallery with what the Germans then called a *Wunderkammer* (an institution that displayed natural curiosities, coins, armor, firearms, etc.), in a complete and integrated whole. In this way, its collection of art, rocks and minerals, maritime plants, clocks, and butterflies set an important precedent for the content of later public museums, creating a norm that was to remain intact well into the mid twentieth century.

By the end of the eighteenth century, the idea of the national museum had become part of the collective imagination. An indication of its increasing popularity through the latter half of the century can be seen in the choice of a museum as a first subject chosen for the prestigious Prix de Rome in 1778–9. According to contest instructions, this museum was to have three departments: the Sciences, the Liberal Arts, and Natural History, as well as a print room and an area for object conservation — the very foundations of today's public museums. However, there was no separate room for antiquities.

Perhaps the greatest public art museum to emerge from the period was the Louvre in Paris — a massive collection of art and artifacts housed in the by-then deserted royal palace. That the emergence of the Louvre as a significant public institution coincided with the French Revolution should come as little surprise; the public museum remains one of the finest and lasting achievements of the Enlightenment project of democracy embodied in that struggle. Further, the rise of the middle class and its subsequent appropriation of national treasures from the diminished aristocracy meant that art was now decisively in the hands of the public — a situation very different from that which artists had confronted before this revolutionary period, and one with huge ramifications for art making in the nineteenth century.

■ 6.15 François Boucher, *Diana after the Hunt* c. 1750
Oil on canvas, 3 ft 1 in x 4 ft 4 in (0.94 x 1.32 m)
Musée Cognacq-Jay, Paris. © DACS 1996

THE NEOCLASSICAL ARTIST

Asked to justify the tastes and aspirations of her age, a mid-eighteenth-century aristocrat, one Madame du Châtelet, was quoted as saying: "We must begin by saying to ourselves that we have nothing else to do in the world but seek pleasant sensations and feelings." It appears that artists such as Watteau, Jean-Honoré Fragonard (1732–1806), and François Boucher (1703–70; Fig. **6.15**) were sympathetic to such a view, and consequently their life's work displays the playfulness of a secure society. There were, however, others who believed that art could and should deliver more than just gratuitous imagery, and it is from this simple premise that some of the rhetoric of Modernism began to flourish.

Let us consider the issue of art's role in society a little more carefully. Despite the indubitable expertise and panache of artists such as Watteau, it is doubtful that their works could convince any viewer of the merits of Rococo art over, say, that of the Renaissance. Surely art is supposed to be something much more serious and profound than Rococo works suggest? Perhaps the legacy of religious art has made the average viewer particularly sensitive to the vitality and contemplative power of visual images, or maybe today's society is deeply committed to the belief that art and artists provide an important window onto the complexities of the world. These are both valid points, but within this framework is an underlying assumption that there is a moral purpose to art making — that art provides some beneficial and necessary function in and to the world, and that Rococo artists simply evaded this responsibility. This "moral mission" of art forms an important part in the foundations of Modernism, and in the Neoclassical movement of the late eighteenth century those seeds were sown.

To many an observer, Classical society had been the crowning achievement of Western civilization — or so thought a considerable number of artists and philosophers. The art of the Antique supposedly epitomized the perfect equilibrium of freedom and responsibility, rational insight and considered cause, honor and virtue. If one were to catalog the various periods in which the longing for a Classical past was most popular, it would invariably correspond with a significant crisis in the art and art making of the era (and thus with the culture generally). It seems that the cool, analytic character of the Classical period appealed (and still appeals) to those who saw (and see) restraint and sacrifice as admirable virtues in a world plunging head-first into certain chaos. The late eighteenth century was one such period, and as the aristocracy clung to power, so its art embraced the challenging rigor of a new regime: **Neoclassicism**.

There are two ways in which one can resurrect Classical ideals in art: first, through a consideration of the formal characteristics of the past (what the art looked like), and second, by way of a deliberate use of Classical subject matter. This book has pointed to several artists who reworked Classical formal considerations (no small feat in itself, since they relied almost exclusively on Roman copies of Greek statues), most notably Poussin and Carracci. Both artists' emphasis on proportion and symmetry helped perpetuate an ideal world of restraint and clarity; formal constraints were effectively used to parallel similar virtues in the individual. Often, this strength of pictorial vision outweighed considerations of subject matter, which was often left within the confines of the popularized myths (for example, creation, beauty, sacred versus profane love).

What is noticeably absent from these earlier images is the use of legends and narratives from the communities of Sparta and Republican Rome — arguably equal partners with Athens in the history of the Classical world, yet rarely the subject of later painting. This was not mere oversight. If one considers the strikingly different attitudes toward issues of, for example, morality and power held by such societies, such models of behavior would probably have made many a prospective patron uncomfortable — particularly those in power, who had the resources to initiate such lavish commissions in the first place. Both Sparta and Republican Rome prided themselves on their military prowess and their discipline, and understood absolute sacrifice as the most profounded expression of morality. This type of defiant righteousness made many squeamish, as it set precedents for undermining

the general air of peacefulness, and provided an unhealthy influence on the masses. Better for them to think of the kinder virtues than to be uprooted by revolutionary thoughts. However, by the late eighteenth century, the foundations of aristocratic rule were beginning to falter under the strain.

One artist made important connections between the formal construction of his art and the ramifications of his subject matter. His name was Jacques-Louis David, and it might validly be claimed that his work was the first academic art to posit social and political revolt — very modern ideas indeed.

David

David (1748–1825) lived in a France of extremes, in which abject poverty and extravagant affluence coexisted in a constant state of social and economic inequality. Brought up as a painter through the ranks of the French Academy and winner of the prestigious *Prix de Rome*, David was one of the lucky few to reap the considerable rewards of the sanctioned cultural machine. Despite such benefits, he was also in a position to comprehend the further implications of art as propaganda — the way in which such high art only perpetuated certain preconceptions about authority and the role of the individual. The fact that in the end David proved himself as susceptible as any man to hypocrisy should only heighten one's appreciation of the fragility of his vision, since within his art lies a moral authority as vibrant and ultimately as destructive as that which came before. The result of this dynamic is a fascinating example of an artist whose works seem to encapsulate the most significant ideological shifts to occur during his lifetime. In simpler terms, his works record what it meant to be an educated person at this particular point in the history of the world.

One of David's most notable compositions is the *Oath of the Horatii* (Fig. **6.16**) of 1784–5, completed four years before the beginning of the French Revolution. The subject matter is anchored in Republican legend, and it alludes to a series of deaths "through duty," including the Roman virtue of brother killing sister for her love of an enemy. Here the loose philosophizing and lofty aspirations of a Classicist such as Poussin gave way to a straightforward story, portrayed in a shockingly straightforward manner. Despite its obvious technical homage to

■ 6.16 Jacques-Louis David, *Oath of the Horatii* 1784–5
Oil on canvas, approx. 14 ft x 11 ft (4.27 x 3.35 m)
Louvre, Paris

painters such as Poussin and Caravaggio, the *Oath of the Horatii* remains a type of history painting very different from those previously discussed. There is an arresting clarity about David's composition, and the pivotal gathering of the gleaming swords becomes an almost hallucinatory focus — absolute resolution through absolute sacrifice.

There is a certain agreeable severity about this picture: here the Republican virtues that resonate through the storyline find their compositional equivalent in the equally harsh and disciplined execution of the painting. Like Rococo artists before him, David had found an adequate formal language for his sub-

ject, which resulted in a fundamental harmony. Here, "form" and "content" complement and reinforce each other; the viewer not only comprehends the subject but is forced to feel it. The composition shows an uncanny intelligence. The tripartite (three-section) arrangement of the picture plane, made plain through the use of the background arch motif, gives an almost religious authority to the piece. On the left stand the proud Horatii, whose gestures to the gathered swords are reminiscent of the awe and reverence that a worshiper might pay to an icon. In the centre, the swords seem an extension of the father figure on whom all loyalty rests. Last (and in

David's case certainly least), on the right side sit the swooning women (the virtues of compromise and love once embodied in the Rococo persona), envisioned as little more than a weak, piteous huddle. The composition is both brilliant and unsettling, and it bears witness to the changing and violent attitudes of the years that followed.

By 1790, the French aristocracy had fallen, to be replaced with chaos and violence. David's *Death of Marat* (Fig. **6.17**) of 1793 is a keen indictment of the various intrigues and assassinations that followed in the wake of the revolution. Here, the patriot Marat, one of the heroes of the cause, lies stabbed in a bath, its water stained deep red by his blood; the symbolic sword of the Horatii had indeed found a home, but the final resolution was anything but virtuous. The starkness of the scene and the forceful placement of the figure on the immediate foreground plane suggest the Baroque theatricality of Caravaggio, and it points to an uncompromising design and vigilance of execution commonplace in both art and political circles during those early revolutionary years.

Unfortunately for the ever-inflammatory David, the tired analogy of "When one plays with fire, one eventually gets burnt," came true: he soon found himself out of favor with those in power and

■ **6.17** Jacques-Louis David
Death of Marat 1793
Oil on canvas
5 ft 5 in x 4 ft 2½ in (1.65 x 1.28 m)
Musées Royaux, Brussels

■ 6.18 Jacques-Louis David
Napoleon Crossing the Alps 1800
Oil on canvas
8 ft x 7 ft 9 in (2.43 x 2.31 m)
Musée de Versailles

retreated from the scene. But ever the pragmatist, it was not long before David found a new patron in French political circles — a man named Napoleon Bonaparte. David's triumphant *Napoleon Crossing the Alps* (Fig. **6.18**) of 1800 bears witness to the ironic end to a fervent revolutionary — the artist agreeably painting yet another manifestation of élite rule.

AMERICAN NEOCLASSICISM

Classical motifs were by no means confined to painting. Communities often recycle history to suit their specific needs, and in the case of Europe at the turn of the century, popular nostalgia for a more harmonious, democratic, and egalitarian time led many to see Classical society as a reasonable aspiration. The result was a proliferation of Classical references throughout almost all the arts during the period, particularly in revolutionary France and the young United States.

Classical architecture, thought to be suggestive of republican virtue, became very popular in the United States after the Revolutionary War. One of the most prominent figures of the period to be inspired by Classical sources was Thomas Jefferson (1743–1826), third President of the United States (1801–9), whose design for the Virginia State House became the inspiration for much American public architecture.

■ 6.19 Thomas Jefferson
State Capitol, Richmond,
Virginia, 1785–9

■ 6.20 Horatio Greenough
George Washington 1832–41
Marble
11 ft 6 in x 8 ft 6 in x 7 ft 10 in (3.45 x 2.59 x 2.09 m)
National Museum of American Art, Smithsonian Institute

The Virginia State Capitol (1785–9; Fig. **6.19**) was the first Classical temple design executed in the young United States, and it looked for inspiration to French Neoclassical architecture and the Roman ruins at Nîmes, particularly a small temple similar in construction to the Temple of Portunus (see Chapter Two). Jefferson, who designed the Capitol while serving as U.S. Minister to France, saw in Classical architecture a degree of moral integrity, seriousness, and dignified restraint, a "noble simplicity" — traits he envisioned as the hallmarks of the new Republic, and ones that were concurrently being embraced in France.

Sometimes, as in the case of David, form and content worked in unison, producing powerful evocations of the Classical aura. At other times the result was more humorous than inspiring; one such example is the notorious statue of George Washington (Fig. **6.20**) produced by Horatio Greenough in a style reminiscent of Roman portraiture. The artist placed a bust of the first President of the United States on a rather imposing and idealized figure — the Olympian God Zeus! The discrepancy between portrait (individual) and ideal (universal) is at once obvious, and the unfortunate result was little more than grand-scale heroic propaganda with little insight into the nature of the sitter. Here the once grand aspirations of the Neoclassical revival were trivialized to the point of virtual insignificance, signaling the eventual exhaustion of a period and its original lofty aspirations. One may speculate that artists simply tired of "politician-turned-god" imagery, and cynically came to see ideas such as symmetry and proportion as just further ways of supporting other, more pragmatic agendas.

ART AND MAN'S INHUMANITY TO MAN

The transition of power during the French Revolution often led to tragic extremes, and the Europe-wide chaos and bloodshed resulting from the Napoleonic Wars poignantly illustrated the seemingly limitless human capacity for cruelty and vindictiveness. Was this essentially human nature? Was this the "noble savage" who lay in the hearts of all humans? Or was this a glimpse of the world of instinct — the darker side of humanity finally exposed? Among the noise, revelry, and violence of the era, there stood one person who dared to look beyond the accepted facade of progress. His name was Francisco de Goya, and his visions remain some of the most unsettling in all of art.

The life of Francisco de Goya (1746–1828) was a microcosm of the social pressures in which he lived and prospered. In retrospect, it seems rather appropriate that he trained and worked under the patronage of an aristocratic court. He grew up as one of the lucky few who gained the favor of the court through skill, and he commenced a career as court portrait painter in his native Spain. He lived in a country with an unmistakable propensity for Rococo stylings, and his early pictures paid homage to those influences. Yet a painting such as that of the *Family of Charles IV* (Fig. **6.21**) of 1800 is indicative of his increasingly dispassionate eye for personality and humanness. The work is neither a Rococo glorification of the aristocracy nor a stiff Davidian political rendering; it is instead a painting of a family, and despite their formal attire, the group remains a curious, if not humorous, assemblage. This was to be the last gasp of naturalism as the eighteenth century defined it, something less passionately inspired than a Watteau, and more frail and believable than a David. However, naturalism requires more than a simple, penetrating observation to have meaning; there must also be an implicit awareness of the fragility of life.

■ **6.21 Francisco de Goya**
Family of Charles IV 1800
Oil on canvas
9 ft 2¼ in x 11 ft ¼in (2.8 x 3.35 m)
Prado, Madrid

Shortly after the turn of the century, Spain was to witness this folly at first hand, as an insatiable Napoleon and his armies marched on Madrid. What followed in their wake was a series of brutal insurrections and retaliations that signaled the end of the Spanish Enlightenment — a world to which Goya was inextricably bound. Out of this all too familiar bloodbath came one of the most devastating depictions of humanity ever to grace canvas: eighteenth-century rationalism stripped bare in the anguished scream of Goya's victim in the *Third of May 1808* (Fig. **6.22**). Here the insights of a keen observer were let loose on humanity in general, and the view from the edge is none too pretty. There is no blind heroism in this painting, and no discrete symbolic language to be followed. It is neither propaganda nor compassion — it is an insight into Alexander Pope's world of witches and demons that the eighteenth century tried so hard to ignore. Humans are let loose on humans, and the result is death and annihilation. The forces of evil (the soldiers) are faceless and thus universal, and the victim is shrunk to the level of puppet, his arms held outstretched and embracing. What a distance art has traveled from Madame de Châtelet's world of pleasure and indulgence.

As Goya grew old, he began a series of highly personal paintings that vividly illustrate the depths of his insight. It is significant that he was deaf when the so-

■ **6.22 Francisco de Goya**
Third of May 1808 1814
Oil on canvas, 8 ft 8¾ in x 11 ft 4 in (2.66 x 3.45 m)
Prado, Madrid

■ 6.23 Francisco de Goya, *Fight with Clubs* (undated)
Oil on canvas, 4 ft ½ in x 8 ft 8¾ in (1.23 x 2.6 m)
Prado, Madrid

called "black paintings" were executed; the images show a focus and concentration that might be expected from someone whose life had become increasingly enclosed. The massive *Fight with Clubs* (Fig. **6.23**) is one of his most powerful and awful depictions of the self-destructive tendencies implicit within all humans; it is Goya's answer to the "might is right" argument that allows humanity to beat itself senseless. This is "truth to nature" in its extreme, and it is a long way from Diderot's favored Chardin. Yet its poignancy is both uncanny and chilling, suggesting that nature is found not in observation but in introspection. Few realized the implications of Goya's late work at the time, and it was not until the twentieth century that these works were given their due.

While an old and disenchanted Goya dared to view nature from the inside, a heroic facade was being developed by a new group, the Romantics.

ART AND THE HEROIC: ROMANTICISM

Goya's haunting vision of a world of perpetual gloom and unfulfilled desire was by no means an isolated attitude by the second decade of the nineteenth century. It appears that Neoclassicism had run its course; the need to order and aggrandize the world through art had, by the fall of Napoleon in 1815, created a rather rigid and uncompromising monster. Analytic clarity and heroic subjects had simply become tired motifs, and many saw the restrictive conventions of Classicism as no longer appropriate in an age of dynamism and chaos. What was needed instead was a method for expressing all the intangibles that one feels but never knows. In short, it required gifted visionaries whose sensitivity to such nuances granted them privileged status — a position artists were quick to seize.

This declaration on behalf of artists was not quite as gracious and humanitarian as it might at first appear. The world of the artist had been turned upside down by the swift changes of revolution. This forced artists to redefine their role in society: to find new patrons and to compete for status in the free-for-all of post-revolutionary culture. The Romantic attitude fits perfectly in this respect, because it placed enormous emphasis on the subjective experience of the individual in the face of an overwhelming world. This shift of sensibility also coincided with a popular mistrust of the restricting and dogmatic rationalism of the previous century. In the face of such dynamics, the artist became the intermediary between the awesomeness of "nature" (to reuse the eighteenth-century definition) and the fragility of humankind.

Prelude: The Industrial and Scientific Revolutions

The beginning of the nineteenth century ushered in revolutionary changes, not only in the political arena but in all aspects of life. The previous century, called the period of the Enlightenment because of its philosophical embrace of the secular and the scientific over the theological, had paved the way for a series of important discoveries and inventions that were to change the face of Western society. The development of the steam engine by James Watt in 1769 was but one of several industrial innovations of the latter half of the eighteenth century, and with them came a social and economic upheaval called the Industrial Revolution.

The effect of mechanization upon society was far-reaching. One of the first industries to adopt technological innovations was textile manufacture. The establishment of mechanized textile mills through the nineteenth century had a massive impact on population movements, as people in need of work began to flock to mill towns in search of livelihoods more predictable than those to be gained from agricultural laboring. This, combined with a parallel mechanization in farming (the cotton gin in the American South is but one example) meant that traditional laborers were no longer needed in the same capacity in rural areas. The net result was the development of the modern city and its stratifications of labor.

Though it raised standards of living, the industrialization of Europe through the nineteenth century was slow and uneven, and when unregulated in its early years, it allowed for much worker exploitation. This in turn led to developments as diverse as political theories of class structure, which have their roots in the work of Karl Marx and Friedrich Engels, the "realist" writing of Charles Dickens and Victor Hugo, and the rise of urban planning as a discipline. No aspect of human culture that came in contact with this technological and social revolution was left unaffected.

Romanticism in art was no different in this regard: to understand it as simply an aesthetic revolt against Neoclassicism is to underestimate the significance of art as a barometer of its time. Romanticism's embrace of the artistic persona, the sublimity of the natural world, and the exotic was clearly a symptom of a larger crisis taking place in nineteenth-century culture — the apparently irreconcilable gulf that was beginning to open up between the role of the individual and subjective experience, in a world that was becoming increasingly complex and detached.

The Sketch and the *Non Finito* in Romantic Art Theory

A rather instructive example of the emerging Romantic sensibility is the increased interest in the *sketch* as a viable piece of artistic production. The arguments supporting the aesthetic merits of the sketch are in essence identical to those that critically underpin Romanticism, and thus a brief digression into these theories might prove fruitful as an introduction to the nineteenth-century revolt against Classicism. (The arguments presented here are but a brief synopsis of an excellent article on the subject by Wendelin A. Guentner in the summer 1993 edition of the *Art Journal*.)

The debate concerning the relative merits of the sketch as opposed to the finished art work were not new to late eighteenth- and early nineteenth-century critics. Indeed, as far back as the late seventeenth century, the writer Roger de Piles had considered this issue at some length, and it preoccupied French critics through the following century, including Diderot in his Salon reviews of 1765 and 1767. Yet the sketch's critical attachment to Romanticism was perhaps best articulated in British art circles, where it became linked with contemporary ideas on the **sublime**, which in turn had a profound effect on artists of that period.

The notion of the sublime is often linked to the Irish-born philosopher and social critic Edmund Burke, who laid its aesthetic foundations in his *Philosophical Enquiry into the Origin of Our Ideas of the Sublime and Beautiful* (1757). In this highly influential text, Burke examined the quality of grandeur or exaltedness (sublimity) often attributed to nature and humanity's experiences of it, and embraced this sense as a significant component in art. One section of the text, entitled "Infinity in Pleasing Objects," is particularly interesting in its discussion of the merits of unfinished or incomplete experiences. Burke took as an example the fascination with newborn animals as opposed to adults, which he suggested was because newborns arouse the imagination, by posing the promise of something more, of future development, of infinite possibility. He then extended this exhilarating sense of promise to the artist's sketch: "In unfinished sketches of drawing I have often seen something which pleased me beyond the best finishing."

This theory of course flew in the face of Neoclassical wisdom, which saw true art in the whole, the complete, and the considered. Neoclassicism, as demonstrated in the writings of Sir Joshua Reynolds, for example, was anchored in a view of the world as fixed, unchanging, and rationally ordered. This left little room for the imagination, which was often only summarily discussed in literature of that period. Thus it is not surprising that Burke's interest in the imagination soon found an audience among writers and artists disenchanted with the rigid formulas of the academies.

The imaginative potential inherent in the sketch was likewise available to viewers of the landscape in the form of the **non finito** (meaning simply unfinished), in which objects or situations stimulated the imagination. A good example might be a set of ruins, such as a decrepit castle or church, in which viewers, confronted by a sense of incompleteness, are stimulated into accessing their own creative spirit. In other words, a certain lack of determinacy is pleasurable.

Richard Payne Knight, a critic and supporter of Burke, claimed,

> In grasping infinity, the mind exercises the powers…of multiplying without end, and in doing so expands and exalts itself, by which means its feelings and sentiments become sublime.
>
> *Analytical Inquiry in to the Principles of Taste* (1805)

He went on to describe reason, the very hallmark of Neoclassical theory in the Enlightenment, as having "little or nothing to do with taste; for taste depends upon feelings and sentiment, and not upon demonstration or argument." In this specifically Romantic notion of art, a painting is understood to possess an emotional or imaginative potential — the more these faculties are engaged, the more sublime the art.

The previous argument is perhaps best understood in schematic form. Guentner's breakdown of the values associated with both the *sketch* and the *finished work of art*, part of which is presented below, clearly illustrates this dramatic rift between Classical and Romantic ideals:

Sketch	Work of Art
-*preliminary version*	-*final version*
-executed *"in nature," "on the spot"*	-executed *in the studio*
-*becoming* (ephemeral, transitory)	-*being* (eternal, unchanging)
-*instinct* (authenticity, sincerity, honesty)	-*reason* (intellect, discipline, judgment)
-*spontaneity*	-*sustained effort*
-*individual* (private, original)	-*collective* (public, general)
-*active reception* (beholder finishes a sketch)	-*passive reception* (beholder contemplates a finished work)
-*nature*	-*culture*
-*Romantic*	-*Classical*

Of course, some of these traits are not as antithetical as they may first appear. For instance, once the "look" of a *natural* sketch has been determined, it is certainly possible to mimic those supposedly honest and spontaneous gestures back in the studio — making them as conventional as the Classical motifs. Indeed, some of the so-called masters of the "spontaneous" gesture in Romantic art (such as Turner and Constable, who will be discussed shortly) executed much of their work within the safe confines of the studio, amid sketches and compositional experiments. Here the *sublime* meets the *picturesque*, which is really nothing more than the paring down and redesigning of that unruly Romantic vision of nature into something a little more organized and pleasing to look at. Yet despite Romanticism's theoretical shortcomings and self-indulgent air, the Romantic notions of originality, authenticity, and individual genius had a profound effect on nineteenth- and twentieth-century art making, and in this regard Romanticism remains quintessentially Modern.

Géricault's *Raft of the Medusa,* 1818

An instructive example of the emerging Romantic sensibility in grand form is a work by Théodore Géricault (1791–1824), *Raft of the Medusa* (Figs. **6.24** and **6.25**) of 1818. The painting was based on the tragic voyage of the French ship *Medusa*, which in 1816 fell into the hands of a negligent sea captain (appointed by friends in the government), who sailed headfirst into a storm. The result was that a single raft was set adrift on the open seas, crowded with people deemed unworthy of lifeboats. The story created a sensation in Paris, with images of parching thirst and

■ 6.24 Théodore Géricault
Sketch for the Raft of the Medusa
1818
Pen and ink
16⅛ x 23 in (41 x 58.4 cm)
Gemente Museen, Amsterdam

■ 6.25 Théodore Géricault
Raft of the Medusa 1818
Oil on canvas
16 ft 1 in x 23 ft 6 in (4.8 x 7 m)
Louvre, Paris

■ 6.26 Jean-Auguste-Dominique Ingres
La Grande Odalisque (*Harem Girl*) 1814
Oil on canvas, 3 ft ¼ in x 5 ft 3¼ in (0.92 x 1.6 m)
Louvre, Paris

unbearable heat, and even rumors of cannibalism prevailing. In this age of billboards and docu-dramas, it may seem obvious for Géricault to have chosen a monumental scale, 16 feet 1 in by 23 feet 6 in (4.8 x 7 m) for such a controversial subject, but at the time of its execution, this was considered an affront to prevailing Classical decorum. In awarding a contemporary event a level of dignity and importance once reserved for only the most profound myths, Géricault's monumental work also acted as a deliberate critique of the self-proclaimed righteousness of the Classicists.

Yet in spite of its novelty, the painting remained indebted to Classical standards of formal composition. The sweeping diagonals that permeate the scene are at once dynamic and yet balanced, and despite the rough seas and intense lighting, the composition retains absolute harmony of parts. However, Géricault was not simply a passive practitioner of these devices: his considerable formal skills were used for ultimately dramatic ends, as the sweeping thrust of the design accentuates the descisive gesture of the indefatigable sailor and the approaching vessel. It is unfortunate that Géricault died tragically young, aged only thirty-three, for his ability to evoke a certain consciousness of the human condition through paint was singular.

The Delacroix-Ingres Debate

Without doubt, the most famous artistic feud to take place in early nineteenth-century Paris was between the Neoclassicist Jean-Auguste-Dominique Ingres (1780–1867) and the Romanticist Eugène Delacroix (1798–1863). Their quarrels were fierce and public and as a result were often parodied in the newspapers. The battle was, as one might expect, about all those things the Romantics and Classicists could never see eye to eye on: composition versus color, order versus imagination, reason versus instinct. Ingres, a pupil of David, is known mainly for his highly refined, austere, and meticulously painted portraits and mythological scenes. *La Grande Odalisque* of 1814 (Fig. **6.26**) is indicative of his desire to distill a timelessness and completeness in his compositions. Yet, despite first impressions, Ingres was not without his Romantic flourishes. In works such as *La Grande Odalisque*, he took great liberties with anatomical accuracy (such as in the length of the arms, which would surely drop to the floor if she were ever to stand!), lending an air of otherworldiness and subjectivity to what is otherwise a very staid composition. Further, the exotic character of the subject, supposedly a concubine in a Turkish harem, speaks more of

6.27 Eugène Delacroix, *Death of Sardanapalus* 1826
Oil on canvas
12 ft 1 in x 16 ft 3 in (3.68 x 4.95 m)
Louvre, Paris

the Romantic desire for the unusual and the unfamiliar than it does of any Neoclassical concern for Antique virtues embedded in the Classical tradition.

Perhaps the most painterly of the Romantic artists, Delacroix combined a typical Romantic interest in the exotic with a liberated handling of materials and color to produce some of the most captivating images of his era. His propensity for intense color and gestural paint activity can be seen in the *Death of Sardanapalus* (Fig. **6.27**) of 1826, in which his handling of materials and the wildly organic forms seem to reiterate the intense violence and passion of the scene. Here, as in all great art, a direct connection between form and content was developed, and the result was a painting that not only describes the horror of a slaughter in the name of vanity but in some ways mimics its very energy.

The element of the exotic, a subject popularized by artists of that period and evident in work as diverse as Ingres and Delacroix, points to a general trend in nineteenth-century art referred to as *Orientalism*. According to critics such as Edward Said, the "Orientalizing" trend in Romantic art corresponded to a general impression among artists of that period that Arab culture (suggesting the Islamic peoples of North Africa, the Middle East, and Persia) represented a life of instinctive hedonism and violence, simplicity and sexual abandon — in other words the embodiment of Romantic naturalism over Neoclassical constraint. Yet it was also a brutal racial stereotype masquerading as an aesthetic disposition. This may have had something to do with the political climate of the time, which tended to pit Eastern against Western values in the daily dispatches from the Turkish-Greek War. Romantics such as the poet Lord Byron and the painter Delacroix supported the Greek cause, yet it is also clear that the fierceness of the Turkish troops left an indelible mark on their psyches. This, combined with a relentless European expansionism into North Africa, provided the necessary ingredients for such blatant and damaging stereotypes — which were not only acknowledged but embraced by many of the period's better artists. In this regard at least, the Romantic period, despite its claims to being radical and favoring progress, toed the political and social line of bias in nineteenth-century Europe.

Friedrich

Society's relationship with the environment changed with the Romantics. Gone were the confident, restrictive renderings of Poussin and David. Instead, the world was portrayed as vindictive, threatening, and sublime; nature had now become not the product of human intellect but an allegory of the troubled, tumultuous world of the human psyche. As revolution and social upheaval captivated the imagination of whole communities and set minds adrift in a seemingly endless sea of possibilities, nature became a reminder of the relative insignificance of existence in the face of an overwhelming and amoral universe. One of the truly superb depictions of the sublimity of nature is a work by Caspar David Friedrich (1774–1840), the *Polar Sea* (Fig. **6.28**) of 1824. Here the individual (and all humanity for that matter) reads as little more than a footnote in the violent convulsions of nature. The ship, once a mighty symbol of conquest, lies crushed by the sheer weight of an ice pack. In the face of such a scene, even David's heroic Horatii could do little to save the day. There is no heroism here and no morality play — just the ambivalent work of a world both grand and ultimately unmerciful. Nature, it seems, was the great equalizer in many an artist's eyes, and in this regard the landscape took on its own sense of urgency.

■ 6.28 Caspar David Friedrich, *Polar Sea* 1824
Oil on canvas, 3 ft 2½ in x 4 ft 2½ in (0.97 x 1.28 m)
Kunsthalle, Hamburg

■ 6.29 J. M. W. Turner
*Snow Storm: Hannibal and his Army
Crossing the Alps* 1812
Oil on canvas
4 ft 9 in x 7 ft 9 in (1.45 x 2.36 m)
Tate Gallery, London

■ 6.30 John Constable
Hampstead Heath 1821
Oil, sketch
10 x 12 in (25.4 x 30.5 cm)
City Art Galleries, Manchester

■ 6.31 John Constable, *Haywain* 1821
Oil on canvas, 4 ft 3¼ in x 6 ft 1 in (1.3 x 1.85 m)
National Gallery, London

Turner and Constable

Two other artists are worthy of mention with regard to the new attitude toward nature: the British painters J. M. W. Turner (1775–1851) and John Constable (1776–1837). Like Friedrich's, Turner's conception of nature can be best understood with the aid of two Romantic critical terms — the "sublime" and the "picturesque." Both artists and writers responded to the *sublimity* of all that was awesome in landscape: the grandeur of mountains and storms or the emptiness of the plains. The *picturesque* was homelier, a landscape of cultivation with brightly clad rural laborers and abundant vegetation set against a backdrop of rolling hills. These two modes were dominant in the output of Turner and contemporary landscape painters all over Europe. Yet Turner also used the expressive freedom gained in his landscapes of the sublime to dramatize grand subjects of the past. As a result, the mixture reflects a view of landscape both heroic and often merciless (Fig. **6.29**). Perhaps more than any other feature, it is the searing, almost mater-

ial presence of light that makes Turner's paintings so tangibly different from those of his contemporaries. Here light is seen as nature's divine instrument — a force that decomposes or solidifies forms at will and which is as wild and unharnessed as the environment it illuminates.

Constable, on the other hand, was the quintessential empiricist, believing all landscape painting to be the patient result of observing facts. To this end, he produced countless works that examined transient moments — the effect of light through clouds, breezes through trees, etc. To him, the sky was also the key, but he applied a meteorologist's precision to the recording of phenomena, believing that the wonder of nature did not require the dramatic embellishments so glorified in the work of Turner. Constable's *Hampstead Heath* (Fig. **6.30**) and the *Haywain* (Fig. **6.31**) of 1821 exemplify such patient observation, and the result, while perhaps less dramatic than the work of Turner, eloquently captures a similar devotional attitude toward the world that is typically early nineteenth century.

Gothic Art and the Pre-Raphaelites

Romantics too had specific historical precedents in mind for giving credence to their aims. As a reaction to the Classicism of the academies, Romantic artists dismissed the conventions of the Renaissance; instead they turned their attention to less refined and more expressive art. Early Christian art, and in particular that of the Middle Ages, became an important source for imaginative wanderings. Soon, like the Neoclassicists before them, many Romantic artists began to reconstruct works from the past to express the conditions of their own age. The British seemed particularly fond of the idiosyncrasies of the Gothic era. A building project that made this connection quite clear was the formidable Houses of Parliament in London (Figs. **6.32** and **6.33**), with their direct associations with medieval forms.

Members of the Pre-Raphaelite movement, as the name implies, desired an art in keeping with the spiritual aims of the pre-High Renaissance era. To this end, the Pre-Raphaelites abandoned the techniques they had received in training at the Royal Academy, where the precepts laid down in Reynolds' *Discourses* were still observed. Instead the young Pre-Raphaelites developed a style of painting with vivid colors applied onto a canvas prepared with brilliant white underpainting. The result was a jewel-like intensity that, while not imitating the methods of the early Italians (the one Pre-Raphaelite attempt at mural painting was a technical disaster), seemed to return to the directness and supposed honesty of

■ **6.32 Charles Berry and A. W. N. Pugin**
The Houses of Parliament, London, 1836–60
Length 940 ft (286.51 m)

■ 6.33 Interior view of The Houses of Parliament, London, 1836–60

■ 6.34 Dante Gabriel Rossetti
Ecce Ancilla Domini 1850
Oil on canvas
28½ x 16½ in (72.4 x 41.9 cm)
Tate Gallery, London

early Italian art. The group favored subjects from medieval mythology and from Shakespeare, as well as attempting to revitalize religious painting. *Ecce Ancilla Domini* (Fig. **6.34**) of 1850 by Dante Gabriel Rossetti (1828–82) challenged pictorial convention with its deliberately distorted perspective and creamy fresco-like coloration. However, there is more to Rossetti's version of the Annunication than imitation of art before Raphael: the expression of the young Virgin Mary is not that of an idealized type but a vivid and thoroughly modern portrayal of a deeply troubled adolescent.

The world had seen much, perhaps too much, in the century and a half between Watteau and Friedrich. It had gone from aristocratic pleasure and Classical restraint to fear and trembling, and art was its quivering voice in the chaos. The artists had lost patronage but gained autonomy, and now they faced their biggest challenge: to find a voice as loud and overwhelming as the industrial age. This would require a strategy — or even better, a whole new way of looking at the role of art. This was to be the beginning of Modernism, the subject of the next chapter.

SUMMARY

The eighteenth and early nineteenth centuries were a period of unprecedented political and social upheaval throughout the Western world. As the decadence of the ruling aristocracies gave way to equally convulsive revolutionary excesses, artists found themselves reconsidering their traditional role in the greater cultural arena. As art production shifted from large decorative projects and commissioned portraiture to the more personal interests of the artists involved, there was likewise a significant reappraisal of the meaning of art as a potent aesthetic, emotional, and even political catalyst. The issue of nature, both that of human consciousness and of the environment in which humanity functions, also came under the increased scrutiny of thinkers and artists alike, as the rationalism of the previous era gave way to a more personal, speculative mode of thought. It was during this necessary re-evaluation that the modern notion of the artist as a distinct, autonomous voice within culture began to arise.

Suggested Reading

The period between 1700 and 1830 is rich with biographers and historians, and its documents provide singular insights into the processes by and conditions under which art was produced.

Eitner, Lorenz: *Neoclassicism and Romanticism 1750–1850, Sources and Documents. Volume One: Englightenment/Revolution* (Englewood Cliffs, NJ: Prentice-Hall, 1970). A good collection of material.

Guentner, Wendelin A.: "British Aesthetic Theory 1780–1830," *Art Journal*, summer 1993, p. 40 ff.

Held, Julius S. and Posner, Donald: *17th and 18th Century Art* (Englewood Cliffs, NJ, and New York: Prentice-Hall and Abrams). A useful survey of the period.

Levey, Michael: *Rococo to Revolution: Major Trends in Eighteenth-Century Painting* (London, New York, and Toronto: Oxford University Press, 1977). Another useful survey of the period.

Vaughan, William: *Romantic Art* (London, New York, and Toronto: Oxford University Press, 1978). A thorough and enlightening introduction to the modern world and its particular artistic sensibility in the early nineteenth century.

Pronunciation Guide

François Boucher   **FRAN**-swah boo-**SHAY**

Jean-Baptiste-Siméon Chardin   zhan ba-**TEEST** see-may-**OHN** shar-**DAN**

Jacques-Louis David   zhahk lwee dah-**VEED**

Eugène Delacroix   oo-**ZHAN** duh-luh-**KRWAH**

Diderot   dee-**DROH**

Jean-Honoré Fragonard   zhahn oh-nor-**AY** frag-uh-**NAR**

Théodore Géricault   tay-aw-**DAWR** zhay-ree-**KOH**

Jean-Baptiste Greuze   zhan ba-**TEEST** grooz

Jules Hardouin-Mansart   zhool ar-**DWAN** mahn-**SAR**

Horatii   huh-**RAY**-shee-eye

Jean-Auguste-Dominique Ingres   zhan aw-**GOOST** daw-mee-**NEEK AN**-gruh

Rococo   ruh-**KOH**-koh

Rousseau   roo-**SOH**

Louis le Vau   lwee luh-**VOH**

Versailles   ver-**SY**

Antoine Watteau   an-**TWAN** wah-**TOH**

Glossary

journalistic art criticism (*page 294*) A form of writing on art based primarily on direct observation, deliberation, and brief critique, rather than using works as the basis of a more complex theoretical argument. The mainstay of most art critics today, the style was first used by Denis Diderot in his reviews of the Paris Biennials between 1759 and 1781.

Neoclassicism (*page 298*) The term used to describe the revival of Classical conventions such as symmetry, a reliance on draftsmanship over color (in painting), and the evocation of a determined and disciplined order to the world.

non finito (*page 307*) Meaning literally unfinished or not finished, it is a term used by late eighteenth-century theoreticians to describe the duality of potential in a sketch or unfinished work of art.

Rococo (*page 288*) Deriving from *rocaille*, a delicate and ornate form of shell and rock work used to decorate walls and floors, the term refers to a period in European art c. 1700, when technical exuberance and pleasurable sensations were popular, signaling a shift away from the rigid formulas of the Baroque Classicists.

Romanticism (*page 306*) A movement in early nineteenth-century culture against earlier rationalism and Classicism. It sought to elevate the fantastic, the sublime, and the pleasurable and asserted the primacy of the individual's experience and self-conscious isolation of the artist after the decline of individual patronage.

sublime (*page 306*) First coined by Edmund Burke in 1757, it describes the quality of grandeur or exaltedness found in nature that held aesthetic potential for the artist. The pictorial conventions that developed out of it are often described as the picturesque.

7

THE MODERN WORLD AND ITS ART

■ 7.1 Claude Monet
Regatta at Argenteuil (detail) 1872
Oil on canvas
19 x 29½ in (48 x 75 cm)
Musée d'Orsay, Paris

Art never expresses anything but itself.
OSCAR WILDE, *The Critic as Artist*

The most fundamental appreciation of art is always contingent upon a series of value judgments (the tools one uses to assess the merit of a work). These value judgments are in turn inextricably linked to a wide range of interests and social conditions (one's "historical condition"), and thus any evaluation of art is itself an expression of its age. This cycle helps explain the subtle differences in taste and values between generations and cultures, since each sector develops around a particular set of conditions unique to its age.

In earlier discussions, much time has been spent sorting out the wide variety of historical factors that have contributed to the common understanding and appreciation of art, and by placing art and art practice within the context of its contemporary value system, it has become apparent that art often carries implicit notions about the state of being human during its time. Since artists have traditionally produced work for specific viewers (Church, state, aristocracy, or the marketplace), it seems only logical that in some way art should reflect the interests of its clients, who were in turn significant players in the daily events and dominant interests of the age.

Suppose artists were to sever their direct links to this patronage system. Would art still be an accurate gauge of the human community, or would it simply become the irrelevant toy of each artist, without direct association with or responsibility to its age? One might also inquire as to why artists would want to divorce themselves from society in the first place, particularly since they often gain a considerable amount of prestige and financial reward for their work. Further, if the artist no longer produces work for a specific patron, the issue of subject matter becomes at once essential: what does one create when one is working only for oneself? These basic questions about the nature of artistic practice outside the realm of traditional patronage are the legacy of Modernism, and if they can be answered, the importance of Modernism to an appreciation of art will become clear.

THE IDEOLOGICAL FERMENT

To appreciate the significance of the decline of patronage and the rise of the modern artist, it is necessary to consider how radically the world changed between the French Revolution and the mid nineteenth century. The invention of various mechanized techniques for the production of goods enabled massive industrial expansion to take place in western Europe and North America. Items that once took weeks, even months, to produce were now assembled in hours, replacing traditional cottage industries and old-fashioned craft guilds with factories and an increasingly urban labor force. What a miracle was the machine! Not only did it produce goods at an extraordinary rate: it also helped establish a vital middle class, who prospered in this new spirit of optimism and unprecedented freedom. The world was full of hope, and progress was in the air.

Artists were quick to pick up on this spirit of progress. This in turn forced many artists to reconsider their function in society — a position now the subject of heated debate as society moved ever further from the traditions of Church and Crown, and the call for grand decorative programs shrank. What, then, was the role of the artist in society? And further, did the artist have any mission or specific voice to offer the public? The answer, as far as artists were concerned, was a resounding yes, and this paved the way for the rise of the "avant-garde."

Theories of Progress in Art and Culture

The term **avant-garde** simply means "before the rest," and it implies the role of heroic exploration, of blazing a trail for others less adventurous. That this appelation has, for better or worse, come to identify Modernism, should explain something about the lofty goals and aspirations of artists during the period. When the great Romantic poet Percy Bysshe Shelley

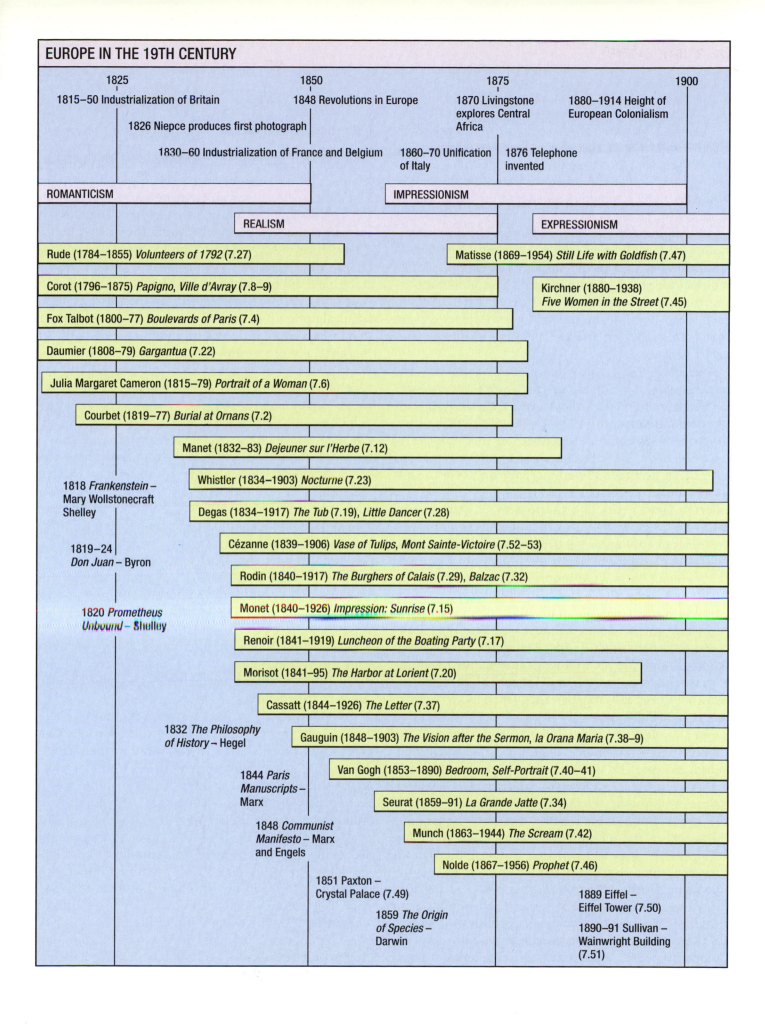

EUROPE IN THE 19TH CENTURY

1825	1850	1875	1900

1815–50 Industrialization of Britain

1848 Revolutions in Europe

1870 Livingstone explores Central Africa

1880–1914 Height of European Colonialism

1826 Niepce produces first photograph

1830–60 Industrialization of France and Belgium

1860–70 Unification of Italy

1876 Telephone invented

ROMANTICISM

IMPRESSIONISM

REALISM

EXPRESSIONISM

Rude (1784–1855) *Volunteers of 1792* (7.27)

Matisse (1869–1954) *Still Life with Goldfish* (7.47)

Corot (1796–1875) *Papigno, Ville d'Avray* (7.8–9)

Kirchner (1880–1938) *Five Women in the Street* (7.45)

Fox Talbot (1800–77) *Boulevards of Paris* (7.4)

Daumier (1808–79) *Gargantua* (7.22)

Julia Margaret Cameron (1815–79) *Portrait of a Woman* (7.6)

Courbet (1819–77) *Burial at Ornans* (7.2)

Manet (1832–83) *Dejeuner sur l'Herbe* (7.12)

1818 *Frankenstein* – Mary Wollstonecraft Shelley

Whistler (1834–1903) *Nocturne* (7.23)

Degas (1834–1917) *The Tub* (7.19), *Little Dancer* (7.28)

Cézanne (1839–1906) *Vase of Tulips, Mont Sainte-Victoire* (7.52–53)

1819–24 *Don Juan* – Byron

Rodin (1840–1917) *The Burghers of Calais* (7.29), *Balzac* (7.32)

1820 *Prometheus Unbound* – Shelley

Monet (1840–1926) *Impression: Sunrise* (7.15)

Renoir (1841–1919) *Luncheon of the Boating Party* (7.17)

Morisot (1841–95) *The Harbor at Lorient* (7.20)

Cassatt (1844–1926) *The Letter* (7.37)

1832 *The Philosophy of History* – Hegel

Gauguin (1848–1903) *The Vision after the Sermon, Ia Orana Maria* (7.38–9)

1844 *Paris Manuscripts* – Marx

Van Gogh (1853–1890) *Bedroom, Self-Portrait* (7.40–41)

Seurat (1859–91) *La Grande Jatte* (7.34)

1848 *Communist Manifesto* – Marx and Engels

Munch (1863–1944) *The Scream* (7.42)

Nolde (1867–1956) *Prophet* (7.46)

1851 Paxton – Crystal Palace (7.49)

1889 Eiffel – Eiffel Tower (7.50)

1859 *The Origin of Species* – Darwin

1890–91 Sullivan – Wainwright Building (7.51)

(1792–1822) declared that "Poets are the unacknowledged legislators of the world," he was engaging in more than simple self-aggrandizement: he was suggesting that art has the power to transform the world. This was indeed a significant departure from earlier concepts.

To comprehend the ramifications of this new attitude — the confidence Shelley's dictum embodied — it is necessary to consider some of the complex foundational ideas that anchored artistic production during the nineteenth century. Thus, it is necessary to seek some sense of the pervading intellectual climate that both supported and enriched the artistic debates of the period.

One of the most influential theories of the Modern period was developed in the work of a late-Enlightenment figure, the German Idealist philosopher Immanuel Kant (1724–1804). His notion of the *disinterested viewer*, as described in his *Critique of Judgment*, was, he claimed, the essential component behind an aesthetic experience. By disinterest, Kant by no means suggested a lack of interest, but rather that the viewer should come to a work without predisposition, expectation, or inclination. Suppose you were asked to view a painting of a landscape. Upon first glance, the scene might remind you of a particular place, perhaps your home, and as a result you might feel positively disposed, even nostalgic, towards the work. Kant did not deny the power of such a response, but he claimed that it was based on sentiment rather than aesthetics. Beauty, in Kant's mind, is something intrinsic to a work through its organization and execution, and not anchored to elements external to the visual experience (such as symbolism, iconography, history). The idea of the disinterested viewer found considerable support during the Modern age, when subject matter became increasingly subsumed into the dynamics of picture making, and artists concerned themselves more with how they painted things than what they were actually painting.

Another philosopher who exerted tremendous influence on the nineteenth-century intellectual and cultural stage was G. F. W. Hegel, whose theory of a *dialectic* through history suggested that progress is the inevitable result of the ongoing clash of contradictory principles. His famous equation of *being* (the ultimate thesis of life) and *non being* (its antithesis), finding synthesis in the dynamic process of *becoming*, underpinned his belief in progress as a fundamental component to human existence — and supported a vision of culture moving towards ever more complex, resolved, and humane conditions. There was even a place for heroes in all this. However deterministic this formula first appears, Hegel acknowledged that it was possible for individuals to participate in pushing history towards its inevitable end in spirit. The answer lay in great figures who possessed the leadership capable of transforming whole societies — in other words, statesmen and other political figures.

Others were less convinced, as they believed the political arena to be too much compromised by social dynamics, power struggles, and political expedients to be capable of promoting profound change. Hegel, like Kant before him, believed that art, philosophy, and religion were equal but separate paths to the fulfilment of the spirit. In the writings of Friedrich Schelling (1775–1854) and others after Hegel, art was elevated above these other faculties because it was seen as fundamentally removed from the constrictive social dynamics that hamper revolutionary change. Here Shelley's pronouncement found its philosophical support: the artist, once the slave of Church and state, has through intellectual speculation been reconfigured as a kind of Modern savior!

To many, the argument was convincing. To lend even greater credence to this optimistic view of the progress and destiny of mankind, in 1859 the biologist Charles Darwin released his treatise *On the Origin of Species* which, though controversial from the outset, appeared nevertheless to provide conclusive evidence that nature was indeed moving toward more complex and efficient entities. Such theories also led to greater political speculation.

By the middle of the nineteenth century, Karl Marx and Friedrich Engels had formulated a radical criticism of Hegel's earlier theory. Rather than believing in an abstract spirit coming to self-consciousness, Marx and Engels saw changes in the material reality of the life experienced by mankind. The domination of different classes, rather than the proximity of theory to spiritual ideals, became the key to their analysis. Using the language of contemporary economic thought, known as political economy, Marx and Engels developed a theory called "historical materialism" in which the goal, rather than Hegel's realization of an abstract spirit of mankind in the real world, was the liberation of the worker. For many artists, the heroic and revolutionary nature of such speculation and, further, the need for certain "world historical individuals" (to borrow a phrase from Hegel) to drive the mechanism forward were enticing. Perhaps the first artist whose works revealed the effects of this ideological ferment was Gustave Courbet.

Courbet

Gustave Courbet (1819–77) is today known (perhaps misleadingly) as a "realist" for his essentially unsentimental portrayal of life in the mid-nineteenth century. One of the most famous of his early works is his vast *Burial at Ornans* (Fig. **7.2**) of 1849. Its acute description of this simple yet profound ceremony seems to have provoked very specific, sometimes vehement, responses in the years immediately after its unveiling, and as a result the realism was thought to be motivated by little more than socialist concerns. The negative reaction to this subject matter should not come as a surprise, as throughout the history of Western art few artists had ever considered the plight and devotion of the peasant as a topic worthy of serious attention — other than for overtly sentimental or moralizing reasons. However, it would be misleading to view Courbet as principally a politically motivated painter; in fact, his work asserted a very modern notion that an artist is first and foremost a social barometer of his/her age and context.

In 1861, Courbet wrote: "An epoch can be reproduced only by its own artists. I mean artists who have lived in it. I hold that the artists of one century are fundamentally incompetent to represent the things of a past or future century...It is in this sense that I deny the existence of an historical art applied to the past." This was, of course, an affront to the academic standards of Neoclassicism, but it was also an artistic call to arms for expression tied directly to the events, traumas, and psychology of the age — art as a dynamic, if sometimes uncertain, voice within culture, rather than a decorative or didactic tool. This opinion was not well received in critical circles, since most influential writers and "taste-makers" still viewed art as a tool for moral elevation and profound teaching, and consequently saw everyday events as simplistic and unworthy subject matter. As a result, *Burial at Ornans* was rejected at the Universal Exposition of 1855. Courbet responded by setting up his own show in a tent next to the official exhibition. In the process, he sealed his reputation as a master of self-promotion (again a posture considered unworthy of an artist in earlier times) and a politically astute artist.

■ 7.2 Gustave Courbet, *Burial at Ornans* 1849
Oil on canvas, 10 ft 3 in x 21 ft 8¾ in (3.12 x 6.62 m)
Louvre, Paris

How does such a dramatically different view of art alter the way in which the artist, and thus the viewer, comes to appreciate the meaning of a work of art? Here, a simple comparison might prove useful, based on the important reciprocal relationship between contemporary ideas in other fields of human inquiry and those in the visual arts. If one compares Courbet's *Stone Breakers* (Fig. **7.3**) of 1849 with Jacques-Louis David's *Oath of the Horatii* (see Fig. 6.16), it seems quite apparent that the artists in question constructed their paintings with very different intentions. David demanded that his composition evoke the same characteristic sensibility as the tale he told. Thus the rigid geometry and severe handling of forms further accentuate the impression of ultimate sacrifice. In short, form (the stark, angular composition and its reserved handling) and content (a tale of heroic denial and stoic discipline) merge into a unified and consistent whole. This relationship between form and content was no less important to Courbet, but his choice of conventions to accentuate his message is telling. Though Courbet understood and even utilized several traditional compositional devices in his work (notice how the implied diagonals created by the picks counter the opposing sloping diagonal of the background), the seemingly natural gestures of the figures give the impression of an authentic and perhaps more "natural" space. Rather than developing an architectural framework or other mathematically derived pictorial structure, Courbet's painting enables the viewer to enter into the scene with few external or otherwise presumed considerations other than the labors of the two men. As a result, one's concentration is thrust upon these two solitary figures and their brute activity; if there is any heroism present, it must rest with the travails of the workers, and the elevation of the here and now. Painted only a year after the 1848 revolt in France, it speaks of an art for the masses and a creative process intimately linked to the stresses of the street. This is what "realism" meant to Courbet.

■ 7.3 Gustave Courbet, *Stone Breakers* 1849
Oil on canvas, 5 ft 3 in x 8 ft 6 in (1.60 x 2.59 m)
Formerly Gemäldegalerie, Dresden (Destroyed 1945)

■ 7.4 William Fox Talbot, "A View of the Boulevards of Paris," 1843
A salt print from a calotype negative

PHOTOGRAPHY AND PAINTING

One of the traditional functions of art in Western society is to suggest or re-create aspects of the world one normally perceives — to provide a window onto the world, or at least imply that what is seen in art abides by most of the rules of everyday perception. Despite often dramatic changes in philosophy, subject matter, and even taste since the Renaissance, there was always a consistent and underlying assumption in the West that art functioned within the confines of representing forms. But suppose someone was to invent a machine that could not only document the world effectively but do it more accurately than any human. Would this discovery diminish the importance and status of art in culture, or would it force artists to reconsider the nature of art in an increasingly industrial and mechanized age? By the middle of the nineteenth century, the advent of the camera signaled a new era for art, and it forever changed the way in which artists and viewers were to look at the world through images.

The working premise behind photography (a word derived from the Greek, meaning to write or describe with light) had in fact existed for several centuries before it was finally fixed on paper. Initiated during the Renaissance and further developed through the Baroque period, a device called a *camera obscura* (see Fig. 5.54), used by Vermeer in the seventeenth century, was employed in the study of perspective. It was made of a simple enclosed box with a tiny hole in one end, which allowed external light to pass through and project an image onto the interior wall. The inverted image was then traced by artists, who used the projected image to obtain a more "lifelike" representation of the world. The problem was how to fix this image in a permanent state.

Early Photographic Developments: Niépce, Daguerre, and Fox Talbot

The early advances in **photography** belong as much to the history of science and technology in the nineteenth century as they do to art — or perhaps even more so. It starts with J. N. Niépce (1765–1883), a French inventor who between 1813 and 1827 committed himself to improving the recently invented lithographic process (see pages 340–342). The process was initially tied to traditional chalk drawing, which proved time consuming and not particularly accurate when used to copy items such as engravings. Niépce sought to replace this cumbersome method for transferring images to lithographic stones by using light. In 1829 he began a partnership with Louis Daguerre, (1787–1851), a former scene painter who had only a few years earlier developed the *Diorama*. Daguerre had used the traditional camera obscura in the production of his panoramas and, like his associate, became increasingly obsessed with the thought of fixing the inverted image permanently onto a panel. Niépce died in 1833, but his experiments proved instrumental in Daguerre's subsequent development of the first **daguerreotype**.

The breakthrough came in 1837, when Daguerre successfully captured light on a silvered copper plate. By exposing this plate to the vapours of mercury and then bathing the plate in salted hot water, he was able to fix the effect of light and create an image. Though the exposure time was unmanageably long and the chemicals nasty, the invention set off a wave of refinements and spin-off inventions that permanently altered the concept of "pictures."

■ 7.5 Maxime du Camp, *Temple of Ramses*, 1850
Victoria & Albert Museum, London

While Daguerre was busy with his silver salts in France, in Britain William Henry Fox Talbot (1800–1877) was simultaneously attempting to fix images on light-sensitive paper. In 1835, he succeeded in producing the first *Talbotype* or *calotype*, by using gallic acid as his developer. Once the image (which appeared in negative) was fixed on paper, Fox Talbot applied a layer of wax to its surface, making it translucent. Light was then again projected through this *negative* and used to make *positive* prints.

Fox Talbot's *View of the Boulevards of Paris* (Fig. **7.4** on page 325) of 1843, made from the calotype process, gives some indication of the quality of photographic images at the time. One of the first things that strikes the viewer's eye is the image's lack of refinement or clarity. There are two reasons for this loss of definition: the relative crudity of the calotype process, and the still rather lengthy exposure time. The resultant *blurring* of elements (noticeably the trees in this print) was to prove of great interest to painters during the period, who saw in the new medium a new pictorial convention for motion. Fox Talbot noticed other, less technical, and more aesthetic dimensions to these early photographic prints.

Aesthetics in Early Photography

When Fox Talbot set about documenting the streets of Paris in photographs, he composed in a manner not unlike that of a painter. Yet when the prints were developed, he became increasingly aware of the camera's ability to seize upon the scene's less obvious stories — the posters, signboards, and other discreet information that were part of the urban landscape. He wrote, with regards to this print: "A whole forest of chimneys borders the horizon: for the instrument chronicles whatever it sees, and certainly would delineate a chimney pot or a chimney sweeper with the same impartiality as it would the Apollo Belvedere." Fox Talbot referred to this quality as "fascinating irrelevancy," and though he appears to have enjoyed such incidentals, others were not equally convinced. Contemporary critics claimed that, without a level of compositional discretion accompanied by an ability to edit out peripheral (read commonplace) information, how could photographers rightfully claim any artistic virtue to their work?

There emerged two, opposed critical positions with regards to the camera's apparent disinterest: one

In other words, photographs needed to be tidied up. As a result, many of the best prints of the 1850s and 1860s are of architecture — a subject that possesses a strong sense of pattern, symmetry, and clear purpose and which can be composed in an attractive manner. Maxime du Camp's *Temple of Ramses* (Fig. **7.5**)) of 1850 is an excellent example of this trend towards compositional clarity, an element considerably enhanced through the 1850s by the discoveries of orthoscopic lenses and albumen paper (negatives coated in egg white, which gave exquisite detail).

Photographers of that period also turned to such traditional painting genres as portraiture, still life, and landscape for inspiration. Julia Margaret Cameron's *Portrait of a Woman (Mrs Duckworth)* (Fig. **7.6**) of 1867 and Adolphe Braun's *Still Life with Deer and Wildfowl* (Fig. **7.7**) of 1865 are good examples of the trend towards "art" photography that surfaced during the mid nineteenth century, and it suggests that artists

■ **7.6 Julia Margaret Cameron**
Portrait of a Woman (Mrs. Duckworth), 1867
Victoria & Albert Museum, London

■ **7.7 Adolphe Braun**
Still Life with Deer and Wildfowl, 1865
Carbon photograph. The Metropolitan Museum of Art, New York
David Hunter McAlpin fund, 1947 (47.149.54)

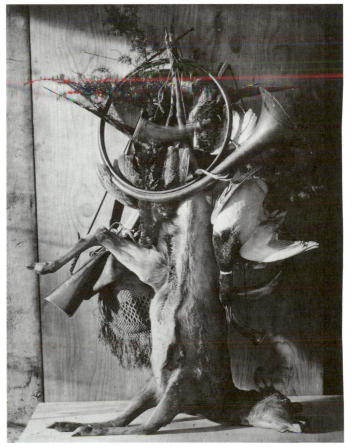

overtly political, the other more strictly formal. The political ramifications of photography were explored, in fact, not by a photographer but by the painter and printmaker Honoré Daumier (1808–79). An astute observer of the political and social culture of his time, he often cited a gap between what he called "official culture" and that which occurred on the street. He saw in photography and its objective, documenting eye the potential to elevate the status of the "irrelevant" poor within official culture — to make the invisible visible, so to speak.

However, photography was first and foremost an instrument of the market during its early years — and the market was part and parcel of official culture. One of the predictable results of this arrangement was the dismissal of those "fascinating irrelevancies" as unseemly, unaesthetic, and certainly unmarketable.

working in the medium were often more comfortable mimicking the conventions of painting than they were exploring the unique qualities inherent in photography.

The refinement of the photographic image through the nineteenth century sent shock waves through the art community. The repercussions of such accessible, accurate "do-it-yourself machines" for the art world, which prided itself on the craft of representation, were predictably significant. The issue of craft, in which an artist painstakingly studies nature and learns to represent it (consider Reynolds' discourses on art, Chapter Six, pages 290–293) was now in jeopardy, since this new technology could do it better, more economically, and in less time than the painter. There were those who attempted to mimic "high art" subjects and composition through the photographic medium, but often these images lacked the consistent internal harmony the viewer had come to expect from a painting. However, the effects of photography were soon to influence even the most traditionally minded artists.

Corot and the Influence of Photography on Painting

Jean-Baptiste-Camille Corot (1796–1875) is an excellent example of a painter who "resaw" his subject in terms of the photograph. His early works reflect an interest in capturing a specific place and time — an idea that would find its greatest expression in the late Impressionists. A painting such as *Papigno* (Fig. **7.8**) of

■ 7.8 Camille Corot, *Papigno* 1826
Oil on canvas, 13 x 15¼ in (33 x 38.7 cm)
Fritz Nathan Collection, Zürich

■ 7.9 Camille Corot, *Ville d'Avray* 1870
Oil on canvas, 21⅝ x 31½ in (55 x 80 cm)
The Metropolitan Museum of Art, New York
Bequest of Catherine Lorillard Wolfe, 1887

1826 is indicative of Corot's desire to order and solidify his experience of a dynamic environment into a well-orchestrated painting. Particularly notable about these early works, the uncanny stillness of the landscape (reminiscent of Poussin) seems more in line with still-life painting than the natural world. Nevertheless, the combination of rigorous visual observation and sensitivity to natural light makes these simple scenes arresting to the eye.

Like his predecessor Poussin, Corot spent much of his time in Italy, but he returned home to the outskirts of Paris toward the end of his life. There he came into contact with a group of inventive photographers who were also captivated by the landscape. By the 1860s the exposure time for a photograph had dwindled down to mere seconds, which made it workable for documenting human subjects. However, even one second of exposure time became an issue for those interested in photographing the natural world. A simple phenomenon such as wind or the passage of light through leaves changed the position

of objects constantly, and the result was a photograph with three notable characteristics: first, blurred areas, caused by the movement of forms during exposure; second, the disintegration of some forms due to strong sunlight, which breaks down solid forms and creates a feathery appearance throughout, called *halation*; and third, the combination of *blurring* and halation that creates an integration of all areas of the field, in turn unifying the plane.

The concept of blurring should come as little surprise to those familiar with even the simplest of modern cameras, and anyone who has walked through a light forest on a sunny day will understand the concept of halation. The combination of these two phenomena provided Corot and other artists with a new set of conventions for describing the natural world. Corot's *Ville d'Avray* (Fig. **7.9**) of 1870 demonstrates such an assimilation of photographic devices into traditional painting, and it paved the way for an even more revolutionary departure from convention — with the group now known as the Impressionists.

THE ARTIST AT MID-CENTURY

Nineteenth-Century Color Theory

Photography was by no means the only innovation to find its way into the realms of art. During the early nineteenth century the fields of physics and optics also paved the way for developments in the understanding of color. In 1839 the French thinker Eugène Chevreul published his *Principles of Harmonies and Contrasts of Color and Their Application to the Arts*, a text that was to influence a whole generation of artists (both Monet and Seurat had firsthand knowledge of this work). In his treatise, Chevreul claimed that colors in proximity to one another influence and modify how each is perceived. This means that viewers see color only in relation to its environment, as each sensation of color is directly related to its position among other colors. Chevreul also stated that any color seen alone appears to be surrounded by a specific complementary color, somewhat like a faint halo. (Try staring at a red dot for a minute, and then quickly look away. Notice how you now observe a green or opposite color ghost in its place.) To see what this meant to artists at the time, a brief look at a color wheel (Fig. **7.10**) will be helpful.

■ **7.10 Color wheel**

According to nineteenth-century color theory, the relationship between colors was explained in terms of a schematic wheel, with the colors blue, red, and yellow providing the backbone for all other combinations; because of the necessity of using these three colors in the mixing of all other colors, they are called "primary." Half-way between red and yellow on the wheel is the color orange, which is produced by mixing equal portions of the primaries on either side. Given this configuration, the colors closest to each primary will then have a greater saturation of that color in their mix (red-orange, red-violet). An examination of the color that lies directly opposite any "hue" (the property that gives a color its name) on this wheel makes it apparent that this complementary possesses none of the color traits of its opposite. Take the color red, for instance. According to the wheel, its complementary or opposite is green, which is made up of equal parts of yellow and blue — and no red. Now consider this phenomenon in the light of Chevreul's claim that each color possesses a faint halo of its complementary when isolated. One obvious (though amazing) corollary is that each color has implicit characteristics of every other hue in its makeup.

Interesting though all this might be, such treatises are of value to artists only when they can be practically applied. One implication drawn from the findings was that artists could use colors (usually referred to as "chroma," with regard to the purity of the colors and the amount of their saturation in the paint) that were dramatically more intense in close proximity. When such high chroma color applications were allowed a degree of space between them, the result was an intensified experience of each; when placed in closer proximity, the vivid colors neutralized each other. This idea is exemplified in pictorial form in a work by Pierre-Auguste Renoir (1841–1919), *Railway Bridge at Chatou* (Fig. **7.11**) of 1881, in which a variety of intense colors was used to create a dazzling yet still remarkably harmonious painting.

Before the mid nineteenth century, an artist was to all intents and purposes confined to the studio, since each color had to be carefully prepared, the pigment ground and mixed with safflower or some other available oil. This put obvious restrictions on any artists interested in natural light; they would have to make sketches in watercolor — or have a very good memory! The production of the squeezable tin tube, which was sealed at one end, filled with paint, and then capped at the other, gave artists unprecedented freedom to execute work in virtually any locale.

The Modernity of Manet

The transition from artists such as Courbet and Corot to the Impressionists appears, in retrospect, very predictable. A key figure was Édouard Manet (1832–83), whose monumental and controversial work *Le Déjeuner sur l'herbe* (*Luncheon on the Grass*) (Fig. **7.12**) of 1863 suggests a new attitude toward the problem of making an image. At first glance, this work appears to have much in common with the history of Western painting already discussed, yet there are some noteworthy departures.

The first and perhaps most apparent difference between this image and its predecessors is the purposeful disregard of volume in the painting. Since the Renaissance, Western artists had been concerned with rendering three-dimensional forms on a two-dimensional surface, and thus they utilized a series of conventions to give the illusion of forms in space (chiaroscuro, perspective). Though Manet still implied

space within the confines of the picture plane, the figures he handled with broad, sweeping areas of undifferentiated color, denying the traditional modeling that would grant these figures volume.

The subject matter of *Le Déjeuner sur l'herbe* remains one of the most enigmatic, if captivating aspects of the work. The forthright glance of the central female nude seems specifically designed to draw the viewer into the scene, yet the relationship between figures and specifically the context of the nude in relation to the two decidedly dressed men created a stir from its inception. Even at the Salon des Refusés (where images not chosen in the Paris Biennials could be viewed), the work was viewed as scandalous, and today its iconography is still not without its critics. One contemporary wrote of it: "A commonplace woman...as naked as can be, shamelessly lolls between two dandies dressed to the teeth. These latter look like schoolboys on a holiday, perpetrating an outrage to play the man, and I search in vain for the meaning of this unbecoming rebus...This is a young man's practical joke, a shameful open sore." Is this a commentary on the preoccupations and leisure activities of the middle class, a mildly

■ **7.12 Édouard Manet**
Déjeuner sur l' Herbe 1863
Oil on canvas
7 ft ¾ in x 8 ft 10⅜ in
(2.15 x 2.7 m)
Louvre, Paris

erotic picture of two couples caught in a private moment, or simply some artists and their models? In any event, this is a very modern picture, focused in the present and involved with subjects that came to personify the Modern attitude.

From reports, it appears that Manet was certainly conscious of the novelty of the work, yet he remained convinced that its importance lay not in its subject matter but in its painting. Indeed, the unconventional array and placement of figures only reiterate the notion that this is first and foremost a painting about painting.

Perhaps this needs explaining. Today, the notion of a work of art's formal arrangement acting in part as a type of inner or self-critique is quite common, since after all it is through art's conventional language that the viewer accesses its information. Manet's painting is an early example of this very modern approach to art making. Take, for instance, the unorthodox relationships set up between the viewer and the painting. First, there is an undeniable debt to traditional allegorical painting in the choice of figures and setting, yet the title of the work posits little more than the

acceptance of its contemporaneity, its here and now, and certainly not any of the higher or finer virtues associated with the earlier allegories of a Titian or a Watteau. Yet the formal poses of the figures contradict any suggestion of this being a simple representation of middle-class Parisians out on a jaunt in the woods. Indeed, the clash between the clothed and the unclothed, the dramatic warmth of the flesh offsetting the cool lushness of the landscape and drapery, the polarity of title and its historical debt, all point to the implausibility of this as either an allegory or an accurate representation of everyday life. Instead, the viewer is left with a sense of the artist's freedom to pick and choose at will — for the sake of the picture, for its aesthetic effect, for the sake of art. Here Manet positions himself as one of the first "pure painters" of the Modern period, in which once sacred aspects of subject matter and symbolic content are subordinate to the act of painting and a regard for the material properties of the medium.

Manet was adept at recontextualizing the subject matter and compositions of other artists. A particular preoccupation was Goya, and in Manet's reconstitution of the Spaniard's work the revolutionary character of the artist's painting becomes apparent. Manet's decisive contribution to "the new art" can be assessed by comparing the *Balcony* (Fig. **7.13**) of 1869 with Goya's *Majas on the Balcony* (Fig. **7.14**) of 1810–15. Immediately, one is taken by the apparent flatness of Manet's painting, particularly when compared with the atmospheric handling of space so evident in the Goya. Manet's heightened color scheme and rigid **positive-negative space** design (positive referring to the shapes of forms representing the subject matter, negative to the open spaces surrounding them, often called the background) contradict many of the traditional notions of space "in" the painting — which is another way of saying that the composition reasserts the surface, rather than actively trying to deny it (as was previously popular). Manet's figures

■ 7.13 Édouard Manet, *The Balcony* 1868–9
Oil on canvas, 5 ft 7 in x 4 ft 1 in (1.7 x 1.24 m)
Musée d'Orsay, Paris

■ 7.14 Francisco de Goya
Majas on the Balcony 1810–15
Oil on canvas, 6 ft 4¾ in x 4 ft 1½ in (1.95 x 1.26 m)
The Metropolitan Museum of Art, New York

are not easily assimilated into the depths of the painting; they operate as much as flat forms of color as they do as protagonists in some social affair. This does not mean that Manet was unconcerned about the content of his work — the penetrating glances and preoccupied dispositions of his subjects prove that he most certainly was. Rather, Manet may best be understood as an artist of his time, rethinking the nature of painting in an era of unsurpassed expansion. When Courbet remarked that Manet's paintings were "as flat as playing cards," he could never have imagined how prophetic those words would come to be.

IMPRESSIONISM

There are few movements in art that so exquisitely parallel the developments of their time as **Impressionism**. The term is something of a misnomer, and it derives from one specific painting — *Impression: Sunrise* (Fig. **7.15**) of 1872 by Claude Monet (1840–1926). It was in the adept hands of Monet that the vision of a world created by light and color found perhaps its greatest expression. To appreciate fully the radical nature of Monet's and his fellow Impressionists' work, it is necessary once again to consider the artists within the context of traditional Western two-dimensional visual culture.

Since Giotto's "re-engagement" of Classical conventions for the depiction of space and volume on a flat plane, painters had been interested mainly in naturalism as applied to form, rather than to the quality of light and color. The reasons for such a bias in the Western tradition are themselves rooted in assumptions about the nature of art and existence in which painting was seen as the masterful illusion of three dimensions in two. The problem with any serious consideration of the naturalistic effects of color and light is that both factors tend to destroy the perception of depth and to disintegrate form, which results in flat painting. Though such a depiction of form through the experience of light and color might seem more truthful to perception, for almost five centuries painting was preoccupied with a different kind of truth. In a world in which people saw the intellect as living proof of God's divine order, it should come as little surprise that rationally deduced conventions

■ **7.15** Claude Monet, *Impression: Sunrise* 1872
Oil on canvas, 19½ x 24½ in (49.5 x 62.2 cm)
Musée Marmottan, Paris

■ 7.16 Claude Monet, *Regatta at Argenteuil* 1872
Oil on canvas, 19 x 29½ in (48 x 75 cm), Musée d'Orsay, Paris

such as perspective and symmetrical composition found greater favor with artists. By the middle of the nineteenth century, however, the world had changed, and so too had its perception of naturalism.

Monet

Monet's *Impression: Sunrise* is a kind of painting very different from those Western culture had experienced. Gone was the concrete form carefully executed to give the suggestion that it existed in a defined and measurable space. Instead, the work appeared as a series of "color events" taking place on the surface of the canvas, in which forms were articulated through their response to light. Here, the simple recognition of halation as a perceptual reality opened the door to a revolutionary new way of looking. Impressionism had two distinct effects on painting: it elevated color to the status of subject matter, and it reasserted painting's relationship to the flat surface. But perhaps what is most interesting about these departures is how they followed a predictable evolution toward self-critique and the questioning of perception inherent in painting that had been developing since the Renaissance; in other words, Impressionism was at once the heir to a tradition and a departure from it.

Monet was one of the first artists to work almost exclusively out of doors. With a tube of paint in his hand, he was liberated from the confines of the studio, and set to work at understanding the one natural phenomenon still virgin territory in the nineteenth century — the effect of natural light on forms. Light in fact meant color, since one perceives light only through its effects on color, and color was one area that the new photographic medium could not, in the late nineteenth century, yet restore. So vital was the proper understanding of color to artists such as Monet that they forbade the use of black in their paintings — since black corresponded in scientific terms to the absence of color and thus did not exist in nature.

There is also a degree of self-imposed naïveté implicit within Impressionist art. The history of Western painting until Monet had been predominantly about what one knew, rather than what one saw. Artists used pictorial conventions with the aim of producing a very particular kind of experience — one in which viewers became God, and the world was organized around their gaze. Of course, the world never actually appeared this way to anyone in everyday experience, and thus it is fair to claim that painting was as much about a culture's projection of ideas onto the world as it was about an authentic, disinterested representation. Impressionism sought to bring painting in line with commonsense visual experience, and as a result, traditional conventions were replaced with a more spontaneous depiction of nature's dynamics in oil paint. In short, construction gave way to impression.

Monet's *Regatta at Argenteuil* (Fig. **7.16** on page 335) of 1872 was executed in the same year as *Impression: Sunrise* and demonstrates the radical strides the artist was making from one painting to the next. What is perhaps most captivating about this work is his commitment to showing the process of painting. Take, for instance, the vibrant array of color found in the reflection on the water's surface: rather than subtly blending his color through a series of glazes (as was traditionally done), Monet let each sensation of light have a physical, painterly correspondent. As a result, viewers are more aware of the artist's efforts to describe a sensation than of the image itself.

This process is called **mark making**, and it takes as its premise the fact that the gestures, scribbles, and gouges produced by an artist during the execution of a work are part of the work's subject matter. The implication of such an obvious work method is that now, instead of simply looking through a window onto the world, one is forced to look at the world through the artist's physical experience of his/her subject. Paint is a wonderful carrier of messages when allowed to exist undiluted; its paste-like consistency takes brush marks and other gestures and transforms them into intimate suggestions of the artist's method of work. Thus in Impressionist painting the viewer is privy not only to the artist's sensation of the natural world but also to the very experience of painting that sensation.

There is, however, a degree of irony in all this, for in attempting to view the world in a more objective,

■ 7.17 Pierre-Auguste Renoir, *Luncheon of the Boating Party* 1881
Oil on canvas, 4 ft 3 in x 5 ft 8 in (1.29 x 1.72 m), Phillips Collection, Washington, D.C.

more truthful, and less "conventional" manner, artists such as Monet seemed to produce decidedly more intimate, subjective, and egocentric views of the world. Yet this is also what makes their work definitively modern and their efforts all the more engaging.

Varieties of Impressionist Experience

In 1874 a group of artists, spearheaded by Monet, organized a show of work at the Café Guerbois in Paris, after being denied entry to the fashionable Salons because of their unconventional approach to painting. *Impression: Sunrise* seems to have provoked the most vehement of outcries from critics, who labeled the entire group "Impressionists" (by no means a compliment at the time). Despite sometimes overt differences in attitudes between artists who took part in the initial and subsequent "Impressionist" exhibitions, the label stuck.

Pierre-Auguste Renoir shared Monet's enthusiasm for the effects of light and freedom of paint handling but was much more conservative in his tastes. Renoir was one of those rare characters in art who seemed genuinely content to explore and elevate the status of everyday joy and harmony without moralizing baggage. A painting such as his *Luncheon of the Boating Party* (Fig. **7.17**) of 1881 is a delightful depiction of *joie de vivre* in those seemingly endless forty years of peace and prosperity between the Franco-Prussian War and the First World War. But it is in a painting such as *Nude in the Sunlight* (Fig. **7.18**) of 1876 that Renoir's unparalleled ability to unleash the sensual potential of light becomes apparent. The skirting and flickering of light on translucent skin are heightened by the liberated handling of the paint, which gives the entire painting a hazy and diffused ambience.

The idea of an "impressionistic glance" not only lay in the liberation of color and an increased emphasis on the artist's response to his or her environment, but also had repercussions in the way in which artists composed. One such artist, convinced that painting could be manipulated to suit the "natural view," was Edgar Degas (1834–1917). Some of his most captivating work was done in chalk pastel — a medium that effectively combines a variety of mark-making devices usually associated with drawing and dramatically intense color.

The Tub (Fig. **7.19**) of 1886 exhibits Degas's formidable drawing skills and keen eye for essentials.

■ 7.18 Pierre-Auguste Renoir
Nude in the Sunlight 1876
Oil on canvas, 32 x 25 in (81 x 63.5 cm)
Musée d'Orsay, Paris

However, what is perhaps most intriguing about this image is its rather unorthodox perspectival composition. The very fact that one perceives the viewpoint as an oddity is in itself illuminating; the naturalness of such a view (one gets the distinct impression of having opened a closed door and caught this woman in the midst of a bath) is an open critique of the traditional notion that the viewers hold a privileged position in the world as described in art. There is also more than just a hint of the influence of photography in such work; Degas's disposition toward cropping elements around the extremities of his scenes reminds the viewer more of snapshots than of the ordered world of traditional painting. In *The Tub* the viewer is privy to this scene only as a passer-by, given a glimpse into a world without a predetermined storyline. Here, the innocent glance produces an impression as powerful as any specific truth to stimuli.

■ 7.19 Edgar Degas
The Tub 1886
Pastel on paper
27½ x 27½ in (70 x 70 cm)
Louvre, Paris

■ 7.20 Berthe Morisot
The Harbor at Lorient 1869
Oil on canvas, 17⅛ x 28¾ in
(43.5 x 73 cm)
National Gallery of Art,
Washington, D.C.
Alisa Mellon Bruce Collection
© 1995 Board of Trustees

■ **7.21 Mary Cassatt**
Mother and Child 1889
Oil on canvas
29 x 23½ in (73.7 x 59.7 cm)
Cincinnati Art Museum
John J. Emery Endowment 1928

Degas was also a notoriously tough critic — particularly when it came to his contemporaries. One artist who succeeded in impressing him, however, was the Impressionist Berthe Morisot (1841–95), whose work he claimed "concealed the purest draftsmanship." In the beautiful *Harbor at Lorient* (Fig. **7.20**) of 1869, she demonstrated her capacity to fuse an open and vital compositional arrangement with a loose but delicate application of paint.

The American Mary Cassatt (1844–1926) was also closely associated with Degas, and her work combines the often contradictory sensibilities of drawing and color with singular insight. *Mother and Child* (Fig. **7.21**) of 1889 is typical of Cassatt's work, which drew heavily on the everyday relations between mothers and their children. Here, she took Manet's initial experiments in presenting large areas of undifferentiated color to new heights; now volume is implied almost exclusively through the sensitive handling of line that forms the shapes (such as under the woman's arm and the child's wrist). Even the simple background is articulated almost exclusively through line, but these lines retain a certain unpredictable and organic quality that is always associated with Impressionist painting. The result is an interesting merging of Monet's light and mark making with Manet's flattening of forms, in a satisfying and sensitive portrayal of domestic life.

THE ART OF LITHOGRAPHY

The nineteenth century was unprecedented in its rate of invention and expansion; no field of technology was unmoved by the insatiable pull of progress. Printmaking was no exception. The advent and mastery of **lithography** □ by artists during the nineteenth century was one of the technical and artistic highlights of the period; it was given its extensive use during and directly after the Impressionist period.

Perhaps the most adventurous artist to use the lithographic medium during the mid nineteenth century was Honoré Daumier (1808–79), whose marriage of political outrage and energized draftsmanship made for arguably some of the most profound social commentary of the era. By the 1820s, lithography had become a popular method for producing small leaflets and journals in what was a politically turbulent time in France. The cost was relatively low, and the technical demands of printing could be kept to a limited number of practitioners. Daumier proved particularly adept at satire, and his work soon found a wide acceptance among the readers of the political magazines. One of his most notorious images from the 1830s (which was never published in a journal but which nevertheless landed him in jail for six months) was *Gargantua* (Fig. **7.22**) a scathing indictment of King Louis-Philippe as a pear-headed glutton with the legs of an ass.

By the 1850s, Daumier's popular "one franc" lithographs were in such high demand that he no longer had time to plan his drawings in advance of their execution on lithographic stone. The result was a series of remarkably fresh and vibrant prints, such as *A Queen Prepares for her Great Speech*, which capture the satirist at his most artistically assured. The drawing in these late works possesses an immediacy and facility rare in early lithography, and it set a precedent for other artists in their exploration of the expressive, rather than the technical, possibilities afforded by the medium.

As the century advanced, artists took lithography in different directions. James Abbot McNeill Whistler (1834–1903) worked with a London printer on a process called *lithotint*, in which layers of delicate tusche washes were painted directly onto the litho stone surface and printed in subtle tonalities. The result, evident in Whistler's brilliant *Nocturne* (Fig. **7.23**) of 1878, is a misty, moody ambience of remarkable subtlety and simplicity.

Another artist often associated with lithography is Henri de Toulouse-Lautrec (1864–1901). Almost single-handedly, he launched the tired and predictable genre of nineteenth-century poster design into the realm of art, combining bold and gestural lines with

■ 7.22 Honoré Daumier
Gargantua, 1831
Lithograph
Bibliothèque Nationale, Paris

■ 7.23 James McNeill Whistler
Nocturne (The Thames at Battersea), 1878
Lithotint, 6¾ x 10⅛ in (17 x 25.8 cm)
Cleveland Museum of Art

FOCUS ON

Lithography

The term lithography derives from the Greek, meaning stone writing. Unlike the three other graphic techniques (intaglio, relief, and silk-screen), lithography's invention and early development are well documented. The process was invented in Munich in the 1790s by Alois Senefelder (1771–1834), an actor-playwright who needed a cheap way of reproducing his plays. His initial intention was to write in reverse on a copper plate covered with a homemade resist of wax, soap, and lampblack. The idea was then to etch the plate in acid and pull a print from it (the intaglio process). However, writing in reverse is tough work, and Senefelder decided to practice on whatever was available — including a piece of polished limestone he was using as an ink slab. According to traditional accounts, Senefelder was in the middle of practicing his backwards writing when a housekeeper entered the studio requiring a laundry list.

■ 7.25 Illustration of lithographic press

■ 7.24 Photograph of Senefelder's pole press from 1797
Photo: Deutsches Museum, Munich

Without a writing instrument nearby, Senefelder hastily wrote up a list with his crayon of hardened resist on a nearby piece of limestone. Afterwards, perhaps on a whim, he decided to sponge bath the stone in nitric acid and water, which bit into the stone everywhere except where the resist had been applied. The difference in relief was barely discernible, about the thickness of a playing card, but when it was rolled with ink, it provided a clear relief print of the list.

Next came Senefelder's invention, in 1799, of the lithographic *pole press*, which, in an attempt to prevent paper slippage, utilized a clamp to secure a "scraper bar" against the back of the printing paper (Fig. **7.24**). The paper rested against the inked surface of the limestone slab, which when pulled under the scraper made a print. Later, a roller was introduced to help move the slab (Fig. **7.25**). Finally, changes in the inking process were introduced. Senefelder had originally used a letterpress tampon to apply ink to his stone, but because of its softness and the shallowness of the relief, ink often stuck not only to the intended relief areas but to the bitten sections as well. To circumvent this problem, he applied ink with a stiff roller, which effectively distributed ink onto the relief and left the negative or bitten empty. Later that year, Senefelder, confident that the processes had commercial potential, filed for a patent on his "chemical printing" method in Munich. Albeit still crude, lithography — "stone writing" — was born.

Lithography flourished during the nineteenth century because of its relative immediacy, the variety of techniques and effects that could be employed, and the quality of reproduction. The first lithographs often had the look of etchings, as artists wrestled with the potential of the new printing medium. Yet in the hands of artists such as Goya and Delacroix the expressive potential of lithography was finally realized. Changes in the hardness of grease crayons and in the ink-like resist called *tusche* enabled artists to achieve a wide variety of values and atmospheric effects previously unavailable in etching.

flat areas of vibrant color to produce images that were the perfect embodiment of Paris night life — lively, energetic, theatrical, and sometimes melancholic. His *Seated Clownesse* (Fig. **7.26**) of 1896 is indicative of his lithographic style. Here he employed three stones (red, yellow, and black) and the *spray* technique (flicking tusche from a brush to make a uniform pattern of very small dots on the stone) to produce an engaging image of cabaret life — of bright lights, theatre, and lonely souls.

■ **7.26** Henri de Toulouse-Lautrec, *The Seated Clownesse*, from the series *Elles*, 1896
Color lithograph, 28 x 22 in (71.1 x 55.9 cm)
The Metropolitan Museum of Art, New York, The Alfred Stieglitz Collection, 1949 (49.55.50)

NINETEENTH-CENTURY SCULPTURE

As was previously discussed in connection with Impressionism, the necessary and predictable path toward a revolutionary new form of art making seems to lie in the questioning of previously established conventions. Painting questioned the idea of illusion, and the discrepancy between what one saw and what one thought one saw. In this way, the concerns of nineteenth-century sculptors paralleled attitudes in the two-dimensional arts, but sculpture's established set of conventions forced it in other directions.

Rude

A work by François Rude (1784–1855), *Volunteers of 1792* (known as *La Marseillaise*) from the Arc de Triomphe (Fig. **7.27**) of 1833–6, is indicative of the prevailing interests in sculptural art mid-century. The emotional and exuberant subject matter is most certainly Romantic in attitude, yet compared with much of the painting of the period, it pales in comparison (compare it with Géricault's *Raft of the Medusa* [Fig. 6.25]). The reasons for this are as much embedded in the nature of sculpture as it was understood in the nineteenth century as they are an indictment of Rude's work, and they say a lot about the accepted sculptural conventions of the time. Despite a move toward greater naturalism in the painting of the period, it is interesting to note how derivative *La Marseillaise* appears.

The reasons for this often frustrating recapitulation of supposedly "eternal" standards in sculpture between Bernini and the late nineteenth century can be directly tied to practical considerations. One of the most immediate determining factors behind the execution of a sculptural project is the market — sculpture has been traditionally tied to large-scale commission work. Figurative sculpture is unlike painting in that it requires a substantial amount of room in which to be displayed; this places the work economically within the range of a very select group (such as the Church or state) with the resources to buy and house it. The cost of basic materials and labor could be so great that few artists could afford to produce work or experiment of their own accord — they were financially bound to commission work, even as late as the 1830s.

A second factor of some significance in the development of a specific sculptural language was the necessary consideration of the work's architectural or environmental surroundings. Until the nineteenth century, sculpture was often tied to architectural considerations. Rude's work was a direct heir to such a tradition, as relief sculpture is inextricably linked to the wall, and thus must be set within the confines of a greater architectural environment. This practical reality had a determining effect on the work produced, with everything from subject matter to scale needing to be considered within the context of larger issues. This helps explain why Rude's figures continued the lineage of ideal form that dates back to Classical

■ **7.27 François Rude**
Volunteers of 1792 (La Marseillaise) 1833–6
Stone
Approx. 42 ft x 62 ft (12.8 x 18.9 m)
Arc de Triomphe, Paris

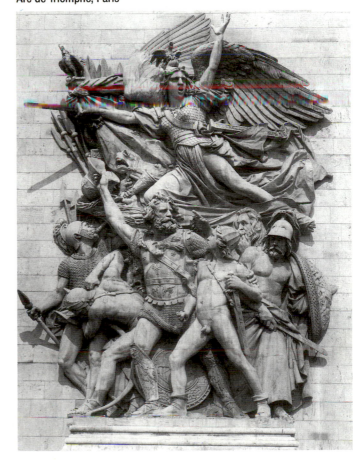

Greece: heroic figure modeling seems most appropriate within the realm of sanctioned heroes, which is the territory of Church and state.

Perhaps the most apparent, though often ignored, convention employed by sculptors during this period was the **pedestal**. It was the accepted standard for the display of sculpture as early as Archaic Greece and was considered an inevitability in sculpture by the nineteenth century, not a convention to be challenged. A pedestal removes the object from the space and scale of the viewer; it elevates and sanctifies the object as "other," "different," and usually "heroic." Thus any appreciation of a sculptural form often came with the implicit acceptance of the majesty and sanctity of the figure, and as with perspective and chiaroscuro in painting, a seemingly arbitrary convention soon became an essential characteristic of the medium.

Degas

It is arguable that the first radical departure from such accepted norms in sculpture came, ironically, in the work of a painter — Edgar Degas's *Little Fourteen-Year-Old Dancer* (Fig. **7.28**) of 1881. It is the only sculpture Degas ever exhibited, and though it exists in bronze reproduction at museums throughout the world, the original was of colored wax. The idea seems to have been to produce both a gesture and a coloration that were at once natural and convincing. Degas colored his wax to simulate the skin of a fourteen-year-old dance student, and the various accoutrements (the tutu made from gauze and tulle, silk wrapped around the figure as a bodice, and real hair attached to her head) accentuate the enormous gulf that had developed between the perception of naturalism and the nature of sculpture before this work. Degas's dancer possessed no pedestal as part of the object, so that the form is grounded on its base as a human would stand — again placing it within the context and even the psychological space of the viewer. It is also not idealized. Many critics were openly hostile to its appearance, and it seems that many writers, while willing to accept the realism of a Courbet, were not yet able to see such naturalism in the ideal world of sculptural forms.

■ 7.28 Edgar Degas
Little Fourteen-Year-Old Dancer c. 1881
Wax, silk, satin ribbon, and hair
Height 3 ft 3 in (0.99 m)
Collection of Mr. and Mrs. Paul Mellon, Upperville, Virginia

■ 7.29 Auguste Rodin, *The Burghers of Calais* 1884–6,
Bronze, 6 ft 10½ in x 7 ft 11 in x 6 ft 6 in (2.09 x 2.41 x 1.98 m)
Hirshhorn Museum and Sculpture Garden, Smithsonian Institute

Rodin

Degas's *Little Dancer* was an affront to most of what
sculpture had held dear since the Renaissance: it did
not idealize, it used color rather than stone or bronze,
it broke with the pedestal, and it was unapologetically
naturalistic. However, it was in the hands of a sculptor that the conventional language of sculpture was to
undergo its greatest transition. Auguste Rodin (1840–
1917) was perhaps the most gifted sculptor in
Western art since Bernini, and his work spanned six
crucial decades in the development of modern art.

Rodin's *Burghers of Calais* (Fig. **7.29**) of 1884–6
was commissioned by the port city of Calais to honor
six of its citizens who, in 1347, willingly allowed
themselves to be taken hostage by the invading
English in the hope that their city might be spared.
Upon first impression, this sculpture has few of the
qualities one has come to expect from public monuments. Consider the *Burghers* in the light of François
Rude's monument to Marshal Ney (Fig. **7.30**) of 1853
— a typical example of public sculpture then (and
still) popular. Rodin's decidedly intense depiction of
the human condition is at once a radical departure

from the norm. The modeling of the figure responds as much to the materials in which the sculptor worked as it does to any anatomical accuracy. In this way, Rodin paralleled the Impressionist interest in developing a relationship between the materials one used and the image one hoped to capture, a tendency eloquently captured in his drawings (Fig. **7.31**). Here, the sensitivity of the cast bronze (see box page 65) replicates all the imprints and the wrestlings with the original clay and plaster surfaces; the dialogue between the artist's creative activity and the serious-ness of the subject matter creates a work of tremen-dous psychological penetration rather than generic glorification. Gone too is the lofty pedestal — the con-vention by which artists had traditionally distanced and monumentalized public figures. Instead, these figures engage one's space in a most personal and inti-

■ 7.31 Auguste Rodin
Dancing Figure 1905
Graphite with orange wash
12⅞ x 9⅞ in (32.6 x 25 cm)
National Gallery of Art, Washington, D.C.
Gift of Mrs. John W. Simpson

■ 7.30 François Rude
Monument to Marshall Ney 1853
Bronze
Height 8 ft 9 in (2.67 m)
Place de L'Observatoire, Paris

■ 7.33 Detail of *Monument to Balzac* 1897–8

One of the most celebrated sculptures produced by Rodin is his monument to the French writer Balzac (Figs. **7.32** and **7.33**) of 1897–8. Here, many of his germinating ideas came to full maturity, and the result is a hauntingly enigmatic expression of genius. Perhaps more than any other work Rodin executed, this monolith pointed sculpture's way into the twentieth century, as a pivot between nineteenth-century representation and the need for modern artists to share some of themselves through the material process itself. The most obvious difference between this work and the *Burghers* is the crudeness of its execution. It appears that Rodin was as much concerned with leaving evidence of his work methods (including chisel marks, soft modeling work, etc.) as he was interested in producing a likeness of the French novelist. Rodin hoped to create an object that did not simply reproduce Balzac in three-dimensional form but truly embodied his genius. Thus the rough-hewn look of the figure emerging out of his heavy cloak is more than a simple representation of an artist of incredible energy; it mimics such personality traits through the very work process itself. Here material, artist, and subject matter become one unified expression — a sensibility, it seems, whose time had come.

■ 7.32 Auguste Rodin
Monument to Balzac 1897–8
Plaster
Height 9 ft 10 ins (2.99 m)
Musée Rodin, Paris

mate manner, forcing the viewer to relate to this work on a fundamentally physical level. The result is a public sculpture that functions on a plane altogether different from that of its predecessors, as the public subject and the artistic gesture fused into a demanding image of sacrifice.

THE LIBERATION OF COLOR

As Chevreul's color theory became common knowledge in art circles and the photograph proved itself increasingly adept at representing reality on a two-dimensional plane, many painters began excursions into color as a means of unlocking the potential still believed to be manifest in painting. The debate about the nature of painting had been engaged as long as painting itself, but it was often fought in and around two prominent positions; in the days of the French Academy it was the "Poussinists" versus the "Rubenists" — or for simplicity's sake, drawing versus color.

Drawing was traditionally based on conventions used to delineate space and structure in a painting. Drawing helps create order in a work — an order many artists saw manifest in nature itself, via the grace of God through creation. The very thought of an untamed experience of the world, full of sense experience, was most probably unnerving to many an artist until the nineteenth century. This helps explain why color often had a role subsidiary to drawing in painting. To many, color confused order and often dispersed space, and thus could be used only in moderation. Monet had shown how one could understand nature through an accurate and disinterested approach to color, and quickly other artists began similar investigations.

■ 7.34 Georges Seurat
A Sunday on La Grande Jatte — 1884 1884–6
Oil on canvas
6 ft 9 in x 10 ft ⅜ in (2.06 x 3.05 m)
The Art Institute of Chicago
Helen Birch Bartlett Memorial Collection, 1926.224

Color has two specific effects on a two-dimensional image: it can disperse volume, and, if used in broader applications, it creates the impression of pattern. Both work in competition with drawing conventions such as perspective for the viewer's interest, and as a result often disturb one's appreciation of illusionistic space.

Seurat

One of the most interesting investigations into the relationship between color theory and painting came in the work of Georges Seurat (1859–91). Seurat perhaps most closely understood the repercussions of Chevreul's theories for artists, and his work stands out as the clearest expression of the influence of theory on art making in the late nineteenth century.

Seurat's *A Sunday on La Grande Jatte* (Fig. **7.34**) of 1884–6 took almost two years to complete and is the most exhaustive example of his theory of "divisionism." He applied his paint in small, carefully selected "dots" of chromatically intense color. He then applied Chevreul's method of neutralizing color by placing these dots in direct proximity to other colors, allowing their resonance to dissipate into a larger field; where he wanted each color to retain its identity, he simply nullified most of the visual competition. Seurat also effectively used Chevreul's notion of the "negative after-image," which he mimicked by placing his

■ 7.35 Detail of *La Grande Jatte* 1884–6

complementary pairs in direct conflict with one another (note the red interspersed among the field of green in the detail of *La Grand Jatte* [Fig. **7.35**]). The result is a field of view that visually vibrates, much like the flickering of natural light. Here science and art merge in a truly nineteenth-century interpretation of the world.

It is hard to tell where Seurat might have gone with his great talent had he not died at the early age of thirty-two. His method of applying contemporary theory to painting had its admirers almost immediately, and soon many artists had moved well beyond his initial discoveries. Yet color theory was by no means the only influence to take hold with colorists during the late years of the century; artists were looking to new sources for inspiration and found them in the Japanese print.

The Influence of Japanese Prints

After centuries of self-imposed isolation from the rest of the world, Japan, with its rich culture, was opened to the West in 1853, when Commodore Perry's "black ships" were granted then unprecedented docking privileges on the island. Before long, trade had brought an assortment of Japanese treasures to Western markets, including the highly sought-after Japanese porcelain. Such delicate merchandise required careful packing, and the Japanese traders used whatever was accessible — straw, wood chips, and old printed paper. Some of the first two-dimensional images from Japan to arrive in the West came through this rather unlikely route, but the timing could not have been better.

Traditional Japanese printmaking was based mainly on the woodblock technique, which was capable of producing a high-quality, clear image with very simple tools. The process involves the inking of cut-out wood forms, which are reassembled and through pressure then transferred onto paper. The woodblock method is also a relief form of printing, which means that only the raised areas of the block are printed. One repercussion of this technique is that images produced in print are often quite uniformly flat and strongly articulated as shapes. Take, for instance, Eisui's *Courtesan Yasooi of Matsuba-ya with a Camellia* (Fig. **7.36**), an image probably typical of those filtering into the West during the period. The degree of outline that articulates such forms and the repetition

■ 7.36 Eisui, *The Courtesan Yasooi of Matsuba-ya with a Camellia* late 1790s
Obon color print. Tokyo, National Museum

of pattern over large areas of space were understandably very new to Western eyes.

In the Japanese print, artists such as Manet and Cassatt (Fig. **7.37**) saw a degree of flatness, pattern, undifferentiated color, and internal design that was in sympathy with their own investigations. Further, the Japanese print showed a way of creating art on a two-dimensional surface without the tired conventions of perspective and atmospheric space that had been a part of Western painting since the Renaissance.

■ 7.37 Mary Cassatt
The Letter 1891
Color print with dry paint, soft ground etching and aquatint
13⅝ in x 8¹⁵/₁₆ in (34.5 x 22.8 cm)
Philadelphia Museum of Art
Louis E. Stern Collection (63–181–22)

Gauguin

Several artists were indebted to woodblock prints; some artists copied directly from the images. Two of the most famous painters to develop the dramatic flattening of space and saturated areas of color were Vincent van Gogh (1853–90) and Paul Gauguin (1848–1903). However, each artist also brought to this new set of conventions a very specific attitude about the nature of color and its psychological effect on the viewer.

Gauguin's *Vision after the Sermon* (Fig. **7.38**) of 1888 is a striking example of his willingness to let color inform the viewer in less than traditional ways. Here color is not a matter of simply transcribing natural events with a sensitive eye (as was the case with the Impressionists) but another way of generating subject matter. Like many of his contemporaries after Impressionism, Gauguin desired color that was liberated from its role as representation, and as a result functioned with a degree of symbolism and intent on the part of the artist (hence the rather loose term

■ 7.38 Paul Gauguin
The Vision after the Sermon 1888
Oil on canvas
28¾ x 36½ in (73 x 92.7 cm)
National Gallery of Scotland, Edinburgh

IA ORANA MARIA

■ 7.39 Paul Gauguin
Ia Orana Maria 1891
Oil on canvas
44¾ x 34½ in (113.6 x 87.6 cm)
The Metropolitan Museum of Art, New York
Bequest of Samuel A. Lewisohn, 1951

"**Post-Impressionist**" to describe those artists who consciously rejected the naturalism of the Impressionists). The *Vision* shows an obvious indebtedness to Japanese sources in its flat areas of vibrant color and denial of perspectival motifs, but it is also a religious painting done by an inherently Western artist. Gauguin's use of the flat red field (at once a revolutionary departure from Impressionist naturalism) makes demands on the viewer that are not simply perceptual but decidedly psychological in nature. One understands "red" not only as the color of an apple but as a suggestion of warmth, passion, carnality, and a host of other notions. Humans are no more capable of separating feelings from perception of color than they are able to have a truly objective thought. Gauguin understood this implicitly and used painting as an arena for investigating humanity's more private instincts.

Gauguin drew from other sources besides woodblock prints: he actively collected works from non-Western (Polynesian, West Indian) and folk traditions (Brittany) in his attempt to find a symbolic language capable of transcending traditional Western painting. In these he saw a freshness of approach and a more forthright dissemination of ideas without the compromising conventions of the trained artist. Gauguin and his "**Symbolist**" colleagues saw the history of Western art since the Renaissance as tragically flawed by its desire to work from observation — empiricism as applied to art. By demanding greater freedom from observation in his work, Gauguin also gave the viewer a degree of autonomy to suggest a more personal meaning — often unavailable in earlier art.

Gauguin's desire to cross cultural and conventional barriers can be seen in his *Ia Orana Maria* (Fig. **7.39** on page 353) of 1891, in which a traditional Madonna and Child subject is placed in a Polynesian scene, accentuated by an abundance of pattern and saturated, flat color. Here the viewer is an active participant in the creation of meaning, rather than a silent receiver, and the result is eminently more satisfying.

Van Gogh and Munch

The tragic life of Vincent van Gogh is so well documented that it often obscures the revolutionary quality of his work. Like Gauguin, van Gogh wished to release color in painting from empirical notions, but unlike Gauguin he spent his life painting from observation. However, through van Gogh's eyes the simplest, most commonplace scene is transformed into an enticing, if often hallucinatory, experience. Take, for

■ 7.40 Vincent van Gogh, *Bedroom* 1888
Oil on canvas, 28¾ x 36 in (73.6 x 92.3 cm)
The Art Institute of Chicago, Helen Birch Bartlett Memorial Collection

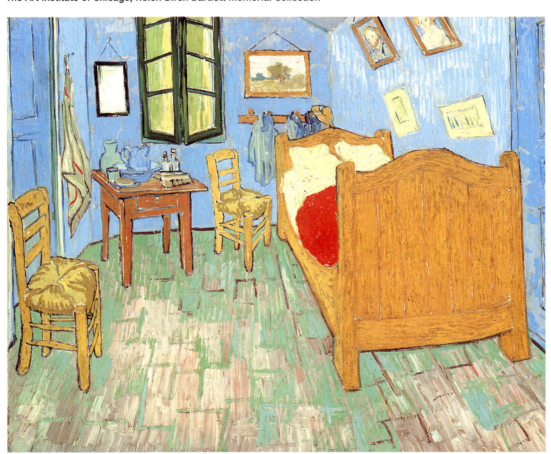

The implications of such blatant subjectivity for later art can be seen by comparing a van Gogh *Self-Portrait* (Fig. **7.41**) of 1886–7 with *The Scream* (Fig. **7.42**) of 1893 by the Norwegian painter Edvard Munch (1863–1944). Van Gogh's paint handling does not simply describe through color: it physically forms his features. The chisel-like quality of his brushwork distorts the face into a mask of material, each stroke a convulsive attempt to address observed reality in terms of paint. In *The Scream*, perhaps the most angst-ridden image in the history of Western art, the viewer is granted only remnants of the natural world. Instead, the painting becomes a battleground for the pressures and anxieties of modern life that seem as natural and as omnipresent as the real world, and in desperate need of a visual equivalent not realized in a simple observation.

■ 7.42 Edvard Munch, *The Scream* 1893
Tempera and casein on cardboard, 36 x 29 in (91.4 x 73.7 cm)
© The Munch-Museum/The Munch-Ellingsen-Group/DACS 1996
Photo courtesy of National Gallery, Norway

■ 7.41 Vincent van Gogh, *Self-Portrait* c. 1886–7
Oil on artist's board mounted on cradled panel
16½ x 13¼ in (41 x 32.5 cm)
The Art Institute of Chicago
The Joseph Winterbottom Collection, 1954.326

instance, his *Bedroom* (Fig. **7.40**) of 1888, in which a subject with seemingly little pictorial merit is elevated to the status of self-portrait.

Van Gogh's sources are at once apparent: the ambiguous space, the large areas of flat color, the heightened palette, and the strong character of outline all follow precedents in previously described woodblock prints. But to this pictorial strategy van Gogh added something specifically his own — an emotional application of paint. No longer was color applied in flat, sweeping gestures; instead it was understood first and foremost as oil paint, which has its own material qualities. Here van Gogh drew even further away from established conventions, heightening not the appreciation of nature in some supposedly objective form but the intrinsic personality of the artist wresting with his subject. The result was an even greater shift toward the primacy of the artist's subjective experience in the vision of the painting.

Munch found this vocabulary by exploring the conventions themselves: lines once used in painting to represent nature now actively broke it down, and color was released from its function as a descriptive device to resonate with the sounds of the troubled mind (Fig. **7.43**). This was to be the new naturalism of the late nineteenth century and a premonition of the twentieth, as many people found it increasingly difficult to divorce subjective experience from objective reality — a vivid signal of the growing dislocation of human consciousness from mechanized society. If Monet's work can be said to have grown out of an interest in natural observation, Munch's *Scream* attests to the increasing inability of artists to see anything outside the daily traumas associated with being human. Significantly, during this period of peace and prosperity Sigmund Freud developed his theory of repression and neurosis as both personal and social disorders — ideas with their pictorial equivalent in the work of artists such as Munch.

Subjectivity and Expression

The term **Expressionism** has been traditionally used to describe artists whose work is involved not so much with a description of nature (implicit within the terms "Impression-ist," "Real-ist," etc.) but with the expression of less tangible and often psychological states through images. Often such work maintains the suggestion of a specific subject: for example, the work by Ernst Ludwig Kirchner (1880–1938) *Five Women in the Street* (Fig. **7.45**) of 1913–15. Through devices not often associated with observation (aggressive paint handling, bright unnatural color), artists were able to

▲ **7.43** Edvard Munch,
The Kiss 1902
Woodcut, printed in color,
18⅜ x 18⁹⁄₁₆ in (46.7 x 46.4 cm)
Collection The Museum of
Modern Art, New York
Gift of Abby Aldrich Rockefeller

▶ **7.44** Ernst Ludwig Kirchner
Three Figures 1909
Woodcut
Albertina Graphische Summlung,
Vienna

■ 7.45 Ernst Ludwig Kirchner, *Five Women in the Street,* 1913–15
Oil on canvas, 47½ x 35½ in (120.6 x 90.2 cm). Rheinischer Bildarchiv, Cologne Museum, Ludwig

produce images about the various states of being rather than of the historically static, singular "being." They even pirated less refined techniques such as the woodcut print, which they saw as raw, physical, and very graphic.

Like many an artist before them, Expressionists such as Kirchner (Fig. **7.44**) and Emil Nolde (1867–1956) (Fig. **7.46**) capitalized on the materials and techniques of other cultures in an attempt to free their images from the tired clichés of the Western tradition. In appreciating non-Western and naïve work, artists (often mistakenly) saw what they considered a more pure and less repressed expression, and took from these cultures freely. In Expressionist art, reality is understood as the production of each individual, with all the idiosyncrasies inherent in being human. With vibrant color, disfiguring drawing, and sometimes violent applications of material, Expressionists championed the egocentric vision.

Matisse

There was also a contrary side to this revolution of color and material consciousness interesting painters at the turn of the century, and it would be a mistake to see such innovations as limited to the expression of anxiety and alienation. If color can emotionally harass, it can also entice, and the most lyrical and subtle of the colorists of the period was most certainly Henri Matisse (1869–1954), who seems light years apart from the moody pictures of Munch and Kirchner.

Loosely associated with the artists André Derain and Maurice de Vlaminck between 1905 and 1907 in a movement called **Fauvism** (the Wild Beasts), Matisse began to develop a psychology of color of particular sensitivity. A delightful example of Matisse's playfulness with established painting conventions is his *Still Life with Goldfish* (Fig. **7.47**) of 1911. Matisse wrote that painting was not about static truths (the kind he saw evident in the work of Seurat), nor a record of a passing sensation (the Impressionists), but about expressing a "nearly religious feeling toward life." In an artist's statement published in *La Grand Revue*, Paris, December 1908, he wrote:

■ **7.46 Emil Nolde**
Prophet 1912
Woodcut
12¾ x 8⅞ in (32.4 x 23 cm)
National Gallery of Art, Washington, D.C.
Rosenwald Collection © Nolde-Stiftung Seebüll

> *I am unable to distinguish between the feeling I have for life and my way of expressing it… Expression to my way of thinking does not consist of the passion mirrored upon a human face or betrayed by a violent gesture. The whole arrangement of my picture is expressive… Composition is the art of arranging in a decorative manner the various elements at the painter's disposal for the expression of his feelings.*

Matisse saw the interrelationship of colors in composition as the fundamental problem for the contemporary painter, and his painstaking synthesis of color in his arrangements attests to his ability to bring harmony and tranquility to a part of culture that was beginning to anticipate a series of major convulsions.

Matisse's unabashed use of large areas of color often gives the impression of an intricate pattern, in which each element is sharply defined and articulated

■ 7.47 Henri Matisse
Still Life with Goldfish 1911
Oil on canvas, 4 ft 10 in x 3 ft 2⅜ in (1.47 x 0.97 m)
Pushkin Museum, Moscow
© Succession H. Matisse/DACS 1996

■ 7.48 Henri Matisse, *Harmony in Red* 1909
Oil on canvas
5 ft 11¼ in x 8 ft ⅞ in (1.81 x 2.46 m)
The Hermitage, St. Peterburg, © Succession H. Matisse/DACS 1996

through bold outline — a method that forces the image to sit flush to the surface of the painting. *Harmony in Red* (the *Red Room*) (Fig. **7.48**) of 1909 is a good example of Matisse's unequaled ability to compose disparate objects in a coherent and seemingly effortless whole. Here, the large areas of red pattern (tablecloth and wall) are neatly offset by the strength of the green in the window (green is, of course, red's complementary color), and the figure (the white and deep blue falling on either side of the red in tone) — each of which helps balance one's perception of the scene. Further, the organic quality of the patterned wallpaper and tablecloth is carefully kept in check by the strong vertical–horizontal grid set up by the windowsill and chairs. What is truly remarkable about this sort of work is how deceptively facile it appears upon first glance; the technical problems are so convincingly solved that the viewer feels only resolution and harmony, rather than struggle and self-consciousness. Here, Matisse is decidedly different from the Expressionists, working feverishly to avoid discord on any level.

OF STEEL AND SKYSCRAPERS

The fine arts were not the only aspects of the larger cultural machine to show signs of revolutionary change between 1850 and 1900. Architecture also underwent tremendous reconsideration at the hands of both engineers and architects.

The Technological Advance

Perhaps the most noteworthy technical breakthrough to come about in the late nineteenth century was the development of structural steel, which enabled structures to be built higher and more safely than ever before. Until the commercial manufacture of steel in the nineteenth century, architects had been forced to consider the tremendous weight of masonry walls when calculating the height of a building; the higher the building, the more the weight resting upon the lower walls, which resulted in the structural necessity of building thicker supporting walls at the foundation, which then ate up interior space. Even with the time-honored use of the buttressing system, it was difficult

to fashion a tall structure with any sizable interior space. Steel changed all that. Arranged in a grid format around a series of reinforced columns, steel was both flexible and incredibly strong, so that it could carry an extraordinary amount of the building's load without the visual bulk associated with masonry — hence the term *load-bearing steel frame*. As a result, storey after storey could be built upon a relatively streamlined foundation, which gave unity and uniformity to the structure as a whole.

The Crystal Palace and the Eiffel Tower

One of the repercussions of budding nationalism in the nineteenth century was a new brand of cultural and technological chauvinism called the Exposition. One of the earliest was the Great Exhibition in London of 1851, which was intended to be a showcase for "Works of Industry of All Nations." The architectural problem was how to house such a massive amount of technology under one roof. The solution was, for lack of a better term, a giant greenhouse, covering over 17 acres (6.8 hectares) and reaching a height of 108 feet (11 m). The architect was in fact a

■ 7.49 Joseph Paxton
Crystal Palace, Hyde Park, London 1851
destroyed by fire 1936
Contemporary lithograph
New York Public Library
Aston, Lennox, and Tilden Foundations

■ **7.50 Gustav Eiffel, Eiffel Tower, Paris 1889**
Wrought iron on a reinforced concrete base
Original height 984 ft (299.9 m)

designer of greenhouses named Joseph Paxton (1803–65), and his cast iron and glass Crystal Palace (Fig. **7.49**), built in a mere nine months, was to become a model for subsequent buildings of prefabricated design.

By contemporary accounts, the Crystal Palace was considered a marvel of construction but something of an anomaly as a building. Paxton had no qualms about this, arguing that its underlying architectural principle was not aesthetic but practical: the maximum size of fabricated glass in the 1850s was four feet (1.3 m) and for purposes of load, no element could weigh more than a ton (101 kg), which in turn restricted the span of the cast iron to 24 feet (7 m). The result was an unabashedly utilitarian building in keeping with the spirit of the time, and a "skeleton and skin" design that was mimicked well into the twentieth century.

London was not the only city to sponsor an Exposition. The Paris World's Fair of 1889 (celebrating the hundredth anniversary of the French Revolution) also provided an architectural and technological highlight: Gustav Eiffel's (1832–1923) famous tower (Fig. **7.50**). It outraged many a taxpayer with its cost (over a million dollars at 1880s currency rates), and for that, many claimed, all they got was a skeleton of steel. It was the quintessential modern building, which pandered neither to architectural convention nor to contemporary taste but instead embraced innovation and technological advance. It remained the tallest structure in the world until 1932. Rather than being a functional building, the Eiffel Tower served purely as a monument and observation deck. It is important to remember that this structure predated both the skyscraper and the airplane, so a view of the world from 984 feet (300 m) up was unprecedented at the time. This must have had a profound effect on the average citizens, who now envisioned their world as an assemblage of lines and flat borders of color — the horizontalization of their known experience.

Skyscrapers

The birth of the modern skyscraper relied on yet another innovation, again tied to steel: reinforced concrete. Simply put, reinforced concrete is concrete poured into a steel rod skeleton welded together on site; this reinforces the strength and overall resiliency

■ 7.51 Louis Sullivan
The Wainwright Building, St. Louis, 1890–1

of the concrete. The combination of reinforced concrete and the load-bearing steel frame enabled architects such as Louis Sullivan (1856–1924) to create unified multi-storeyed buildings, fittingly called skyscrapers.

Sullivan's Wainwright Building (Fig. **7.51**) of 1890–91 in St Louis is a good example of the dramatic departures such technical innovations precipitated in architecture. Sullivan envisioned his buildings as analogous to the human body, the facade being the flesh or muscle stretching over the skeletal steel gridwork. Here, the facade reflects its internal construction rather than being self-sustaining in the manner of previous building designs. As an adherent to the "form follows function" argument (the belief that good or truthful design must follow a structure's utilitarian requirements), Sullivan built with obvious sympathy for the idea that images or objects must reflect their own structural or internal makeup — an idea popular among artists of the period.

The skyscraper was also the tangible result of the effects of increased urbanization during the end of the last century. The concept came at the right time, as cities became increasingly crowded, real-estate costs soared, and old methods of building would have been virtually impossible to finance. The skyscraper enabled businesses to stay located in the city, employing more workers in less space than ever before. So in this regard, the form following function formula of Sullivan and his colleagues not only reflected aesthetics but once again had decidedly social ramifications.

NATURE IN FLUX

Monet was perhaps the first artist seriously to question the value of traditional painting conventions based on systems rather than on actual observation. He attempted to see nature as a collection of visual stimuli of which light was the unifying and consistent feature. The result was a form of painting that more closely mimicked one's actual experience of light as color, and its effect on the perception of forms in space. However, Monet still adhered to a more subtle convention — that one's gaze upon the world was static, though nature might indeed be in flux. When looking at paintings, one often takes for granted the fact that one's view of the world (the illusionistic world inside the painting) is static and fixed. The gaze is steady and absolute, with items supposedly closest to the viewer's vantage point in sharper focus than those in the background. But is this the way the eyes actually see? And furthermore, is such a view representative of the artist's vision of the world?

The artist most responsible for taking the dramatic leap into the world of unfixed perception was Paul Cézanne (1839–1906), and his questioning of some of the most basic assumptions about observation resulted in arguably the most revolutionary development in painting since the Renaissance.

To obtain a better understanding of the nature of Cézanne's departure from traditional norms, a simple experiment might be useful. Place one of your fingers about 6 in (15 cm) away from your nose, and stare at

■ 7.52 Paul Cézanne, *Vase of Tulips* c. 1890–2
Oil on canvas, 23½ x 16⅝ in (59.6 x 42.3 cm)
The Art Institute of Chicago
Mr. and Mrs. Lewis Larned Coburn Memorial Collection, 1933.423

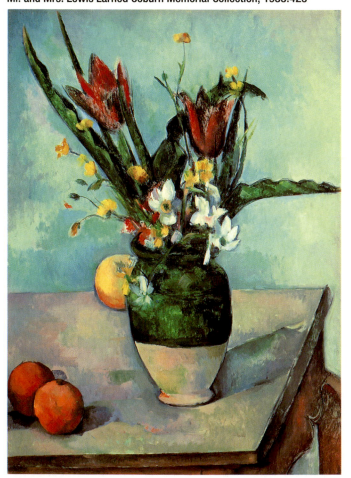

it. You will note that, in order to register the form of your finger clearly, your eyes blur all background visual information into a flat pattern of color. Now reverse the process, and register any item in the background. Your finger, now out of focus, dissipates into a "ghost" — suggested rather than clearly articulated. This is the nature of perception, and it implies that visual concentration upon one form often requires the active disintegration of another. This should not come as much of a surprise, as such a manner of seeing is one of the ways in which humanity orders the world — a survival mechanism, if you will.

Now flip back through this book to any of the Western paintings executed since the Renaissance, and you will note that the views represented abide by a very different principle of perception. In traditional painting, figures, trees, and other items can be seen in conjunction with each other in a manner that could not in reality be received by the eye at the same time. This is one of the miracles of painting: viewers are given the powers of observation and order they neither possess nor experience in the real world. It is perhaps an engaging idea, but it is certainly not an accurate representation of what or how an individual sees. Cézanne desired a painting that not only mimicked the dynamics of the natural world around him but addressed the nature of human perception as well.

Cézanne

Cézanne's early experiments were relatively conservative in nature when compared with his breakthrough work at the turn of the century. Yet even in earlier works there is a persistent questioning of space that culminates in what might be called "wandering perspective" — the design simply does not correspond to established conventions. Take, for instance, the *Vase of Tulips* (Fig. **7.52**) of 1890–92. The table is at a peculiar and unreliable angle: it is hard to believe that the fruit and the vase could actually have sat on that surface. The distortion is, however, so evident that one finds it difficult to believe that an artist of Cézanne's stature could simply have erred in observation. On the contrary, this obvious internal inconsistency is perhaps a more truthful representation of the still life — not of a vase and some fruit on a table but of the very act of looking at these items. Cézanne once claimed that he was never able to see the same

■ 7.53 Paul Cézanne, *Mont Sainte-Victoire seen from Les Lauves* 1902–4
Oil on canvas, 27⅞ x 36⅛ in (70.5 x 92 cm)
Philadelphia Museum of Art
George W. Eikins Collection

scene twice; every time he blinked, shifted, reorganized his focus, or even scanned a view, his image would alter. Thus his paintings quickly became experiments in documenting the process of perception, complete with all its inconsistencies. The result is a significant distortion in the interior space of the painting, which, when combined with the flat massing of color throughout the work, diminishes the viewer's ability to perceive illusionistic depth.

Cézanne's most radical paintings, produced toward the end of his life, were based almost entirely on one solitary motif: Mont Sainte-Victoire (Fig. **7.53**). The traditional landscape subject not only provided him with an infinite variety of natural occurrences (wind, sunlight, cloud cover, etc.) but gave him the opportunity to integrate the idiosyncrasies of human perception with an equally unreliable source — his immediate environment. The result is a style of painting that seems to fold and unfold as one's eye scans the surface. Each perceived color only partially implicates its descriptive source: the dynamic activities of the wind, the splattering of light, the eye's desire to focus, the tilt of the head, the fatigue in the back, and most importantly the act of painting itself, all contribute to the active disintegration of form.

In Cézanne's work, one's consciousness of the vulnerability of perception is tantamount to truth in painting. In this way, Cézanne's paintings are about time — change and flux that are truly understood only by those with the courage and patience to recognize their effect. But Cézanne also hoped to invest a degree of order in the chaos he saw manifest in looking. As a result, like those before him, he unapologetically implied a strong underlying structural order in his paintings (note the unmistakable vertical–horizontal orientation of the marks). Apparently, even within the chaos of such a vision, Cézanne still believed that

order could and indeed should prevail — and this was a matter of conviction.

Cézanne saw the act of perception as the true subject of painting, and he wrestled with the repercussions of this position for the process of creating art. But he was categorically tied to the world of observation, and thus, even in repeated motifs such as Mont Sainte-Victoire, there is never a true "system" in his painting — each piece acquired the nuances of the day filtered through Cézanne's eyes. However, a systematic dissection of the world was not long in coming, primarily in the hands of young painters who understood the enormous repercussions of Cézanne's vision. The breakthrough came in 1907, and the artist was a Spaniard named Pablo Picasso (1881–1973).

■ 7.54 Pablo Picasso, *Les Demoiselles d'Avignon* Paris (June–July 1907). Oil on canvas 8 ft x 7 ft 8 in (2.44 x 2.37 m). The Museum of Modern Art, New York. Acquired through the Lillie P. Bliss Bequest. Photograph © 1996 The Museum of Modern Art, New York. © DACS 1996

The Break: Picasso's *Demoiselles d'Avignon*, 1907

Les Demoiselles d'Avignon (Fig. **7.54**) has long been considered a revolutionary work in the history of Western art. It was initially designed to be a moralizing tale about desire, vanity, and the corruption of the flesh, and at least in that respect it seems hardly new. But this is no didactic painting in the traditional sense of the word, and it certainly does not operate within the confines of conventional representation. There is almost no space within the interior of the scene: everything is pushed up against the front plane, and depth is collapsed. Here the human figures no longer claim privileged status, carefully articulated as in the past to define them as separate from the dynamics of the world; instead, their mutilated bodies have become intersecting planes of flatly rendered flesh. Further, those faces — the most essential generators of individuality and meaning within the bodies — have become macabre masks, ideally suited to the demands of the painting. This is certainly not a typical painting of a brothel.

Les Demoiselles is rooted in two pictorial sources: late nineteenth-century painting and African masks. The assimilation of previous painting advances reads something like a *Who's Who* of art: the viewer acknowledges Cézanne's shifting planes that corresponded to the non-fixed quality or insecurity of his perception, Manet's large areas of undifferentiated color that flatten space, and the strong outline reminiscent of Gauguin and van Gogh. What is most dramatic about this work is the violence with which Picasso assaulted the image, and further that he was willing to take on the sanctified image of the human body to do it. Never before in the history of Western art had an artist so openly mutilated the image of the body, as if the environment was itself a weapon that destroys and reorganizes at will. Here the dynamic tensions in nature and the artist's insecurity of perception meet the symbol of a static, controllable, egocentric world — the human body — and in the end the force of history seems too great.

Much has been written on the parallels between the disintegration of volume in turn-of-the-century painting and the equally revolutionary findings in science at the time, and this raises some interesting considerations. In 1905 a then little-known physicist named Albert Einstein published his now-famous *Special Theory of Relativity*, in which he presented his

■ **7.55 Ceremonial Mask, Ivory Coast, Africa**
Black wood
9⁷/₁₆ x 6½ in (24.5 x 16.5 cm)
Musée de l'Homme, Paris

controversial equation $E = mc^2$. This formula presented a coherent argument for a world in flux, with energy exchanging on every level at every second. This put in crisis the very idea of fixed being, and with it came the discomforting possibility that notions such as self, soul, and ego were simply conventions to make life easier to live. Though Picasso was certainly not influenced by or even interested in such findings, the parallels are indeed uncanny.

Picasso's use of African masks as a pictorial source serves an important visual function in the painting, but it also demonstrates how such images often carry other implicit connections to their age. In African masks (see Fig. **7.55**) Picasso saw the radical flattening of features and bold descriptive markings that corresponded rather well to his own predisposition for depicting forms, and it solved the tricky problem of dealing with the face. But it would be wrong to see such overt allusion as a form of respect or even appreciation for the motif's function or origin. Picasso saw such work simply as powerful imagery, ready to be used. In this way, artists such as Picasso paralleled many of the less articulated attitudes of Europe toward the African continent at the turn of the century — a source of raw material, cheap labor, and exotic subject matter, with little knowledge of the cultures that informed such work — a cultural phenomenon that parallels the Orientalist tendencies of the Romantic artists. This is not meant to be an indictment of such work; rather it helps explain how artists are often implicitly bound to their world, and their work is the carrier of those contradictions.

Les Demoiselles was still a long way from the systematic treatment of the painting surface that marked Picasso's later work (see Chapter Nine for a discussion of Cubism). In fact, it seems to pose more questions than it answers, and it would take time to comprehend fully the repercussions of such a departure from the norm. Yet it remains the most visible breakthrough into twentieth-century art, and it started a dialogue that resonates in the present day.

SUMMARY

Cultural historians have come to view the nineteenth century as a period obsessed with the seemingly endless possibilities afforded by mechanization and progress, while simultaneously reeling from what some have aptly called the "shock of de-Christianization." As a result, the art of the era possesses these dual, often contradictory, characteristics of unbridled enthusiasm and an increasingly disturbed psyche. The role of the artist, once chiseled in the stone of patronage and representation, also underwent dramatic changes: the advent of photography, optics, color theory, art for art's sake, and a rising middle class all contributed to a view of the artist as autonomous, adventurous, heroic, moral — or more commonly avant-garde. This in turn led to a radical reconsidering of time-honored conventions for art production, including a move away from the pedestal in sculpture, a consideration of material properties in painting, and a general assumption that the artist's responsibility was to act as a catalyst for change. This implicitly moral, hierarchical view of art making was considered fundamental to the notion of being modern. Current iconography owes much to the thoughts and cultural artifacts of the nineteenth century.

Suggested Reading

Several studies relate modern art to the complex web of social and intellectual upheavals in which it evolved.

Boimé, A.: *A Social History of Modern Art* (Chicago: University of Chicago Press, 1987). One of the best of the recent studies.

Hamilton, G.H.: *Painting and Sculpture in Europe 1880–1940* (Harmondsworth and New York: Penguin Books, 3rd edn 1981). A thorough overview of the period.

Jeffrey, I.: *Photography: A Concise History* (London and New York: Thames & Hudson, 1981). A good introduction to early photography.

Pool, Phoebe: *Impressionism* (London and New York: Oxford University Press, 1967).

Pronunciation Guide

Paul Cézanne   say-**ZAHN**
Eugène Chevreul   oo-**ZHAN** shev-**ROOL**
Camille Corot   kah-**MEEL** kaw-**ROH**
Gustave Courbet   **GOO**-stahv koor-**BAY**
daguerreotype   duh-**GER**-uh-**teye(p)**
Honoré Daumier   oh-nor-**AY** doh-**MYAY**
Edgar Degas   ed-**GAR** day-**GAH**
Eiusi   ay-**OO**-see
Paul Gauguin   goh-**GAN**
Édouard Manet   ay-**DWAHR** mah-**NAY**
Claude Monet   klawd moh-**NAY**
Edvard Munch   **ED**-vard muungk
Pablo Picasso   **PAHB**-loh pee-**KAH**-soh
Oscar Rejlander   **AHS**-ker **RAY**-lan-der
Pierre-Auguste Renoir   pyer aw-**GOOST REN**-wahr
Auguste Rodin   aw-**GOOST** roh-**DAN**
Georges Seurat   zhorzh suh-**RAH**
Toulouse-Lautrec   too-**LOOZ** loh-**TREK**

Glossary

avant-garde (*page 320*) From the French, "before the rest," this was a term applied to artists of various persuasions to imply a self-appointed role as explorer or adventurer. It has implicit connotations of heroic will and the artist as savior of society, ideas in keeping with the progressive doctrines of the Romantics and the Idealists of the nineteenth century.

daguerreotype (*page 326*) A chemically derived silver-plated copper sheet invented in 1837 by Louis Daguerre that produced a clearer photographic image in far less exposure time. This invention meant that people could be documented clearly in photographs. It had enormous repercussions for both photography and painting.

Expressionism (*page 356*) A term historically applied to art that is involved not so much with a faithful, seemingly objective description of nature (implicit within the terms *Impressionism*, *Realism*, etc.) but with the expression of less tangible and often psychological states. Typical devices are aggressive paint handling and the use of bright, unnatural color.

Fauvism (*page 358*) An art movement of the first decade of the twentieth century, in which artists made bold use of color to express the inner qualities rather than the superficial appearance of objects.

Impressionism (*page 334*) An art movement that took its name from one particular painting by Claude Monet, *Impression: Sunrise* of 1872. Arising out of the naturalism of the Realists (such as Courbet), as well as an interest in the transitory experience of light and color on objects, Impressionism did two distinct things to painting: it elevated color to the status of subject matter, liberating the artist's marks from previous craft constraints, and it inadvertently asserted painting's relationship to the flat surface.

lithography (*page 340*) Meaning "stone writing," it is a printing process in which resists are applied to a stone slab, then the surface is exposed to nitric acid. The unbitten relief areas are then rolled with ink, paper is applied and the stone is run through a press to produce an image.

mark making (*page 336*) The gestures, scribbles, and gouges produced by an artist during the execution of a work that are left visible to the viewer, thus becoming an essential part of the overall subject matter.

pedestal (*page 344*) A sculptural device used to separate an object from the space and scale of the viewer; it elevates and sanctifies the object as "other," "different," and usually "heroic." The removal of the pedestal thus implies a movement back into the physical, tangible world of the viewer.

photography (*page 325*) From the Greek, meaning to write or describe with light, the term was first applied to a technical process in 1826 when Nicéphore Niépce first placed light-sensitive silver salts onto a surface, enabling a truthful reproduction of a projected image to be made. Though the initial exposure time was a lengthy eight hours, it set off a wave of pioneering developments that eventually made the medium accessible, practical, and affordable.

positive-negative space (*page 333*) An element of design in which positive refers to the shapes of forms representing the subject matter, and negative to the open spaces surrounding the subject, often called the background. The term is used in both two- and three-dimensional art to describe the relationship between parts of a work.

Post-Impressionist (*page 353*) An art movement of the mid-nineteenth and early twentieth century in which artists such as van Gogh and Gauguin rejected the naturalism of the Impressionists.

Symbolist (*page 354*) A literary and artistic movement, c. 1885–1910, characterized by a reaction against realism and the use of evocative but often private symbols.

8

ART IN THE AMERICAS

*Colonies do not cease to be colonies because
they are independent.*

BENJAMIN DISRAELI

Since art, like all forms of communication, possesses the characteristics of language, it often runs the risk of being misunderstood by those who are not fluent in the subjects, contexts, or even materials of other cultures. Each time an image, object, or monument enters into a cultural context that is not its own, it must inevitably go through a process of translation to make it intelligible to the inheriting community. This book has charted this type of transformation taking place; the influence of Japanese prints and African masks on the early Modernism of the last chapter are but two examples. Since no two communities share an identical set of circumstances or conditions, their lives and thus their art develop around a set of understood ideas and images specific to their locale. When outside images enter, the process of acceptance and assimilation creates what might be called a hybrid form, possessing characteristics of both cultures.

Certain communities are more susceptible to such cross-fertilization than others, and often it is the forced imposition of one culture upon another that creates the most dramatic deviations. In this way, the history of art (like the history of all ideas and all cultures) can be seen as a series of mutations, with the dominant view most often exerting the strongest force. There is no better place to witness the truth of such a dynamic than in the Americas. Since the second half of Chapter Nine will concentrate almost exclusively on art making in the United States, it is essential at this point to consider the rich and varied history of art and art making in the Americas as a whole.

ART IN THE NOMADIC COMMUNITIES

The Americas are a land of immigrants. Even the earliest indigenous peoples were once nomads, crossing the frozen Bering Strait from north Asia into the new continent in search of better lands and herds. It appears that there was no sign of human life in the Americas until those first settlers came, in or around 10,000 BC. They were Paleolithic in social organization and habit, moving with the hunt and presumably making little that they could not haul with them. Slowly but surely, these nomadic groups moved south and east, into Central and South America. The last of the indigenous peoples to cross over into the Americas were most likely the Inuit and Eskimo of modern Canada and Alaska, who retain a distinct physical resemblance to their Asian ancestors. No artifacts survive from the earliest of the Paleolithic tribes that later populated the southern expanses of the continent, but several more northern indigenous communities continued to exist in an undisturbed state well into the twentieth century, affording valuable insights into art making in the early Americas.

In considering the practical realities of art making in a Paleolithic context (see Chapter One pages 40–43), it was noted that the criteria were often simple: items had to be transportable and thus small in scale; they usually bore a direct relationship to issues of basic survival for the community (sustenance and procreation) and were thus designed around a set of guiding principles that were generally understood as "truth" to explain existence (a myth structure and a corresponding visual language or "iconography").

Such imagery can be seen in a turn-of-the-century painted buffalo hide decorated with images of the hunt (Fig. **8.2**). It seems the artists responsible for this work understood the desirability of flat design for translating events or ideas on a surface; here pictures became a formal kind of language, reminiscent of handwriting. Horses, warriors, and buffalo were all rendered as generalized shapes (sometimes referred to as "idea-forms"), which merged actual representation with a corresponding concept. The artist created not simply a representation of an event but a symbolic language capable of merging the physical reality of the hunt with the community's consciousness of its position in the world. In other words, events were seen within the context of the larger mysteries of life, and thus the concept of naturalism seems meaningless in such discussions.

■ 8.2 *Painted Buffalo Robe* 1909
Royal Ontario Museum, Toronto
Edward Morris Collection

The abundance of herds throughout the continent meant that any move toward a more settled, agricultural existence was slow in coming — if it came at all. In Europe and Asia the primary reason behind the shift to agriculture had been the recurring problem of keeping up with the wandering food supply (the herds), and thus Neolithic culture (the foundation of civilization) was more a practical solution than a moral decision. In the Americas, the abundance of natural food resources, combined with the adaptive qualities of the peoples, meant that organized communities could and often did develop without agriculture, with social structures as complex as their European and Asian counterparts. However, several of the largest indigenous communities did turn to and subsequently thrived on agriculture, which in turn led to a more stable social organization and the specialization of labor.

To make art, one must have materials with which to work, and often the materials have a profound

■ 8.3 *Tlingit Mask* c. 1850
McMichael Canadian Collection, Kleinburg

effect on the images and the workmanship of the objects in question. Take, for instance, a mask (Fig. **8.3**) created by the Tlingit Indians of the northwest coast, who utilized materials as native to them as the development of their myths. The materials (seashell for teeth, cedar for the face, huckleberry dye for coloration, and human hair) formed an important, if often overlooked, link to the subject matter itself. In

■ 8.4 *Stoney Ceremonial Headdress* c. 1900
Height 5 ft 8 in (1.72 m)
Courtesy of the Glenbow Museum, Calgary, Alberta, Canada

Tlingit society, as in many other native communities, the preoccupation with transformation — of individual into animal and back into individual — was vital to the overall myth structure, one that both paralleled natural processes of the world around them and gave meaning to existence.

Ceremony is one such way of visualizing myths, and the mask, which disguises the human in another persona, provides a pivotal role in the playing out of this world view. In this case, the function of the mask (implying transformation) and its form (the materials gathered from the immediate vicinity) produce an image with direct connotations to the lives and environment of its audience. If ceremony can be seen as a celebration of and meditation on a village's life, it seems both fitting and right that its various costumes and props also provide a visual bond to its world. In self-sufficient communities such as the Tlingit, the strength of this relationship between the natural world and human ideas gives their objects an unmistakable presence.

Ceremony has historically played a vital role in every community's self-expression. In nomadic communities, the necessity of quick migration had a profound effect on the objects and visual images produced for such occasions. In such communities, music and dance often played a primary role in ceremony, and visual imagery was used to heighten the effect of the other activities. Thus costume became an important vehicle for visual expression in communities such as those of the Plains Indians.

In the Stoney Indian community, the wearer of the ceremonial headdress (Fig. **8.4**), played a vital role in its creation. The designs were passed down not from elder to apprentice (as is traditionally the case in Western art) but from God, the Great Being, to warrior in a dream. Everything, from the materials to the design was considered in the light of the dream, exemplifying the direct link between the making of the object and its meaning. In many such pieces, the idea of transformation (metamorphosis) is present; in this example, the use of an eagle feather was both a homage to the Great Spirit embodied in the bird and a visual cue for the warrior's flight into and through battle. The sight of a young brave with headdress and ornamental leggings moving at full gallop must have elicited an overwhelming psychological response in those watching. That must have been the intention.

EARLY CIVILIZATIONS

Not all early American communities needed to migrate with their herds, and, as with Neolithic culture elsewhere, a more stable lifestyle usually sparked an increase in architecture and monumental sculpture, and with it a specialized workforce. The subsequent refinement of skills and surplus of goods culminated in several substantial city complexes — none more impressive than Teotihuacán (Fig. **8.5**). It is located about 35 miles (56 km) northeast of present-day Mexico City, and during its heyday (100 BC–AD 650) it was the largest city in the New World, with well over 200,000 residents.

The shift from nomadic to civic life has historically had a profound effect on how a culture understands and expresses itself. Teotihuacán's massive population (probably developed through the combination of its assimilation of smaller communities and its ideal location near food and water supplies) created both a workforce capable of large-scale construction and a class of specialized craftspeople to put into practice such interests. As is the case in most communities, the largest building projects executed at Teotihuacán were religious in nature, reflecting the concerns of the community for the appeasement of the gods.

Perhaps the most ambitious of these architectural projects were the Pyramids of the Sun and Moon, which are reminiscent of the pyramid constructions

■ **8.5** **View of Teotihuacán**
100 BC to 650 AD
Showing Pyramids of the Sun and Moon

■ 8.6 View of Macchu Picchu c. 1500
Inca

■ 8.7 Detail of masonry work from
Ollantaytambo, Peru
Contemporary to Macchu Picchu

of Ancient Egypt. The form probably derived from two sources — the burial mound and the mountain — but unlike the pyramids in Egypt, those here appear never to have been used as burial chambers. Instead, the monuments speak of life and death in more subtle ways, reflecting the passing of time and the workings of nature through a careful consideration of the structure's relationship to its environment. For instance, the Pyramid of the Sun was designed to fall into direct line with the position of the sun at the summer solstice — the point in the seasons at which life gives way to death, and light to darkness (resembling the alignment encountered in the discussions of Stonehenge, Fig. 1.7, in Chapter One [see page 46], where the design was fixed upon the winter solstice). Even the number of steps was carefully considered within the context of the calendar, numbering 365, with the last step being the summit. The stepped outline of the pyramid also implies ascent, as if the viewer is welcomed as a participant to engage with the structure. The Pyramids of the Sun and Moon remain primary to the layout of the city, which fans out to encompass an area of over 13 square miles (34 sq. km). Following the orientation of the pyramids, the layout of Teotihuacán was organized to precise astronomical observations, and in this regard it remains one of the most sophisticated examples of urban design intact from that era.

Another remarkable urban design is the spectacular Macchu Picchu (Fig. **8.6** on page 377), built by the Incas in the late fifteenth and early sixteenth centuries in the Peruvian Andes. Though the Incas were better known for their warring than for their domestic interests, the great skill apparent in the masonry at Macchu Picchu points to a community not out of touch with design and structural considerations. How Inca masons were able to join such huge pieces of rock without mortar in their construction of the walls (Fig. **8.7** on page 377) remains a mystery; presumably painstaking effort and technical perfection were common factors in Inca construction.

Little remains today of the once famous Inca sculpture and jewelry. The reasons for this are both economic and aesthetic, and they center around one material: gold. An object such as the *Seated Female Figure* (Fig. **8.8**) from Cauca, Colombia, seems to be indicative of Inca sculpture, which was often small and portable and made from the soft gold of the Andes mountains. It was most likely a cult figure, and with its accentuated breasts and crotch, it probably functioned as a fertility goddess. After the Spanish conquest of Central and South America, most of these objects, once essential expressions of Inca culture, were melted down for their gold — the currency of the age in Europe.

On the surface, the decision to destroy objects for their crude material worth appears to be solely a matter of economics, but implicit in such activity was the underlying assurance that these items were not art and thus had no value beyond their weight in gold. To the self-proclaimed Spanish art critics of the New World (who were often either military men or clergy), the exaggerated features, sexually charged imagery, and "pagan" subject matter did not abide by the set conventions of Europe that marked one item as more worthy of the label "art" than another. In short, much of the legacy of the Inca, as well as Mexican Aztec, material culture was melted down to make Spanish coinage.

■ 8.8 *Seated Female Figure* (Quimbaya) c. 11th to 14th century
From Cauca, Colombia
Gold
Height 11½ in (29.2 cm)
Museo Arqueológico de América, Madrid

TWO WORLDS COLLIDE

The colonization of the Americas by Europeans had an enormous effect on the course of art making in the Americas. In the relationship between conqueror and conquered, those in power dictated the values and thus the art of the communities. Through slaughter and treaty, the ravenous European states carved up indigenous culture to suit their own material needs, while ironically trying to "save" the native peoples from Hell by introducing a God who was as foreign to them as the gun. Such impositions took time, and often ideas and images did not translate effectively. As a result, the mixing of two disparate cultures resulted in a number of fascinating deviations.

Some of the first images produced by Westerners in the "New World" were supposedly anthropological in nature, using drawings, paintings, and prints as a way of documenting events and individuals for an anxiously waiting European public. These images, produced and accepted as accurate representations of the Americas, are extraordinary examples of how one's notions of "realism" are often filtered through preconceptions and stereotypes.

Take, for instance, a print of an Iroquois (Fig. **8.9**), published in the late eighteenth century, which depicts the Indian as a bloodthirsty savage, equipped (one might say overequipped) with the accoutrements of war: an ax, a war club, and even a musket for good measure. The costuming is particularly interesting, as the artist deemed it appropriate to give his subject snowshoes though he is dressed in summer attire. No doubt the Iroquois did wear snowshoes, used war clubs and even appropriated the occasional musket, but the artist's conscious exploitation of the exotic over the actual, and the violent over the social, only further reinforced a common European stereotype of the native community as "savage" — less civilized and therefore necessary to control. Here again, the popular understanding of art as disinterested representation is refuted: realism and reality are based as much upon one's feelings about an event as they are upon steadfast observation. As the old adage reminds us, we see what we want to see, and no doubt our jaundiced view of this image now is also a reflection of our own current interests and values.

One thing the indigenous peoples of the Americas

and their European conquerors had in common was the centrality of visual art in religious teaching and ceremony. The first Christians brought with them not only the Bible but also an established iconography, which they hoped to transplant into native communities. In the more urban centers, such as Mexico City and Asunción, the considerable European population that had immigrated to the colonies during the seventeenth through nineteenth centuries gave Church officials strict control over the artistic enterprises through commissions; in the more isolated regions of the colonies, the strength of the native pictorial traditions provided a very different context for Christian symbolism. Perhaps the most celebrated examples of such cross-fertilization in artistic traditions are the **Santos** figures of Mexico and New Mexico, which effectively demonstrate the intriguing results of such a collision.

■ 8.9 *Iroquois allant à la découverte* 1796
Etching by J. Laroque after a drawing by J. Grasset St. Sauveur, Paris Public Archives of Canada, Ottawa

The word *santos* simply means saints, and it refers to the devotional images produced for households in the converted regions of Mexico and New Mexico from around 1540 onwards. The spread of Christianity through these communities was immensely

■ 8.10 *La Santisima Trinidad* (Holy Trinity) (undated)
Wood and pigment
Height 10 ins (25.4 cm)
The Taylor Museum, Colorado Springs

successful, and soon there arose a need for religious imagery capable of visually translating biblical scenes. However, the isolation of many of these areas from established trade routes made the acquisition of Spanish art impractical and often economically unfeasible. The inevitable result was the emergence of devotional images produced by local artists who carried over many of the technical and material interests of the area. The *Holy Trinity* (Fig. **8.10**) is one such example of a New Mexican *bulto* (a Santos figure constructed in three dimensions), carved in native cottonwood, primed with *yeso* (a local variety of gesso made by mixing animal glue, water, and baked gypsum powder together), and then painted with locally derived vegetable and earth pigments.

What is perhaps most interesting about these Santos images is how they engaged the traditional Christian iconography. Often, as in the case of the *Holy Trinity*, the images make visually explicit many of the contradictions implicit within the Christian dogma, and accentuate some of the more literal interpretations of the Scriptures. The threefold nature of the Christian God, as Father, Son, and Holy Spirit, is a puzzling abstraction to most Christians, and it should come as little surprise to find artists wrestling with its meaning over the centuries. Though today the Trinity is most generally represented with both Christ and God in human form and the Holy Spirit as a Dove, this was not always the case. The three-headed deity, of which the Christian image of the Holy Trinity is a direct heir, was actually an accepted motif in Europe during the Middle Ages but was banned in 1745 as an heretical image. However, such edicts were often slow in making their presence felt in the New World, and the image, which also had precedents in the earlier devotional images of the indigenous culture of the region, remained an essential part of the local iconography.

Most of the religious art executed in the New World was produced in the colonies with direct affiliation to the Catholic Church, such as those ruled by Portugal, Spain, and France. The Dutch and British, both of whom had interests in the Americas, were officially Protestant and thus had little interest in or regard for Church art.

New France was settled much later than the Spanish colonies, primarily along the St. Lawrence River and basin, and certain aspects of its religious art offer further unique insights into the relationship

■ 8.11 Anon
Ex-Voto "Les Trois Naufrages" (Ex-voto of the *Three Castaways*) 1754
Oil on panel
The Museum of Ste. Anne de Beaupré, Quebec City

between a place, its culture, and its images. The votive painting is a particular genre of religious art that commemorates the mercy of God or the saints in the saving of a life or rescue of an endangered worshiper, and it has its roots in early European art. However, by the eighteenth century there were few who still practiced the art, and fewer still who found themselves in such harrowing positions as to necessitate divine intervention. New France was different: its climate was often severe and merciless, and working in the woods and on the seas made many a colonist a likely candidate for heavenly help.

The ex-voto of the *Three Castaways* (Fig. **8.11**) is typical of such votive paintings, executed by a local artist in an uncompromising fashion. In this scene, two men and three women were crossing the St. Lawrence River when their boat overturned. Both men were able to climb aboard the hull of the boat and secure one of the three drowning women — the others perished. Above appears St. Anne, from whom the unfortunate group seek comfort and to whom they recommend their souls. The painting was com-missioned by the survivors, as stated on the inscription, in recognition of divine intervention on their behalf.

It appears that there was a direct correlation between the severity of the environment and the degree of respect and even reverence a culture paid to it through expressions such as art, and in the case of the early settlers in regions such as New France, prosperity and stability were often equated with notions of mercy and awe. This might help explain the later authority of landscape painting in such regions throughout the nineteenth and twentieth centuries.

A significant amount of the New World was colonized by Britain, a country whose chief interests lay predominantly in the northeast region of North America. Unlike the production of art by their competitors, the French, Spanish, and Portuguese, that in British North America had almost no links with the devotional needs of the community; instead, it rested on the fancies of the marketplace, both in the colonies and in the "old country." As in the established art market of the Dutch Golden Age, the artists of British

North America produced work covering a wide range of interests, including still life, portraiture, landscape, and genre scenes, which appealed to the domestic interests of their clientele.

In 1776, the American Revolutionary War severed direct political and economic links with Britain, but it had little effect on the overall production of art. Tastes remained rather puritan, with small-scale portraits and landscape painting being most popular and commanding the highest prices. Sculpture (apart from large government monuments) and large-scale religious art had almost no market in such societies, and as a result little of any substance was produced during the period.

One of the first American artists to emerge into significance from the postrevolutionary era was John Singleton Copley (1738–1815), whose early portraits, such as that of *Nathaniel Hurd* (Fig. **8.12**) of c. 1765, exhibit a propensity for close observation and spartan design. A comparison between Copley's portraiture and that of a British contemporary (for example, Reynolds' *Portrait of the Artist*, Fig. 6.12, of 1773) points to the reserve with which the American handled both his materials and his subject. In producing work that so capably mimicked the qualities of his efficient, disciplined, and moralizing young nation, Copley responded not so much to the idiosyncrasies of his subjects as to a pervasive attitude in the young United States.

■ 8.12 John Singleton Copley
Portrait of Nathaniel Hurd c. 1765
Oil on canvas
30 x 25½ in (76.2 x 65 cm)
The Cleveland Museum of Art
Gift of the John Huntington Art and Polytechnic Trust, 15.534

THE EARLY AFRICAN-AMERICAN EXPERIENCE

America must have seemed a land of endless possibilities for those who could harvest its resources. However, such enterprise required cheap labor, and few colonists were willing to engage in such demeaning work. The secret to success seemed to lie in the ability to identify and secure a source of labor that required little or no maintenance, could be forced to provide services below the standards of the ordinary citizen, and could be morally justified to the greater community. Such a resource was found in the peoples of Africa, who were bought and sold as slaves.

The African Legacy

The Atlantic slave trade provided a steady supply of forced labor to most of the New World, from Brazil to New York, and in the process displaced and nearly destroyed several age-old African communities. The slave traders preyed specifically on African communities that lived in urban environments, due primarily to the practical considerations of capturing and transport. This meant that people chosen for export to the Americas were often part of a highly complex and developed social structure, vital to any rich artistic heritage. Of the numerous African traditions destroyed during these inhuman raids, the cultures of the Yoruba, Kongo, Dahomean, Mande, and Ejagham were hardest hit. The Yoruba and the Kongo, two of the most advanced communities to suffer at the hands of the traders, were destined for North America and the Caribbean.

The Yoruba were arguably the most complex and urban African society in existence when the slave traders first dropped anchor in Africa. Their cities were efficient and densely populated, with a highly specialized labor force organized around the needs of the community. (As late as the middle of the nineteenth century, after years of persecution at the hands of competitors and slave traders, the city of Abeokuta still had a thriving population of over 200,000.)

As is the case in any organized society, Yoruba religious ritual was based on a series of assumptions about the workings of the world and the elemental forces to which each individual is bound. An example of a Yoruban deity is Ogún, the "hard god," the god of war and of iron. Ogún possesses a complex duality and ambivalence (much like Shiva in the Hindu pantheon), embodied in the activities of the blacksmith, who transforms iron. As a material, iron is understood as both a liberating and a destructive force in nature, the material of tools such as the machete and the hoe, which clear the forest, and of the knife, a weapon of war and death. Here, the use of iron as the artist's material not only describes or initiates an expression; it embodies the experience, with all its innate complexities.

The forced migration of Yoruba culture to areas such as Cuba did not stifle such motifs, but circumstances significantly altered their manifestations in

■ 8.14 *Caldero de ogún* (Ogún cauldron), Cuban, 1970 Iron

art. Take, for instance, two liturgical pieces devoted to Ogún: one produced at the turn of the century in Ilesha, Nigeria (Fig. **8.13**), the other a recent work from an anonymous artist in western Cuba (Fig. **8.14**).

The Nigerian example, a piece of jewelry worn in religious festivals, is in keeping with traditional visual manifestations of the god, who is commonly symbolized by both the blacksmith and his fire. Each of the roughly hewn tools that decorate the pendant acts as a visual reminder of the process of transformation implicit within the blacksmith's craft, while also suggesting the ambivalence of Ogún's nature through the assortment and often contradictory uses of the tools (dagger and spoon shapes displayed side by side).

The Cuban devotional cauldron (*caldero de ogún*) is made of cast iron and holds an assortment of everyday objects of the same material, such as nails, chains, bracelets, and so forth, as if containing a simmering broth of metal. The items, ranging from horseshoes to arrows, parallel the visual operations implicit in the Ilesha pendant, focusing on the contradictory nature of the iron creations. In this case, the artist has made accommodations to the New World, utilizing found, prefabricated objects. Yet despite the differences in appearance between the two objects, there remains a commitment to the materials as content — not simply illustrating an idea but existing as the idea. In recent years the *caldero de ogún* has found its way into the Cuban communities of New York and Miami, continuing one of many such traditions that arrived with the first slaves.

■ 8.13 From the Oginnin Ajirotitu Forge, Ilesha *Amula ogún* (Ogún pendant) c. 1900–25. Brass and Iron

■ 8.15 Chalices quilt c. 1860
7 ft 3 in x 6 ft 3 in (2.21 x 1.91 cm)
The American Museum in Bath
Gift of Mrs. W. Webster Downer

Few of the early slaves were given any say in the religion they were to follow in the New World. In areas such as Haiti, they were forcibly baptized by law and given cheap reproductions of images of the various saints to help them understand Catholicism. Predictably, such a collision of Western and African religious and pictorial traditions created a set of hybrid forms and ideas similar to those already noted as a fundamental characteristic in the art of the Americas. One example is the transformation of St. James, the patron saint of Spain, who was popularly envisioned as a soldier clad in armor, iron sword in hand, trampling Saracens under his feet. Such imagery had a profound effect on the slaves, who drew distinct parallels between such violent imagery and the notion of death by iron associated with both

the Yoruban and Dahomean Ogún. The banner motif, often illustrated alongside representations of the warrior saints, also had direct visual parallels in African society, and it was not long before the format of these Christian religious banners took on new meanings.

This appropriation and assimilation of the banner format can be seen in a *vodun* (voodoo) flag dedicated to the unified spirits of both Ogún (Ogoun) and St. James, produced in Haiti around 1945 (Fig. **8.16**). Unlike the coloration of the Christian banners from which they were stylistically derived, that of such flags was often enhanced by the use of reflective materials such as sequins and bright, chromatically rich fabrics. The decorative embellishment hints that they might also have derived inspiration from traditional costuming used in religious parades; banners of

■ 8.16 Adam Leontus, *St. James/Ogún Flag* c. 1945
Gold sequins sewn on crimson silk
Haitian

among the waste of the plantation. It is indeed a testimony to the vision and conviction of these early African-American artists that, despite almost impossible conditions and few materials, they kept their rich visual tradition alive.

By 1900 African-American communities began to thrive in urban centers such as New York, Philadelphia, and Washington, assisted by a steady migration of rural black families to the large labor pools in the industrial northeast. The combination of access to schooling and supplies, and the tenuous integration of the American black into mainstream white conservative European culture, had an enormous effect on the community's artists. A few black artists traveled and studied abroad, assimilating the advances in Impressionism and Expressionism and reworking such conventions to suit their own vision. The *Banjo Lesson* (Fig. **8.17**) by Henry O. Tanner (1859–1937)

■ 8.17 Henry Tanner, *Banjo Lesson* c. 1893
Oil on canvas, 48 x 35 in (122 x 89 cm)
The Hampton Institute, Hampton, Virginia

a similar design and makeup can still be seen today in Mardi Gras celebrations.

The most prolific visual art produced within slave communities was in areas with strong ties to the Catholic Church (the Caribbean and South America). It seems that such societies condoned the use and production of images to enhance religious teachings, and hence the fascinating mutations. In North America, most early slave art centered around crafts, such as basket weaving, quilt making, and pottery. The relative lack of activity in painting and sculpture in these slave lands can be attributed to both the prominence of Protestantism in the region (and in particular in the strongly anti-pictorial Baptist community of the South) and the rich craft tradition from which African-Americans drew both inspiration and technical proficiency. As a result, many of the early items produced in North America were utilitarian in nature, but with a regard for pattern and color missing from the often austere colonial aesthetic, such as a coverlet (Fig. **8.15**) produced in the second half of the nineteenth century on a plantation in Texas. Often, such work was produced from shreds and scraps — virtually anything the artists could scavenge from

■ 8.18 Jacob Lawrence, *One of the Largest Race Riots Occurred in East St. Louis* (1940–1)
Panel 52 from *The Migration Series*
(1940–41; text and title revised by the artist in 1993)
Tempera on gesso on composition board
12 x 18 in (30.5 x 45.7 cm)
Collection, The Museum of Modern Art, New York
Gift of Mrs. David M. Levy

exemplifies the integration of then current pictorial strategies (the emphasis on mark making, strong outline, and paint application) into the work of a black American painter — perhaps the premier American painter working in Paris during the time.

The Harlem Renaissance

In time, such popular painting ideas found their way into the art communities in America. This in turn created a generation of sophisticated artists nurtured on both contemporary European trends and traditional black motifs. One of the pre-eminent hubs for such activity was Harlem, which provided an essential focus for black culture during the first decades of the twentieth century. During this period, a number of artists associated with the "Harlem Renaissance" came into national prominence, including the prolific Jacob Lawrence (b. 1917).

Lawrence was acutely aware of his position as both an artist and a member of a disenfranchised group. He used the conventions of modern painting as a springboard for his own brand of social commentary. A work such as *One of the Largest Race Riots Occurred in East St. Louis* (Fig. **8.18**), from the *Migration of the Negro* series of 1940–41, exhibits Lawrence's assimilation of Modernist ideas, such as the flattening out of the space and the graphic potential of undifferentiated planes of color, but these conventions were kept in check by an overwhelming need to create an intelligible narrative for the viewer. The choice of such Modernist strategies for the description of events was conscious and noteworthy: Lawrence embraced ideas that themselves derived from African conventions and, like Picasso, used them for more personal ends. They combine to produce work that is at once both contemporary and relevant — a piece of Modernist art with didactic aims.

A REVERENCE FOR THE LAND

The circumstances behind the immigration of Africans and Europeans to the Americas were so different that they were bound to have an effect on the art each group produced. To an immigrant leaving a Europe of increased congestion and industrial squalor, the Americas must have seemed like a natural oasis. The vastness of the terrain and its untainted majesty must have been a profound inspiration to many settlers, engendering an admiration that was bound to find its way into art. In the young United States, landscape painting quickly took on nationalistic pretensions: it was identifiably different, non-European, and thus considered a unique expression. Furthermore, natural beauty, which in the eyes of many of these early artists triggered an understanding of the unity of all things, was also deemed morally good, and as a result, landscape assumed the weight of transcendental and nationalistic fervor — hence the term **Transcendentalists**.

Three American Landscapists: Cole, Homer, O'Keeffe

The group of artists that best epitomizes this rapture with the natural world was known as the Hudson River School. Of its members, the painter Thomas Cole (1801–48) is perhaps best known. Cole's *Schroon Mountain, Adirondacks* (Fig. **8.19**) of 1838 is representative of his mature work. Stylistically, there is very little to differentiate it from the European landscape tradition from which it sprang: the sweeping panorama is certainly reminiscent of earlier Dutch Baroque painting. What is different is the vibrancy of

■ 8.19 Thomas Cole, *Schroon Mountain, Adirondacks* 1838
Oil on canvas, 3 ft 3⅜ in x 5 ft 3 in (1 x 1.6 m)
The Cleveland Museum of Art
Hinman B. Hurlbut Collection, 1335.17

the color, particularly the autumn hues and the blue northern light of the Adirondacks. The simple appearance of the landscape energized such work with a freshness and grandeur that one has come to take for granted in North America, but during this period taste was still in the hands of the Europeans — and certainly not those of the colonists. As one might expect, these images were far more popular at home than abroad. This might help explain the reverence and implicit patriotism that surround the work. Take, for instance, the proclamation by the painter Asher Durand that every American family should own a painting of the American landscape, which should be hung above the family Bible. Here the suggestion of religious awe and the wonder of God's creative power manifest in nature are addressed in terms of the landscape. The artist's representation of the landscape offered to fill a visual void in the religious meditations of a fundamentally image-suspicious community.

Winslow Homer (1836–1910), arguably the best-known American landscape painter of the late nineteenth and early twentieth centuries, was brought up within the myth of the American landscape, yet his work retained the intimacy of human contact often overlooked in the grandeur of earlier paintings. This intimacy was produced by placing humans as active, even equal participants in the unfolding of nature — something the Transcendentalists would have found an unwarranted distraction. The result is not, as one might assume, sublime (as was the case with the Romantic landscapists) but on the contrary a picture of harmony and precious balance — not sentimental, but sympathetic to the fragile human condition in the larger scheme of things. Homer's *Gulf Stream* (Fig. **8.20**) of 1899 focuses one's attention on the human subject as an essential participant in the overall meaning of the scene; the viewer relates not so much to the blind anger of the sea but to how such anger monumentalizes the fisherman as a symbol of human dignity and simple, everyday triumph. As Americans slowly but surely gained control of their majestic wilderness, such imagery found an increasingly sympathetic audience in a population that saw its identity related more to marketable human attributes such as

■ 8.20 **Winslow Homer**
Gulf Stream 1899
Watercolor, 11⅜ x 20 in (28.9 x 50.9 cm)
The Metropolitan Museum of Art, New York

discipline and effort than to an awe for what they could not conquer. In this way, Homer's choice of subject matter was indeed a testimony to its age.

Georgia O'Keeffe (1887–1986) was just beginning her career when Winslow Homer died, and her work belongs more to the legacy of American Modernism than it does in any strict sense to the American landscape tradition. Yet O'Keeffe's lifelong preoccupation with the natural world, and in particular the stark landscapes of Texas and New Mexico, makes her contribution to the landscape genre in the twentieth century unique.

Born in Wisconsin and educated in Chicago and New York, O'Keeffe first came in contact with the American Southwest during a teaching engagement in Amarillo, Texas. During this period, her drawings caught the eye of the influential photographer and art dealer Alfred Stieglitz, whose "291" Gallery was the center of avant-garde art in New York. Stunned by what he considered the unabashed feminine sensibility of her landscapes, he began exhibiting her work in 1916, beginning what would be a thirty-year professional and personal relationship.

O'Keeffe's *Black Hollyhock, Blue Larkspur* (Fig. **8.21**) of 1929 is representative of much of her mature work. Here, close-up observation of the natural world begins to yield to abstraction, as the petals of flowers take on a sensuousness often attributed to human skin. Much has been made of the apparent sexuality of O'Keeffe's work and her choice of subjects (flowers being the sexual organs of plants), yet she strenuously

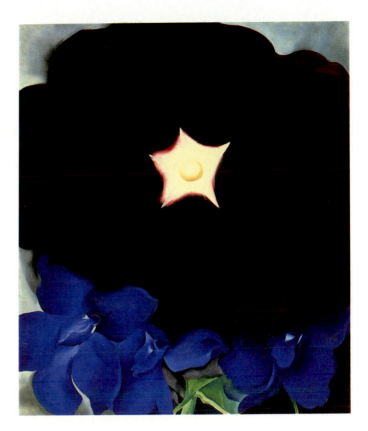

■ 8.21 Georgia O'Keeffe
Black Hollyhock, Blue Larkspur 1929
Oil on canvas, 36 x 30 in (91.4 x 76.2 cm)
The Metropolitan Museum of Art, New York
George A. Hearn Fund, 1934 (34.51)

denied that this was her intent. Her work suggests a view of nature different from that of her male contemporaries — one of flux, of lushness, or reproductive potential, and of internal harmony, sensibilities that artists and critics such as Judy Chicago and Germaine Greer later celebrated as the very essence of a woman's experience of nature.

The Group of Seven and the Canadian Landscape Tradition

The United States was not the only nation in the Americas to develop great regard for the landscape genre. Indeed, there were some areas on the continent in which geography and climate posed a very real threat to human safety and stability, and again this manifested itself in an almost religious attitude toward the landscape. Canada is a young nation by almost any standards, and its cultural expressions

---

FOCUS ON

Watercolor

Watercolor is a transparent medium made of pigment mixed with a binder of gum. The pigment/binder base is then mixed with varying amounts of water (the greater the amount, the more transparent the paint) and applied to white paper. Once the watercolor is drawn into the paper, its effect is often permanent; thus it is a technically challenging medium, though also perhaps the most spontaneous.

Gouache, sometimes called "Body Color," is simply watercolor mixed with an opaque pigment, often "Body White," to create a look similar to tempera. In many cases, gouache and watercolor are used simultaneously in a work, creating both transparent and opaque areas of color.

■ 8.22 Tom Thomson
Autumn Foliage 1916
Oil on wood
10½ x 8½ in (26.7 x 21.5 cm)
National Gallery of Canada, Ottawa

developed around two equally contentious issues: what Canada was and what Canada was not. The answer to what Canada was seemed to lie in the exposing of a people who struggled and continued to survive in a landscape of awesome beauty and little mercy. This, like any generalization about national identity, was a myth, as most Canadians lived not in the Shield or the tundra but in farming communities and cities along the southern border. But myths are constructed for very important reasons: they help a community understand and develop its distinctive identity, and in Canada the landscape helped mold that identity. Furthermore, it helped express what Canada was not — the United States. In producing work about a place and a light and a consciousness very different from its neighbor's, the young nation developed a cultural vision identifiably its own.

The **Group of Seven** embodied this Canadian sense of identity in art. They were a loose association of artists who painted together from around 1911 through the early 1920s and who shared a desire to express the national landscape "as it was" rather than

■ 8.23 A. Y. Jackson, *Frozen Lake, Early Spring, Algonquin Park* 1914
Oil on canvas, 32 x 39 in (81.4 x 99.4 cm)
National Gallery of Canada, Ottawa. Bequest of Dr. J. M. MacCallum, Toronto, 1944

through the tired conventions of European painting, which seemed to make the Canadian landscape look like a scene from the Dutch Baroque. To do so, they employed a variety of more contemporary conventions, such as thicker applications of paint to imply the importance of the artist's experience of place through the process of painting, a heightened interest in color, and a desire to paint almost exclusively outdoors.

Their choice of seasons seems appropriately Canadian: the brilliance of autumn with its singular chromatic intensity, seen here in *Autumn Foliage* (Fig. **8.22**) by Tom Thomson (1877–1917), and in the pastel hues of late winter snow, envisioned in *Frozen Lake, Early Spring, Algonquin Park* (Fig. **8.23**) by A. Y. Jackson (1882–1974). Here, the palette — one that parallels the unique quality of northern light on the Canadian soil — takes on a distinctiveness all its own: vibrant, intense, geographically specific.

Thomson, a self-trained artist who came to painting late in life, was in fact a professional outdoorsman by training and was therefore acutely aware of the subtle nuances at work in the natural world. This consciousness, perhaps even self-consciousness of the artist within the environment, is the essence of the Modernist landscape painter. Yet in Thomson's work one is ultimately seized by the apparent rightness and ease, the very naturalness of his craft in the face of this dispassionate world. The recurring motifs of the hardrock Canadian Shield, the lonely white pine, the crispness of winter light, and the ferocity of autumn winds all came to embody a very Canadian response to the problem of communal identity.

This point was not lost on the artists themselves. In an exhibition of paintings by the Group of Seven in 1921, the artists summed up their desires for the landscape genre: "These pictures...express Canadian experience, and appeal to that experience in the onlooker. Someday, we think, the land will return the compliment and believe in the artist...as a real civilizing factor in the national life." The parallels between the American Hudson River School and the aims of the Group of Seven are striking, and they are a reminder of how art and art making are often invested with a series of meanings and justifications that fall outside the confines of simple composition and technical virtuosity. In both cases, seemingly neutral and disinterested subject matter became a vessel for a national consciousness.

■ **8.24 Emily Carr**
Landscape with Tree 1917–19
Oil on canvas, 21¼ x 17 in (53.9 x 43 cm)
Collection of Glenbow Museum, Alberta (56.23.5)

Emily Carr (1871–1945), though never officially a member of the Group of Seven, likewise sought a sense of regional consciousness in her depictions of Vancouver Island and the British Columbia coast. Often compared to the American Georgia O'Keeffe in her highly individual and sensitive portrayal of the natural world, the Canadian Carr is also noted for her compassionate observations on the decline of the indigenous communities of the West. Carr was also sympathetic to the overwhelming power and majesty of her natural subjects — of spiraling Douglas fir trees swaying in coastal breezes and ocean mists bathing towering mountains. The elemental quality of these works (Fig. **8.24**) is also reminiscent of O'Keeffe, which has led some scholars to suggest a specifically feminine sensibility at work. Also like O'Keeffe, Carr would have denied this. Intuitively feminist or not, her work remains some of the period's most powerful landscape painting and added a vision of nature unique to the Canadian tradition.

THE ARTIST AS SOCIAL CRITIC

Sometimes, as was the case with landscape painting in Canada and the United States, art embodies a popular vision; at other times it can become a tool of revolt and challenge. The way in which artists approach the problem of "intent" can have a tremendous effect on both the work methods and the outcome of their art. Take, for instance, the issue of how a landscape painter and an artist involved in political commentary attack and justify meaning in their works of art. A good example here might be the Group of Seven — artists who saw the landscape as a vehicle for larger issues, such as identity and a sense of place. The emphasis with this kind of intent is on discovery, brought about by the intimate contemplation of one's world. When this kind of insight occurs, the result is an image charged with qualities that come to "embody" larger concerns. With the Hudson River School and the Group of Seven, this embodiment took on nationalist pretensions, since the intense contemplation of their immediate geography "implied" that the work was about a specific locale and a specific, identifiably different people. Thus, through a long process distinct from the subject itself, the work may become a channel for political ideas. In such cases, political or social relevance is "projected" onto the subject as a way of extrapolating the greater meaning of the art for the culture. Such a road is long, treacherous, and impractical for a political artist, whose message may get lost among the bravado of the paint and the beauty of the subject matter. Instead, the political artists' intent is to provide commentary, communicating an idea as clearly and directly to their audience as the subject permits.

Political artists have always functioned in the gray area between the established pictorial conventions of their age and a desperate need to communicate. During the Renaissance and Baroque eras, the two could go hand in hand, as the premise behind conventions such as perspective and chiaroscuro was to order the natural world in a clear and logical fashion. However, as such conventions fell out of favor, the images themselves changed, making instant communication and understanding a more difficult and often less desirable motivation. In some cases, the two did merge with success, but in times of turmoil many an artist fell back on old conventions in order to be understood — the events simply necessitated a clear, intelligible voice. Such was the case with the Mexican muralists, who produced some of their most important work in the early to mid twentieth century.

The Mexican Muralists

The Mexican Revolution began in 1911 with the fall of the dictator Díaz and inspired almost two decades of revolt, bloodshed, and some lasting and significant reforms for its people. The turbulence of the age had an enormous effect on many of the country's young painters, who saw the traditional art of the academies as incompatible with their social consciousness, nationalistic fervor, and socialist aims. In response, their choice of format was the mural, which had a rich history in the religious art of Mexico. It also had a decidedly populist component, decorating exterior facades and thus being accessible to all, not hidden away in a collection or a museum. The artists even rediscovered fresco, which gave the compositions a permanence and coloration unlike any other form of painting. The result was imagery rich in content, political in motivation, and indebted to historical conventions.

Diego Rivera (1886–1957) was one of the first of the young Mexican muralists after the fall of Díaz to establish a reputation for insightful, uncompromising images of revolt and social commentary. His *Night of the Rich* (Fig. **8.25**) of 1923–8, part of a massive cycle of twenty-four frescoes illustrating the class struggle in Mexico, combines a clear, intelligible narrative detailing the excesses of the rich with an idiosyncratic depiction of volume that derived from an investigation of pre-Columbian figures (Fig. **8.26**), which littered his homeland. In this manner, Rivera's art opened itself up to nationalist interpretations, either directly through images or indirectly by suggesting a collective Mexican past by way of a specific conventional language — sentiments in keeping with the young nation's desire for self-determination. Here, the fresco muralist of Mexico had parallels with the landscape painter of Canada during the early decades of the twentieth century, as each attempted to assert a voice of difference and individuality through his or her art.

José Clemente Orozco (1883–1949) was another Mexican muralist who rose to some prominence during the post-Díaz period. His figures show little of the

■ 8.25 Diego Rivera
Night of the Rich 1923–8
Fresco
The Ministry of Education,
Mexico City

■ 8.26 Massive stone head, Olmec, Ancient Mexico
University Museum of Anthropology, Jallapa, Mexico

■ 8.27 José Clemente Orozco
Victims 1936
Fresco
University of Guadalajara

overt political interests of Rivera, instead concentrating on a more personal expression of the human condition. The result was a body of work that can be both poignant and subtle, as his *Victims* (Fig. **8.27**) of 1936 attests. There is a clarity and vigor to Orozco's work, and his images seem to embody suffering rather than simply illustrating its results. In *Victims*, the slashing gestures of paint seem to lacerate the bodies as much as describe them, and as a result the viewer empathizes with the participants rather than simply reading the work as a set of instructions. Here, the personalities of Rivera and Orozco differed and it was their particular intent that dictated to a very large extent the choices they made in their art.

8.28 Frida Kahlo
The Two Fridas 1939
Oil on canvas, 5 ft 7 in x 5 ft 7 in (1.7 x 1.7 m)
Museo de Arte Moderno, Mexico City

Though the Mexican artist Frida Kahlo (1907–54) is most celebrated for her wrenching self-portraits (such as the *Two Fridas* [Fig. **8.28**]), she also exhibited considerable skill in examining the decidedly political dimensions of human psychology. She was a close friend of Trotsky and, like her husband Rivera, a devoted member of the Communist Party, and many of her most personal works are vivid expressions of political will. Her *Marxism Will Give Health to the Sick* (Fig. **8.29**) of 1954, the year of her death, is indicative of her personal embrace of politics and her belief in the revolutionary potential of artistic activity. Yet her paintings, unlike those of the muralists, remained intimate in both size and subject matter throughout her career. Jewel-like and imaginative, the paintings suggest tragedy and triumph in graphic and uncompromising terms. In addressing her own pain and suffering with such force of conviction, her highly autobiographical work can be said to take on political dimensions.

8.29 Frida Kahlo
Marxism Will Give Health to the Sick 1954
Oil on masonite, 30 x 24 in (76.2 x 60.9 cm)
Frida Kahlo Museum, Mexico City

American Documentary Photography

Politically motivated art was by no means limited to Mexico during these years, as an unprecedented economic depression caused many to reconsider the political and social structures of their respective nations. In the United States, photography proved a particularly effective vehicle for social commentary, and many of the period's most compelling images were produced by way of the camera.

One of the first American photographers to use the camera as a tool for social change was Lewis Hine (1874–1940), whose work chronicling the abuses of child labor between 1905 and 1918 set an important precedent for future documentary photographers. *Child in Carolina Cotton Mill* (Fig. **8.30**) reveals Hine's particular blend of social critique and aesthetic control, in which even the most desperate of conditions were rendered with a keen eye to composition. When later critics found this marriage of exploitation and beauty somewhat problematic, Hine retorted that in using "more pictorial personalities" (such as doe-eyed

children) he was celebrating the human spirit's resilience to hardship and injustice. By the early 1930s, however, Hine's work was being criticized on another front — for its Modernist sympathies.

During the 1920s, much had been made of the inroads of Modernism into American documentary photography, particularly its "mechanistic aesthetic," which emphasized clear architectural composition and the industrial subject. With the stock market crash of 1929, much of what modern society endorsed — namely industrialization and standardization — became immediately suspect, creating a backlash that moved towards the "honest efforts of simple folk." The result was the "pastoral" documentary of the 1930s, celebrating the poor rural farmer and migrant worker as the noble embodiments of the American way. At their worst, these images were exploitative and condescendingly degrading; at their best, as in the work of Dorothea Lange (1895–1965), the images transcend their historical circumstance to speak of human tragedy and injustice in a convincing and dignified manner. Images such as Lange's *Migrant*

■ 8.30 Lewis Hine
Child in Carolina Cotton Mill 1905
Gelatin-silver print on masonite,
10½ x 13½ in (26.7 x 34.3 cm)
Print made by Hine Foundation
of Photo League Collection,
The Museum of Modern Art,
New York Purchase

■ 8.31 Dorothea Lange
Migrant Mother, Nipomo, California 1936
Gelatin-silver print
Library of Congress, Washington D.C.

Mother, Nipomo, California (Fig. **8.31**) of 1936 are indicative of Depression Era documentary photography and remain among the most profound representations of the human spirit in American art.

The American continent was a land of promise and often a land of escape for its first settlers. It brought into close proximity cultures and peoples who would have had little to do with each other in their previous homes. The sometimes volatile mixing of cultural ideas and their conventions led to a rich, dynamic legacy of art in the Americas. It also contributed to an overall prosperity of which the world was soon to take notice. After years of artists and ideas germinating in the Old World and then being transplanted to the New, the time was about to come when the tide would start to flow the other way.

SUMMARY

An examination of the art of the Americas reveals the extent to which art, like all culturally significant ideas, deviates and changes as its original context shifts. The history of the art of the Americas is a history of integration: as the ideas of one dominant community surface (often through force), so too do the conventional languages of its culture manipulate (as they are manipulated by) the existing status quo. As a result, the images of the post-Columbian Americas remain an eclectic array of hybrid visual ideas, providing a fascinating glimpse into the evolution and deterioration of cultures, nations, and ethnic communities. Here, and perhaps most vividly through art, we are witness to the exhilarating and often tragic consequences of the cross-fertilization of Western and indigenous cultures.

Glossary

Group of Seven (page 391) A loose affiliation of Canadian painters between 1913 and the mid-1920s whose work centered around the northern landscape as the source for a national art movement different from the art of their neighbors to the south and that of Europe.

Santos (page 379) The Spanish for "saints," the term refers to the devotional images produced for households in the converted regions of Mexico and New Mexico from around 1540 onwards. A *bulto* (a Santos figure constructed in three dimensions) is often carved in native cottonwood, primed with *yeso* (a local variety of gesso made by mixing animal glue, water, and baked gypsum powder together), and then painted with locally derived vegetable and earth pigments.

Transcendentalists (page 387) A group of American landscape painters who considered the painting of nature as a meditation on the absolute. By using the American landscape as the source for such work, there was an implicit degree of nationalism inherent in both the rhetoric and the criticism of the movement.

Suggested Reading

Readings in the art of the Americas are quite new in most cases, since serious scholarship on the subject has only recently surfaced (a vivid indication of art history's ties to the European tradition).

Driskell, David: *Two Centuries of Black American Art* (Los Angeles and New York: Alfred A. Knopf/Los Angeles County Museum of Art, 1976). An informative introduction to African-American art.

Kubler, George: *Art and Architecture in Ancient America* (Harmondsworth: Penguin Books, 1975). A useful introduction to pre-Columbian art.

McCoubrey, John: *American Art 1700–1960* (Englewood Cliffs, NJ: Prentice-Hall, 1965).

Reid, Dennis: *A Concise History of Canadian Painting* (Oxford and Toronto: Oxford University Press, 1973).

Thompson, Robert Farris: *Flash of the Spirit: African and African-American Art and Philosophy* (New York: Vintage Books, 1984). A highly recommended text on the African-American experience.

Weismann, E. W.: *Art and Time in Mexico* (New York: Harper & Row, Icon Editions, 1985).

Pronunciation Guide

José Clemente Orozco   hoh-**ZAY** kluh-**MEN**-tay oh-**RAWS**-koh
Frida Kahlo   **FREE**-duh **KAH**-loh
Georgia O'Keeffe   **JOR**-jah oh-**KEEF**
Ollantaytambo   **oh**-yahn-ty-**TAHM**-boh
Macchu Picchu   **MAH**-choo **PEEK**-choo
Diego Rivera   DEE-**AY**-goh rih-**VAIR**-uh
Teotihuacán   tay-oh-**tee**-wah-**KAHN**
Tlingit   **KLING**-kuht

9

ART IN THE TWENTIETH CENTURY

9.1 Joan Mitchell
Low Water (detail) 1969
Oil on canvas
9 ft 4 in x 6 ft 7 in (2.84 x 2 m)
Carnegie Museum, Pittsburgh
Patrons Art Fund, 70.63.2

*I want to express my feelings
rather than illustrate them.*

JACKSON POLLOCK

It has been said that the nature of art and art making has changed more in the twentieth century than it did in the preceding 20,000 years. In this regard, art has simply paralleled the social and technological upheavals of which it is a part, so though it is certainly true that the creative and critical outpourings of the twentieth century are without precedent in the history of culture, they must always be viewed in the light of the greater dynamic in which they inevitably function.

The twentieth century will be remembered as the century of technological evolution: the automobile, the airplane, the atomic bomb. Art also faced up to a world that operated on very different principles from those of the happy years of Impressionism, as mass industry and global strife made notions of basic survival and human dignity uncertainties. In this quagmire of anxiety, self-absorption, and constant titillation, the once resonant voice of art and the artist seemed horribly nostalgic and sentimental. As the Marxist critic Theodor Adorno noted with regard to Expressionist painting after the Second World War: in the face of the gas chambers and mass graves of Dachau, there can be only silence — any attempt at expression would simply be meaningless. One can easily go on from these circumstances to include the ever-present excesses of neon, billboards, and loudspeakers, all of which scream in a world already deaf from the clamor. However, in the early years of the century, the notion of excess was still in its infancy, and minds relished the opportunities afforded by progress.

FLATNESS AS AN IDEA

The discussion of the avant-garde in Chapter Seven ended with a particular painting, which apparently signaled a new attitude in art. The painting was *Les Demoiselles d'Avignon* (see Fig. 7.54), and its painter, Pablo Picasso, was still a young man in search of a personal statement in painting. Soon after his breakthrough piece, he began a series of what he called "investigations" in collaboration with another eager young artist, the Frenchman Georges Braque (1882–1963). The term investigation is appropriate in addressing such an artistic enterprise, for it implies an almost scientific dissection of the established "truths" of painting, and at least to some extent their subsequent work was a reflection of such skepticism.

What exactly were Braque and Picasso skeptical of? Primarily of the age-old conventions of observing illusionistic space on a flat plane. There had been works, particularly in the late paintings of Paul Cézanne, that challenged the notion that the world of perception could be fixed, but this was not enough. Painting is an art of conventions, and anyone wishing to challenge the previous language has to do more than just destroy it: he/she has to replace it with another, or else there is no art. Cézanne, despite the radical quality of his late work, still adhered to the principles of observation and thus affirmed the notion that painting was about representation. Taking the visual hint from Cézanne, Picasso and Braque began seriously questioning the legitimacy of such claims and sought to replace the old "system" of painting with a revitalized, new vision. Their approach was called Cubism.

Cubism

Cubism was never a term that either artist really liked; it was mockingly suggested by a rather conservative critic who claimed that the paintings looked as if they were made up of "little cubes." At first glance, Cubism appears to be a purposeful distortion of visual experience, as if the artists consciously tried to shatter and splinter their subjects into an incredibly cramped space. But this is only partially true, and it is more a result of visual priorities than outright mischief.

Compare a pre-Cubist painting such as Picasso's *Les Demoiselles d'Avignon* with a more traditionally inspired work by a contemporary, Pierre Bonnard (1867–1947). His *Dressing Room Mirror* (Fig. **9.2**) of 1908 is an exquisite example of the colorist's adherence to the pictorial values of Impressionism, by which his work was inspired. The sensuality of his brushwork is kept in check by the overall needs of the composition — one that places volume and an articulated space over all other concerns. In doing so,

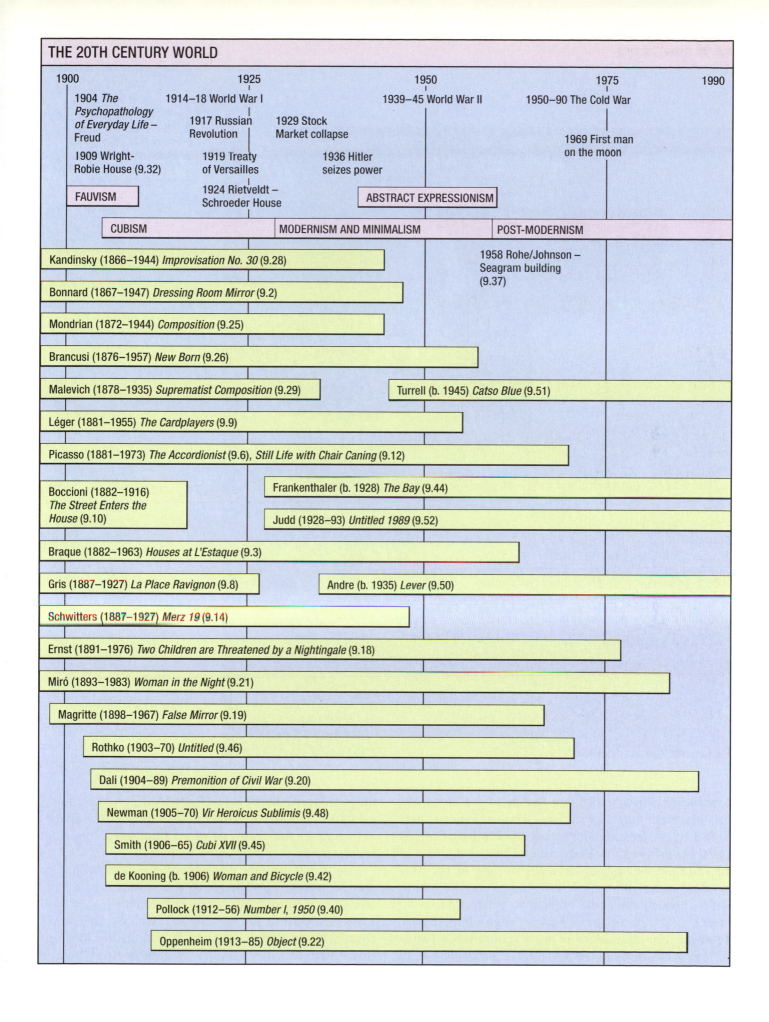

THE 20TH CENTURY WORLD

1900   1925   1950   1975   1990

1904 *The Psychopathology of Everyday Life* – Freud

1914–18 World War I

1917 Russian Revolution

1929 Stock Market collapse

1939–45 World War II

1950–90 The Cold War

1909 Wright-Robie House (9.32)

1919 Treaty of Versailles

1936 Hitler seizes power

1969 First man on the moon

1924 Rietveldt – Schroeder House

FAUVISM

ABSTRACT EXPRESSIONISM

CUBISM

MODERNISM AND MINIMALISM

POST-MODERNISM

Kandinsky (1866–1944) *Improvisation No. 30* (9.28)

1958 Rohe/Johnson – Seagram building (9.37)

Bonnard (1867–1947) *Dressing Room Mirror* (9.2)

Mondrian (1872–1944) *Composition* (9.25)

Brancusi (1876–1957) *New Born* (9.26)

Malevich (1878–1935) *Suprematist Composition* (9.29)

Turrell (b. 1945) *Catso Blue* (9.51)

Léger (1881–1955) *The Cardplayers* (9.9)

Picasso (1881–1973) *The Accordionist* (9.6), *Still Life with Chair Caning* (9.12)

Boccioni (1882–1916) *The Street Enters the House* (9.10)

Frankenthaler (b. 1928) *The Bay* (9.44)

Judd (1928–93) *Untitled 1989* (9.52)

Braque (1882–1963) *Houses at L'Estaque* (9.3)

Gris (1887–1927) *La Place Ravignon* (9.8)

Andre (b. 1935) *Lever* (9.50)

Schwitters (1887–1927) *Merz 19* (9.14)

Ernst (1891–1976) *Two Children are Threatened by a Nightingale* (9.18)

Miró (1893–1983) *Woman in the Night* (9.21)

Magritte (1898–1967) *False Mirror* (9.19)

Rothko (1903–70) *Untitled* (9.46)

Dali (1904–89) *Premonition of Civil War* (9.20)

Newman (1905–70) *Vir Heroicus Sublimis* (9.48)

Smith (1906–65) *Cubi XVII* (9.45)

de Kooning (b. 1906) *Woman and Bicycle* (9.42)

Pollock (1912–56) *Number I, 1950* (9.40)

Oppenheim (1913–85) *Object* (9.22)

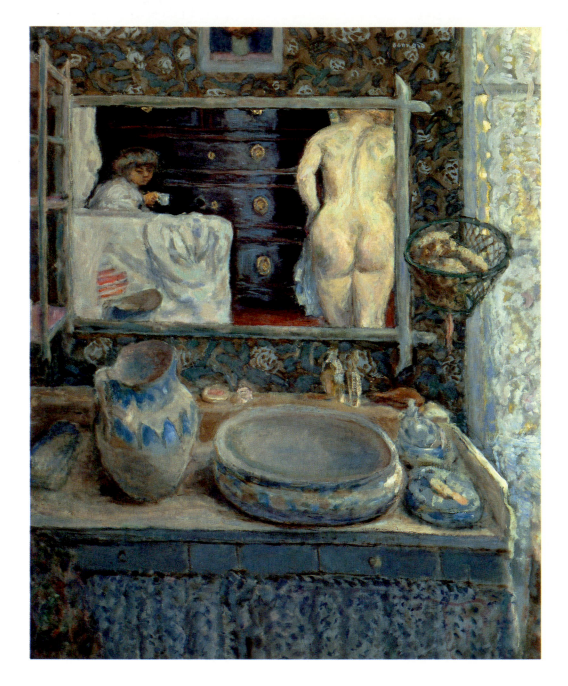

■ 9.2 Pierre Bonnard
Dressing Room Mirror 1908
Oil on canvas
3 ft 4 in x 3 ft 2 in (1.01 x 0.96 m)
Pushkin Museum, Moscow

Bonnard set up a traditional forum in which to discuss his predominant concern — color. What is perhaps most interesting about this work (apart from its painterly prowess) is Bonnard's acknowledgment of the multiple viewpoint; his recurring use of the mirror motif as a tool for more fully describing the nature of his three-dimensional objects on a flat plane is an effective, if not original, way of describing forms. However, the boundaries of such spontaneous painting from nature allowed for only a small degree of movement on this revolutionary front, and Bonnard's profound interest in natural light and color always kept him in the realm of more traditional modes of representation.

The Cubist Braque was apparently more willing to sacrifice volume and space in order to assert the surface of his painting. His *Houses at L'Estaque* (Fig. **9.3**) of 1908, produced in the same year as Bonnard's *Dressing Room Mirror*, shows little concern for illusionistic space. On the contrary, it appears that Braque

■ 9.3 Georges Braque
Houses at L'Estaque 1908
Oil on canvas
28¾ x 23⅝ in (73 x 59.5 cm)
Kunstmuseum, Bern
The Hermann and Margrit Rupf
Endowment Collection
© DACS 1996

went out of his way to contradict traditional methods of organizing space: his perspective lines do not correspond with each other, and his use of light and shade is consistently irregular.

As early as 1908, Braque had already begun to formulate a coherent system for painting, based on an inversion of conventions formerly responsible for the depiction of illusionistic space on a flat plane. The idea of illusionistic space, produced by the conventions of perspective and volume, was established during the Renaissance and thereafter went unchallenged until the twentieth century. The Cubists in effect "reinvented" painting through a decidedly twentieth-century temperament.

The idea of flatness takes its premise from the notion that "truth" in painting must correspond to two primary features of the activity: the physical reality of the two-dimensional plane and the shifting nature of perception. To make flatness an "idea," it was necessary to reconsider how an artist arrived at a

■ 9.4 Pablo Picasso
Portrait of Gertrude Stein 1906
Oil on canvas
39¼ x 32 in (99.7 x 81.3 cm)
The Metropolitan Museum of Art,
New York
Bequest of Gertrude Stein 1946
© DACS 1996

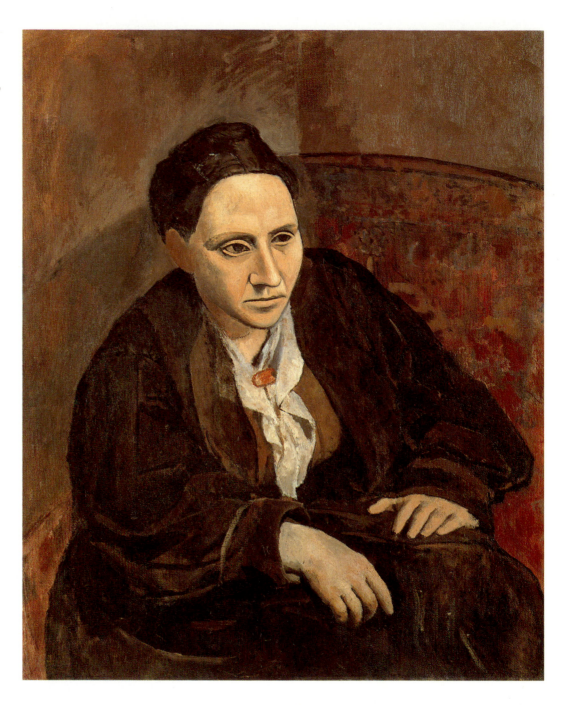

satisfactory representation of the world on a two-dimensional plane, without adhering to old conventions that held little relevance in a modern world.

A series of examples may prove helpful in illustrating this concept. The evolution of Picasso's Cubist portraiture between 1906 and 1911 shows the steady dissection of his perceptual experience down to its most basic parts. In following Picasso's development from his *Portrait of Gertrude Stein* (Fig. **9.4**) of 1906,

through the *Girl with a Mandolin* (Fig. **9.5**) of 1910, to his *Accordionist* (Fig. **9.6**) of 1911, one can see a clear movement away from natural appearance and traditional conventions for the depiction of volume. In *Girl with a Mandolin*, the viewer witnesses the body as a fragmented, dislocated, yet still identifiable assemblage of forms, existing in a shallow space reminiscent of relief sculpture. There remain references to volume (and thus to the conventions that made such illusionism possible) throughout the work, particularly in the neck, breasts, and arms, yet even these are greatly diminished by the dissection and splitting of the face and shoulders. Further, Picasso's collapse of the middle and background into the immediate vicinity of the figure enhances the dispersion of the body across the picture plane. The result: a picture that hugs the surface.

How did artists achieve such a seemingly systematic destruction of space on the two-dimensional plane? The easiest and perhaps most helpful answer is that they simply reversed the conventions responsible for producing illusionistic space and in doing so achieved a kind of art that embodied the prevalent ideas of its age. Take, for instance, the accepted technique of exhibiting a consistent and often directed

■ 9.5 Pablo Picasso, *Girl with a Mandolin,* (Fanny Teller) 1910
Oil on canvas, 39½ x 29 in (100.3 x 73.6 cm)
The Museum of Modern Art, New York. Nelson A. Rockefeller Bequest
Photograph © 1996 The Museum of Modern Art, New York.
© DACS 1996

■ 9.6 Pablo Picasso
The Accordionist 1911
Oil on canvas
51¼ x 35¼ in (130.2 x 89.5 cm)
Solomon R. Guggenheim Museum, New York
Gift, Solomon R. Guggenheim, 1937. © DACS 1996

light source for depicting volume — the kind that illuminated the interiors of paintings by Masaccio, Caravaggio, Rembrandt, and the Impressionists. This convention took as its premise the general assumption that a consistent and predictable light source produces a series of highlights and shadows that imply depth and volume in a regular fashion — hence the viewer's "belief" in the illusionistic space. Picasso and Braque equated this convention with the suggestion of a space they so emphatically dismissed as inaccurate and untruthful. However, if a consistent light source was of primary importance for the depiction of space, an inconsistent light source could be used to flatten dramatically such a space and such an illusion.

In the extended arm of the figure in the *Girl with a Mandolin*, Picasso was toying with the notion that a consistent light suggests space. The upper arm is defined by a light source that emerges from the side of the painting, illuminating the exterior surface of the arm; the modeling is thus consistent in its approach with more traditional forms of painting. However, if Picasso was interested in defining the arm as a round appendage with volume, he would most certainly have gone to the trouble of wrapping the elbow with the same light that graces the outside surface of the upper arm. Instead, the outside aspect of the joint is described in shadow, as if the light source had suddenly shifted direction completely. The forearm continues such an inconsistency of directed light, painted flush to the canvas, while the mandolin, supposedly on the same external plane as the upper arm, is shrouded in shadow. This deliberate "misuse" of the light source is effective precisely because it is so consistently inconsistent (hence the suggestion of a system or organized method, and not a random, thoughtless activity). By the summer of 1911, the process of dispersing volume across the plane was complete, as Picasso's *Accordionist* gives only the slightest hints of the origin of its subject.

In Picasso's *Man with a Hat* (Fig. **9.7**) of 1912, the radical ideas germinating in his *Girl with a Mandolin* came to full maturity. Here, the earlier experiments in light and shade were pared down to a synthesized and harmonious whole. Also, by then Picasso had developed a form of shorthand for representing not the subject in front of him but the very act of perceiving a three-dimensional form. In this case, a head is depicted in both frontal and profile positions simultaneously, as if the viewer is scanning the subject from one direction to the other. Here, the side of the nose and the two eyes share the same facade, creating a hybrid kind of representation unlike anything that had come before it in Western art. This is Cézanne's doubt taken to its logical conclusion, as now the figure lies flush to the surface, like the skin of an orange peeled from its fruit. Perhaps an even better analogy is that of a map, in which surfaces that are conveniently projected flat, though still very much a representation of the world, are certainly not reality as one usually envisions it.

Cubism dismantled the methods of earlier art by attacking its sacred conventions, and though the techniques of Cubism soon found immense popularity

■ 9.7 Pablo Picasso, *Man with a Hat* Paris (after December 3, 1912) Pasted paper, charcoal and ink on paper 24½ x 18⅝ in (62.2 x 47.3 cm). The Museum of Modern Art, New York. Purchase. Photograph © 1996 The Museum of Modern Art, New York. © DACS 1996

with artists, during its most radical early years it successfully destroyed centuries of assumptions about the nature of painting. If one places such an artistic investigation within the greater context of all forms of human inquiry, Cubism can best be understood as a child of its time. Its radical posturing and disregard for established truths were part of a more general cultural and intellectual overhaul taking place in the first decade of the new century — epitomized not only by Cubist art but also by Einstein's relativity theories, Lenin's Communist ideals, and Henry Ford's assembly-line productivity. In those days, it was called progress.

Many mimicked the work of Picasso and Braque during those first years, but few attained the forcefulness of vision that so often accompanies new discoveries and so rarely guides those who follow. Some, such as Juan Gris (1887–1927), assimilated the basic

■ 9.8 Juan Gris
La Place Ravignon
(*Still Life Before an Open Window*) 1915
Oil on canvas
45⅞ x 35⅛ in (116.3 x 89.3 cm)
Philadelphia Museum of Art
Louise and Walter Arensberg Collection

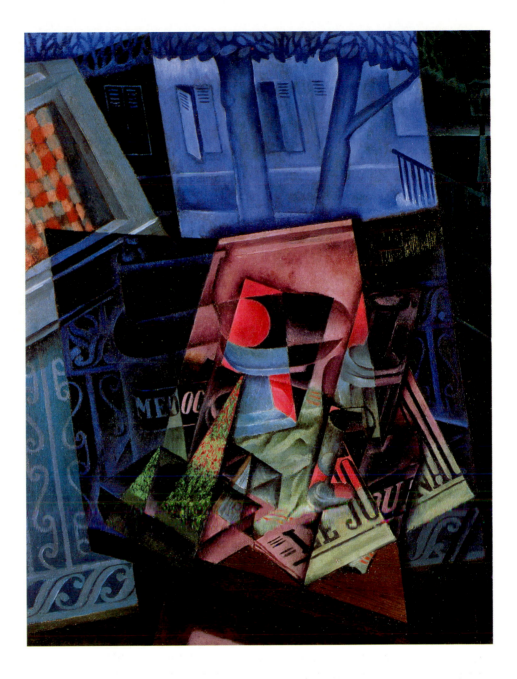

tenets of Cubism thoroughly, making remarkably poetic paintings within the constraints of Cubist geometry and fractures (Fig. **9.8**). Others, such as Fernand Léger (1881–1955), saw the radical dismantling of the figure in space as an opportunity to investigate other interests that lay outside the boundaries of pure observation. Léger's figures are rendered with the mechanical prowess and shiny, predictable surfaces of machines — efficient, steady, and disciplined at all times. *The Cardplayers* (Fig. **9.9**) of 1917 exemplifies the then persuasive argument for an art that

placed observation behind the new pictorial strategies for the flattening of space. This attitude was tantamount to an outright dismissal of the earlier Impressionist wish for an art of "looking" rather than "thinking," and at least in this regard it is not inappropriate to see parallels between the theoretical projections of Renaissance art and the conventions of Cubism: both sought to organize painting around governing principles first and naturalism second.

Art functions as a manifestation of an individual's experience of the world; every expression needs a

■ 9.9 Fernand Léger, *The Cardplayers* 1917
Oil on canvas, 4 ft 2⅞ in x 6 ft 4in (1.29 x 1.93 m)
Rijksmuseum Kroller-Müller. © ADAGP/SPADEM, Paris and DACS, London 1996

language or commonly accepted communication system to be understood. As a result of this dialogue between people and their world, there develops a series of "constructions" (strategies) whose popularity (or appropriateness) is determined by larger historical conditions. Accepted visual ideas, such as linear perspective, chiaroscuro, and even color theory, have been called "conventions" — pictorial expressions developed around a kind of "truth" that seems as changeable as the seasons. Cubism is no exception to this rule, and its visual language soon became a vessel of other, less obvious agendas also popular at the time.

Perhaps the most interesting use of the Cubist visual shorthand (at least from a political perspective) was the art of the Futurists, whose works were characterized by speed, dislocation, automation, and anarchy (in no specific order).

Futurism

Futurist painting is a fascinating example of how seemingly innocuous pictorial conventions can take on larger than life political and social agendas. The **Futurists** were for the most part a collection of Modernist Italian painters who saw the destruction of the old and the glorification of the new as the hallmarks of a truly modern artist. They went so far as to draw up a list of "club rules" governing their art and thoughts, the most famous of which was the *Futurist Technical Manifesto* of 1910, which consisted of nine declarations and an additional four demands. In it, they declared, among other things, that all forms of imitation should be despised and all forms of innovation glorified (declaration number 1), that it was essential to rebel against the notions of good taste and harmony (number 2), that art critics were useless (number 3), and that the title "madman" should be looked upon as a badge of honor (number 5).

Perhaps the most talented Futurist artist to emerge from the group was Umberto Boccioni (1882–1916), whose work and interests spanned both painting and sculpture. In *The Street Enters the House* (Fig. **9.10**) of 1911, he was obviously indebted to Cubist inventions for the depiction of a fractured space and the breaking down of forms across the picture plane. But to this he added something Braque and Picasso had noticeably shied away from: color — the kind that illuminated and even decomposed forms in Impressionist painting with its resonance and brilliance. In such work, forms, light, and color melt into a frenzy of simultaneous activities, each actively pursuing the other for clarity and visual authority. The result is something like visual noise, in which each gesture or diminished form takes on the personality of a boisterous shout in a turbulent crowd.

Yet it appears that the radical Boccioni's treatment of forms within this Cubist space was actually much more conservative than that of his less political friends Picasso and Braque, and he never completely abandoned the descriptive character of his work. In his sculptural work (Fig. **9.11**) he also maintained an awkward balance between the radical character of Cubist conventions and his desire to produce a likeness. In this case, it appears that the environment is the culprit, pushing and reshaping the body at will. The work looks like an icon to motion and progress and, ironically, also necessarily refers back to the whole history of figurative sculpture it supposedly

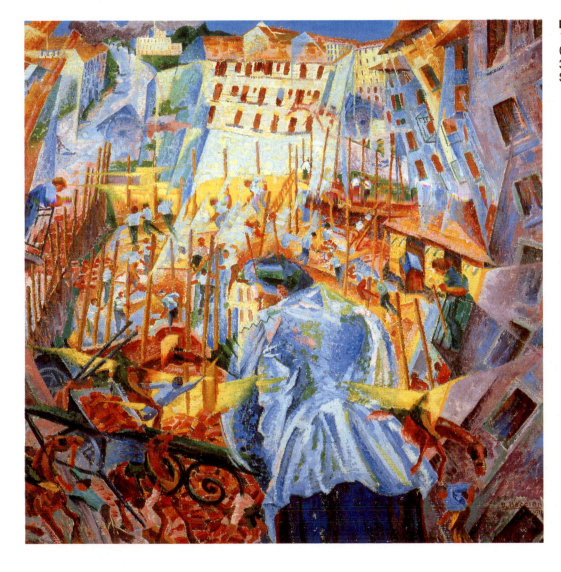

■ **9.10** Umberto Boccioni
The Street Enters the House 1911
Oil on canvas
3 ft 3⅜ in x 3 ft 3⅝ in (1 x 1 m)
Sprengel Museum, Hanover

disdains. Perhaps the greatest irony of all was Boccioni's welcome embrace of the First World War as a "cleansing" of culture. When war was declared, he, like many of his Futurist comrades, immediately enlisted, and shortly after he was killed. Thus, with the horrors of the First World War, Futurism died too, and with it the aspirations of a world governed by the omnipotent machine.

COLLAGE AS AN IDEA

In the winter of 1911–12, Picasso painted his *Still Life with Chair Caning* (Fig. **9.12**), which again challenged the traditions of earlier art. This rather inconspicuous work has remained one of the most influential paintings of the twentieth century in that it was the first to incorporate **collage** into the mainstream of artistic expression. Collage is so common today, in everything from kindergarten art to the New York galleries, that one takes it for granted, but the technique is less than ninety years old.

Collage, which simply means "gluing," is a way of introducing actual items or their facsimiles into a painting as subject matter. It enabled the artist to use materials as part of the piece, rather than having to go to the trouble of representing them (and in the case of Cubism, such representations or illusions were considered illegitimate in the first place).

Picasso's initial attempt to embellish both his subject and his surface is in retrospect quite charming in its wit; the supposed chair caning is, on closer inspection, not caning at all but a piece of oil cloth with a printed surface to simulate (read represent) the actual material. Thus what one initially considers most "real" is in fact the most false, and thus the Cubist conventions, which lie outside the confines of representation, are perhaps most real since they have pretenses to imitation. The result is a push and pull dialogue within the piece, as the viewer's notion of "real" continuously shifts back and forth from the artist's hand to the appropriated materials. The final wrapping or "framing" of the work in rope further reiterates the "objectness" of the painting, pulling the eye around the perimeter and making the viewer aware of the surface edge. Here, Picasso challenges the viewer to deal with the contradictory notions of painting as image versus painting as object, and the result is a dynamic and energized experience.

• Painting was by no means the only art discipline to succumb to the charm and efficiency of collage. Soon, sculpture too freed itself from centuries of restrictive technical conventions with the collage aesthetic — once more thanks to Pablo Picasso. The notion of *assemblage*, whereby items rather than flat shapes are assembled to produce a completely new object, was a logical outgrowth of Picasso's earlier Cubist explorations with collage. His *Still Life* (Fig. **9.13**) of 1914 exhibits many of the characteristics already noted in his painting, but it is his unrestrained use of what appears little more than refuse as the impetus for art making that was indeed radical. This in turn freed sculpture from its traditional reliance on craft, notably the painstaking techniques for casting in bronze and carving in stone. Assemblage was instrumental in separating sculpture from the time constraints and tedious technical considerations that so often blocked an artist's spontaneity. The result was nothing short of spectacular.

■ 9.12 Pablo Picasso, *Still Life with Chair Caning* 1912
Oil and pasted oilcloth, rope
Oval 10⅝ x 13¾ ins (27 x 34.9 cm)
Musée Picasso, Paris
© DACS 1996

Collage seemed to hold unlimited promise for artists interested in incorporating fragments of every-day life directly into their work. Items such as news-paper, cardboard, advertisements, and mechanical reproductions found their way into the art of the age, paralleling the proliferation of mass imagery in the public domain brought on by the advances in indus-trial printing technology. Of course, collage could, and often did, have a decidedly anti-academic side to it as well, as the notion of "refuse turned art" tended to infuriate those who held art up as a bastion of painstaking craft and subtlety.

The German artist Kurt Schwitters (1887–1948) is perhaps best known for his "Merz" pictures, in which a series of remarkable collages forms the backbone.

Merz 19 (Fig. **9.14**) of 1920 is indicative of Schwitters' sensitivity to discarded material, out of which he con-structed a sense of meaning and dignity in visual form. The shifting planes and shallow space of this collage have obvious pictorial precedents in Cubist art, but nowhere in Picasso or Braque does one experience the sense of loss, isolation, and abandon-ment inherent in the torn scraps of handwriting and of tickets — passing fragments of people's lives — that confront the viewer on the picture surface. Schwitters' collages thus acted as a kind of quiet social portrait in those humiliating days after the First World War, and it is to his credit that these fragments of loss and dislocation were composed with such dignity and affection.

■ 9.13 Pablo Picasso, *Still Life* 1914
Painted wood and upholstery fringe, width 18⁷⁄₈ in (47.8 cm)
Tate Gallery, London. © DACS 1996

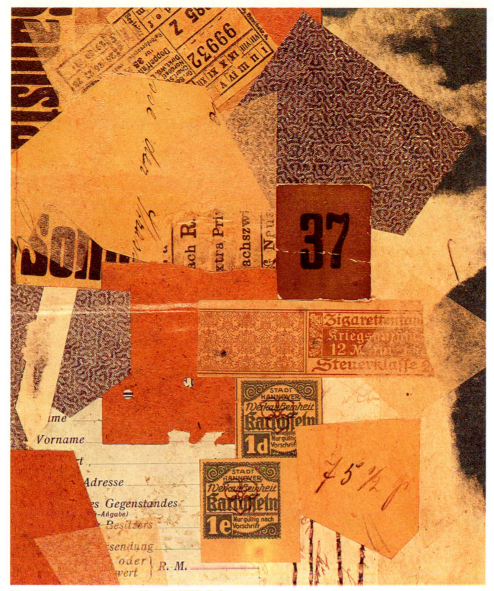

9.14 Kurt Schwitters, *Merz 19* 1920. Collage on paper
7¼ x 5⅞ in (18.4 x 14.7 cm). Yale University Art Gallery, New Haven, Connecticut. © DACS 1996

RETHINKING ANOTHER OLD IDEA

To appreciate fully the nature of twentieth-century art making, it is necessary to consider the enormous effect two disparate phenomena had on visual culture: Cubism and the First World War. While Cubism questioned earlier conventions in art, the brutal reality of war gave abstraction its edge.

To those who survived the First World War, it came to embody the collapse of traditional Western culture: 60 million men had been mobilized; 9 million were killed; total civilian casualties were close to 30 million. It is estimated that one out of every two households in Europe lost a loved one, and that approximately half a generation of young men were annihilated.

What had started as an exercise in honor and chivalry ended as mass destruction, and machines formerly admired proved themselves as efficient at killing and maiming as they were at producing cars and clothes.

The First World War forced many to reconsider the kind of value system and culture that could have permitted such an atrocity in the first place. As the war dragged on, more and more artists felt themselves compromised by the act of making art — at least the kind of work that seemed so much a part of the larger, hypocrisy-ridden cultural machine. For many, to continue meant a drastic re-evaluation of the role of art for themselves and their society. The result was a radically new way of looking at the world and at art — one that survives to this day.

Dada and Its Legacy

It is not to the more established artists that one must look for an idea of the nature of art making during those lost years of the war, but to the generation that lost so many of its own — the younger and less settled members of the avant-garde.

Ironically, one of the first art centers to show signs of radical activity was Zurich, in neutral Switzerland. Here, a collection of artists, including poets, actors, painters, and sculptors, gathered to "form" (in the loosest of senses) **Dada**, a nonsensical name meant to be in keeping with the spirit of the group (Fig. **9.15**). Together, they attacked most of Western culture's sacred cows, and in the process invented such novel forms as simultaneous poetry (a variety of poems recited by various readers at the same time), phonetic poems (verses based exclusively on sounds), automatic writing, and art by chance (in which shapes and lines are dictated by accident, or even the roll of dice). If all this seems anarchic, it is important to remember that Dada was born as much out of anger as it was from a legitimate artistic alternative. Like the phenomenon of "punk rock" that surfaced sixty years later, Dada set out to disturb and destroy many of art's most highly valued ideas, seeing them as complicit with the very value system that had promoted and glorified such destruction. (Remember, art not only expresses the nuances of its age but also helps define the parameters of meaning and acceptability.)

At times, Dada bordered on outright nihilism, notably in some of the infamous Dada gestures. Take, for instance the story of the American Dadaist Arthur Cravan, who once challenged the heavyweight boxing champion Jack Johnson to a fight, stripped during a lecture on art he gave to a prestigious social club, and in true Dada style set out for Mexico from New York harbor in a row boat — and was never seen again. Such exhibitions, though at least partly the eccentric antics of an artist bent on notoriety, were nonetheless the foundations for later performance art, in which the artist becomes the sole vehicle for expression.

There are, of course, thousands of historical precedents for performance art, ranging from the Catholic mass to war dances. Unlike theatre, performance is executed within the confines of tangible, experiential time and space rather than "through" an artificial construct. In other words, both the artist and the

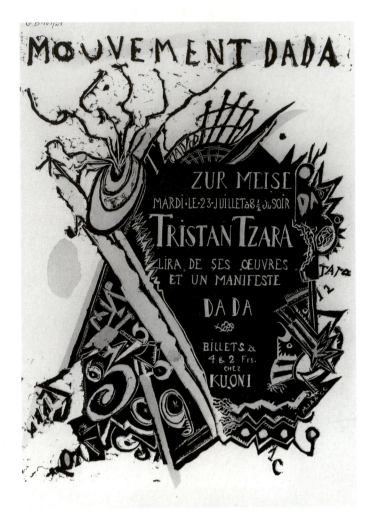

■ 9.15 Marcel Janco, *Mouvement DADA, Zur Meise* 1918 Lithograph poster, 18¾ x 12⅞ in (47.6 x 32.5 cm) © DACS 1996

viewer are placed in the same perceptual and spatial experience.

One of the most noted practitioners of performance work throughout the 1960s and 1970s was Chris Burden (b. 1946), whose often conspicuously violent acts directed at himself are a direct heir to the original Dada gesture. *Trans-Fixed* (Fig. **9.16**) of 1974 is indicative of Burden's mature work: here the mediating (and Burden would say comforting) structure of traditional art making (the materials that are used to make art objects) is sacrificed for a more immediate, less removed form of experience. This type of work resolutely disputes the commonly held notion that art and artists must operate within the confines of a museum or commercial gallery; instead, it draws attention to the art act over the art object (which in this case is nothing more than two nails) taking the art out of mainstream culture. In *Trans-Fixed*, Burden draws explicit parallels to the pictorial tradition of the crucifix, using himself as art object, material, activity, and artist in one sweeping gesture. (Burden was nailed to the hood of a Volkswagen with two nails through his palms. The car was backed out into a speedway, revved for a period of two minutes, and then returned to its housing.)

This notion of creative autonomy, inherent in later performance work, made such activity popular with many Dada artists. Also, its cross-disciplinary nature (performance can include sound, video, costumes, and a host of other media) was an open attack on the widely held belief that mixing media — particularly "high art" with popular culture — was in decidedly poor taste. This, of course, gets to the heart of the matter: the rather conspicuous dose of vaudeville

■ 9.16 Chris Burden, *Trans-Fixed* 1974
Performance in Venice, California, April 23, 1974
Courtesy of the artist

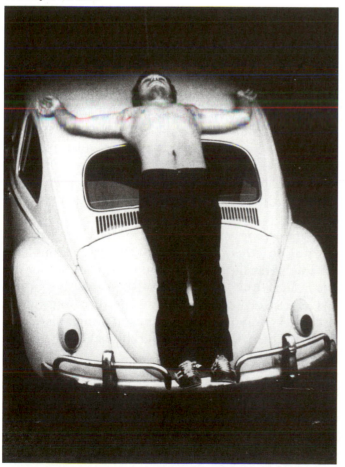

inherent in early Dada performance work clearly illustrates many an artist's distrust of the more traditional forms of expression. Culture, at least in the eyes of the Dada artists, had failed its citizens. Viewed from the muddy trenches of the Great War, art looked no different from politics or the notion of good guys and bad guys. If art was an expression of its age, few thought the vision worthy of any praise. The tradition of performance was born out of such a situation, but it was by no means the only constructive idea to mature during the heights of Dada; the rather limited assortment of happy or inspiring sights to greet the artist of the postwar period pushed many an adventurous soul to begin documenting less well-traveled territory — the unconscious.

The issue of trust — in a vision, a world, or even a method connected with art — was of paramount concern for many younger artists shortly after the war. They began to look skeptically at the very social and intellectual systems that they, and the rest of the Western world, had been so eager to embrace since the Renaissance. The foundation of most time-honored institutions has been the ability of humans to understand, control, and evaluate the world around them — and then use this information to produce a more humane, compassionate world for all. The crisis of 1914–18 mocked such outright optimism in human rationality; it did not take a genius to see the carnage as a definitive rebuff to those who saw progress as the wellspring of happiness.

Humans are first and foremost social animals, defined and manipulated by pressures of which they are rarely conscious. By the turn of the century, Western rationalism was not simply a popular method or intellectual construct for testing ideas, it had become the very substance of human consciousness. In this forum, truth was truth only if it fitted within the boundaries of the system, and when the supposedly infallible system showed its first signs of stress, many began to question whether the very view of reality had been tarnished in the process. Dada recognized this instinctively and set about developing an art program free of previous systems (or so its exponents thought). The problem was how to produce an art free of all social and intellectual baggage, since art had always involved a process of selection and refinement that was based on thought. The answer came in the simple acknowledgment of chance as an acceptable part of art making — an idea that would have seemed ludicrous to an artist of the stature of Cézanne only fifteen years earlier. But then again, Cézanne did not have the opportunity to see Western culture turn upon itself, as this younger generation had.

Arp and Ernst

The main practitioner of the art of chance was Jean (Hans) Arp (1887–1966), a Dada artist less bent on the grand gesture than on establishing a liberating (and in his eyes moral) work method for his art. The result can be seen in his *Collage Arranged According to the Laws of Chance* (Fig. **9.17**) of 1916–17. Here, the actual work method is perhaps more noteworthy

■ **9.17 Jean Arp,**
Collage Arranged According to the Laws of Chance 1916–17.
Torn and pasted paper, 19⅛ x 13⅝ in (48.6 x 34.6 cm)
The Museum of Modern Art, New York. Purchase. Photograph © 1996
The Museum of Modern Art, New York. © DACS 1996

than the image it produced (though Arp would have vehemently disagreed), and it hints at a much larger issue in later art making: the supposed unlocking of the unconsious.

Arp steadfastly believed that the unconscious existed and could be triggered, but unearthing it required a radically different approach to art making. To produce this image, Arp simply dropped pieces of torn paper in a random manner onto a field of background color, and then glued the shapes down exactly where they fell. Such a method denies all possibility of craft concerns, technical prowess, or even the simplest discretionary gesture on the part of the artist; all aspects of its production are left to chance — or perhaps, more correctly, to the innate laws of nature. Thus these works were seen as a triggering mechanism to the unconscious, an activity in harmony with nature rather than against it.

One might ask how true such work is to the notion of chance, particularly considering the significant amount of decision making still apparent in the activity (what color paper to use, what pieces to exclude, which images to exhibit, etc.). No doubt Arp could never bring himself to produce a completely random, chance art — his very acknowledgement of it as "art" required a process of conscious decision making (another in the list of perlexing paradoxes). Yet, the importance of Arp's work lies in its acceptance of the uncontrolable event as at least as real and truthful as all the intellectual conventions on which the Western tradition was grounded. At a time at which many of those intellectual and cultural ideals were being poisoned by the lethal stench of mustard gas, the unconscious might indeed have seemed like a breath of fresh air.

If Arp's work was not an end in itself, it at least led the way to other, more complex investigations into the role of art in unlocking the secrets of the human unconscious. Max Ernst (1891–1976) was one of the first artists to use the freedoms afforded him by his Dada background to investigate, and even reassemble, the world of appearances. Using collage, he effectively produced odd assemblages out of bits and pieces of commercial print and throw-away culture. Yet unlike Schwitters (who used collage as a form of commentary on cultural decay and the powerlessness of earlier art), Ernst seemed content to create images that can only be compared with the dream state — tangible, vivid, and yet absurd.

■ 9.18 Max Ernst, *Two Children are Threatened by a Nightingale* 1924
Oil on wood with wood construction, 27½ x 22½ x 4½ in
(69.8 x 57.1 x 11.4 cm). The Museum of Modern Art, New York.
Photograph © 1996 The Museum of Modern Art, New York.
© SPADEM/ADAGP, Paris and DACS, London 1996

Today, it seems that every child goes through a period of gluing cut-out heads on magazine bodies; such nonsensical arrangements often make us laugh. During the early 1920s, this activity was serious; it was a radical new way of connecting disparate items into a new pictorial whole. As with Arp's "chance" collages, the idea behind such work was to stimulate responses that lay outside normal, everyday understanding. Ernst's assemblages reach out not so much to rational faculties as to that special place inside each individual that is neither familiar nor controlable — the unconscious.

Ernst's *Two Children are Threatened by a Nightingale* (Fig. **9.18**) of 1924 reveals these seemingly "irrational" compositions, in which the scene has no precedents in everyday reality. Instead, it draws inspiration from dreams — imagery as powerful and persuasive as anything in the conscious, but untainted by social conditions. Ernst searched the world of the everyday for possible clues to unlock the unconscious, and by reassembling and distorting common fragments, he believed he could parallel the processes of dreams. To this end, he invented *frottage*, which is simply the transferring of surface designs through rubbing charcoal and graphite on paper. In this way, the most common items such as wood were transformed into mysterious images, resembling everything from faces to landscapes.

UNLOCKING THE UNCONSCIOUS: SURREALISM AND ITS LEGACY

As the work of Arp and Ernst attests, several prominent artists began investigating less traditional avenues as a new source of subject matter and a fresh approach to the creative process during the post-war period. The unconscious provided the avant-garde artists with images and ideas rooted not so much in the past as in the mysterious present, and for at least a few years the human mind appeared a wellspring of source material. Furthermore, by the 1920s the work of the psychoanalyst Sigmund Freud had opened the way to discussion of human sexuality and neurotic behavior — topics rich in forbidden imagery. Yet most of all, directing one's energies toward the "interior landscape" was a practical way for many artists to avoid the humiliating realities they were forced

to face almost daily in those anxious years between the two wars. From this background came the "Surrealist" movement, which, though originally conceived as a radical literary group, soon came to embrace the visual arts as well.

Surrealism was Dada without the cynicism. One of the great ironies of Dada was the built-in nihilism of its radical dismissal of culture; as it was commonly put, the true Dadaist was against even Dada. At least in this sense, Surrealism pointed a way out for committed artists, by rather optimistically forecasting the unconscious as the new threshold of revelation and liberation for a stagnant culture. To unlock such fleeting and temperamental subjects, many artists began experimenting with dream states and accepted chance

■ 9.19 René Magritte, *The False Mirror* (*Le Faux Miroir*) 1928.
Oil on canvas, 21¼ x 31⅞ in (54 x 80.9 cm). The Museum of Modern Art, New York.
Purchase. Photograph © 1996 The Museum of Modern Art, New York.© DACS 1996

as both a tool of inspiration and an applied method for developing imagery in their art.

The writings of the psychoanalysts Sigmund Freud and Carl Jung were important catalysts for the Surrealists. Both men had spent their professional lives in the pursuit of the unconscious, and their findings were at once alarming and exhilarating. Freud saw the human mind as a complex array of sexual tensions and multiple repressions that inevitably led to neurosis, which was at the heart of social relations, governing the perception of self and reflected in the very construction of human societies. Freud's view of labor (the selling of one's time for money) and its connection to psychological illness is significant in that it correlates the postponement of fundamental desires (what he called the pleasure principle) brought on by the need to work with a capitalist economic system. In this way, sexual repression is seen as a catalyst, and indeed an anchoring for the alienation many feel in the high capitalism of the twentieth century, bringing about not simply individual but also collective neurosis. This, of course, delighted many of the more politically radical Surrealists, who saw the cultural taboo of sexuality as a provocative challenge to the status quo — in both art and society.

In the writings of Jung, a student of Freud, the parallels between Surrealism and psychoanalysis found their most deliberate course. Jung was convinced that social and interpersonal relations are the very foundations of the unconscious. Since all humans develop social constructs as a matter of survival, Jung thought it was possible for different, even isolated cultures to share a basic unconscious structure. He noted the existence of a variety of cross-cultural myths and symbols (the cross, the triangle, the circle) that have been found in the most isolated of societies — communities that appeared to have had no physical contact with one another. Jung believed this to be the function of an inherent visual language rooted in the unconscious and released through creative activities. He called this basic vocabulary of images, sounds, and stories "archetypes" and was convinced that all humans shared an intuitive level of understanding through the contemplation of such forms. Of course, the problem was how to recognize archetypes, and further how to trigger an unmediated response to such imagery without falling back on rational faculties.

The answer came in an idea called **synchronicity**, a method of bringing two or more disparate elements into direct contact with one another, to create a visual entity with few parallels in ordinary life (juxtaposition). Jung believed synchronicity to be an effective tool in activating the unconscious, and it often found its way into the work methods of Surrealist artists.

Surrealist Painting

The paintings of René Magritte (1898–1967) are excellent visual examples of synchronicity. In the *False Mirror* (Fig. **9.19**) of 1928 he juxtaposed an eye and the sky to produce a new image, which effectively subverts any rational explanation. The end result is a kind of visual and intellectual discord, which is supposed to trigger an unconscious response.

Salvador Dali (1904–89) was another practitioner of distorted reality, and his obsessive paintings appear as almost direct translations of nightmares and hallucinations. At their best, Dali's images can have a paralyzing effect on the viewer, as his *Premonition of Civil War* (Fig. **9.20**) of 1936 attests. Here, images expand, change identity, and decompose in a series of exotic transformations that have all the coherence of a vivid nightmare.

Both Magritte and Dali chose to work within the constraints of traditional picture making in producing such images. By utilizing such conventions as perspective and modeling with light and shade, they effectively distorted commonsense reality in a manner that mimics the visual experiences born out of the dream state. Since each artist desired his work to

■ 9.20 Salvador Dali
Premonition of Civil War 1936
Oil on canvas
43¼ x 33⅛ in (109.8 x 84.2 cm)
Philadelphia Museum of Art
Louise and Walter Arensberg
Collection
© DEMART PRO ARTE BV/DACS 1996

■ 9.21 Joan Miró, *Woman in the Night* 1945
Oil on canvas, 4 ft 3⅛ in x 5 ft 3¾ in (1.3 x 1.6 m)
Solomon R. Guggenheim Museum, New York. Gift, Evelyn Sharp, 1977. © ADAGP, Paris and DACS, London 1996

function in that gray area between the known and the unknown, the familiar and the unfamiliar, the use of more traditional picture making allowed them greater freedom to explore the possibilities inherent in distortion.

The popularity of the human unconscious as subject matter led to a general proliferation of quirky and otherwise uninspired "trick art" — an unfortunate label that still persists in some discussions of Surrealism today. At its best, it provided viewers with a disarming look into a world of confusion and neurosis; at its worst, it became a tedious and predictable sleight of hand, or as one critic put it, "a never-ending opera of self-indulgence." What many an artist passed as dream imagery seemed little more than an exercise in manipulating realist techniques — a work method many thought had died in the trenches along with all the other traditions. There were, however, artists who

managed to avoid the predictability of dream illustration, and perhaps none was better than Joan Miró (1893–1983).

Miró is one of those rare figures in art whose work bridges several prevalent sensibilities in one coherent vision. Never a "card-carrying" Surrealist and always somewhat suspicious of the group's self-importance, Miró nonetheless embraced the idea of change and metamorphosis as a feature of one's view of the world. To this he added a distinctly Cubist sensibility toward space and a splash of his own Spanish iconography to produce a body of work that merges the affairs of the conscious and the unconscious in a neat package. *Woman in the Night* (Fig. **9.21**) of 1945 shows Miró playfully indulging in a variety of invented shapes and characters, which seem to grow out of a seemingly spontaneous arrangement of black circle forms. The emphasis here is not so much on a naturalistic representation that is then distorted as on producing forms as idiosyncratic and undigested as the unconscious itself. Miró was not simply a sensitive transmitter of child-like imaginings; his thorough understanding of the languages of twentieth-century art makes his work function on a formal as well as an intuitive level.

Take, for instance, his dispersion of space across the surface of the canvas: the apparently random collection of black dots is held together through a variety of thin linear gestures, which are repeated throughout the painting as a unifying motif. In this way, Miró implied an inner order and logic within the playfulness and supposed spontaneity of the scene, creating a harmony and a stasis in what could have been a series of idle wanderings. Here one witnesses the successful integration of the tradition of formal painting (to which Cubism is heir) into the more romantic vocabulary of the Surrealists, and in this manner Miró pointed a way for the next generation of artists.

Surrealist Sculpture

Surrealist strategies of juxtaposition and distortion, most noted in the work of painters and poets, proved equally effective in other media. *Object (Luncheon in Fur)* (Fig. **9.22**) of 1936 by Meret Oppenheim (1913–85) is a good example of the Surrealist method of upsetting a common sense understanding of the world in sculptural form, and evoking the bizarre workings of the haunting subconscious in the process. Here surfaces once smooth and ceramic are presented fur-like and animate, the kind of violent juxtaposition often experienced in dreams.

Another sculptor committed to issues often associated with Surrealism was Alberto Giacometti, (1901–66) whose *Palace at 4 a.m.* (Fig. **9.23**) of 1932–3 remains one of the most enigmatic and disconcerting images of the period. The skeletal stage-set palace provides a cold and vacuous architectural backdrop for a series of isolated objects: an armless woman,

■ **9.22 Meret Oppenheim**
Object (Le Déjeuner en Fourrure) 1936
Fur-covered cup, saucer, and spoon: cup 4³⁄₈ in
(10.9 cm) diameter; saucer 9³⁄₈ in (23.7 cm)
diameter; spoon 8 in (2.2 cm) long; overall
height 2⁷⁄₈ in (7.3 cm)
The Museum of Modern Art, New York.
Purchase. Photograph © 1996 The Museum of
Modern Art, New York. © DACS 1996

■ **9.23 Alberto Giacometti**
Palace at 4 a.m. 1932–33
Construction of wood (matchsticks), glass, wire,
and string, height 25 in (63.5 cm)
The Museum of Modern Art, New York. Purchase
Photograph © 1996 The Museum of Modern Art,
New York. © DACS 1996

a spinal column, a bird skeleton in flight, and an abstract form situated against a vertical slab. According to Giacometti, the sources of the scene are autobiographic and linked to memory. For instance, the armless, fertility-like figure represents his mother; the spinal column is a symbolic portrait of a woman from a failed relationship, and the bird represents the bird that sang at 4 a.m. on the night before the couple broke up. The collision of highly personal subject matter with the hallucinatory quality of memory makes for a profoundly isolated and mysterious arrangement. Though Giacometti later abandoned this method for a more deliberately figurative style, his early Surrealist musings remain some of the most captivating and believable interpretations of the subconscious produced during the period.

THE QUEST FOR A PURER ART

Between 1900 and 1945, many different approaches to art making ran simultaneously: Cubism, Fauvism, Futurism, Expressionism, Dada, Surrealism, and a host of lesser movements claimed a degree of sovereignty at one time or another, only to be assimilated by or deviate into another movement. Yet the question remains: if one is willing to accept the premise that art visually reflects the tensions and ideas of its age, how does one reconcile the disparate nature of many of the activities? Further, how does an intelligent viewer determine standards of quality amid all the confusion?

Just as various doctors might recommend surgery,

■ **9.24 Piet Mondrian,** *The Gray Tree* **1912**
Oil on canvas, 27¼ x 42⅜ in (70.5 x 107.5 cm). Gemeentemuseum, The Hague

medication, or merely rest to cure the same illness, depending on their education, their personal idiosyncrasies, and even their cultural background, so, during the first half of the twentieth century, the various arts attempted to cure what they perceived as a sick culture.

Despite repeated attempts to overthrow the traditional reverence afforded the art object, there were still artists who invested their work with an enormous amount of spiritual weight. The trick was to uncover the good that lay inside the bad and the polluted, and to do this required a dramatic paring down of forms and images to their bare essentials. This rather formidable task was the life's work of the artists Piet Mondrian (1872–1944), Constantin Brancusi (1876–1957), Wassily Kandinsky (1866–1944), and Kazimir Malevich (1878–1935).

Abstract Art

Mondrian's first excursion into twentieth-century painting came as a result of his interest in Cubism. His initial experiments in fracturing space and asserting the picture plane relied heavily on a vertical–horizontal configuration — nature seen through God's imposed grid system (Fig. **9.24**). Eventually, the grid format acquired the symbolic equivalence of a universal order, assuming compositional authority over all other forms in his work. A series of calculated black lines came to embody an entire world view, in which the vertical–horizontal orientation of the composition mimicked humanity's most basic gravitational experience of the world (humans as vertical, earth as horizontal). Even the shape of the painting (the perfect square) suggested a supreme and all-inclusive order.

Having engaged in this selective paring down of visual experience, Mondrian then considered color. In the light of his desire to exclude extraneous information from his paintings for a clearer view of the world, it seems appropriate that he was equally selective in his choice of palette. The result was a combination of primaries — red, blue, and yellow — within the confines of his superimposed ordering system (Fig. **9.25**). All color can be derived from the mixing of the primaries, which is another way of saying that the primaries are the essential building blocks of perception. Together, the steady combination of primary color and a rigid grid pattern became the painterly equivalent of life itself — all experiences pared down to their

■ **9.25 Piet Mondrian**
Composition in a Square 1929
Oil on canvas, 19¾ x 19¾ in (50 x 50 cm)
Yale University Art Gallery, New Haven, Connecticut
Gift of the Collection Société Anonyme

purest visual approximations. Mondrian aspired to painting that, like Einstein's theory of relativity, could become the blueprint for a new, more truthful experience of life through art. He saw these works as deeply spiritual and as a source for renewal at a time at which the world seemed in complete disarray.

The closest kindred spirit to Mondrian in sculpture was Constantin Brancusi. Romanian by birth and trained as a master stonecutter, he arrived in Paris in 1904 and quickly assimilated both the technical and visual aspects of the aging Rodin's sculpture. His initial attempts, of 1908, are reminiscent of both Rodin and even Michelangelo in their desire to unlock their captive subject matter from within the marble confines.

The idea that natural materials such as wood and marble suggest certain subjects to their makers has a long tradition in many cultures, and most probably developed as a way of compromising with sometimes less than adequate starting materials (such as odd-shaped wood or fractured stone). In Brancusi's work, this old-fashioned relationship between the ever-sensitive artist and his/her suggestive materials took on

■ 9.26 Constantin Brancusi, *New Born* 1915
Marble, limestone base, 6 x 8½ in (15.2 x 21.5 cm)
Philadelphia Museum of Art
The Louise and Walter Arensberg Collection. © DACS 1996

heightened significance, and soon the work became more distilled and pared down. His famous *New Born* (Fig. **9.26**) of 1915 shows many of the characteristics of his mature work: an emphasis on the primacy of the form, a deletion of representational elements that might individualize the subject, and a suggestion of purity.

Despite the level of synthesis and obvious disregard of representational elements, Brancusi refuted the notion that such forms were abstract. In a statement that sounds reminiscent of the Neo-Platonists, Brancusi proclaimed, "...that which they call abstract is the most realist...what is real is not the exterior form but the idea, the essence of things." Here art had come full circle, as an artist of the twentieth century embraced the Greek notion of pure essences privy to the artist. Many have gone so far as to claim that the genius of Brancusi lay in his ability to run with the Classical notion of essences and push it to its logical conclusion. In the process, he created a body of work that convincingly suggests a world of forms and objects that exists above the corruptions and distorted realities of the everyday (Fig. **9.27**).

Wassily Kandinsky was another artist who saw the breakthroughs of Cubism as a chance to distil a purer art from the confines of representation. Like Mondrian and Brancusi, he isolated the elements of his craft, which were in painting line, color, gesture,

and the relationship of the image to the surface; everything else was incidental. In this manner, emotional states and their expressions were freed from their age-old reliance on representation, which in Kandinsky's eyes diluted the authority and power of an individual's most basic human experiences.

Like many of his predecessors, Kandinsky came to abstraction via representational painting, and in many of the early abstractions (which he often called improvizations), elements from observation remain, though in somewhat schematic form (Fig. **9.28**). What is different about these works is the conscious disengagement of color from its traditional role as a descriptive tool in the development of a naturalistic scene.

Kandinsky discovered the "inherent expressive properties of color" outside their relation to the "real" world one evening, after a long day of painting, when he was confronted by an image of "extraordinary beauty, full of an inner radiance" — the very thing he was struggling to create in his own landscapes. Upon closer inspection, he was astonished to learn that the image he so admired was actually one of his earlier paintings, accidentally placed upside down, destroying its original representational scene. From this moment, the story goes, color became the subject of almost religious reverence for Kandinsky, as he was increasingly convinced that the path to the heart and soul lay not in painting pictures "of things" but in isolating the purer expressions embodied in color and line.

The religious icons of Kandinsky's native Russia also became a significant source in the development of his "spiritual" (his word) painting. Kandinsky had grown up seeing the traditional icon painting of Orthodox Christianity, with its highly convincing (even hallucinatory) arrangement of pictorial devices that transcend simple representation. The religious overtones in both his painting and his writing seem to verify that he saw his work operating on a similar plane.

Perhaps the most tragic player in this story of artistic autonomy and "pure" art is the Russian Kazimir Malevich, whose career is a sad reminder of the devastating effects authoritarian politics have on artistic and intellectual freedom. Working initially in the dynamic and art-conscious atmosphere of pre-revolutionary Moscow, Malevich quickly immersed himself in the prevailing ideas and attitudes of his time; by

9.28 Wassily Kandinsky, *Improvisation No. 30* (Cannons) 1913
Oil on canvas, 3 ft 7⅝ in x 3 ft 7⅝ in (1.1 x 1.1 m)
The Art Institute of Chicago. A.J.E. Memorial Collection
© ADAGP, Paris and DACS, London 1996

9.27 Constantin Brancusi, *Bird in Space* 1928
Bronze (unique cast), 43 x 8½ x 6½ in (137.2 x 21.6 x
16.5 cm). The Museum of Modern Art, New York. Given
anonymously. Photograph © 1996 The Museum of
Modern Art, New York.© DACS 1996

9.29 Kazimir Malevich
Suprematist Composition: White on White c. 1918
Oil on canvas, 31½ x 31½ in (79.4 x 79.4 cm)
The Museum of Modern Art, New York
Photograph © 1996 The Museum of Modern Art, New York

■ 9.30 El Lissitzky, *Beat the Whites with the Red Wedge* 1920
Lithograph, 20⅞ x 27½ in (53 x 70 cm)
Lenin Library, Moscow

1915 he had successfully worked his way through Impressionism, Expressionism, and Cubism and was beginning to explore new avenues. He called his one-man "school" **Suprematism** and based his paintings on the primacy of the square — a shape impossible in the world of nature and thus in his eyes full of metaphysical connotations. These were arguably the most radical paintings to come out of the young legacy of abstraction in their simplicity and clarity.

In Malevich's *Suprematist Composition: White on White* (Fig. **9.29** on page 427) of c. 1918, one square floats within the confines of the outer square edge, each differentiated by only the slightest change of value. In this simple geometry Malevich saw the essence of all art, stripped bare of the impediments of representation, which had historically obscured the trans-

cendent quality of pure visual sensation. After completing this work, Malevich asserted, "I have broken the blue boundary, I have emerged into white. Beside me, comrade pilots, swim the sea of infinity. I have established the semaphore of Suprematism. Swim! The free white sea of infinity lies before you."

Malevich believed that art was meant to be useless (meaning without use), and thus it should not seek to satisfy material needs. In his eyes, it was important for an artist to keep a certain amount of autonomy from everyday events in order to nurture pure, unrestrained images. It was here that he found himself at odds with many of his Russian colleagues from before the October Revolution of 1917. Though a supporter of the Revolution and its aims, he was suspicious of any art that was too directly tied to the political agendas of the day. As a consequence, Malevich and his philosophy of art were pitted against the more utilitarian "people's art" of the **Russian Constructivists**, who attempted to merge avant-garde sensibilities with everyday life in the cause of Communism (as in, for example, the street poster *Beat the Whites with the Red Wedge* of 1920 by El Lissitzky [1890–1941; Fig. **9.30**]).

At first, both attitudes coexisted in a spirit of artistic freedom, but as Lenin consolidated his power throughout the region, the once seemingly endless supply of funding for the arts began to fail amid economic despair. By the early 1920s, only those artists whose work reflected the "correct" revolutionary spirit (read the aims of the government) were able to secure much-needed funds, leaving those who operated outside these boundaries of art making to fend for themselves. In other countries, this arrangement might have seemed workable, even commonplace, as artists have always relied on some sector of the marketplace for their income, but in the Soviet Union, the Revolution had all but wiped out that sector of society that had been capable of supporting, and willing to support, such "useless" work. This left virtually no outlet for Malevich's radically apolitical Suprematist paintings, and with the death of Lenin and the rise of Stalin, the situation worsened.

Stalin's interest in what he called "agri-culture," a nationalist art program based on the glorification of the worker and the land, further demoted the avant-garde artist from political grace. Indeed, avant-garde art, a bastion of radical politics in pre-revolutionary Russia, was by the late 1920s looked upon with suspicion — a suspicion that often resulted in extended visits to the nearest gulag. Malevich was not unmoved by the traumas that surrounded both himself and his work, and by the end of his life he found himself retreating back toward the safer political confines of his earlier representation.

MODERNISM IN ARCHITECTURE

Following the development of reinforced concrete and structural steel, the embodiment of late nineteenth-century architectural progress was the Sullivan *skyscraper*. Its unique marriage of recent technical advances with urban planning realities provided Modern architects with a radically new aesthetic with which to usher in the twentieth century.

■ 9.31 North America and Europe in the late twentieth century

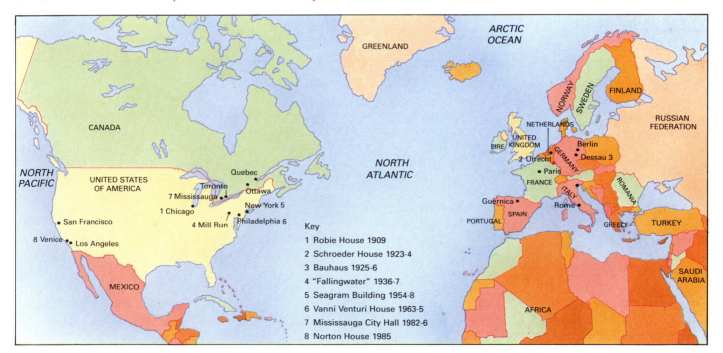

Key
1 Robie House 1909
2 Schroeder House 1923-4
3 Bauhaus 1925-6
4 "Fallingwater" 1936-7
5 Seagram Building 1954-8
6 Vanni Venturi House 1963-5
7 Mississauga City Hall 1982-6
8 Norton House 1985

■ **9.32** Frank Lloyd Wright
Exterior of Robie House, Chicago, 1909

■ **9.33** Frank Lloyd Wright
"Fallingwater" (Kaufmann House), Bear Run, Pennsylvania, 1936–7

Frank Lloyd Wright's Organic Theory of Architecture

Beautiful buildings are more than scientific. They are true organisms, spiritually conceived, works of art, using the best technology by inspiration rather than ideosyncrasies of mere taste or any averaging by the committee mind.

from Frank Lloyd Wright, *A Testament*

■ 9.34 Floor plan of Robie House

One of the first Americans to follow Sullivan's lead into the twentieth century was the architect Frank Lloyd Wright (1867–1959), who worked with Sullivan in his Chicago office between 1888 and 1893. From contemporary accounts, Wright appeared particularly adept at residential design, and thus he was given most of the firm's non-business accounts. In 1893, Wright left Sullivan's firm and began a lifelong professional commitment to residential architecture.

Wright is best known for his "context-sensitive" residential designs, which attempted to integrate materials and layout in the immediate natural environment. The Robie House (Fig. **9.32**) of 1909 is often referred to as an example of his "Prairie style" in that its design asserts the horizontal (mimicking the landscape of the American Mid-West) rather than the vertical, as was the case with Sullivan's skyscrapers. The structural key to this design is the *cantilever*, "the horizontal projection of an architectural member out into space without external support." Technically, these projections stay in place by way of the principle of counterbalance. In the Robie House, Wright used the central chimney mass as his visual and structural anchor, and in using extremely strong yet relatively light steel (in the projection) and reinforced concrete (in the anchoring) he successfully collapsed the traditional notions of interior and exterior spaces into a more organic whole.

The interior plan of the Robie House (Fig. **9.34**) also provides an indication of Wright's radical organic design. Unlike typical residential housing of the period, in which rooms were laid out as autonomous, boxed-in units, Wright allowed for the floor plan to move around the central axis in an open, unobstructed, and communal manner. Further, the interior design does not mask the exterior structure (as was the case in older houses) but visually reasserts it, supporting the notion of an overall continuity and harmony of parts.

In Wright's most famous work, the Kaufmann House — which is generally referred to as "Fallingwater" (Fig. **9.33**) — the principles first asserted in the Robie House reached their full maturity. Here the previous horizontal cantilevering projections are stacked in a manner suggestive of rock slabs — a configuration clearly meant to mimic the Pennsylvania landscape in which the house is situated. Wright even used local quarried stone in the construction of the chimney facings; the matching of naturally exposed rock and dressed stone thus further reinforces the visual connection between building and site. The result is a work that seeks harmony with its environment, rather than overpowering it.

De Stijl Architecture

By 1910, Wright's architecture (and specifically the Robie House) had caught the attention of prominent European architects, among them the Dutchman Gerrit Rietveldt (1888–1964). Like Piet Mondrian, Rietveldt was a member of the *De Stijl* (The Style) movement, founded in Amsterdam in 1917. Repulsed by the carnage of the First World War and its destructive value system, De Stijl artists committed themselves to abstraction in the most utopian of senses. Rietveldt, like his associates, saw his work as fundamentally ethical. He steadfastly believed that quality abstract design could transcend the morass of the everyday and exalt a more pure state of being — all that was needed was an "ultimate style" of art and architecture that could be mass produced and made available to all.

The architectural result of De Stijl theory was Rietveldt's quintessentially Modern Schroeder House (Fig. **9.35**) of 1923–4. Here many of the concepts first articulated by Wright in his Robie House reached their abstract pinnacle: the house collapses the exterior-interior relationship into a fully integrated space and surround. The Schroeder House is a brilliant example of the visual and spatial *equilibrium* so often sought by abstract artists; here solid collides with void, vertical is matched by horizontal, cement is countered by glass, three-dimensional forms evolve from two-dimensional planes. The result, or so Rietveldt and his associates hoped, was a kind of aesthetic purity that could help harmonize a fractured world.

■ **9.35 Gerrit Rietveldt**
Schroeder House, Utrecht,
The Netherlands, 1923–4

The Bauhaus

If this search for a purer art ever had an institutional manifestation, it was certainly in the guise of the **Bauhaus**. The term Bauhaus, German for "building house," was chosen by the movement's founder, the architect Walter Gropius (1883–1969), from the idea of the medieval common lodgings in which craftspeople engaged in the construction of cathedrals lived. The term is significant in that it asserted a collective vision of art making, in which the subjective experience of the individual artist and the autonomy of the object gave way to the notion of a community of workers and the integration of all items into a unified and, in Gropius' view, universal totality.

This aesthetic philosophy of valuing the clean, the unornamented, and the supposedly objective over the highly personal, idiosyncratic, and subjective experience was yet another reiteration of the general mood of suspicion that permeated much of 1920s art; the nineteenth-century belief in the centrality of individual experience was seen by many, Gropius included, as having been at the heart of the tragic First World War. Gropius' design concept, best reflected in the school itself (Fig. **9.36**) possesses neither a regional nor a national architectural identity — attributes one has come to expect from important structures.

■ **9.36 Walter Gropius**
Bauhaus, Dessau, Germany, 1925–26
Photograph courtesy, The Museum
of Modern Art, New York

Instead, its mechancial, perhaps even industrial, appearance asserts a purity of design outside the boundaries of individual preference and toward a more universal, "world-community"-embracing view of the future of architecture. To this end, Bauhaus design went far beyond straightforward architectural concerns: everything, from rugs to lighting to furniture, was considered in terms of the total experience.

The Bauhaus survived as an active art and design center until 1933. In that year the National Socialists under Hitler shut its doors, accusing it of degeneracy, and a movement of exceptional educational and artistic energy disbanded.

There were many artists who, like Gropius, Mondrian, Brancusi, and Kandinsky, carried on the traditional line that art could be a vehicle for special, universal, even sacred experiences — even after the horrific outbreak of the Second World War. However, by the middle of the twentieth century few apparently still believed that traditional art conventions could carry the burden of an increasingly alientated soul. As movies, radio, and print carried the daily horrors of a world once again under siege, and the name Hitler became a household word, the efforts of avant-garde artists to make even a small contribution amid the carnage appeared a rather nostalgic dream — at least in Europe.

The International Style

After the collapse of the Bauhaus in 1933, its director, the architect Mies van der Rohe (1886–1959), was soon forced to emigrate to the United States. He took with him a Bauhausian sense of Modern architecture that valued clarity of design and minimum of decoration as ethical standards for building. He found a sympathetic audience in the American architectural community, particularly in the architect and theorist Philip Johnson (b. 1906), who in 1932 had coined the term **International Style** to describe the new aesthetic in an exhibition of contemporary architecture at New York's Museum of Modern Art.

This notion of *pure design* (which itself suggests a very Modernist turning away from history) proved appealing to many architects. Mies van der Rohe is best known for his "less is more" approach to design, in which modularity, an economy of means, and a decidedly puritan sensibility towards embellishment became the standard. The rejection of traditional

■ 9.37 Mies van der Rohe and Philip Johnson Seagram Building, New York 1954–8

building materials such as stone and wood for steel and glass is yet another reflection of the style's utopian Modernism, and for better or worse it paved the way for almost three decades of uniform urban design.

The "less is more" aesthetic can be seen in Mies van der Rohe and Philip Johnson's Seagram Building (Fig. **9.37**) of 1958. The architectural archetype of the "corporate cathedrals" of the 1950s and 1960s, the Seagram Building embodied the late Modernist sensibility towards materials (fabricated bronze and amber colored glass on the facade) and the Platonic legacy of ideal or pure design (suggested by its modular construction and uniformity). In this way, the *International Style* skyscraper was the inevitable result of *progress* (the anchoring ideology of the Modern age), as it was understood in architectural terms.

THE AVANT-GARDE IN AMERICA

One of the repercussions of the Second World War was the exodus of prominent European artists to the safer shores of America. They brought with them an assortment of current trends, including aspects of Dada, Surrealism, and a variety of abstract programs. In a new land, a once euphoric avant-garde found a sustaining second wind, away from the despair, cynicism, and creative frustration of war-torn Europe. The new center of Modern art was New York, which displaced an occupied Paris and became the melting pot of European art and American artists. The result was nothing short of spectacular.

Assuming that Modern art is born out of innovation and experiment (and according to most artists, this is certainly the case), one might ask what was left for the generation of young American artists to discover after the likes of Mondrian and the Surrealists. After all, by 1945 art had been effectively pared down to the sparest of elements, and even chance accidents were now standard fare in most progressive work. Yet Modernist art remained rather timid in its ambitions for the audience, and it was here that the boldness and self-assurance of the American landscape made its presence known, creating the most unabashedly heroic period in twentieth-century art.

To create any myth of heroes effectively, it is first necessary to lay out strict criteria or boundaries by which to measure prospective candidates. In post-war America, the critics Clement Greenberg and Harold Rosenberg were primarily responsible for setting such standards. Both came to contemporary art from more politically volatile concerns, but as with so many other intellectuals during the heights of the "Red scare," the lack of enthusiasm for "radical" ideas pushed them into less conspicuous fields.

Greenberg's "Avant-Garde and Kitsch" (*Partisan Review*, VI: 6, Fall 1939) paved the way for later American art when he wrote, "Today, the medium is the public content of the abstract painter's craft." Greenberg believed that formal considerations were the heart and soul of Modernist art, and thus painting, sculpture, photography, and other forms of visual art were most valid and truly radical when they openly exhibited a direct relation to the physical factors behind their creation. Greenberg has been labeled a formalist critic, because of his insistence that great art acknowledge its physical parameters. Thus a great painting would first and foremost set up a dialogue between the subject and the physical realities of the edge, surface, and paint material. As early as Cubism, the subject had become transformed by these considerations, to the point at which traditional notions of painting as an illusionary window onto the world had been overcome by a new ideal, which reiterated the **non-illusionistic** or "truthful" aspects of the work. To this rather bland formula, Greenberg added the notion of the artist's hand, which could also be the vehicle for more intriguing subject matter.

To understand fully the ramifications of the "artist's mark" and its important relation to American Abstract art, it is perhaps appropriate at this point to examine the work of an artist Greenberg particularly admired: the tumultuous Jackson Pollock.

Abstract Expressionism

Pollock (1912–56) remains one of the most celebrated (and in his day, the most ridiculed) artists in American history. His seemingly random and incoherent method of painting elicited the mockery of conservative critics and the public alike, who saw his work as a joke produced by a man out of control (Fig. **9.38**). What appeared at stake for those critics was the very validity of the craft of painting, since Pollock's "drip" method seemed without technical skill or even much thought. Of course, this was not the case, but it is true that Pollock's use of materials had its precedents in the spontaneous and the accidental experiments of European Surrealism and its celebrated attempts to unlock the unconscious — freeing the artist from restrictive technical conventions. Pollock was aware of these developments by way of the works of expatriate Europeans living in New York during the late 1930s — in particular, Archile Gorky (1904–48; Fig. **9.39**). Yet for all the radical tendencies supposedly inherent in Pollock's work (Fig. **9.40**), there were elements as old as time embodied within those drips.

A seldom mentioned yet noteworthy parallel to Pollock's spontaneous gesture is the Zen Buddhist method of meditative ink painting, which was discussed in Chapter Three. The idea behind virtually every aspect of this method was an attempt to reunite opposites, or opposing forces at work in the act of creation. The relationship between the artist's hand

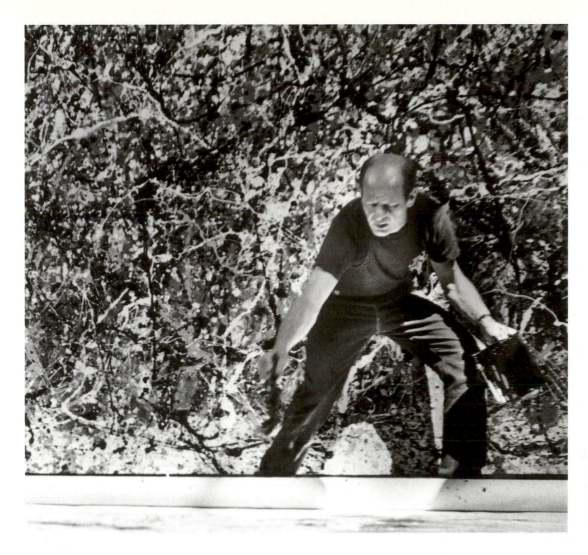

(which attempts to bring order and ideas to the work) and the natural behavior of the materials (the inherent ink splashes and paper bleeds that work against an imposed order by producing a wide range of unpredictable events) was thus used as a working metaphor for the spiritual and psychological conflicts that people confront daily (the polarities of nature and nurture, planning and chance, male and female, aggressive and passive, etc.). By the late 1940s, such ideas were beginning to be fashionable in the United States, arriving with the GIs stationed in the Orient after the war. Though it is difficult to know to what extent Pollock was influenced by or even aware of these notions, his few statements exhibited a striking sympathy for such ideas.

As the celebrated photograph of Pollock in his East Hampton studio (see Fig. 9.38) attests, he did not always use conventional painting tools to produce his marks; in fact, he often preferred working with sticks rather than brushes, and even poured paint right out of the can to keep his control of it to a minimum. The idea was to let the materials respond naturally to the motions of the artist's hand, and by working on the floor on large areas of canvas, Pollock achieved a convincing visual re-creation of a body in motion.

Pollock talked of the feeling of being "in" his paintings, like an active participant in an unfolding drama rather than an omniscient creator. In part, this almost uncanny feeling of motion and energy can be attributed to his willingness to enlarge the parameters of modern painting beyond the easel scale of a Picasso. The vastness of some of Pollock's canvases allowed him literally to dance with paint as an extension of his body, leaving a trail of motion within a complex web of color and line.

Despite the overwhelming desire to read Pollock's paintings as simply raw documents of primal energy, it would be misleading to see paintings such as *Lavender Mist* (see Fig. 9.40) as only expressive outpourings. The label **Abstract Expressionism** has been commonly applied to many of the first-generation American abstract painters after the Second World War, due to the primacy of gesture and color over all other pictorial concerns. No doubt this is a vital

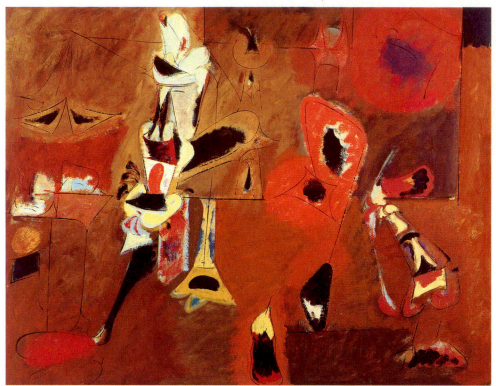

■ 9.39 Archile Gorky
Agony 1947
Oil on canvas
3 ft 4 in x 4 ft 2½ in (1.01 x 1.28 m)
The Museum of Modern Art,
New York. A. Conger Goodyear Fund
Photograph © 1996 The Museum of
Modern Art, New York

■ 9.40 Jackson Pollock
Number 1, 1950 (Lavender Mist) 1950
Oil, enamel, and aluminum on canvas
7 ft 3 in x 9 ft 10 in (2.21 x 2.99 m)
National Gallery of Art, Washington, D.C.
Alisa Mellon Bruce Fund

feature of Pollock's work, but it fails to recognize the importance of the formal issues these paintings address.

The all-over application of paint and the dispersal of depth across the surface of the picture plane directly relate to the earlier investigations of the Cubists and Mondrian. The gestures of paint force one's eyes to travel in and out of shallow space and across the whole area of the canvas — gone completely is "window onto the world" illusionism, replaced by a seemingly endless universe of movement "on" the surface plane. Also, the viewer is made aware of the limits of this plane, since the surface design is often pushed in a uniform manner to the boundaries of the painting's edge. Here, in these straightforward and uncompromisingly intelligent paintings, the critic Clement Greenberg's ideal of an art that embraced the truth of its "objectness" and the spirit of its making becomes a reality — the pictorial marriage of form and content in a convincing, though deceptively complex body of work.

The critic Harold Rosenberg formulated the celebrated analogy of "the Coonskins and the Redcoats" with regard to the rise of American abstract art. In this rather romantic scenario, the Americans were, of course, the coonskins, who, though less refined than their European counterparts, would nonetheless overrun the decadent and bankrupt traditions across the sea. What both Rosenberg and Greenberg (who proposed the term "American Style Painting") were attempting to address was a seemingly new kind of energy embodied in American art after 1945. Though the criteria were never steadfast, generally speaking the work was: large in scale (which was poetically related to the expansive American landscape, even though most of the artists were urban New Yorkers and thus probably more influenced by billboards), devoid of overt representational imagery, paying close attention to the formal qualities inherent in the medium, and ripe with an unprecedented degree of rhetorical baggage.

There were some, such as Franz Kline (1911–62), whose work followed a more violent and gestural course, mimicking both architecture and calligraphy in a few dramatic strokes (Fig. **9.41**). Others, such as the Dutch expatriate Willem De Kooning (b. 1906) continued to paint on the borders of the figurative tradition, desecrating images under a convulsion of painterly gestures. His most famous works from the

■ 9.41 Franz Kline, *Vawdavitch* 1955
Oil on canvas, 5 ft 2 in x 6 ft 8 in (1.57 x 2.03 m)
Private Collection, New York

1950s are his provocative "Woman" paintings, which walk a fine line between exuberant, almost rapturous, painting and violent dismemberment (Fig. **9.42**). This is Picasso's *Demoiselles* taken to the extreme — the critic Robert Hughes has referred to it as the "Breck" shampoo girl of the 1950s with fangs.

What is perhaps most disconcerting about such work is the authority and power of De Kooning's mark making — his painting becomes violence manifest. There are several critics who, with some justification, have come to view the abstraction of a Pollock or a De Kooning as saturated with unsettling assumptions about art making as the domain of the virile male — aggressive, violent, heroic, misogynist.

Women too embraced the new freedom of gestural painting as a way of freeing themselves from the restrictive confines of the earlier pictorial traditions from which they had been excluded. Joan Mitchell

■ 9.42 Willem De Kooning
Woman and Bicycle 1952–3
Oil on canvas
6 ft 4½ in x 4 ft 1 in
(1.94 x 1.24 m)
Collection of Whitney Museum
of American Art, New York
Purchase © Willem De
Kooning/ARS, NY and DACS,
London 1996

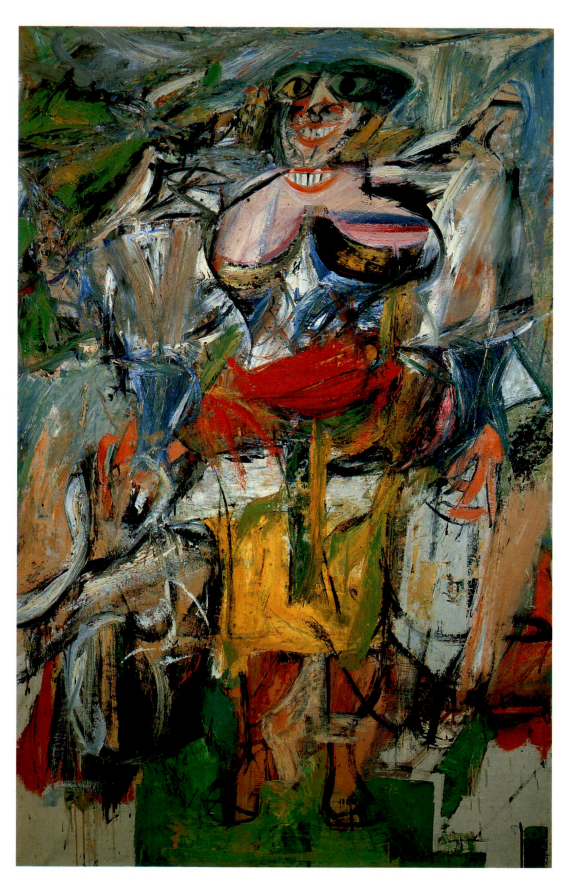

■ 9.43 Joan Mitchell
Low Water 1969
Oil on canvas
9 ft 4 in x 6 ft 7 in (2.84 x 2 m)
Carnegie Museum, Pittsburgh
Patrons Art Fund

(b. 1926) was one of the pioneering women painters of the post-war era, and despite differences in gender her work exhibits many of the visual characteristics of her male counterparts (Fig. **9.43**). Others, such as Helen Frankenthaler (b. 1928), exploited the more lyrical possibilities of gesture afforded by the direct staining of her canvases with thin washes of paint (Fig. **9.44**). Whether the "lyrical" slow curve and thinly veiled mark of a Frankenthaler are more innately feminine than the crisper, more defined gesture of a Mitchell is open to debate — the issue will be taken up at greater length in Chapter 10, pages 477–484.

Though painting was not alone among the visual arts in its embrace of the new abstraction, it was certainly the most suited. Considerations such as color

■ 9.44 Helen Frankenthaler, *The Bay* 1963
Acrylic on canvas, 6 ft 8¾ in x 6 ft 9½ in (2.05 x 2.07 m)
© The Detroit Institute of Art. Gift of Dr. and Mrs. Hilbert H. DeLawter

and gesture (which, of all the various visual conventions utilized in art making, appeared most directly tied to emotional responses in the viewer), which by 1950 were an integral part of the painter's vocabulary, seemed difficult to translate into other fields of art. However, there were some notable exceptions, such as the sculptor David Smith (1906–65). Originally trained as a painter, Smith put himself through school with his skills as a welder. Interested in collage as a way of building images, he soon seized the opportuni-

ties afforded by welding to begin assembling three-dimensional constructions. From this point on, he abandoned the suggestive and atmospheric qualities of painting for the physical demands of sculpture.

Cubi XVII (Fig. **9.45**) of 1963 is one of many pieces executed by the artist in steel — a material not often associated with great art at the time. Why steel instead of casting elements in bronze or carving in stone, as was traditional? Smith was deeply influenced by the assemblage constructions of Picasso, which he saw as a successful three-dimensional solution to collage. His first works combined metal elements, using welding techniques as the collage artist uses glue, slowly layering information. However, many materials did not possess the strength or resilience necessary to produce works with the degree of ease and spontaneity implicit in collage. The answer came in steel, an industrial material of great strength that could be fabricated and assembled into a variety of interesting configurations without worry of collapse. *Cubi XVII*'s rather precarious posture suggests the speed and energy of collage, but in a far more tangible, physical manner. Yet Smith recognized that sculpture too has its surfaces, and he began grinding or sometimes painting his work to bring more visual information to bear upon the piece. In *Cubi XVII*, the auto grinder became the rough equivalent of Pollock's sticks, circulating visual energy around the piece as light reflects off its surfaces. With Smith's acceptance of the formal characteristics of traditional sculpture (volume, the engaging of space and materials), combined with a highly personal investment in the work through his use of gesture, it is little wonder that Greenberg saw him as one of the foremost artists of the post-war period.

Mark Rothko and Barnett Newman

Gesture and luscious material handling were not the only attributes of abstract painting embraced by the avant-garde in post-war America. There were artists who invested their energies in unifying the picture plane in a more resonant, less overtly physical manner, producing eloquent expressions of harmony, balance, and equilibrium. Due in part to the large areas of undifferentiated color in many of the works, this loose association of artists has come to be known as the "color field painters." They included the likes of Mark Rothko (1903–70) and Barnett Newman (1905–70).

Rothko's *Untitled* (Fig. **9.46**) of 1960 is indicative of his mature work, with flooded fields of resonant color bleeding to the extremities of the surface's edge, suggesting everything from landscape to the dream state. The relationship between colors, fluctuating between harmony and discord, gives these works an undeniable moodiness and solemn quality often associated with great religious art. This point was not lost on Rothko, who said, "The most important tool the artist fashions through constant practice is faith in his ability to produce miracles when they are needed.

■ **9.45 David Smith**
Cubi XVII 1963
Stainless steel
Height 9 ft (2.74 m)
Dallas Museum of Art
Eugene and Margaret
McDermott Fund

■ 9.46 Mark Rothko
Untitled 1960
Oil on canvas
5 ft 9 in x 4 ft 2½ in (1.75 x 1.27 m)
The Museum of Modern Art,
San Francisco
Acquired through a gift of
Peggy Guggenheim

▶ 9.47 Mark Rothko
View of The Rothko Chapel,
Houston 1965–6
Oil on canvas
North, Northeast, and
East paintings

Pictures must be miraculous." (*Possibilities*, I, 1947, p.84). Here is yet another example of a work of art that traverses the expanse between formal concerns popular since Cubism and the desire for an exalted, universal subject matter accessible to all with a meditative and patient eye. Rothko's evocative paintings lend themselves readily to the introspective viewer and, like other religious works, function most effectively when granted a quiet, traffic-free setting for their contemplation. To facilitate such demands,

Rothko was given what was perhaps the last great religious commission in Modernism, maybe even Western art — the production of a series of paintings for a non-denominational chapel outside Houston (Fig. **9.47**), which has been aptly described as one of the most solemn places on earth.

A word on "untitled" works. Over the past half-century, many artists have made the conscious decision to leave their art titleless. This does two things: first, it implies that there is no one correct meaning to the work, and second, it invites the viewer to be an active participant in the process of art making — both of which require explanation.

The notion of a single correct meaning in a work of art has always been contingent upon the viewer's ability to recognize the subject matter and on his/her intimate knowledge of the artist, his/her ideas, the context of the piece, the specific historical context, etc. This, of course, is impossible; the infinite combination of personalities, experiences, cultural prejudices, and their subsequent influences makes the argument of a single "true" meaning a fallacy. In traditional representation, this gulf between one universal "meaning" and various individual "meanings," though it still existed, was minimized to some extent by the viewer's instant recognition of the subject, which when placed within the context of the title, helped restrict the subject "matter" into a more channeled number of possibilities. In non-representational work such as Rothko's, the absence of easily identifiable images on which to hang presumed meaning forces the viewer to consider more personal explanations for its content. In this way, the viewer creates

meaning in the work; in other words, the traditional proposition "this is what I am experiencing" becomes "what is this I am experiencing?".

The untitled work is obviously not for every artist, since its reliance on the viewer's active participation minimizes the artist's own voice (hence its unpopularity with politically motivated artists, who often use their work as a platform for issues). In the case of Mark Rothko, the openness of meaning afforded by the untitled label seems absolutely appropriate when one considers his desire to address a more intuited range of emotions in his audience.

Like Rothko, Barnett Newman believed that art could still carry the weight of human consciousness and renewal, but his stricter adherence to formal issues has made his paintings less accessible to the average viewing public. *Vir Heroicus Sublimis* (Fig. **9.48**) of 1950–51 operates first and foremost as a painting about painting; that is, the artist has concentrated the audience's visual energies upon the physical relationship of the surface (a uniformly flat application of saturated red) to the edges of the canvas, which is further accentuated by the thin vertical

■ 9.48 Barnett Newman, *Vir Heroicus Sublimis* 1950–1
Oil on canvas, 7 ft 11⅜ in x 17 ft 9¼ ins (2.42 x 5.41 m)
Collection, The Museum of Modern Art, New York
Gift of Mr. and Mrs. Ben Heller

lines (what he called "zips") that act as parallels to those edges. Newman saw these vertical zips on the horizontal plane as functioning on two distinct levels: first, as a formal device to reassert the presence of the outside edge, and second, as a body metaphor. The vertical marks on the horizontal plane mimic the fundamental way in which humans interact with their world, and in this way a highly abstract formal painting comes to embody a variety of more personal attributes. Put another way, Newman's suggestion of the body (even if highly abstracted) as a straightforward formal device enables what might on first glance appear little more than a spartan canvas to take on highly personal, even universal characteristics — body and world unified in harmony and stasis. Within this context, Newman's grandiose choice of title (*Man the Heroic and Sublime*) serves a vital function in suggesting a deeper significance to what on the surface may appear little more than a formal exercise.

The Advent of Minimalism

Barnett Newman is quoted as saying that American abstract art was "asserting man's natural desire for the exalted...a concern with the absolute emotions." Looking back at *Vir Heroicus Sublimis*, it is perhaps fair to say that a chasm existed between what was said about the art and what the art actually looked like during the heights of American post-war abstraction. The rhetoric that surrounded such self-proclaimed "heroic" work was dense and often intolerable to

those artists a generation younger who were forced to grow up under its formidable weight. The subsequent backlash signaled the beginnings of a crisis in art making, as increasingly artists began questioning the authority of their elders and, more importantly, stopped believing the heroism. Some of the younger artists openly confronted the ideals of Modernism, criticizing both its message and its ability to change the world in any significant way. These were the Pop Artists, who helped usher in the current Postmodern era (see Chapter Ten, page 459).

Before a movement can truly be said to have ended, it must first show the signs of exhaustion. One of the most basic tenets of Modernism was the belief in innovation; artists, like their colleagues in science and business, had openly embraced the notion of innovation as progressive and thus good (or "modern"). Yet there are only so many variables available to the artist in producing art, and eventually this seemingly endless supply of new combinations was going to run out. Abstract Expressionism had pushed the limits of art making almost to the edge; it was now simply a matter of pushing it over. This last phase of Modernism has aptly been described as **Minimalism**.

When the painter Frank Stella (b. 1936), one of the most influential of the Minimalist artists, was asked to express his thoughts as he was producing his series of "black paintings" in 1959–60, he claimed he wanted to "paint a picture no one could write about." *Die Fahne Hoch!* (Fig. **9.49**) of 1959 is the result of that approach — an image that defies both the easy symbolism and the heroic stature of its predecessors in Abstract Expressionism. Stella's painting consists of little more than an arrangement of flatly applied black enamel lines on raw canvas; they radiate from the center in a predictable, uniform manner. All components of the painting work in remarkable harmony and coherence.

Instead of using traditional oil paint, which dries to a rich, suggestive black, Stella chose an industrial enamel, which dries absolutely flat and is absorbed into the canvas. The canvas is left unprimed, without

■ 9.49 Frank Stella, *Die Fahne Hoch!* 1959
Black enamel on canvas, 10 ft 1½ in x 6 ft 1 in (3.08 x 1.85 m)
Collection of Whitney Museum of American Art, New York
© DACS 1996

its typical application of gesso or lead white to protect the surface. Visually, this decision helps bind the canvas to the paint as one complete object, and it also reasserts the painting as a form rather than simply a surface — a piece of stretched material over a rectangular frame, which creates edges. The result is a work that successfully destroys any vestige of illusion by methodically dissipating space, as the bar-like black stripes push the eye away from the center of the picture plane, bringing attention to the edge. Gone is the space, gone is the illusionism, gone are practically all suggestions of subject matter other than the apparent "objectness" of the painting. This is what might be referred to as a self-enclosed work — an image that is internally consistent and requires no information outside the boundaries of its own edges to function. Here, painting has collapsed into sculpture, referring more to three-dimensional concerns than earlier painting conventions.

Minimalism was primarily a sculptural movement, and it put tremendous emphasis on structural unity, synthesis of parts, and absolute intelligibility. Carl Andre (b. 1935) worked as a studio mate of Stella's during the early 1960s, yet his vision was even less grounded in traditional forms. His first works involved both stacking and carving wood, which implied architecture and also totemic sculpture. But the referential quality of this early sculpture seemed too closely tied to history and to craft for Andre's temperament, and soon carving (which implied the artist's hand) gave way to simple, regular stacking.

Andre's next move was away from the vertical plane, toward the horizontal, which hugged the earth and denied figurative and architectural associations. *Lever* (Fig. **9.50**) of 1966 consists of 137 unconnected commercial firebricks assembled across the floor, and it sums up Andre's interests during the mid 1960s: sequence, horizontality, the assertion of gravity, and a steadfast denial of craft or expression. When it was first shown, in 1966, it immediately caused an outcry from public and critics alike, who saw no "merit" in a row of bricks.

How does a viewer make sense of a row of bricks? And furthermore, what would possess an artist to produce this kind of work? First, it is important to acknowledge that, if *Lever* is art, it necessarily opens itself up to a dialogue with history, since all art, even the most radical, relies on that history as a point of departure. In this regard, there is much of interest in

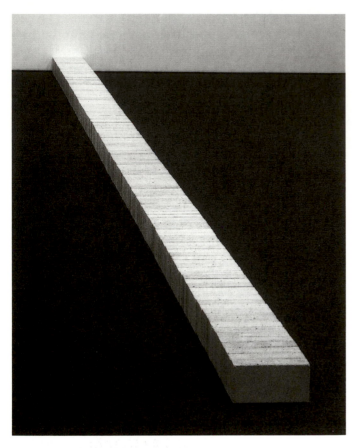

such claims is that the Minimalists remain some of the most informed and critically aware artists of the twentieth century, whose decision to produce anti-craft work was the result of choice and thought, rather than a lack of skill or conceptual immaturity. Andre, like other Minimalists, questions the validity of technique and craft, which were viewed as romantic, nostalgic nonsense in a world of automation and conformity. Without technique, the viewer is forced to consider the intrinsic merits of the piece as a visual phenomenon — a conceptual cuing device, if you will. Since one cannot be distracted by seductive technical work that suggests the artist's hand and thus an external subject matter, one is forced to deal with it on other terms. In addressing those visual concerns, Minimalist art enters into a dialogue not only with other art but also with the history of speculation that surrounds the very idea of merit.

■ 9.50 Carl Andre, *Lever* 1966
137 firebricks, assembled: 4½ x 8⅞ x 348 in (11.4 x 22.5 x 883.9 cm)
each brick: 4½ x 8⅞ x 2½ in (11.4 x 22.5 x 6.4 cm)
National Gallery of Art, Ottawa
© Carl Andre/DACS, London/VAGA, New York 1996

■ 9.51 James Turrell
Catso Blue (original) 1967 recreated by the artist in 1987
Light projection
Collection Lannan Foundation, Los Angeles

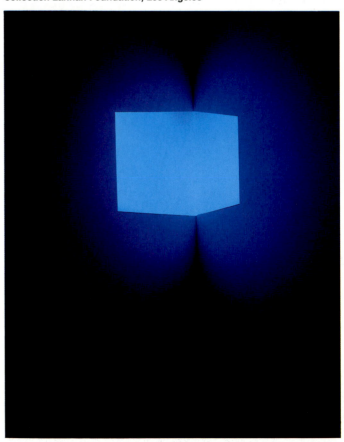

Lever, since it seems to provoke comparisons with traditional sculpture — traditional sculpture is vertical, often figurative, and even in its most radical form material-oriented, whereas *Lever* is horizontal, anti-figurative, component-like (each piece having attributes of the whole), and conspicuously without technical prowess (compare David Smith's *Cubi XVII* [see Fig. 9.45]). Taken within this context, Andre's line of bricks appears an affront to traditional values in sculpture, and when viewed within the context of sculpture in a museum, say, it acts as an informed critique of that tradition.

Can that alone make it art? Perhaps the most troubling aspect of this work for most viewers is its lack of technique; the simple fact that anyone could have assembled it insults the traditional view of artists as skilled technicians, whose work comes as a result of years of arduous training. What is most ironic about

Another artist concerned with the primacy of vision and phenomena over materiality is James Turrell (b. 1943) whose "light sculptures" of the 1960s pushed the traditional physical boundaries of a work of art to its near breaking point. Light, implied in art through pictorial conventions such as shading in painting and observed as highlight and shadow in sculpture, is here taken as a separate and fundamental component of the perceptual experience — visually present and yet materially absent. Like his Minimalist colleagues, Turrell clearly places emphasis on the viewer's pure experience of phenomena over concerns of craft or expression. He once stated that he wanted to "make light inhabit a space so it feels materially present," and in works such as *Catso Blue* (Fig. **9.51**) of 1967 one may begin to comprehend his conviction. There is an ephemeral quality to this art that differs dramatically from that of Andre — a quasi-spiritual component inherent in the notion of granting materiality (form) to the immaterial (light). In embracing a kind of perceptual idealism, these supposedly sterile and neutered objects of Minimalism take on a kind of humanity and reverence often reserved for religious art.

Donald Judd (1928–93) was an early Minimalist who had continued to pursue an art that openly criticized aspects of Cubism that so influenced twentieth-century art. In Cubism, the audience is granted a simultaneous view of all angles of the perceptual field — different views brought together to form a visual approximation of the process of observing the whole. Judd wanted an art that could be understood at once, in an instantaneous rather than a fractured manner. The result is work whose components are interchangeable, machine-assembled, modular, and thus absolutely predictable.

Untitled (Fig. **9.52**) of 1989 is typical of Judd's obsession with modular construction, and it purposefully leaves little of significance to the imagination. Here, the subjectivity of the viewer, so important to the Abstract Expressionists, dissipates into an absolute view — coherent, static, whole. Judd and his compatriots claimed that such art had ethical ramifications: that it embodied universality, not individualism. This is sculpture pared down to its most fundamental characteristics, and if the view is none too inspiring, it is perhaps because Minimalism appears as an art without a voice.

■ 9.52 Donald Judd
Untitled 1989
Copper, red plexiglass
each 9 x 40 x 31 in (23 x 101.6 x 78.7 cm)
Courtesy Paula Cooper Gallery, New York

In the muteness of Judd's sculpture, the final exhaustion of the Modernist ideal became increasingly apparent. Decades of relentless innovation had led to a virtual vacuum, but to turn back was to admit defeat. Minimalism closed the door on Modernist optimism once and for all in its sterile fabrications. Now it seems more a question of how to go forward when everything appears to have been done. This is the crisis of today's art.

THE END OF AN ERA

As an idea or movement, Modernism was intimately linked to a series of popular assumptions about the world that surfaced in the late nineteenth and early twentieth centuries. The machine age had promised, and had often delivered, a better life for those held so tightly in its grasp. However, as today's accoutrements of civilized warfare so dramatically attest, the machine is little more than an extension of human conscience and frailty — no better, no worse, but certainly imperfect. Art too had openly embraced innovation and progress as cures for a complacent culture, and soon the mystique of the artist as an explorer of the great unknown took on heroic proportions. Modernist art actively sought to separate itself from everyday pedestrian concerns in order to focus on creating a visual strategy that could point the way for future generations. Yet deep within this complexity of ideas there existed one underlying assumption: that the evolutionary theories of science proved that progress was inevitable, and thus could be transferred to all fields of human endeavor. Thus innovation, despite an occasional setback, became a motive for art making, and as with science, notions of art as a process of almost religious discovery or exploration soon became an integral part of artists' vocabulary.

Modernist art certainly did not save the world, and even at the best of times it was terminally myopic — but at least it was a conviction. At a time at which cynicism has become increasingly fashionable, perhaps one can take solace from the knowledge that there are, or were, people who believe/d that ideas can/could save the world.

One of the most eloquent obituaries for the Modernist movement was written by the critic Peter Schjedahl in a recent article on abstract painting:

> Art as a substitute religion (and it was no less than this for Rothko as well as Mondrian) has disappointed us, and there is a general understanding, I think, that artistic grandeur is not worth the terrible human cost required to attain it. It would be a shame, however, to let our present cynicism be retroactive, denigrating the great work created in the last tide of faith. Rothko lacked the wisdom of the 1980s, which is that to believe in anything these days is messy and dangerous — and that does give us an edge on him.
>
> Quoted in Suzi Gablik, *Has Modernism Failed?*

SUMMARY

Like the culture that gives it meaning, the art of the twentieth century is the focus of considerable debate and will continue to be so for the foreseeable future. Perhaps it is the current lack of historical distance that makes any process of evaluation treacherous, but it also suggests that the revolutionary attitudes inherent in the idea of Modernism are perhaps still current.

Within the sixty years that separate Cubism from Minimalism, Modernist art traveled its precarious path through two world wars, the Depression, the advent of nuclear bombs, and the Cold War. Its flat paintings and environmental sculptures, its embrace of nature, chance, and the unconscious, its paradoxical deification and suspicion of the machine, and its rejection of traditional standards of quality and values, all parallel the twentieth century's struggle for definition and meaning. If the underlying attitude that permeates the words and work of these artists now seems sadly out of date, perhaps it is because the viewer now lacks the necessary faith that artists can indeed bring about change; that they can not only reflect their world but actively participate in its creation. If cynicism prevails, it is our loss, and will certainly remain their strength.

Pronunciation Guide

Bauhaus **BOW**-hows
Umberto Boccioni   oom-**BER**-toh bah-**CHOH**-nee
Pierre Bonnard   pyer boh-**NAHR**
Georges Braque   zhorzh brahk
collage   koh-**LAHZH**
Helen Frankenthaler   **FRANG**-kuhn-**thaw**-lur
Sigmund Freud   **SIG**-muhnd froyd
Alberto Giacometti   al-**BER**-toh jah-kuh-**MET**-ee
Juan Gris   hwan grees
Carl Jung   yuung
Wassily Kandinsky   **VAS**-uh-lee kan-**DIN**-skee
Fernand Léger   fer-**NAN** lay-**ZHAY**
René Magritte   ruh-**NAY** mah-**GREET**
Joan Miró   mee-**ROH**
Meret Oppenheim   mer-**ET AH**-pen-**heye(m)**

Glossary

Abstract Expressionism (*page 435*) A common appelation for first-generation American abstract painting after the Second World War, due to the primacy of gesture and color while keeping consistent with the aims of formalism (the all-over application of paint and the dispersal of depth across the surface of the picture plane).

Bauhaus (*page 432*) Derived from the German "building house," it was a school of art and design developed under the guidance and aesthetic philosophy of the architect/designer Walter Gropius. Active in the 1920s and early 1930s, it attempted a collective vision of art making, in which the traditional subjective experience of the artist and the autonomy of the object were relinquished in favor of a more communal attitude to the problem of design. It put emphasis on pure, unornamented structures devoid of subjective or regional idiosyncrasies.

collage (*page 413*) Meaning "gluing," it is a method of applying extraneous material (and thus subject matter) to an art work. It has been used to reiterate objects and ideas from the real world, as well as to suggest history, nostalgia, and the build up of superficial material culture.

Constructivism (*page 429*) Founded in revolutionary Russia, the movement attempted to reconcile advanced Modernist aesthetics with the goals of Communism.

Cubism (*page 402*) The first art movement of the twentieth century systematically to reconsider the conventions of painting since the Renaissance. It was an attempt to represent fully and exhaustively on a flat surface all aspects of what the artist saw in three dimensions.

Dada (*page 416*) A radical art movement initiated in Zurich during the First World War as an affront to what it saw as the hypocrisy of conventional culture. Its exponents attempted to set new standards for art and art making by abandoning traditional picture making in favor of performance work and other non-traditional gestures. It also used chance as an important part of the art process, in the hopes of producing work free of the trappings of rational culture.

De Stijl (*page 431*) A Utopian collective founded in the Netherlands after World War I which prized the ethical potential of Modernist design and architecture. Among its most noted members were the architect Rietveldt and the painter Mondrian.

Futurism (*page 410*) A Modernist-anarchist association of predominantly Italian artists, who championed change and automation as liberating characteristics of a new age. The movement was to deteriorate after World War I.

International Style (*page 433*) A form of later Modern architecture based on modular design, an emphasis on steel and glass, and little or no embellishment. The style is best epitomized in the corporate skyscraper.

Minimalism (*page 444*) A painting and sculpture movement of the 1960s based on the primacy of the art object in its purest formal condition.

non-illusionistic painting (*page 434*) A term used to identify paintings that refers essentially to their physical and material character. Such work attempts to deny conventional pictorial constructs (such as perspective, chiaroscuro) for organizing space; hence its non-illusionism.

Suprematism (*page 428*) A one-man school founded by Russian Kazimir Malevich, it prized artistic autonomy and geometric purity as gateways to the metaphysical experience.

Surrealism (*page 419*) A literary and visual art movement interested in unleashing and exploring the potential of the human psyche. Loosely based on both Freud's and Jung's investigations into the mind, it is also direct heir to earlier Dada strategies of the unlocking of the unconscious by the use of chance.

Synchronicity (*page 421*) First articulated by psychoanalyst Carl Jung, it is the collision of elements not often associated with one another, that create a discord in rational understanding and thus precipitate unconscious activity. Surrealist artists were to mimic this principle in their work.

Suggested Reading

Chipp, H.B.: *Theories of Modern Art: A Source Book of and by Artists and Critics* (Berkeley: University of California Press, 1968). For those who want to read about what the artists and critics thought about their work and that of others.

Heard, George Hamilton: *Painting and Sculpture in Europe, 1880–1940* (Harmondsworth and New York: Penguin Books, 1981). A comprehensive and thorough introduction to twentieth-century art.

Lucie-Smith, Edward: *Late Modern: The Visual Arts since 1945* (Oxford, New York, and Toronto: Oxford University Press, 1980). Provides a closer look at post-war art.

Read, Herbert: *A Concise History of Modern Painting* and *A Concise History of Modern Sculpture* (both Oxford, New York, and Toronto: Oxford University Press, 1974). Popular single-volume introductions.

Rosenblum, Robert: *Cubism and Twentieth-Century Art* (Englewood Cliffs, NJ, and New York: Prentice Hall & Abrams, 1976). A fascinating read on the enormous influence of Cubism on future art.

Stangos, Nikos: *Concepts of Modern Art* (New York and London: Thames & Hudson, 1981). An informative and insightful look at post-war art.

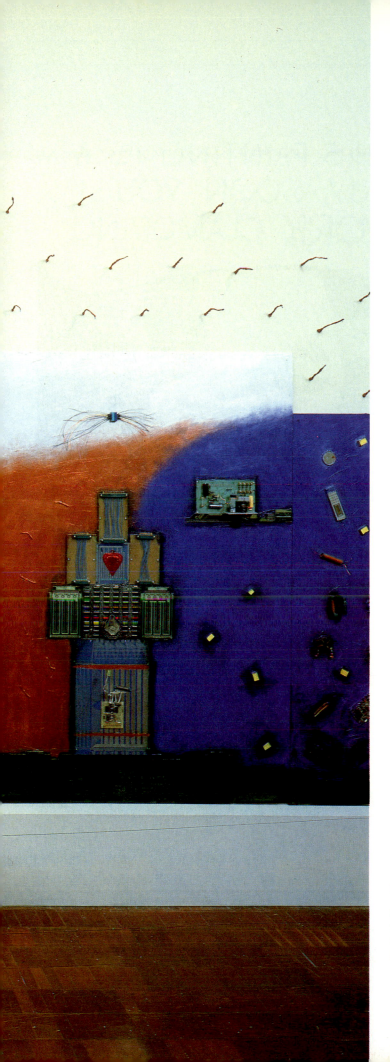

10

CONTEMPORARY ART, ISSUES, AND IDEAS

■ 10.1 Betye Saar
Mojotech (detail) 1988
Installation
24 ft 6 in x 6 ft 4 in (7.46 x 1.93 m)
From *The Migrations of Meaning* organized
by the INTAR Gallery, New York

■ 10.2 Roy Lichtenstein
Masterpiece 1962
Oil on canvas
4 ft 6 in x 4 ft 6 in (1.37 x 1.37 m)
Private Collection, New York
© Roy Lichtenstein/DACS 1996

PRELUDE: IRONY AND THE DECLINE OF THE MODERN

The real answer to the question of whether or not modernism has failed can only be given, in the end, by changing the basic dimensions in which we measure not only happiness and unhappiness in our society, but also success and failure.

SUZI GABLIK, *Has Modernism Failed?*
(New York and London: Thames & Hudson, 1984, p.128)

In 1962, the American artist Roy Lichtenstein painted *Masterpiece* (Fig. **10.2**), a work that functions both on the level of "serious" art and as a critique of that tradition. Derived from comic strip images and mimicking the commercial "ben day dot" printing configuration popular in cheap reproductions, the work seems to rejoice in its easy accessibility and popular appeal. It is about popular culture, art as a commodity, and the gulf between high and low art. It is also about the hypocrisy and failings of Modernist culture in the age of the media blitz. It has been fittingly called **Pop Art**.

This work is very different from the Pollocks and Rothkos of the previous chapter. It espouses few of the heroic standards of the previous generation of American painters, who invested their work with an enormous amount of personal and cultural significance (Fig. **10.3**). To the Abstract Expressionists, art had been about very specific things: autonomy, artistic will, the search for a universal or archetypal language, and a respect for the formal tradition and the physical realities of the materials, epitomized in the work of Jackson Pollock (Fig. **10.4** on page 455). This was quintessential Modernism, born of progress and sustained by will; it was also a myth that was beginning to show signs of terminal exhaustion by the late 1950s.

By the early 1960s, there were those (such as Frank Stella, James Turrell, and Donald Judd) who still embraced formal abstraction as a vital and necessary form of investigation, but even these artists recognized that the romantic rhetoric of the previous generation had outstripped the work (hence Stella's claim that he "wanted to paint something that no one could write about").

Despite their apparently radical nature, the works of Pollock, Newman, and Rothko were now firmly entrenched as part of "high American culture," showing in exclusive galleries and selling for considerable amounts of money. They were sanctioned by being placed alongside other "masterpieces" in important public museums, and their images now appeared on everything from postcards to backdrops for fashion advertisements. In short, the blood, sweat, and tears that had been so much a part of the Abstract Expressionist persona had proven itself to be no more radical or difficult to neutralize than any other form of culture; it simply became a precious object, invested with value and thus part of the larger mechanism of the marketplace.

■ **10.3 Ad Reinhardt**
The Rescue of Art
Cartoon published in Newsweek, 12 August, 1946

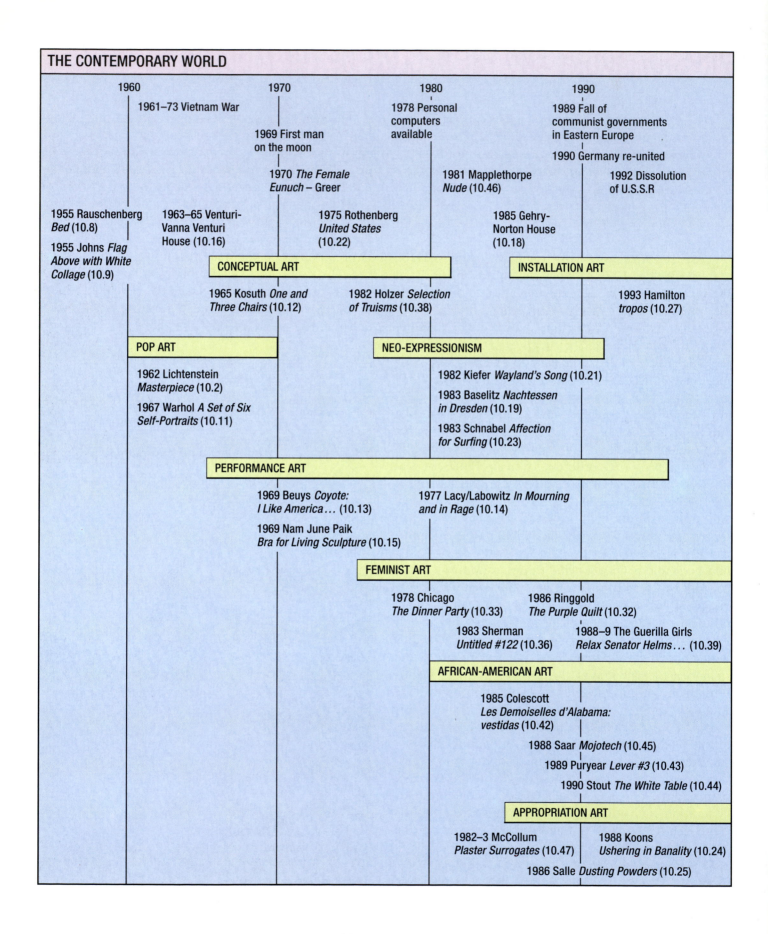

THE CONTEMPORARY WORLD

1960 — 1970 — 1980 — 1990

1961–73 Vietnam War

1969 First man on the moon

1978 Personal computers available

1989 Fall of communist governments in Eastern Europe

1990 Germany re-united

1970 *The Female Eunuch* – Greer

1981 Mapplethorpe *Nude* (10.46)

1992 Dissolution of U.S.S.R

1955 Rauschenberg *Bed* (10.8)

1955 Johns *Flag Above with White Collage* (10.9)

1963–65 Venturi-Vanna Venturi House (10.16)

1975 Rothenberg *United States* (10.22)

1985 Gehry-Norton House (10.18)

CONCEPTUAL ART

INSTALLATION ART

1965 Kosuth *One and Three Chairs* (10.12)

1982 Holzer *Selection of Truisms* (10.38)

1993 Hamilton *tropos* (10.27)

POP ART

NEO-EXPRESSIONISM

1962 Lichtenstein *Masterpiece* (10.2)

1967 Warhol *A Set of Six Self-Portraits* (10.11)

1982 Kiefer *Wayland's Song* (10.21)

1983 Baselitz *Nachtessen in Dresden* (10.19)

1983 Schnabel *Affection for Surfing* (10.23)

PERFORMANCE ART

1969 Beuys *Coyote: I Like America...* (10.13)

1969 Nam June Paik *Bra for Living Sculpture* (10.15)

1977 Lacy/Labowitz *In Mourning and in Rage* (10.14)

FEMINIST ART

1978 Chicago *The Dinner Party* (10.33)

1986 Ringgold *The Purple Quilt* (10.32)

1983 Sherman *Untitled #122* (10.36)

1988–9 The Guerilla Girls *Relax Senator Helms...* (10.39)

AFRICAN-AMERICAN ART

1985 Colescott *Les Demoiselles d'Alabama: vestidas* (10.42)

1988 Saar *Mojotech* (10.45)

1989 Puryear *Lever #3* (10.43)

1990 Stout *The White Table* (10.44)

APPROPRIATION ART

1982–3 McCollum *Plaster Surrogates* (10.47)

1988 Koons *Ushering in Banality* (10.24)

1986 Salle *Dusting Powders* (10.25)

■ 10.4 Jackson Pollock
Convergence 1952
Oil on canvas
8 ft x 13 ft (2.43 x 3.06 m)
Albright-Knox Art Gallery, Buffalo, New York
Gift of Seymour H. Knox, 1956

The Lesson of Duchamp

Early in the century, few members of the avant-garde challenged the accepted notion of art as a specifically sacred, romantic endeavor. Seeing art as a decidedly social construction and recognizing how seemingly arbitrary foundations of quality have often been, one particularly innovative and skeptical individual, Marcel Duchamp, used his art as a form of Modernist critique.

Duchamp (1887–1968) was trained as a painter and during the early 1910s produced a series of Futuro-Cubist paintings culminating in his *Nude Descending a Staircase* (Fig. **10.5**) of 1912.

● Shortly after this he began his breakthrough series of what he called "ready-mades" — objects in and of this world reassembled or recontextualized to alter their meaning. For example, his *Bicycle Wheel* (Fig. **10.6**), originally of 1913 and reproduced in a limited edition in 1951, consists of a bicycle wheel positioned upright on a simple stool. Both items are accepted as viable art materials by the artist without the typical alterations that might have made them appear more personal or idiosyncratic — more art-like. Instead, one is simply given an assemblage of parts, put together in an unorthodox manner.

As a consequence of its peculiarity, the *Bicycle Wheel* presents the viewer with a number of puzzling suggestions. Is it art? What constitutes the designation art? How does the context in which this piece functions (a gallery or other art space) change or affect its meaning? And to what extent are the subjective experience of the artist and his use of materials important parts of the idea of art? Such work

■   10.5 Marcel Duchamp
Nude Descending a Staircase No. 2
1912
Oil on canvas
58 x 35 in (147 x 89 cm)
Philadelphia Museum of Art
The Louise and Walter Arensberg
Collection. © DACS 1996

stretches the traditional boundaries of art by implicating the viewer in the process of the piece's construction and meaning. *Bicycle Wheel*, like other Duchamp ready-mades, asks serious questions about how the viewer comes to understand something, and how art is as much a matter of *context* as it is of *content*. Such simple items also suggest that the sacred aesthetic experience traditionally demanded of art can be expanded to embrace objects and ideas from every part of life. All that can be said for certain is that there are no clear answers to be had from these ready-

■ 10.6 Marcel Duchamp
Bicycle Wheel (3rd version after lost original of 1913)
Assemblage: metal wheel, 25¹/₂ in (64.8 cm) diameter, mounted on painted wood stool, 23³/₄ in (60.3 cm) high, overall, 50¹/₂ x 25¹/₂ x 16⁵/₈ in (128 x 64.8 x 42 cm)
The Museum of Modern Art, New York
The Sidney and Harriet Janis Collection. © DACS 1996

L.H.O.O.Q.

■ 10.7 Marcel Duchamp
La boite en valide (L.H.O.O.Q.) 1919
Rectified readymade, pencil on reproduction
7³/₄ x 4⁷/₈ in (19.7 x 12.2 cm)
Collection of Mrs. Mary Sisler
© DACS 1996

mades, only challenging, even disturbing questions — questions few in the early part of the century were willing to answer.

Though Duchamp was only loosely associated with Dada, his work shows certain underlying sympathies with Dadaist anger and aims. His *L.H.O.O.Q* (Fig. **10.7**) of 1919 is a deliciously nasty attack on high culture through one of its sanctioned icons, the *Mona Lisa* (the initials L.H.O.O.Q. pronounced together in French produce the phrase "She's got a hot ass," or "she has a willing ass"). The witty imposition of an almost childlike mustache and beard drawing not

■ 10.8 Robert Rauschenberg
Bed 1955
Mixed Media
74 x 31 in (188 x 78.7 cm)
Collection Leo Castelli Gallery, New York

only "defaces" the portrait but also suggests a rather floating sexuality in the subject. The idea of androgyny, fluctuating between defined social constructions, both sexually and culturally, was a recurring critical theme for Duchamp for the next decade, when he "gave up" art to concentrate on chess. However, in these pivotal works, he initiated a level of critical inquiry and skepticism that dramatically affected the idea of art making in the late twentieth century.

Rauschenberg and Johns

During the heights of 1950s abstraction in New York, there emerged two young artists of Duchampian temperament who with cold detachment began to reconsider the uneasy relationship between high and low or popular art so mocked by Clement Greenberg. Their work forms an important bridge between the lofty heights of Abstract Expressionism and the later cynicism and hypercriticality of Pop Art. Their names are Robert Rauschenberg (b. 1925) and Jasper Johns (b. 1930).

Rauschenberg's *Bed* (Fig. **10.8**) of 1955 was one of a series of works done on/with found materials, collected from around the artist's neighborhood. Upon first glance, it is difficult not to view the painting in the light of Abstract Expressionist ideals: the application of paint seems satisfyingly akin to the meaty gestures of a De Kooning, dripping freely and mimicking the experience of the artist's hand. Indeed, most of the attributes of American Abstract painting seem at least suggested within the context of this work; the only problem is that all this so-called "high art" activity is taking place on an old quilted cover and pillow. It is here that Rauschenberg made his decisive break from that tradition. The conventions of abstract painting are placed within the context of the discarded object, a strategy that elevates the mundane or the everyday while simultaneously questioning the assumed sacredness of the art object.

This process is called "recontextualization" in that it reconstitutes certain images or devices outside their traditional frame of reference. Take, for instance, the bed: it is as if the artist has taken an element understood as both functional and oriented on the horizontal (we see the bedspread on a bed, we lie under it) and, by turning it upon the vertical and divorcing it from its original function, made it appear new and strange. In doing so, commercial, discarded material culture is elevated to high art, and conversely the high-art conventions of Abstract Expressionism appear as little more than crude encrustations on its surface. The result is work that seems to waver between an outright criticism of Abstract Expressionism and an embrace of such a conventional language.

Jasper Johns' *Flag Above with White Collage* (Fig. **10.9**), also of 1955, shows a similar cool ambivalence toward the recent history of painting from which it emerges. Johns' use of the flag motif is at once a brilliant, witty play on "Greenbergian" formalism (painting referring first and foremost to its physical and material characteristics). Applied in encaustic (a technique of painting with pigment suspended in molten wax, which creates a translucent, slightly matt surface), perhaps the most vivid and universally understood symbol of American national *identity* (read culture) is rendered flat, neutered, recontextualized, and formally correct. It is at once the height of formal abstraction and the dissolving of such high principles into mainstream, digestible culture. Flags are graphic, meant to be perceived quickly and understood within the context of a host of historical and social messages. High art, on the other hand, is about looking slowly, about craft, elevated subject matter, and whatever else might be invested in the work. Art is *supposed* to take time, rise above pop culture, be "significant." Here, that slippery relationship has been brought to a finely honed edge, as the commercial and the precious slowly collapse into one fitting embodiment of the times.

The Pop Sensibility: Lichtenstein and Warhol

By the year 1960, art had found itself being challenged for the public's visual attention, engaged in a fight it could not possibly win. Televisions were now commonplace, and billboards and neon littered the cityscape. Indeed, the whole visual environment of the Western world had become a hyper-intense, synthetic experience of endless perceptual stimulation — a situation that dwarfed even the heroic scale and vivid palette of Abstract Expressionism. Furthermore, there was a general feeling among most of the younger members of the avant-garde that Modernism had failed in its attempts to elevate consciousness and provide a radical, progressive role model for the larger community. No doubt art and art making had mimicked the upheavals of Western culture credibly and effectively, yet through it all, avant-garde art had not been able to effect change outside the boundaries of its own discourse.

Perhaps the most disheartening aspect of the whole Modernist era (particularly for the generation of artists that arose out of the shadow of heroic American abstract painting) was the absolute lack of reasonable alternatives afforded to them for positive change and innovation after drip painting and color fields. Thus, while the Minimalists were taking formalist art to its logical conclusion, there appeared on the scene a group of young, disenchanted artists who began openly to criticize the rhetoric and failings of the Modernist view. By embracing the mundane and the commercial and dismissing the heroic and the masterpiece, they came to be called Pop Artists.

Masterpiece (see Fig. 10.2) by Roy Lichtenstein (b. 1923) is a good example of what such a critique looks

■ **10.9** Jasper Johns, *Flag Above with White Collage* 1955
Encaustic with collage
22½ x 19¼ in (57.1 x 48.9 cm)
Loan, Oeffentliche Kunstsammlung Basel, Kunstmuseum
© Jasper Johns/DACS, London/VAGA, NY 1996

like as an art image. In terms of its formal makeup, it adheres to many of the tenets of Modernist painting: the flatness of the plane is asserted by the use of uniform black borders, it engages large areas of undifferentiated color, and in a delightful bit of tongue-in-cheek, it is even overtly self-referential (since the internal dialogue revolves around the issue of painting). What is missing is equally important here: material is applied in a generic, non-specific manner rather than as an assortment of grand, juicy, autobiographic gestures; the subject matter is not heroic or elevated but blatantly òvert, accessible, and crassly focused on the marketplace; and the rendering is not subjective but follows very specific commercial conventions for imaging figures in space. In short, Lichtenstein removed virtually every last vestige of the subjective, heroic condition of art making that had been implicit in Modernist culture since Manet.

Again, the discussion comes back to the issue of form and content, as Lichtenstein has been very careful to maintain certain painting conventions in order to criticize others. For instance, despite the numerous radical changes from earlier images taking place in the painting, this work still adheres to traditional oil on canvas construction — historically the materials of Western painting. This way, the work opens itself up to a more fruitful and obvious dialogue with the tradition from which it emerges. Even the square format suggests artists such as Mondrian, who elevated the shape to a status of almost religious significance. It is this tradition that Lichtenstein hopes to comment upon, and by suggesting some affinity to it through this limited shared visual language, the work functions as a witty, critical evaluation of the state of art making after the likes of Jackson Pollock (Fig. **10.10**).

Lichtenstein has continued to maintain a formal dialogue with Modernist art, reworking such images as Monet's cathedral and haystack series, and even Picasso's Cubist works through the arbitrating and neutralizing filter of the "ben day dot" configuration. Other Pop Artists have been less concerned with such critical directions, relying instead on exercising the Pop "sensibility" to its extreme. Of these, no artist so fully embodied Pop Art as Andy Warhol (1930–87).

Warhol's mechanized lifestyle and constant flirtation with the social élite made him the very personification of the Pop attributes of alienation, commodity fetish, fashion, and the neutralized individual. He once said, "I want to become a machine," and by mimicking the reproductive characteristics of the marketplace, he became a living parody of the Modernist dream.

■ 10.10 Roy Lichtenstein
Big Painting Number Six 1965
Oil on canvas
Collection of Robert Scull, New York
© Roy Lichtenstein/DACS 1996

Like Lichtenstein, Warhol used commercial art processes as a means of paralleling artistic and mass-reproductive methods. His use of silk screening (a printing technique usually associated with cheap mechanical reproductions) on a traditional canvas ground is an immediate affront to the great subjective gestures of abstract painting: **screen printing** is absolutely flat, consistent, and generic, and in this way it both reasserts the flatness of the plane and simultaneously destroys the notion of the artist's hand as a significant part of the work.

Warhol's *Set of Six Self-Portraits* (Fig. **10.11**) of 1967 is indicative of his approach to image making: flat applications of highly saturated color, repeated in series as if to suggest endless mechanical reproduction. Gone is the notion of a singular, precious creation; instead, Warhol grants the viewer mechanical ghosts, desensitized images not once, or even twice, but three times removed from true experience — mimicking the leveling effect of the mass media on one's perception of the world. Warhol even went so far as to have many of his works produced in factory-like environments, denying himself any contact with the finished product. Even the traditional notion of the artist's signature was reconsidered in terms of sterile mechanization: instead of signing his name on the back of the paintings, as was tradition, he often used a rubber stamp. In this way, he rejoiced in the demystification of what was once a sacred, highly personal experience. In Warhol the artist as hero turns unapologetically into the cult of personality.

ART AFTER POP: SOME CONSIDERATIONS

In the work of Lichtenstein and Warhol, it is possible to see the beginnings of a **Postmodern** sensibility. By breaking down the boundaries between high and low art and criticizing the artistic persona and myth of the sacred object, they were in essence calling into question the continued viability of the Modernist movement. In the eyes of many Pop artists, Modernism (as a method of looking at the world) was collapsing under the weight of commercialism and pluralism. In short, Modernism was no longer capable of producing meaningful representations of the contemporary world.

There is certainly no shortage of theories that attempt to explain the phenomenon of Postmodernism, which is perhaps another way of saying that no one is a hundred percent sure what it means — other than by defining it as the art of the period "after Modernism." Postmodernism implies a new historical period — a new way of thinking about the world, not simply a change in artistic direction.

Some cultural theorists explain the move away from Modernism in terms of a *paradigm shift*, a fundamental change in the way in which one looks at the world. Most people would agree that the West's unbridled enthusiasm for progress and innovation at any cost has been tempered since c. 1980, and few would be so presumptuous as to claim that humanity is any more moral or socially responsible for having pursued this course. However, this is only a part of the complex dynamic; issues of race, gender, and the politics of inclusivity, ideas that were rarely a part of the Modernist view of the world (since the Modernists were supposedly involved with something far grander than politics), have become significant features of today's cultural landscape. Clearly, Modernism had a difficult time addressing these important cultural ideas in a straightforward manner, opting instead for a kind of "social message through association" ethic. Being avant-garde supposedly *implied* a kind of moral posturing, and thus abstract painting, many argued, did (in a roundabout way) carry a social message.

Pop Art demonstrates a particularly cynical side of the emerging Postmodernist argument: the representation of a world of ruthless commodity fetishism, in which a desensitized, glassy-eyed public is fed brightly packaged nonsense. It is a world of alienation and value-relativism, a period of endless titillation and a society of countless victims. In this environment, the aesthetics of mass production and banality often seem to take precedence over issues of personal conviction and self-imposed struggle. Thus Pop Art can be understood as both a representation and a searing critique of contemporary society.

Expanding the Field: Conceptual Art

The end of Modernism is difficult to pinpoint; indeed, there are those who believe that there is still much to gain by continuing the artistic legacy and that it is far from exhausted. Nevertheless, during the 1960s and 1970s, more and more artists challenged the status quo by moving their creative activities in directions outside the traditional constraints of both media (painting and sculpture) and venue (the gallery). The result was the rise of **Conceptualism**, which had a massive effect on later art.

Conceptual art prized the creative impulse over the construction of the object, and in this way it is reminiscent (at least in spirit) of Plato and his view of the crassness of the material world. Conceptual art elevates the idea above the object, considering the thought process the pure embodiment of art. Sol Lewitt (b. 1928), an early exponent of Conceptual art, explained the premise as follows: "In Conceptual art the Idea or concept is the most important aspect of the work...all planning and decision are made beforehand and their execution is a perfunctory affair. The idea becomes the machine that makes the art."

An example of this method is Lewitt's *Ten Thousand Lines About 10 Inches (25 cm) Long, Covering a Wall Evenly*, a work that exists as an idea only. If you were interested in "buying" the piece, you would receive only a certificate enabling you to hire a draftsman to execute the work on a wall of your choice. The art can also be dismantled at will — simply by painting on top of it (or it could be stored by slipping it in a file folder!). In the Conceptualist's mind, it is the idea that is the fundamental component; hence the actual execution, which might change from locale to locale, poses little risk to the integrity of the art.

■ 10.12 Joseph Kosuth, *One and Three Chairs* 1965
Wooden folding chair, height 32⅜ in (82.3 cm)
Photograph of chair, 36 x 24 in (91.4 x 61 cm)
Photographic enlargement of dictionary definition of chair, 24 x 25 in (61 x 63.5 cm)
Collection, The Museum of Modern Art, New York. Larry Aldrich Foundation Fund

This might seem like a pointless exercise, but implicit in Conceptual musings is both a critique of the *production of commodities* so much a part of Modern art, and an elevation of thought over action, or idea over process.

Despite the many variations that have occurred in painting and sculpture over the years, one thing has remained constant: they exist as objects, and objects can be bought and sold. Further, since art is understood as a looking-glass into the human condition, people *value* it. This, for better or worse, makes much of what is considered art a commodity, which can be purchased and exchanged in the marketplace. Even the most difficult and revolutionary of Modern works possess this material nature, which means that, despite all the avant-garde claims to the contrary, Modern art is still intimately tied to the marketplace.

Modern art's awkward (and often hypocritical) relationship to the material and consumer forces of the world was particularly disconcerting for many of the young artists coming to maturity after Abstract Expressionism. Conceptual art can thus be seen as an attempt to break free from the production of such cultural commodities, in the hopes of producing a purer art — an art with the kind of integrity Modernism had once espoused. Yet the Conceptualists proved themselves no less immune to the pressures of the marketplace and the gallery system than other artists. Lewitt's *Ten Thousand Lines*, for instance, has apparently changed hands for the tidy sum of $30,000, proving that even ideas can be packaged into commodities.

Conceptual art was by no means limited to investigations of creative process: many artists began to examine the system in which one may come to understand the world — namely the relationship between language and art. A good example of this kind of visual critique is *One and Three Chairs* (Fig. **10.12**) of 1965 by Joseph Kosuth (b. 1945) which serves as a kind of linguistic meditation on the nature of reality. The work consists of a folding chair, situated between a photograph of the object and an enlarged dictionary definition. Both the image and the definition are what linguists refer to as *signifiers*; that is, they express the idea or *signified* of the chair. Together, signifier and signified complete a *sign*, which refers to the actual object resting on the floor — namely the chair, which linguists call the *referent*. The general theory that supports this concept is called semiotics, and its application in areas such as art is usually referred to as **Structuralism**. Yet both definition and photograph are likewise objects in their own right, referring not only to the chair but to photography and the written English language as well. In other words, they stand as expressions of the chair and not the chair (hence the enigmatic title *One and Three Chairs*). Thus Kosuth's work effectively draws the viewer's attention to the slippery linguistic operations implicit in an image, calling into question how accurate any representation really is when its language structure operates according to its own rules.

Performance and Video Art

As the previous discussion of Conceptualism points out, by the mid 1960s many artists were seeking alternative strategies for the production of art. Both Pop Art and Minimalism contributed to this migration, first by collapsing the traditional boundaries between high and low art and by calling into question the art community's reliance on the commercial marketplace. There were, of course, precedents for this kind of critique. The theatrical gestures of the Dada period bore witness to a dramatic reevaluation of the codes and conventions of artistic practice, and Dada set an important precedent for the rise of **Performance art** in the 1960s and 1970s. Like its predecessor, Performance art was both an attempt to collapse boundaries between artistic disciplines and a method of circumventing the easy commodification of the art object (by producing no object at all). Yet it is also the logical extension of late Modernism in its emphasis on the artistic *gesture* and the primacy of the *act* over the physical result. In this way, Performance art, despite its myriad of interpretations, embodies a very Modern kind of cultural space.

During the heights of Pop Art, several artists experimented with making art in "real time." These performances, called *Happenings*, grew out of the intimate confines of the artists' studios and were seen as a logical extension of the explorations many of the partici-

pants were engaged in with their pictorial work. One way of understanding the often chaotic structure of these Happenings is to consider the collage sensibility of Pop Art applied to movement, sound, and costume. A good example of the frenetic quality of these performances is the *Car Crash* of 1960 by Jim Dine (b. 1935) in which he attempted subjectively to reconstruct the sensation of an actual crash. Instead of a plot-line and a logical narrative sequence, the audience/viewer is confronted with a collage of sights, smells, gestures and sounds, mimicking the way in which one experiences a work of art, rather than presenting events as they might appear in conventional theater.

If influence is indeed the test of an individual's artistic importance, clearly the Performance artist/shaman/activist Joseph Beuys (d. 1986) was one of the seminal figures of late twentieth-century art. Like that of his contemporary Andy Warhol, Beuys' persona, developed and groomed over several years and by way of provocative gestures, was an integral part of his art.

According to legend (as the facts seem somewhat dubious), Beuys, as a young German fighter pilot, was shot down over the frozen Crimea during the Second World War. Dragging himself from the burning wreckage, he fell unconscious, left to freeze in brutal winter conditions. Thanks to a band of wandering Tartars, he was saved by being wrapped in insulating layers of felt and animal fat, which protected him from the hostile environment. These rudimentary elements, namely fat and felt, were to become Beuys' symbolic materials through his life, and his work in Performance and **Installation art** addressed issues of healing in both a personal and collective manner.

One of Beuys' most famous Performance pieces was *Coyote: I Like America and America Likes Me* (Fig. **10.13**) of 1969. The "exhibition" was his first trip to America, and he incorporated the experience into the performance by using a gallery as an arena for cultural acclimatization. The performance involved his being whisked from the plane and delivered directly to the gallery, where he spent three weeks living with a wild coyote (symbolic of America), with only a cane and a felt blanket to protect and comfort himself. The performance thus became an exercise in trust, symbolic of old world meeting new and the potential for mutual harmony — in short the kind of interaction one would normally associate with shamanistic practices. Further, it was taking place in *historical time*

■ 10.13 Joseph Beuys
Coyote: I Like America and America Likes Me 1969
Performance at the Rene Block Gallery, New York
Copyright 1974 Caroline Tisdall
Courtesy Ronald Feldman Fine Arts, New York

■ 10.14 Suzanne Lacy and Leslie Labowitz
In Mourning and in Rage 1977
Photograph of performance
Photo: Susan R. Mogal

(meaning in the present or experiential time as opposed to theatrical time), which suggests a kind of experience different from that of theater. It is, in short, an extension of the traditional working of visual art without the objects, or, as some have put it, the objectification of the artist.

Performance art also lends itself to collaborative efforts. *In Mourning and in Rage* (Fig. **10.14**) performed in 1977 by Suzanne Lacy (b. 1945) and Leslie Labowitz (b. 1946) was an examination and protest of media and violence that points to the political advantages afforded by a medium not bound to the gallery space. The performance, which took place outside Los Angeles City Hall, was meant to call attention to the sensational media coverage of the Hillside Strangler murders. It was also the first of many collaborations between Lacy and Labowitz (who studied under Beuys), and it underscores the potential of Performance art as a tool for social critique. It comes as little surprise that the most interesting and thought-provoking work being done in this area today is by feminist and minority artists.

■ 10.15 Nam June Paik
Photograph from performance of *Bra for Living Sculpture* 1969
Copyright Peter Moore, collection Charlotte Moorman

The conventional line between theater and the visual arts was not the only one to be blurred during the period: with the advances in technology through the 1960s, video became a potent vehicle for artistic expression. Perhaps the most noted of the early practitioners in video is the Korean-American Nam June Paik (b. 1932), whose work includes video monitors in connection with installation work. In his video work, the typical television-style narrative sequencing is often subverted, replaced by information in a manner that mimics the visual strategies employed in the viewing of a traditional work of art. In works such as *Bra for Living Sculpture* (Fig. **10.15**) of 1969, monitors mounted on the cellist Charlotte Moorman were wired to respond to the musical vibrations of the cello strings. When the musican played, the images quivered and/or changed, creating a series of jarring juxtapositions in the minds of viewers — the public sphere (broadcast media) is forced to collide with the private experience (the body), implicit sensuality (the isolation of the breasts) is offset by explicit banality (the monitor images), etc. In this way, Paik's installations offer up for contemplation the complex role of technology in how one "sees" the world, embracing video for its obvious creative advantages, while remaining quick to expose its manipulative character.

Predictably, the line between video and performance has itself become blurred in recent years. The work of Laurie Anderson (b. 1942), whose performances include video and music, is a good example of the creative possibilities afforded by such an interdisciplinary mix. In her performances, slide projections, animation, synthesized keyboards, violin and voice, elaborate lighting, and costuming provide the conventional backdrop for an array of meditations on gender and power, personal and public.

There is also a decidedly populist side to Anderson's embrace of technology and the more accessible forms of artistic language (such as pop music, with which she scored a hit with *O Superman* in 1981). Anderson has often criticized the insularity of the American art world and supports the notion that popular media can provide an effective channel for artistic expression. Others argue (perhaps rightly) that the popular media, driven as they are by consumer interests, will only further co-opt the new and the inventive (i.e. contemporary art) for their own purposes — namely selling goods and supporting the status quo. Ironically, critics claim that, despite Anderson's earnest attempts to raise public consciousness through the popular media, she has in the process become a victim of this very phenomenon — her signature style has been co-opted by the "music video" industry. The transition is enough to make even the strong-stomached wince: here the challenging and evocative methods of Anderson are used to support the lyrics of Bon Jovi and the Beastie Boys, and the radical potential of the media is lost in a sea of nonsense.

THE RISE OF POSTMODERNISM

The New Architecture

Less is not more, less is a bore. ROBERT VENTURI

The term **Postmodernism** was first coined by the architectural critic Charles Jencks in relation to the rejection by certain architects of International Style architecture in the late 1970s. International Style architecture was supposedly the crowning achievement of Modernist building design, a perfect structural system based on the glass box. Its roots were in the Bauhaus, with which it shared a sympathy for clean, unornamented design. It was elegant, refined, proportionally considered; in fact, it was the architectural embodiment of formalist Modernism.

Yet the fact remains that, despite the many architectural achievements that came out of the International Style, it was dogmatically restrictive and, if public opinion is worth anything, was bordering on being anti-human in its boxlike sterility. One of the first concerted attacks on the "glass box" was made by the architect and theorist Robert Venturi (b. 1925) in his work *Complexity and Contradiction in Architecture* written in 1966. In it, he criticized the tired regularity of the International Style, while suggesting methods of enriching it by considering new and different architectural languages, including Pop Art, "Route 66" culture, and sixteenth-century Mannerism. What Venturi most embraced was the idea of an American architecture in touch with the realities of the age, namely pluralism and commercialism.

One of the earliest buildings by Venturi in keeping with the principles set out in his "gentle" manifesto was the Vanna Venturi House (Fig. **10.16**), which he built for his mother in 1963–5. Though nowhere near as radical in its dismissal of Modernist conventions as

■ **10.16 Robert Venturi**
Vanna Venturi House, Chestnut Hill, Pennsylvania, 1963–5

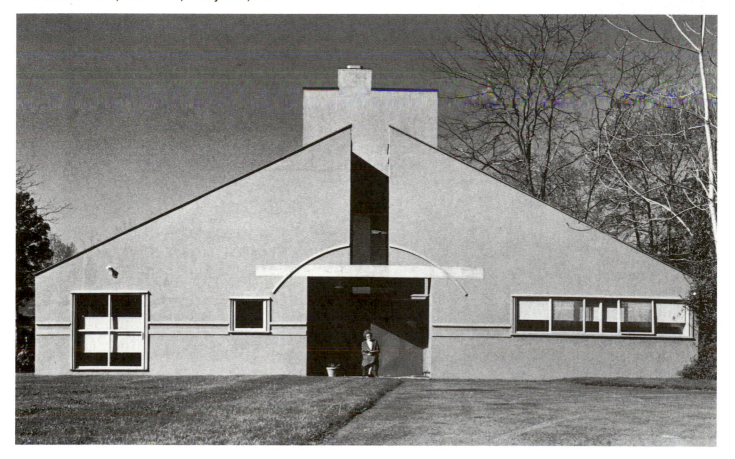

later works became, its quasi-International Style only accentuated the design's departure from established norms. The general impression, that of planar design with punched-out windows, is of Miesian Modernism. However, there are noticeable irregularities, made conspicuously present in the facade, which suggest a clear breaking away from the predictability of the International Style. One of the dynamics at work is an internal, architectural conversation about the idea of "house": the pitched roof and ribbon windows are clear references to the traditional housing unit, while the offset chimney, void entrance, broken arch, and pediment give it an air of eccentricity. The architectural critic Charles Jencks sees such obvious distortions in the conventional language of Miesian Modernism as clearly paralleling the strategies of Pop artists. He writes, "These distortions and amplifications were used by Venturi like the giant shifts in scale of the Pop artists. They made the house seem "too big" or "too small" depending on perspective, just as did the amplifications of Warhol and Oldenburg..."

■ 10.18 Frank O. Gehry & Associates
Norton House, Venice, California, 1985
© Tim Street-Porter/Esto

Here then is one architectural manifestation of the Postmodern sensibility: *the amplification and distortion of an established code*. But this was by no means the only theoretical position employed by architects anxious to rid themselves of the tyranny of the glass box: the *denial of innovation* and *appropriation of previous artistic mannerisms* also had a considerable impact on today's notion of architecture.

Mississauga City Hall (Fig. **10.17**) of 1982–6, designed by Edward Jones and Michael Kirkland, is an excellent example of the Postmodern sensibility applied to architecture. Gone is the glass and steel symmetry of the International Style, replaced with an assortment of building forms derived from various historical contexts. The architects have reconsidered the historical concept of the municipal building and have drawn at will from a variety of sources, such as medieval clock towers. This is indeed a form of historical pirating, as items, even building materials, have been reassembled outside their original context to produce a new architectural form.

Consider the re-emergence of brick and stone as building materials — items many had thought were

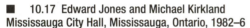

■ 10.17 Edward Jones and Michael Kirkland
Mississauga City Hall, Mississauga, Ontario, 1982–6

obsolete and nostalgic in the late twentieth century. This might say something about the issue of innovation and many an individual's desire to be free of such aesthetic constraint. For if virtually all options for innovation are exhausted, there remain only two possible avenues for an artist: one is to accept that what one creates is a recapitulation of or direct copy from past forms and styles; the other is simply to stop producing work.

This is not to say that the physical results of borrowing and collaging disparate entities is not of considerable interest; indeed, for some, the liveliness of current architecture is a breath of fresh air from the predictable, distilled forms of the International Style. A particularly witty and somewhat quirky example of the Postmodern aesthetic in domestic form is the Norton House (Fig. **10.18**) of 1985 by Frank Gehry. The house, which overlooks Venice Beach in California, is as eclectic and eccentric as the community itself. Of particular interest is Gehry's lively use of color tiles as a decorative device on the facade, an act of embellishment that would have found few friends among the International Stylists. Equally witty is the study, which is suspended in front of the house and connected by a ladder staircase — a form that mimics the lifeguard stands on the beach. It is the quintessential Postmodern beach house with just the right amount of individuality, and it points to an inventive use and recombination of architectural principles that are now the hallmark of the age.

NEO-EXPRESSIONISM AND THE RETURN OF THE FIGURE

We are unable to focus our attention on the present, as though we have become unable to, or incapable of, achieving aesthetic representations of our current experience.

FREDERIC JAMESON

The idea of innovation has not always been part of art making. For centuries, artists did quite well without feeling they needed to keep up with the relentless pace of the marketplace. In this regard, innovation, as a Modernist idea, has slowly given way over the past two decades to an endless assortment of historical allusions, as artists and architects alike become stylistic nomads, in search of a conventional language they can use in their work. This has led to an abundance of stylistic variations — many of which look remarkably like earlier art. Such is the case with the Neo-Expressionists.

Neo-Expressionism is, as the name implies, a reworking of the early twentieth-century Expressionist vocabulary. It aims at penetrating the human psyche with high-key, violent applications of paint that are often used in a semi-naturalistic, subjective manner. Take, for instance, *Nachtessen in Dresden* (Fig. **10.19**) of 1983, by the German artist Georg Baselitz (b. 1938). It is a massive oil painting of dislocated, inverted figures. This is about as far away from Minimalism as it is possible to get in its unapologetic embrace of what was once considered a spent or dead conventional language. The Italian artist Sandro Chia (b. 1946) also develops his images around a set of already established conventions, which in the case of his *Rabbit for Dinner* (Fig. **10.20**) of 1981 mimic the bright, excited color and emphasis on motion found in the work of the earlier Italian Futurists. Chia has been quoted as saying, "Today there are only mannerisms, and I am simply an historical nomad."

In the case of both the Italian "Transavant-gardia" and German Neo-Expressionists, a considerable amount of the pictorial allusion is derived from earlier, often overtly nationalistic sources. Sometimes, it is the very notion of history itself that comes under scrutiny. *Wayland's Song* (*Wolundlied*) (Fig. **10.21**) of 1982 by Anselm Kiefer (b. 1945) is part of the artist's ongoing re-evaluation of German consciousness after the Second World War. Born in 1945, the year the war ended, Kiefer has been obsessed with reclaiming a personal history from among the ruins and conspicuous silence of the previous generation.

Kiefer's "burnt landscapes" of straw and emulsion scattered on photographs are at once nostalgic and heroic. His use of lead, the material of alchemy (a "science" that attempted to turn lead and other base materials into gold), speaks of a distant rebirth and

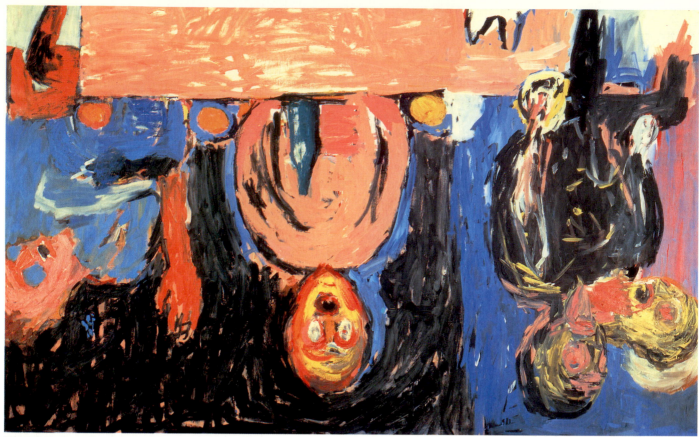

■ 10.19 Georg Baselitz, *Nachtessen in Dresden* 1983
Oil on canvas, 9 ft 2 in x 14 ft 9 in (2.8 x 4.5 m). Saatchi Collection, London

■ 10.20 Sandro Chia, *Rabbit for Dinner* 1981
Oil on canvas. Stedelijk Museum, Amsterdam

flight; the wing rises out of the landscape of history as a symbol of both hope and resurrection, while its lead construction speaks only of impotence and frustration. These are massive paintings, whose heroic scale only furthers the suggestion of a monument implicit within the subject matter. Often, the titles of Kiefer's paintings refer to specific German campaigns during the Second World War or to ancient German mythology. In this way, Kiefer has brought back nationalism and nostalgia to today's painting — ideas both enchanting and troubling. This reliance on visual sources that are at once aggressive, dominating, and sentimental has a darker side: of the major figures in German and Italian Neo-Expressionism, not one is a woman.

The return to the figure in North America has paralleled in many ways the work of the Europeans, but the wider variety of source material has meant that the appelation Neo-Expressionist does not fit well. Arising out of the Minimalist aesthetic, painters such as Susan Rothenberg (b. 1945) have attempted to re-engage imagery into the formal considerations of late abstraction. In Rothenberg's *United States* (Fig. **10.22**), the contour of the horse both acts as a line gesture, pushing one's eye to the edges of the canvas, and suggests a banner motif, simplifying the subject matter

■ 10.21 Anselm Kiefer, *Wayland's Song (Wolundlied)* 1982. Oil, emulsion, straw, photography (on projection paper) on canvas, with lead wing, 9 ft 2 in x 12 ft 6 in (2.8 x 3.8 m) Saatchi Collection, London

■ **10.22** Susan Rothenberg, *United States* 1975
Acrylic and tempera on canvas, 9 ft 6 in x 15 ft 9 in (2.89 x 4.8 m)
Saatchi Collection, London

into a schematic, intelligible whole. Other artists, such as Julian Schnabel (b. 1951), have countered the purity of Minimalism with a form of "Maximalism" or an "everything but the kitchen sink" mentality (Fig. **10.23**). Here, broken crockery, discarded wood, and Bondo all become the materials of high art; the few suggestions of imagery in the work evolve slowly in one's consciousness from a captivating variety of surface events. The implication of an archaeological site turned up on a wall is interesting here; the rich surfaces are as much topographical maps as they are illusionistic space, and in this way they are a fitting 1980s commentary on discarded and indeed discardable culture.

The Art of Appropriation

While some artists have reinvested the act of art making with meaning, others have followed the more critical path of the Pop artists. One practitioner of the

Duchamp-Warhol school of hypercriticality is Jeff Koons (b. 1955), whose *Ushering in Banality* (Fig. **10.24**) of 1988 posits an almost Warholian wavering between known and unknown, real and artificial, craft and kitsch. In this case, an overtly cute, Disneyland-type scene is recontextualized by the use of polychrome wood — the traditional material of medieval religious sculpture. The labor-intensive craft involved in such carving thus acts as a direct counter to the kitsch nature of the subject matter — the uneasy elevation of the crass to the status of high art. There is an undeniable sense of anxiety implicit in such work, as the viewer's equilibrium and sense of order, of good and bad, of right and wrong, is kept off balance. In this way, Koons' work mimics the confusing state of affairs that confronts the average person daily.

The paintings of David Salle (b. 1952) are yet another manifestation of this trend towards collapsing meaning/s in a work of art. Salle's *Dusting Powders*

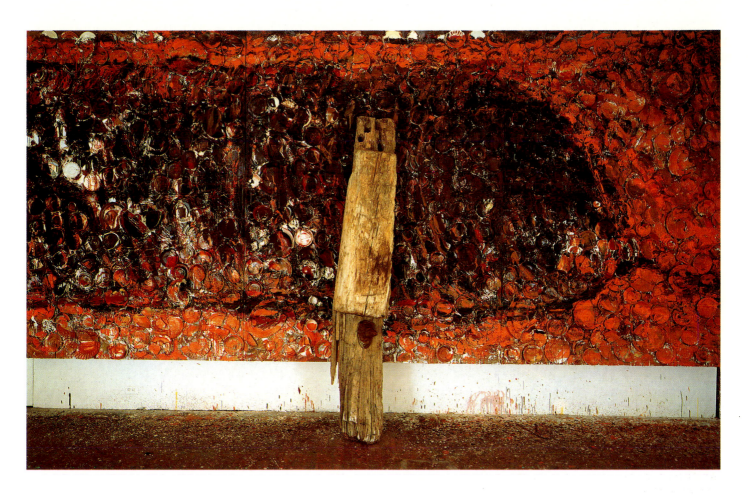

■ 10.23 Julian Schnabel
Affection for Surfing 1983
Oil, plates, wood, Bondo on wood
9 ft x 19 ft x 2 ft (2.77 x 5.8 x 0.61 m)
The Pace Gallery, New York

■ 10.24 Jeff Koons
Ushering in Banality 1988
Polychromed wood, edition of 3
3 ft 2 in x 5 ft 2 in x 2 ft 6 in
(0.9 x 1.57 x 0.76 m)
Sonnabend Gallery, New York

■ 10.25 David Salle, *Dusting Powders* 1986
Acrylic and oil on canvas with wooden chair fragments, 9 ft x 13 ft (2.74 x 3.96 m). Gerald S. Elliot Collection

(Fig. **10.25**) of 1986 is indicative of his pictorial strategy. Here elements with little or no material or symbolic relation are brought together in the same field of vision. For instance, an inventory of images that appear in the painting includes a repeated photo silkscreen of an African Bush tribe, a still from a pornographic film, schematic drawings of an outboard motorboat, an umbrella, a windmill, a quasi-representational portrait with superimposed Medusa hair, and finally for good measure bits of a broken wooden chair glued to the surface — in other words a series of disparate events that frustrate the viewer's ability to make sense or meaning from the collection. The same is true of Salle's rather libertine use of pictorial conventions. The painting's surface, once an arena for the subjective, expressive musings of the Modern artist (such as Jackson Pollock), is presented here as a

catalogue of styles — the photographic meets the schematic, and the illusionistic crashes into the material. The result is an assemblage of pictorial codes that contradict and neutralize each other's communicative power.

Perhaps what is most disconcerting about Salle's painting is his ability to neutralize the meanings inherent in his images. Though on the surface such a pictorial strategy may appear simply an extension of the earlier Surrealist use of juxtaposition (such as the paintings of Magritte), the results clearly could not be more different. Surrealism sought to invent and elevate meanings through unconscious triggers; Salle's work diminishes such connections to the point of almost extinguishing them. These are paintings that, to borrow from Shakespeare's *Macbeth*, are "full of sound and fury, signifying nothing."

Installation Art

One of the most exciting aspects of the art scene of the mid 1990s is the embrace of whole environments, even those outside the typical gallery or museum space, in the construction of works of art. The principle of *Installation art*, like that of Performance art, is both new and very old, as it has precedents in numerous activities through the history of Western culture. In theory, Installation art is that which builds a work around a specific site or critical position, rather than making autonomous objects that hang as individual entities on a wall. Given this rather loose definition, it is possible to see the work of a museum curator as that of an installation artist, since the selection of art, the exhibition's layout, its pedagogical aids, and its catalogue combine to produce a specific kind of artistic experience — one that the curator exploits in order to present his or her ideological position. Indeed, the interior of a cathedral is nothing if not an installation of objects, designed for that space and meant to support the theology of the day. Installation art's current popularity may owe something to a general distrust these days of making discrete objects (which easily enter into the marketplace), but it also provides the artist with unparalleled opportunities of combining a variety of media (painting, sculpture, video, performance) into a richly layered tapestry of meanings.

One of the most prolific and interesting installation artists is the American Bruce Nauman (b. 1941), whose work in both video and installation is some of the most potent, if disconcerting art produced in the late twentieth century. His *Hanging Carousel* (stainless steel version; Fig. **10.26**) of 1988 is one in a series of powerful installations he produced in the late 1980s and early 1990s — some of which utilized video as a fundamental component in the creation of his environments. Here a group of taxidermy mounts, frighteningly lifeless, neutered, and yet embryonic in appearance, revolves around a central pole. The effectiveness of this work lies not so much in its exposing of modern culture's crude desire for trophies and the barbaric spectacle of the hunt but the way in which Nauman has activated and agitated the gallery space. Photographs cannot adequately convey the masterful unease such a work implants in the viewer; there is something both captivating and horrible in the experiencing of disembodied carcases, which, hanging from their necks, spin endlessly.

■ **10.26** Bruce Nauman
Hanging Carousel (stainless steel version) 1988
Stainless steel, cast aluminum, polyurethane
18 ft (5.5 m) diameter
Leo Castelli Gallery, New York
© Bruce Nauman/ARS, NY and DACS, London 1996

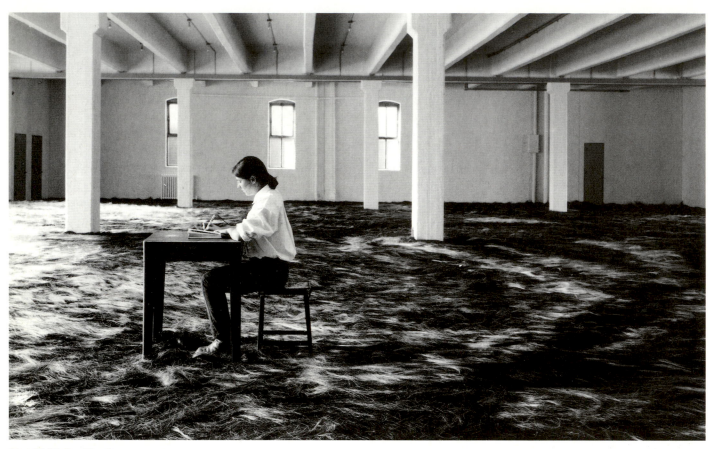

■ 10.27 Ann Hamilton
tropos October 7, 1993–June 19, 1994
Courtesy of Dia Center for the Arts

Ann Hamilton (b. 1956) also uses the installation format, yet her work focuses primarily on sensation, or, as some critics have put it, on presenting the unspeakable. She is quoted as saying: "The problem with language is that it is made out of words... Language is not an experience. You have to trust the things you can't name...you feel through your body, you take in the world through your skin." Hamilton's works are notoriously ambitious in both scale and scope, and often require the help and support of both volunteers and skilled craftspeople in their production. She is also known as a meticulous researcher, sensitive to materials and refreshingly non-dogmatic in her politics.

The result is works such as *tropos* (Fig. **10.27**) of 1993–4, installed at the Dia Center in New York. The installation, being primarily about sensation (the word *tropos* refers to a natural-born inclination, an innate tendency to react in a definite manner towards stimuli), is (predictably) difficult to describe. In the most simple terms, it is a 3,000 square foot (278.7m²) room, carpeted wall to wall with woven animal hair and lit only by diffused light from covered windows. In the middle of the room sits a spotlighted attendant at a metal desk, who silently burns text out of a book with a wood-burning tool. In the background there is an audiotape of barely discernible speech that floats in and out of the silence. The smell is that of burned paper and musty animal hair, and a light smoke drifts across the room. What does it mean? In considering Hamilton's work, perhaps this is the wrong question to ask. The work attempts to circumvent common-sense rationalizations by producing environments that are both hauntingly enigmatic and yet vaguely reminiscent. Smell, texture, sound, images, and their peculiar interrelationships all conjure memories, or dispositions toward the work that lie outside traditional methods of understanding them. In this way, Hamilton's installations have an air of mystery that is both captivating and entrancing.

WOMEN'S ART AND FEMINIST CRITICISM

Why has it been necessary to negate so large a part of the history of art, to dismiss so many artists, to denigrate so many works of art simply because the artists were women? What does this reveal about the structures and ideologies of art history...?

ROZSIKA PARKER and GRISELDA POLLOCK,
Old Mistresses: Women, Art, and Ideology
(New York: 1981, pp. 132–3)

A History Lesson

Artemisia Gentileschi's (1593–1652) *Judith and Maidservant with the Head of Holofernes* (Fig. **10.28**) of c. 1620–25 is one of the great examples of the Caravaggesque in Italian Baroque painting; its dramatic chiaroscuro and emotional content make it the stuff of

■ 10.28 **Artemesia Gentileschi**
Judith and Maidservant with the Head of Holofernes c. 1625
Oil on canvas, 6 ft ½ in x 4 ft 7¾ in (1.84 x 1.4 m)
© The Detroit Institute of Art. Gift of Leslie H. Green 1952

■ 10.29 Judith Leyster
The Gay Cavalier c. 1628–9
Oil on canvas, 35⅛ x 29 in (89.3 x 73.7 cm)
Philadelphia Museum of Art. The John G. Johnson Collection (J.440)

true Counter-Reformation spirit. Yet despite its considerable merit and technical proficiency, it owes its singular status in art history circles almost excusively to one important characteristic; it was painted by a woman.

It is rare indeed in art history books for the work of a woman to be compared favorably with that of a man. There are, of course, some exceptions: genre scenes by Judith Leyster (1609–90) in the Dutch Baroque (Fig. **10.29**), society portraits by Élisabeth Vigée-Lebrun (1755–1842; Fig. **10.30**), and the intimate Rococo stylings of Rosalba Carriera (1675–1757; Fig. **10.31**) have all achieved a degree of consideration in surveys of the period. However, the percentage of male to female artists in the history books is so outrageously high that one is left with three possible explanations; one, that there have been very few

■ 10.30 Élisabeth Vigée-Lebrun
Portrait of Marie-Gabrielle de Gramont, Duchesse de Caderousse 1784
Oil on oak panel, 41⅜ x 29⅞ in (105 x 76 cm)
The Nelson-Atkins Museum of Art, Kansas City, Missouri
Acquired through the generosity of Mrs. Rex L. Dively; Mary Barton
Stripp Kemper and Rufus Crosby Kemper, Jr. in memory of Mary Jane
Barton Stripp and Enid Jackson Kemper; The Nelson Gallery
Foundation; Mrs. Herbert O. Peet; Mrs. George Reuland through the
W.J. Bruce Charitable Trust; and the Estate of Helen F. Spencer, by
exchange (86–20)

like all matters of social and cultural significance, tied tightly to a complex set of problems.

The first possible justification — that, throughout history, there have simply been far fewer women producing art, and consequently there exist far fewer examples of works by women in prominent collections and museums — is certainly borne out by statistics, but the more important question is, why is this so? It appears that art making, like politics, medicine, philosophy, and jurisprudence, has historically been the domain of men, and since men set the standards for social behavior, it is not surprising that women found themselves playing a secondary role in valued cultural fields, such as the visual arts. This, of course, leads to the second hypothesis — the issue of quality: the work of women artists has been of inferior quality

■ 10.31 Rosalba Carriera
Louis XV as a Young Man 1721
Pastel on paper
18½ x 14 in (47 x 35.6 cm)
**Courtesy of Museum of Fine Arts, Boston
The Forsyth Wickes Collection**

women artists; two, that the work produced by women artists was of consistently poorer quality; or three, that the work produced by women artists fell outside the categories of high art. Each of these explanations has had an effect on the focus of recent feminist criticism, which has attempted to understand and evaluate this blatant discrepancy of numbers between male and female artists, and their speculations on the political nature of art making have shaken contemporary art and art history.

Where were all the women artists? There is no simple answer to this question, since gender issues are, and therefore lacks sufficient merit to be considered alongside the work of men. This is a most interesting proposition and, though flawed, it has been used repeatedly in art historical circles to ignore the contributions of women.

In order to produce work of quality, most artists, particularly those brought up in the age of the academies, spent a considerable amount of their training in a studio, studying everything from anatomy to color mixing and aesthetics. The result was generation after generation of artists schooled under the strict quality control of a governing body — a governing body that also had control over the admission of women to its program. Though one can be sure that many women possessed the skills to study at an academy, few were ever granted the opportunity.

Consider again Zoffany's portrait of members of the Royal Academy (see Fig. 6.9). Those women lucky enough to study at the Academy were constrained by the moral standards of the day — a morality that forbade women to look at a nude and thus to work in the life drawing studios. In this respect, the issue of quality, seemingly so important to some art historians, becomes shrouded in a number of gender attitudes commonplace at the time. If some of the women artists from the past produced works that seem less "convincing" than those of their male counterparts, it is perhaps because they were handicapped from the very outset — the system of art training never allowed women equal access to the study of art. This also makes the accomplishments of artists such as Angelica Kaufmann and Élisabeth Vigée-Lebrun that much more remarkable, bearing in mind the less than ideal social milieu in which they operated.

If women are no less inclined to create visual expressions than men and yet few examples of their output exist, perhaps it is the definition of art itself that needs reworking. If it is acknowledged that the arena of "high art" (sanctioned as such by men, of course) was limited to men, by looking at the so-called "domestic arts," one may consider a completely different set of artistic principles — ones governed almost exclusively by women. This path has been extremely fruitful for elevating the status of many historical women artists whose work necessarily falls outside traditional definitions of art. Items such as quilts, basketry, needlepoint, and clothing have all recently been the stuff of exhibitions of women's art in prominent museums. This reclamation of domestic crafts by women as mainstream "high art" was particularly popular during the 1970s and 1980s, as evidenced in the narrative, often politically motivated, quilts by Faith Ringgold (b. 1934; Fig. 10.32). This critical strategy has fittingly been labeled "inclusive," as it attempts to broaden the boundaries of "high art" to embrace the creative output of women artists who were not afforded the luxury of operating in the same artistic context as their male counterparts.

First-Generation Feminist Art and Criticism

Critical opinion about the role of women's art and feminist discourse often falls into two camps: first- and second-generation criticism. Roughly speaking, these strategies follow a logical progression from an inclusive view of art to that of re-examining the very foundations of the art historical canon.

Typical of so-called first-generation women artists is Judy Chicago (b. 1939), whose Dinner Party (Fig. 10.33) of 1978 possesses several characteristics popular in early feminist art: an embrace of traditional domestic arts such as stitching, weaving, and china painting, the use of the woman's body (in particular the genitalia, which act as the site of difference between women and men), and the use of famous and not-so-famous women from history as subject matter (Fig. 10.34). Such an installation celebrates the significance of women's culture and biological "difference" — a difference that makes women's art unique in both sensibility and production. As a huge collaborative enterprise (300 men and women worked five years to complete the piece), it also acts as a pointed critique of the age-old idea of the artist as solitary genius, embracing a more communal experience of art making — mimicking the social nature of traditional domestic arts such as quilting (see Fig. 10.32).

First-generation feminist art criticism shares many attitudes with the work of Ringgold and Chicago, including a more inclusive view of art and an interest in the role of the female body. Crucial to the reception of women's art in the 1970s were the works of the art historians Linda Nochlin and Ann Sutherland Harris (who in 1976 put together Women Artists 1550–1950, an exhibition and accompanying catalogue that brought to light the achievements of women artists through Western art history) and the critic Germaine Greer (whose Obstacle Race: The Fortune of Women

■ 10.32 Faith Ringgold
The Purple Quilt 1986
Acrylic on cotton, tie-dyed, printed and pieced fabric
7 ft 7 in x 6 ft (2.31 x 1.83 m)
Bernice Steinbaum Gallery, New York

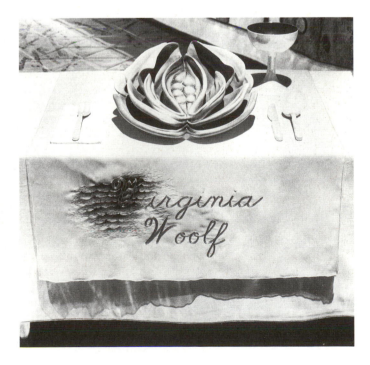

Painters and Their Work of 1979 espoused the contention that there were indeed "great" works of art produced by women), who attempted to open up the art historical canon, placing the work of men and women side by side.

There were, however, problems with such an approach from the very outset, since any attempt to include women's art in "mainstream" art history meant that women artists, who were not granted the same privileges as their male counterparts, were being evaluated on the same terms. To elevate the role and production of women artists through the ages, it was going to be necessary to reconsider the very structures of quality in art. This approach has proven itself fruitful not only for feminist critics but also for other under-represented groups, such as African-Americans and Third World artists, who have historically been excluded from consideration in art circles due to the incompatibility of their work with Western standards.

The Second Generation

Two of the most prominent exponents of second-generation feminist criticism have been Rozsika Parker and Griselda Pollock, whose 1981 *Old Mistresses: Women, Art, and Ideology* shows the subtle but all-important relationships that tie the production of art to a series of power and ideological issues — issues that determine the values of a community and consequently the notion of quality in art. By deconstructing the old model to expose its ingrained sexism, such vital research has forced many scholars and artists to rethink their traditional assumptions.

■ 10.36 Cindy Sherman
Untitled #122 1983
Color photograph, 34⅝ x 20⅝ in (87.9 x 52.3 cm)
Pamela and Arnold Lehman, Baltimore

■ 10.35 Cindy Sherman
Untitled #74 1980
Color photograph, 20 x 24 in (50.8 x 60.9 cm)
Iris and Ben Feldman, New York

■ 10.37 Barbara Kruger
Untitled ("We Won't Play Nature to Your Culture") 1984
Photograph, 6 ft x 4 ft (1.83 x 1.22 m)
Courtesy Mary Bodne Gallery, New York

Several women artists have taken up this approach, questioning the legitimacy of previous programs and searching for suitable representations. One of the more interesting contemporary artists dealing with issues of representation is Cindy Sherman (b. 1954), whose self-portraits such as *Untitled #74* (Fig. **10.35**) of 1980 and *Untitled #122* (Fig. **10.36**) of 1983 are disturbingly inviting images of media-induced "types." Using herself as both creator and subject, her suggestions of woman as a victim of characterization appear almost tragic; the hollowness of such facades speaks of the collapse of individuality into the oppressive desire to conform.

The work of Barbara Kruger (b. 1945), such as *Untitled ("We Won't Play Nature to Your Culture")* (Fig. **10.37**) of 1984, takes a more confrontational approach, utilizing the conventions of graphic design to provoke response in the viewer. Here issues of control and the oppression of a woman's body are represented with the same media-induced stylings that are traditionally used to "type" woman — the quick slogan and the digestible image both mimic the advertisement and aggressively confront the viewer (who is often suggested as either victim or villain).

The Conceptual artist Jenny Holzer (b. 1950) is another who uses the strategies of the mass media as a fundamental component in her work. In her *Selection of Truisms* (Fig. **10.38**) of 1982, Holzer presents a series of opinions as assertions, truncating and simplifying complex issues into an authoritative "big brother" voice and in the process mimicking the stylings of the advertising and political spinmasters. The flat and direct quality of their presentation is both disconcerting and effective; the "Truisms" are at once part of the media landscape while purposefully dislocated from its commercial aims.

Recent figures suggest that, though women artists make up a sizable proportion of the art community, there is still a considerable lack of women's art being shown in commercial galleries. Radical feminist art groups such as the Guerrilla Girls have attempted to expose such inadequacies through a series of events and advertising campaigns (Fig. **10.39**) designed to expose the continued omission of women from art circles. Such pressure tactics are launched not so much at the art historical canon, or even art making

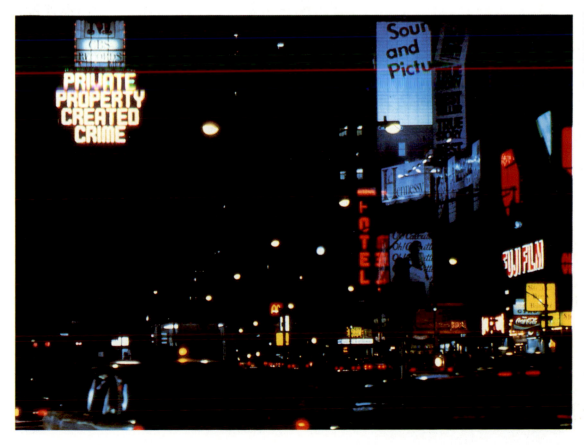

■ **10.38** Jenny Holzer Selection from *Truisms* Spectator Board, Times Square, New York, 1982. Courtesy Barbara Gladstone Gallery, New York

■ 10.39 The Guerrilla Girls, *Relax Senator Helms, The Art World is Your Kind of Place* 1988–9
Silk screen, 17½ x 22¼ in (44.5 x 56.5 cm)
Courtesy, The Guerrilla Girls

RELAX SENATOR HELMS, THE ART WORLD IS YOUR KIND OF PLACE!

- The number of blacks at an art opening is about the same as at one of your garden parties.
- Many museum trustees are at least as conservative as Ronald Lauder.
- Because aesthetic quality stands above all, there's never been a need for Affirmative Action in museums or galleries.
- Most art collectors, like most successful artists, are white males.
- Women artists have their place: after all, they earn less than 1/3 of what male artists earn.
- Museums are separate but equal. No female black painter or sculptor has been in a Whitney Biennial since 1973. Instead, they can show at the Studio Museum in Harlem or the Women's Museum in Washington.
- Since most women artists don't make a living from their work and there's no maternity leave or childcare in the art world, they rarely choose both career and motherhood.
- The sexual imagery in most respected works of art is the expression of wholesome heterosexual males.
- Unsullied by government interference, art is one of the last unregulated markets. Why, there isn't even any self-regulation!
- The majority of exposed penises in major museums belong to the Baby Jesus.

Please send $ and comments to: **GUERRILLA GIRLS** CONSCIENCE OF THE ART WORLD
532 LAGUARDIA PL. #237
NEW YORK, N.Y. 10012

for that matter, as at the institutions and galleries that inevitably make or break an artist's career. As part of a larger reorganization of institutions and attitudes, the sometimes controversial antics of the Guerrilla Girls have been pivotal in the current art debate.

Though still relatively young as critical movements go, feminist art and criticism have been essential in broadening the narrow parameters of art and exposing culture's unspoken relation to issues of gender and power. Their influence can be seen in the work of a variety of disenfranchised groups, and by the intelligence of their reasoning, they have become the anchors of a more inclusive, sensitive view of the role of creative activity in the community. Perhaps more than any other critical and social program of the late twentieth century, feminism has provided the most solid foundations for a new view of art, and one that will pave the way into the twenty-first century. At least in this regard, suspicions about art's being terminally exhausted seem to have been greatly exaggerated.

ETHNICITY AND REVISIONISM

The word quality is used as if it were synonymous with skin pigmentation and ancestry, but is stated publicly as signifying an unsullied and courageous color-blind standard.
    HOWARDENA PINDELL "Breaking of the Silence,"
    New Art Examiner, October 1990, p. 19

The term "**revisionism**" has come to reflect a strategy of correction: something in the past is deemed to have been wrongly perceived and that perception is to be reconsidered. As a community, we often "rethink" ideas in the hope that, by re-evaluating an apparent "truth" or traditional assumption, we might finally get it right. Since this phenomenon is part of basic human inquiry, it should come as little surprise to find many artists taking a hard look at the relative merits and inconsistencies of art history as it has been explained to them. Of course, the history of Western art is predominantly the history of white male Europeans, and consequently it has been those cast outside the "mainstream" who have found themselves most intimately linked to the notion of revisionism. By visually and critically evaluating the exclusive nature of assumptions about masterpieces and great artists, revisionist thinkers have begun an important process of broadening the boundaries of "art."

Art and Criticism in the African-American Community

Many African-American artists have attempted to merge Western pictorial conventions with issues of race and identity, though perhaps none better than Romare Bearden (d. 1988). His collages (Figs. **10.40** and **10.41**) embrace a flattened space and overall design reminiscent of Cubism, but they further accentuate the fragmentation and dislocation of a people — a collection of parts rather than a functional, organic,

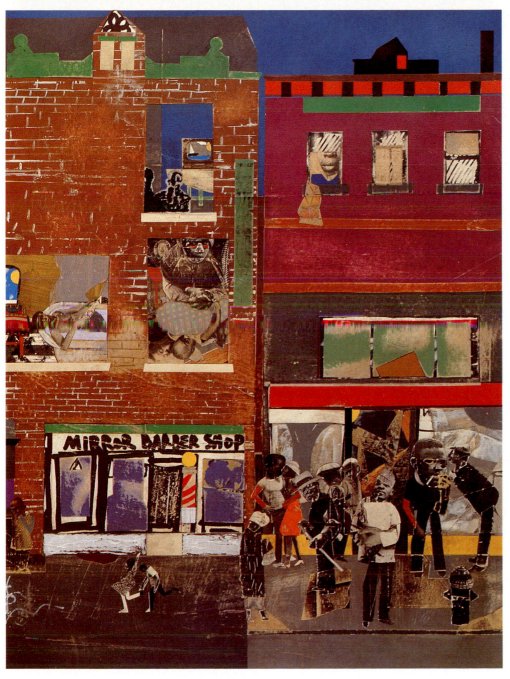

■ 10.40 Romare Bearden
The Block
Cut and pasted papers on masonite
Six panels
Overall 4 ft x 18 ft (1.22 x 5.49 m)
The Metropolitan Museum of Art,
New York
Gift of Mr. and Mrs. Samuel Shore, 1978
(1978.61.1–6)

■ 10.41 Detail showing Block #6
from *The Block*
4 ft x 3 ft (1.24 x 0.91 m)

■ 10.42 Robert Colescott
Les Demoiselles d'Alabama: vestidas 1985
Acrylic on canvas
8 ft x 7 ft 8 in (2.43 x 2.3 m)
Phyllis Kind Gallery, New York

▶ 10.43 Martin Puryear
Lever #3 1989
Ponderosa pine, painted
7 ft ½ in x 13 ft 6 in x 1 ft 1 in (2.15 x 4.1 x 0.33 m)
Courtesy of Margo Leavin Gallery, Los Angeles

and psychologically whole being. It is ironic to note that such "modern" conventions as flattened space were partly derived from African sources; here they resurface as a fitting representation of the ongoing struggle for identity and cultural wholeness in the black community.

Robert Colescott (b. 1925) is an African-American artist who has been at the forefront of a visual examination of the "canonized" Western pictorial tradition since the mid-1970s. His poignant and witty *Les Demoiselles d'Alabama* (Fig. **10.42**) of 1985 is typical of his visual strategy; here he quotes directly from Pablo Picasso's *Les Demoiselles d'Avignon* (see Fig. 7.54) of 1907 (a vital Modernist document), cleverly replacing the three central proto-Cubist figures with African-American women. The direct evocation of Picasso is important here, and the figures mimic almost exactly the poses of the originals, only now the once-discomforting objects of desire (Picasso's idea was for his painting to be a moralizing tale about brothels and sexually transmitted disease) are transformed into slightly raw, humorous caricatures of blacks and their attendant white counterparts. (Note how even the knife-like piece of still-life fruit in Picasso's image is rendered in the Colescott as watermelon — part of the traditional diet of the slave.) A multiplicity of ideas is generated by such a work, but perhaps the clearest of voices rises from one specific issue: the damning silence that traditionally followed discussions on the cultural significance granted to the African-American experience in art history. It is here, among the masterpieces of the Western tradition, that Colescott illuminates this undeniable absence; here, art is seen as embodying not only a host of higher ideals but also some implicit notions about race relations and stereotypes.

The notable absence of many groups from the art historical canon has paralleled a similar lack of status afforded such individuals in all aspects of society. Just as the feminist movement successfully launched a campaign of critical inquiry into the "cult of masterpieces," so other disenfranchised groups have also benefited from this form of critique, including African-Americans, Hispanic Americans, and indigenous Americans. The result has been the emergence of a brand of art and criticism often tied to issues of domination, identity, and cultural difference.

■ 10.44 Renée Stout
The White Table 1990
Mixed media
76½ x 60 x 14½ in (194 x 152.4 x 36.8 cm)
From *The Migrations of Meaning*, curated by Judithe McWillie and Inverna Lockpez, and organized by the INTAR Gallery, New York

As was pointed out in Chapter Eight, the African-American contribution to American art and culture has been both rich and varied, enveloping the craft traditions of the American South and the more pictorial and religious preoccupations of the Caribbean. Black artists such as Faith Ringgold (see page 480) have paid direct homage to such craft interests by mimicking many of the formal features of that tradition. The sculptor Martin Puryear (b. 1941; Fig. **10.43** on page 487) also evokes a rich material consciousness in his elegant, simple forms. His enthusiastic embracing of methods and techniques from the pre-industrial era speaks eloquently of the history of objects and images produced by those who had no access to the "miracle" of heavy machinery and technical innovations. Consequently, his work speaks of nurturing, of slow and methodical labor, and of a deeply felt sensitivity to materials — all elements of a visual tradition outside the increasingly progressive nature of Modern art. Indeed, one of the major criticisms launched at Puryear's work is its sometimes "excessive craftsmanship" — a quintessentially Modernist prejudice that fine craftsmanship in some way denies the piece a radical posture. In this manner, Puryear's merging of late Modernist formal sculpture with craft traditions that derive from as far back as the first slaves from Africa appears both quietly articulate and sincere.

There are likewise African-American artists currently producing work involving a reinterpretation of, and reinvestment in, traditional African-American aesthetics such as vodun. Renée Stout is one such artist. The *White Table* (Fig. **10.44**) represents her symbolic working out, in installation format, of the pain of learning of racial discrimination at the school in which she once worked. Her choice of elements, including a central doll figure and an assortment of highly personal fetish items, parallels the symbolic healing strategies of the vodun culture discussed in Chapter Eight. The concept of *nkisi* (black traditional healing) is never far from these works' source, and Stout's use of elemental substances such as menstrual blood (kept in a vial in the doll), sorrel buds (for health), and garlic, suggests a conscious attempt to reintroduce mysticism and healing, so central to this work and yet so foreign to much of Modern art, back into the fabric of artistic practice. Perhaps more importantly, the *White Table* is a reinvestment in those practices that are the source of a specifically African-

■ 10.45 Betye Saar, *Mojotech* 1988
Installation, 24 ft 6 in x 6 ft 4 in (7.46 x 1.93 m)
From *The Migrations of Meaning*, organized by the INTAR Gallery,
New York

American history and experience.

The work of the installation artist Betye Saar (b. 1926) parallels that of Renée Stout in its open embrace and celebration of the diverse artistic traditions that make up African-American visual culture in the 1990s. Her work combines elements from an eclectic array of sources, including Christian and African religious art, inner city popular culture, even garage sales, as a means of addressing the contemporary situation.

Saar's *Mojotech* (Fig. **10.45**) of 1988 has an aesthetic and symbolic outlook similar to that of African-American folk art traditions, which often place great spiritual significance in the *reanimating* of everyday objects. On the central low pedestal or altar form, Saar has carefully placed the interior workings of an old radio, which has been wrapped in animal fur. This collision of textures and types might at first suggest the visual strategies of Surrealism, but given its situation among other bits of urban detritus, the combination seems more mysterious than disjunctive. It is as if the circuits and electrical nature of the appliance are granted, through the artist's intervention, an animalistic vitality. Even the title *Mojotech* refers to this animating of world: *mojo* is a name often given to traditional vodun practices in the American South, while *tech* clearly refers to the technological age — in which humans are often kept at a safe distance from any meaningful personal or spiritual interaction. Given this dynamic, there is something liberating in viewing these works: they impart potentiality and presence rather than cynicism and irony — which seems to be the trademark of much of the "hot" art these days.

■ 10.46 Robert Mapplethorpe
Nude 1981
Gelatin-silver print, 20 x 16 in (51 x 41 cm)
Robert Miller Gallery, New York

SOME CLOSING THOUGHTS ON PUBLIC FUNDING AND CENSORSHIP

The public funding of art considered obscene or pornographic is an issue central to much of the right-wing media's hostility towards recent art. Since this book exists primarily because we, as a cultural community, have invested value in art as a fundamental human activity, worthy of not only individual but public support, it should come as no surprise that the following comments reflect a specific and heartfelt position. I make no apologies for this. Indeed, if the contents of this book have not convinced you of the essential value of art and artists — even difficult and controversial ones, I have failed.

Many readers may not be aware of the complexities involved in the exhibiting of art in today's galleries and museums. An active artist, interested in exhibiting his or her work in a public space, has a limited number of recognized venues available for such purposes: a commercial gallery, a non-profit space, a cooperative space, or a museum. Each exhibition environment has its good points, yet each presents a set of constraints that may or may not be in sympathy with those of the artist.

The commercial gallery space is highly prized by artists as a "reputation maker" and has the resources to promote work, but it often conforms to the tastes of that same marketplace. The result is that all but the most adventurous galleries stay clear of work that has the potential to offend its clientele. This presents few problems for an abstract painter, but it may prove costly for an artist who chooses to criticize that marketplace and those individuals who have most benefited from its competition. Such an artist may therefore choose instead to produce work for exhibition in a non-profit space, which exists through donations, foundation, and governmental grants. Such spaces are often showcases for younger artists, or for work that shows little commercial potential. Given the current artistic climate, which includes a considerable amount of installation, performance, and multi-media work, much of the most interesting work falls within this category of the "commercially dubious." Indeed, some of the most captivating artists working today stand at a suspicious distance from the marketplace, choosing instead to commit themselves to strategies that criticize today's value system. Non-profit spaces thus exist as one of the few viable exhibition environments for such artists — without such venues, their work would simply not be shown.

Museums operate on much the same principle, only at significantly higher stakes. As bastions of culture in the community, museums must walk a fine line between supporting the cultural legacy as it is understood (i.e. showing the Rembrandts and van Goghs that everyone loves) and challenging the public with work that comments upon the contemporary situation. Behind all this there is the issue of money: it takes a great deal of money to keep a museum's doors open, and even more to mount exhibitions. Where does this revenue come from? Admissions, donations, and grants — again usually from governmental agencies.

Here we can begin to anticipate a problem: public money, raised from people's taxes, is potentially available through granting agencies to fund exhibitions for which public sentiment may be weak. Indeed, in the case of the recent National Endowment for the Arts crisis concerning the photographic works of Robert Mapplethorpe (1946–89; Fig. **10.46**) and Andres Serrano, the issue threatened (and continues to threaten) everything from ballet to jazz, and installation art to opera. The argument, innocent enough on the surface but chilling in its repercussions, goes something like this: *taxpayers should not have to support art that openly defies public mores. If artists want to produce indecent work, let them do it with their own money, instead of mocking the very constituency that funds them.* Implicit within these remarks is a series of assumptions about art, morals, decency (and thus indecency), and the rights of the taxpayer that have huge ramifications not only for art making but for freedom and democracy.

Taxpayers should not have to support art: this suggests that the production and display of the arts is ornamental and not critical to society. Further, it suggests that those who enjoy the arts should pay for the pleasure, as we apparently do for everything else we enjoy. Implicit in this are two questionable assumptions: that the only function art provides is a kind of intellectual entertainment and that it is the domain of the rich. As this book has made clear, art is much more than entertainment — it is a culture's self-reflection, and sometimes the view is not pretty. Without available avenues for cultural self-reflection, a society is for all intents and purposes dehumanized, and history teaches all too well the horrors that often accompany such a flagrant dismissal of art as a tool in a culture's self-awareness. (Nazi Germany and Stalinist Russia attempted to thwart their culture's reflective potential.) If art is indeed a method used by the community to think about itself, the assertion that it is somehow ornamental, the plaything of the idle rich, is both absurd and dangerous.

...that openly defies public mores is likewise ridiculous and insidious in its simplicity. First, the term "public mores" suggests that we collectively believe the same things and operate with the same assumptions about life, despite the apparent plurality of opinions that seems to exist in a healthy democracy. This argument is central to the Mapplethorpe and Serrano debacle, since both artists' works were considered obscene — Mapplethorpe's homoerotic photographs called pornographic and Serrano's photograph of a crucifix submerged in urine blasphemous. The story is by now familiar: learning that the exhibitions were funded in part by the National Endowment for the Arts (a Federal funding agency), groups from the religious and political right began a vitriolic publicity campaign against both the art and the agency. It appears that it is not art per se that is at issue with these right-wing groups but art that either describes a lifestyle different from their own or criticizes their values (God forbid). The implication is that only art that openly embraces the values of the so-called status quo should be given the opportunity to be exhibited in public spaces. Again the ghosts of recent totalitarianism lurk just beneath the surface of this argument, as both Hitler and Stalin used such tactics as a way of controlling (silencing) dissident voices. Ironically, such a fear of art's ability to comment on and even sway the social agenda of the culture contradicts the earlier declaration that art is of secondary importance; it is a begrudging declaration of art's power and its essential contribution to human discourse.

Finally, *...let them* (artists and institutions) *do it with their own money, instead of mocking the very constituency that funds them.* Without adequate state support, institutions are put in the unenviable position of choosing between staging only high-priced "blockbuster" exhibitions that have profit potential or closing their doors to the public. *Unconstrained funding* (as opposed to constrained, such as corporate funding, which often supports only projects that are in sympathy with company philosophy) is then essential in keeping such institutions above the self-serving dictates of the powerbrokers and special-interest groups. Without this mechanism in place, artists and museums are at the mercy of a marketplace and a political arena that does not take kindly to those who criticize its values.

The United States government spends more taxpayers' money yearly on military marching bands than it does on the arts. The United States ranks an embarrassing *last* per capita in the industrialized world in public funding of the arts. During the thirty years of the National Endowment for the Arts only a handful of the thousands of artists' grants have ever been considered controversial. And finally, the ability not only to tolerate but to embrace dissent as a fundamental component of a democracy anchors the very notion of Western culture. These should not, and indeed cannot, be lost in the hyperbole that threatens the ability of the visual arts to make an active and continued contribution to society.

CONCLUSIONS

The current reexamination of the art historical canon and its hierarchy of quality has had dramatic repercussions on visual discourse; everything from art school curriculums to government funding and museum acquisitions has been in some way affected by this important and healthy debate. At the heart of such matters is the problematic relationship between taste and values, and further how those seemingly colorblind values suggest very specific and ongoing social and political constructions. This simple (and some would say even obvious) acknowledgment that cultural institutions have in the past reflected very specific biases on the basis of race or gender has had a liberating effect on the work and reception granted to disadvantaged individuals or communities. Yet the question remains: how do such groups, once tracked into the mainstream through such validating mechanisms as periodicals and major museum shows, retain their autonomy and legitimacy as a separate and distinct voice — particularly in a marketplace that values novelty over integrity?

■ 10.47 Allan McCollum
Plaster Surrogates 1982–3
Enamel on Solid-Cast Hydrostone
Installation: Marion Goodman Gallery, New York City, 1983

An interesting example of such a flattening capability, implicit within the very idea of an art marketplace, can clearly be seen in the increasing popularity of the Mexican artist Frida Kahlo (see Chapter Eight) — an artist whose lifetime's work had been all but forgotten until the late 1980s, when feminist scholars and historians saved her from virtual obscurity. Poignant and expressive in their search for a personal feminine identity in the male-dominated Mexican art world of the 1930s, Kahlo's paintings have recently taken on the trappings of feminist icons, and she has become something of a cult heroine. Yet once such an artist is deified, he or she can be conveniently commodified, and it was not long before Kahlo's works appeared on everything from album covers to T-shirts, and even pop stars such as Madonna began citing Kahlo as an inspiration. Though one may claim that such exposure is long overdue, the speedy transition of Kahlo from forgotten artist to cult heroine has destroyed much of the initial radical stance these works once embodied. If it is indeed the uncompromising content of such works that makes them at once arresting to a Western public, it is the market that ultimately neutralizes and trivializes the voices of

formerly neglected artists into something a little more digestible.

In the light of this discussion, one may ask how artists actually "beat the system." How do artists, posturing as radical voices, avoid almost certain complicity with a system bent on commodifying almost any gesture? One answer comes in the rather depressing and cynical guise of what some artists proclaim as a "hovering" or "rear-guard" (as opposed to avantgarde) strategy. *Plaster Surrogates* (Fig. **10.47**), a series of "pseudo-artifacts" that Allan McCollum constructed to look like painting, are in actuality nothing more than cheap, mass-produced plaster casts. His "orchestration of a charade" (his words) isolates this policy of giving the viewer everything and nothing, where close examination thwarts an original desire to look at these images. In this manner, such work hovers between anticipation and outright banality, paralleling the artificial nature of much visual experience. The work's apparently radical nature lies specifically in its ready acceptance of self-perpetuated boredom — and further, humanity's collective inability to distinguish truth from falsehood.

If hovering seems a pessimistic pictorial strategy,

it nonetheless has many subscribers, particularly amongst younger artists attempting to reconcile art with the traumas of today's world. However, one may question whether the current fashion of embracing banality and cynicism is indeed a fruitful strategy for the generation of art or simply a posture. Already the catchphrase of the 1990s seems to be "reenchantment," and 1980s irony is replaced by a desire for sincerity and collective action. Time will tell.

Suggested Reading

Many of the best sources for information on artists and art criticism in the contemporary world come by way of periodicals and exhibition catalogues. The following is a partial overview of influential and informative sources:

Periodicals:
Artforum (New York)
Art in America (New York)
Art Journal (New York)
C Magazine (Toronto)
Flash Art (Italy)
New Art Examiner (Chicago)
October (MIT Press)

Survey exhibitions of Contemporary Art with extensive catalogues:
Carnegie International (Pittsburgh)
Documenta (Kassel, Germany)
Whitney Biennial of American Art (New York)
Venice Biennale (Venice, Italy)
Sao Paulo Biennale (Sao Paulo, Brazil)

Pronunciation Guide

Georg Baselitz   gay-**ORK BAH**-zuh-**lits**
Joseph Beuys   boys
Marcel Duchamp   mar-**SEL** doo-**SHAHM**
Anselm Kiefer   **AN**-selm **KEE**-fur
Roy Lichtenstein   **LIK**-ten-**steye(n)**
Bruce Nauman   broos **NAW**-muhn
Nam June Paik   nam juun pagk
Betye Saar   **BET**-ee sahr
David Salle   **DAY**-vuhd sal
Renee Stout   ruh-**NAY** stowt

Glossary

Conceptualism   (*page 462*) A late 1960s and 1970s movement which prized the concept or idea over the making of the art object. In direct reaction to the rise of the art market and the commodification of art during the period, artists rejected producing saleable objects.

Installation Art   (*page 464*) The construction of an environment as opposed to individual objects characterizes installation art. Popular today as a means of extending the gallery experience, installation emerged as one of a number of artistic solutions to the problem of making art after the decline of Modernism.

Neo-expressionism   (*page 469*) A movement of painters in the early 1980s who have embraced many of the pictorial conventions of earlier German Expressionism. The work is noted for its violent paint application, agitated color, and highly subjective subject matter.

Performance Art   (*page 464*) The extension of the traditional visual arts into actual time and space. The artist and viewer thus become participants in the artwork.

Pop Art   (*page 453*) A 1960s movement which drew its content from the commercial marketplace. It is noted for its critical opposition to many of the sacred tenets of Modernism, such as originality and progress, embracing instead the repeatable look of the mass-produced and commercial.

Postmodernism   (*page 467*) Meaning literally "after Modernism" it is a speculative term embraced by most contemporary commentators to describe the cultural climate after the rise of Pop Art. It is characterized by irony, the acceptance of appropriation, and an overall dismissal of the formal program of Modernism.

Revisionism   (*page 484*) A critical position which attempts to analyze and dismantle the previous art program (such as Modernism) on the basis of its value system.

screen printing   (*page 461*) A printing process in which ink is dragged through a stencil attached to a stretched piece of silk. Its flat and commercial-looking qualities made it a favorite of the Pop artists.

Structuralism   (*page 464*) A linguistic theory which stresses language as a socially generated system.

GLOSSARY

Abstract Expressionism   A common appelation for first-generation American abstract painting after the Second World War, due to the primacy of gesture and color while keeping consistent with the aims of formalism (the all-over application of paint and the dispersal of depth across the surface of the picture plane).

arabesque   Meaning "Arab-like," it is commonly used to describe Islamic ornamental work, which combines vegetal and geometric configurations into a unified composition. The result is a balance of hard-edged and curvilinear marks, which, like the *yin and yang* of Taoism, combine to produce a visual equivalent of harmony in life and conduct.

arch   A structural device that allows an opening in a wall, roof, etc. to exist without supports. The arch consists of a series of carefully cut stones, called *voussoirs*, which butt one against another to create a semicircle. The central voussoir, called the *keystone*, exerts pressure down through the arch, holding the form in place.

architecture   Commonly defined as the art of designing space. Its roots are in the Greek "arch" (meaning higher or better) and "tecture" (meaning construction or building), but the term is popularly used to address virtually all facets of the organization of spaces (landscapes and interiors, for example, as well as buildings).

architrave   See Doric order.

atmospheric perspective   A convention for developing depth within a painting by making objects appear less defined as they recede in space. Often, this was combined with a slow transition toward the color blue in the background that was supposed to mimic our perception of faraway scenes.

audience   The viewers of an object who complete the process of communication between themselves, the artist, and the art, thus an intrinsic part of the art-making process. Each member of an audience brings to bear a multitude of personal experiences and learning upon the work in question, and as a result the message a work gives is never absolutely identical to any two individuals. There is, in essence, a constant process of re-creation every time an individual enters into a dialogue with a piece.

avant-garde   From the French "before the rest," this was a term applied to artists of various persuasions to imply a self-appointed role as explorer or adventurer, blazing a trail for others in the community to follow. It has implicit connotations of heroic will and the artist as savior of society, ideas in keeping with the progressive doctrines of the Romantics and the Idealists of the nineteenth century.

Baroque   A term used to identify the period in Western art from c. 1600 to c. 1750. Its linguistic origins indicate something complex, intricate, or irregular, and it most likely refers to the increase in emotional content and exuberant composition after the restraint of the Renaissance.

basilica   An early form of Christian church architecture based on Roman secular designs which set precedents for later Christian building projects. It possessed an outer courtyard or atrium, a long central hall or nave with side aisles, an intersecting transept at one end, and a second-level clerestory which enabled a uniform lighting of the interior.

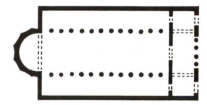

Bauhaus   Derived from the German "building house," it was a school of art and design developed under the guidance and aesthetic philosophy of the architect/designer Walter Gropius. Active in the 1920s and early 1930s, it attempted a collective vision of art making, in which the traditional subjective experience of the artist and the autonomy of the object were relinquished in favor of a more communal attitude to the problem of design. It put emphasis on pure, unornamented structures devoid of subjective or regional idiosyncrasies.

black-figure style   The painting in early Greek pottery of figures in black slip on terracotta surfaces, which were then scratched into with styluses to articulate forms. See also *red-figure style*.

bronze casting   A method of replicating a form through the production of a shell, usually of clay, into which a molten copper-tin alloy is poured. The most popular method for bronze casting is the lost-wax technique, in which an object is formed in wax and covered in clay, and then the wax model is melted away, leaving a perfect impression.

calligraphy Literally the art of writing, it is the written word or words as a visual document. Often painted, it can take on visual characteristics much like a painting, embodying a series of other visual and cultural issues.

calligraphy

capital See Doric order.

chiaroscuro From the Italian "light and shade," it is a technique for suggesting three dimensions by modeling figures in highlight and shadow. Its more dramatic cousin *tenebroso*, which implies a more theatrical use of light with deep shadow, is also used to describe such a visual effect. Artists often will use a directed or "raking" light source, which produces predictable shadows, to achieve this effect.

civilization Derived from Latin words for citizen and town dweller, it has come to imply the social interrelations between people and ideas, rather than concrete events and objects.

closed-form Sculptural forms that keep a certain visual connection to their original block shape; generally sculptures which have little articulation and do not visually activate the surrounding space, giving the appearance of being self-enclosed. See also *open-form*.

collage Meaning "gluing," it is a method of applying extraneous material (and thus subject matter) to an art work. It has been used to reiterate objects and ideas from the real world (Picasso), as well as to suggest history, nostalgia, and the build-up of superficial material culture (Schwitters). Collage usually implies two-dimensional art such as drawing, whereas "assemblage" often refers to three-dimensional strategies.

Conceptualism A late 1960s and 1970s movement which prized the concept or idea over the making of the art object. In direct reaction to the rise of the art market and the commodification of art during the period, artists rejected producing saleable objects.

Constructivism Founded in revolutionary Russia, the movement attempted to reconcile advanced Modernist aesthetics with the goals of Communism.

contour drawing A method of rendering an item on a two-dimensional plane using its external edges as a guide. Often, these edges will suggest volume, mimicking the folds and undulations of the surface, and hence it is an effective way of creating illusionistic space.

contrapposto A figure pose first developed by Polyclitus with his *Doryphorus* (Fig. **2.27**) model in Classical Greece, it combines a "fixed" or "engaged" leg with a "free" leg — a motion that creates a sway in the hips and is subsequently counterbalanced by the upper torso. During the Renaissance, such a pose took on greater importance as the harmonious embodiment of the active and contemplative lives which direct all human conduct, and thus was considered an ideal form.

conventions The specific communicative tools or strategies used to form a cultural code. In art, these tools range from a symbolic use of color to forms of perspective or even the shape or dimensions of a piece. Conventions are also inherently social in nature; they come into existence through common agreement and are maintained through custom.

Corinthian order A Greek architectural order notable for its modelled acanthus leaf motif and rounded capitals.

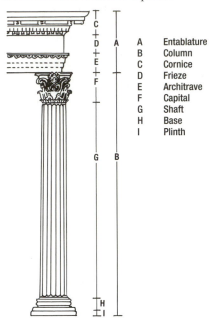

A	Entablature
B	Column
C	Cornice
D	Frieze
E	Architrave
F	Capital
G	Shaft
H	Base
I	Plinth

Cubism The first art movement of the twentieth century systematically to reconsider the conventions of painting since the Renaissance. Such work is epitomized by the severe flattening of the space across the picture plane, a consistently inconsistent light source, and an imploding of the traditional fore-, middle- and background areas in painting composition.

cuneiform Mesopotamian script derived from pictures arranged in a narrative order named after the wedge-shaped marks created by the writing styles. The ancestor of the modern Western script, it is the logical extension of earlier two-dimensional designs.

Dada A radical art movement initiated in Zurich during the First World War as an affront to conventional wisdom and traditional culture. Born from outrage at the apparent hypocrisy of European culture, it attempted to set new standards for art and art making by abandoning traditional picture making in favor of performance work and other non-traditional gestures. It also used chance as an important part of the art process, in the hopes of producing work free of the trappings of rational culture.

daguerreotype   A chemically derived silver-plated copper sheet invented in 1837 by Louis Dagguerre that produced a clearer image in far less exposure time. This invention meant that people could be documented clearly in photographs (the natural movements of a human and the long exposure time made it almost impossible to photograph individuals before this point). This discovery had enormous repercussions for both photography and painting.

De Stijl   A Utopian collective founded in the Netherlands after World War I which prized the ethical potential of Modernist design and architecture. Among its most noted members were the architect Rietveldt and the painter Mondrian.

dome   In structural terms, a dome is simply the intersection of several arches around a central axis. In its earliest use, the dome rested directly on a cylindrical wall called a *drum* but as building projects increased in size, the drum was replaced by the *pendentive* — a triangular shaped segment of vaulting that effectively transfers the stress away from under the dome.

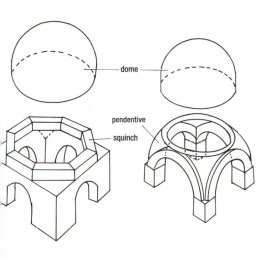

Doric order   The first architectural system developed by the Greeks, it had its roots in earlier timber *post and lintel* design. Like the older timber forms (which were essentially long sections of fallen tree propped up to support an overhang), Doric columns rest directly on the floor or *stylobate*, and taper like tree trunks as they move upwards. The top or head of the column (called the *capital*) mediates between the cylindrical shape of the column and the angular forms of the supporting structure, called the *entablature*, which is comprised of three distinct parts. The band of rectangular blocks immediately supported by the columns is called the *architrave*. Above it stands the *frieze*, which consists of alternating blocks of relief sculpture or painting (the *metope*) and vertical bands (the *triglyph*). Above this is the crowning *pediment* — a triangular-shaped construction which forms the roof. All other Classical building design emerged from the Doric order.

empiricism   A philosophical position holding that one can gain knowledge and insights into existence through the close observation of nature. Originating in the writings of Aristotle, it had sweeping implications for the study of science in the Middle Ages. Its effect on art making can be seen in the high degree of naturalism and close observation in the works of many northern Renaissance artists.

engaged columns   Non-structural decorations used on exterior walls in Roman temples to give the appearance of true vertical columns which support the entablature. A practical solution to

the problem of integrating the earlier Greek temple design with the Roman interest in defining interior spaces (which walls provide).

entablature   See Doric order.

etching   Derived from the old High German word *azzen* or the Dutch *etsen*, to eat, it is a printmaking process that involves the drawing of lines into a resist already painted on a metal plate. Drawing removes the resist, exposing the metal, which is then submersed in acid (called "biting"). The exposed metal is then eaten into, leaving a series of lines "etched" in the metal. When the plate is inked (the artist applies ink to the whole plate surface, then wipes away the excess on the surface, leaving ink in the small etched grooves) printing will faithfully reproduce the original lines.

Expressionism   A term historically applied to art that is involved not so much with a faithful, seemingly objective description of nature (implicit within the terms *Impressionism*, *Realism*, etc.) but with the expression of less tangible and often psychological states through images. Through devices not often associated with observation (aggressive paint handling, bright unnatural color) Expressionist artists believed they were more capable of producing intimate, egocentric visions of their world. Often, such artists would pirate less refined techniques such as the woodcut print, which they saw as raw, physical and very graphic. In appreciating non-Western and naïve work, artists (often mistakenly) saw what they considered a more pure and less repressed expression, and took from these cultures freely. In Expressionist art, reality is understood as the production of each individual, with all of the idiosyncrasies inherent in being human.

Fauvism   An art movement of the first decade of the twentieth century in which artists made bold use of color to express the inner qualities rather than the superficial appearance of objects.

flying buttress   A supporting armature used on Gothic cathedrals to take the strain of the vast vaulted ceilings. The buttress distributed the mass of the building away from the walls to the area around the foundation, allowing architects to build higher and more structurally sound churches, with more window space and thus greater light in the interior.

foreshortening   A convention for depicting illusionistic space in painting. The technique involves the visual contraction of an object as it moves back in space.

fresco   A painting method by which colored pigments immersed in water are applied to fresh plaster, which absorbs the paint and dries rockhard. This method was particularly popular for decorating interior spaces during the Renaissance.

frieze   See Doric order.

Futurism   A Modernist-anarchist association of predominantly Italian artists, who championed change and automation as liberating characteristics of a new age. The movement was to deteriorate after World War I.

gouache   Sometimes called "Body Color," gouache is simply *watercolor* mixed with an opaque pigment, often "Body White," to create a look similar to *tempera*.

Group of Seven   A loose affiliation of Canadian painters between 1913 and the mid 1920s whose work centered around the northern landscape as the source for a national art movement different from the art of their neighbors to the south and that of Europe.

icon   Literally meaning image, the term is generally used to describe representations of the Christian pantheon, particularly those with metaphysical connotations produced under Orthodox Christianity.

iconoclasm   The practice of denying representational imagery in a community, often on moral or religious grounds. The term literally means image-breaking, the destruction of an already produced image. In religious art, this concept often parallels ideas on the blasphemy of figurative art as a direct confrontation to the creative powers of God — usually associated with monotheistic faiths such as Judaism, Christianity, and Islam.

iconography   The meanings and symbolic associations attributed to a figure or idea.

ideal-forms   Generalized shapes which combine actual representation with a corresponding concept. Together, the artist creates not simply a reproduction of a specific event but a symbolic language capable of merging such a physical reality with the community's consciousness of its world (sometimes also referred to as pictographs).

idealism   To imbue an item (often the human figure) with a greater degree of stature and significance by observing not specific features of the individual but rather the more universal and distinguished characteristics of the human form as accepted by a given culture.

ideal measurement   A system for the development of images/objects based on an external source (natural or supernatural) deemed central to a given community. Thus an item such as a bird or a rock could be utilized as the fundamental unit for determining the size of a figure.

impasto   A thick application of paint, usually in layers, producing a rough, textured surface.

Impressionism   An art movement named specifically after one particular painting by Claude Monet, *Impression: Sunrise* (Fig. **7.15**) of 1872. Arising out of the naturalism of the Realists (such as Courbet), as well as an interest in the transitory experience of light and color on objects, Impressionism did two distinct things to painting: it elevated color to the status of subject matter, liberating the artist's marks from previous craft constraints, and it inadvertently asserted painting's relationship to the flat surface.

intent   The interests of the artist as perceived by the audience, or why an artwork was made. This becomes an important issue in objects that have little referential character (such as paintings).

International Style   A form of later Modern architecture based on modular design, an emphasis on steel and glass, and little or no embellishment. The style is best epitomized in the corporate skyscraper.

Installation Art   The construction of an environment as opposed to individual objects characterizes installation art. Popular today as a means of extending the gallery experience, installation emerged as one of a number of artistic solutions to the problem of making art after the decline of Modernism.

Ionic order   A more refined and slender version of the earlier Doric design, its most noteworthy feature is the double-scroll *volute*, which acts as a mediation point between the entablature and the column.

kouros   A generic term for early Greek figurative sculpture (the female types called "koré," the male "kouros"), many of which exhibit features evident in earlier Egyptian models, including a stiff frontal posture and relatively little articulation of joints.

line speed   The ability of line (depending on its characteristic thickness or relative angularity) to suggest motion in a drawing or painting.

linear perspective   A geometric system for defining items in space, probably first invented by the Romans and then rediscovered by Brunelleschi in the early fifteenth century. It implies that all lines receding back into space have as their point of origin a central vanishing point or points, depending on the circumstances. Implicit within this method is a certain centrality in the viewer's gaze (particularly in one-point perspective), which parallels the Renaissance belief in the centrality of human existence.

lithography   A method of making prints from a flat surface, usually a stone or metal plate (in offset lithography); often used in early newspapers. An image is drawn onto the surface with an oil-based crayon (litho crayon), which resists water when the surface is wiped with a wet sponge. An oil based ink is then rolled across the surface and adheres only to the oil of the crayon drawing, leaving the damp areas of the plate clean (since oil and water do not mix). Paper is then placed on top of the stone, and run through a press, producing an image. The process became popular among artists around the middle of the nineteenth century for its similarity to drawing and the sensitivity of mark such prints possessed.

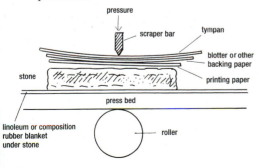

Mannerism   A transitional period between the High Renaissance and the advent of the Baroque (c. 1600) characterized by stylistic virtuosity and compositional complexity over conventions of restraint and idealism.

mark making   The gestures, scribbles, and gouges produced by an artist during the execution of a work that are left visible to the viewer, thus becoming an essential part of the overall subject matter. Since paint is extremely tactile, it can become a carrier of physical messages and events when allowed to exist undiluted; its paste-like consistency takes brush marks and other gestures and transforms them into intimate suggestions of the artist's method of work.

metal engraving   The process by which a multiple of an image is produced by scoring a metal plate with a burin to create lines. Ink is rubbed into the scored surface and dampened paper is then pressed against the surface, pushing the paper into the ink-filled troughs, which creates the print.

metope   See Doric order.

Minimalism   A painting and sculpture movement of the 1960s based on the primacy of the art object in its purest formal condition.

mosaic   The art of creating images using colored stone, terracotta, and glass *tesserae*. This art form was originally used to decorate the floors and walls of buildings.

motif   A recurring image or theme.

mural   A large-scale painting often applied to a wall or other architectural surface.

narrative   The progression of an idea from one image to another, often implying a passage of time. To arrange images in narrative, it is necessary clearly to identify a direction of movement, suggesting a possible entrance into the plot, as well as an exit.

naturalism   An attempt to imitate the world of everyday perception, or as things exist naturally. Art that draws from the world as it exists in perception,

without idealization (often opposed to the precepts of Classicism, which forms ideals from natural phenomena).

Neo-Classicism   The term used to describe the revival of Classical conventions such as symmetry, a reliance on draftsmanship over color (in painting), and the evocation of a determined and disciplined order to the world. The development of the movement corresponds with the prevailing revolutionary attitude in Europe and America against the excesses of the state and the aristocracy (hence its deliberate critique of the preceding Rococo period).

Neo-expressionism   A movement of painters in the early 1980s who have embraced many of the pictorial conventions of earlier German Expressionism. The work is noted for its violent paint application, agitated color, and highly subjective subject matter.

non-finito   Meaning literally unfinished or not finished, it is a term used by late eighteenth-century theoreticians to describe the duality of potential in a sketch or unfinished work of art.

non-illusionistic painting   A term used to identify paintings that refers essentially to their physical and material character. Such work attempts to deny conventional pictorial constructs (such as perspective, chiaroscuro) for organizing space; hence its non-illusionism.

open-form   Sculptural work that engages its surrounding space as an extension of the sculpture, activating the area around the figure and interacting with the viewer's space. Many such pieces show little suggestion of their original source shape. See also *closed-form*.

pedestal   A sculptural device used to separate an object from the space and scale of the viewer; it elevates and sanctifies the object as "other," "different," and usually "heroic." The removal of the pedestal thus implies a movement back into the physical, tangible world of the viewer.

pediment   See Doric order.

perfect proportion   A system of determining the scale of a figure based on an interrelationship of parts within the body (the figure thus becomes its own gauge for ideal measurement). Proportion supports the idea of an internal harmony, rather than imposing a set of standards or restrictions on the body, gathered from external considerations.

Performance Art   The extension of the traditional visual arts into actual time and space. The artist and viewer thus become participants in the artwork.

photography   From the Greek, meaning to write or describe with light, the term was first applied to a technical process in 1826 when Nicéphore Niépce first placed light-sensitive silver salts onto a surface, enabling a truthful reproduction of a projected image to be made. Though the initial exposure time was a lengthy eight hours, it set off a wave of pioneering developments that eventually made the medium accessible, practical, and affordable.

Pop Art   A 1960s movement which drew its content from the commercial marketplace. It is noted for its critical opposition to many of the sacred tenets of Modernism, such as originality and progress, embracing instead the repeatable look of the mass-produced and commercial.

prehistoric   Meaning before historical documentation.

primitive   A value judgment used to identify and label the visual artifacts produced by certain traditional cultures in recent times as less sophisticated, and thus of poorer quality.

positive-negative space   An element of design in which positive refers to the shapes of forms representing the subject matter, and negative to the open spaces surrounding the subject, often called the background. The term is used in both two- and three-dimensional art to describe the relationship between parts of a work.

post and lintel construction   Any vertical form (post) that supports the horizontal (lintel) on its crown, from which the later convention of the supported ceiling was derived.

Post-Impressionism   An art movement of the late nineteenth and early twentieth century in which artists such as van Gogh and Gauguin rejected the naturalism of the *Impressionists*.

Postmodernism   Meaning literally "after Modernism" it is a speculative term embraced by most contemporary commentators to describe the cultural climate after the rise of Pop Art. It is characterized by irony, the acceptance of appropriation, and an overall dismissal of the formal program of Modernism.

realism   A commonly accepted understanding of one's world. The art of reality is an expression of how one understands the world, and not necessarily contingent upon what one sees (see *naturalism*). In this sense, most visual artifacts address the nature of reality as seen through the eyes of an historical period.

red-figure style   The opposite procedure of the *black-figure style* evolving in the mid sixth century BC, here the artist paints the background areas in black slip, leaving figures in terracotta, which are then articulated through painted lines, giving them a greater sense of form and detail.

relief   Often achieved through carving or casting, it is the rise of material above a two-dimensional plane, or the cavity created below the plane, which enables forms to be articulated through light and shadow.

Renaissance   Meaning "rebirth," it is generally used to define the period in European culture between 1400 and 1600, when there was a renewed interest in Classical scholarship and art.

repoussoir figure   One or more silhouetted figures situated in the immediate foreground, facing away from the viewer, creating a sense of space in the middleground area. This convention gives the work an increased sense of intimacy, since the viewer's gaze is somewhat blocked by the suggestion of these foreground figures.

Revisionism   A critical position which attempts to analyze and dismantle the previous art program (such as Modernism) on the basis of its value system.

ribbed vault   This is constructed by way of a series of intersecting pointed arches that, when assembled, provide a structural skeleton (ribs) of a vaulted ceiling.

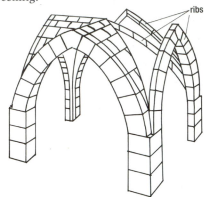

Rococo   Deriving from *rocaille*, a delicate and ornate form of shell and rock work used to decorate walls and floors, the term refers to a period in European art c. 1700, when technical exuberance and pleasurable sensations were popular, signaling a shift away from the rigid formulas of the Baroque Classicists.

Romanticism   A movement in early nineteenth-century culture against earlier rationalism and Classicism. It sought to elevate the fantastic, the sublime, and the pleasurable (ideas bound to the psyche rather than learned through rational processes) and asserted the primacy of human beings' relationship to their world, and the isolation of the artist after the decline of individual patronage.

Santos   The Spanish for "saints," the term refers to the devotional images produced for households in the converted regions of Mexico and New Mexico from around 1540 onwards. A *bulto* (a Santos figure constructed in three dimensions) is often carved in native cottonwood, primed with *yeso* (a local variety of gesso made by mixing animal glue, water, and baked gypsum powder together), and then painted with locally derived vegetable and earth pigments.

scale diminution   Used in painting, it is the reduction in scale of an object as its position from the picture plane changes. Together with *foreshortening*, it is used to suggest space.

screen printing   A printing process in which ink is dragged through a stencil attached to a stretched piece of silk. Its flat and commercial-looking qualities made it a favorite of the Pop artists.

sculpture   Objects produced in the round, possessing volume and interacting with real space. They have the ability to be viewed from any angle, a process which mimics our experience of the world. Also, like our own bodies, they occupy tangible space.

self-referentiality   An object or image that appears to serve no practical or obvious function, and as a result the viewer is forced to consider it in terms of its own intrinsic characteristics. An object is referential when it shows obvious relations to other external functions.

solid shape drawing   Color applied uniformly across a plane, making the image appear solid and separate from its surroundings.

Structuralism   A linguistic theory which stresses language as a socially generated system.

stylobate   See Doric order.

sublime   First coined by Edmund Burke in 1757, it describes the quality of grandeur or exaltedness found in nature that held aesthetic potential for the artist. The pictorial conventions that developed out of it are often described as the picturesque.

Suprematism   A one-man school founded by Russian Kazimir Malevich, it prized artistic autonomy and geometric purity as gateways to the metaphysical experience.

Surrealism   A literary and visual art movement interested in unleashing and exploring the potential of the human psyche. Loosely based on both Freud's and Jung's investigations into the mind, it is also direct heir to earlier Dada strategies of unlocking of the unconscious by the use of chance.

symbol   A set of communally accepted meanings associated with a form.

Symbolism   A literary and artistic movement c. 1885–1910 characterized by a reaction against realism and the use of evocative but often private symbols.

symmetry   A compositional device to produce balance between parts through offsetting items on either side of center (almost like a mirror). The result is an image or building that appears in perfect equilibrium.

synchronicity   First articulated by psychoanalyst Carl Jung, it is the collision of elements not often associated with one another, that create a discord in rational understanding and thus precipitate unconscious activity. Surrealist artists were to mimic this principle in their work.

Transcendentalists   A group of American landscape painters who considered the painting of nature as a meditation on the absolute. By using the American landscape as the source for such work, there was an implicit degree of nationalism inherent in both the rhetoric and the criticism of the movement.

tempera   The mixing of pigment with a binder (historically egg yolk) creates tempera paint. During the Renaissance, the use of oil instead of egg yolk resulted in the development of oil paint.

triglyph   See Doric order.

undercutting   In sculpture, the technique of creating deep cuts in stone to produce shadow; the result suggests movement and dynamism, as the surface is transformed by light and shade capable of expressing the most dramatic of gestures.

volute   See Ionic order.

watercolor   A transparent medium made of pigment mixed with a binder of gum. The pigment/binder is then mixed with varying amounts of water and applied to white paper.

wood engraving   A relief printmaking method whereby areas not to be printed are carved out of a flat wood surface, leaving the intended image raised to take ink. A roller of ink is applied to the surface, paper placed on top, and then pressure applied, transferring the image onto the paper.

yin and yang   Described as the unity of opposites popular in Taoism and Buddhism, this circle symbol combines its halves to create a perfect harmonious whole — the decline of one is supported by the rise of the other (implying such opposites as intuition versus rationality, etc.). Harmony is thus attained when one finds the perfect equilibrium between these two polar qualities. The artistic ideal is then achieved through the relationship between artist and materials, or rational conception and the accidents of nature.

SUGGESTED READING

General

Norma Broude and Mary D. Garrard, *Feminism and Art History: Questioning the Litany*. New York: Harper & Row, 1982.

John Fleming, Hugh Honour and Nikolaus Pevsner, *The Penguin Dictionary of Architecture*. Harmondsworth: Penguin Books, 1980.

Hugh Honour and John Fleming, *The Visual Arts: A History*, 3rd edition. Englewood Cliffs, N.J.: Prentice-Hall, 1991.

H. W. Janson, *History of Art*, 4th edition. New York: Harry N. Abrams Inc., 1991.

Sherman Lee, *A History of Far Eastern Art*. New York: Harry N. Abrams Inc., 1982.

Linda Nochlin, *Women, Art, and Power and Other Essays*. New York: Harper & Row, 1988.

Henry M. Sayre, *Writing About Art*. Englewood Cliffs, N.J.: Prentice-Hall, 1989.

CHAPTER 1
The Beginnings of Art

Cyril Aldred, *Egyptian Art in the Days of the Pharaohs 3100–320 BC*. New York: Oxford University Press, 1980.

Pierre Amiet, *The Ancient Art of the Near East*. New York: Harry N. Abrams Inc., 1980.

H. A. Groenwegen-Frankfort and Bernard Ashmole, *Art of the Ancient World*. Englewood Cliffs, N.J.: Prentice-Hall, 1972.

CHAPTER 2
The Art of the Classical World

John Boardman, *Greek Art*. London: Thames and Hudson, 1985.

John Boardman, J. Griffin and O. Murray, *The Oxford History of the Classical World. Volume One: Greece and the Hellenistic World. Volume Two: The Roman World*. Oxford and New York: Oxford University Press, 1988.

Denys Haynes, *Greek Art and the Idea of Freedom*. London and New York: Thames and Hudson, 1981.

J. J. Pollitt, *The Art of Greece 1400–31 BC*. Englewood Cliffs, N.J.: Prentice-Hall, 1965.

J. J. Pollitt, *The Art of Rome c. 753 BC–AD 337*. New York: Cambridge University Press, 1983.

Martin Robertson, *History of Greek Art*. Cambridge: Cambridge University Press, 1975.

Anne Sheppard, *Aesthetics*. Oxford and New York: Oxford University Press, 1988.

Donald Strong, *Roman Art*. Harmondsworth: Penguin Books, 1988.

CHAPTER 3
Art and Religion

C. Davis-Weyer, *Early Medieval Art 300–1150*. Englewood Cliffs, N.J.: Prentice-Hall, 1971.

Richard Etthighausen and Oleg Grabar, *The Art and Architecture of Islam, 650–1250*. New York: Viking Penguin, 1987.

Michael Gough, *The Origins of Christian Art*. London: Thames and Hudson, 1973.

Oleg Grabar, *The Formation of Islamic Art*. New Haven: Yale University Press, 1973.

Susan Huntington, *Art of Ancient India: Buddhist, Hindu, Jain*. New York: Weatherhill, 1985.

Cyril Mango, *The Art of the Byzantine Empire 312–1453*. Englewood Cliffs, N.J.: Prentice-Hall, 1972.

A. C. Moore, *Iconography of Religions*. London: SCM Press, 1977.

B. Rowland, *The Evolutions of the Buddha Image*. New York: Harry N. Abrams Inc., 1963.

CHAPTER 4
Issues and Ideas in Renaissance Art

M. Baxandall, *Painting and Experience in Fifteenth Century Italy*, 2nd edition. London and New York: Oxford University Press, 1988.

A. Chastel, *A Chronicle of Italian Renaissance Painting*. Ithaca: Cornell University Press, 1983.

S. J. Freedberg, *Painting in Italy 1500–1600*. Harmondsworth and New York: Penguin Books, 1971.

T. G. Frisch, *Gothic Art 1140–ca. 1450*. Toronto: University of Toronto Press, 1987.

Creighton Gilbert, *Italian Art 1400–1500*. Englewood Cliffs, N.J.: Prentice-Hall, 1980.

James Snyder, *Medieval Art: Painting, Sculpture, Architecture, 4th–14th Century*. New York: Harry N. Abrams Inc., 1989.

James Snyder, *Northern Renaissance Art*. New York: Harry N. Abrams Inc., 1985.

Wolfgang Stechow, *Northern Renaissance Art 1400–1600*. Englewood Cliffs, N.J.: Prentice-Hall, 1966.

Lawrence Wright, *Perspective in Perspective*. London: Routledge and Kegan Paul, 1983.

CHAPTER 5
Art Issues, and Innovations in the Baroque Era

Anthony Blunt, *Art and Architecture in France 1500–1700*. Harmondsworth and New York: Penguin Books, 1973.

R. Enggass and J. Brown, *Italy and Spain 1600–1750*. Englewood Cliffs, N.J.: Prentice-Hall, 1970.

Julius Held and Donald Posner, *Seventeenth and Eighteenth Century Art: Baroque Painting, Sculpture, Architecture*. New York: Harry N. Abrams Inc., 1971.

A. Hyatt Mayor, *Prints and People*. Princeton: Princeton University Press, 1971.

J. C. Rich, *The Materials and Methods of Sculpture*. New York: Oxford University Press, 1947; reprinted New York: Dover Books, 1975.

Jakob Rosenberg, Seymour Slive and E. H. ter Kuile, *Dutch Art and*

Architecture 1600–1800. Harmondsworth: Penguin Books, 1977.

D. Saff and D. Sacilotto, Printmaking: History and Process. New York: Holt, Rinehart and Winston, 1978.

Simon Schama, The Embarassment of Riches: An Interpretation of Dutch Culture in the Golden Age. New York: Alfred A. Knopf, 1987.

Rudolf Wittkower, Art and Architecture in Italy 1600–1750. Harmondsworth and New York: Penguin Books, 1973.

CHAPTER 6
Reason and Revolution
Thomas E. Crow, Painters and Public Life in Eighteenth-Century Paris. New Haven: Yale University Press, 1985.

Lorenz Eitner, Neoclassicism and Romanticism 1750–1850. Englewood Cliffs, N.J.: Prentice-Hall, 1970.

Wendelin A. Guenter, "British Aesthetic Theory 1780–1830." Art Journal, Summer 1993.

Michael Levey, Rococo to Revolution: Major Trends in Eighteenth-Century Painting. London, New York and Toronto: Oxford University Press, 1977.

William Vaughan, Romantic Art. London, New York and Toronto: Oxford University Press, 1978.

CHAPTER 7
The Modern World and Its Art
H. H. Arnason, History of Modern Art. New York: Harry N. Abrams Inc., 1986.

A. Boimé, A Social History of Modern Art. Chicago: Chicago University Press, 1987.

T. J. Clark, The Painting of Modern Life: Paris in the Art of Manet and His Followers. Princeton: Princeton University Press, 1986.

Jean-Luc Daval, Photography: History of an Art. New York: Rizzoli, 1982.

G. H. Hamilton, Painting and Sculpture in Europe 1880–1940, 3rd edition. Harmondsworth and New York: Penguin Books, 1981.

Elizabeth G. Holt, From the Classicists to the Impressionists. Garden City, N.Y.: Doubleday, 1966.

Ian Jeffry, Photography: A Concise History. London and New York: Thames and Hudson, 1981.

Phoebe Pool, Impressionism. London and New York: Oxford University Press, 1967.

Robert Rosenblum and H. W. Janson, Nineteenth-Century Art. New York: Harry N. Abrams Inc., 1984.

CHAPTER 8
Art in the Americas
Matthew Baigell, A Concise History of American Painting and Sculpture. New York: Harper & Row, 1984.

David Driskell, Two Centuries of Black American Art. Los Angeles and New York: Los Angeles County Museum of Art and Alfred A. Knopf, 1976.

Robert Farris Thompson, African Art in Motion: Icon and Act. Berkeley: University of California Press, 1974.

Robert Farris Thompson, Flash of the Spirit: African and Afro-American Art and Philosophy. New York: Vintage Books, 1984.

George Kubler, Art and Architecture in Ancient America. Harmondsworth: Penguin Books, 1975.

John McCoubrey, American Art 1700–1960. Englewood Cliffs, N.J.: Prentice-Hall, 1965.

Dennis Reid, A Concise History of Canadian Painting. Oxford and Toronto: Oxford University Press, 1973.

E. W. Weismann, Art and Time in Mexico. New York: Harper & Row, Icon Editions, 1985.

CHAPTER 9
Art in the Twentieth Century
H. B. Chipps, Theories of Modern Art: A Source Book of and by Artists and Critics. Berkeley: University of California Press, 1968.

Edward Fry, Cubism. London: Thames and Hudson, 1966.

Silvio Gaggi, Modern-Postmodern: A Study in Twentieth-Century Arts and Ideas. Philadelphia: University of Pennsylvania Press, 1989.

George Hamilton Heard, Painting and Sculpture in Europe 1880–1940. Harmondsworth and New York: Penguin Books, 1981.

Robert Hughes, The Shock of the New. New York: Alfred A. Knopf, 1981.

Kim Levin, Beyond Modernism: Essays on Art from the '70s to '80s. New York: Harper & Row, 1988.

Edward Lucie-Smith, Late Modern: The Visual Arts Since 1945. Oxford, New York and Toronto: Oxford University Press, 1980.

Edward Lucie-Smith, Movements in Art Since 1945. New York: Thames and Hudson, 1984.

Herbert Read, A Concise History of Modern Painting. Oxford, New York and Toronto: Oxford University Press, 1974.

Herbert Read, A Concise History of Modern Sculpture. Oxford, New York and Toronto: Oxford University Press, 1974.

Robert Rosenblum, Cubism and Twentieth-Century Art. Englewood Cliffs, N.J.: Prentice-Hall and Harry N. Abrams Inc., 1976.

Peter Seiz, Art in Our Times. New York: Harry N. Abrams Inc., 1981.

Howard Smagula, Currents: Contemporary Directions in the Visual Arts. Englewood Cliffs, N.J.: Prentice-Hall, 1983.

Nikos Stangos, Concepts of Modern Art. New York and London: Thames and Hudson, 1981.

CHAPTER 10
Contemporary Art, Issues, and Ideas
Suzi Gablik, Has Modernism Failed? New York and London: Thames and Hudson, 1984.

Rozsika Parker and Griselda Pollock, Old Mistresses: Women, Art, and Ideology. New York: 1981.

Periodicals:
Artforum (New York)
Art in America (New York)
Art Journal (New York)
C Magazine (Toronto)
Flash Art (Italy)
New Art Examiner (Chicago)
October (MIT Press)

Survey exhibitions of Contemporary Art with extensive catalogues:
Carnegie International (Pittsburgh)
Documenta (Kassel, Germany)
Whitney Biennial of American Art (New York)
Venice Biennale (Venice, Italy)
Sao Paulo Biennale (Sao Paulo, Brazil)

CREDITS

The author and publishers wish to thank the artists, museums, galleries, collectors, and other owners who have kindly allowed works to be reproduced in this book. In general, museums have supplied their own photographs; other sources, photographers, and copyright holders are listed below.

I.1 Photo: Vatican Museum
I.2 Hulton Picture Library, London
I.3 Photo: Calvin Klein
I.4 J. P. Tarcher
I.22 Photo: Hans Petersen
I.24 Vatican Museum
I.27 Photographie, Paris
1.1 Zefa Picture Library, London
1.3,1.4,1.5 Color Foto Hinz, Allschwill
1.6 Arlette Mellaart
1.7 Skyscan Balloon Photography, Cheltenham
1.9 Zefa Picture Library, London
1.15 Hirmer Fotoarchiv, Munich
1.16 Zefa Picture Library, London
1.17 Photo: Fleming/Honour
1.18 Zefa Picture Library, London
1.19 Kurt Lange, Obersdort/Allgau
1.20 Hirmer Fotoarchiv, Munich
1.21 Spectrum Picture Library, London
1.22 Hirmer Fotoarchiv, Munich
1.23 R.M.N.
1.24 Hirmer Fotoarchiv, Munich
1.25 Hirmer (Neg. 622.5050)
1.26 Hirmer (Neg. 624.1052)
1.29 National Museum, New Delhi (Neg. 331)
1.31 TAP Service, Athens
1.32 Ancient Art and Architecture Collection, London
2.1 Scala, Florence
2.2 Photo: Vatican Museum
2.3,2.5 Archivi Alinari, Florence
2.8 Photo: D.A.I. Athens, Ker.7750.
2.9 TAP Service, Athens
2.10,2.11,2.13,2.14 Hirmer Fotoarchiv, Munich
2.15 Photo: Devos, Boulogne-sur-Mer
2.18 Fototeca Unione, Rome
2.19 John Donat Photography, London
2.21 Hirmer Fotoarchiv, Munich
2.22 John Donat Photography, London
2.25 Hirmer Fotoarchiv, Munich
2.26,2.27 Archivi Alinari, Florence
2.28 Photos: left: Bulloz, Paris; 0257573-8732 right: Lauros-Giraudon, Paris
2.29 Archivi Alinari, Florence
2.30 Deutsches Archäologisches Institut, Rome
2.31 Archivi Alinari, Florence
2.33 D.A.I. Athens
2.34 Fototeca Unione, Rome (Neg 11299).
2.36 Hirmer Fotoarchiv, Munich
2.37 Archivi Alinari, Florence
2.38,2.39 Fototeca Unione, Rome
2.40 Hirmer Fotoarchiv, Munich
2.41,2.42,2.43,2.44 Archivi Alinari, Florence
2.45 Leonard von Matt, Buochs
2.46,2.47 Scala, Florence
3.3,3.4 Israel Museum, Jerusalem
3.5 Photo: Yale University Art Gallery, Connecticut

3.6 Israel Museum, Jerusalem
3.7 Photo: Vatican Museum
3.8,3.9 Pontificia Commissione per L'Archeologia cristiana
3.13 Kenneth J. Conant
3.14,3.17 Sonia Halliday, Weston Turville
3.18 Corinium Museum, Gloucester
3.19 Scala, Florence
3.20 Hirmer Fotoarchiv, Munich
3.21,3.22 Photographs: Vadim Grippenreiter
3.23 Viollet, Paris
3.24 Clive Hicks, London
3.25 Bulloz, Paris 027968-60516
3.26 Giraudon, Paris
3.30,3.32 A.F. Kersting, London
3.33 Sonia Halliday, Western Turville
3.37 V & A, London
3.38 Left: Spectrum Picture Library, London, right: Barnabys Picture Library, London
3.39 Spectrum Picture Library, London
3.40 Zefa Picture Library, London
3.41 Photo: Picterse-Davison International, Dublin
3.42 Ashmolean Museum, Oxford
3.44 Sonia Halliday, Western Turville
3.46 Foto: Wetstein & Kauf, Zurich
3.47 A.F. Kersting, London
3.53 Mansell Collection, London
3.54 British Library, London
3.56 Werner Former Archive, London
4.4 Hermann Wehmeyer, Hildesheim
4.8,4.9,4.10,4.11,4.12,4.13,4.14 Scala, Florence
4.15 Mansell Collection, London
4.16,4.18,4.19,4.20 Scala, Florence
4.21 Archivi Alinari, Florence
4.22 Quattrone Mario Fotostudio, Florence
4.24 Mansell Collection, London
4.25,4.26 British Library, London
4.28 Giraudon, Paris
4.32,4.33 Archivi Alinari, Florence
4.34,4.36 Scala, Florence
4.37 Archivi Alinari, Florence
4.42 Scala, Florence
4.44 A.F. Kersting, London
4.45 Spectrum Picture Library, London
4.46 R.M.N
4.50 Foto: Blauel/Gnamm - Artothek, Peissenberg
4.54 MAS, Barcelona
5.1 R.M.N.
5.4 British Library, London
5.7,5.8,5.9,5.10,5.11 Scala, Florence
5.12 R.M.N.
5.13,5.14 Scala, Florence
5.15,5.16,5.17 Archivi Alinari, Florence
5.18 Scala, Florence
5.20 Archivi Alinari, Florence
5.21 Scala, Florence
5.22,5.23 Archivi Alinari, Florence
5.24,5.25 Scala, Florence
5.26,5.27 R.M.N.
5.28 Photo: Studio Bassett
5.31 Bridgeman Art Library, London
5.32 Oronoz, Madrid
5.36 Artothek, Peissenberg
5.38 Bridgeman Art Library, London
5.40 Scala, Florence
5.41 Artothek, Peissenberg
5.43,5.44,5.52 R.M.N.
6.1 Bridgeman Art Library, London
6.2 Giraudon, Paris
6.3 Scala, Florence
6.5,6.7,6.8 R.M.N.

6.11 Reproduced by permission of Lord St. Oswald and the National Trust
6.13,6.14 R.M.N.
6.15 Cliches Musées de la Ville de Paris, © by SPADEM 1995
6.16,6.18 R.M.N
6.19 Virginia State Library
6.21 MAS, Barcelona
6.22 Scala, Florence
6.22 Bridgeman Art Library, London
6.23 MAS, Barcelona
6.24 Photo: Amsterdam Historische Museum
6.25,6.26,6.27 R.M.N.
6.28 Ralph Kleinhempel, Hamburg
6.32 A.F. Kersting, London
6.33 John Bethell, St. Albans
7.1,7.2 R.M.N.
7.3 Bridgeman Art Library, London
7.4 Photo: Fox Talbot Museum, Chippenham
7.8 Giraudon, Paris
7.10 Tintometer Ltd., Salisbury
7.11 Bridgeman Art Library, London
7.12,7.13,7.15,7.16,7.18,7.19 R.M.N.
7.27 Bulloz - 027986-60044
7.28 Photo courtesy Tate Gallery, London
7.30 Giraudon, Paris
7.47,7.48 Bridgeman Art Library, London
7.50 ©ND-Roger-Viollet, Paris
8.5 Zefa Picture Library, London
8.6 South American Pictures, Woodbridge
8.7 J. Allan Cash, Ealing
8.22 Photo by Wellard
8.23 Courtesy Dr. Naomi Jackson Groves
8.25 Bob Schalkwijk, Mexico
8.26 Werner Forman
8.28,8.29 Bob Schalkwijk
9.2 Bridgeman Art Library, London
9.12 Photo: Giraudon, Paris
9.14 Photo: Joseph Szaszfai
9.15 Photo: Kunsthaus, Zurich
9.30 Photo: Stedlijk Van Abbesmuseum, Eindhoven
9.32 Photo: Wayne Andrews/Esto
9.35 Photo: Centraal Museum, Utrecht
9.37 Esto, New York
9.44 Photo: Geoffrey Clements, New York
9.47 Photo: Hickey and Robertson
9.51 Photo: Henry Art Gallery, Washington
10.1 Photo: William Nettles
10.2 Photo: copyright Sonia Llopez
10.7 Photo: Musée National d'Art Moderne, Paris
10.8 Photo: Leo Castelli Gallery, New York
10.9 Photo: Colorphoto Hans Hinz
10.10 Bridgeman Art Library, London
10.13 Photo: Caroline Tisdall
10.15 Photo: Estate of Peter Moore, New York.5/13/69-A4
10.16 Photo: Rollin R. La France
10.17 ©Robert Burley, Design Archive, Ontario
10.18 Photo: © Tim Street-Porter/Esto
10.25 Photo: Gagosian Gallery, New York
10.27 Photo: Thibault Jeanson
10.28 Photo: ©The Detroit Institute of Arts 1995
10.29 Photo: Donald Woodman
10.35,10.36 Photos: Metro Pictures, New York
10.38 Photo: Barbara Gladstone Gallery, New York
10.45 Photo: William Nettles
10.47 Photo: Serpentine Gallery, London

INDEX

① It seems as if the artists of the past were not as "emotionally tortured" as the ones of modern day art. Is that true?

② Did modern artists want fame and recognition?

③ Should we redifine art? Why is should we consider geometric lines on canvas art?